# THE GRACES OF INTERIOR PRAYER

A Treatise on Mystical Theology

FR. AUGUSTIN POULAIN, SJ

Originally published in French as *Des Grâces d'Oraison* in 1901.
First English edition appeared in 1910.

The present copy has been retypeset, reprinted, and republished by
Caritas Publishing on June 3, 2016, the Solemnity of the Sacred Heart of Jesus.

The original *Approbation of His Eminence Cardinal Steinhuber*, the *Author's Preface to the Sixth Edition*, and the *Introduction to the Tenth French Edition* by Bainvel, have been moved to the back of the book. And an *About the Author* has been added.

Cover art: adapted from *St. Dominic in Prayer*, by El Greco

ISBN: 978-1-945275-01-2

Library of Congress Control Number: 2016938463

## Reviews of *The Graces of Interior Prayer*

"The fruit of over forty years of patient labour... it has already passed through many editions in the author's own country, has been translated into many languages, and has received the express approval and blessing of the Holy Father; and we are glad now to welcome it in its English dress, in the hope it may do in England the good work it has done elsewhere... Père Poulain's book is a description of the highroad of prayer and a chart for the use of the traveller. He gives the sign-posts and the stopping-places; he warns us of the dangerous corners; from the experience of those who have traversed the country he gives rules of guidance for those who will follow after. For these more than for anyone else he has laboured, and for these in proportion as they have themselves made progress in the journey." —*The Tablet.*

"A first-class text-book of Mystical Theology... nothing important is omitted... has a good bibliographical index... is well translated.... May it soon be found in every monastic and clerical library and on the shelves of the educated layman."
—*The Universe.*

"The translation is admirably done and the fulness of treatment of a supremely difficult subject in all its possible bearings is beyond praise... A carefully drawn up bibliography of mystical writers adds value to an already extremely useful book. No community, whether of men or women, should be without this book." —*Catholic Book-Notes.*

"A perfect storehouse of information on the whole subject of prayer... this is a work which should be treasured by all who aspire, as we all lawfully may, to know something experimentally here below of that Union of God which is to be our happiness hereafter. The translation is excellently done." —*The Month.*

"This valuable book... ought without doubt to find a place in all theological libraries... As a work deserving close study from clergy and religious orders it is invaluable, and as a work of reference it will be also of much use to the studious Catholic layman." —*The Catholic Times.*

# THE GRACES

# OF

# INTERIOR PRAYER

*To FRC,*

*who is a cedar of Lebanon rooted in Living Waters,*

*imbibing deeply of ever-ancient, ever-new Tradition,*

*the publisher dedicates this 2016 reprint.*

*Nihil Obstat*
*Joannes P. Arendzen, D.D., Ph.D., M.A.*
*Censor deputatus*

*Imprimatur*
*E. Morrogh Bernard*
*Vicarius generalis*

*Westmonasterii*
*die 19a Octobris 1949*

# CONTENTS



## PART I

## MYSTICISM: SOME PRELIMINARY QUESTIONS



## PART II

## SOME GENERAL IDEAS ABOUT THE MYSTIC UNION

## PART III

### A STUDY OF EACH OF THE DEGREES OF THE MYSTIC UNION SEPARATELY

## PART IV

### REVELATIONS AND VISIONS

## PART V

## THE TRIALS THAT ARE SENT TO CONTEMPLATIVES



## PART VI

## MYSTICISM: SOME SUPPLEMENTARY QUESTIONS

# APPROBATION OF HIS HOLINESS POPE PIUS X

[*Translation*]

REVEREND FATHER,

The Holy Father has confided to me the agreeable mission of conveying to you his warm and sincere thanks for the remarkable treatise on Mystical Theology entitled: *Les Grâces d'Oraison*, the fifth edition of which you have just published. His Holiness is rejoiced at the fruitful result of your long years of study, spent in observing the ways of grace in souls aspiring to perfection. He is happy to see that now, thanks to you, directors of consciences possess a work of great worth and high utility. You not only rely on the incontestable doctrine of the old masters who have treated this very difficult subject, but you present these teachings, which constitute your authorities, under the form that our age requires. While wishing your work a great success and abundant spiritual fruits, His Holiness grants to your Paternity the Apostolic Benediction.

In acquainting you with this favour, I am happy to assure you of the sentiments of high esteem with which I am,

Yours very affectionately in the Lord,

✠ CARDINAL MERRY DEL VAL.

Rome, *April* 2, 1907

# PREFACE TO THE ENGLISH TRANSLATION

The work of which this is a version was received with so much favour on its first appearance that it has been translated into several other European languages, and it is hoped that its somewhat learned title may not keep it out of the hands of many whom it is well fitted to serve. It is an example of modern scientific methods applied to a subject— mysticism—which critics outside the Church commonly regard as a mere form of brain-weakness peculiar to pious persons, and over which even Catholics are sometimes apt to shake their heads. Is there to be found in the interior life of devout souls, in their intercourse with their Maker, a life more intimate still—a secret door opening into a world still further withdrawn from sense, where very few may enter, but where the chosen ones have a sight and feeling of God, and enjoy His presence not less, but more really than we apprehend objects with our bodily senses? This is clearly a question of no little importance, and one which should not be without interest for a day like our own when we hear so much of Occultism and Theosophy and Spiritualism in its different branches—all of them attempts in their own way to pass material bounds and explore the region beyond.

But Père Poulain's book is much more than an examination of spiritual marvels. It is a survey of the Kingdom of Prayer in all its length and breadth, in its lowest as well as its most perfect forms. The interior life is seen to be a process, an orderly evolution, of which we can outline the laws and mark the successive stages. Even in its highest development we are permitted, as it were, to watch the first sprouting of the wings, then their gradual growth and freer play, until at last, with gathered strength and unerring aim, they bear the soul towards God beyond the range of our sight.

There are comparatively few problems of the ascetical life which do not fall in some degree within the scope of this treatise—the helps and hindrances of prayer, interior trials, scruples, discouragement, presumption. On all these topics the teaching of the author, deduced, be it observed, from the words or actions of the saints which he cites, seems to us eminently helpful and sane. Not unfrequently it lurks in unexpected places, in what appear to be casual remarks, in brief comments on some unusual point of theory or practice, but it will not escape the eye of a careful reader; and, above all, it will be treasured by those who are entrusted in whatever way with that most difficult and delicate of tasks, the direction of souls.

The experiences of those who have climbed the highest peaks of Perfection, their successes, even their mistakes, cannot fail to be useful even to those who are still stumbling on its lower slopes, or only gazing wistfully upwards from its base.

It will be understood that Père Poulain is at no pains to conceal the hardships and dangers of the ascent, when we say that he discusses the cases of saints who have been haunted by the temptation to self-destruction, and devotes a chapter to the prophecies of others which have not been fulfilled in the event.

And yet no one, we think, can rise from a deliberate perusal of this work, or of any considerable portion of it, without having gained a larger idea of the Divine Goodness and Power, and also of the capacity of God's creature, man. It is surprising to find that our nature, even its mortal state, can bear the strain of so strait a union with the Divinity, can become so privy to His secrets, and can look, unblinded, at such close quarters, almost on the very Face of God.

Finally, it is an encouragement to be told that a sound asceticism does not forbid poor sinners to desire even these extraordinary forms, and to believe that Our Father, Who is in heaven, and Who will not give His children a stone instead of bread, will grant even these gifts to those who ask Him aright.

DANIEL CONSIDINE, S. J.

WIMBLEDON COLLEGE,
WIMBLEDON

# AUTHOR'S PREFACE TO THE FIRST EDITION

**1.—Aim.** I had often dreamed of writing a quite small and purely practical treatise on Mysticism. I wished as far as possible to give very clear and very accurate *descriptions,* as well as very plain *rules of conduct.* Have the mystics always achieved this? Have we never suffered from their obscurity, their vagueness?

Such was my ideal, and it was very difficult of realisation. But I have, at any rate, made the attempt, and the reader will see how near I have come to attainment.

**2.—Course adopted.** It will be seen that I have followed what may be called the *descriptive school.* There is another, the *speculative school,* which endeavours to systematise all facts theologically by connecting them with the study of grace, of man's faculties, of the gifts of the Holy Spirit, etc. The first is that of the saints, or great contemplatives who have observed the extraordinary graces which they have found in themselves. The second has been created by eminent theologians, and it requires a profound knowledge of scholasticism.

If I do not associate myself with this latter school it is not from contempt. It deals with many high and interesting questions. But the readers whom I have in view do not desire these things. I am writing especially for those souls who are beginning to receive the mystic graces and who do not know how to find their way in this new world. And I address myself to those also who are *drawing near* and who have entered into the adjacent states.

The same difficulties present themselves to these souls also.

Now such persons require something really practical. They wish for very exact pictures—I was about to say photographs—in which they can recognise themselves *immediately.* They also require rules of conduct reduced to a few striking formulae, easy to *remember and to apply.*

Certain theologians would require more than this. They will perhaps see in this little book a mere manual, resembling those treatises on practical medicine which do not lose themselves in high biological theory, but merely teach us how to make a *rapid diagnosis* of each disease and *lay down the proper treatment.* But alas! I confess that I should think myself very happy to have attained such a difficult end!

Another reason for remaining in the realms of the practical is that the speculative school has produced masterpieces which could probably not be surpassed. One would prefer to re-edit their immense labours rather than begin the work all over again.* It does not appear to me that mysticism can make any advance on that side.

But it is quite otherwise with regard to *descriptions.* In the course of the centuries we find these becoming continually more and more exact. Writers arrive gradually, although very slowly, at distinguishing, one from another, states which had previously been confused; and they find happier comparisons by which to depict them. In this respect mysticism participates in the forward movement which is to be seen in all the descriptive sciences. There is no reason to believe that this progress will be arrested. Our successors will do better than ourselves. And it is in this direction that the future of mysticism lies.

I have indicated several points upon which new researches will be necessary.† But, as no method should be carried to extremes, I shall here and there allow myself certain remarks which will be of interest to the learned only.

But I shall relegate these, as a rule, to a footnote, or I shall warn the reader that they may be omitted.

Many of these remarks are made with the object of initiating the reader into the language of ancient treatises, translating it into a more modern and sometimes a more accurate form. Failing these explanations, some of the old writers cannot be read with profit. Their shades of thought escape us; we are misled by words which they employ in a sense now no longer ours.

3.—**Precautions taken.** In the absence of other qualities, this book will, I think, possess that of being a conscientious piece of work. For the last forty years I have studied these questions steadily in view of it. I have read quantities of treatises, ranging from duodecimos to folios. I have interrogated at great length numbers of persons possessing the graces of interior prayer, and others who were under the illusion that this was so in their case also. An acquaintance with these last is also useful.

If the reader detects any error, or finds me too obscure, I beg him to tell me so quite frankly. I am not afraid of objections and contradictions. They have almost always taught me something, if it were only that I could make some distinction clearer.

4.—In this treatise no **ascetic counsels,** properly so called, will be found. I have contented myself as far as possible with giving rules of conduct suitable for the extraordinary ways. I am concerned with mysticism, not with asceticism. I speak of the things that God as King performs in certain souls, and not of those which these souls should themselves accomplish in order that God may reign

* See in the Bibliographical Index at the end of this work the authors who have written in Latin.

† We must not say that the day for such inquiry is past, that the last word on mysticism has been said. No human science can ever have said its last word. In our days the descriptive sciences (and mysticism is one of them) never cease to accumulate facts. Hence their wonderful progress. The great mystics have understood this necessity instinctively. Their books are primarily collections of observed facts. But we must not suppose that they have described every detail, that they have answered every question (see the word *Research* in the Analytical Index.)

within them. Here, however, are some general remarks which may prevent illusions and misunderstandings.

1° The mystic graces do not lift the soul out of the ordinary conditions of Christian life, or free it from the necessity of aiming at perfection.—Whatever the state, whatever the road by which the soul is led, the way to show our love for God and to incline towards Him successfully, consists in avoiding sin, in the exercise of the practices of virtue; in renunciation and humiliation; in self-conquest, so that the heart may be emptied of self and a way made plain for grace; in a generous performance of the duties of our state. The paths of duty, of renunciation, and of humility are for all alike: there are no exceptions. If some are kept treading them longer than others, these are they to whom God grants the most abundant graces. We should look with suspicion upon a spiritual path that tended to divert the soul from these highways trodden by Christ and followed by all the saints.

2° *Mystical graces are not sanctity.*—They are merely powerful means of sanctification; but they must be received with humility and corresponded to with generosity. It is not always easy to use them aright. And the souls that are favoured with these gifts fear them even while they desire them. In everything else they love to walk in the ordinary ways, to remain in the ranks, so to speak, so long as God does not constrain them to come out of them. One of the surest signs of the Spirit of God is an instinctive horror of any singularity of conduct, of exceptions, of privileges, of all that distinguishes the soul from other souls and attracts attention to her.

3° *To pass our time in dreaming of the mystic ways* is a dangerous error. If a desire for extraordinary graces of union is not forbidden as a general principle, if it may, theoretically speaking, be good, yet illusions are very easy and are not of rare occurrence. Certain souls flatter their self-love by making ready for these graces, as if there could be any preparation other than fidelity to all the duties of our state, than the practice of the ordinary virtues, than the perfecting of our most common actions. By chimerical aspirations after blessings which are not in accordance with their actual dispositions, certain souls lose the graces of sanctity which God had destined for them. The practical course is to perfect ourselves in the ways in which our feet have been set; it is to correspond to the graces that we possess to-day. The souls called by God to the higher ways are precisely those who, acknowledging themselves to be the most unworthy, are chiefly occupied with the task of doing their very best in the ordinary paths. St. Teresa, speaking of herself, says: "She always desired virtues more than anything else; and this it is that she has charged her nuns to desire, saying to them that the most humble and mortified will be the most spiritual" (*First Letter* to Father Rodrigo Alvarez, S. J. *Life,* p. 450). Read also not only St. Francis of Sales, but St. Alphonsus Alvarez, or St. Teresa, especially in the *Way of Perfection;* or, again, Blessed Margaret Mary's letters and her Instructions to Novices; and we shall see everywhere that this is a fundamental doctrine of the true mystics, no less than of the ascetics.

4° One of the *great advantages of St. Ignatius' method of spirituality* is that it is a system of good sense and of action, a practical spirituality; and nothing could be more opposed to the illusion of chimerical desires and a vague sentimentality. It is in full accord here with true mysticism. And it is so also in a more positive way, by helping the soul to mount up with the aid of grace towards the highest sanctity by the gospel paths of renunciation and in the spirit of humility. Fixing its gaze lovingly upon the divine Master and Model, it removes all obstacles to the divine action, and prepares the soul in a marvellous way to feel its most delicate touches. One remark may be a discreet invitation to yield ourselves up to the breathing of the Holy Spirit. One method of prayer brings the soul, so to speak, to an active and reposeful expectation of the divine call.* This rule is as much or more applicable to cases of extraordinary prayer, and that other applies to these cases only. But St. Ignatius' method has not the drawbacks of certain so-called easy or simplified systems which tend more or less to carry the rules of mysticism into asceticism and seem to recommend for the common way that expectant or passive attitude which is only suited to the extraordinary states.

5° For all spiritual questions it is *necessary to have a director.* The more extraordinary the ways by which the soul is led, the greater, as a rule, is the need of direction. I do not insist upon this point; the ascetical authors do so sufficiently. (See chap. xxvi.) I pray God that this book may accomplish the only end that I had in view: the good of souls. May it awaken within them an attraction for prayer and the need to unite themselves closely with the divine Master. If through ignorance they have placed any obstacles in the way of grace, may these pages reveal to them the precious vocation to which they are called by the divine Goodness. May they again, in their turn, enlighten others; may the souls raised to the fruitful joys of the mystic life become more and more numerous in the Church, especially amongst those who have been consecrated to God. *Emmitte spiritum tuum... et renovabis faciem terrae.*

Paris, *January 29th*, 1901.
*Feast of St. Francis of Sales.*

* See Suarez, *De Religione Societatis Jesu,* Book IX, ch. vi, No. 9.

# THE GRACES OF INTERIOR PRAYER

## PART I

MYSTICISM: SOME PRELIMINARY QUESTIONS

## CHAPTER I

### PRINCIPAL DEFINITIONS

**1.—Fundamental distinction.** Before reviewing the various degrees of mental prayer, they must be divided into two main categories—the prayer termed *ordinary,* and *mystic* or *extraordinary* prayer.

We apply the word mystic to those supernatural acts or states which our own industry is powerless to produce, *even in a low degree, even momentarily.*

**2.—Explanation**. There are other supernatural acts which can be the result of our own efforts. For instance, the man who wishes to make an act of contrition, hope or love of God, is sure to succeed if he corresponds to grace; and he can always do so.

And it is the same with a host of meritorious actions: relieving the wants of the poor, self-mortification, prayer, etc. Preachers exhort all Christians to these acts; which would be an absurdity if they did not depend upon our own will.

This does not prevent these acts from depending upon divine grace also; *but this grace is never refused,* because God desires to give us means of acquiring merit. So it is with an engine-driver on his locomotive—two actions are about to be combined. It rests with the man to start or to stop his engine by the turning of a lever. But all that he does by this slight movement is to bring an enormous power into play—that of steam under high pressure. The motive-power lies, not in his feeble arm, but in the steam; but this latter is always at his disposal.*

**3.**—On the other hand, there are many supernatural phenomena which always evade our endeavours. Strive as I may to make energetic acts of the will in order to prophesy, or to see God or my guardian angel or Satan; and nothing, absolutely nothing, will result unless God intervenes in a special manner. I shall not even, as the above definition says, succeed in a *low degree or momentarily.*

This is what we call a mystic state.

Ordinary prayer may be compared to the atmosphere that surrounds our globe. The birds move about in it at will. Thanks to its aid, they can rise above the earth, and they mount higher in proportion to the strength of their wing-beats.

But this atmosphere has its limits. Above, lie those vast expanses that stretch away to the stars and beyond. Try as they may, they cannot penetrate thither, *even by redoubling their efforts.* The eagle is as powerless as the rest. God alone can transport them to this region; were He to do so, they would lie passive in His hand, there would be no further need to use their wings. They would have to discard their former methods of operation and adopt new ones. This upper region, where the wing no longer has any power, is a figure of the mystic state. It resembles it also by its peace, its silence. Far from the turmoil of earth we enter into a space empty of all created things. God dwells there alone.†

**4.**—And so mystic theology becomes defined: it is the science of the study of the mystic states.

**5.**—**Consequence**. From the above definition it follows that a supernatural state should not be described as mystic if it differs only in *intensity* or in *duration* from that which anyone can produce at will.

**6.**—By way of an **application**, let us put this question. Are we in the mystic state by the mere fact that we feel a sudden and very ardent fervour in our prayer?

By no means. It is true that this fervour does not usually depend upon our own will. We cannot, alas! procure it at pleasure, or we should never suffer from aridity. But there is a part of the definition not yet verified. In order that such a state should be mystic, as has been said, it must not be procurable at will, *even in a low degree, even momentarily.* But we can all, when we choose, procure in a low degree, or momentarily, a sentiment of love for God; of devotion, that is to say. So that fervour and divine love do not necessarily belong to the mystic state. It is

* This comparison must not be taken in too strict a sense. I am obliged to leave out of the question the preventing grace that aids us at will.

† Certain persons will prefer an historic definition and one that is more easily grasped; the following suffices for many discussions. We will give the name mystic to the states that St. Teresa describes in the latter part of her *Life,* beginning at chapter xiv, and in the last four mansions of the *Interior Castle.*

possible that it should be ordinary prayer, *as to kind,* even when the love becomes ardent.

**7.**—From this application we see the utility of the words "even in a low degree, even momentarily," which I have inserted in the definition. They help us to a clear solution of certain difficulties. In introducing them into the definition, I have merely given expression, however, to an idea which was implied by all writers when they said that it is *absolutely impossible* to procure the mystic states for ourselves.

**8.**—The preceding definition is that which **St. Teresa** gives in a little treatise addressed, under the form of her *Second Letter,* to Father Rodrigo Alvarez.* She begins to define the mystic states by employing the synonymous term of *supernatural* states of prayer: "*Supernatural,*—so I call that which *no skill* or effort of ours, however much we labour, can attain to, though we should prepare ourselves for it, and that preparation must be of great service" (*Relation,* viii, 3, *Life,* p. 455). She shows elsewhere that she has this definition in mind when she says: "This is a thing supernatural, and which we cannot acquire with all the diligences we use" (*Way of Perfection,* ch. xxxi, p. 93). In her other works the saint describes the mystic states without first giving any general definition concerning them.

**9.**—We can make the above definition **still more exact**, and say: we give the name of *mystic* to supernatural states containing a *knowledge* of a kind that our own efforts and our own exertions could never succeed in producing.

We saw just now that love cannot effect *a specific difference* between ordinary prayer and the mystic state (see Suarez, *De Orat.,* Book II, ch. ix, No. 13). Even in Heaven it will not be of a new species, but only of a greater intensity. The difference, then, must be drawn from the kind of knowledge that we receive. If we read St. Teresa and other great mystic writers, we shall see that this is also their belief.

**10.—Divers designations of the mystic states.** We must be acquainted with these designations if we wish to read the old writers. These terms require explanation, for they include some abbreviations which have often led to misunderstandings. The names are as follows:

**11.**—1°. **Supernatural states of prayer.** This is the expression that St. Teresa makes use of. She is employing an abridged form of words here, in order to say: *manifestly* supernatural states. On the other hand, many of the old writers called the nonmystic prayers: natural prayers. This is, again, an abbreviation, signifying: states that *appear* natural.

**12.—Explanation**. In ordinary prayer the acts are already supernatural and meritorious. But if faith did not teach me this, I should not be aware of it.

* For the sequence of these letters, or *Relations,* see the *Biographical Index* relating to St. Teresa at the end of this volume.

Nothing suggests this fact to me. And so when I devoutly pronounce the name of Jesus, my faculties *apparently* produce a natural act only, one similar to that of the child who repeats its mother's name.

In the mystic state, on the other hand, something shows us more or less clearly that God is intervening.

To take a clear and simple case: at Lourdes, Bernadette has an apparition of the Blessed Virgin; and not only is the fact supernatural, but it is *manifestly* so. It is, therefore, a mystic fact.

So, too, the term *infused* prayer signifies *manifestly infused:* that is to say, evidently supernatural.

**13.**—2°. **Extraordinary states.** This expression may be understood in two ways. It is often intended to signify that our faculties are operating in a new manner, which is unknown to them in the natural course of life. It is, then, the *manner of operation* that is styled extraordinary.

And it is in the same sense that we speak of the *ordinary* and the extraordinary supernatural. The first is when the acts are apparently natural: to say an *Ave Maria,* for example.

At other times the words "extraordinary state" are taken as synonymous with rare or infrequent, and it is often understood as being a question of rarity, not amongst the really pious, but amongst the generality of Christians. But whatever the standpoint from which we set out, this expression is regarded as synonymous with the mystic state.

**14.**—3°. **Passive states.** By this we merely wish to say that we receive something from another source, and render count of it to ourselves.* It is an abbreviation; in order properly to express the fact that our activity takes a part in this reception, we should have said *passivo-actif.* In a strictly passive state we should receive without doing anything at all.

St. Thomas likewise says that our material senses, sight and hearing, are passive faculties (I, q. 78, a. 3); and yet they react.

The word *passive* has another drawback: by itself it is vague, for it does not say what things are received, and these might be very various. But it becomes exact from the moment that we begin to regard it as a synonym for *mystic,* having previously defined this last word.

The passiveness is so much the greater as the mystic state is higher, because God's part in it is then more accentuated. But the activity is augmented at the same time.

* Some writers wrongly extend this term "passive" to states that are simply bordering on the mystic state, but in which the soul finds a difficulty in discoursing. By this reckoning all aridity should be called a passive state. But no; a *suppression* is not enough, there must be some *reception* of knowledge. Certain quietists also carried this suggestion still farther by giving the title of passive to mental prayer in which reasoning is *voluntarily* put an end to. So that the word passive is no longer for them even approximately synonymous with mysticism.

So, on the other hand, ordinary prayer is described as *acting.*

**15.—We must not confound** *mystic* with *ascetic* theology. The last-named has an aim quite different to that of mysticism. It is concerned with the virtues. It points out their nature, their kind, the means for their acquirement, the obstacles, the exaggerations, or the counterfeits to which they are liable, etc. Their point of contact with mysticism is this: that both alike treat of prayer. But ascetic theology confines itself by agreement to the study of the ordinary ways of prayer; that is to say, the prayer that depends, like the virtues, upon man's own exertions.

A great confusion of ideas is consequently involved when *The Imitation* is referred to as a mystical work. No; it is, first and foremost, an ascetic work.

It is true that good Catholic writers have sometimes used the word *mystic* as signifying *ascetic.* But we should be prevented from doing this for the future by the following reasons: 1° that we should be perpetuating an ambiguity. The word *ascetic* is clear and exact. Why, then, substitute for it another which is equivocal? 2° The word mystic cannot be justified if it is employed in the sense of ascetic. For it supposes a science which contains an element of mystery. Now, there is none in the teaching of abnegation and humility. Is it desired to indicate that it is a question of the mysterious action of grace? But in that case, dogmatic theology should also take the name of mystic.

So, too, there are writers who confound the words *mystic* and *seraphic.* If a poem speaks of divine love, they describe it as mystic. But why mix up such different ideas?

**16.**—The word **mystic** is much used by modern **literary men** in many senses; and these all differ from the true sense given above. It is not always easy to know what they mean to imply by their use of the term, for they omit to give any definition; but the following appears to be deducible from their vague descriptions.

They call a man a mystic 1° when he is strongly enamoured of any ideal, human or divine; 2° when he can give no clear explanation of the exalted grounds of his love. If he is called a mystic, it is because of this mystery, of this obscurity, of this intuitive and uncommunicable knowledge.

To sum up, the name of mystic is most commonly given to anyone who is at the same time enthusiastic and obscure, not living like all the rest of the world, taking dreams for realities. On this principle it would be applicable to an enigmatic writer, a Utopian, preaching a social or aesthetic creed, etc.

The rationalistic school of Cousin regarded Christians as mystics because of their acceptance of the supernatural. This change of names enabled him to attack Christianity without doing so too apparently.

Nearer to our own days, many philosophers class indiscriminately as mystics all ascetic Christians, Buddhists, and Moslems when they display an ardent religious spirit and a desire for union with the Supreme Being. What significations for one single word!

In this book I shall take the word *mystic* in the restricted sense in which St. Teresa and St. John of the Cross employ it. It is the one in most common use in the Church.

# CHAPTER II

## Of the Four Degrees of Ordinary Prayer And of the Last Two in Particular

**1.**—In ordinary prayer there are **four degrees**: 1° *vocal* prayer, which is a recitation; 2° *meditation*, also called *methodical* or discursive prayer. This last term indicates a chain of quite distinct reflections or arguments. We can include in this degree *meditated readings* and the *slow recitation* of a vocal prayer, accompanied by some reflections which help us to penetrate its meaning; 3° *affective* prayer; 4° the prayer of *simple regard* or of *simplicity*.

I shall say nothing of the first two degrees. They are outside my subject, and are explained at great length in a number of excellent treatises with which the reader is familiar, so that he will not wish me to traverse the same ground again.

### § 1. The Third and Fourth Degrees of Ordinary Prayer: Affective Prayer and the Prayer of Simplicity. Definition of These Two States.*

**2.**—We call **affective prayer** that mental prayer in which the affections are numerous or occupy much more space than the considerations and the arguments.

Not that the considerations are absent (we must necessarily go on thinking), but they are less varied, less prolonged.

In this degree we generally find as a foundation some *dominant idea* which does not, however, exclude a host of other secondary and less perceptible ideas. It is accompanied by very ardent affections.

* It must not be concluded that I regard these two degrees as identical because I consider them in the same chapter. I merely wish to avoid repetitions, as much the same things are to be said about them both.

This degree differs from meditation, therefore, merely as from the greater to the less. It is a discourse, only less varied and less apparent and leaving more room for sentiments of love, praise, gratitude, respect, submission, contrition, etc., and also for practical resolutions. The *deduction* of truths is partly replaced by *intuition.* From the intellectual point of view the soul becomes simplified.

This simplification may be greater or less. In a word, the degree is more or less marked and elevated according to the individual case.

**3.**—But the simplification can be carried farther still, and may extend, in a certain measure, to the will, which then becomes satisfied with very little variety in the affections. There is nothing to prevent them from being very ardent at times, but they are usually produced without many words. This is what we call the **prayer of simplicity** or of *simple regard.*

It can be *defined* thus: a mental prayer where 1° intuition in a great measure replaces reasoning; 2° the affections and resolutions show little variety and are expressed in few words.

When this state has reached its full development, not only do certain acts, of which I have just spoken, become rare, but the attempt to produce them results in a feeling of impotence and distaste. And it is then the same also with those representations of the imagination which would aid other persons in their prayer.

**4.**—The preceding definition is primarily negative, because it consists in saying what it is that has in part disappeared: the discursive act and the variety of words. It will be well to complete it by describing its **positive side** thus: in the prayer of simplicity there is a thought or a sentiment that returns incessantly and easily (although with little or no development) amongst many other, thoughts, whether useful or no.

This *dominant thought* does not go as far as to be continuous. It merely returns frequently and of its own accord. We may compare it to the strands which thread the pearls of a necklace, or the beads of a Rosary, and which are only visible here and there. Or, again, it is like the fragment of cork, that, earned away by the torrent, plunges ceaselessly, appears and disappears. The prayer of simple regard is really only a slow sequence of single glances cast upon one and the same object.

This degree only differs from the preceding degrees as the greater differs from the less. The persistence of one principal idea, however, and the vivid impression that it produces, point as a rule to an increased action on God's part.

**5.**—An **exaggerated picture** of the prayer of simplicity has been drawn at times. It has been so described as to lead us to suppose that the intellect and the will continue inactive before a single idea; one showing, that is to say, neither interruptions nor the least modifications. In this case the *multiplicity* of acts would have disappeared *entirely* and during the whole time that the prayer lasted; whereas it has only diminished notably and for a certain time—long enough to draw attention to it. The simplicity is approximate only and liable to interruption.

We shall see that this is so, even in the mystic states. In the prayer of quiet, the principal act is often accompanied by other acts, though on different levels of consciousness; a crowd of little thoughts pass and repass though but half perceived.

Those who appear to believe that the simplicity and the immobility are absolute, and last for a considerable time, forget to state whether they have ever met with such cases in practice, or if they have imagined them, *a priori*, in the study. For it would be a more extraordinary state than the mystic states themselves. Suarez considers it unlikely that there should not be a certain renewal of ideas, and especially of sentiments (*De Orat.*, Book II, ch. x, Nos. 12, 13). He concludes thus: "I think that it is in this sense only that contemplation can habitually be prolonged; but that it is very rare for the simple act to continue for long."

Scaramelli, on the other hand, seems to consider that the absence of considerations has reached an extreme degree when he says: "To know truths by a simple glance of the soul, is a mode of knowledge *above our human intelligence*, whose property it is to seek after truth by reasoning... it is a *superhuman* mode" (Tr. 2, Nos. 156, 69, 143). We can begin by replying that it is less a question here of seeking truth than of enjoying it. And then we shall see by examples (No. **26**) that this state, stripped of all exaggerations, and as it actually exists in real life, is very human.

Let us not invent chimerical states, and then substitute them for the real ones. Otherwise, in practice, our treatises will be useless. No one will be able to recognise his own state in our descriptions.

This exaggerated way of imagining the prayer of simple regard also leads to its being classed wrongly amongst the mystic states. For we are so struck by the exceptional character with which it is endowed, that we feel obliged to find it a place far above the modest prayer of meditation.

**6.**—Many writers include the prayer of simplicity in affective prayer, which they thus regard as exhibiting **two degrees of elevation**. And in this case, between them and us, it is a mere question of words.

**7.**—Before these two states could really constitute separate **degrees of prayer**, they must be capable of being prolonged for more than a few minutes at a time; they should continue, for instance, for an hour or more. For a very brief space, nothing is easier than for the mind to formulate ardent affections or to operate in a simple manner. Everybody can do it.

It is on this account that these states, although requiring the co-operation of grace, are not called mystic (see the definition, ch. i, No. 1).

We can express this reason differently, by saying that the name "mystic" has never been given to an exercise having the appearance of a purely natural operation. Now, this is the case with these degrees of prayer.

**8.—Various names**. The two states which we have just defined have sometimes been called the *prayer of the heart,* in order to indicate that the considerations do not predominate in them.

I believe that the term affective prayer was created by Alvarez de Paz (*Opera,* Vol. III, *De Inquisitione pacis,* 1616). He devotes to this degree three hundred folio pages, full of pious aspirations. Some later writers have adopted this language. Others have employed different terms; others, again, include in their classifications neither the name nor the thing. We see from this circumstance how slowly the science of prayer has come to distinguish the facts that it observes and to coin its own language.

The term, prayer of *simplicity,* which is very clear, seems to have been invented by Bossuet.*

This state, again, has been called *active recollection* or *active repose* (as opposed to mystic or *passive* repose), *active quietude* (as opposed to true quietude, that which is understood in St. Teresa's sense, and which is quite different), *active silence* (as opposed to the passive prayer of silence), and, most frequently, *ordinary* or *acquired contemplation* (see ch. iv, No. **6**).

St. Francis of Sales called it the prayer of *simple committal to God.*† This expression requires to be properly understood. It does not mean that we are to come to our prayer without preparation, doing nothing on our own side and committing to God the care of doing everything. But it supposes that God acts, and that we yield ourselves to this action, in spite of our natural tendency to prefer our own more restless action as being more pleasing to the natural faculties.

* After mentioning meditation. "The soul," he says, "by her fidelity in mortification and recollection usually receives a purer and more interior prayer, which we may call the prayer of *simplicity,* and which consists in a *simple interior gaze,* regard, or loving attention, directed towards *some divine object,* whether God in Himself or one of His perfections; it may be Our Lord Jesus Christ, or some one of His Mysteries or *some other Christian truth.* The soul, discarding all reasoning, then employs a gentle contemplation by which she is maintained in peace" (No. 3). This passage gives a very good definition of the kind of prayer that we are speaking of, and the various objects to which it can be applied.

This diversity of subjects shows that Bossuet has not St. Teresa's prayer of quiet in view, as some writers have believed; for the prayer has God alone for its object, except in a very subordinate way. The same thing follows from the fact that he does not attribute an experimental knowledge of God's presence to the degree that he describes, but only a simple *"remembrance by faith,"* as though one should say interiorly, *"I believe* that my God is present" (Nos. 4, 9). Further, he has informed us that this state is the "ordinary" consequence of meditation (No. 3), which is not true of the mystic union. Finally he asks all of his readers to practise this exercise on the first rising in the morning. It depends, therefore, upon their own will, and consequently is not mystic.

The above passage occurs in a work that was composed for the Order of the Visitation at Meaux, and entitled, *Manière courte pour faire l'oraison enfoi.* In vol. VII of the Vives-Lachat edition a less obscure title has been given to it, *Méthode facile pour passer lajournée dans l'oraison,* etc.

† These words occur without commentary in a letter written by the saint to St. Jane Frances de Chantal (March, 1615, Migne ed., Vol. V, col. 961, 965). They are also indicated by this latter when she is giving a clear description of the prayer of simplicity (*Reponses sur le Coutumier,* art. 24; Migne edition of the saint's works, Vol. II, col. 236).

**9.**—All these different names given to the prayer of simplicity have led to an error on the part of certain writers; for they have supposed them to correspond to different degrees. But if we look closely at their descriptions, making abstraction from the names, we perceive that the differences which they point out bear upon insignificant shades only. At most, these might serve to distinguish variations in one and the same degree. The multitude of classifications merely embarrasses the mind instead of assisting it.

Besides, *a priori,* it is easy to prove that ordinary **prayer cannot comprise any general degrees other than those** enumerated. There are two cases only. Either we reason, and then it is meditation, or we do not reason, and then it is affective prayer or the prayer of simplicity. All must necessarily enter one or other of these categories.

**10.—Transitions**. The preceding states may be linked one with another and, again, with meditation by a series of insensible transitions; whereas in the simplification of acts there may be either more or less.

It is a prejudice, then, to believe that there is a wall, as it were, erected between these simpler ways and the set methods of prayer. These last are not a prison from which we are forbidden to emerge. They are rather an open garden. We can remain in it if we like the regular walks, the ribbon-borders, where every plant has its own place. But these paths merge into woods, where those who are so inclined may wander in greater freedom, penetrating farther into the forest. St. Ignatius, at the conclusion of his stay at Manresa, wrote out a collection of methods; but he certainly meditated upon their subjects in a much simpler and higher manner than did those to whom he explained them later on. He kept to the spirit rather than to the letter.

**11.**—In respect of the diminution of the reasonings, the prayer of simplicity leads on by a **gentle ascent** to the mystic states. And these latter are really prayers of simple regard, although we give them another name in order to avoid confusion. And so we get evidence here of *the law of continuity,* a law that we must not take in too narrow a sense, and that we express in this way: *Natura non facit saltus* (Nature does not proceed by sudden bounds).

It is true that in the mystic state we have a new gift, but we still find an approximate continuity in this gift also. For it is usually granted only in a low degree to beginners. So that the transitions are gradual.

**12.—Analogies**. In the natural order we find conditions of soul that are analogous to the prayer of simplicity.

The mother watching over her child's cradle thinks of him lovingly for hours together, but with interruptions, and she does this without any arguments.

Two friends have not always new ideas to interchange. And yet they can remain in each other's society for long periods of time, enjoying the happiness of being together in tranquillity and *silence.*

In the case of a child who is unhappy because he is separated from his family, the impression is intense and persistent, but without any reasonings; his grief is no less strong, however, so far from being so is it that he sometimes loses sleep and the health is affected.

So, too, when a man falls in love, he thinks day and night of the object of his passion; but this thought, this sentiment, often shows *no variety.* It is always the same confused image, the same thought, happy or sad, that reappears, and each time that it presents itself he finds satisfaction in it *without experiencing any need of change.*

Finally, the artist remains motionless before some beautiful spectacle in nature or wonderful Old Master.

**13.**—To sum up: in all great preoccupations or in strong enactions of sorrow, joy, or admiration, we get personal proof of this double fact to which we have just called attention in the prayer of simplicity—namely, that the idea or the memory by which we are impressed is not absolutely continuous, but only very frequent, and that when it reappears it is without any appreciable development.

**14.**—The examples just given, not only serve to convey a clear idea of the nature of the prayer of simplicity, but they show, *a priori,* that **it must exist**.

This existence is clearly established by experience (see extracts at the end of chapter). But it will be as well to offer a further proof to those who decline to recognise anything between ordinary meditation and the mystic state.

This is the argument. We have just proved the existence, in the natural order, of states of soul presenting exactly the same characteristics as those which we have taken as the definition of the prayer of simplicity. Only that the mind is occupied with earthly things instead of divine. Now, as grace works in accordance with the plan of nature, being content at first to elevate it secretly *without changing its outward appearance,* it follows that there should be quite similar states in the supernatural order.

### § 2. Various Details.

**15.—General aspect of the spiritual life**. When these simplifications of the soul make their appearance during prayer, the same thing occurs with the other exercises of the interior life. The examination of conscience, for instance, takes place more intuitively, more rapidly, and by a single glance.

**16.—Object** of these prayers. They can be applied to all those subjects that used to offer themselves for meditation: God, Jesus Christ, His mysteries or interior states, the Blessed Virgin, the saints, or such truths as man's last end, our own nothingness, the vanity of all things, etc. (Bossuet, *loc. cit.,* 8, note).

**17.**—The prayer of simplicity, however, has often a *tendency* to simplify itself even with regard to its object, which thus at time becomes to a certain extent unique. The soul is then drawn to content herself with *thinking of God* or of *His presence* in a confused and general manner. It is an affectionate remembrance of God. If this be consoling, the soul feels a sacred flame which burns on gently within her and takes the place of reasonings.

This very special state, the one approaching most nearly to mystic states, is called the **prayer of loving attention to God**. It is important to note that, in this case, other subjects are not excluded; they are merely of a secondary importance. They are intertwined with another and a more persistent subject—the thought of God. This mingling will become still more evident in the prayer of quiet.

This prayer of loving attention to God is nothing else than the exercise of the presence of God, so much recommended by all ascetical writers, only it has this peculiarity, that it is confused and with few or no reasonings. It is not a *meditation* upon the presence of God.

The quietists exaggerated the simplicity of this state.* They went too far also in supposing that all prayer of simple regard must have the confused thought of God for its object. This is one of its kinds only.

Some good writers, such as Courbon, have perpetuated the same error in their classifications. Without actually saying so, or being aware of it, they reduced all prayer of simplicity to this one special variety. Any Christian truth can, however, be considered in this simple way.

**18.—Use of the imagination.** If we feel the need of employing it, nothing hinders our calling in its aid. But it will not then multiply imageries. The picture will usually be blurred and without details.

In the course of the day it may even do us a service in the following manner. If in my morning prayer I have thought of one of Our Lord's virtues, contemplating such or such a scene in His life, it will be sufficient to conjure up this picture amidst my various occupations, and I shall then not only remember Him, but also the virtue in question. This is a sweet and simple manner of prayer.

**19.—Distractions.** Distractions may occur in these states as in discursive prayer.† It is a labour to repulse them. Yet, notwithstanding, these states have been called the *prayer of repose;* but this is merely an allusion to the diminution of reasoning.

**20.—Efforts.** The prayer of simplicity, then, requires efforts at times, especially in order to curtail distractions, just as this is so with the prayer of quiet itself. Everything depends upon the force with which the wind of grace blows. It is the same with meditation. When the vessel's sails are not unfurled, the oars must take their place.

* Even Bossuet seems to force the note slightly in the work quoted from above (8, note), except in No. 8. Further, he goes too far in suggesting that the virtues are born as of themselves from the simple thought of God present. It is excessive to say of this degree, which, after all, is merely ordinary prayer, "The less the creature labours, so much the more powerfully does God operate" (No. 3). Although God does not wish to be hampered in His operations, He expects at least to be aided.

† See St. Teresa's *Life,* ch. ix.

We see, therefore, that, compared with meditation, the prayer of simple regard is not what inertia and absence of effort are to labour, except occasionally and in appearance only; it is merely what uniformity is to variety. In both cases there is action, and energetic action at times. This is often present in intuition when it is well directed and rendered fruitful, just as it is in acts of reasoning.

**21.—Sufferings**. These states are produced, sometimes with consolations, sometimes with aridity (for this last case, see ch. xv). If there is aridity and the soul is unable to meditate, this inaction may be extremely painful. But the soul often suffers, even when the prayer of simplicity is partly consoling. For our own curiosity prefers a variety of ideas, our faculties feel the need of movement like children whom we cannot keep still. The imagination becomes irritated at not being called upon, and goes to seek its diversion elsewhere. And, finally, there is the trial of having to fight against distractions.

In the prayer of quiet, similar sufferings often occur, I will explain them with greater detail when dealing with this state later on.

It is very important to realise that upon quitting the degree of meditation, we enter upon a path which is far from being strewn with roses only, as many people suppose.* Crosses abound. If we are ignorant of this main truth, we shall quickly fall into anxieties and discouragement during our periods of aridity. And then we shall be tempted to abandon our prayer in virtue of such false principles as the following: "If God approved of my praying, or of my praying in any particular manner, He would give me proof of His approval by consolations." Or, "It is simply losing time to continue in such a purgatory, when I might develop my activities so well in another direction" (see ch. xxiv, **58** *bis*).

We often constrain ourselves to continue in a friend's company, even when our subjects of conversation are exhausted. We ought not to depart from God because He seems to hide Himself.

**22.—Question**. How can we say that a state of aridity belongs rather to the prayer of simplicity than to the way of meditation? In both cases there are distractions and incapacity for reasoning; is it not the same thing, therefore?

No. There is this difference, that in the prayer of simplicity there is one dominant thought which returns persistently (see No. 4).

**23.—Fatigue**. This varies from one person to another. It is less in proportion as the action of grace is greater.

**24.—Various degrees of facility**. All alike have not the same facility for affective prayer, and especially for the prayer of simple regard. For a few

* Father de Caussade truly says: "There is nothing more sublime than contemplation as we find it in books; nothing more beautiful or grander than passive prayer in theory. But in practice there is nothing more humiliating, more crucifying" (*Inst. spir., dial.* XII). This writer is probably speaking of the mystic state, but his remarks apply even more to the prayer that we are now considering.

moments together, this latter is quite easy to any soul of good will. For after painfully amassing considerations, the soul is inclined to enjoy them tranquilly, for a few minutes at any rate, and to content herself with a general and confused view of things.

But it is especially important to inquire which are the persons who possess this facility for a longer time. The *complexion of mind,* the *kind of occupations* or of *intellectual culture* may dispose towards it, and then a merely ordinary supply of grace is sufficient. But at other times a stronger grace is required,* on account of the obstacles presented by a certain type of mind, or of the great perfection to which it is approaching. Let us now come to the details.

**25.—Sooner or later** many persons arrive at this manner of prayer, and by a natural process, so to speak. When anyone has made twenty meditations upon death, for instance, the considerations to which he might apply himself upon this subject and all that arises from it, do not interest him any more; he is almost weary of them; or, rather, these considerations would be useless to him. They are present in his memory, and he embraces them *at a glance.* He comes at last to form *general impressions.*† And if we take pleasure in these truths, they return easily to the mind; and this is one of the characteristics of the prayer of simplicity (No. **4**).

It is the same also if we revert daily to two or three virtues, the need of which is more particularly felt.

Or, again, we have formed a habit of connecting all our thoughts with some one saying, or central idea, such as the Passion or the Blessed Sacrament, and we rest in this thought without any great developments. So that, unless we possess a nature overflowing with activity, we come easily enough to the prayer of simple regard, provided that we lend ourselves to it.

St. J.-B. de la Salle, who gives a very good description of this state in his *Explication de la methode d'Oraison* (Part II, ch. i, § 1), alludes to this *progressive* simplification of the soul when, at the conclusion of his explanations upon the "three different ways of applying ourselves to prayer by dwelling upon a mystery, such as the holy presence of God," he says: "They can be brought approximately to the three states of the spiritual life. Conversations by discourse and multiplied reasonings, to that of the beginners; some few reflections, persisted in for a long time, to that of the proficients (or the more advanced); and simple attention to that of the perfect."

* But even so we are not in a mystic state. For this grace merely prolongs or reinforces an act that we can produce at will.

† Hugh of St.-Victor is alluding to the contemplation which is thus acquired when he gives the following definition, adopted by Richard of St.-Victor: "Contemplation is a penetrating gaze, which without any effort embraces several objects simultaneously" (Richard, *De contempl.*, Book I, ch. iv, Migne ed., col. 67).

It is my conviction that many of those who practise mental prayer daily, come, at the end of several years, to the prayer of simplicity, although often without being aware of it.

**26.**—Let us now see who they are that arrive there **fairly rapidly**: 1°. Those who, like St. Teresa,* are endowed with but little memory or imagination. They must perforce be satisfied with small things, and they have no inclination to make any great efforts to acquire that with which nature has dowered them so sparingly.

The prayer of simple regard, on the other hand, is very difficult for those in whom these two faculties are highly developed or who have a restless temperament. A flood of memories, images, and sensible emotions come to them. They find more pleasure in this variety than in a state which is peaceful and monotonous as the desert.

**27.**—2°. It is the same with unlettered, simple souls when they wish to pray mentally, instead of being satisfied with vocal prayers. They have no taste for high considerations. Possessed of but few ideas, only to be nearer to God is happiness to them. It is sufficient for them to love Him. This is the prayer of Magdalen at Our Lord's feet.†

On the other hand, St. Teresa reproaches certain of her confessors, who were great preachers or learned theologians, with their tendency to employ their hours of prayer in composing real sermons, full of texts from Holy Scripture (*Life,* ch. xv). This tendency in certain preachers can be explained. Having the art of developing a subject and the habit of expounding the truths of religion with many considerations and much imagery, they find it easy and pleasant to act in the same manner during prayer. They continue preaching, but to themselves.

Father Balthasar Alvarez knew this temptation to substitute study for prayer, and he dissuaded persons from it, saying: "If we do not emerge from this prayer with fresh thoughts, at least we possess more virtues and are on better terms with God" (*Life,* From the French of Louis du Pont, ch. xli).

**28.**—3°. Loving natures feel attracted towards all practices in which acts of love preponderate over acts of the understanding. And, moreover, the memory of the object love returns frequently of itself.

**29.**—4°. *Women* are generally inclined to a very simple form of mental prayer. St. J. F. de Chantal writes: "Our blessed Father used to say that women had not

* "God never endowed me with the gift of making reflections with the understanding, or with that of using the imagination to any good purpose; my imagination is so sluggish that even if I would think of or picture to myself, as I used to labour to picture, Our Lord's Humanity, I never could do it" (*Life,* ch. iv, 10 and ix, 7).

† St. Francis of Sales makes use of this comparison while applying it more particularly to supernatural ways of prayer. "Behold her" (Magdalen), "I beseech thee, Theotimus: she sighs not, she stirs not, she prays not... and this Divine Love, jealous of this love-sleep and repose of this well-beloved, chides Martha for wanting to awaken her" (*Treatise on the Love of God,* Book VI, ch. viii, Dam Mackey, O.S.B., p. 256).

much capacity for *lofty considerations;* but the we must, however, make all who enter religion begin with these considerations when they are not accustomed to this holy exercise, for that it is very important to impress the truths of religion firmly on their minds at the beginning" (*Réponses sur le Coutumier,* art. 24, Migne ed., col. 233).

And, in fact, if we question women as to the subject of their prayer, we discover that everything is usually summed up in a few words. Instead of making long arguments, they have a happy facility for *continuing for a long time under the impression* of some one idea, and this is very profitable. It is true that in convents, the subject for the morning's meditation is read overnight. But when the hour of prayer comes, it often happens that the nuns do not succeed in developing it; at times, even, there is no inclination to make use of it at all.

**30.**—5°. In the *Contemplative Orders,* where much time is given to prayer, it very soon comes to be simplified. If a continued exercise of the understanding were necessary, the head would quickly become weary.

**31.**—St. Francis of Sales and St. J. F. de Chantal wished all their spiritual daughters to understand the prayer of simplicity and to practise it as far as possible. The results corresponded to this direction. St. J. F. de Chantal wrote: "The more I see, the more I am convinced that Our Lord leads *nearly all* the sisters of the Visitation to the prayer of *simple union,* a simple abiding in the presence of God" (*Réponses sur le Coutumier,* art. 24, translated in the *Life* of St. J. F. de Chantal, Bougaud, Vol. I, p. 446). And elsewhere: "The almost universal attraction of the sisters of the Visitation is a *very simple attention to the presence of God,* and I might well omit the *almost,* for I have remarked that all who apply themselves to prayer as they should, are drawn to it from the very first, and that all who perform their duty with regard to self-mortification and the exercise of the virtues, *arrive there at last.* Many are drawn to it from the outset, and it seems as if God made use of this sole means in order to make us reach the goal and our soul's perfect union with Him. Finally, I hold that this manner of prayer is essential to our little Congregation; and that it is a great gift from God for which we should be infinitely grateful" (*Letter to a Superior,* ed. Plon, Vol. III, p. 337. *Life* by Mgr. Bougaud, ch. xviii).*

* Certain writers have been mistaken in interpreting these passages as referring to the prayer of quiet (understood in St. Teresa's sense). The context of the first quotation clearly proves that it is a question of the prayer of simplicity. For instance, the saint says that great aridities occur in this state, and that "the poor soul can only suffer" (Migne ed., Vol. II, col. 235). This characteristic is not found in the prayer of quiet. And then she says: "The most usual and useful subjects are the Life, Death, Passion, and Resurrection of Our Lord." Now the prayer of quiet is occupied almost wholly with the possession of God.

Let us further remember that the saint published her Réponses in 1632, twenty-two years after the founding of the Congregation, which then numbered fifty-five Houses. Now positive proof would be required before we could admit that almost all the members of such a numerous Society were raised to extraordinary states. It is a question, then, of ordinary prayer, as a whole; a certain number of Sisters only attaining like their saintly Foundress to the mystic state.

The saint says again: "Mgr. de Langres said that he considered that this attraction is so markedly the attraction of the daughters of the Visitation, that he did not think that anyone could really have the Visitation spirit if she was without this attraction to a happy and holy interior simplicity" (*Œuvres,* ed. Plon., 1875, Vol. II. *Entretien* 36, *sur la fidélité à suivre l'attrait de la grâce pendant l'oraison*).

**32.**—If, on the other hand, which God forbid, the **Directors** of a Community were prejudiced and had an aversion for this kind of prayer, the result would probably be that they would make it less common. This would not be so, I admit, if the persons concerned merely resisted the attraction in good faith and through obedience. They would then escape with the loss only of their peace of soul during the prolonged struggle. But we go beyond this as a rule. Not knowing that we are receiving a gift at God's hands, we take no interest in it, and become careless over the removal of the obstacles that it encounters in our lives. It is this negligence that God punishes by diminishing His graces. The director has been the occasion only; the real fault lies with us.

**32** *bis.*—* 6°. The brevity of the prayer or other circumstances may have the effect of facilitating simple prayers—*at certain moments,* at any rate. Here are some examples: (*a*) Those who make a short visit to the Blessed Sacrament do not, as a rule, think of going through any set meditation or of reciting a vocal prayer. They continue tranquilly and lovingly in the thought that God or Our Blessed Lord is there present. This is already the prayer of *simple regard,* although of short duration. We have not here the more complicated case of a daily half-hour or hour of prayer (see 52). (*b*) It is often the same during the thanksgiving after Communion, when the Mass has been preceded by mental prayer. For a certain fatigue has resulted, which tends to repose and justifies it. (*c*) Nuns who recite a Latin Office without understanding it can neither occupy their minds with what they are reading nor follow any other connected train of thought, but they often think of God in a confused way, and with love. This will be the prayer of simplicity.

**33.**—We have now said enough to show that our **natural dispositions** and mode of life have an influence upon the nature of our prayer. We shall not be surprised, therefore, to find that one person should have passed on at once to affective prayer, having had hardly any acquaintance with the prayer of meditation, and that another should have arrived at certain other degrees without having first gone through all those that were intermediary.

**34.**—In order to **facilitate the practice of affective prayer**, it is as well to do as St. Ignatius did, and to take as subjects for prayer, not the abstract virtues, but the historic facts that teach these virtues. When we meditate on any Mystery of Our Lord's life, it is easy to make the affections predominate by

* In my second preface [p. 572, No. 1] I explained my reason for introducing numbers bis.

testifying our respect, love, gratitude or compassion to Our Saviour or His Blessed Mother, and holding "colloquies" with them.

We can also establish a certain order in the sentiments that we try to excite. To produce affections is really to make interior acts of certain virtues; we shall therefore draw up a list of virtues appropriate to our needs. We begin, for instance, by acts of faith, hope, or charity towards God and our neighbour. We then go on to contempt of self, resignation, zeal, love of regularity, etc.; or the four ends of the holy sacrifice of the Mass: adoration, thanksgiving, petitions for pardon and for graces.

### § 3. Advantages of These Prayers. Real or Apparent Drawbacks.

**35.**—The advantages of **affective prayer**. If we compare it with prayer in which the considerations predominate, we see that it is usually superior; for, all other things being equal, *its effect upon the conduct is greater,* and it leads more quickly to perfection.

1°. The difficulty arising in the practice of the virtues proceeds, as a rule, less from a want of knowledge than from a lack of faith, hope, or love. The will is weak; we must begin, therefore, by arousing its activity.

2°. And then the virtues are acquired by a repetition of their acts rather than by reflections; and, finally, these acts are more meritorious than those of the understanding.

**35** *bis.*—3°. In this kind of prayer we not only throw off the inertia of the will, but we dwell on certain sentiments and develop them. Now, present-day psychologists have shown the great importance of feelings from the point of view of action.* A mere idea is not usually sufficient to urge us to action. "Motor-ideas" (*idées-forces*) are ideas accompanied by one or more feelings.† Example: The simple thought of death does not drive men to be converted, unless at the same time they experience the terror of knowing it to be imminent. If we are overtaken by a feeling of slothfulness when we ought to rise in the morning or perform some tiresome duty, it is not sufficient to see that we are wrong; we remain inert. But if we are afraid of being reproved, we act at once without arguing the matter; and thus one feeling triumphs over another. This is understood in the Religious Orders; you find small rules with regard to supervision which may be rather irksome, but which prevent slackness. The fear of an admonition intensifies the feeling of duty.

* We have many feelings, as we have many tastes, habits, needs, and passions. The one are the expressions of the other.

† In his *Exercises* St. Ignatius seeks to give, not only strong convictions, but energetical feelings.

4°. Union with God, wherein holiness lies, is, above all, a union of the will. A method in which the acts of the will are more numerous or more interior, leads most rapidly to the goal,* the soul's activity being less absorbed by the reason.

We must not exaggerate this doctrine, however, by despising the considerations. For they are indispensable in order to excite the will, more especially in the case of a soul that is not yet penetrated with a horror of sin and has not understood that certain virtues, such as prompt obedience, mortification, meekness, and devotion, are essential. The motives for their practice must be insisted upon. If the acts of the will are the end, those of the understanding are the means. Prayer is a banquet, whence the soul derives her strength; but it is the understanding that serves up the viands.

In order to reconcile these conflicting requirements, all we have to do is to avoid giving the considerations the principal part.

**36.**—The advantages of the **prayer of simplicity**. In order to judge whether it is superior to the preceding degrees, let us examine it from the point of view of the three elements that it contains: knowledge, affections, and resolutions. The conclusion will be that it may be advantageous or the reverse, according to the individual case, and that it must not therefore be adopted blindly when we have the power of choice.

**37.**—From the point of view of **knowledge**, the prayer of simplicity is not always better than discursive prayer. If it is to have its full utility, the person must be *instructed* with regard to the duties of the spiritual life, *habituated* to their practice, and in *actual dispositions* to make use of what he has learned and to sanctify himself.

If these conditions are fulfilled, a host of useful memories will come back to the mind during the prayer. The ideas are not really fewer, nor less deep than in meditation; but they present themselves in a simpler, more condensed, more intuitive form, and the need to translate them into words is less felt. It is just as a man, who is well versed in any science, takes in a crowd of facts at one glance. You would not call that an inferiority.

This advantage does not accrue if the person is not instructed in the virtues, as happens with *beginners*. The mind finds nothing to gather up. And, on the other hand, as they make no effort to enter deeply into the subject of the meditation, they learn almost nothing during the time of prayer. We must not expect that God will make up for our deficiencies. For in this degree He does not usually intervene, like a professor, to teach us new truths. He is content to

* "It is very important," says Father Rodriguez, "*to continue for a long time in the affectionate movements* of the will: and the masters of the spiritual life say that prayer arrives at a sovereign degree of perfection when we no longer try to excite the love of God in our hearts by way of meditation, but when the heart, penetrated with this love, for which it yearned, rejoices in it and reposes in it as the goal of all its endeavours and desires" (*Practice of Christian Perfection: On Prayer,* ch. xii).

aid us, by means of ordinary grace, to *remember* acquired truths.* And so, with those whose knowledge of spiritual things is not of a high order, these prayers will be a means of progress with regard to the will, not with regard to instruction.

**38.**—But because these kinds of prayer afford less instruction than meditation, it does not follow that they are to be forbidden if God seems to be calling the soul to practise them. For it is very easy to give instruction outside the hours of prayer, by readings, sermons, and conversations. There will thus be certain hours for study, and others, again, in which the soul can give herself up to the Divine love. And the readings will also furnish useful material for the time of prayer.

**39.**—2°. **Affections**. Under this aspect the prayer of simplicity has the same advantages as affective prayer, and for the same reasons.

**40.**—3°. **Resolutions** and the practice of the virtues. From this point of view, the prayer of simplicity is as powerful as meditation, provided that the person is instructed and established in virtue. For it produces acts of the love of God. Now this love will incite the soul to abnegation. It would be gross ignorance to believe that we could stop short at fine sentiments. The true love of God shows itself by *detachment* from all that is not God: by detachment from our comforts and by devotion to others, detachment from the world's esteem, etc. These practical conclusions will be drawn spontaneously, so to speak, even during our prayers. For the sake of depreciating the prayer of simplicity, do not let us regard it as some fantastic thing in which we love God without perceiving or desiring the requirements of this love. Let us stick to the concrete. The word simplicity must not, as I have already said, be taken in its absolute sense. If the person is not well grounded in the necessity for abnegation, let him be instructed apart from his prayer, as in the case of other things.

**41.—First objection**. Many writers do not make the above restriction when they speak of the prayer of simple regard, which they describe under the name of contemplation (see ch. iv. They proclaim its absolute superiority over discursive prayer, and they are not, therefore, in full accord with you.

**42.—Reply.** The divergence is probably apparent only, and this may proceed from three causes:—

1°. Without drawing attention to it, these writers are studying this state from the *philosophic* standpoint; and then their thesis is correct. For they merely intend to say that intuition is superior to reason, and that a mode of knowledge resembling that of the angels is more perfect than that which is habitual to man.

* Some writers fall into exaggerations when they speak of the "admirable lights" that the soul receives in this prayer (see ch. xvi, 36. Literature is inclined to embellish everything. But if these authors had wished to be quite accurate, they would have said that when speaking thus they had certain exceptional souls in view.

But what I, on the other hand, have looked at, is the *practical side,* which is the most useful: progress in the spiritual life, that is to say.

2°. Or, again, these writers rightly regard the prayer of simplicity as being, in certain respects, a preparation for mystic prayers. This is an advantage, but it does not follow that this state is *always* more fruitful than its predecessor. It will be so only if we are thoroughly acquainted with our road and if our goodwill is maintained and fortified.

3°. Finally these writers often imply that the simple regard is produced by a great abundance of light, and that the contrary occurs in discursive prayer. But it is not always so, and we can perfectly imagine that the reverse should be the case. In order to compare two different degrees, we must not take one in its state of light and warmth, and the other in its dark and cold state.

**43.**—There is a **second objection** to affective prayer, and to the prayer of simplicity in particular, and this one is quite a classic: namely, that we waste our time, that we remain in a state of idleness.

**44.**—**Reply.** This is so in appearance only, and is due to superficial observation. We do *exactly the same things as in meditation.* The soul works, therefore, only more simply, more gently, less visibly at first sight, but the work done is no less real.*

Let us not confuse these prayers, which aim at the definite goal of our sanctification, with reverie. This latter is a state of relaxation of our energies, in which we abandon ourselves, like a ship without a rudder, to every current, whether of images or feelings. It results in nothing; it is simply repose.

But let us study a case where the objection appears to have more force: that of the prayer of loving attention to God, which, as we have seen (17), is one special kind of the prayer of simplicity. Let us suppose that for some appreciable time—a quarter of an hour, for instance—this prayer is made without any difficulty or admixture of anything else, with the exception of a few distractions. We should then be content to love God without adding any other special acts, such as acts of humility, petitions, etc., and also without making any practical applications or receiving any light upon our conduct. This extreme case is probably not realisable, but we will imagine it. I say that, even then, it is not time lost, if, as I have supposed (**37**), we are sufficiently well-grounded in spiritual matters.

In fact, in order to regulate our conduct satisfactorily outside the time of prayer, two things are necessary: to know what we ought to do in some particular case, and to have the will and the strength to carry it out. In the prayer of meditation we pursue both these ends simultaneously; but nothing hinders our separating the two operations; and this is just what occurs in the state that we are now examining. We have, in part, relegated the instructions to

* For those who confuse the prayer of simplicity with Quietist practices see 60 (second and third rule) and ch. iv., 10.

some other time, and we are satisfied to give free play to the will by penetrating ourselves with the love of God, which must necessarily include general dispositions to self-devotion and sacrifice.

Let us add that the vitality given to the will by the prayer of simplicity will not, perhaps, be perceived at once. So under the sun's action, a vast work of growth goes on in the meadows and forests; and yet all these hidden sources of life do their part slowly and in silence. All those million molecules of sap circulate like a crowd of workmen engaged in the construction of a house. So with the prayer of simplicity, the soul is a field exposed to the Divine Sun. The growth carried on is a silent one, but it is a real work. We shall see that something analogous, but more striking, occurs in the mystic state.

**44** *bis.*—Since the above objection is unfounded, how can we explain its being so widespread, and why does it arise so readily to the mind? Here are some reasons.

1°. It is the result of a prejudice. We often imagine that work is identical with noise. But is the artist whose brush travels silently over the canvas less busy than the blacksmith who deafens us with his activity?

We fancy that we are thinking and accomplishing a great deal when we are conscious of a wealth of words and of material images. But if this activity of the inferior order diminishes, as often happens when our prayer becomes higher, it is then more difficult to take note of our thoughts, and so we wrongly conclude that we have almost ceased to think and have sunk into a state of sloth. A certain void is indeed produced, for particular things have diminished; but these are merely the gross auxiliaries of thought, the form that it has borrowed from the senses, and not thought itself. This latter has become more spiritual, but less easy of apprehension. A bottle seems empty when only filled with air; and so does the sky when it is clear and cloudless. And yet air is not nothingness.

2°. Here is a second prejudice: It is supposed that, in order to act in a holy manner, it is absolutely necessary to formulate very distinct resolutions in prayer. But many persons do not feel the need of this. All that is necessary is that they should develop general dispositions to generosity. They continue for a long time under their influence, and then, at the proper moment, the general impulse of all their faculties carries them promptly and, as it were, instinctively to action. Even when a man wishes to forecast everything in detail, how many unforeseen actions are still performed each day, resulting from a totality of circumstances that it would be difficult to analyse!

We must clearly understand that our *numerous and quite distinct* reflexions do not constitute our only sources of action. We have a striking example of this fact in the imitative instinct. We are carried away, almost forcibly at times, to imitate those to whom we are attracted or whose company we frequent; and this without any reasoning. This obscure but efficacious tendency is utilised in the spiritual life when we read the lives of the saints or take the Life and Passion of Our Lord as a subject of prayer. If we love our Divine Master ardently, we then feel ourselves impelled to become better, to imitate His virtues, to unite ourselves to His sufferings. It is well, I admit, to strengthen this instinctive action by reasoning, if we can do so without difficulty. But it is not necessary for everyone; and this is a point to be remembered. It is this, so it seems to me, of which the opponents of the prayer of simplicity have not taken sufficient notice.

It is the same with our habits, our passions, and our various needs. They cause us to act more or less automatically; and therefore all prayer, in which the desire to please God grows stronger, will become almost unconsciously the source of a host of virtuous actions. It will create the necessary disposition of mind without resorting much to distinct resolutions. When we think of the sea, we always picture to ourselves a succession of waves, which rise, follow one another, and then subside; but this is the surface only. They cover immense depths. But our imagination does not weave its dreams about them, because those things only take hold of it that have well-differentiated parts. It is the same when I observe my soul. The distinct acts are the things that seem of importance in her. But these are, on the contrary, mere surface groupings, visible but transient. Underneath lies the intimate, the permanent, and the great source of action.

From what has just been said we must not conclude that definite resolutions are useless, but simply that we ought not to be disturbed when we experience difficulty in producing them.

3°. The fact that the prayer of simplicity is sometimes called the prayer of repose has helped to promote the above objection; for the name seems to indicate a state of idleness. But this would be to exaggerate the meaning that the word repose was intended to convey. Father de Caussade explains it: "We must know that the mind and the heart do not rest as the body rests, by ceasing to act, but rather by continuing to act in a simpler, gentler manner which delights the soul" (*Dialogues,* Book II, preliminary *Dialogue*). He adds the comparison of the miser or ambitious man, who, "when they allow their hearts and minds to rest," do not cease to act and are not idle, but go on thinking of the object of their affection and growing more and more attached to it.

4°. Finally, this objection is naturally provoked when the expression, prayer of simplicity, is taken too literally. As I have explained (5), I do not pretend that the simplicity is rigorous and that it lasts for an hour at a time. There are many moments when the faculties are employed as in ordinary meditation, and where they work, therefore, in the usual way. Why, then, do we still call this exercise by the name of prayer of simplicity? It is because there are no words to describe these blendings of the various states and all their thousand shades. We are forced to name it by its *general tendency,* by some characteristic that strikes the attention at certain moments.

The opponents of the prayer of simplicity forget all these restrictions, however evident they may be. They conjure up an ideal state, one that is superhuman and deprived of all that makes it useful. And then it is fair game for their condemnations. But let us take things as they exist in real life.

**45.—Continuation of the objection**. Agreed, then, it will be said, that the soul is usefully occupied in this prayer. But is it the *best* way of spending our time? Is not meditation more profitable?

**46.—Reply**. I have shown above that this is not so, provided that certain conditions are fulfilled (**37**). Do not let us judge of the efficacy of a method by the complication of the means that it employs. David had nothing but his sling in his contest with Goliath; but he knew how to use it. If he had been obliged to wear Saul's cuirasse, casque, and buckler, he would have been greatly hampered.

But let us even admit that at certain times the prayer of simplicity may be so mingled with distractions that it appears to be of little utility. Would it then be better to return to meditation, properly so called?

Yes, if you can do so. But, as a rule, not only would the soul feel distaste, but she would experience a great difficulty. This, as we shall see shortly (**54**), is an unequivocal sign that the prayer of simple regard is the result of a divine action. And if this is so, it is clear that this occupation is the better, even when we fail to explain how. Otherwise God would be inviting us, or even constraining us, to a state that is less favourable to the production of virtues.

**47.—Unfavourably disposed directors**. When directors offer the objection that I have just discussed, it is sometimes the fault of the penitent, who does not express himself clearly. For instance, he will say: "I hardly do anything in my prayer," or, "I am satisfied with just loving God in it." The director, unless he has studied these questions, does not know how to supplement this information, and can only reply: "Since your prayer is without any real profit to you, return to meditation."

Hence we see the necessity of instructing penitents, so that they may learn how to explain their state of soul clearly.

**48.**—We come to the same conclusion when we see that persons who are given to prayer are apt to put the same objections to themselves. As long as it has not been explained to them why the way that they are in is good, they are racked with apprehensions. They constantly resist their attractions. Thence follow **interior sufferings**. It is a duty to give them back their peace of mind by dispelling their prejudices. If, for instance, their only facility is for a vague and loving attention to God, we must teach them to be content with it.

**49.—Another difficulty**. Novices, and even some formed Religious, are obliged to give an account of their prayer, either privately to their Superior or director, or sometimes in public. And this, if their prayer is very simple, becomes an anxiety to them. Seeing others indulging in magnificent developments, they are ashamed of their apparent poverty; and instead of passing the hours devoted to prayer in loving God, without very many distinct ideas, they struggle to produce beautiful thoughts. St. Jane Frances de Chantal condemns this conduct (see the quotations, **80**, 4°); also Boudon (*Le Règne del Dieu en l'Oraison mentale,* Book I, ch. iii).

If a description of your prayer takes two sentences only, do not try to say more about it; the Superior should not be surprised.

**50.**—Can it be said that the acts of love which are made during the prayer of *the simple presence of God* **contain implicitly** and in an eminent degree the acts of the other virtues?

Not always; not even in the prayer of quiet, which is, however, higher than it. This expression, which we find in some ancient writers, should not be taken too literally. They mean to say that divine love is the source of the other virtues, that it gives a disposition to practise them; but it is not itself their actual equivalent, for each virtue has its special object which differs from that of charity.

Or, again, these writers suppose, without actually stating it, that the simplicity of this prayer is approximate only, and that reflexions upon the various virtues and their motives may be found here, although in an obscure manner.

The quietists, on the contrary, took literally this maxim, that their contemplation, reduced almost to nothing, was a unique act, comprising "eminently" all the others, and consequently dispensing with all the others. They sought in this way to justify their simplifications which were carried to excess.

There is a simple and natural way of avoiding illusions on this point. It is: not to analyse our prayers incessantly, but to watch our external conduct. If interior acts of certain virtues have been produced, at least implicitly, during our prayer, they will make themselves apparent afterwards—spontaneously, as it were—when the occasion offers. If there is a seed, it will develop.

**51.**—We have compared methodical prayer with that of simplicity. Some persons resort to **exaggerated arguments** for the sake of dispensing themselves from the first. "What a complication!" they say. "When confronted with a subject, I could never force myself to apply the *three powers* of the soul (the memory, the understanding, and the will) to it successively. I want to go straight to God. How could I ever resign myself to that string of *preludes, compositions of place, colloquies,* etc.* The paraphernalia is too cumbrous; it

* These operations are found under different names in all the methods.

The teaching of these processes is not, as has been sometimes supposed, the chief object of St. Ignatius' *Exercises.* This book is intended for a thirty days' Retreat, and presupposes a man with a certain desire to be generous towards God, but kept back either by ignorance with regard to the means to be taken, or by his weakness. The *Exercises* are skilfully combined for his gradual development in generosity, and, if he is capable of it, his being led on to heroism. This ingenious plan may escape the notice of a superficial reader; it is only really understood by those who submit to it, even to its apparently most insignificant details. This arrangement, where everything is ordered with reference to a special object, gives its character to the book, and makes it unlike any that went before.

With St. Ignatius, instruction in mental prayer is but a secondary object, or a means. We can imagine that a man might go through the *Exercises* and afterwards confine himself to vocal prayer, but he would, weighs the soul down, I have no sympathy with those preachers who give retreats and think themselves obliged to teach us so many learned operations which were never heard of in ancient times."

I reply that all these things are more complicated in theory than in practice; as is the case with all treatises on rhetoric or logic. We find many learned words that really express perfectly simple operations which we are performing every day of our lives without giving any attention to them. But we do them better when we have an explicit knowledge of their meaning and have isolated them by analysis. Preachers and authors are right, therefore, in teaching them, in distinguishing these different acts and giving them names which help to make the distinction permanent. This done, I like to believe that they remember to inform you that *in practice you can proceed in the way that suits you best.*

Nothing, for instance, obliges you, as you suppose, to employ the three faculties *successively*. If this seems complicated to you, then use them all simultaneously. It will be a very simple method of prayer, and I defy you to simplify it further. For in all mental prayer we are obliged to remember, to think, and to will.

I could show that the other words which have alarmed you, express acts that have been known from time immemorial, and that you yourselves perform them instinctively. Only you separate them very slightly or not at all, and are scarcely conscious of them. However, since this simplification succeeds in your case, no one thinks of condemning it. But others will prefer to unravel these acts, and they must be allowed to do so.

To sum up, it is useful to have learnt the theory; and it is necessary to have liberty in applying it.

### § 4. Rules of Conduct for Daily Mental Prayer.

**52.—Marks of a vocation**. The first problem that a Director is often obliged to solve is the following: Given a person who habitually practises affective prayer or the prayer of simple regard, what are the signs by which he can decide that this prayer is in all probability due to God's action, and that the soul must consequently be allowed to continue in this way? We are supposing that it is a question of a daily half-hour or hour (see **7**).

**53.**—There are **two signs** which are necessary and sufficient: *success* and the *profit* derived afterwards from the prayer. *

notwithstanding this, have obtained the principal result of this long retreat. The important point is reformation of life.

The truth is that he has learnt at the same time how to pray; and that he has thus acquired a powerful means of ensuring perseverance in well doing.

* As a rule these signs may be applied to a spiritual exercise of any kind whatever, when we have previously satisfied ourselves that it is good in itself. This is precisely the case here.

First, success in prayer. There should be a *facility* for this exercise, and the soul should succeed with it at least, *as well as with meditation.*

Next, as to the profit derived from it outside our prayer. This prayer should excite, in no less a degree, at any rate, than in meditation, a sincere desire for perfection and the practice of virtue. This characteristic does not make itself patent in a day.

The more these signs are accentuated, the more manifest will be the divine action.

Note well that I have not said that the success and the profit should be considerable, but only that these should be as much as in the case of the former methods. We must compare the soul with herself, not with others who are led by a different way.

**54.—Two supplementary signs**. The fact of its being God's call will be placed beyond doubt, if the facility is accompanied by one of the two following sentiments: a persistent *attraction* for these prayers; and *difficulty* and *distaste* for meditation.

These signs would not appear to be indispensable.*

Many writers, I own, seem to admit the contrary. But perhaps they have not thought of distinguishing between the strictly necessary conditions and those which are supererogatory. Or, again, they suppose, implicitly, that in practice these sentiments are almost always united, that they form one inseparable whole, as it were. Perhaps they are right.†

However this may be, the two first signs alone should suffice to prevent us from disturbing those who practise these prayers. If anyone is succeeding in a holy occupation and profiting by it, what reason can we give for turning him aside from it? In the natural order, when a person consults us with regard to entering some honourable profession, we say he is acting wisely if he adopts one for which he has an *aptitude* and which is *profitable* to him. By analogy we ought to act in the same way in the choice of things appertaining to the supernatural order.

Courbon calls our attention to the fact that in these passings from one degree to the other, three dangers are to be avoided: the first, that of being unwilling to quit the degree in which we have hitherto been; the second, of quitting it too late; the third, of quitting it too soon (Part II, ch. i).

* Such is Bossuet's advice: "I am quite persuaded that in giving ourselves up to faith alone, which of its nature is not discursive or reasoning, we can cause the discourses to cease, *without being powerless to make them.* This state is good and in conformity to St. Paul's teaching; for he did not ask for reasonings but for faith alone. When I find a Christian, therefore, who, *without being in this state of inability to discourse* or *without thinking himself to be in it, prays without discoursing,* I shall have nothing to say to him except this: that he should have confidence and live on in peace" (Letter to Mme. de Maisonfort, Vivès-Lachat ed.. Vol. XXVII, p. 322).

† I say perhaps, because it is a question of fact, which can only be decided by experience. And no writer has discussed it.

**55.**—When anyone believes himself to be in the prayer of simplicity, an **embarrassing situation** may arise: that in which the simple prayer is very arid and beset with many distractions. The two first signs mentioned above are scarcely apparent any more. What do the other two, then, prove? Does the powerlessness that is experienced proceed from God's action? Should we not rather attribute it to negligence, sloth, or general fatigue?

**56.—Reply.** We shall always know what to do when it is a question of fatigue, and should remedy it as best we can by the usual means.

But as for the charge of idleness, we must not be in too much of a hurry to make it. As has been said (**53**), from the moment that efforts to meditate cease to give better results, either during the time of prayer or in the external conduct, there is no cause for anxiety. And this is so more obviously still if the person, whom we suppose to be sincere and of good-will, declares that in order to apply himself to a variety of reasonings, efforts exhausting from their continuity would be required. To refuse to make a slight effort would be sloth, but this is no longer so when we recoil before some crushing burden. We do not say, "I will not," but "I cannot."

**57.—Objection.** Yes; but is not this last statement usually based upon an illusion? Such an impossibility may be apparent only? It is simply torpor. They would overcome it if they would rouse themselves and take their spiritual progress strongly to heart. Perhaps it is just this that God desires?

**58.—Reply.** To urge people on to exertion is all very well as a general argument. The call to effort is excellent, always provided, however, that the result obtained is better, and the fatigue temporary only. But in the case of many persons, these double conditions would not be fulfilled. They would have been disquieted without any serious advantage, and by striving to avoid sloth will have become so jaded as to be unable to do anything more. This is what we arrive at by a system of: *exert yourself, no matter what results.*

The same difficulty occurs with regard to study and mortification. When anyone believes that he is really doing as much as he can, he is often led to ask himself if he could not do more. And yet we must pause somewhere. Unhappily, there is no chalk line showing the boundary where wisdom advises us to stop short. This is a question of moral appreciation, of good-will and sincerity before God. Love God, and you will find the wise medium.

**59.—Another case.** Sometimes the person does not know how to explain in what his mental prayer consists. What should the Director do? He should not seek for a clearness that is impossible of attainment. It is enough if he knows that the person is honestly doing what he can, in his prayer, and whether he derives any good from it. Such a method is simple and sufficient.

**60.—Three rules of conduct** with regard to difficulty in meditation. They apply to the prayer of simplicity. All writers agree in admitting them.

We inquired just now how we were to know if God has called the soul to this state. We will suppose that the reply is in the affirmative, and we have therefore to decide upon a line of conduct.

*First rule,* concerning those acts for which no inclination or facility is experienced *during prayer* (reflections, vocal prayer, petitions, etc.): never to force ourselves to produce them, but to rest content with the prayer of simplicity (which by supposition is successful).

The motive of this rule is, that to act differently would be to thwart the action of grace.

*Second rule,* concerning those acts for which, on the contrary, we have a facility *during prayer:* to yield to this inclination instead of insisting upon continuing inactive.

The reason is that all our faculties are not too many when we want to attain to God. When we can do so, let us make use of the intellect, the memory, and imagination. We only discard these powers when we find a difficulty in exercising them.

To sum up, there are two contrary excesses to be avoided: forcing ourselves to perform a variety of acts, seeing in these acts the ideal prayer; and compelling ourselves systematically to repose, as the quietists do.

With regard to these questions, see St. Francis of Sales' replies to St. J. F. de Chantal (*Life* of the saint, by Mgr. Bougaud, Vol. I, ch. xviii; *Life* of Father Balthasar Alvarez, from the French of Louis du Pont, especially ch. xli. See also Extracts, No. **83**).

*Third rule* to be followed outside the time of prayer, properly so called: to profit by all opportunities either of getting instruction or of arousing the will; and thus to supplement anything that might be lacking in the prayer itself.

**61.**—The second rule can be laid down in another form: namely, that **we must not make any efforts** to introduce ourselves into the prayer of simplicity. This is what the orthodox writers of the seventeenth century expressed by saying that we should "not meddle with it" (ne pas s'y ingérer). The quietists held the contrary opinion.

We ought not, therefore, to say to ourselves: "*I will try* systematically to suppress all distinct acts, even those that I could make easily, such as various acts of praise, thanksgiving, repentance, petition, love, etc.; and I will compel myself to be content with the simple attention to God with a gaze of love." Besides the fact that it would be very difficult to carry out if we were not impelled to it by grace, these efforts, produced solely by our own exertions, would lead to a prayer which would be of no advantage to us. It is profitable only if it is the result of divine influence. We should then fall into a deplorable state of lukewarmness; we should no longer think of practising the different virtues outside of our hours of prayer.

And this error would be still more grave if a whole community of religious were *pressed* to make *efforts* in order to introduce themselves into this degree of prayer. In fact, we have seen that in order to practise it as a frequent state we must be called thereto by God (**52**). It follows, therefore, that we must not force anyone to it, and, above all, a whole community. The members have not all, usually, the same vocation with regard to prayer; do not let us divert them from their own way. It is enough that these souls should have sufficient instruction to keep them from impeding the divine grace *if it should please God to act.* We should therefore confine ourselves to giving them this instruction.

**62.**—In order **to apply** the rules given above, it might be well to imbue ourselves with those still more detailed which will be given in chapter xiv, on the ligature. They are drawn up, it is true, with reference to the prayer of quiet, but that is analogous, only more clearly accentuated than this prayer.*

We will merely say that when anyone has become aware that he is often in the prayer of simplicity, he should have no scruples about curtailing certain vocal prayers *which are not of obligation* if he finds a difficulty in continuing them, or if he sees that by replacing them with a less varied prayer he unites himself better to God. "In prayer," says St. Thomas, "we should make use of vocal prayers and other outward signs of the same sort only in so far as they excite interior devotion. But if, by these exercises, the mind is distracted, or if we experience a certain restraint (*si mens qualitercumque impediatur*), we must give them up. This is especially the case with those who find themselves sufficiently disposed to devotion without having any need of such preliminaries" (2. 2. q. 83, a. 12, c).

There are persons who think they are acting rightly by forcing themselves to a variety of acts in mental prayer. St. Ignatius gives the opposite advice. "If any particular point causes me to experience the grace which I am seeking, I must remain there calmly until my devotion is satisfied, without caring for anything more" (*Exercises, First week,* add. 4). The souls who are called thereto by God are thus directed gently onwards to affective prayer or the prayer of simplicity. For this continued dwelling upon one thought has not merely the effect of making us enter into it more profoundly; it leads us to perform it with greater *affection* or *intuition.* And so he also recommends a return to anything (such as considerations or affections) which in the preceding meditation should have brought most consolation or compunction (*First week, Exercise* 3. See also *Annot.* 2; *Fourth week, notant.* 2; 2nd manner of prayer, and then rule 2). It is a remarkable thing, and one that leads necessarily to the same end, that the saint wishes a considerable part of the five daily meditations to be made up of repetitions. He includes two a day at the beginning of the first week, and three

* St. John of the Cross tells us that the rules which he has given for passive or "perfect" contemplation are applicable, not to it alone, but to another kind which is less elevated also; that is to say, "to the whole of that time in which Our Lord communicates the simple, general, and loving attention, of which I have made mention before, or when the soul, assisted by grace, is established in that state" (*Ascent of Mount Carmel,* Book II, ch. xxxii, p. 204).

during the two following weeks. The last is always an "application of the senses."*

**63.—Efforts.** Certain writers recommend occasional pauses in mental prayer, which advice resolves itself into making efforts to arrive at the prayer of simplicity. But this counsel should be taken with a restriction: the pauses should come so easily that they are rather accepted than induced.† For this kind of prayer must be left to come spontaneously without any actual effort on our part (**60**). And this will be so if God calls us to it, and if our prejudices oppose no obstacle in the way of the divine action.

Obviously, also, the pauses consist, not in doing nothing, but in acting with a greater simplicity.

**64.**—When we are in these degrees, should we **prepare the subject** of our prayer?

In the case of affective prayer, there can be no doubt of it. For it deals with special subjects which may vary from day to day.

In the case of the prayer of simple regard, we should clearly say the same if the subject is often changed. There is difficulty only when it always consists in the prayer of loving attention to God. I say that in nearly every case it is better to advise that the subject should be prepared beforehand; because, as I have already said, this loving remembrance of God is not so exclusive but that a crowd of other, secondary, ideas may mingle with it. It is necessary to supply food for this activity.

There is an exception in one case only: where *long experience* has shown that such prepared subjects are *absolutely useless,* while our own thoughts furnish us with sufficient occupation, and the practical conclusion with regard to conduct follows spontaneously. But this condition must be of rare occurrence, save in certain mystic states. The prayer of simplicity has no such pretensions.

Even in this extreme case it would be better to come to prayer with something equivalent to a preparation. It is not necessary to make a different one every day. It is sufficient to have some thoughts in readiness, and to be able to make use of them, if necessary, during the first few moments, at any rate.

* And thus we come more and more to operate "cum affectu et simplici intuitu," as Fr. Louis de la Palma, provincial of Madrid, says, in his *Praxis vitæ spiritualis,* 1634. See also Suarez, *De relig., Soc. Jesu* (Book IX, ch. vi, No. 11).

† Bossuet is often quoted as urging these pauses (*États d'oraison,* Vol. VII, No. 10). But the context shows that he is referring to those that are produced spontaneously. Like Fr. Balthasar Alvarez, whose teaching he is summing up, he is thinking of the mystic state only. Now in this state, the repose is merely accepted. And Fr. B. Alvarez also explains his meaning elsewhere. "To discontinue the reasonings upon particular truths, for the time being, is not to tempt God... These reasonings, possible at other times, are not so then" (*Life,* ch. xli, *second difficulty*). Courbon (Part III, end of ch. vi) advises these pauses, but in quite a different case. He is speaking of vocal prayer only, and suggests certain pauses in order to avoid a mere routine recital and to favour recollection. I think Fr. de Caussade (*Instruct.,* Part II, dial. v) insists too much upon this method of pauses and their being made systematically.

St. Francis of Sales had to consider this question. Mother Mary of the Trinity, prioress of the Carmelites of Dijon, had advised St. J. F. de Chantal not to go on preparing her meditation.* She probably believed her to have arrived at the prayer of simplicity. The Bishop of Geneva disapproved of this direction, however. In a letter of June 11th, 1610, that is to say, shortly before St. J. F. de Chantal gave up living in the world, he wrote to her thus: "To make a practice of making no preparation seems to me to be going too far... this may be done usefully at times, but that it should be the rule does not, I confess, appeal to me."

**65.**—Courbon mentions a **temptation** that may assail those who have attained to the prayer of simplicity. This is "to devote little or no time to prayer, on the pretext that they are always at prayer, no matter what their occupations may be." They even fancy "that they pray better as they come and go about their work."

But these persons must understand "that the loving attention in which their prayer consists needs fortifying, because it is continually diminishing in process of time, just as a spring becomes gradually weakened by use. For *this attention is assailed* by a multitude of others which it is impossible to avoid while we are in action. It therefore requires to be brought back again and re-established; and this all takes place during the hours which are specially consecrated to prayer" (Part III, ch. ix).

### § 5. General Survey of the History of Mental Prayer.

**66.**—Before the fifteenth century, or even the sixteenth, the usage of methodical mental prayer—prayer, that is to say, where the *subject, method,* and *duration* are determined—is not traceable in the Church.†

In order to avoid all misunderstandings I insist upon this point: that it is solely a question here of methodical mental prayer, and not of that without fixed rules; made when you choose, for as long as you feel the attraction, or on a subject chosen according to the inspiration of the moment. It is clear that from all times persons have reflected with this freedom on the truths of salvation, and

* *Life* of the Saint by Mgr. Bougaud, Vol. I, ch. x, 2nd ed.

† The Carthusians, however, appear to have had a time set apart for mental prayer from the first (see *Patrologia latina,* Migne ed., Vol. CLIII, col. 699, 701, *Guigonis consuetudines*). *Points for meditation* are suggested at the close of the fifteenth century by Jean Mombaer of Brussels (Mauburnus), died in Paris 1502 (*Meditatorium membrum,* 3). He belonged to the pious association of the *Brothers of the Common Life,* founded by Gerard de Groote at the end of the fourteenth century, and which spread from the Low Countries to Germany and Italy. Thomas à Kempis belonged to the Canons regular of this brotherhood.

Father Faber (*Growth in Holiness,* ch. xv, p. 261) has formed a very strange idea of the mental prayer of the old Fathers and the saints of the desert, when he says that the method of St. Sulpice claims to be "a more faithful transcript" of it than that of St. Ignatius. I think that both are very far removed from it. He quotes no documents in support of his theory.

have sought to recollect themselves in God without the recitation of formulas. This, I admit, was mental prayer, but of a different kind.

This matter settled, here are some proofs of my proposition.

It seems that the prayer of the **old Orders** consisted in penetrating the mind with ideas inspired by the Divine Office and Holy Scripture; then in free moments it reverted peacefully to these thoughts without any preconceived plan. The rules of Orders before the sixteenth century contain no definite instructions regarding prayer, apart from the Divine Office. By the word *oratio,* they intend to signify vocal prayers. We must guard against interpreting this word in accordance with our modern ideas (see the collection of rules published by Holstenius, Librarian of the Vatican: *Codex regularum,* Rome, 1666).

Take the primitive rule of the Carmelites, for instance. Composed by St. Albert, Patriarch of Jerusalem, it was confirmed and modified by Pope Innocent IV in 1248. It was re-established by St. Teresa for the reformed Carmelites; but she had to make the addition of two hours' mental prayer. The old rule was satisfied with saying: "The religious shall be always in their cells, or near them, *meditating and occupying their thoughts day and night* in the law of God, and watching in prayer, unless otherwise employed in just and reasonable duties, and the recitation of the Divine Office" (*Book of the Foundations,* p. 316). And the real meaning of the passage is simply to secure recollection and reflexion upon divine things without determining the means to be adopted: whether reading, vocal prayer, etc. For if it was a question of meditation in the modern signification of the word, nobody could have been required to practise it uninterruptedly "day and night," and some method would have had to be laid down. This wide interpretation is that given by the Theology of Salamanca, composed by the Carmelite Fathers. They hold that this rule is kept even by the study of scholastic and moral theology and all sciences bearing upon them (*Cursus theol. mor.,* Tract XXXI, ch. ix, punct. 9, Num. 63).*

**66** *bis.*—With regard to the Order of **St. Dominic**, a Father Provincial has been good enough to give me the following information. In the early traditions of the Order, there is never any question of individual prayers, at specified hours and of fixed durations (see two thirteenth-century writers, Blessed Humbert de Romans and Gerard de Fraschet, *Vitae fratrum*). It is in 1505, nearly three hundred years after the foundation of the Order, that a change appears at the Chapter of Milan. Henceforward there is to be mental prayer in the Choir, in community, for half an hour in the morning and as much in the evening. From 1569 onwards twelve successive Chapters considered it necessary to repeat this direction, making it ever more and more urgent. That

* In his commentary on the Rule of St. Benedict (*P.L.* LXVI) Dom Martène says: "With the ancients, to meditate often signifies a simple reading (as in the second rule of the Holy Fathers, ch. v), or to apply oneself to some pious study" (col. 414, rule 8).

of 1868 deprives the offender of any participation in the merits of the Order for the day of omission, unless he has been prevented by illness or being on a journey. That of Rome (1670) requires the subject of the meditation to be read aloud at the beginning of the exercise.

As for the **Franciscans**, we find instructions on the subject in a seventeenth-century treatise: *Commentaria in statuta et constitutiones fratrum minorum,* by Fr. Sanctorus de Melfi, who wrote it by the order of his General (Rome, 1643). He thus sums up the legislation laid down by the general Chapter of 1594,* renewed by that of 1642: "We command that after Compline all Religious, whether lay-brothers, scholastics, or priests, shall apply themselves to mental prayer for the space of half an hour, and that they devote the same time to it after Matins. This exercise will be preceded by a short reading in some spiritual book which shall serve as material for the meditation" (ch. v, stat. II, p. 394 and following).

This order at the end of the sixteenth century cannot, evidently, have created a sudden change. It implies, then, that for some time past (we do not know how long) the practice of mental prayer had spread to certain Houses or families of the Order. But it supposes also that this usage was not yet universal or obligatory. An evolution was in process. It would be interesting if these historical questions could be elucidated by specialists.

**67.**—These customs of the old Orders are due to many **causes**. The first is that the vocal prayer was long in many monasteries, and in this case it would have been extremely fatiguing to have had to go on to meditate afterwards by learned methods.

Another cause is that the effects of meditation were provided for by rules which ensured a persistent state of recollection, and by frequent prayers forming a series of stepping-stones throughout the whole course of the day. The commentator on the Rule of St. Benedict (Migne edition, Vol. LXVI, col. 414, B), says: "In the old monastic rules we find no definite hour assigned to mental prayer, because in all places and at all times they were thinking upon Heavenly things." In a word, there was an atmosphere, a continuous *life* of prayer, which was less the result of one particular exercise than of everything taken as a whole. But for those, on the contrary, who mix much with the world, it is generally necessary to give a more definite form to certain religious exercises or to certain of their elements, such as the preparation and the resolution, in order to bring the mind back to the recollection of divine things. In fact, we find these forms playing an important part in the more modern Congregations of men or women who have suppressed or curtailed the recitation of the Office in common.

* The Franciscan *Codex redactus* gives still earlier orders concerning "mental prayer": 1553 (Salamanca), 1579 (Paris), 1590 (Naples), 1593 (Valladolid). An obscure passage, dated 1475 (Naples), and another, slightly clearer, of 1532 (Messina), are also quoted.

Finally, the mode of prayer of the ancients is explained by the intellectual life of their time. Possessing very few books, they did not vary their readings as we do. They accustomed themselves to live with very few ideas, just as is the case now in the changeless East and the Convents of the Greek Rite. In old days the soul was less complicated, slower than our own, and their prayer felt the effects of this condition.

Great changes took place in the West after the Renaissance, when human thought became, I will not say deeper, but more restless, a movement that has always gone on becoming more accentuated.

**68.—St. Ignatius** himself had no idea of changing the universal usage. As soon as a man entered the Order, he made him follow his *Exercises* in silence for a month. Afterwards the obligatory morning prayer consisted solely in half an hour of vocal prayer and the recitation of the Little Office of the Blessed Virgin. The professed religious were only invited in a general way to consecrate the largest possible part of their free time to prayer. This custom lasted for thirty years; and then mental prayer was gradually introduced.

**69.**—In the seventeenth century the **method of St.-Sulpice** became celebrated. It has passed through two considerably different phases, as M. Letourneau, Curé of St. Sulpice, has pointed out in his book, which is well furnished with facts, references, and authorities: *Méthode d'Oraison mentale du séminaire de St. Sulpice* (Lecoffre, 1903).

The first version, which we owe to M. Olier (1656), resembles M. de Condren's manner of prayer, who himself took it from Cardinal Berulle (*ibid.*, Appendix, p. 322). It was almost wholly an affective prayer, supposing men who were already instructed and who only needed to have their wills aroused.* Without seeking to develop a subject, you "adore Jesus Christ in one of His Mysteries," and then strive to enter into a "participation" of His sentiments (*ibid.*, ch. i, pp. 6, 7).

The second version is due to M. Tronson. He made a change which, while perhaps appearing insignificant at first sight, was really of profound importance. He wished to make the exercise more practical and to adapt it to the needs of the seminarists who are beginners with regard to prayer. And he therefore transformed M. Olier's affective prayer into true meditation, adding considerations and strengthening the petitions (*ibid.*, ch. ii).

* "In the presence of these subjects of prayer," says M. de Berulle, "we confess our unworthiness *and our powerlessness* to sound their depths by thought, being satisfied to *regard* them with humility in order to honour and revere them *until it shall please God* to consider our baseness and poverty, and to give us His light by which to understand these subjects." M. Olier says: "In this participation God communicates His gift *only* by the hidden operations of His Spirit. The soul that experiences some secret operations in her heart, *should abide in repose and silence... without wishing to act by herself or* to make any efforts which should disturb the pure and holy operations of the Holy Spirit within her" (*ibid.*, p. 8). M. Tronson, on the contrary, says that this part of prayer "should chiefly take the form of petitions" (p. 136).

**70.**—Because there was a long period when methodical mental prayer was not in use in the Church, we must not conclude that it is useless, or wish to suppress it under pretext of restoring the former spirituality. The methods have been an **advance,** and this advance has been brought about, naturally and necessarily, by changes in the temper of the human mind, as I have showed above.

In our days we have to avoid two opposite exaggerations—one of being the slave of methods, the other of despising them; one of wishing to impose them upon everybody alike, the other of dissuading everyone from them. The truth lies between the two courses: recommend the methods to those who can make use of and derive profit from them.*

We have an example of this breadth of mind in a piece of advice given by Fr. Achille Gagliardi, S.J., who was the first commentator of St. Ignatius' *Exercises*, and who is an authority in the matter. Speaking of the particular Examen, he says: "This examen is very important for all, but it is otherwise in the case of that *strict method* which consists in marking a series of dots in columns. This is useless and even harmful to the scrupulous and those who are lacking in memory or imagination; let them perform this examen in another way" (*Commentarii;* premium, § 2).

**71.**—The prayer **of simplicity** has evidently been practised from all times. But the art of explaining it has progressed but slowly. It has often been described in an obscure or too brief manner, or without distinguishing it clearly from the mystic union. It would be interesting to disentangle the course of the development of these explanations.

We find, at any rate, that gradually, during the first half of the seventeenth century, the idea of this degree passes from learned books into pious treatises of a popular character. This is probably owing to St. Jane Frances de Chantal's teachings, which were spread in all directions by her spiritual daughters.

But the tares of quietism grow alongside of the good seed. In 1687 the Church is obliged to intervene, that the prayer of simplicity may not be perverted by exaggeration, and she condemns quietism.

It is greatly to be desired that in our days some slight idea, at least, of this degree should be given in books or instructions for novices, instead of letting it be supposed that there is nothing between making acts of reasoning in prayer and being lifted up in an ecstasy. How many directors or mistresses of novices

* Suarez wisely steers a middle course between the extremes of too much or too little. "In order," he says, "that man, on his side, may accomplish all that is possible, it is necessary for him to assist himself by *counsels and rules*. But the object of these aids is not to make a prisoner of him, or to impose a restriction, so to speak, upon the Holy Spirit, who must be free to move His creatures as it shall please Him. They merely teach us how to set to work when the Holy Spirit does not prevent the action by a special grace; and further, when the grace is given, they make us capable of receiving it, of feeling and following it" (*De religione Soc. Jesu*, Book IX, ch. vi, No. 3).

have never heard of this intermediary! And how can they, then direct, either for the present or the future, those numberless souls who come to this state? They will be inclined to say to them: "Since you have not reached the mystic state, you must continue in that of meditation."

St. John of the Cross denounces these incomplete directions (*Ascent of Mt. Carmel,* Prologue; *Living Flame,* stanza 3, § 4 and 12. See also my ch. xxvi); and he does so in very strong terms. But I do not insist upon this point, for I shall be told that reproaches bearing upon persons who are regarded as being highly enlightened, can only be tolerated on the part of a saint! They may even add under their breath that the saint himself is too exacting here. We will not argue the matter.

It is with the object of remedying this state of affairs to some extent that I have dealt with the prayer of simplicity at such length. I regard this chapter alone as being no less useful than the mystic portion, properly so called, of which I am soon to speak.

## EXTRACTS*

### § 1. Existence† and Nature of the Prayer of Simplicity

**72.**—St. J. F. de Chantal:

1°.‡ "My spirit in its extreme summit is in a *very simple unity;* it does not unite, for when it desires to make acts of union, which it too often wishes to do on certain occasions, it feels a strain, and perceives clearly that *it cannot unite itself, but only remain united:* the soul would not willingly stir thence. She neither thinks nor does anything, unless it be *a certain deepening of her desire,* which goes on, as it were imperceptibly, *that God should do with her and with all creatures, in all things, all that He wills.*§ She would do *this only* for the morning exercise, for that of Holy Mass, for the preparation for Holy Communion, as a thanksgiving for all benefits; in fine, for all things she would

* I will arrange the extracts in this work as far as possible in the chronological order of their authors. It will often, however, be useful to begin with St. Teresa, or some writer, giving a decisive passage.

† This existence is proved by the extracts that are to follow, and by those that establish (ch. iv) the existence of *acquired contemplation.* For this last, in virtue of the definitions that have been admitted, is none other than the prayer of simplicity.

‡ In writing these lines the saint may perhaps have been thinking of a higher state than the prayer of simplicity. In any case we can apply this passage to this last state. The following passages are more conclusive.

§ The saint here particularises to a certain extent the occupation of this prayer, according to her own attraction; or again, this state was attended with suffering, and then it frequently gave rise to acts of conformity to the will of God.

merely abide in this *very simple unity of spirit* with God, without *extending her outlook elsewhere*" (Letter of June 29th, 1621, to St. Francis of Sales. Plon ed., Vol. I, of the *Letters*).

2°. "You have indeed given me cause to blush in asking me about my prayer. Alas! my daughter, as a rule it is nothing but distractions with some suffering. For what else can a poor, pitiful spirit, filled with a thousand matters, do? I tell you in confidence and simply, that it is about *twenty years* since God took from me all power to accomplish anything in prayer with the understanding, and consideration or meditation; and that *all that I can do* is to suffer and to stay my spirit very simply in God, cleaving to this operation by an entire committal, without making acts, unless I should be incited thereto by His motion, there awaiting what it shall please His goodness to give me" (Blaise ed., *Letter* 282, to a Superior).

3°. Various kinds. Advice to directors:

"There are various degrees in this manner of prayer, as in all the others; some persons possessing *this unique simplicity and repose* in a much more eminent degree than the others, and receiving divers lights in it... This attraction is so well adapted to us that those souls that are drawn away from it seem to leave their centre; they lose their freedom of mind and sink into a condition of constraint and perplexity which robs them of their peace" (*Réponses sur le Coutumier,* art. 24; Migne ed., col. 237).

4°. Of the arid kind:

"It often happens that the souls who are in this way, are tormented with many *distractions,* and that they remain without any sensible support, Our Lord withdrawing from them *the sentiments of His sweet Presence and all kinds of aids and interior lights;* so that they remain in a state of *total impotence and insensibility,* although it may sometimes amount to less than this. This is a source of some astonishment to souls who are not yet very experienced; but they must remain firm, and rest in God above all sight and feeling; *suffering,* receiving, and cherishing equally all the ways and operations that it shall please God to perform in them... With the supreme summit of their spirit they should unite themselves with God *and lose themselves wholly in Him,* finding by this means peace in the midst of conflict and repose in labour" (*ibid.,* col. 237).

5°. The same subject. Not to be bent on self-analysis:

"There are souls amongst those whom God leads by this *way of simplicity,* whom His divine goodness strips so extraordinarily of all satisfaction, desire, and feeling, that they have difficulty in *enduring* and in *expressing* themselves, because what passes in their interior life is so slight, so delicate, and so imperceptible, being all at the extreme summit of the spirit, that *they do not know how to speak of it.* And these souls sometimes suffer greatly if their Superiors are not acquainted with their way, because, fearing to be useless and to be wasting time, *they wish to achieve something,* and rack their brains with reflections, so as to be able to observe what is going on within them; this is very prejudicial to them, and causes them to fall into great perplexities of mind which are difficult to unravel, unless they submit to discard these reflections entirely and to *suffer with patience* the pain that they feel, which pain is often due merely to their always wishing to be doing something, and *not being content with what they have, and this disturbs their peace of mind* and causes them to lose that very simple and very delicate interior occupation of their will" (*Letter to a Superior,* Plon. ed., Vol. III, p. 338).

6°. Prejudices regarding the prayer of simplicity:

"Our blessed Father used to call it very holy and salutary, and said that it contained all that could be desired for God's service. But, notwithstanding, I know that it is strongly opposed by those whom God leads by the way of reasoning, and many of our sisters have been troubled in this manner, being told that they are idle and wasting time. But, without wishing to be wanting in the respect that I owe to these persons, I assure you, my very dear sisters, that you should not turn aside from your road for such talk. For our blessed Father, who perfectly understood all kinds of prayer, as is seen in his writings, has always approved of this one, and also said that, while others eat *divers* viands at the Saviour's table, we [should] repose our souls and all our affections on His loving breast by a very simple trust. With such a solid counsel [to rest upon] we must stand firm, and faithfully follow this way as soon as we are drawn thereto. For we must not go thither of ourselves, but with humility and patience await the hour which our divine Saviour has determined for introducing us to this happiness. For in order to go to God and to attain to Him, we must allow ourselves to be led by His Spirit. That which is of His choosing is always the best for us" (*Réponses sur le Coutumier,* art. 24, Migne ed., col. 236).

Speaking of the "prayer of the simple presence of God," she says: "The advice of religious persons is usually much opposed to this, which is a great source of trouble to the daughters [of the Visitation] and sometimes to those who rule over them" (Letter to Mother Favre, Nov. 10th, 1630, Plon. ed., 1878, Vol. III, Letter 1053; Migne ed., Vol. II, col. 1602). See also above, No. *31.*

**73.**—St. Ignatius (Second letter to Sister Rejadella, Venice, 1536):

"All meditation where the understanding works, fatigues the body. There are *other meditations,* equally in the order of God, which are restful, full of peace for the understanding, without labour for the interior faculties of the soul, and which are performed without either physical or interior effort."

Having been consulted with regard to the exercises that were to be required of the Scholastics of his Order, St. Ignatius replied that they must not be overburdened with meditations. First and foremost, two very simple, short but frequently repeated exercises were to be required of them: the loving attention to God, as present with us, and the offering of their works. "This will be easy... and if they are well disposed they will in this way draw down visits from God which, in spite of their brief duration, will produce great results" (Reply to Fr.

Brandon: *Letters* of St. Ignatius, Vol. II of the 1875 Madrid ed., appendix, p. 560).

**74.**—Fr. Nouet (*Conduite de l'Homme d'Oraison*):

"When the man of prayer has made considerable progress in meditation, he passes insensibly to affective prayer, which, being between meditation and contemplation, as the dawn is between the night and the day, possesses something both of the one and of the other. In its beginnings it contains more of meditation, because it still makes use of reasoning, although but little in comparison with the time it devotes to the affections; because, having acquired much light by the prolonged use of considerations and reasonings, *it enters at once into its subject,* and sees *all its developments without much difficulty,* whence it is that the will is soon moved. Hence it arises that in proportion as it perfects itself, it discards reasonings, and being content with a simple glance, with a sweet remembrance of God and of Jesus Christ, His only Son, it produces many loving affections according to the various motions that it receives from the Holy Ghost. But when it has arrived at the highest point of perfection, it simplifies its affections equally with its lights; so that the soul will remain sometimes for an hour, sometimes for a day, sometimes more, in the same sentiments of love, or contrition or reverence, or some other movement the impression of which she has received" (Book IV, ch. i).

**75.**—Fr. Grou, on "The way of simplicity." By this he means one of its kinds, the loving attention to God:

"Instead of the complicated and fatiguing exercise of the memory, the understanding, and the will, which faculties are applied now to one subject, now to another, in meditation, God often brings the soul into a simple prayer, in which the mind has no other object than a confused and general idea of God; the heart no other feeling than a sweet and peaceful taste of God, which nourishes it without any effort, as infants are nourished by milk. The soul then perceives so little of her operations, so subtle are they and delicate, that *it seems to her that she is slothful* and plunged into a kind of sleep... And, finally, He detaches her from a multitude of practices of which she had made use before to sustain her piety, but which, like so many fetters, would now only hamper her and lead her away from her simplicity" (*Intérieure de Jésus et de Marie,* Vol. I, ch. xl; Fr. Cadres' ed.).*

* Fr. Grou's biographer tells us that he was here describing his own habitual state (*ibid.,* pp. liv, lv).

I might have quoted another passage on the same state of prayer, taken from the *Manual of Interior Souls* (the chapter on simplicity), by the same author. But it contains some exaggerated expressions, like the following: "The soul is not occupied with anything," "she does not know if she is praying," "hours are passed thus without distaste." This last case does not by any means occur with everybody.

**76.**—Fr. de Clorivière. After describing affective prayer (*Opuscule sur la Prière,* Book II, ch. xx), he goes on to the following degree, which he calls the prayer of recollection:

"New graces are the reward of souls who are faithful in responding to God's designs... They are, as it were, imperceptibly raised to a more perfect state. Their love, although more ardent, no longer affords them the same consolation, because it is more enlightened. They see clearly, they feel that it is neither the *multiplicity* nor the *variety* of their acts that render them more pleasing to God; that the *simpler* their acts are, the greater is their perfection and the more do they bring the soul into that calm in which God is pleased to act... Little by little they withdraw from the *multiplicity* of acts which has no longer the same attraction for them, and which would rather tend to dissipation than to bring them to God, by preventing them from following the leading of the Holy Spirit" (Book II, ch. xxiv). See also chapter vii. In chapter xxxi the writer interprets Bossuet's work on the prayer of simplicity, in the same way that I have done (ch. i, 8).

**77.**—St. Teresa describes affective prayer without, however, giving it a name:

"As to those who, like myself, cannot... [make much use of their understanding] I have no advice to give, except that they are to have patience, until Our Lord shall send them both matter and light; for they can do so little of themselves, that their understanding is a hindrance to them rather than a help. To those, then, that can make use of their understanding, I say that they are not to spend the whole time in that way... they must not, when prayer is sweet, suppose that there never will be Sunday or a time when no work ought to be done. *They think it lost time to do otherwise;* but I think that loss their greatest gain. Let them rather, as I have said, place themselves in the presence of Christ, and, without fatiguing the understanding, *converse with Him,* and in Him rejoice, without wearying themselves in searching out reasons; but let them rather lay their necessities before Him, and the just reasons there are why He should not suffer us in His presence —at one time this, at another time that— lest the soul should be wearied by always eating of the same food" (*Life*, ch. xiii, 16, 17).

**77** *bis.*—Fr. Bainvel, S.J.:

"We must act in our prayer... But to act is not necessarily to make distinct or classified acts. The heart may be fragrant with some one person or thing, and *we keep silence,* because we are afraid lest in unlocking it the fragrance may evaporate... When we begin, it may perhaps be necessary to divide, analyse, explain now one kind of acts and now another. Little by little we act without separating the component parts of our actions; we proceed by undivided and sometimes very complex processes, *the analysis of which may be difficult.* Let us recall the difference between reading and spelling, between reading with the eyes and reading when pronouncing the words... We cease to spell as soon as we know how to read; a hurried reader prefers to read with his eyes, without pronouncing. Thus, when the act of faith or love is difficult to make, it may be excellent to formulate it, even in words; when it comes of itself, as it were, and when the man lives it, it may be better to say nothing. When we are not able to meditate, we can aim at calling upon the three faculties to act in turn; when we meditate well, we make these act without thinking about it, or distinguishing their acts or the parts that they play" (unpublished *Opuscule* on *l'Oraison,* 3rd Lesson).

### § 2. First Rule of Conduct: Not to Make Efforts in Order to Produce These Acts, If Difficulty is Experienced in So Doing (**60**).

**78.**—St. John of the Cross:

1°. "This passage, then, [from *meditation* to *contemplation*] takes place when the *discursive* acts and meditation fail, when sensible sweetness and the first fervours cease... At this time, then, the direction of the soul must be wholly different from what it was at first. If formerly it was supplied with matter for meditation and it did meditate, now that matter must be withheld and meditation must cease, because, as I have said, it cannot meditate, do what it will, and distractions are the result... He [God] is now secretly and quietly infusing wisdom into the soul, together with the loving knowledge of Himself, independently of these *divers* acts, without their being *multiplied* or *elicited*" (*Living Flame,* stanza III, line 3, § 5, 6).

2°. "There are souls who, instead of *abandoning themselves to the care and protection of God,* hinder Him rather by their *indiscreet behaviour,* or resist Him like little children, who, when their mothers would carry them in their arms, struggle and cry that they *may be allowed to walk.* These souls make no progress, or if they do, it is comparable only to the walking of an infant child. I purpose [in this treatise], by His help, to furnish some directions, so that they may understand the matter for themselves, or at least submit to the guidance of God" (*Ascent of Mt. Carmel,* Prologue).

**79.**—St. Francis of Sales:

1°. He composed for the use of the Visitation a *Spiritual Directory of daily actions.* He gives here a great number of little exercises, intentions, ejaculatory prayers, etc., corresponding to the different hours of the day, and concludes article 12 with the following *Advice:*

"The Directory proposes a *large number* of exercises, it is true; and it is, moreover, good and suitable *at the beginning* to keep the mind regulated and occupied; but when, in progress of time, souls have become practised in this *multiplicity* of interior acts, and when they are formed, trained, and their rough edges taken off, then these exercises must be combined into one exercise of greater *simplicity,* namely, either the love of trust, or of the union and reunion of the heart to the will of God, as the exercise of union shows; so that this *multiplicity* converts itself into *unity.* But it lies with the Superior to know and discern the interior attraction, and the state of each one of her daughters in particular, in order that she may lead them all according to God's good pleasure. And further, if even in the noviciate there are certain souls who are afraid of subjecting their minds too much to fixed exercises, provided that this fear does not proceed from caprice, presumption, contempt, or chagrin, it is for the prudent mistress to lead them by another way, although, as a rule, this one is useful, as experience shows" (*Works,* Migne ed., Vol. V, col. 169).

2°. "Let those who understand nothing of it [the Latin of the Divine Office] keep themselves simply attentive to God, making loving outpourings, while the other choir says the versicle, and they make the pauses" (*Directory* of the Visitation, art. 4).

3°. Speaking of the interior exercises ordered by the Directory:

"When, in progress of time, souls have practised this *multiplicity* of interior acts, these exercises must be *united* in an exercise of greater *simplicity,* so that this *multiplicity* is converted into *unity*" (*ibid.,* end of art. 12).

**80.**—St. Jane Frances de Chantal:

1°. "God, in this state, is the special agent who directs and teaches; the soul is the person who receives the highly spiritual gifts that are made to her, these being the grace of being *attentive* [to God's voice] and *divine* love together. And since His goodness deals henceforth with the soul as a giver, the soul should go to God with a trustful heart, *without particularising* other acts than those to which *she feels herself moved* by Him, remaining passive, as it were, *without making any effort of herself,* with this regard of simple quietude, like one who should open his eyes with an infantine glance with a simple attention, in order thus to join love to love. If we wish to act, and to leave this very simple and tranquil loving attention which is without reflections, we hinder the blessings which God communicates by this, the only attention that He requires" (*Opuscules,* Plon ed., Vol. III, p. 278).

2°. "If in prayer the soul feels some of those touches, by which God shows that He desires to communicate Himself to her, we should then discontinue all action, and stop quite short, in order to give place to His coming, and not to prevent it by unseasonable actions, but to dispose to receive it with interior silence and a profound respect" (*ibid.,* p. 262).

3°. On the thought of the Mysteries of Our Lord's Life, the saint wrote to St. Francis of Sales:

"I have often been troubled, seeing that all preachers and good books teach that we should consider and meditate upon the benefits that we have received from Our Lord, His greatness, the mysteries of our Redemption, especially when they are brought before us by the Church. And yet the soul that is in this state of *simple regard* and idleness, desiring to make the attempt, *can in no wise achieve it,* which is often a cause of great distress to her. But it seems to me none the less that *she does it in an excellent manner,* which is a simple memory and very delicate representation of the mystery, with sweet and delectable affections." St. Francis replied: "Let the soul dwell upon the mysteries after the manner that God has given to her to do, for preachers and spiritual books have no intention of advising us to do otherwise" (*Life* of the saint, by Mère de Chaugy, Book III, ch. xxiv, and the saint's *Works,* Migne ed., Vol. II, col. 857).

4°. "When at prayer we are drawn to great *simplicity,* we must not be disquieted because, about the great feasts, we are not taken up with thoughts of these great mysteries, for *we must always follow our attraction.* Out of prayer we may make reflections, and look simply at or read these mysteries; for although we make no high considerations about them, we nevertheless feel in ourselves certain sweet affections of imitation, of joy or others. And for prayer, *the great secret is always to follow therein the attraction given us...* Souls drawn to *simplicity* in prayer should take great care to cut off a certain eagerness, which often makes us desirous of doing and multiplying acts during it... But as we must never of ourselves attempt this kind of prayer, so we must follow the attraction as soon as God gives it" (*Entretien* XXXVI, Plon. (1875 ed.), Vol. II, p. 350 and fol. English: *Exhortations, Conferences,* etc., by the Sisters of the Visitation, Conference XXXV).

**81.**—Bossuet:

"All that unites us to God, all that causes us to taste Him, to delight in Him, to rejoice in His glory, and to love Him so purely that we find our happiness in Him, and, not satisfied with reflections, with thoughts, with affections and resolutions, leads us solidly to *the practice* of detachment from self and from created things; all this is good, all this is true prayer. We must take care not to *torment our heads,* or *over-excite our hearts;* but to take whatever offers itself to the soul's sight with humility and simplicity, *without those violent efforts* which are rather imaginary than real and *well grounded;* allowing ourselves to be drawn gently to God, abandoning ourselves to the promptings of our own spirit" (Opuscule, *De la meilleure manière de faire oraison.* Vivès-Lachat ed., Vol. VII, p. 501).

**82.**—A thought of the Blessed Curé d'Ars:

"We do not need to do so much talking in order to pray well. We know that Almighty God is there, in the Tabernacle; we open our hearts to Him, *we take delight in His holy Presence;* this is the best prayer" *Vie,* by M. Monnin, Book V, ch. iv).

**82** *bis.*—Fr. de Smedt:

"*Arid contemplation,* which perhaps we might be allowed to call the *prayer of patience...* Consists in a peaceful waiting before God, without any very distinct thought or feeling, except a general feeling of satisfaction in thus doing Him honour by our presence, like those noble courtiers whose whole duty is to stand at certain times in their sovereign's presence" (*Notre vie surnaturalle,* Vol. II, part 2, sect. 3, sub-sect. 2, art. 1, chap. iv, par. 2).

### § 3. Second Rule: Not to Make Efforts in Order to Hinder Acts—Third Rule.

**83.**—St. Alphonsus Liguori inveighs against certain mystics who forget this rule, and who, before the soul arrives at the mystic state, proscribe in a general way all "the acts of the will; those of love, oblation, resignation, etc." He concludes thus, adopting Fr. Segneri's remarks: "When God does not speak, the soul must use all possible means to unite herself to God: meditations, when they are necessary; affections, prayers, resolutions; provided that those acts are produced without constraint; we must be satisfied, then, with those towards which the soul feels herself sweetly inclined" (*Homo apost.,* Appendix I, No. 7).

**84.**—St. Teresa's doctrine is the same. Her words refer here, it is true, to the beginnings of supernatural prayer. But they would apply *a fortiori* to the prayer of simplicity. She devotes nearly a whole chapter to this question, and sums up her thought thus: "The mind must act until it is called to recollection by love" (*Interior Castle,* Fourth Mansion; ch. iii, 5). Since "God gave us faculties that we might make use of them, each of them will receive its proper reward. Do not let us, then, try to charm them to sleep; let us *permit them to do their work* until divinely called to something higher" (*ibid.,* 6).

**85.**—St. John of the Cross upon the third rule:

After recommending that the repose of the spirit in the prayer of simplicity and the mystic state should be accepted, he adds:

"At other times, however, in all our acts of devotion and of good works, we must make use of good recollections and meditations, so that we may feel an increase of profit and devotion; most especially applying ourselves to the life, passion, and death of Jesus Christ Our Lord, that our life and conduct may be an imitation of His" (*Ascent of Mt. Carmel,* Book II, ch. xxxii, p. 204)

# PART II

## SOME GENERAL IDEAS ABOUT THE MYSTIC UNION

## CHAPTER III

### THE VARIOUS KINDS OF MYSTICAL GRACES

**1.—Two groups.** In Chapter I we discriminated between the mystical graces and those of the ordinary way. We must now divide the first into their respective kinds. From the outset we have to recognise two quite distinct groups amongst them.

In order to understand this clearly, let us remember that in Heaven we shall receive two kinds of gifts which will not have the same importance. On the one hand, we shall have the *beatific vision,* which will put us into possession of God; on the other, we shall behold the saints, the angels, and other *creatures.* These, in the language of the theologians, constitute relatively the first object and second object of beatitude.

**2.**—And in the same way, on earth we can distinguish two sorts of mystical graces, according to the **nature of the object** that is supernaturally offered to our understanding.

The characteristic of the states of the *first group* consists in this, that it is *God Himself,* and God alone, who manifests Himself. We call them the *mystic union,* or, again, *mystical* (or infused) *contemplation* of the Divinity.*

In the *second group* the manifestation has to do with some *created object.* We shall see Our Lord's Sacred Humanity, for instance, or the Blessed Virgin or an angel, or some past or future fact, etc. We find here *visions* (of created things) and *revelations;* in other words, *apparitions* and *supernatural utterances.* To these are added miraculous corporeal phenomena, such as those that are observed in the case of ecstatics.

* Taken alone, the words *mystical contemplation* might apply even to revelations and visions; but St. Teresa and St. John of the Cross and many others have adopted the contrary usage.

**3.**—It is necessary to make a **clear distinction** between these two categories of graces; first, because we shall have to describe them separately; and secondly, because we must hold them in very different estimation. The graces of union with God are by far the most useful and the most sure (see ch. xxi, **44**).

**4.**—**Names** given to these two groups. It has been proposed to give the name *deific* (*indéiques*) to those graces by means of which we *penetrate into the Divinity.** The others, which have for their end something that is *outside of God, God,* would be termed *ex-deific* (*exdéiques*). Nothing so contributes to clearness of thought as the practice of bestowing *very short* and *sharply contrasting* names upon things which we are inclined to confuse.

Following Scaramelli, many writers have designated these two groups by the words *confused contemplation* and *distinct contemplation.* They thus refer, not to the object of the knowledge, but to the manner of knowing it. This second point of view seems of less importance than the first. And this language also implies that the revelations always consist in very definite knowledge, which is incorrect.

**5.**—**The four stages** or degrees of the mystic union. From the following chapter onwards I shall have to allude to them. I take them as St. Teresa described them in her last work, *The Interior Castle.* In her *Life,* written by herself, the differences are perhaps less easily distinguished. We have:

1°. The *incomplete* mystic union, or the *prayer of quiet* (from the Latin *quies,* repose, which expresses the *impression* experienced in this state);

2°. The *full* or *semi-ecstatic union,* called also by St. Teresa, the prayer of union;

3°. The *ecstatic union* or *ecstasy;*

4°. The *transforming* or *deifying* union, or the *spiritual marriage* of the soul with God.

**6.**—**Analogies** and differences between these graces. As we shall see later on by the descriptions, the three first degrees are fundamentally but one and the same grace, which we can call the *non-transforming union.* They constitute respectively the *weak* state, the *medium* state, and the *strong* state of the grace. In a word, they are, above all, three degrees of *intensity.* In the prayer of quiet, the soul is a vessel only half filled with the Divine nectar; at times it may contain but a few drops. In the full union, it is *filled* to the brim. In ecstasy, it runs over and is in a state of ebullition.

And so there is a unity between these three degrees. It is well to remember this when reading St. Teresa, as it will guide us through the numerous descriptive details that she supplies (see ch. vii, 3).

* Dante has created an analogous word. Desiring to express that the Seraphim plunged into God, he invents a word, and says that they *s'india* (sink themselves) in God (*Paradiso,* Cant. IV, line 28).

As to the spiritual marriage, we shall see that it does not bring the preceding states to perfection by strengthening, but rather by modifying them.

**7.**—What we have just said of the three first degrees gives a fair idea of the marks that distinguish them one from the other. In the same way, we do not need any elaborate explanations in order to grasp the differences existing between a hill, a mountain, and a chain of mountains; or between a house, a mansion, and a palace.*

But there is a way of being still more precise, by defining the lines of demarcation and choosing them in such a way as to be easily discernible. In order to do this, let us characterise each degree by one of its effects.

**8.**—Here are the **definitions** that can be applied to the three degrees below the spiritual marriage. The mystic union will be called:

1°. The *prayer of quiet,* when the divine action is not strong enough to hinder distractions; or, briefly, when the imagination still preserves its liberty;

2°. *Full union,* when it possesses the two following characteristics: (*a*) its strength is so great that the soul is *fully* occupied with the divine object; not diverted, that is to say, by any other thought; in a word, it has no distractions; (*b*) on the other hand, the senses continue to act more or less, so that it is possible, by a greater or lesser effort, to put ourselves into relations with the exterior world, by speaking, walking, etc.; it is possible to come out from our prayer;

3°. *Ecstasy* (and this is the universally accepted definition) is when the divine action has a considerable force, and all outside communications with the senses are interrupted, or almost entirely so. Thus we are no longer capable of any movements, such as are voluntary at least, nor are we able to come out of our prayer at will.

We see that these definitions have nothing vague about them: each degree is differentiated from its predecessor by a new *fact,* and this fact is directly and easily discernible. Leaving the intensity out of the question, the full union differs from the prayer of quiet by the absence of distractions, and ecstasy differs from full union by the complete alienation of the sensible faculties.

It is far from being the case that mystics have confined themselves to this scientific method in their classifications.

**9.**—Such, then, is the non-transforming mystic union, divided up into three well-defined types. But we must not exaggerate this idea of separation; and let us say at once that it is possible to pass from one type to another by imperceptible **transitions**.

* St. Teresa employs another imagery; The prayer of quiet is a "spark" and ecstasy a "conflagration" (see ch. xii, 12, 4°). It only remains to describe the intermediate state state by saying, for instance, "the full union is a flame."

The result is that, in practice, we often hesitate to classify a grace decidedly under such or such a one of these denominations. We can merely say: it is very near to this or that type.

Thus, in the scale of colours, we think of blue, green, and yellow as being quite distinct things, well-defined types. But this does not prevent their being connected by an unbroken chain of intermediate shades. We can only describe these shades by attaching them to the fundamental colours as closely as may be. We say, for example, it is a green inclining to yellow. It is impossible to proceed otherwise; and besides, this language is quite sufficiently clear.

**10.—Other kinds**. We shall see that all the other kinds referred to by the mystics (prayers of *silence, supernatural sleep, inebriation, jubilation, wound of love,* etc.) are only different *ways of being* of the four preceding degrees. They are not successive degrees. By treating them as such, mysticism is wrongly complicated (see ch. xxx).

**11.—History of the individual soul**. St. Teresa has thought of the four preceding degrees as being real stages, *successive* periods, spiritual ages or graduated states, that is to say; always, of course, excepting those special cases where God intervenes. The soul *generally* remains for some time in each state before passing on to the next; and the passage is difficult. And thus many souls stop on the road.

In the *Interior Castle,* the saint gives the name of *Mansions* to the periods corresponding to each degree of prayer. By this she does not mean that during these phases the soul remains uninterruptedly in one special prayer without any goings back. It is sufficient to have the prayer sometimes, but without passing beyond it.

**12.**—Those who remain stationary would do well to ponder a thought that should engender humility: it is that God has perhaps called them to mount up higher. Every seed contains in itself the power of development; if it comes to nothing, it is that it has encountered some obstacle. St. Teresa suggests that this obstacle is often imputable to us.* And therefore, instead of feeling a certain pride because we have arrived at the prayer of quiet, we ought to ask ourselves fearfully why we have not gone beyond it.

**13.—General aspect**. Already in ordinary prayer we have found that there were four degrees (ch. ii) which usually were also halting places. The degrees of the *mystic union* follow those of the *ordinary* union. The spiritual marriage, which is the supreme degree here below, is itself only the foretaste of a yet higher state, the *beatific union* of eternity.

* Speaking of raptures: "When I come to these wonders of God's greatness (I mean when I come to speak of them), I cannot but feel keenly grieved at seeing what we lose *by our own fault.* It is true, His Majesty grants these favours to whom He chooses, yet if we were to seek Him as He seeks us, *He would give them to all of us.* He only longs for souls on whom He may bestow them, for His gifts diminish not His riches" (*Interior Castle,* Sixth Mansion, ch. iv, 16).

**14.—Slightly different classifications.** The Ven. Mary of the Incarnation, Ursuline, reckons three halting places only, because she amalgamates the second and the third (*Histoire,* by the Abbé Chapôt, Part IV, ch. iv; or *Vie,* by an Ursuline of Nantes, ch. xx).

St. John of the Cross does not think of distinguishing between the first three degrees. His one desire is to reach the last, the spiritual marriage. All that lies before this state seems to form but one whole. It is of small moment to him whether there are separate hostels on this road; he wishes the soul to sojourn there for the shortest possible time. So that, as far as he is concerned, the true mystic halting places are reduced to two: (1°) the transforming union, and (2°) all that leads to it.

And, further, St. Teresa's three first degrees seem to him to be chiefly a time of probation. He expresses this idea by giving to them all collectively the name of the soul's *second purgation.* He also calls it the *night of the spirit* (see ch. xv). And this is certainly not because we are deprived of light; but because these lights are but darknesses, and often painful darknesses, when compared with the full radiance which awaits us at the end.

**15.**—Questions of **terminology**. The state that I have called *full union* is sometimes referred to by St. Teresa as the *prayer of union,* without any descriptive adjective. She was probably afraid of coining a new word, and so she preferred to particularise that of *union,* which had a far wider significance. This method has one drawback: language is deprived of a general term which is not replaced by another, and which, moreover, is perpetually wanted. The saint herself has not been able to avoid employing it in many other cases.*

For one thing, this restriction applied to the word *union* might seem to suggest that in the first degree of the mystic state—in the prayer of quiet, that is to say—*union* with God is not yet experienced. This would be a gross error, one into which St. Teresa, however, did not fall, since she calls the prayer of quiet "a close *union* with God" (*Life,* ch. xiv, 3); only this union of the powers is imperfect, distractions wage war against it. The soul is not "yet altogether absorbed in God" (*ibid.,* ch. xv; 3).

Following Scaramelli, many writers have wished to avoid the drawbacks that I have just pointed out. And they have therefore added a qualifying term to the word union. They say *simple union,* without explaining what they mean by this term. It might be objected that the union with God which the soul experiences in the ordinary way, and which is constantly written about in ascetical works, is still more deserving of this name; it is in some respects far simpler. And if we are by way of speaking of the mystic states only, it is the prayer of quiet which

* On the other hand, no inconvenience, in French at any rate, has followed the Saint's action in restricting the sense of the word *quietude* to one special state. For this word has disappeared from current language, and has been replaced by the word repose. In Latin, on the contrary, in order to avoid an ambiguity, the expression *oratio quietis* has needed a qualification.

should be called the *simple union.* In fact, (1°) it is a union; (2°) a mystic union; (3°) it is the lowest degree of this series, and therefore the *simplest* union.

I have adopted the expression: full union. In her *Life,* chapter xvii, 7, St. Teresa makes use of the equivalent term, saying: *perfect union* (*entera union*). She does this when speaking of a closely allied state, of which she says: "There is another kind of union which, though not a *perfect union,* is yet more so than the one of which I have just spoken." She had just expressed the same idea with regard to the union to which we are now referring, saying: "This state of prayer seems to me to be a most distinct union of the *whole soul* with God" (*ibid..,* 5).

It has been suggested to me that this expression, *full union,* was not a happy one, because it would apply with greater truth to ecstasy or to the spiritual marriage. But the same thing might be said with regard to the word quietude, which signifies *state of repose;* from the points of view both of the soul and of the body, ecstasy would have the first right to this name. But it has been instinctively felt that a good reason existed for applying it to the first degree of the mystic union. The intention was to compare this state, not with those that follow, but with those that went before. And the impression that the soul experiences as she passes from meditation to the prayer of quiet is thus rendered. She says to herself: What repose! It is this that strikes her. She is not thinking of what will follow later on. And equally, when the soul passes from the prayer of quiet to the next degree, she says also: What *plenitude!* And we wish to give it a name that indicates this new sentiment also. The same argument might be used with regard to the expression: affective prayer. For all the subsequent degrees are affective. And yet we reserve this name for the state that *first* makes this ardent affection felt; and in the same way the name of prayer of simple regard is given to the first state that exhibits simplicity.

# CHAPTER IV

## HISTORICAL EXPLANATION OF THE WORD CONTEMPLATION

**1.—Difficulty**. If we want to understand the ancient writers, we must be acquainted with a word that they constantly employ—namely, contemplation. And the first thing to remember is this, that they do not all give it exactly the same signification; if we do not notice this fact we shall group together a number of passages which, when closely looked into, will be found to contradict each other.

**2.**—Let us first suppose that the word *contemplation* is employed **without any qualification**.

When it is thus used as the opposite of the word *action,* it often signifies all kinds of prayer, including discursive prayer and the recitation of the Office. And, further, it refers to the contemplative life; that is to say, the whole of a life wherein prayer plays a large part. It is the contrast between Martha and Mary. This is one first signification.

**3.—Classical definition**. If the word contemplation is opposed to the word *meditation,* the sense is already restricted. It even seems at first sight to have a clear and distinct meaning. Various authors appear to be of this opinion when they give it the following definition: *It is a simple regard, accompanied by love;* or this other equivalent: *It is a simple and amorous gaze.** But is not such a phrase open to various interpretations? Alas! yes.† For the simplicity of acts, of which it is a question here, can be understood in a wider or narrower sense without the reader's knowing which is intended. Is the simplicity complete, or only considerable? Does it bear upon acts of the imagination, or of the memory,

* It is understood that this must be more than momentary.

† The same must be said with regard to the expression *prayer of simple regard,* which is synonymous with contemplation, according to the definition that I have just given.

or of the understanding, and including a simplification of the will? Each person understands it in his own way.*

**4.**—Thus with some authors there is **no intermediary** between meditation and contemplation. This reverts perhaps to the classification that includes *affective prayer* in the last-named state. And the preceding definition may give countenance to this view. For the understanding then is *simplified;* its *regard is more simple.* The will alone has retained its *multiplicity of acts.* This is the second sense of the word contemplation, but it is somewhat rare.

Others, such as Alvarez de Paz, allow contemplation to begin only when the will itself has become simplified; in a word, the first step is that which we have rightly named the *prayer of simplicity.* It is clear that affective prayer is not, in his eyes, a part of contemplation, because, he explains the two states in separate and successive treatises; we have thus a third interpretation of the word. It is this that Courbon has adopted (Part III, ch. I). St. John of the Cross requires that there shall be something further still: a latent mystic state. I shall explain this presently, when speaking of the first *obscure night* (fourth sense).

With St. Teresa, the sense is yet more restricted. It applies only to the manifestly mystic states† (fifth sense).

**5.**—Here, then, are **five different significations** for the same word. Conclusion: when anyone quotes an author who is speaking of contemplation, we must always ask ourselves what, taking the context into consideration, he really had in view.

It is also the same, unhappily, with many other expressions in the language of mysticism. For instance, *quietude, union, silence, sleep, recollection,* etc. Authors are far from all understanding them in exactly the same way, especially those before St. Teresa, or who lived at about the same period.

**6.—Qualifying terms.** In order to avoid these ambiguities, many writers have added qualifying adjectives to the word contemplation. They distinguish two kinds of contemplation. That which they call *infused, passive, extraordinary,* or *eminent,* is nothing else than the mystic state (see ch. iii, 2). The other, called *acquired, active,* or *ordinary,* is defined as follows by Scaramelli, who is the echo here of all his predecessors: "It is that contemplation which, with the aid of grace, we can acquire by our own endeavour, and particularly by a long practice

* I do not include here another sense again, which St. Ignatius gives to the word contemplation in his *Exercises.* He applies this name to a mental prayer bearing upon some historic fact. By the methods that he counsels, he inclines the soul to a simple and amorous gaze; but he does not insist upon that simplicity which characterises the other kinds of contemplation. It is still possible to reason; it is regard, but not necessarily simple regard, as the old definition requires it to be.

† "In these two things (vocal and mental prayer) we may do something with God's assistance, but in *contemplation,* just now mentioned, *nothing at all.* His Majesty it is that doth all" (*Way of Perfection,* ch. xxv, p. 6).

of meditation; although, strictly speaking, it is not due to all these efforts" (Tr. 2, No. 69).*

In plainer language, it is the prayer of simplicity. That prayer, which has been described by different names, is always the same intermediary between meditation and the mystic state.†

**7.—History** of this expression. I do not think that the expression, "acquired contemplation," was employed before the seventeenth century, except by Denis the Carthusian (*De Fonte lucis,* ch. viii, fifteenth century). It occurs in 1609, in a Spanish work by Fr. Thomas of Jesus, who regards this word as being one that is in use amongst the mystics (*preface*). The other writers of the early part of the seventeenth century, such as Suarez, the Ven. Louis du Pont, St. Francis of Sales, and Alvarez de Paz, are not acquainted with the term.

**8.**—Cardinal Brancati, writing towards the end of the seventeenth century, proves that the Fathers were acquainted with acquired contemplation, **although they did not give it a special name**, and that they had therefore distinguished it from infused contemplation. For at times their writings are urgent upon the subject of a simple regard, as something that is dependent upon our own will, while at others they imply that it is not so dependent. Now, this resolves itself into admitting two contemplations of opposite characters, and these characters are exactly those by which we define the acquired and the infused contemplations (*Op.* 3, ch. x).

Two later writers, Lopez de Ezquerra and Fr. Honoré de Ste-Marie, have proved this same thesis at great length. The first-named insists strongly upon the existence of acquired contemplation, and quotes passages from twenty-five of the Fathers (*Prologue,* No. 14), and is very severe upon those who regard this prayer as a modern invention (Nos. 10, 11, 15), The second says: "Although the Fathers and ecclesiastical writers of the first eleven centuries did not know these two kinds of contemplation under the names acquired or infused, active or passive, they have none the less spoken of the two modes of contemplation

* St. Alphonsus Liguori: "As Fr. Segneri says in his golden book, *La Concordia,* ordinary meditation usually succeeds after some time in producing that contemplation which is called acquired, and which consists in perceiving at a glance truths that we only discovered before by a long *discourse*" (*Homo apost.,* Appendix I, No. 7). The saint is not speaking of affective prayer, which he doubtless includes in *meditation.* Between this and "infused contemplation," he places the state to which I have just referred, and which he also calls active recollection, and then one of his special cases which he names contemplative repose (*otium contemplativum*); it is the loving attention to God (see ch. ii, 17).

Boudon includes both these kinds in this definition: "Contemplation is a simple and affectionate regarding of an object without *discourse or enquiry.* All creatures seen with the eye of faith can become subjects for contemplation, with this difference, that meditation seeks for that which contemplation already possesses" (*Le Règne de Dieu dans l 'oraison mentale.* Vol. I, ch. viii).

† I have said elsewhere (ch. ii, 72, note) that it amounts to the same thing, whether we prove the existence of the prayer of simplicity or that of acquired contemplation. This last point will be established presently.

which these names signify" (*Tradition,* etc., Vol. I, Part II, d. 3, a. 3). Fr. Honoré develops this idea by the aid of a large number of quotations.

He adds that Richard of St.-Victor (*De gratia contemplationis,* Book V, ch. i, Migne ed., col. 167) is the first to have dealt *very explicitly* with acquired contemplation; but neither does he give it any special name. Richard sums up his theory in chapter ii. Studying the different degrees of Christian contemplation (he is not concerned with any other; col. 169 A), he distinguishes three degrees, the last of which is ecstasy, and he says: "The first degree is obtained by *human industry,* the third by divine grace *only,* and the intermediary degree by a blending of both these actions" (col. 170 B).

**9.**—The **Quietists**. A few words must be said here concerning certain errors in relation to perfection and prayer.

By the word contemplation, the quietists of the seventeenth century unanimously understood the prayer of simplicity, but carried to absurd lengths (see Molinos, prop. 23, Falconi, Malaval, d'Estival).

They also made use of exaggerated expressions in order to describe its good effects. Molinos says: "By *acquired* contemplation we arrive at a state in which we commit no kind of sin, neither mortal nor venial" (Prop. 57). Mme. Guyon proclaimed that the supreme degree of her prayer was superior to ecstasy and other divine manifestations; which is simply puerile.* This conclusion was a consequence of their fundamental principle† that *all action is an imperfection,* and that the immobility of our faculties must therefore be the *ideal,* towards which all our endeavours should tend. Hence the name of *quietists,* which expresses their exaggerated tendency to repose. This absurd principle once admitted, we can understand how greatly they would esteem a state of prayer in which the soul becomes simplified and its action less. But this esteem started from a false premise which has had more than one unfortunate result.

**10.**—But because the prayer of simple regard has been thus extolled by the quietists, we need not conclude that it is dangerous,‡ for we should then fall blindly into a snare set for us by the Devil. When he cannot make a direct attack upon practices that are inspired by God, he tries to bring them into discredit by exaggerations or an admixture of falsehood. These practices thus become suspected even by well-intentioned persons who have not the leisure or the talent to separate the good grain from the tares.

* She had the presumption to declare that "the majority of saints, such as St. Teresa, had never reached her level (*Les Torrents,* Part IV, ch. iii, Nos. 5, 7, 10). She regards their "passive way of illumination" as a simple step in the direction of the "naked faith," the "total death" in which she finds herself. But God does not require of them (of these souls) *"such an exalted perfection"* (No. 3).

† I shall speak of this again later (ch. xxvii). Dom Mackey reminds us that Molinos claimed to base this principle upon St. Francis de Sales' teaching (*Words* of the saint. Vol. V, p. lvii).

‡ This happened after the condemnation of Molinos (1687). The Sacred Congregation of the Inquisition pronounced to the contrary in this same year (Terzago, p. 21).

The prayer of the quietists cannot be confused with the real prayer of simplicity. In the first case, all activity is suppressed as far as possible; in the second, we make use of it to the best of our powers. In one we think of nothing at all; in the other we apply ourselves to some idea, or feeling, or act of the will. These are very clear distinctions, both as to tendencies and results.

# CHAPTER V

## FIRST FUNDAMENTAL CHARACTER OF THE MYSTIC UNION: GOD'S PRESENCE FELT

**1.—The course to be followed** *when expounding the mystic states.* We are acquainted with their general definition, and the names of the four degrees of extraordinary union with God (ch. iii); but we still know nothing of the inmost nature of this union. This is what we must now explain. Lucidity has always seemed difficult of attainment in these matters.

Two opposite courses present themselves. The one consists in a study of the details, describing one set of special states, and leaving it to the reader to construct the general idea.

The other begins with *this general aspect,* and descends subsequently to the details.

Those who prefer the first method have only to read St. Teresa's beautiful descriptions. I have adopted the second one, as more expeditious.

The ordinary man prefers speed to everything else. Details do not usually interest him, but only the main lines. So you begin by offering him the one thing that he demands. He seems to say: Try in an hour to make me understand exactly what mysticism is. This can be done.

The method, however, is not a new one. In fact, the majority of Latin treatises of the seventeenth and the eighteenth centuries begin with generalities on contemplation. It remains to be seen whether they have always chosen the most important characteristics, and not those easiest of comprehension.

**2.**—The **inmost nature of the mystic union**. This is shown in the two following theses.

**3.—First thesis**. (*1°*) *The mystic states which have God for their object attract attention at the outset by the impression of recollection and union which they cause us to experience. Hence the name of mystic union.* (2°) *Their real point of difference from the recollection of ordinary prayer is this: that in the mystic state, God is not satisfied merely to help us to* **think of** *Him and to* **remind** *us of His presence: He gives us an experimental, intellectual knowledge of this presence. He* *makes us feel that we really enter into communication with Him.* (3°) *In the lower degrees, however (prayer of quiet), God only does this in a somewhat obscure manner. The manifestation increases in distinctness as the union becomes of a higher order.*

**4.—Explanation**. The present thesis does not seek to define the exact *physiognomy* of the knowledge that is received. This will be the object of the following thesis. For the moment, it is sufficient to understand what an abyss separates ordinary prayer from the mystic union. There is a profound difference between *thinking* of a person and *feeling* him near us.

And so when we feel that someone is near us, we say that we have an experimental knowledge of his presence.

In ordinary prayer, we have only an abstract knowledge of God's presence.

**5.—Demonstration**. I do not pause at the first part of this thesis because it is universally admitted; and it is the same when the second part when it is a question of full union and ecstasy, because two explicit passages from St. Teresa are quoted by everybody. The saint here explains how some ignorant directors had maintained to her that God is not present in the soul. She adds that in receiving the prayer of union she had *experimental* proof to the contrary (see Extracts.)

But we must show that it is the same with the prayer of quiet also. I do not know that this has ever been openly denied before our days.* But several authors seem to have ignored it. And yet St. Teresa is quite as definite upon this point. Twelve conclusive passages can be cited (see Extracts at the end of the chapter). I will add to these some quotations taken from other authors. Their statements are fully confirmed by experience.

* In his book, *The Life of Union with God* (1900, No. 127), and in *The Mystical State* (1903, No. 107), M. Saudreau regards it as possible that God should *sometimes* make His presence felt in the mystic union. But he does not see in this an essential and characteristic fact. In his more recent book (*Les faits extraordinaires de la vie spirituelle*) this writer goes still farther. He tries to prove by metaphysical arguments that the direct sentiment of the presence is impossible. According to him, it can only be known indirectly; we feel something else: peace, love, etc., just as in ordinary prayer, although with greater force, and we conclude from this that God is present. The author seeks to entice me into the field of speculative theology and the philosophic theory of knowledge, the difficulties of which have caused so many disputes. But I have always said that I leave these questions to those who are abler than I (see Preface 1, No. 2°). I work with a view to practical utility, merely trying to speak the language of the authorized mystics, and to make their thought accessible to all. In chapter xxxi, 28 *bis*, however, there will be found a manner of seeing things which is not touched by M. Saudreau's arguments.

As to the passages that I have brought in support of my thesis, he disputes their value, declaring that they amount to nothing more than a manner of speaking. And yet the natural sense cannot be discarded without solid reasons other than this: It is not in accordance with my system.

This writer has wished me to suppress my chapters v and vi. Now it is a remarkable fact that in letters from souls favoured with these graces, which several directors have been kind enough to communicate to me (suppressing the names), those two chapters are said to be precisely those that struck them most, and gave them an exact picture of their state.

It is of little importance that, in the works of Dionysius the Areopagite and other primitive writers, this thesis is rather hinted at than expressed. It suffices that St. Teresa, followed by so many others, gives it to us explicitly. In mystic as in dogmatic theology, formulas become more exact as the centuries go by. The primitive mystics often content themselves with rapid outlines, or they enlarge complacently upon the more evident but less important characteristics. Thus they are especially struck with the fact that the knowledge is sublime and obscure, and that the love is ardent and unreasoned.

Farther on I will give a direct refutation to an error opposed to this thesis (**19**).

**6.**—It would be impossible to insist too strongly upon the **importance** of the proposition just established. Those who are ignorant of this fundamental truth have no accurate conception of mysticism. For them everything will remain obscure and incomprehensible.

**7.—The degree of evidence that it affords**. The third part of the thesis says that at times the reality of the divine presence in the prayer of quiet is only apparent in a somewhat obscure way. This point is not contested. We shall see presently (**15**) that this is so especially with beginners; such little light as God gives them being in part veiled by their prejudices or ignorance.

But, for the moment, it is not our business to study the measure in which a beginner attains to a consciousness of his state; the important thing is to say in what this state *actually* consists, and what a man who is *already instructed*, and whose attention is awakened, comes really to find there.

**8.—The difference between divine love and the mystic union**. We may say that this latter *begets* divine love, that it is a union with God by love. But if we stopped here, we should not have said everything. We must add that this love is called forth by a known, experimental *possession* of God. This is where it differs from love which is felt in the ordinary way of prayer.

Divine love does not of itself make God known as being present in the soul, except by deduction. You would have the same feeling for absent friends. You are united to them in memory and in heart; but to clasp their hand is a very different thing.

**9.—Objection**. And yet when divine love becomes very ardent, we are led to say: I feel that God is working within me. And this leads us to add immediately: Therefore He is within me. And so we declare God's presence within us?

**10.—Answer**. No doubt; but you only arrive at this point by reasoning. By *way of experience*, you know only one thing—that your soul is inflamed with love. By a rapid deduction you then say to yourself that God alone could be the author of such a state, and by a second argument you conclude that He is present. But in the mystic union the soul proceeds quite otherwise. She has an experimental knowledge, analogous to that of the senses which do not reason; the soul, then, *perceives;* she does not *conclude*.

To sum up, the ardour of the divine love does not suffice to determine that a state is mystic. You may say, if you like, that it is *seraphic*, which is quite different.

**11.—Comparisons** with the ordinary exercise of the presence of God. The analogy between them is twofold: 1° the object is the same—God present; 2° the two exercises deserve the name of the prayer of repose, although in varying degrees.

But there are profound differences. The thesis has told us that, in the one, the soul *thinks* of God; in the other, it *really feels* Him. The first is the result of a simple act of faith;* the second adds to this an experimental knowledge. We can can have the former at will; the latter only when it pleases God to manifest Himself.

**12.—A confusion to be avoided**. In spite of the fundamental differences which have just been pointed out, some authors, though a few only, such as Cardinal Brancati, have confounded the prayer of quiet (interpreted, let it be clearly understood, in the sense in which St. Teresa uses the word) with the ordinary exercise of the presence of God, and even with the prayer of simplicity. This means that they have not taken account of the second proposition in my first fundamental thesis. They are thus reduced to making the difference between the ordinary state and the mystic state a mere question of intensity.

**13.—Cause of this confusion**. What has misled them is, doubtless, that, in order to form an idea of the prayer of quiet, they were content to have recourse to the etymology of the word (which simply signifies *repose*). Therefore all *tranquil* prayer, so they said to themselves, must be called the prayer of quiet.

But the question should be put differently and from the standpoint of history. The sense of a word is fixed by usage; there are shades of meaning which etymology does not show. They ought to have said: St. Teresa has attached a *special* signification to this word. What is this signification? When compared with the older meaning, does it involve any restriction in the sense?

There is no doubt as to the answer. The saint has *restricted* the sense of the word quiet, and language has become more precise with regard to it. Before her day, each author understood it in his own way, and sometimes gave it only a vague signification.

At the time of St. Francis of Sales the change was too recent to be invariably adopted. The language of mysticism was far from being fixed; and, the holy doctor and St. J. F. de Chantal take the word quiet, sometimes in its ancient, wide sense (in which case it included even the prayer of simplicity), sometimes in the new and restricted sense adopted by St. Teresa. How many readers are there who have never suspected† this!

* Scaramelli, Tr. III, No. 26.

† This was so with Mgr. Bougaud in his *Life of St. Jane Frances de Chantal.*

**14.—The dispositions required for a high degree of contemplation.** We understand now why the learned have not more aptitude for entering into the mystic state than the unlettered.

This could scarcely be explicable if these states consisted merely in having profound or subtle ideas about God. On the contrary, theologians and men of genius would then present a very favourable disposition; grace, following in the train of nature, would have almost nothing to do in order to raise them to a high degree of contemplation.

But the thesis has taught us that it is a question of an experimental knowledge. Hence the natural power of the intellect, or the amount of learning, do not come into it at all. A peasant receives the impressions of sense just as vividly as an academician.

On the other hand, scholars regain their place of superiority when it is a question of theoretical discussions. But this is not mental prayer.

**15.—Doubts of beginners.** If we lay the preceding and following theses before them, they will make no objection. The truth will appear evident to them.

But if they have not read any mystic writings, if they have not been taught the exact manner of interpreting what they experience, it will be very difficult for them to arrive *by themselves* at the truth. This is because, in the prayer of quiet, God as yet only manifests Himself obscurely (7). The evidence that He gives of His presence is not yet strong enough to triumph over certain preconceived ideas which I am going to point out. On one side they are impelled to say: "It is God. He is there." But on the other hand they think they have strong reasons for rejecting such a thought. Their minds become confused, and they no longer know what to believe.

**16.**—It is particularly **during the time that the prayer of quiet lasts** that the soul instinctively believes in the presence of God. It is *afterwards* that she begins to reason and falls back into uncertainty.

Let us note well that this uncertainty does not bear upon the existence of a particular spiritual impression (which I shall describe farther on), but only upon its cause. The beginner says: "I have experienced something extraordinary, and probably supernatural. It is an impression of a special kind, and one of which I have hitherto known nothing, and of which the majority of Christians know nothing either. It contains a religious sentiment and it unites me to God. This is indisputable; but what a strange way to pray!" The delicate point is the daring to admit to ourselves that it is God Himself of whom we were thus conscious, and that we were really in touch with Him. And so we find reasons alternately for either opinion.

**17.—Preconceived ideas.** There are several kinds of preconceived ideas which suffice to veil the knowledge of God's presence. One is due to a feeling of *humility* and prudence. We say to ourselves: "Is it possible that God should grant me so great a grace? No, I must find some other explanation." And we hope to discover one eventually.

The *second preconceived idea* common to beginners is due to their *ignorance of mysticism.* It consists in believing that the graces of interior prayer are quite different from those which they are now experiencing. The *Lives* of the saints have nearly always spoken to them of visions. This is how they also ought to begin, so they think. They ought to see Our Lord, the Blessed Virgin, and the angels. If they imagine anything else—the manifestation of God Himself, for instance—they picture it in quite another manner. It should be resplendent, showing the three Divine Persons or certain of their attributes. It should also cause a vehement, overflowing love, such as the saints had in their raptures. But this contemplation has quite other characteristics, being obscure, confused, tranquil. It cannot, therefore, be God who is manifesting Himself.

Another prejudice found amongst beginners will be explained later on (ch. viii, 7).

**18.**—Thence follow **interior sufferings**. For if it is not God who makes Himself felt, whence can such a state proceed? Is it the devil? Is it disease? And the soul is full of anxiety. She consults directors. But sometimes these directors themselves are ignorant of mysticism, and are no less embarrassed than the penitent. Sometimes, too, the soul explains her interior state so badly that they can hardly be blamed for believing her to be subject to illusions.

The great remedy is either to discover a wise director who is versed in mysticism, or to read a book in which there is a good description of this state. The soul will then recover her peace (see also ch. ii, **48**).

**19.**—**The error** diametrically opposed to the above thesis consists in admitting the following proposition: the mystic states (or their inferior degrees, at any rate) do not contain any new fact, any element of a distinct order, any mode of operation *specifically* different from those of ordinary prayer. They only differ by the *intensity* of certain elements: a more sustained attention, a more clearly felt peace and joy, a deeper understanding of the truths of religion, a more ardent love. Freethinkers are obliged to imagine things in this way to facilitate their purely naturalistic explanations.

But as the same idea may have occurred to Catholics, it will be useful to give a direct refutation of this conception of mysticism (whether it be considered as bearing upon mysticism as a whole, or only upon the inferior degrees).

1° When ancient writers agree in saying that we cannot attain to the mystic states by our own efforts, they speak of an absolute, *total* impossibility; in a word, we cannot procure them for ourselves even in *a low degree* (ch. i, **1**). Now, this would not be so if the ordinary state of mental prayer were *only a low degree* of the mystic states.

2° Mysticism has always been held to contain a large element of mystery; this is shown by the etymology of the name. The writings of the mystics abundantly justify this idea. Any impartial person studying the great descriptive writers, such as Ruysbroeck, Blessed Angela of Foligno, St. Teresa, St. John of the Cross, the Ven. Mary of the Incarnation (Ursuline), Ven. Marina de Escobar, etc., must feel that where prayer is concerned they speak of things with which ordinary Christians have not the least acquaintance: they are even tempted to call them unintelligible.

From the moment that we could teach the substance of the science in these words—"See what all pious people experience in their prayer, and then intensify it in your thoughts"—there would no longer be any difficulty to solve in mysticism. A man who has never seen a mountain finds no difficulty in imagining one, because he has, at any rate, seen a hill. It would be the same thing here.

And for the same reason an explanation of mysticism could be compressed into five lines. Why, then, should ancient writers have been at pains to indite such huge volumes, excusing themselves all the time for undertaking a task that was above human capacity?

But this is explained if the mystic state is an enigma, if it contains a *new fact,* and is not merely the intensification of an old fact known by everybody.

3° If in mysticism we descend from the general view to the details, we shall see that the above thesis gives the key to many difficulties which are to be met with in the old writers—for instance, in their descriptions or their terminology: we shall have more than one proof of this; which the opposite system cannot succeed in giving.

Let us quote some examples at once:

(*a*) It is certain that St. Teresa, when describing the prayer which she calls quietude, did not merely intend to speak of a remembrance of God or of a high idea of the Divinity. This fact is self-evident. But it must be denied unless we accept the thesis (see Extracts). Let anyone in the same way read Blessed Angela of Foligno over again, and try to interpret her visions as being anything else save an experimental knowledge!

(*b*) So, too, we should have to say that a large number of writers have been wrong in distinguishing two kinds of contemplation, the acquired and the infused. Why, indeed, embarrass oneself with learned terms if between these two things it is only a question of the degree of intensity with which they are experienced?

4° We shall see farther on that there is an intellectual vision of Jesus Christ and the saints (ch. xx). Their presence is made known to the soul, but without the manifestation of any material form. So, by analogy, we must admit that there is in the same way an experimental and intellectual knowledge of the presence of God.

5° If we admit that mystic contemplation differs from the ordinary state only by the vividness of the light and the love, it is a contradiction to say afterwards that there are mystic states which are very weak and hardly perceptible. And yet all writers agree that this is so.

6° We have seen (**18**) that when a soul begins to receive the mystic graces in a very evident way, she feels surprise and even anxiety. Now, the contrary should occur if the system that I am impugning were the true one. "If the basis of the mystic state," (says a recent writer) "were but a knowledge and a love of God, felt with an intensity which may vary in strength, we do not see what could disquiet the souls that are led by these ways. Such effects, being good in themselves, cannot instil anxiety into the conscience. The soul that feels them is happy in them; she feels herself drawn towards God, and this can only strengthen her and inspire her with confidence" (M. l'Abbé Caudron, *Revue du Clergé Français,* June 1st, 1906). What surprises and distresses the soul is the feeling that she is entering a wholly new world. It is this, too, that alarms certain directors who would otherwise have no objections.

**20.—Question**. We can imagine that a soul might never experience the sensible (felt) presence of which the thesis speaks, and still, however, have vivid lights upon certain mysteries of religion, such as the Incarnation, the Redemption, and the Holy Eucharist, with the result that she is filled with a very ardent love. Can we say that such a soul is in the mystic state when she receives these graces?

**21.—Answer**. No, not if these lights are not revelations in the strict sense of the term. And this by reason of our definition of mystic acts (ch. i, **1**). We do not give this name to lights which only differ in intensity from those which everybody can produce. All that can be said is that the prayer just referred to deserves the name of ordinary as to kind, and of extraordinary as to elevation. It is a high and an excellent way, but different from that which is described by St. Teresa and her school. Is this a common way, or does it even ever exist in practice? The question cannot be solved *a priori.* The facts must be observed. But this would necessitate numerous and difficult inquiries which no one has as yet thought of making.

**21** *bis.*—I have been asked why I do not hear speak of the feelings of love which accompany the mystic union, but defer the matter to chapter xi. These feelings, I am told, form an essential part of this union; they are one of its fundamental elements. It would therefore seem that they should be spoken of at the beginning.

My reply is that one cannot speak of everything at once. And then these feelings are merely the consequence of the knowledge of a new kind which characterizes the mystic union. It is this knowledge which is the really fundamental element, the necessary starting-point of the description. We must begin by concentrating our attention on this all-important and difficult subject.

# EXTRACTS*

## § 1. Passages in Which the Prayer of Quiet is Spoken of Explicitly, and in Which it is Stated That the Presence of God is Really Felt in It.

**22.**—St. Teresa†:

1° "It is impossible to persuade it [the soul] now that God *was not with it,* till it turns back upon itself and beholds its own failings and imperfections. Then it fears for everything; and it is well it should do so" (*Life,* ch. xv, 23).

2° She relates what she herself experienced at twenty years of age, before her definite conversion: "I used to have at times, as I have said, though it used to pass quickly away,—certain *commencements* of that which I am now going to describe... and sometimes even when I was reading,—*a feeling of the presence of God* would come over me unexpectedly, so that I *could in no wise doubt, either that He was within me,* or that I was wholly absorbed in Him. It was not by way of vision; I believe it was what is called mystical theology" (*Life,* ch. x, 1).‡

3° "God... will have the soul comprehend that His Majesty is *so near it,* that it... may speak to Him itself, and not with a loud crying, because so near is He already, that He understands even the movements of its lips... and [He will] also have us understand what His *presence* bringeth about" (*Life,* ch. xiv, 7, 8).

4° "For the soul is already ascending out of its wretched state, and *some little knowledge of the blissfulness of glory* is communicated to it" (*ibid.,* 6). One cannot see what the significance of this last sentence could be, if it was not a question of a real possession of God, and therefore a presence that is felt.

5° "So, in the beginning, when I attained to some degree of supernatural prayer—I speak of the prayer of quiet—I laboured to remove from myself every

* Let us remember that we can defer reading these extracts until later (second preface).

† If anyone were to deny that these passages prove the thesis, he would have to give a perverted and wrong interpretation to an expression that occurs repeatedly: *to feel the presence of God.* It would have to be taken merely as indicating affective movements, joy, sweetness, love, etc. But if this had been the saint's intention, if she spoke in such an unnatural way, the context would finally show us that this was so. She would not compare the soul to holy Simeon (see 6°). He knew by a special light that the Son of God was really in his arms. He did not conclude it by a simple impression of sweetness.

‡ I have known readers to be embarrassed by this last sentence, which appeared to them inaccurate. As a matter of fact, it would seem that the saint should not have said that a state of soul is mystic theology, but that it is studied in theology.

The saint did not mean anything else, but she expresses herself in the language of former days, which was borrowed from scholasticism. Modern writers speak differently. They consider each science objectively, as a group of truths consigned to a written treatise, leaving out of the question the minds that applied themselves to these truths.

The scholastics, on the contrary, regarded all science subjectively, such as it exists in the thinker's mind; they define it as a habitus, a state of mind. This language was still employed in the seventeenth century.

thought of bodily objects;... I thought, however, that I had *a sense of the presence of God:* this was true, and I contrived to be in a state of recollection before Him" (*Life*, ch. xxii, 3).*

6° "... It is the settling of a soul in peace, or rather Our Lord,† to speak more properly, puts it in peace, by His Presence, as He did just Simeon: for all the faculties are calmed. The *soul understands* after a manner far different from *understanding by the exterior senses,* that *she is now joined near to her God,* for that within a very little more she will attain to the being made one with Him by *union...* But the *child Himself* made Himself known to him [just Simeon]: just so the soul understands Him here, though not with like clarity; for she herself knows not how she understands, but that she seeth herself in the Kingdom (at least, *near* the King who is to give it her)... they [the faculties] can think *near whom* they stand; for two of them [the understanding and the memory] are free... They [those who are in the prayer of quiet] are *so near,* that they perceive they are understood by signs. They are *in the palace, close by* their King, and see that He already begins here to bestow on them His Kingdom" (*Way of Perfection,* ch. xxxi, pp. 93, 4).

7° "When His Majesty... begins to contract an amity with the soul... there is raised in the interior of the soul so great a suavity that makes her *perceive very plainly* that Our Lord is *very near* to her. I call [it] *Prayer of quiet,* for the repose it causeth in all the powers: so that the party seems to *possess God* as he most desires... though she [the soul] perfectly sees not the Master that teaches us, yet plainly understands He is *with* her" (*Conceptions of the Love of God,* ch. iv, pp. 308, 9).

8° *Second Letter to Fr. Rodrigo Alvarez.* The saint here expounds the theory, dear to several of her predecessors, that all the mystic states are founded upon the existence of *spiritual senses;* this expression indicating the faculty of perceiving a spiritual being *experimentally* (see the next chapter).

9° In the prayer of quiet, "the soul is like a child that sucks still, who lying at his mother's breast, she, to please him, without his moving his lips, spirts her milk into his mouth: just so here; for... our Lord is pleased that, without her forethinking thereon, she should understand that she is conversing with Him...

* In the *Life,* ch. xxvii, 6, there is a passage which I do not insert here, although at first sight it seems to support the thesis. She is speaking of "the prayer of union and of quiet." In reality the saint is probably speaking not of that which occurs *during* these states, but in the intervals between them. It is a more ardent devotion, manifesting the presence of God *in an indirect way.* "We seem to feel that He hears us *by the effects* and the spiritual impressions of great love and faith of which we are then conscious, as well as by the good resolutions, accompanied by sweetness, which we then make... God is understood to be present there, *by the effects* He works in the soul."

† In order to understand certain passages from St. Teresa, we should know that in translating *Nuestro Señor,* by Our Lord, we do not give the exact shade ot the Spanish expression. When the context does not modify the sense of these expressions, the first, the Spanish, refers to God Himself, equally with *el Señor,* while the second, the English, refers to the Humanity of Jesus Christ.

Let her not desire to know how she enjoys it, and what that is which she enjoys; but let her then neglect herself, for *He that stands by her* will not neglect to see what is best for her" (*Way of Perfection,* ch. xxxi, pp. 95, 6).

10° "The soul.. feels great delight at being *so near* to God" (*Interior Castle,* Fourth Mansion, ch. iii, 12).

11° Referring to the way in which we should act when transiently deprived of the mystic union, the saint says: "When the fire in our hearts... does not burn and we *do not feel the presence of God,* we must search for Him as He would have us do, like the Bride in the Canticles, and we must ask all creatures: 'Who it was that made them?' as St. Augustine (either in his Meditations or his Confessions) tells us that he did. Thus we shall not stand like blockheads, wasting our time in the hope of again receiving what we before enjoyed. At first it may be that Our Lord will not renew His gift again for a year, or even for many years" (*Interior Castle,* Sixth Mansion, ch. vii, 11).

12° Speaking of a state which is still removed from ecstasy, but which overtakes the soul in the midst of her occupations, when the mind is not recollected, not even thinking of God: "The soul makes amorous complaints to its Bridegroom, even uttering them aloud; nor can it help itself, for it knows that, though He is present, He will not manifest Himself so that it may enjoy Him" (*Interior Castle,* Sixth Mansion, ch. ii, 3).

**23.**—Fr. Balthasar Alvarez, speaking of the prayer of quiet:

"Since it is God who calls certain souls to the prayer of quiet, it is no doubt pleasing to Him that they employ themselves, then, not in desiring or expecting revelations, but in contemplating His perfections, and producing affections in His holy presence" (*Life,* translated from the French of L. Du Pont, Vol. II, ch. xli, p. 170; Second difficulty).

**24.**—St. Francis of Sales:

"The soul who in this sweet repose enjoys this delicate sense of the divine *presence*" (*Treatise on the Love of God,* Book VI, ch. viii, p. 255).

"Now it fares in like manner with the soul who is in rest and quiet before God: for she sucks in a manner insensibly the delights of *His presence,* without any discourse... She sees her spouse *present* with so sweet a view that reasonings would be to her unprofitable and superfluous. Nor does the soul in this repose stand in need of the *memory,* for she has her lover *present.* Nor has she need of the imagination, for why should we represent in an exterior or interior image Him whose *presence* we are possessed of?... O Eternal God! when by Thy sweet *presence* Thou dost cast odoriferous perfumes into our hearts... the will... as the spiritual sense of smell, remains delightfully engaged in enjoying [in the French, *sentir*], without adverting to it, the incomparable good of having its God *present*" (*ibid.*, ix).

**25.**—The Ven. Louis du Pont (*Vie du P. Balthasar Alvarez*). Fr. du Pont reviews the different degrees of mystic prayer, and sees in them only the development of one and the same grace, called by different names. He adds:

"This prayer is called the *prayer of the presence of God,* of repose or recollection, and of silence... All prayer, then, supposes the presence of God; but the prayer of which I speak has received this name for a reason peculiar to itself; it is, that in this prayer the soul, illuminated by the Divine light, discovers, *without any reasoning* or difficulty, God *present,* near her, or within her, insomuch that she seems to see, to hear, and to *feel* Him. Thus Moses, as the great Apostle relates, stood firm before Pharaoh, because he believed he saw the invisible God present to defend him" (*Life of Balthasar Alvarez,* from the French of Louis du Pont, Vol. I, ch. xiv, p. 155).

**25** *bis.*—Alvarez de Paz:

1° On the prayer of quiet: "The soul sees herself *near* God; she sees herself loved and esteemed, the object of a special providence, like a very dear daughter... In this degree, the knowledge of God *present* and taking notice of the soul can only be called darkness instead of light, if it is compared with the great brightness of the following degrees... The soul understands, as it were experimentally, that which she only knew before by faith—namely, that she is seen of God, tenderly loved by Him; *quite near* to Him who is prompt to benefit her, and grant her desires. Also she rejoices and is at rest, like the child, who after having wept, is taken into his mother's arms and allowed to suck her milk" (*De inquis. pacis,* Book V, Part III, ch. iv).

2° Let us now give this passage on the full union: "It is a very precious gift by which God manifests Himself in the depths and inmost centre of the soul with a *very strong light;* He shows Himself *present,* regarding the soul and tenderly loving her... The mind knows Him, now as a certain All in which is all good, now as having one or more special perfections" (*ibid.*, ch. v).

**26.**—St. Alphonsus Rodriguez, speaking of himself:

"This person is accustomed to practise the exercise of the presence of God in three ways. The first is by the way of the memory... The second is by the way of the understanding; the soul knows *without any reasoning* (because she has passed this degree) how God is in her. By this knowledge she comes to *feel the presence* of God within her, God giving her the grace of communicating Himself to her in this manner. This *feeling of the presence of God* is not obtained by way of the imagination; but it is in her as a certitude received from on high; she has a *spiritual and experimental certitude,* that God is in the soul and in all places. This presence of God is called an *intellectual presence.* As a rule, it lasts a long time; the farther the soul advances in God's service, the more *continuous* is it, and the more *felt,* God daily communicating Himself more to the soul if she disposes herself thereto by a generous mortification... It has often happened to this person that, without any effort on his part, without his even thinking of it, this sovereign Master has placed Himself sensibly before him, as a man should place himself suddenly before another, without this latter being aware of it, etc." (*Vie* de St. Alphonse, from his Mémoires, No. 40. Also quoted by Fr. Nouet, *Conduite de l'homme d'Oraison,* Book IV, ch. vi).

**27.**—Fr. Lallemant:

"When, after a long cultivation of purity of heart, God would enter into a soul and *manifest Himself to it openly by the gift of His holy presence...* the soul finds itself so delighted with its new state, that it feels as if it had never known or loved God before" (*Doct. Spir.* 7th *principe.*, ch. iv, art. ii, § 1, Eng.: *Spiritual Doctrine,* edited by F. W. Faber, d. d.).

**28.**—Fr. Nouet (*La conduits de l'homme d'Oraison*):

After having spoken of the *active* presence of God, which depends "to some extent upon the man's industry and will," he adds that there is "a passive but transient *presence* of God, and also an habitual passive *presence* of God which is the man's state. As to the transient *presence,* when the soul is favoured with it, it is not by her own choice or industry, but by a supernatural light that is infused when she is thinking of it least. Sometimes, when entering into prayer or some other exercise, with dryness and disgust, after suffering this pain, she suddenly perceives that the Bridegroom is *present,* and this presence, with regard to which she feels a great certainty, causes a loving and reverent trembling... Often the perception of this presence holds her in a loving admiration, and often also her faculties remain held as though by a sweet sleep, in which she tastes incredible delights... We see by this how desirable is this visit of the Bridegroom, even when it lasts no more than a quarter of an hour; but when it is stable and in a way habitual, it is much more precious... This presence [whether transient or not] operates in such wise as to make us *perceive, feel,* and know with certainty that *God is in the soul* and that the soul is in God" (Book IV, ch. vi).

**29.**—Scaramelli (*Directorum Mysticum,* Treatise 3):

"The infused prayer of *repose* is nothing else than a certain calm, a repose and an interior sweetness, which have their birth in the most secret depths of the soul and at times overflow upon the senses and bodily faculties, and which results from the soul *not only approaching God, but also feeling His presence.* The reader must not imagine that this degree of prayer proceeds from any act of *simple faith* produced by the aid of ordinary grace, in virtue of which the soul *believes* that God is present: because this act, as is manifest and as is proved by experience, would be unable to produce the great effects of repose, sweetness, and peace to which we have referred. These proceed from the gift of wisdom which brings the soul near to God, *making Him present* by His light, so that not only does she *believe* in His presence, but she actually *feels it with a very sweet spiritual sensation*" (No. 26).

"From this *perception of God present* is born a great calm, a great peace, a joyousness full of sweetness, which rise up from the soul's inmost centre—that is to say, from the place where God *makes His sweet presence felt by the soul*" (No. 28).

"In order to determine whether anyone possesses this prayer, we must observe whether the soul knows God to be *present* by a certain *experimental knowledge* that causes her to *feel* and *taste His presence,* and whether, without any fatigue, she feels the calm, the repose, and the interior peace, in the spiritual faculties, at any rate. If this is so, the soul is already raised by God to this degree of prayer" (No. 32).

**30.**—Fr. Rousseau (a Dominican of the eighteenth century), speaking of the first degree of infused contemplation, says:

"The manner of praying in this degree and in the succeeding degrees is to find ourselves in *a certain presence of God,* which is very simple and very far removed above *another presence* of God, in which beginners find themselves at times" (Letter XX).

**31.**—Fr. de Clorivière, describing the prayer of quiet:

1° "When the soul presents herself at prayer, even if she should come to it with the design of occupying herself with some special subject, she at once finds herself, without knowing how, *recollected* within herself *with a sweet feeling of the presence of Our Lord.* This feeling, it is true, is not very distinct; but the *peace* and the sweetness that accompany it convince the soul that He whom she loves *is near,* that He *comes Himself* to give her proofs of His love, and that she should then think of nothing else than of the happiness that is offered to her." The soul is then "an infant half asleep upon its mother's knees, which, pressed against her breast, with scarcely any movement of the lips... receives the milk that flows gently into its mouth and becomes its sustenance. St. Teresa and St. Francis of Sales make use of this comparison... Such is the soul's disposition in the prayer of quiet, feeling, although in a confused manner, that the celestial Bridegroom deigns in a manner to *take her in His arms.* She dares aspire to a yet closer union, or, rather, it is the Bridegroom Himself who suggests this desire to her heart... She then does nothing, she can do nothing else than rejoice in the blessing that she possesses" (*Considérations,* etc., Part II, ch. xxxiii).

2° However, "the soul's powers are not always in the same degree of drowsiness. Sometimes the memory remains free, with the imagination... The will alone enjoys the sweetness of the Bridegroom's *presence.* Also it *quite frequently* happens that it does this in a hardly perceptible way. The Lord then makes His *presence* felt at the point or summit of the will only, in the most spiritual part of this faculty. His action takes place in the most secret region of the soul, which has but a *slight knowledge* of it; but this knowledge, slight as it is, is sufficient, when the soul is faithful and courageous, to maintain her in calm... It often happens that God, touched by the soul's secret desires and the patience with which she awaits Him, will come *Himself* to console her, and will make her enter into a more profound repose by a new feeling *of His presence,* a feeling which, rising from the soul's depths, as from the sanctuary in which it resides, will spread through all her faculties and will sometimes pass on into the exterior senses. If it pleases the Lord to remain always hidden, He will give the soul strength to bear this painful state, and will cause her to derive the greatest benefit from it. This trial, far from depressing the soul, will only augment her desire to unite herself with Him; she will confess her weakness, and call upon Him to come to the help of her helplessness, and to draw her that she may run after Him to the odour of His ointments" (*Canticle of Canticles,* 1, 3; *ibid.,* ch. xxxiv).

3° There are a number of documents in existence in which Fr. de Clorivière describes his own prayer from the age of thirty onwards. We see here that the quietude of which he speaks above was his ordinary state. "As soon as he began to pray, he became recollected and penetrated with an *interior feeling of the presence of God.*" This prayer "appeared to him to come from on high and to be far above his own efforts" (*Histioire du R. P. de Clorivière,* by Father Terrien, 1891, Book I, ch. v; Book II, ch. iv).

**32.**—M. Ribet:

"The prayer of quiet, then, is a *feeling of the presence* of God which has its birth in the secret recesses of the soul, and in it the will reposes and takes its delight" (*La mystique divine,* Vol. I, ch. xii, No. 1).

"At the first stages of supernatural prayer... God reveals Himself only by *His presence*" (*ibid.,* ch. ix, No. 1). Speaking of the lowest degree of infused contemplation, he says:

"When God wills to raise a soul to mystic communications, He withdraws her from exterior things, turns her, so to speak, entirely inwards, and draws her by a delicious sentiment of His *presence* in her innermost depths... According to St. Teresa, this supernatural concentration of the soul seems to give her new senses, by which to *prove and taste the presence* of God, as she has exterior senses by which to *put herself into communication with material things*"; (*ibid.,* ch. xi, No. 1). The same idea is repeated in many passages.

**33.**—Mère Thérèse Couderc, foundress of the Congregation of Our Lady of the Cenacle:

"The more we are united to God, the more we desire this union. But what is this taste of God? It is more difficult to describe it than to experience it when grace gives it. We can say, however, that it is a sweet *sentiment of the presence of God* and of His love, causing the soul to feel a great happiness and to become recollected in Him to the point that she finds a difficulty in distracting herself... I am often obliged to do violence to myself in recreation, so as to let nothing of this appear... All other pleasure than that of *tasting* God becomes insipid to me" (*Histoire de la Congrégation,* by P. Longhaye, p. 178).

**34.**—Fr. Duplanchy:

"Without giving a definition here of extraordinary contemplation, which it belongs to mysticism to do, we will point out the two characteristic notes which distinguish it from contemplation or ordinary prayer: 1° an inner perception... of a *very special presence* of God...; 2° a suspension, complete or only partial,* of

* By partial suspension we must understand here that which only partly prevents distractions.

acts of the intellect, the memory, the imagination, and the exterior senses which might prevent the will from possessing this ineffable divine *presence* in perfect peace.

"All prayer or contemplation which is not accompanied by these two characteristic notes, *no matter how great its perfection* and whatever its effects, does not go beyond ordinary or acquired prayer" (see the word *Ascetic* in Vacant's *Dictionnaire de Théologie,* Vol. I, col. 2041).

In the same dictionary Canon Lejeune admits our thesis under the word *Contemplation.*

Abbé Gombault speaks in the same way in an article on Mysticism, published in *La Science Catholique* (Dec. 1st, 1907). Here is his conclusion: "This *experimental* knowledge of the divine *presence* in mystic prayer is so clearly testified to by all contemplatives, that it is useless to demonstrate it by quotations" (p. 35).

See also various Extracts in the next chapter.

For the states below ecstasy, I make use especially of passages from St. Teresa and her successors. I give my reasons in ch. xxx, 2 and 2 *bis,* when giving a general survey of the history of mysticism.

### § 2. Passages Where the Mystic States Are Spoken of as a Whole, Without Distinguishing Their Degrees. They Apply, Therefore, Implicitly to the Prayer of Quiet.

**34** *bis.*—Tauler:

"After the man has entirely freed himself from all attachment to things both within and without, and has learnt to rely on nought [in himself] but his own nothingness, nothing then prevents him from turning towards this pure and very simple good, which is the all-good and all-powerful God. In this union... the man does not attain to God by images or meditations, nor by a higher mental effort, nor as a taste or a light. But it is *truly Himself* that he receives inwardly, and in a manner that greatly surpasses all the savour, all the light of created beings, all reason, all measure, all intelligence" (*Institutions,* ch. xxvi).

**34** *ter.*—Walter Hilton. He speaks of union with Jesus. But the context indicates that it is a question of union with the Divinity:

"The soul seeth that her love is nought, therefore she desireth His love, for that is enough. Therefore she prayeth and desireth that the love of God should touch her with His blessed light, that she may see a little of Him by His gracious *presence,* for then should she love Him; and so by this way cometh the gift of love, *which is God,* into a soul... [There is a] special grace made spiritually by the touching of His gracious presence, as He worketh in His perfect love...; for in imperfect lovers love worketh at a distance by human affections; but in perfect lovers love worketh *nearly* by her own spiritual affections... [ch. v]... Every reasonable soul ought to covet with all its power to approach to Jesus and to be united to Him through feeling of His gracious invisible *presence.* How that *presence* is felt may better be known by experience than by any writing... Verily I think nothing can make the soul of a lover full of mirth, but the gracious *presence* of Jesus as He can show Himself to a pure soul. [ch. xi]. [The soul] thinketh that it *toucheth* Jesus, and through virtue of that unspeakable touching it is made whole and stable in itself" (*Scale of Perfection,* Book II, Part III, chs. v, xi, xiv).

**35.**—Gerson (*On the Magnificat.*)

He explains the *sapientia christianorum* of which Dionysius the Areopagite speaks: "A difficulty still remains, and it is the only one. We have to explain how we *make experiment* of the union [with God.] We may say that this *experimental union* is a simple and actual *perception* of God, proceeding from sanctifying grace, which begins here below and perfects itself in Heaven by grace consummated. It is, then, a foretaste and pledge of eternal glory and felicity... We thus arrive at an exact, condensed definition of *mystic theology,* by saying: It is an *experimental perception* of God" (Tr. 7, ch. ii).

See the following chapter (No. 45) for another similar definition by the same writer.

**36.**—Ven. John of Saint-Samson:

"*Mystic theology,* taken in its essence, is nothing other than God ineffably *perceived*" (*Maximes,* edited by Fr. Sernin, ch. xxi).

**37.**—Philippus a SS. Trinitate, describing the mystic union generally, which he calls the beginning of celestial beatitude:

1° "Perfect men find this beginning here below in the intimate union with God, which gives them at one and the same time *an experimental knowledge of His presence* and a love that rejoices in it" (Summa..., Part III, tr. 1, disc. 1, art. 5).

2° "The actual union of fruition* is the effect or the act of charity, not of him who goes out towards God *absent,* but of him who cleaves to God present: the first act would be merely desire; the second is satisfaction, fruition" (Part III, tr. 1, art. 4).

**38.**—A vision of the Ven. Marina de Escobar:

The vision of the divine ladder: "One day I saw a ladder, that sprang from the breast of Jesus Christ, present in Heaven, and descended to the earth. At the top it was very narrow, and at the bottom very wide. I tried to turn away my attention, fearing to be deceived by my imagination; but the greater my efforts, the more God obliged me to look. This ladder seemed to be of very pure gold; its steps were resplendent; and I understood that *it represented Heaven.* A multitude of angels ascended and descended by these steps, and others were all round about it. All the steps were thronged with the souls of the blessed, everywhere, below and in the

* Many writers call the mystic union the union of fruition. They wish to express by this name that God and His presence are really *experienced,* and to point out that it is more than a mere union of will and of love.

middle and above. All possessed God according to their merits... *Near the lowest step* I also saw a number of souls that are *still living upon earth,* and that by contemplation *enjoyed these eternal blessings in so far as is possible here below.* There were more women than men" (*Vida,* Vol. I, Book ch. xi, § 5, a. d. 1622.)

**39.**—Antonius a Spiritu Sancto:

Ordinarily "God is hidden from him who has habitual grace and charity; he can neither have experimental knowledge of His *presence* nor perceive it without a special favour. But by this union of fruition God manifests Himself to truly purified minds in such a manner that they perceive and taste *this presence directly and experimentally* by the knowledge and embrace of love. The real union of fruition of the contemplative soul with God is an *experimental and immediate* perception of God, produced in the intelligence and the will by the *real presence* of God. It is not the beatific vision; the mind, however, knows the divine *presence,* not only by faith, but through the gift of wisdom, by taste and experience" (Tr. IV, Nos. 10, 11).

**40.**—Fr. Meynard:

After having said that the mystic union is often called a union of fruition, although it is inferior to that of Heaven: "The union of fruition is an ardent and profound feeling of God *present in us...* The soul knows that *God is there, and she feels Him by a sweet experience:* it is a beginning of the happiness of Heaven" (Tr. II, No. 278).

**41.**—Fr. Mathieu Rousset, O.P.:

"The experimental knowledge of God's indwelling and *presence* within us is the *foundation,* the *raison d'etre,* of what we call the mystic life. It is an incomparable grace. It is also a grace that is not very common, even amongst those who are occupied with spirituality; a great number know nothing about it... And if one day its existence is revealed to them, no less astonished than Jacob awaking from sleep, they might, like him, exclaim; 'Indeed, the Lord is in this place and I knew it not' " (*La Doctrine spirituelle,* Vol. II, Book I, ch. xv, 1902 edition).

**41** *bis.*—Fr. Route, S.J.:

"We know the Catholic doctrine: in the mystic union, which is a *direct apprehension* of God, God acts immediately upon the soul in order to communicate Himself to her; and it is God, *not an image of God,* not the illusion of God, that the soul perceives and attains to" (*Les Études* for Aug. 5th, 1908, p. 371).

### § 3. Passages Describing a State Which at Least is Lower Than Ecstasy.

**42.**—Fr. Balthasar Alvarez (quoted by the Ven. Louis du Pont):

"Having placed myself in prayer, *I felt that God was there.* I saw Him; neither with *my bodily eyes,* nor through *my imagination:* nevertheless His *presence* was certain to me, and the sight I had of it was far more powerful than that of the imagination, or of the corporal eyes... It communicates such peace, and so deep a consolation, that it seems as if God had brought the soul into His eternal kingdom... It seems to her that she knows nothing, and feels no curiosity whatever, content with what she possesses without seeing it" (*Life* of Fr. Balthasar Alvarez, Vol. I, ch. xv, p. 172).

**43.**—St. Bernard:

"Be most careful not to allow yourself to think that there is anything imaginary, on the one hand, or corporeal on the other hand, in this mingling of the Word with the soul of the believer... That union, then, is made in the Spirit... A soul in this condition, with such feelings and so beloved, will be far from content that her Bridegroom should manifest Himself to her in the manner which is common to all; that is, by the things which are made, or even in the manner peculiar to a few, namely, by dreams and visions; such a soul desires that by a special privilege He should descend from on high into her, and pervade her wholly in the deepest affections, and to the very ground of the heart. She desires that He whom she loves should not show Himself to her in an *outward* shape, but should be, as it were, inpoured into her; that He should not merely appear to her, but should enter into and dominate her; *nor* is it doubtful that her happiness is so much the greater, as He is within rather than without... I am not, however, able to describe the manner in which God manifests Himself as He is, although in this manner of manifestation He declares Himself no other than He is. For, however full of reverence and devotion souls may be, He will not continue His *Presence* in them permanently and precisely thus, nor with complete uniformity to all individuals. For according as the desires of a soul vary, so the delight felt in the Divine Presence must needs vary also; and that heavenly sweetness strikes in divers ways upon the palate of the soul, according to the variation of its desires and longings" (*In Cant.*, Sermo XXXI, No. 6, 7. English: *Cantica Canticorum,* translated by S. J. Eules).

See also a passage from St. Bernard in ch. xxv, **24.**

**44.**—Richard of St.-Victor, commenting upon this verse of the Canticle of Canticles: "In my bed by night I sought Him whom my soul loveth: I sought Him and found Him not." He describes the desire of contemplation, and says, incidentally, in what it consists:

"The Bride is right in saying that she seeks in the darkness (that of the Spirit); for she does not possess the Bridegroom fully and does not feel *His presence.* It is true that He is present in essence, and also as the object of desire, since this desire [which is due to His grace] implies His presence; but this presence does not make Him visible. The obscurity has not yet disappeared, the light that *manifests His presence* has not yet shone out. Also the Bride laments this night; she bewails being obliged to seek the Bridegroom in it and not to find Him. She calls on the light, the grace which will make Him fully *present;* she desires to be seen by Him and to see Him. This great favour, this experience of the *presence* and the spiritual sweetness, is referred to in these words: 'I sought Him whom my soul loveth.'... Alas! the Bridegroom does not always discover Himself immediately when we seek Him and desire Him. He delays, in order to prove our constancy and in our own interest; for when a thing has cost us much trouble we are more attached to it and keep it with greater care: desires that are too quickly satisfied become weaker: the others go on growing stronger" (ch. i).

**45.**—St. Gertrude (the episode of the fountain):

"It happened on a certain day, between the Festival of the Resurrection and Ascension, that I went into the court before Prime,* and seated myself near the fountain,— and I began to consider the beauty of the place, which charmed me on account of the clear and flowing stream, the verdure of the trees which surrounded it, and the flight of the birds, and particularly of the doves,—above all the sweet calm,—apart from all, and considering within myself what would make this place most useful to me, I thought that it would be the friendship† of a wise and intimate companion, who would sweeten my solitude or render it useful to others, when Thou, my Lord and my God, who art a torrent of inestimable pleasure, after having inspired me with the first impulse of this desire, Thou didst will to be also the end of it, inspiring me with the thought that if, by continual gratitude, I returned Thy graces to Thee, as a stream returns to its source; if, increasing in the love of virtue, I put forth, like the trees, the flowers of good works; furthermore, if, despising the things of earth, I fly upwards, freely, like the birds, and thus free my senses from the distraction of exterior things,—my soul would then be empty, and my heart would be an agreeable abode for Thee.

"As I was occupied with the recollection of these things during the same day, having knelt after Vespers for my evening prayer before retiring to rest, this passage of the Gospel came suddenly to my mind: 'If any man love Me, he will keep My word, and My Father will love him, and We will come to him and will make our abode with him' (St. John xiv. 23). At these words my worthless heart *perceived* Thee, O my most sweet God and my delight, *present therein...*, although my mind takes pleasure in wandering after and in distracting itself with perishable things, yet... when I return into my heart, I *find Thee there;* so that I cannot complain that Thou hast left me, even for a moment, from that time until this year, which is the ninth since I received this grace, except once when I perceived that Thou didst leave me for the space of eleven days... and it

* It was in 1281, the time from which the saint dated what she regarded as her conversion, She was then twenty-six years of age. She often entered into communication with Our Lord's sacred Humanity. But here she is speaking particularly of the Divinity, as is seen from a passage from St Bernard, that she quotes, and from the last lines of the chapter.

† Later on the author of *The Imitation* will say: "When Jesus is present, all is well, and nothing seemeth difficult; but when Jesus is absent, everything is hard... *Without a friend thou canst not well live;* and if Jesus is not thy friend above all others, thou shalt be sad and desolate indeed" (Book II, ch. viii, 1, 3).

appeared to me that this happened on account of a worldly conversation... Then Thy sweetest humanity and Thy stupendous charity moved Thee to seek me, when I had reached such a pitch of madness, that I thought no more of the greatness of the treasure I had lost, and for the loss of which I do not remember to have felt any grief at that time, nor even to have had the desire of recovering it, I cannot now be sufficiently amazed at the mania which possessed my soul... Draw and unite me entirely to Thyself, that I may remain inseparably attached to Thee, even when I am obliged to attend to exterior duties for the good of my neighbour, and that afterwards I may return again to seek Thee within me, when I have accomplished them for Thy glory in the most perfect manner possible, even as the winds, when agitated by a tempest, return again to their former calm when it has ceased; that Thou mayest find me as zealous in labouring for Thee as Thou hast been assiduous in helping me; and that by this means Thou mayest elevate me to the highest degree of perfection, to which Thy justice can permit Thy mercy to raise so carnal and rebellious a creature" (St. Gertrude, *Life and Revelations,* by Sister M. Frances Clare, Part II, ch. iii, pp. 76-9).

**46.**—Blessed Margaret Mary:

"This divine Saviour said to me: that He would endow me with a new grace, still greater than all those that He had hitherto bestowed on me, which was that I should *never* lose sight of Him, *having Him always intimately present:* a favour which I regard as the crown of all those that I have hitherto received of His infinite mercy, as since that time I have had this divine Saviour *intimately present* without any interruption... This divine *presence* inspires such respect in me that when I am alone I am obliged to prostrate myself upon the earth and to annihilate myself, so to speak, in the *presence* of my Saviour and my God... I find also that all these graces are accompanied by an unalterable peace, an interior joy, and especially by an ever more ardent desire to be humiliated, despised, annihilated, and overwhelmed with all kinds of sufferings, in order to become a little less unworthy to be the least of the servants of Jesus Christ" (Second Letter to Fr. Rolin, Vol. II of the second Paray ed., 1876, p. 323).

### § 4. The Presence of God Felt in the Full Union and Following States.

**47.**—St. Teresa:

1° On the *full union:* "God *visits* the soul in a manner which prevents it doubting, when returning to itself, that *He was within it and that it dwelt in Him.* So firmly is it convinced of this truth, that, although years may pass before this favour recurs, the soul can never forget it nor doubt the fact... I knew someone who was unaware of God being in all things by *presence,* power, and essence, yet was *firmly convinced* of it by a divine favour of this sort. She asked a half-instructed person of the kind I spoke of to tell her in what way God dwelt within us: he was as ignorant on the subject as she had been before Our Lord revealed the truth to her, and answered that the Almighty was only present in us by grace. Yet *so strong was her conviction of the truth* learnt during her prayer, that she questioned other spiritual persons on the subject, who confirmed her in the true doctrine, much to her joy" (*Interior Castle,* Fifth Mansion, ch. i. 8, 9).

2° On *ecstasy:*

"The soul is represented as being *close* to God, and there abides a conviction thereof so certain and strong that it cannot possibly help believing so... In the beginning it happened to me that I was ignorant of one thing—I did not know that God is in all things; and when He seemed to me to be so near I thought it impossible. Not to believe that He was *present* was not in my power, for it seemed to me, as it were, evident that I felt there His very *presence.* Some unlearned men used to say to me that He was present only by His grace. I could not believe that, because, as I am saying, He seemed to me to be present Himself; so I was distressed" (*Life,* ch. xviii, 19, 20).

"When a soul [by ecstasy] sees itself *so near* unto God" (*Life,* ch. xix, 22).

Whether in a rapture or during the prayer of union, "Our Lord unites the spirit to Himself and makes it both blind and dumb, like St. Paul after his conversion... for the supreme delight of the spirit is to realise *its nearness* to God" (*Interior Castle,* Seventh Mansion, ch. i, 8).

3° On the *spiritual marriage.* "Unless she first deserts God, I believe He will never fail to make her sensible of His *presence*" (*ibid.*, 12).

See also several of the Extracts to the chapter on Ecstasy.

### § 5. On the Certainty Given By the Prayer of Quiet and the Full Union.

**48.**—St. Teresa:

"But as in these days women have fallen into great delusions and deceits of Satan, I began to be afraid because the joy and sweetness which I felt were so great and very often beyond my power to avoid. On the other hand, I felt within myself a very *deep conviction that God was with me, especially when I was in prayer.* I saw, too, that I grew better and stronger thereby. But if I was a little distracted, *I began to be afraid,* and to imagine that *perhaps* it was Satan that suspended my understanding, making me think it to be good, in order to withdraw me from mental prayer, hinder my meditation on The Passion, and debar me the use of my understanding; this seemed to me, who did not comprehend the matter, to be a grievous loss" (*Life,* ch. xxiii, 2, 3).*

* This took place in 1555, when the saint began to receive the mystic graces again. She was then forty years of age.

# CHAPTER VI

## SECOND FUNDAMENTAL CHARACTER OF THE MYSTIC UNION: THE INTERIOR POSSESSION OF GOD: THE MANNER IN WHICH IT IS FELT

**1.—The spiritual senses.** The first thesis has told us that in the mystical union we have an experimental knowledge of the presence of God. We shall now add that this knowledge is the result of an impression, a spiritual *sensation** of a special kind.

Hence a question arises: Can this spiritual sensation be compared to anything that is already known, to one or more of those sensations by which we prove the *presence* and the nature of material objects? Or must we say that there is no existing analogy with the natural order?

In other words, does the soul possess *intellectual spiritual senses,* having *some resemblance* to the bodily senses, so that, in an *analogous* manner and in divers ways, she is able to perceive the *presence* of pure spirits, and the presence of God in particular? This is the question to be dealt with now, and our general conception of the mystic states will thus become more exact.

**2.**—By the spiritual senses we do not, of course, mean the **imaginative senses**— the faculty, that is to say, by which the imagination *imitates* and recalls to our minds colours, sounds, etc. This would not be the way to enter into real correspondence with pure spirit, but at the most with corporeal objects, such as

* This very clear expression is employed by Scaramelli. See the Extracts in the preceding chapter (**29**). Fr. de la Reguera had equally made use of it a short time before. Speaking of what he calls God's penetration (*illapsus*) into the soul, an expression which he regards as synonymous with the full mystic union (No. 728), he says: "This contemplative union does not consist only in the union that is common to all the just; there is an added *spiritual* and experimental *sensation* of God's presence which has penetrated the soul. On this point the approved mystics and, generally speaking. *all authors* are in agreement, while employing at times equivocal terms" (Vol. I, No. 735).

the material symbols which represent these spirits. It is a question here of a purely intellectual imitation.*

**3.—There is a spiritual sight.** We know this even without studying mysticism. Faith teaches us that eternal happiness will consist in *seeing* God. And by this word we mean to signify a mode of knowledge of *such a kind that we are instinctively led to compare it with bodily sight.* Otherwise the word would have no exact meaning.

So in Heaven the angels and the Blessed *see* one another. A host of comparisons describing Heaven are derived from light, and therefore allude to sight. Even the devils see themselves and are seen.

**4.—There is a spiritual hearing.** For the saints and the Blessed speak to one another. It is true that for this they have no need to utter sounds, to employ definite language; it is sufficient that they should *desire to communicate their thoughts.* But this communication may be called speech on the part of the transmitter, and *hearing* on the part of the receiver.

In the same way God has often spoken intellectually to the prophets and to other saintly souls. In Heaven He speaks to the angels when He gives them His direct commands. We shall hear Him also; for love constrains Him to enter into relations with His friends in all possible ways. God will not enclose Himself in an eternal silence while the elect are chanting His glory.

**5.—Is there a spiritual touch?**—Here it is the mystics who will reply, and by an affirmative: if it is a question of God, that is to say, for with regard to the angels we have no data to go upon.

The ignorant will exclaim here also. If we tell them that in contemplation we attain sometimes to the *sight* and the *hearing* of God, they will accept it easily enough, because no ideas and words are employed save those to which they are accustomed. But that there should be another way of attaining to God, and that the best means of giving an idea of it should be to compare it to a touch, is a fact which surprises them above measure. But it is this precisely which is a part of

* We thus make acts of pure intelligence, but of a totally different kind from those that we observe in the natural order, with the exception, however, of the experimental knowledge that we obtain of the acts of our own faculties.

Thus an angel's intelligence is capable of two operations of very different kinds: it either perceives an abstract truth, such as a moral or philosophic maxim, or it has an experimental knowledge of an existing object, such as another angel or one of his own thoughts.

We have no words by which to express these two subdivisions of the one identical faculty. The second, the experimental intellectual faculty, might perhaps have been styled the *super-sense,* which would show that it has an analogy with our senses, and also that it is of a superior order. On the other hand, the word *understanding* would continue to be employed when it is a question of abstract knowledge, of ideas, judgments, or arguments. Such is usually the signification given to it by St. Teresa when she explains that the understanding acts or does not act in certain prayers. She is not contradicting herself, therefore, when at one and the same time she says that the understanding does not act, and yet she admits that the mind is occupied. It is then the super-sense only that acts.

the second fundamental truth of mysticism. Those who do not accept it in its entirety will not have a really exact idea of the states of union, and their general conception of these states will consequently suffer.

However, bearing in mind their predispositions, I will divide the thesis into three parts. In the two first I will content myself with statements which no one could think of disputing. I shall not introduce the words *touch* or *spiritual senses,* keeping them for the third part only, as a useful supplement. They are, as a matter of fact, striking pictures and interpretations of things which are experienced; but we can do without them if need be, and so the mistrust that they might excite will not reflect on the essential part of the thesis.*

**6.—Is there such a thing as a spiritual taste and a spiritual sense of smell?** Again the mystic answers yes, and we must not be surprised. For in the corporeal order the senses of taste and smell are only a special kind of touch; so that if we admit the sense of touch in the spiritual order we can have no difficulty about admitting these other senses also. They also are interpretations of certain shades of union.

7.—With the mystics, the words to *see* God, to *hear,* and to *touch* Him are not mere metaphors. They express something more: some close **analogy.**† We now come to the thesis which indicates the second fundamental character of the mystic union.

**8.—Second thesis.** 1° *In the States inferior to ecstasy we cannot say that God is* **seen** *save in exceptional cases. We are not instinctively led to translate our experiences by the word* SIGHT.

2° *On the other hand, that which constitutes the common basis of all the various degrees of the mystic union is that the spiritual impression by which God makes known His presence, manifests Him in the manner, as it were, of something* INTERIOR *which penetrates the soul; it is a sensation of* IMBIBITION (saturation), *of* FUSION, *of* IMMERSION.

3° *For the sake of greater clearness, we can depict what is felt by describing the sensation by the name of* INTERIOR TOUCH.

* Even presented thus, my description will not perhaps be accepted by certain minds, on account of their philosophic systems. To these I offer another ground of understanding. I will say to them: "At least admit that I give an exact description of the *appearance* of the phenomena, and only make your reservations with regard to the real basis of the thing. Briefly, between two evils, I choose the least; between a radical negation and a partial negation I suggest the second as preferable, in the absence of something better; it diminishes our divergences of ideas considerably, and sharply defines our respective positions."

† By metaphor, we mean either a distant or a restricted resemblance to a single quantity: as when we speak of a warrior as a *lion,* or say that we are recipients of a *torrent* of abuse. Analogy, on the other hand, is a very close resemblance, as when we say that God has intelligence, will, justice, etc. Primarily, it is true, the words are confined to the mental representation of things that we have observed in the creature. Then we apply them to God, although they are not verified in Him in exactly the same way. We intend to indicate that there is a strong resemblance, and it is the same when we speak of the spiritual senses.

**9.**—Demonstration of the first part of the thesis: namely, that God is not ordinarily *seen* either in the prayer of quiet or in that of full union. Experience proves this superabundantly; and St. Teresa states it distinctly (see Extracts, No. **22**).

This truth stands out also in the expressions which various writers employ to describe the inferior states. All their comparisons are drawn from other things than sight. They say that we *repose* in God, that we are in His arms or on His bosom, that we plunge into Him as into an ocean, that He floods the soul (*illapsus divinus*), etc.. If God unveiled His Face a little, they would not fail to tell us so, for it would be more easy to understand.

**10.**—This fact also shows us why the majority of those who possess the prayer of quiet find such a **difficulty** in making themselves **understood**.

If they could say: "I see God," their language would be perfectly clear. But they realise that this would be inexact. And, on the other hand, a want of instruction prevents them from finding the proper expressions to employ. They are therefore reduced to making use of such vague and perplexed phrases as this: "I feel God in some sort of way."

**11.**—*Demonstration of the* **second part** *of the thesis.* The enunciation of the thesis tells us that the soul feels God as something *interior* that penetrates her. This does not at times prevent God from being felt *at the same time* as something exterior (see ch. xvi, **29**). There are in this case two simultaneous impressions instead of one.

1°. All those who have had experience of the prayer of quiet testify to this feeling of interior possession. They are aware of it more especially when the eyes are closed, because they are not then drawn and distracted by outward things. They perceive that the basis of their prayer consists, not in a better comprehension or formulation of some abstract truth, but in plunging into some, I know not what, divine atmosphere.

2°. Certain words of St. Teresa, quoted in the preceding chapter, state explicitly that God is felt interiorly.

**12.**—**Objection**. It is true that in other extracts from this same chapter, speaking of the prayer of quiet, she contents herself with saying that the soul feels herself *near* to God.

This language can be explained: (*a*) the saint wished especially to indicate that God becomes present. Now for this purpose it was useless to distinguish between feeling Him *in us* or *near us;* (*b*) the comparisons that she used obliged her to be content with the expression *near to,* under pain of weakening the analogy. Thus she was likening the soul to the aged Simeon, when he felt that it was the Saviour whom he held in his arms. In order to follow up the idea she had to say: and so does the soul feel God *near to her.* To give another example. In the *Interior Castle* (First Mansion, ch. i), and previously in the *Way of Perfection* (ch. xxx), she describes the soul as a castle in which God occupies the central mansion or room. Hence, under pain of a mixed metaphor, it was necessary to say that, as the faculties of the soul advance from room to room, they *draw near* to God, and not that they are immersed in Him, which, however, would have been the true representation of the fact. The words *near to* should be taken here as opposed, not to the *interior* of the soul, but to the *innermost place of this interior.*

And, further, upon three occasions the saint employs the words *near to,* even when it is a question of ecstasy, which, however, is a state in which God takes interior possession of the soul. But the foregoing comparison is a constraint upon her, because the soul has not yet arrived at the central mansion (see ch. v, **47**). It is clear, then, that the *near to* must not be taken in a narrow sense.

**13.**—Many persons to whom the mystic state is familiar, have told me that the following **comparison** depicts with great exactness both the interior possession of God, which is its basis, and the physiognomy of the impression by which it makes itself felt.

We may say: it is in exactly the same way that we feel *the presence of our bodies* when we remain motionless and close our eyes. If we then know that the body is there, it is not because we see it or have been told so. It is the result of a special sensation, of an interior impression which makes us feel that the soul permeates and vivifies the body.* It is an extremely simple sensation, and one that we should try in vain to analyse. And so it is with the mystic union; we feel God in us, and in a very simple way.

**14.**—*Demonstration of the* **third part** *of the thesis:* namely, that the feeling experienced can be described by giving the sensation the designation of interior touch.

I have already advised those who might feel startled by this language to omit this third part. It is enough for them to know that the mystic impression, 1° is not of one kind only; 2° that, fundamentally, it resembles neither sight nor speech (see the first part): 3° they will say that this fundamental quality belongs to a third species, refraining from stating precisely whether its analogy is to be found amongst the material sensations. They can call it inexpressible.

Personally, I think that we should speak thus when it is a question of the Humanity of Jesus Christ or of that of the saints, when they are known intellectually. The impression then received cannot, so it seems, be compared to a touch, because the object is felt at a distance; and yet although, for want of another name, it is called a vision, it is neither sight nor speech.

However, those who are surprised by the expressions *touch* or *Divine contact* probably exaggerate the sense which the mystics attach to them. They fancy that these terms imply some metaphysical doctrine on the possibility of the contact of spirits. But no: we simply wish to depict an impression by a comparison, and

* This impression is admitted to be the result of a multitude of sensations which separately would be imperceptible. and which are united in one confused whole. Thus result is called crœnæsthesis [self feeling].

with this end in view we do not pretend to say anything beyond this: that everything happens *as if* there were a touch.

We now come to the proofs:

1° The expression "interior touch" is quite logically led up to by the fact already admitted, that an interior touch is felt. In fact, in the material order we make use of the word touch each time that it is a question of knowing experimentally any object contiguous to us; while if the object is at a distance, we make use of the words *see* and *hear.* And then it is not with the object itself that we enter into immediate relations, but the radiations or vibrations which it sends out to us. Now it is a question here of a spiritual object which is not remote; it manifests itself by uniting itself with us, dissolving into us, as it were. And it is the word touch, therefore, that best expresses the analogy.

We can also say: the words *sight, hearing,* and *touch* designate here purely intellectual acts. But we understand that they express different circumstances. The first shows that the object of the knowledge is the inner nature of the Divine Being Himself; the second that it is one of His thoughts only; the third that it is more especially a uniting, fusing action which He exercises upon the soul.

2° We have the testimony of various authors, such as St. Teresa. In her second letter to Fr. Rodrigo Alvarez, written a year previous to the composition of the *Interior Castle,* the saint takes the exercise of the five spiritual senses as a point of departure for her description of *all* the states of mystic union. For in speaking of the lowest degree, she says: "The *first* prayer of which I was conscious,—in my opinion supernatural,—... is a certain interior recollection of which the soul is sensible; the soul seems to have other senses within itself then, which *bear some likeness* to the interior senses it possesses."* The word *senses,* being in the plural, indicates that it is a question of senses differing amongst themselves, but resembling those of the body. Otherwise she must have said: "There is one sense which resembles the physical senses, but only when they are taken collectively." On the other hand, the saint allows, as I have said, that in the prayer of quiet and in the full union we are not admitted to *see* or *hear* God. It follows, therefore, that the three last senses only can be called into play, that is *to* say, touch and its derivatives (see the Extracts from various authors, No. **26** and following).

3° The idea of touch is expressed by divers comparisons which the mystics have employed.

Thus Mother Mary of the Incarnation, Ursuline, compares the soul that experiences the mystic union to a sponge filled with water (*Vie par une Ursuline de Nantes,* ch. xx, p. 439). If this sponge were endowed with life, it would feel the water which fills it.

* *Life,* Relation VIII, 3, pp. 455-6.

In her *Life,* compiled from her manuscripts by her son (Book IV, ch. ix, p. 687), we find also the comparison of respiration. This comparison depicts the spiritual impress by the analogy of the delicate touch by which we feel that a vivifying air is penetrating into our lungs.

With regard to the idea of immersion, see No. **39** *bis.*

Many writers follow St. John of the Cross in saying that in the mystic state there is a union of *substance with substance.* This, like the word touch, is a mere manner of speech: they employ it as opposed to the knowledge of a remote object, and resort to the same language, as though it were a question of the *contact* of a material object and of the touch which then results. They wish to indicate a special mode of knowledge.*

Others employ the expression *substantial touches.* Here the adjective, which seems useless, is intended to show that it is not a case of a simple *moral* touch, as when we say that God touches the heart of a sinner, or that a preacher touches his audience.

**15.—Objection**. Scaramelli and, after him, Fr. Seraphim (*Theol. myst.,* No. 160) see a separate degree of prayer in the divine *touches.* This would seem to argue that in the other degrees the spiritual touch is not felt, and that it is therefore not the common basis of all mystical union.

I reply that such is not their intention; and Fr. Seraphim states this himself. They make a degree, not of all touches whatsoever, but of one special kind only, those that are *sudden and violent.*

They are wrong, however, in giving the name of degree even to these violent touches and in endeavouring to assign them a fixed place in the series of states of prayer. It is nothing more than a *manner of being* of one of the degrees—namely, ecstasy.

**16.—To sum up**. The physiognomy of the mystic union may be described as follows: during the union, when it is not too exalted, we are like a man placed beside one of his friends, in complete darkness and silence. He does not *see* him, therefore, he does not *hear* him; he only *feels* that he is there by the sense of touch, because he holds his hand in his own. And so he continues to think of him and to love him.†

**17.**—The material touch may, by increasing in strength, become a clasping and an embrace. It is the same with the spiritual touch. In the prayer of quiet, when it is not very strong, it is a simple *imbibition* which is tranquilly enjoyed. But at times the two spirits embrace one another, which is to say that sudden

* Had they aimed at expressing a metaphysical idea, they would first have had to define what they meant by this language. They had no such intention.

† In such a case affection for the friend, unless it were very strong, would not prevent the imagination from straying away from time to time. We must not be astonished, therefore, if it should be the same in the prayer of quiet.

and affectionate claspings * take place between them (see Extracts, No. **40**, and the canticle which follows chapter xxxi).

This superabundance of grace is not, I think, frequent with beginners; and when they at length come to experience it, it is at first only for a few seconds at a time. If afterwards they were to attempt to reproduce this special impression, they would find it impossible to do so.

**18.—How wonderful will be the union enjoyed in Heaven**. From what has gone before it follows that God can be not only seen and heard, but *breathed in, grasped in a sweet embrace.* By this we can see how complete our happiness will be in eternal life; for God will not only show Himself, He will give Himself to us.

Many Christians form a very incomplete idea of Heaven. They know that we shall see God, that we shall rejoice in the magnificent revelation of His infinite nature; but this is all. They picture Him as a stern prince, isolated upon His throne, proudly keeping his subjects at a distance, admitting them only in the character of spectators. But God will do much more than this. He wishes to be the fragrant air that we breathe, the wine that will inebriate us, the life of our life, the impassioned Lover of our souls. He will vouchsafe to us the "kiss of His mouth" and will receive ours in return. He will not be content until He is merged into, almost identified with the beloved soul that has given herself to Him. He desires an intimate and mutual penetration. Heaven is not merely the vision of God, it is fusion with Him, in love and in possession. If this fusion did not take place the soul would suffer an insatiable thirst.† How could the soul behold the Divine beauty, and not go out towards it with her whole desire?

In order that we may catch a glimpse of these wondrous blessings, God grants a foretaste of them to His friends on earth. It was thus that he showed to Abraham, Isaac, and Jacob the promised land wherein the chosen people were one day to dwell.

**19.—The gift of wisdom**. The preceding theses explain why it is that the mystics say that their contemplation is produced more especially by the gift of wisdom, understanding this word as they do, that is to say: as a *sweet-savoured* knowledge of divine things. They rely upon an etymology that is peculiar to the Latin, and derive *sapientia* from *sapere,* which has two very different meanings, to be wise and to taste.‡

* Their existence, as shown by the quotations, is a fresh proof that the term "spiritual touch" conveys the correct idea.

† Bossuet gives a good description of this thirst when speaking of Communion: "Who is there who does not know how, in transports of human love, we would consume the object of our love, devour and *make ourselves one* in all possible ways,... so that we may possess it, *feed upon* it, be made one with it, live by it? And that which is madness, impotence in carnal love, is truth and wisdom in love for Jesus" (*Medit. sur la Cène,* Part I, J. xxiv).

‡ St. Bonaventure says the same: "The word wisdom, taken in its most exact sense, indicates an *experimental knowledge* of God; it is one of the seven gifts of the Holy Spirit which comes into operation

The soul in the mystic union indeed tastes God and rejoices in Him. According to Scaramelli, "this is precisely the office of the gift of wisdom (at least, carried to certain degree) to render God *present* in the soul, and so much the more present as this gift is the more abundant. This gift brings the soul near to God and it causes her to *feel* and *taste* His most sweet presence" (Tr. III, No. 27).

**19** *bis.*—But if mystic contemplation is produced by gifts of the Holy Ghost, the **converse**, namely, that every act produced by certain gifts is mystic, is false. For that would be tantamount to saying that these gifts never operate in ordinary prayer. Now, such a thesis has never been laid down. It is not in conformity with St. Thomas's teaching, which holds that the gifts are not reserved for difficult acts alone. And further, if this proposition were true, mystics would swarm upon our globe. For at confirmation, and even at baptism, every Christian receives these gifts, and no one can hold that they continue in the state of pure habit without any actuation.*

The proposition that I am contesting has, however, been enunciated in a Catholic Review as being as clear as it is simple, and as giving the key to mysticism. But the author has not thought of bringing any documentary evidence in support of his theory.

And even were it true, this doctrine would be practically sterile as far as directors are concerned; it could not furnish them with any *sign,* any means of discernment. For let us suppose that a person, surprised at what he experiences in prayer, and suspecting the presence of the mystic graces, comes to ask our opinion. Instead of laboriously reviewing the various characters described by the mystics, we should have to reply: "The whole question resolves itself into knowing whether certain gifts of the Holy Ghost have operated within you. Which one is it?" He would be astounded. We must have recourse to characters which are immediately verifiable.

when we taste the divine sweetness... This act comprises both knowledge and affection; it begins with one and concludes with the other. For taste, or degustation, is an experimental knowledge of that which is good and sweet" (*Sententiarum,* Book III, dist. 35, a. 1, q. 1).

In certain manifestations, *the gift of understanding* is added to the gift of wisdom, so that the soul may penetrate the truths of religion to their very depths. I do not speak of the *gift of knowledge,* as it has another object. And as all knowledge proceeds by inference, this gift leads us to make certain inferences from the divine source, whether it refer to God or His creatures (see Scaramelii. Tr. II, No. 143).

This doctrine, as to the part played by the gifts of the Holy Spirit, has only a theoretic interest.

Philippus a SS. Trinitate (Tr. III, disc. 3), Vallgornera (q. 3. disp. 3), Antonius a Spiritu Sancto (Tr. III, No. 290) think that "the formal and educed principle of supernatural contemplation is *sometimes* higher than the gifts of the Holy Spirit." Into these speculative discussions I do not enter.

* Suarez says that if the gifts were but rarely exercised, it would he useless that they should be given to us as habits. It would be sufficient, as in the case of prophecy, to receive a direct motion on each occasion. Prophecy is, in fact, not a habit (*De Gratia,* Book VI, ch. x, No. 4). Fr. Billot adds this reason in order to prove that the gifts serve for "the whole Christian life." "Otherwise," he says, "we do not see why God should assign an extraordinary end to a means which is always included in our common justification, and as inseparably bound up with sanctifying grace as charity and the other virtues" (*De Virtutibus Infusis,* q. 68, pp. 170, 169).

**20.**—And, in particular, the gift of wisdom has a **wider scope** than the production of the mystic states. There are, in fact, two ways of tasting an object: the one indirect and inferior, which is to enjoy it in thought and memory; the other direct and superior, which is to possess the actual object itself, to enjoy it really and experimentally. This higher way is that of the mystic union. All Christians become participators in the inferior mode in the Sacrament of Confirmation.

**21.**—**The difficulties of mysticism** are now surmounted, as far as the task of describing them goes. The points that the uninstructed find disconcerting may be reduced, in almost every case, to two. They cannot understand 1° that God should make His presence felt experimentally: 2° that it should take place otherwise than by sight or speech.

If after our explanation there should still be some obscurity in their minds, their best course will be to pass on, admitting these formulas blindly, as is done with the postulates required in certain sciences. Afterwards the other characteristic marks of the mystic action will be easily grasped. At most the ligature (ch. xiv) will astonish them slightly. But the difficulty here will not be to understand it, but to find its true cause. The search after first causes is never, however, an easy one.

The difficult part of descriptive mysticism is thus reduced to very little. There is a short tunnel at starting, upon this road, but when this is passed we are in broad daylight for the rest of the way.

A professor of theology once told me that his idea of mysticism had hitherto been quite wrong, and that he had never therefore had the patience to study it. He had regarded it as a long chain of propositions, unintelligible to the ordinary man, and so intricate that there was nothing between understanding it altogether or not at all.

We shall see that this, happily, is not the case. So courage! we are now out of the tunnel.

**21** *bis.*—The Extracts belonging to this and the preceding chapter are taken from fifty different authors. This, I think, is sufficient to show that, instead of going out after new inventions, I am giving the true tradition. (See also the Extracts in the chapter on Ecstasy).

## EXTRACTS

### § 1. We Know That in the Prayer of Quiet and That of the Full Union, God Makes Himself Present: We Must Now Prove That This Takes Place, as a Rule, Without His Being Seen.

**22.**—St. Teresa:

1° On the presence of God, felt in the *prayer of quiet:* "The soul understands, in a manner different from understanding by the exterior senses, that she is now placed near her God... *This does not happen because she sees Him with the eyes of the body or of the soul;* for as holy Simeon saw the glorious little Infant only under the appearance of poverty,... he might rather have supposed He was the son of some mean person than the Son of the Heavenly Father. But the Child made Himself known to him, and so, in the same way, the soul understands He is there" (*Way of Perfection*, ch. xxxi, p. 176, Dalton's trans., 1901 ed.).

2° On the *prayer of quiet:* "Though she [the soul] perfectly *sees not* the Master that teaches her, yet [she] plainly understands He is with her" (*Conceptions of the Love of God*, ch. iv, p. 309).

3° On the *full union:* "But, you may ask, how can a person who is *incapable of sight* and hearing see or know these things? I reply that she... perceives them clearly afterwards, not by any *vision,* but by a certitude which remains in the heart and which God alone could give... [But] if *we did not see it,* how can we feel so sure about it? That I do not know: it is the work of the Almighty, and I am certain I am speaking the truth" (*Interior Castle*, Fifth Mansion, ch. i, 9).

4° On the *full union:* "So deeply imprinted on the spirit is the sight it has enjoyed of Him, that it only desires to behold Him again. I have already said that, even by the imagination, *nothing is seen* in this prayer that *can be called even imaginary vision.* I speak of it as 'sight' because of the comparison I used" (*Interior Castle*, Sixth Mansion, ch. i, 1).

5° On the *full union:* "Die! die! as the silkworm does when it has fulfilled the office of its creation, and you will *see God* and will be immersed in His greatness, as the little silkworm is enveloped in its cocoon. Understand that when I say: You will see God, I mean *in the manner described, in which He manifests Himself* in this kind of union" (*Interior Castle*, Fifth Mansion, ch. ii, 5).

See also my chapter v, 22, 6°, 7°.

**23.**—Richard of St.-Victor (*De gradibus violentæ charitatis*): "Often in this state God descends from Heaven; often He visits the soul that is lying in darkness and the shadow of death; often the glory of the Lord fills the Tabernacle that shelters the Ark of the Covenant; but He *so makes His presence to be felt that He does not* reveal His Face. He sheds His sweetness inwardly, but He does not make His beauty manifest. He sheds His sweetness, but He does not display His brightness. His sweetness, therefore, is felt, but His beauty is not seen. He is still surrounded with clouds and darkness; His throne is still the pillar of a cloud. Truly, what is felt is exceeding sweet and *full of caresses;* but what is seen is all in darkness, for He does not yet appear in the light. And although He appears in the fire, it is a fire that warms rather than illumines. He indeed inflames the will, but He does not enlighten the understanding. The soul, then, can verily *feel her Beloved* in this state, but, as has been said, *it is not* *permitted to her to see Him;* or, if she sees Him, she sees Him as in the darkness, she sees Him as though hidden behind a cloud, as a riddle, and not face to face; whence it is that she says: Make the light of Thy countenance to shine upon Thy servant" (Migne ed., col. 1218).

**24.**—St. Thomas (in Ps. xxxiii):

"In bodily things, we first see and then we taste; but in spiritual things, *taste comes before sight.* Unless he taste, none knoweth. And this is why it is said: O taste; and then: see."

**25.**—The Ven. Louis du Pont, in his *Memoirs,* quoted by Fr. Nouet, *Conduite de l'homme d'Oraison,* in a chapter entitled: How God makes His presence felt, *without being seen* (Book V, ch. xvii):

"I have experienced, in prayer and at other times, he says, the *presence* of God in divers manners. Sometimes it seems that we see *God present,* not with the eyes of the body, nor in a very bright light, nor merely by reasoning, but in a special way in which the soul suddenly *feels that He* to whom she speaks, He who listens to her and hears her, *is before her.* And then she prays to Him with greater attention and energy. This knowledge is similar to that which one man has of another when, as they converse together, the *light goes out,* and he remains in darkness without seeing or hearing him or feeling any of his movements, and yet he *knows him to be present* and speaks to him as being present with him. St. Dionysius seems to intend to express the same meaning when he says: Enter into the divine obscurity, because in the darkness we see God."

### § 2. There Are Five Spiritual Senses.

**26.**—St. Augustine (*Confessions*):

"But what then is it [O Lord] that I love when I love Thee? Neither the beauty of the body, nor the graceful order of time, nor the brightness of light, so agreeable to these eyes, nor the sweet melody of all sorts of music, nor the fragrant scents of flowers, oil, or spices, nor the sweet taste of manna or honey, nor fair limbs alluring to carnal embraces. None of these things do I love when I love my God. And yet I love a certain light, and a certain voice, and a certain fragrancy, a certain food, and a certain embrace when I love my God, the light, the voice, the fragrancy, the food, and the embrace of my inward man; where that shines to my soul, which no place can contain, and where that sounds which no time can measure, and where that smells which no blast can disperse, and where that relishes which no eating can diminish, and where that is embraced which no satiety can separate. This is what I love when I love my God" (Book X, ch. vi).

**27.**—In St. Bonaventure's *Works,* the author of *De septem itineribus aeternitatis* begins by explaining that "all experimental knowledge is the act of knowing the *presence* of the object"; he bids us note the difference between hearing of a palatable dish and tasting it (dist. 1), and concludes thus:

"As the *experience* of bodily things is gained by the bodily senses, so too the *experience* of spiritual things is gained in the superior part of the soul by the spiritual senses" (6 dist. 2).

The same doctrine had already been taught in the book, *De mente et anima,* attributed to St. Augustine, but really written by an anonymous Cistercian (§ IX, and XLIX).*

**28.**—The Ven. Louis du Pont, in a paragraph entitled: "On the *extraordinary* forms and the divers manners in which God communicates Himself in mental prayer":

"As the body has its five exterior senses, with which it perceives the visible and delectable things of this life, and makes experience of them, so the spirit, with its faculties of understanding and will, has five interior acts corresponding to these senses, which we call seeing, hearing, smelling, tasting, and touching spiritually, with which it perceives the invisible and delectable things of Almighty God, and makes *experience* of them; from which springs the experimental knowledge of God, which incomparably exceeds all the knowledge that proceeds from our reasonings, as the sweetness of honey is much better known by tasting even a little of it than by arguing at great length concerning its nature" (*Méditations*, Introduction, § XI).

**29.**—Fr. Nouet (*Conduite de l'homme d'Oraison*):

"After the opinion of so many saintly and enlightened Fathers, it would be rash to call in question what *all mystic theologians* follow in teaching with regard to the number of the *five spiritual senses...* All the masters of the spiritual life agree on this point, namely, that the most perfect union with God to which the soul can attain in this life consists in this wonderful experience of the interior senses; the main difficulty lies in knowing to which one of the five it properly, in their opinion, belongs. At one time they seem to attribute it to the *touch,* which is the lowest of all the exterior and the highest amongst the interior, senses. St. Thomas, in his Opuscule 61, places it at the highest degree of unitive love, giving the reason that it achieves the closest union with its object... At another time they seem to give the preference to taste..."

Hugh of St.-Victor seems to mix and confuse the supreme touch with taste. For he says: "To attain to God is to seek Him incessantly by desire, to find Him

* Contrary to what has often been done, I do not quote the five examples of spiritual senses described by these two writers. They prove the thesis in appearance only, for they, at most, refer to the *imaginative senses.* Thus, in order to prove the existence of a spiritual sense of smell, they quote St. Paul's words: "We are the good *odour* of Christ" (2 Cor. ii, 15). But this is simply a metaphor. It is the same with the text relating to sight: "*See* ye that I alone am, and there is no other God beside me" (Deut. xxxii, 39). What is *seen* here is the truth of a proposition; it does not follow that mystics acquire the totally new faculty of *seeing a spiritual substance,* or His thoughts.

by knowledge, and to touch Him by taste..."* St. Ambrose employs the interior senses of smell and of hearing to explain this union. Here are his words: "The soul of the just is the bride of the Word. If this soul *burns with desire,* if she *prays without ceasing,* if her whole being goes out towards the Word, then suddenly it seems that she hears His voice *without seeing Him;* that she savours *inwardly* the odour of His Divinity, which thing often comes to those who are strong of faith. Suddenly the soul's *sense of smell* is filled with a spiritual grace, and, being aware of a sweet breath that tells her of the presence of Him whom she seeks, she says: Behold Him whom I *seek* and whom I *desire.* † St. Gregory and St. Bernard ‡ add sight to the sentiments of love" (Book VI, ch. xiv; also Book V, ch. xvii).

The last opinion does not contradict those that went before, because it is only a question of the highest degrees here. The doctrine of the spiritual senses is accepted by P. de Maumigny (*Pratique de l'Oraison*, Vol. II, Part I, ch. iv).

### § 3. In the Mystic Union the Soul attains to God by a Spiritual Touch.

**30.**—Scaramelli (Tr. 3, No. 24), describing the prayer of quiet:

"As the human body touches another body and is touched by it again, as it thus feels the other's presence, and this sometimes with enjoyment; so the soul *touches* a spiritual substance and is *touched* it again and feels the presence with the *sensation* that pertains to spirit and this sometimes with great delight; for example, when it is God who touches her and is present to her."

No. 27. "Our *exterior senses* reveal to us the presence of their objects by means of gross and material sensations; but here the soul perceives the presence of God by a *spiritual sensation* that is delicate, pure, and simple."

No. 120. "Holy Scripture [speaking of the knowledge of God] describes *the spiritual sense of touch,* which is precisely that of which we are about to speak, more clearly than any other sense. And what else can the expressions signify which the just soul, represented by the Bride, employs in the Canticle of Canticles, when she asks for the kisses, and desires the embraces of her Celestial Bridegroom? What can they signify if it be not these *spiritual touches of the Divinity,* plainly expressed in those kisses and those embraces by which she so ardently desires her God? See! She trembles under His touch! (Canticles,

* Lib. *De arca Noe.*

† In Ps. cxviii, Sermon 6.

‡ The five spiritual senses are referred to indirectly by St. Bernard—in the comparisons that he makes use of, for example. Several writers have been in error in attributing to him an explicit passage beginning with these words: "There are five spiritual senses," etc., the reference being to: *De amore,* ch. vi. The context shows that in this passage the ambiguous word *sensus* signifies not five senses, but five virtuous *sentiments,* such as love for our neighbour. And, further, this passage is not St. Bernard's, but from a writer who is connected with him: William of St.-Thierry (*De natura et dignitate amoris*), ch. vi).

v, 4). Is not this to signify that *highly spiritual sensation* which, at the *contact* of her Beloved, suddenly arises in the innermost chamber of her spirit? The soul, then, does not lack the *spiritual sense of touch* by which she perceives spiritual substances, just as by corporeal touch we perceive corporeal substances."

No. 121. "Before going farther, I would suggest a thought which is important for the proper understanding of what I have to say in this chapter and in the remainder of the treatise. Philosophers state that the *experimental* knowledge of an object is knowledge born of the experience or the act of *some one sense* as it touches its object then present. For example: the experimental knowledge of light is that only which results from seeing light. Consequently, a man born blind, who is incapable of seeing it, would not be able to acquire a like *experimental* idea of light, though you discoursed to him on the subject for a year together; so that all he can arrive at is an abstract and incorrect idea. From this we deduce the conclusion that the *experimental* knowledge of God and of divine things is that, and that only, which arises out of the experience of *God's presence* on the part of *one of the soul's spiritual senses;* for example, the knowledge that results in the soul when *she feels God by the sense of touch,* when she is *aware of Him by the spiritual sense of smell.* I say the same of the other spiritual senses."

No. 122. "This granted, let us proceed to explain by the parallel of the material touches which act upon the body, that other *most sweet touch* that God operates in the souls of His beloved ones, showing the nature of this *true and real but purely spiritual sensation by which the soul feels God in the most secret recesses of her being, and tastes Him with a great delight*" (see chs. v, xiii, xiv, by this same writer).

The existence of a perception of God which is compared to touch is equally admitted by the modern writers who follow Scaramelli: Fr. Sraphin (Part II, ch. ix), Verhaege (Book II, § 1, ch. ix), Voss (Part I, ch. vii).

**31.**—Blessed Angela of Foligno:

"In this feeling by which the soul is made certain that God Almighty is within her... the soul feeleth that God who cannot be measured, is *mingled* with her and hath given her His company (*Visions and Instructions* of B. Angela of Foligno, ch. iii, p. 177).

**31** *bis.*—Ruysbroeck:

1° "This vital union with God operates and varies ceaselessly. When, being with Him, we feel our mutual *attainings* and our *embracings,* we perceive also that we are distinct from God; and hence a pressing need not to remain in ourselves. We feel that we *touch* and are *touched,* that we love and are loved. Suddenly we advance and withdraw" (*Speculum,* ch. xx).

2° "When the soul receives the divine *touch,* she seeks to contemplate and to scrutinise her deep places where the *touch* operates... But the divine light, which is its origin, dazzles her eyes, even as the bat is blinded by the sun's rays. Nevertheless, the spirit, incited and impelled thereto by God, and by itself, begins to inquire of itself again: 'What is God? What is this touch? Whence doth it come?' But it is time lost!... The more advanced souls who have penetrated into the door of eternal life come [at least] to feel and to perceive this *touch*" (*L'Ornement des Noces,* Book II, ch. liv). See also his ch. lxxi on the gift of Wisdom, which is "the divine touch."

**32.**—St. John of the Cross:

1° He is speaking of the case where the mystic communications come from God alone, without the medium of the sensible faculties: "These communications, because the work of our Lord Himself, are wholly Divine and supreme, certain *substantial touches* of the Divine union between Himself and the soul; in one of these, because the highest possible degree of prayer, the soul receives greater good than in all the rest. These are those *touches* for which the Bride prayed, saying: 'Let Him kiss me with the kiss of His mouth.' This being a thing that so intimately relates to God, the soul, anxious to approach Him, values and desires one *touch* of the Divinity more than all the other graces which He bestows upon it. Hence the Bride in the *Canticle,* after the many graces there described, is not satisfied, but prays for these Divine *touches*... The evil spirit... [cannot] know of those Divine *touches* in the *substance of the soul,* wrought in loving knowledge *by the substance of God*" (*Obscure Night,* Book II, ch. xxiii, p. 451).

2° "Now, though in the ordinary course these visions cannot be clearly and distinctly seen in this life, *the effect* of them may be felt in the very substance of the soul, through the instrumentality of a loving knowledge, in the most sweet *touch* and union pertaining to the spiritual impressions... The end I have in view [in this treatise] is the Divine Embracing, the Union of the soul with the Divine Substance" (*Ascent of Mt. Carmel,* Book II, ch. xxiv, p. 170).

3° Speaking of God's action in rapture, he compares it to "the whisper of the amorous gales," and says: these words signify "a most sublime and sweet understanding of God and of His attributes, which overflows into the intellect from the *contact* of the attributes of God with the *substance* of the soul... As the touch of the air is felt in the *sense of touch,* and the whisper of it heard in the ear, so also the *contact* of the virtues of the Beloved is *felt* and enjoyed in the *touch* of the soul that is, in the *substance* thereof, through the instrumentality of the will, and the understanding of the attributes of God felt in the hearing of the soul, that is, in the intellect... It then revives and soothes the sense of *touch*... This *touch* of God greatly satisfies and comforts the *substance* of the soul, sweetly fulfilling its desire" (*Spiritual Canticle,* Stanza XIV, p. 80).

4° He repeats the same figures in the *Living Flame of Love* (Stanza II, line 3) when explaining the lines: "O tender hand! O gentle touch! Savouring of everlasting life!"

5° In his Canticle on Ecstasy he exclaims: "I mounted up higher than all science. Would you describe this exalted science? It is a sublime *touching* of the holy and Divine substance."

**32** *bis.*—Father Augustine Baker, O.S.B.:

"There are other unions entirely supernatural, not at all procured, or so much as intended by the soul herself, but graciously and freely conferred by God upon some souls, in the which He, after a wonderful and inconceivable manner, affords them *interior* illuminations and *touches*" (*Sancta Sophia,* Tr. I, sec. 1, ch. iii, 11).

**33.**—Philippus a SS. Trinitate (*Discurs. Prelim.,* art. 8):

1° "In the mystic union, God is perceived by an *interior touch* and an *embrace:* He is *felt* in an undoubted manner by the soul... She verifies this manifestly, because God then gives her the certainty of His *real presence.*"

2° After having spoken of the union through sanctifying grace: "There is another mode of union between the contemplative soul and God; it takes place by a *substantial contact* betwixt Him and the soul. It is then that He *makes Himself felt* as present and united. This union increases in perfection when, in so far as is possible in this life, the soul's spiritual faculties are fixed steadily on God; the intellect, by an almost continuous and, as it were, clear knowledge; the will, by a love containing not only desire, but, in a certain measure, satisfaction, fruition. This statement is not made absolutely, but with certain restrictive terms, because, as a rule, in this life we do not possess an evident knowledge of God, nor a complete satisfaction. This is the union that St. Augustine desired (*Confessions,* Book X, ch. i) when he cried: 'Let me know Thee, O Lord, who knowest me; let me know Thee as also I am known by Thee. O thou virtue of my soul, enter into it and make it fit for Thee, that Thou mayest have it and possess it without spot or wrinkle' " (Part III, tract. 1, disc. 1, art. 1).

**34.**—Antonius a Spiritu Sancto quotes this passage of Philippus a SS. Trinitate and adds: "All the doctors of mysticism say that mystical theology has this kind of union for its chief object" (Tr. IV, Nos. 2, 5). "The presence of God is known here, not by sight, but by a kind of *experimental touch*" (No. 14). "The intellect and the will can possess it, by a vital *sensation* and a very sweet taste, as an object that we can *touch* and *embrace*" (No. 10).

**35.**—De Vallgornera:

1° "This is the definition of mystic theology that can be deduced from several passages in St. Thomas's writings: It is a very perfect and very high contemplation of God and a very sweet love of fruition that we feel when we come to *possess Him intimately*" (No. 6).

2° "The union of fruition implies the *contact* and the *interior existence* of God in the soul. And then, by a new mode and by His grace, God renders Himself *present* as an object that can be *known experimentally* and *possessed interiorly;* just as though our soul, which is intimately present to us as the root and cause of all our operations, were to render herself still more present and manifest, as an object and an intimate object of knowledge;... in this case there would be experimental *knowledge* and *touch*" (No. 866). "It is not only in the state of glory that God is known experimentally, but also in our earthly state. God is known here, obscurely and by faith, it is true; but He can be known by a certain *experimental touch without being seen.* In the same way, we do not see our soul, but we feel her as an object that is present, having experimental knowledge of the fact that she animates the body, that she gives life to it... God makes Himself really present, in a special manner" (No. 868).

**36.**—Fr. Surin, speaking of the soul "admitted to the cabinet of God" and "received to a perfect transformation into God":

"She knows what He is, indeed she even tastes Him by the divine *contact,* of which the mystics speak, and which is a *supernatural* knowledge whereby the soul knows what God is; not from having seen Him, but from having *touched Him.* For of the spiritual senses, tact is the most delicate, although of the corporeal senses it is the most gross. This *experience* of God gives a perception of Him which is more exquisite and which approaches to Him more nearly than any other thing can do; and even the Blessed, who see God, find the fulness of their felicity in that they *touch Him and possess Him... All agree* that the [main] point in mystic theology is for the soul to arrive at *touching* God, as St. Paul has it: *si forte attrectent eum* (Acts xvii, 27)" (*Traité de l'amour de Dieu*, Vol. I, Book III, ch. vi).

**37.**—Fr. Crasset (*Vie de Madame Hélyot*):

"The ordinary cause of this infinitely delicious pleasure is a celestial *taste* and *savour,* combined with the *ineffable touch* which Blosius calls a *substantial touch* of the Divinity. For just as a friend knows his friend by night, *without seeing* him and *without hearing* him, merely by *touching* him, so when God unites Himself directly to the soul, and when He makes Himself felt in the heart by an inner touch, she cannot doubt that she has *touched the Divinity,* although she may not be able to explain in what manner she has done so. As most holy souls have experienced this grace and *speak of it in the same manner,* it cannot be said to be a flight of the imagination, especially considering that the greatest scholastic theologians, such as St. Bonaventure and Gerson without speaking particularly of any others, have written about it learnedly, being taught by study and by their own experience" (Book II, ch. iv, 15).

**37** *bis.*—Fr. Thomassin, in a chapter styled: "On the sight, and especially on the *contact* with the sovereign Good":

1° "God is present in the soul. If she does not precipitate herself outwards by an irrational love of the things of sense, she will find God *present* as intimately as *she is present to herself,* and in a similar manner; not by the sensible faculties, not by the understanding, which, however, can lay hold of absent objects, but by a *certain more intimate means,* giving a conscious presence" (*Dogmata theologica; de Deo,* Book VI, ch. v, No. 9. 1684).

2° "We grasp God by an *interior* and secret *touch;* we feel Him thus, reposing in us, as it were, in a very intimate manner. This incorporeal, or let us rather say divine, contact, is a very hidden art, which we know more perfectly by experience than by reasoning. Just as the soul comes forth from the hands of the

Divine Artificer without any intermediary, and is fashioned by Him thus; so too, since the *contact* is reciprocal, the soul feels God and *touches* Him, if so be that she is not enveloped, as though with a rind, by the love of things exterior and interior" (*ibid.*, No. 8).

**38.**—Honoré de Sainte-Marie (*Tradition,* etc.):

"The most learned masters of the spiritual life are convinced that the mystic union consists principally in the experience of the two interior senses of touch and smell, or of both of these together" (Vol. I, p. 177, Part II, dist. x). See also *Dissertation Apologétique,* p. 114.

**39.**—St. Alphonsus Liguori thus characterises the graces of the mystic union, which he contrasts with revelations and visions: "They are those that consist in confused and general knowledge and in *divine touches* that unite the soul to God" (*Homo Apost.,* Append. I, No. 23).

**39** *bis.*—Impression of immersion in God:

(*a*) Tauler: "The spirit is *submerged* and absorbed in the depths of the divine ocean, so that we can exclaim: God is in me, God is outside of me, God is everywhere round about me. God is everything to me, and I see nought but God" (*Instit.,* ch. xii).

(*b*) The Ven. Blosius: "The soul, *immersed* in God and absorbed into Him, swims, as it were, to and fro in the Godhead and abounds with unspeakable joy... Now does the soul itself, even in this exile, enjoy a foretaste of eternal life" (*A Book of Spiritual Instruction,* ch. xii, section iv, 2).

(*c*) Alvarez de Paz, speaking of the full union: "In this degree the faculties are transported into the sublime sea of the Divinity, *immersed* in God and raised to the highest degree of light and fervour" (*De inquis. pacis,* Book IV, Part III, ch. v).

(*d*) Ven. Marina de Escobar: The angels "hurled me... into the vast sea of... the Essence of the unknown and incomprehensible God. I was *submerged* in it and lost..." (For the remainder, see ch. xviii, No. **67**.) "The soul is then plunged, as it were, in a vast ocean which is God and again God. She can neither find a foothold nor touch the bottom" (*Vida,* Vol. II, Book II, ch. xxxiv).

(*e*) Schram: "In the degree of passive contemplation called passive *penetration* (*illapsus*), an *experimental sensation* of God, which has *penetrated* into the soul, is added to the substantial penetration common to all the just."—"The soul feels herself wholly *saturated* with God, and she finds Him, as it were, in the most intimate *depths of her being*" (Nos. 329, 323, of the 1848 edition; 318, 312 of the old edition).

**39** *ter.*—In his treatise, *Questiones morales selectæ,* Fr. Vermeersch, S.J., Professor of Theology at Louvain, lays down this thesis: "Mystic grace is a contemplation of God, full of extraordinary and ineffable love, with a certain feeling of the *divine presence...* which the mystics describe by the words *interior senses,* and specially call a *touch.*" He adds: "We speak thus, although it is repugnant to some, to a few; for we now rely upon the weightiest authorities;

this is the criterium of the specific distinction between the mystic union and all other unions" (Vol. I, No. 78).

§ 4. The Spiritual Touch Can Become an Embrace.

**40.**—St. Teresa:

"When this most opulent Spouse is pleased to enrich and more eminently to caress souls, He so converts them into Himself that, as a person swooning through excessive delight and pleasure, the soul seems to herself to be *suspended in those divine arms and to rest on that divine side and those divine breasts;* and doth nothing but enjoy, being sustained with divine milk wherewith her Spouse goes feeding her... She seeth herself... caressed by Him who knows how and is able to do it; she knows not what to compare it to, save the caressing of a mother, that, tenderly loving her infant, thus nurseth and fondles him" (*Conceptions of the Love of God,* ch. iv, p. 310).

See also ch. v, **22**, 9°.

**41.**—Blessed Hugh of St.-Victor (*De arrha animæ,* the end). Dialogue between the man and his soul.

"*The Soul:* What is that sweet thing that comes sometimes to touch me at the thought of God? It affects me with such vehemence and sweetness that I begin wholly to go out of myself and to be lifted up, whither I know not. Suddenly I am renewed and changed; it is a state of inexpressible well-being. My consciousness rejoices. I lose the memory of my former trials, my soul rejoices, my mind becomes clearer, my heart is enflamed, my desires are satisfied. I feel myself transported into a new place, I know not where. I grasp something interiorly as if with the *embraces* of love. I do not know what it is, and yet I strive with all my strength to hold it and not to lose it. I struggle deliciously to prevent myself leaving this thing which I desire to *embrace* for ever, and I exult with ineffable intensity, as if I had at last found the goal of all my desires. I seek for nothing more. I wish for nothing more. All my aspiration is to continue at the point that I have reached. Is it my Beloved? Tell me, I pray thee, if this be He, that, when He return, I may conjure Him not to depart and to establish in me His permanent dwelling-place?

"*The Man:* Yes, it is truly thy Beloved who visits thee. But He comes *invisible, hidden,* incomprehensible. He comes to *touch* thee; not to be seen; to intimate His presence to thee, not to be understood; to make thee taste of Him, not to pour Himself out in His entirety; to draw thy affection, not to satisfy thy desire; to bestow the first-fruits of His love, not to communicate it in its fulness. Behold in this the most certain pledge of thy future marriage: that thou art destined to see Him and to possess Him eternally, because He already gives Himself to thee at times to taste; with what sweetness thou knowest. Therefore in the times of His absence thou shalt console thyself; and during His visits thou shalt renew thy courage which is ever in need of heartening. We have spoken at great length, O my soul. In conclusion, I ask thee to think of none but Him, love none but Him, listen to none but Him, take hold of none but Him, possess none but Him.

"*The Soul:* That indeed is what I desire, what I choose; that is what I long for from the depths of my heart" (Migne ed., Vol. II, col. 970).

**42.**—St. Thomas (Opuscule 65):

"The soul, in the preceding degrees, loves and is loved in return; she seeks and she is sought; she calls and is called. But in this, in an admirable and ineffable way, she lifts and is lifted up; *she holds and is herself held;* she clasps and she is *closely embraced,* and by the bond of love she unites herself with God, one with one, alone with Him."

**43.**—St. Gertrude. In this passage it is not a question of Our Lord's Humanity, for in the rest of the chapter she speaks only of the Divinity.

"O *my God,* the only salvation of my soul... I will dare to say that if anything human or Divine can exceed the blessedness of Thy embrace in this vision, as I consider, I may truly say that, unless Thy Divine virtue possessed that person, the soul would never remain in the body after a momentary taste of this blessedness. I render thanks to Thee... that Thou hast deigned to favour me with Thy *caresses*; so that while I sat meditating, or reading the Canonical Hours, or saying the Office of the Dead, Thou hast often during a single Psalm embraced my soul many times with a kiss which far surpasses the most fragrant perfumes or the sweetest honey; and I have often observed Thou didst look on me favourably in the condescending caresses Thou didst give to my soul. But though all these things were filled with an extreme sweetness, I declare, nevertheless, that nothing touched me so much as this majestic look of which I have spoken" (*Life and Revelations* of St. Gertrude, Part II, ch. xxii, pp. 117, 118).

**44.**—Blessed Angela of Foligno:

"The other way in which the rational soul knoweth God Almighty to be with her is by an *embrace* which God giveth her; for never can father or mother embrace their child, nor any person embrace another with so much love as God Almighty embraces the rational soul... and with so great a sweetness and gentleness, that I believe not that any man in the world can speak of or express it, or believe himself to have experienced it"... (*Visions and Instructions,* ch. lii, p. 179).

See another Extract, ch. xxv, 28.

**45.**—Gerson:

"The object of mystic theology is an *experimental* knowledge of God in the *embrace* of unitive love" (*Theol. myst.,* No. 28).

**46.**—Denis the Carthusian (*Opusc. on the discernment of spirits*):

"When the soul has purified herself, when she burns with the fire of charity, when she shines by reason of her virtues, God takes His pleasure greatly in her,

He holds her familiarly like a fair spouse, *clasping* her, *caressing* her, *embracing* her, and communicating His blessings to her abundantly" (art. 18).

**47.**—Ven. Blosius:

1° Some there are who "are inundated in their inmost souls with plenteous sweetness from God, are joined to Him by the internal *embrace* of love in sensible union, and receive from Him most sweet spiritual *embraces* of love" (*A Book of Spiritual Instruction,* Appendix I, ch. i, No. 2).

2° "Lord [what favours dost Thou not accord to] those who in this exile are intimately united to Thee by reason of the great purity of their hearts? What see they? What hear they? *What do they perceive by way of the [spiritual] sense of smell, taste, or otherwise?* No tongue can express it. The tender *embraces,* the delicate kisses that a mother gives to her dear child, or the bridegroom to his beloved bride, are but the feeble image and shadow of those that Thou bestowest upon the chaste soul that loves Thee" (*Instructio vitæ asceticæ,* Part II, ch. vii).

**48.**—St. John of the Cross compares the higher mystic union to an embrace:

"So then in that soul wherein no desire dwells, and out of which all images and forms of created things have been cast, the Beloved dwells most secretly Himself, and the purer the soul and the greater its estrangement from everything but God, the more intimate His converse and the closer His *embrace...* He is there, as it were, asleep, in the embraces of the soul" (*Living Flame,* Stanza IV, line 3).

**49.**—Fr. Sandæus:

"The mystic union is an *experimental* and direct perception of God by a secret *embrace;* a mutual *kiss* between God, who is the Bridegroom, and the soul-spouse. And this implies that God is present" (Book II, *Comm.* 6, Exerc. 15, disq. 3, p. 471).

**50.**—Fr. Surin:

"The sequel of this perfect love is an *embrace...* by which Jesus Christ remains united to the soul and communicates to her a very sweet *touch* of the *Divine* substance, as all the mystic doctors tell us, and as we know *by the experiences* of the souls that are called to these favours... This touch, which is inexplicable by our speech, is very delicate and nevertheless *very real,* inebriating the soul with a super-celestial good. It consists in an actual possession of the sovereign Good of which, however, she has not *sight,* and which leaves such a high idea of this same Good, that the soul can say that she has *touched and felt* that which is above all created things... The principal knowledge of this truth is founded upon the *sense experience* of persons who have had this favour, and whose sincerity cannot be questioned" (*Catech. Spir.,* Vol. I, Part III, ch. vii).

**51.**—Ven. Mary of the Incarnation, Ursuline, speaking of an intellectual vision of the Blessed Trinity:

"The Divine Word, taking possession of my soul and embracing her with an inexplicable love, deigned to unite Himself with her and to take her for His spouse. When I say that He embraced her, it was not after the manner of human embraces, for nothing of that which falls within the cognisance of the senses in any way approaches this divine operation; but we have to express ourselves according to our gross way of speaking, since we are composed of matter. It was by Divine *touches* and by penetrations of Him in me and of me in Him" (*Vie,* by an Ursuline of Nantes, ch. iv).

**52.**—Fr. Nouet (*Conduite de l'homme d'Oraison*):

"God, who was formerly in the soul of the just *as a hidden treasure,* by way of sanctifying grace, now presents Himself to her as *a Treasure that is found.* He enlightens her. He *touches* her, He *embraces* her, He *penetrates* her, He flows into her faculties, *He gives Himself to her, He fills her* with the fulness of His Being. The soul, in return, ravished by His charms and by the spectacle of His beauty, *holds Him, embraces Him, clasps Him* closely, and, all on fire with love, she flows, she plunges, she buries and loses herself deliciously in God with sentiments of inconceivable joy. Thence comes the great diversity of names that are given to the mystic union, such as *kiss, perfume,* celestial rain, unction, Divine inflowing, transformation, love in fruition, deifying love, and several other similar expressions, that denote the different impressions of the unitive love of which we are now speaking" (Book VI, ch. xiv).

**53.**—Fr. Crasset (*Vie de Madame Hélyot*):

"With regard to the acts that she formulated at this time I reply that she produced one act of very perfect love which lasted from the beginning of her prayer unto the end. This is the act of the Blessed in Heaven, and is the most perfect that can be produced on earth; it is *an act of fruition,* which is the repose of the soul in God as in her last end; for this repose is not a mere cessation of desire referring to an absent good that we do not possess, but it is a real union of the soul with her sovereign Good, which she *possesses and which she embraces* after long seeking and desire" (Book II, ch. iv, No. 25).

**54.**—St. Margaret Mary:

"Every morning, when I awake, I seem to feel my God *present,* and my heart unites itself to Him as to its cause and its only plenitude; and this gives me such an ardent thirst to go to prayer, that the few moments that it takes me to dress seem like hours. It is during this time [of prayer] that I use my utmost endeavours to *embrace* Him, this Beloved of my soul; not with the bodily limbs, but with *interior* arms, which are the powers of my soul" (*Vie et Œuvres,* published by the Order of the Visitation at Paray, Vol. I. Note written by St. Margaret Mary, in 1673, at the age of twenty-six, three years after her entry into the Convent.)

**55.**—St. John Vianney, Curé d'Ars:

"The inner life is a bath of love into which the soul plunges. She is, as it were, drowned in love. God holds the inner man as a mother holds her infant's head between her hands, to cover it with kisses and caresses" (*Vie,* by M. Monnin, Book V, ch. iv).

### § 5. The Spiritual Sensation Compared to That of Smell.

**56.**—St. Teresa:

1° On the prayer of quiet. The soul "perceives a *certain fragrance* as we may call it, as if within its inmost depths were a brazier sprinkled with sweet perfumes. Although the spirit neither sees the flame nor knows *where it is,* yet it is *penetrated by the warmth and scented fumes* which are even sometimes felt by the body. Understand me, the soul does not feel any real heat or scent, but something far more delicious, which I use this metaphor to explain. Let those who have never felt this believe that it really occurs to others: the soul is conscious of it and feels it more clearly than could be told" (*Interior Castle,* Fourth Mansion, ch. ii, 6).

2° "For instance, when reciting the Divine Office in choir, without seeing to penetrate the sense, one may be seized with a delightful fervour, as if suddenly encompassed with a *fragrance* powerful enough to diffuse itself through all the senses. I do not assert that there is really any [material] scent, but make use of this comparison because it somewhat resembles the manner by which the Spouse *makes His presence* understood, moving the soul to a delicious desire of enjoying Him, and thus disposing it to heroic acts, and causing it to render Him fervent praise" (*Interior Castle,* Sixth Mansion, ch. ii 14).

3° On the prayer of quiet. [It is] "as if some very sweet ointment were injected into the intimatest part of the soul, after the manner of an exquisite perfume; when we suddenly come into a place where it is very much, exhaling not only from one, but many things, and we know not what it is, nor from which of them the scent comes, but they all please us... This is what the Spouse here saith... Thy breasts are better than wine, which sends forth an odour like that of very precious unguents" (*Conceptions of the Love of God,* ch. iv, p. 309).

**57.**—Cassian (*Conference,* 4):

"It frequently happens, in the divine visits, that we are filled with perfumes, of a sweetness unknown to human skill; so that the soul, overwhelmed with delight, is lifted into a rapture and forgets that she is living in the flesh" (ch. v).

# CHAPTER VII

## The Mystic Union: Its Ten Subsidiary Characters. Description of the First.

**1.—Enumeration.** The two theses given above have taught us the two *principal* characters of the mystic union. This union has ten subsidiary characters, as will now be successively explained. I number them in continuation to the two fundamental characters.

3° It does not depend on our own will;

4° The knowledge of God accompanying it is obscure and confused;

5° The mode of communication is partially incomprehensible;

6° The union is produced neither by reasonings, nor by the consideration of creatures, nor by sensible images;

7° It varies incessantly in intensity;

8° It demands less effort than meditation;

9° It is accompanied by sentiments of love, of repose, of pleasure, and often of suffering;

10° It inclines the soul of itself and very efficaciously to the different virtues;

11° It acts upon the body and is acted upon in return;

12° It impedes to a greater or lesser extent the production of certain interior acts; this is what is called the ligature.

**2.**—In employing the expression **subsidiary** characters, I have not meant to say that they were devoid of importance, but that, theoretically, they were less important than the two others that went before and of which they are, so to speak, the consequences. These two are, in fact, the only characters that make us acquainted with the basis of the employment given by God to the soul in the mystic state. The others indicate the *effects* or the *accompaniments only.*

Certain of these effects, such as divine love, are produced invariably and without any exceptions. Others may occur here or there.

**3.—The unity of the states in the mystic union.** Farther back I was content to say that the four degrees of this union are not disconnected graces, but the progressive development of one and the same grace (ch. iii, 6). We now have proof of this, since these states resemble each other upon so many points. They have the same elements: namely, the twelve characters enumerated above. The differences will come from the degree of perfection with which these characters are found. This proposition is obvious when we read St. Teresa, and take the trouble to compare the descriptions that she gives of each degree (see also ch. xxv, 20). In the same way Fr. du Pont regards all these graces of union as only one considered fundamentally (*Life of Father Balthazar Alvarez,* ch. xiv).

**4.—The third character** has already been given; it is an absolute powerlessness to procure the mystic states for ourselves. It is from this that I have drawn my definition of the states (ch. i). But it is as well to return to it for the sake of adding some complementary details.

I shall not quote from St. Teresa in proof either of this or the two succeeding characters; because we have only to open her *Works* to see that she speaks of them incessantly.

**5.**—The **powerlessness** in question shows itself in six ways:

1° As has just been said, we cannot bring about the mystic union in ourselves when God does not give it; anyone can prove to himself that to will it is not sufficient;

2° In the same way its coming cannot be *foreseen*, whatever preparations we may have tried to make. Beginners are often surprised at the *unexpected* manner of its arrival. They were not thinking of it, or simply striving to lift up their hearts towards God, perhaps without much success. And all of a sudden a state of recollection of a quite special kind took possession of them without their knowing why. They allow themselves to float with the current, because they saw from the first that was a holy occupation. They postponed the task of examining it more closely to another time. Their part lay in consenting to an unforeseen action;

3° If this union is granted to us, we cannot make it *more intense,* however much we may desire to do so. We plunge ourselves in God only in the precise measure in which He wills it;

4° And it is in the same as to the *kind* of mystic union. We shall see that this favour may differ in the matter of its presence. Now, it in no wise depends upon our will to have one kind of union rather than another; consequently we can foresee nothing with regard to it.

5° Those who have this union from time to time only, usually find it ceases *abruptly* as it came; and this without their participation.

6° We cannot make it cease merely by an *interior* act of the will. We can influence it by indirect means only, by walking or seeking much external distraction. In this way we can *diminish* it, or even cause it to cease altogether (see ch. xiii, **8**).

**6.—Advice to directors**. From the last remark it follows that a director is demanding the impossible if he advises or orders anybody in a general way to quit the mystic union and to return to the ordinary way of prayer. All that could be done would be to give up prayer; which is not at all the same thing.

The person directed should show his good-will, however, by *trying* gently to obey. The result, it is true, is a foregone conclusion. But no matter. Obedience may require us to make the attempt, but it cannot exact success.

**7.**—Another consequence of what has gone before is that in the mystic union we feel our absolute **dependence upon the divine will** with regard to this favour: it lies with God alone to give it, to augment it, or to withdraw it.

Nothing can be more calculated to inspire us with sentiments of humility. For we see clearly that ours is a quite secondary part, that of the pauper who stretches out his hand for an alms. In ordinary prayer, on the contrary, we are inclined to attribute the greater part of the success to our own talents.

This dependence, continually felt, produces also a filial fear of God. For we see how easily He can punish us for our infidelities by the instantaneous loss of everything.

**8.—The cause of this powerlessness**. The above theses give us an insight into the reason why the mystic union is not placed at our disposition like ordinary prayer. It is because this union gives us an experimental possession of God. An illustration to make this clear. If one of my friends is hidden behind a wall, I can always think of him when I wish to do so. But if I wish *really* to enter into relation with him, my will is no longer sufficient. The wall must disappear. In like manner God is hidden. With the aid of grace it is always within the power of my will to think of Him, which is ordinary prayer. But it is clear that if I wish really to enter into communication with Him, this will is no longer sufficient. *An obstacle must be removed;* and the Divine Hand alone is powerful to accomplish this.

**9.**—But if we cannot produce the mystic state at will, we can at least **dispose ourselves** to it. And we can do this by the practice of virtue, and also by a life of interior and exterior recollection (see ch. xxviii, **24**).

Sometimes the soul is taken sudden possession of by the mystic union while reading some pious book or hearing God spoken of. In this case the reading or the conversation is not the cause, but the occasion of the grace received. This grace has God for its sole cause; but God takes account of the dispositions in which He finds us.

# CHAPTER VIII

## THE FOURTH AND FIFTH CHARACTERS OF THE MYSTIC UNION

**1.**—The **fourth character** of the mystic union consists in the fact that the knowledge of God, of which it is partly composed, is *obscure* and *confused.*

Hence these expressions: to enter into the divine obscurity (*oratio in Caligne*), or into the *divine darkness,* to contemplate God in the *darkness.*

These names may be applied to all the mystic states. Some authors, however, reserve them for certain ecstatic visions. There is a great deal of opinion in the matter. Certain very sublime visions are called *the great darkness* (see ch. xviii, **24**).

**2.**—Beginners who have read nothing on the subject of mystic contemplation never suspect that it always remains indistinct. They are even convinced of the contrary; and this doubtless by analogy with our exact knowledge concerning material things. Hence their astonishment when the prayer of quiet is first granted to them; they see in it a preliminary state only, out of which some distinct knowledge will soon make its way. This prayer is for them like some great white canvas stretched over the walls of a room. They are waiting until the painter's brush or a magic-lantern slide should throw upon it certain definite figures and colours. Vain expectation! This state continues without perfecting itself further, and terminates in the same way: Beginners feel a little disappointed that God does not organize things more in accordance with the quite natural and more agreeable plan which they have imagined.

**3.**—The **fifth character** of the mystic union consists in this: that the mode of communication is *but half understandable.*

It is for this reason especially that these states have been called mystic. It is desired to convey the idea that they contain something mysterious, and this even for the instructed. There is more than one how and why which have never been cleared up (see St. John of the Cross, *Obscure Night,* Book II, ch. xvii).

**4.**—All the divine communications have this character of manifesting the **divine attribute** of incomprehensibility. They always contain something that we wish to understand better. With regard to God's other attributes, they nearly all continue hidden in the prayer of quiet; but this one, on the contrary, strikes us from the outset.* And it only becomes more apparent as the soul mounts up to higher modes of knowledge.

**5.—Expressions that need interpretation.** I have said that these states are in part incomprehensible. It would be an exaggeration to say that they are totally so. If we seem at times to suggest this, it is a mere manner of speaking. We exaggerate the idea in order to make it more evident. If, strictly speaking, we understood nothing of our state, we should not know that we were in communication with God, or even that we were praying. We might fancy ourselves attacked by some strange malady.

**6.—Example.** St. Teresa often says that "we enjoy favour without knowing what it is" (see *Interior Castle,* Sixth Mansion). We must understand this *abbreviated* phrase thus: we enjoy this favour without *completely* knowing what it is. We know it in part, because we perceive that it is the divine action, and even a certain possession of the Divinity.

**7.**—I have already (**2**) pointed out a **prejudice** common with beginners. Here is another sufficiently resembling the first. They believe that the mystic states present hardly any element of mystery. Meditation and other inferior states were easy to understand. By analogy they fancy that this condition will continue. They forget that a great change has taken place. Hitherto they performed, in appearance, at least, none but natural acts in their prayer. These acts, therefore, could cause them no surprise. But they are now penetrating into a new world: they are manifestly entering into the supernatural, into the divine. This unknown land is full of mysteries.

If, however, we remain for a long time in one degree, we become so accustomed to it that we no longer take any heed of its incomprehensible side. It is the same in the natural order with thousands of the phenomena round about us. While children are for ever asking the why and the how of things, we ended by forgetting that there are any questions to inquire into.

Beginners often hope to be able to accomplish an exhaustive self-analysis, but they finish by proving the uselessness of their efforts.

**8.**—Hence the **disquietudes** to be found in those who have but lately arrived at extraordinary prayer and are not yet instructed in mysticism. All that is mysterious gives rise to distrust.

* Bousset has noticed this (Letter 98 to Sister Cornuau): "God is something so hidden that we can unite ourselves to Him, when He calls us to do so, with a certain transcendency above all particular perceptions... And in this we do not leave God's attributes, but we enter into the obscurity, or, in other words, into the depths and the incomprehensibility of the Divine Being.

"This is doubtless an attribute, and one of the most imposing amongst them. We never so issue forth from God's attributes that we do not enter into them again from another side, and this perhaps more profoundly. All sides seem reduced to seeing clearly that we see nothing, because we see nothing that is worthy of God. To the animal man this seems nothing but a dream, but nevertheless the spiritual man nourishes himself upon it."

**9.**—And just as the soul experiences difficulty in understanding her state, so she finds it **very hard** to **describe** it, especially if she has read no mystic writings. She makes use of such vague expressions as the following: "I feel *something* that draws me to God, and I find in it happiness and repose"; adding: "I understand nothing of it" (see St. John of the Cross, *Obscure Night,* Book II, ch. xvii). At the sound of this last sentence a skilled director will pick up his ears, recognizing here one of the signs of the mystic state. But others will merely conclude that it is some preposterous kind of prayer which had better be changed as soon as possible.

This difficulty in describing our state is due not only to its being partly incomprehensible, but to another character of the mystic union which I shall explain in the next chapter: namely, that it is produced without any sensible images; and yet if we wish to depict it we can only do so by making use of some such images. We are obliged to invent them; if we are not assisted by a book, this task is not easy one (see Extracts, ch. ix, 31, 5°).

## EXTRACTS

**10.**—Dionysius the Areopagite:

"And if anyone, when he has seen God, understands what he is seeing, it is never God that he has seen, but some one of the things of His which exist and are known" (Letter 1).

**11.**—St. John of the Cross:

1° "As the knowledge [in infused contemplation] is general and obscure—the intellect being unable to conceive *distinctly* what it understands—so the will also loves generally and *indistinctly*" (*The Living Flame of Love,* Stanza III, line 3, § 10, p. 276).

2° Addressing certain spiritual directors, the saint says again: "Say not, therefore, that thy penitent is making no progress, or is doing nothing... he thus draws nearer unto God *by not understanding* than by understanding... The intellect, having neither the knowledge nor the power of comprehending God, *advances towards Him by not understanding.* Thus, then, what thou judgest amiss in thy penitent is for his profit: namely, that he does not perplex himself with *distinct perceptions,* but walks onward in perfect faith" (*ibid.,* § 9, p. 276). See also *The Spiritual Canticle,* Stanza I, line 1.

# CHAPTER IX

## The Sixth Character of the Mystic Union

**1.—The sixth character** of the mystic union consists in this, that the contemplation of God is not produced by reasonings, or by the consideration of created things, or by interior images of the sensible order.

This contemplation has, as we have seen, quite another cause: a direct illumination from God, and, to make this still clearer, a supernatural knowledge of His presence, a spiritual sensation comparable to the sense of touch.

The ancient writers convey these various ideas briefly by saying that mystic contemplation takes place without *any intermediary* (*sine medio*), or that it is immediate. We all say as much with regard to communication by touch.

This knowledge without acts of reasoning and without images bears a resemblance to that of angels; and it is sometimes called an *angelic mode* of knowing. But there are differences also, notably that of clearness.

**2.—The exigence of this character**. Everyone allows that the mystic union is not the result of any act of reasoning; and this is why it is called contemplation, which signifies a prayer of simple regard. Even beginners are struck with this difference. They feel that their new prayer no longer resembles the old. The mind no longer travels over a consecutive train of thought, following up, developing. They feel themselves occupied with a sensation, plunged into an atmosphere which they breathe. Nothing more different can be imagined.

So, too, the consideration of created things has nothing to do with it. And, besides, this operation would, as a rule, presuppose acts of reasoning.

It now remains to prove the argument with regard to sensible images. Many theologians have been reluctant to admit that these images do not constitute the efficient cause of mystic contemplation; at most, they will allow this to be so in the case of raptures.

1° The experience of souls given to prayer decides this question absolutely, even as to the prayer of quiet. If we were to ask them what image it is that gives rise to this contemplation, they would be astounded by the strangeness of the question.

When philosophers wish to study the functionings of the human mind in the natural state, they very properly resort to observation. Let them therefore allow mystics to do the same in the supernatural state.

This question does not really admit of argument.

2° In St. Teresa's long descriptions of the prayer of quiet she has never suggested the presence of any imagery. With regard to the higher states, she often speaks of the suspension of "all the faculties," and says that the inferior faculties (the imagination and the power of reasoning) then remain inactive.

3° A large number of passages declare this character plainly. St. John of the Cross comes back to it incessantly, and he even refers to it in a state that is not fully mystic: *the Night of the Senses.* He has selected this last expression to sum up his teaching upon the subject. What he wishes to suggest is precisely this disappearance in prayer of that which is due to sense. Ruysbroeck likewise perpetually describes mystic contemplation by saying that it is above images and forms (distinct concepts).

Scaramelli (Tr. 2, chs. xv and xvi) quotes St. Bernard, Hugh and Richard of St. Victor, St. Bonaventure, Denis the Carthusian, Lyranus, and Alvarez de Paz in proof of this doctrine.*

4° Should anyone refuse to admit this classical thesis, he ought to tell us which are the images of the prayer of quiet that produce union with God. Does the divine action consist in the representation of God the Father as an old man? or the Blessed Trinity as a sphere? or the Divinity as a cloud? Even if some saint had seen these symbols for a brief period of time, does anyone suppose that he could have made them the subject of his constant contemplation? Who would have the patience to apply himself for any length of time to so simple a spectacle?

**3.**—The mystic writers' habit of expressing themselves by the use of images has often been a source of **misunderstanding** on the part of the ordinary man. Seeing that the words marriage and spiritual senses are employed, they say: this language proves that they are not speaking of purely intellectual facts, but merely of pictures constructed by the imagination or by the sensible emotions. It all takes place, therefore, in the inferior faculties.

Not always. The meaning of these expressions must be decided by the context. When we wish to express intellectual things, we are condemned to make use of human language which is very imperfect and derives from

* But Scaramelli is wrong in conceding that this is not so in the lower mystic degrees, that is to say, in the prayer of quiet. He avoids giving any quotations in support of this restriction (they would lead him to the opposite thesis), nor does he fall back upon experience. He is content to reason *a priori* upon a passage of Aristotle, which has no bearing on the matter; for it alludes to natural modes of knowledge only.

Cardinal Brancati has fallen into the opposite exaggeration. He believed that the imagination usually ceased to act in acquired contemplation; in the prayer of simplicity, that is to say (op. 3, ch. xvi, quoted also by Scaramelli, Tr. 3, No. 157).

corporeal objects. This is a necessary evil. In the same way, and for the sake of making themselves easily understood, the sacred writers speak of God's arms, of His countenance, etc. No one dreams, however, of accusing them of believing that God possesses a real body.

**4.—Objection**. But the schoolmen, on the contrary, have insisted upon the principle that our thoughts are always evoked by images.

**5.—Reply.** Yes, this is so in the natural order, and consequently in the operations of the ordinary supernatural which resemble those of nature. But the schoolmen recognise that a higher supernatural state exists, one in which the soul operates after a purely intellectual manner and without any sensible images, whether they be those that excite the intelligence or even, at times, those that accompany its action.

This is why the schoolmen, with St. Augustine (*In Genes.*, Book XII, ch. vii, xxiv), distinguish not two, but three sorts of visions: the corporeal, the imaginative, and the *purely intellectual* (see ch. xx). St. Thomas implies the same doctrine when he distinguishes three ways of attaining to the knowledge of God: the first by the spectacle of the world; the second by supernatural illuminations, preceded by sensible images (Example: the visions of the prophets; or simply the knowledge of the Person and the acts of Jesus Christ and the saints). There also, he says, the soul acts "according to her" natural "mode." Finally, "by the third manner, the soul rejects all the objects of sense, surpassing all things and her own self in her conception of God" (*De Verit.,* a. 15, ad. 3). As to the possibility of these higher acts, see also Suarez (*De Orat.,* Book II, ch. xiv, No. 4).

As to knowing the precise degree of prayer in which the soul thus begins to dispense of images, it is a question which had no sort of interest for dogmatic theology, and which mysticism has taken it upon itself to solve.

**6.—The concomitant action of the faculties.** Here and there, however, some images and acts of reasoning may be found mingling with mystic contemplation and seeming to aid in completing it. But these acts are present as a mere *accompaniment* only, and not as causes.

They may sometimes be attributed solely to the action of grace; but more often they proceed, at least in part, from our own action, which we *add* to God's action. I shall refer to these later on as *additional acts* (**13**).

For instance, it may happen that, while enjoying the divine communications, I may be searching for words and comparisons in order to describe it afterwards. I am thus making acts of the imagination. But they do not belong to the foundation of my mystic state. It is something that I *superimpose* to it.

In entering into the mystic way, contemplative souls do not, therefore, lose the power of raising themselves to God by the considerations of created things and other ordinary means. But, in addition to this, they have an infused light also, and they thus revert in some measure to the desirable state that was once bestowed upon Adam. "Man," says St. Thomas, "in a state of innocence, had a double knowledge of God and of divine things; the one by way of an interior inspiration which he possessed in common with the angels, and the other by means of sensible things; and this is the mode which is proper to mankind. In that contemplation to which he was raised by grace, he resembled the angels" (*De Verit.*, q. 18, a. 2).

**7.—The triple attitude of our faculties.** Let us now see how our three faculties —the understanding, the memory, and the imagination—act with regard to the divine communication. Each of them has its triple manner of operation, which we can sum up the following words: quiescence, concurrence, and strife.

**8.**—1° **Quiescence.** The faculties may be at rest and abstain from trying to add anything to that which they receive. The intellect is content to drink deep draughts of the experimental knowledge vouchsafed to it; it is wise to stop there. The memory and the imagination, having nothing to receive, seem to slumber; and as a rule this is the best thing that they can do.

**9.**—2° **Concurrence.** If the memory and imagination should awake, they sometimes try to aid the prayer. For instance, the imagination goes in search of the words and comparisons that I have referred to above. Its assistance could very well be dispensed with, but it is a great thing not to be at war with such capricious faculties.

As long as this concurrence lasts, we can say that *all the faculties are united to God.* But, with respect to the memory and the imagination, this is so in a very low degree only, as in the case of ordinary meditation. They make additional acts. They see a banquet served up; but as it is not intended for their entertainment they, at any rate, show a certain amount of zeal by bringing their own provisions to the feast.

**10.**—3° **Strife.** The state of quiescence or of concurrence is never of long duration in the prayer of quiet. Distractions soon make their appearance. The three faculties resemble frolicsome children, who are soon weary of sitting quietly at their mother's side. They want to be running about and playing.

From time to time the attention reverts to the divine action which has been continuous, and then loses sight of it once more; the mystic union again becomes unconscious, unperceived. In the same way, a man stands with his eyes open before some extensive landscape. If his thoughts wander, his eyes still continue to receive the impression of the objects before him. And when his attention returns, he feels, though we know not how, that the sensation has not been interrupted. (With regard to distractions in the prayer of quiet, see St. Teresa, *Life,* chs. xv, xvii; *Way of Perfection,* ch. xxxiii; *Interior Castle,* Fourth Mansion, ch. i, 3).

**11.**—Some persons have found that the prayer of quiet was accompanied by **fewer distractions** in its earlier days than afterwards. How is this fact to be explained? One would expect that the divine action would increase in perfection as time went on.

The following, so it seems to me, is the probable explanation. It shows, too, that it would actually be thus in all cases, except for a special intervention of grace. On God's part the action is doubtless the same as at the outset, neither more nor less. But this action combines, as must always happen, with our human nature, and from this side there are reasons why there should be a decline of attention after a certain lapse of time. At first our curiosity is excited, and with it the hope of progress. Little by little these sentiments become deadened, and the imagination then resumes its sway. We experience similar results when we undertake some new study that interests us keenly. Distractions are then few; but they return as soon as our interest begins to flag.

**12.—Is there a remedy for distractions** in the prayer of quiet? St. Teresa states that she had found none.* Distractions are most frequent when the prayer of quiet is present in a low degree only; it is then a great test of patience.

**13.—Additional acts.** I have already made use of this expression. I must give its exact definition.

To begin with, I applied the names *constitutive* or *fundamental* acts of the mystic state to those acts that belong *necessarily* to the state; such as thinking of God, tasting Him, loving Him.

On the other hand, I described as *additional acts* of the mystic state those acts, other than distractions, which are not proper to the state; that is to say, are neither its cause nor its necessary consequence. This term expresses that an *addition* is made, whether voluntarily or not, to the foundation of the mystic union; it is a many-coloured embroidery, applied to a material of a uniform hue.

Thus, to recite an *Ave*, or any vocal prayer whatsoever, during the prayer of quiet, is to make an additional act, since it is not necessary to the existence of this state. And it is the same when we apply ourselves to acts of reasoning or considerations upon various subjects, such as death, sin, etc., none of these things been essential to the mystic union.

Our natural activity leads us to produce these acts, because it often happens that the mystic union is not sufficient to occupy us fully; we want to complete and to assist the divine action. I will explain the proper course to follow later on (ch. xiv, **33**).

And yet these additional acts do not always proceed from our desire for activity. Then they come from the strongly marked divine attraction. God is free, should He choose to do so, to cause the memory, for instance, of one of the mystery of Our Lord's Life, to return to us frequently, through the mystic

* "I know of no remedy for it; and hitherto God has told me of none. If He had, most gladly would I make use of it, for I am, as I say, tormented very often" (*Life*, ch. xvii, 11). The saint is speaking here of a state which is not yet the full union, although very near to it.

union. It is true that it is then an *addition* to the union, but it is one that is not detrimental to it.

My definition does not include distractions amongst the additional acts. These are prejudicial to all prayer. We must not confound them with others, such as vocal prayers, that are good in themselves and may only be inopportune at times.

**14.—Abbreviations to be avoided.** In place of saying: additional acts, some ancient authors have merely said: acts. It is impossible fully to realise all the ill effects that have resulted from this true general expression. For these writers then went on to enunciate such principles as the following: "In supernatural prayer there are often no acts," or, "we must not be afraid of suppressing all acts." If they had said *additional* acts, the propositions would then have had a clear and correct signification. They would then mean: "In supernatural prayer there are often no acts that are *foreign* to it, such as vocal prayer, acts of reasoning, considerations, distinct reflections," or, "we must not be afraid of suppressing all such acts as are extraneous to the foundation of the prayer." But in the over-abbreviated form given to them, these phrases become very inaccurate. The opponents of mysticism have seized upon them eagerly, and have declared that we wish to suppress even the exercise of the thought and the love of God, which things constitute acts, and so reduce the man to the condition of a block of stone.* Some souls of good-will, on the other hand, have declared anxiously that they fail to understand how to occupy themselves aright in the mystic state. And long dissertations have been entered upon in order to explain to them that there are acts and acts. Time would have been saved had this distinction been emphasised by the use of some expressive terms at the beginning.

**15.—Another abbreviated expression to be avoided.** Instead of saying that mystic contemplation, when deprived of additional acts, comprises neither acts of reasoning nor any extraneous ideas, some mystics have employed a stronger expression. They have said: "The person thinks of *nothing*," or, "he loves God and possesses Him without knowing *anything* about it."

These are mere figures of speech.† For all the schoolmen are in agreement on this point, namely, that there is *neither love nor enjoyment without knowledge.*

* Certain freethinkers, wishing to give a definition of mysticism, have not failed to understand it in this sense. For them, the mystic is a man who, instead of developing and elevating his faculties, annihilates them. He is a maniac who seeks to brutalise his intelligence and to render his will inert. And as he still feels a need for action, he turns for direction to sentiment, which is the sole survivor of the reason (see ch. xviii, 41).

What is depicted here is not mysticism, however, but its counterfeit, as invented by the quietists.

And then these good folk, who judge thus superficially of the saints, pass as being profound and well instructed persons!

† Alvarez de Paz is not at all of this opinion (Vol. iii, Book IV, Part III, ch. viii), and he appeals to experience. But he interprets his experience wrongly, and from it deduces a manifest error. It may be

Again, if it were not so in your prayer, if you were not *thinking* of God in it, how would you know whether it is He whom you love and whether you are praying at all?

The right expression is this: "The mind *does nothing,* save that it adheres to the divine action," or, "it thinks of *nothing* material or earthly, of *nothing* that occupied it habitually in the natural order, of *nothing,* either, of all those things that are developed in books of meditations."

According to Bossuet, when St. Teresa says that "the understanding does not act," she merely means to indicate that no discursive acts are made (*Mystici in tuto,* Part I, Book 1, ch. i)*

In the same way, Bossuet explains that we must not abuse St. Francis of Sales' comparison of the statue. "Comparisons must be kept within their proper limits, and it is fatal to push them to extremes. Thus the saint's statue is motionless, not by the cessation of all acts, but only by the cessation of the *most turbulent* acts" (*États d'Orasion,* Book VIII, No. 15).

**16.—Excuses for this language.** How can these writers have come to employ such a manifestly incorrect phraseology? This is easily explained. Suppose that a traveller leaves a country where he has seen a great variety of *objects*—houses, palaces, trees, people and animals—and upon awaking in the morning he finds himself in some vast desert, arid and sandy or upon the high seas. Ask him: What do you see? And instinctively he will reply: *Nothing.* And if you remonstrate with him for this language, if you urge that he sees the sky and also the sand or the sea, he would answer: Very true, but that is what I call nothing *in contrast with the multitude of objects* that I have left behind.

And, in the same way, these writers are expressing their first feelings of astonishment, the first impressions of solitude and silence that this prayer has made upon them. They exaggerate this impression in order to make it more striking and to describe it in a few words.

**17.**—They know quite well that certain *underlying things* have to be *taken for granted* in their words, but these things, in their eyes, are quite evident. The instructed in mysticism often read between the lines also. It was thus that St. Teresa, when still undecided as to her way, read a little treatise, entitled *The Ascent of the Mount* (*Subida del Monte Sion*). She came across this sentence: "In the prayer of quiet one can think of nothing." But she knew how to interpret its

that in certain tempests of love the soul may believe that she feels nothing else than this love, but the love conceals a subtle knowledge: the soul knows that she loves.

* Example: The saint says: "In mystical theology, of which I spoke before, the *understanding ceases from its acts,* because God *suspends it.*" But she then immediately adds a commentary which restricts her statement to certain acts: "For when Our Lord suspends the understanding, and makes it cease from its acts, He puts before it that which *astonishes and occupies it:* so that, *without making any reflections,* it shall comprehend in a moment more than we could comprehend in many years with all the efforts in the world" (*Life,* ch. xii, 8).

meaning, and was greatly consoled at recognising in it her own prayer (*Life*, ch. xxiii, 13).

The uninstructed, however, are less advantageously placed. The study of their own interior operations fails to supply them with facts to supplement the omissions of their teachers. And so here, as with the other over-abbreviated sentences, they see only insoluble enigmas which are an insult to their good sense. Let us bear this disposition in mind, and confine ourselves for the future to the language of strict accuracy.

Authors have wished to cut their explanation short, and their obscurity has resulted in interminable disputes. And then, to elucidate matters, all the treatises have been lengthened out; the question whether it is possible to love without knowledge having been the cause, especially, of the expenditure of a perfect flood of ink.

There is no objection to the use of the abbreviated phrases when we are speaking of things that everyone is familiar with, for the meaning is then obvious. But it is quite otherwise with mysticism. The things that are left to be understood without being expressed will always lead to misunderstandings here. So let us be careful to avoid them.

**18.**—Is there a state of the prayer of quiet in which the will only is united?

No: if the expression is used, it is only upon condition that it is not taken literally. For in its natural sense it means: "We still love God, but without thinking of Him in any way." This would be absurd. If the mind were in no way united; that is to say, if it were no longer at all occupied with the divine object, we should not love Him, and there would be neither love nor possession, and the will would be no more united than the other faculties.

**19.—First objection.** If anyone tastes honey or some rare vintage, it may happen that he is wholly absorbed in this pleasure, without adding any considerations or acts of reasoning. Now, to enjoy pleasure belongs to the will. So the will alone would seem to be affected.

**20.—Reply.** When we speak of anyone being entirely engrossed with this pleasure, the existence of some knowledge is understood, only no notice is taken of it. For the pleasure necessarily proceeds from knowledge. You *know* the honey as being present and acting upon you. But you are *chiefly occupied with the agreeable effect* which results from it.

Taste, like the other senses, is, first and foremost, an instrument *of knowledge.* But these operations of the senses can be accompanied by either pleasure or pain. There are always two acts instead of one: to know and to possess; but the attention can be occupied especially with the second.

**21.—Second objection.** St. Teresa sometimes makes use of the expression: the will alone is united. And it is the same with St. Francis of Sales in his *Treatise on the Love of God** Is this expression accurate?

**22.—Reply.** We must interpret the language in accordance with what we have just said. We have an additional proof of this in the context. For, while saying that the will *alone* operates, they credit it with acts of knowledge which, however, have nothing to do with it; the will, therefore, is really accompanied by knowledge, and consequently is not quite alone (see Extracts, No. 33).

**23.**—When reading these authors, then, **how should we interpret** this expression: the will alone is united? We must look to the context for the sense. Now, St. Teresa applies it to a case where the soul possesses God, although with a certain liberty of the understanding, which preserves some power of arguing, of reasoning (making her say that the understanding is not united), although with a host of small interruptions due to distractions (see Extracts).

St. Francis of Sales has the same idea in his mind at times. At others, on the contrary, he means that the understanding is wholly attentive, without distractions and without additional acts. And then its activity retires into the background, and we are only conscious of the love and the possession which are dependent upon the will; and we say for short: The will alone operates, or alone is united (see Extracts).

If modern writers wish to continue making use of these abbreviated phrases, let them at least remember to tell us what they mean by them! But, for the sake of greater clearness, it is better to avoid using them for the future.

**24.—Prayer of silence.** We have seen that all the mystic unions merit the name of prayer of repose (chs. II, **19**; III, **15**). In the same way we can give them the name of *prayer of silence,* since the noise of arguments and vocal prayers in a great measure disappears. This name begins to be applicable, in a certain degree, even to the prayer of simplicity.

There are some cases, however, when it is applicable to the mystic union in a quite special manner. I mean at those times when neither distractions nor additional acts occur. All sounds are hushed. The soul is wholly immersed in an act of possession which seems to endure without any variation for a certain length of time. It is as though it were crystallised. This is the *silent prayer of quiet.*

This state is also called *spiritual sleep,* or *sleep of the faculties,* in order to indicate that the memory and the imagination slumber—that is to say, that they do not act. The understanding remains awake with regard to God, but it sleeps with regard to all objects apart from Him.

**25.**—We may form some **idea of these states** by an analogous fact of the natural order. Suppose that you are looking at a peaceful scene—such as a rural

* Book VI, chs. viii, ix, and x. These beautiful passages on the prayer of quiet should be read.

landscape. It is in your power, for a few minutes at any rate, to close the awareness of your mind to the memory of all other things, to all acts of the reason, to the formation of any sentence whatsoever. You merely gaze and recognise the presence of the object of your contemplation. This is a very faithful picture of the prayer of silence, of the prayer of quiet, freed from all that is opposed to it.

Add to this such sentiments of love as are found in a mother watching over her sleeping child, and the resemblance is still more striking.

**26.**—It follows, therefore, that we must not make the prayer of silence or the sleep of the powers into special degrees of prayer, neither should we strive to find them a fixed place in the stages of the mystical life. They are simply names given to the different **ways of being** that the mystic union may possess at certain moments (see ch. iii, **10**).

Scaramelli admits that this is so (Tr. 2, No. 149); and yet he has set himself to classify these varieties as successive degrees.

**27.**—**Explanation of certain words.** If we do not want to be led astray by certain writers, we must be acquainted with the terms that they employ: to feel in the *soul's centre,* or in the *depths of the soul.* It does not occur to them to define these expressions, as they considered their signification sufficiently obvious. But they do not all given the same breath of meaning.

There are at least two points upon which they are all agreed, namely: 1° that the words refer to the soul with regard to its reception of the consciousness of the divinity; 2° that it is a question of a knowledge that exists without the co-operation of the senses, or of the sensible faculties, or of the reason. The soul is considered as a sort of sphere, the sensible faculties forming a surface and establishing a means of contact with the exterior world. But this sphere has an interior part also, a *centre* that is removed from the material world.*

Many writers stop short there, and say: all mystic union takes place at the soul's centre, which simply means: apart from sensible images and acts of reasoning.

Others, such as St. John of the Cross (*Living Flame,* Stanza I, line 3), distinguish several degrees of depth in the mystic union, according as the soul is farther removed from the operations of the senses and of the imagination. The last degree, the true centre, that is to say, may be defined by them as the spirit in the enjoyment of the spiritual marriage. This, in other words, is the idea that St. Teresa symbolises by the Mansions of her *Interior Castle* and their leading up to a central chamber, the Throne-room.

We see that a certain latitude exists as to the use of these words. We can do without them. In themselves they are of slight importance.

* In the seventeenth century the words *introversion* and *extroversion* were frequently used in order to express this entering of the soul to its centre, or issuing forth from it.

**28.**—The word *summit,* or *supreme point of the spirit* (*apex mentis*), has the same meaning. The reason is called the superior part of the soul, in opposition to the *sensible* faculties and appetites. The *summit* is commonly regarded as that which is uppermost, and this, in mystic contemplation, is the mind.

Since the words centre and summit have no exact signification in themselves, they must never be employed to define a state of prayer without previously defining them. Otherwise it would merely be to explain one obscure thing by another that is still more obscure.

## EXTRACTS

### § 1. Mystic Contemplation is Not Produced By Sensible Images.

**29.**—Dionysius the Areopagite, to his disciple Timothy:

"But thou, O dear Timothy, by thy persistent commerce with the mystic visions, leave behind both *sensible perceptions* and intellectual efforts, and all objects of *sense* and *intelligence,* and all things not being and being, and be raised aloft unknowingly to the union, as far as attainable, with Him who is above every essence and knowledge. For by the resistless and absolute ecstasy in all purity, from thyself and all, thou wilt be carried on high, to the superessential ray of the Divine darkness, when thou hast cast away all and become *free from all*" (Dionysius the Areopagite.* *Mystic Theology,* ch. i, § 1, p. 130. Translated by Rev. John Parker).

**30.**—Tauler. He explains that the direct preparation for receiving the Holy Spirit consists first in detachment from all that is not God, and then in interior recollection. This preparation is necessary for all Christians. But all do not practise it to the same degree, and thus all do not receive the Holy Spirit in the same manner:

"Some receive it in the sensible faculties, under forms and *images.* Others intellectually, and therefore in a more perfect manner, in the higher faculties, that is to say, far above the senses. Others, finally, receive it also in that secret abyss, in that hidden kingdom, in those delicious depths that are the noblest part of the soul and the likeness of the most Blessed Trinity. It is there that the Holy Spirit has His true abode, and that the man receives His gifts in a wholly divine manner" (First Sermon for Whit-Sunday).

**31.**—St. John of the Cross:

* See Biographical Index, 2. [Translator.]

1. "This interior wisdom, so simple, general, and spiritual, enters not into an intellect entangled and covered over by *any forms or images* subject to sense,... and therefore the imagination and the senses... cannot account for it..." (*The Obscure Night of the Soul,* Book II, ch. xvii, p. 427). And again, "if that [the Divine union] is to be attained, the soul must enter the second night of the spirit... *perfectly detaching* sense and spirit from all sweetness and from all these [imaginary] apprehensions" (*ibid.,* ch. p. 377). See also *Ascent of Mount Carmel,* Book III, ch. i.

2. The name *night of the senses,* which is given by the saint to the state which prepares the soul for the mystic union (see ch. xv), sums up the whole of his teaching on this point. He wishes to indicate the gradual disappearance in prayer of all that is due to sense.

3. "If it attempts to seek them [sweetness and fervour], not only will it not find them, but it will meet with aridity, because it turns away from the *peaceful and tranquil good* secretly bestowed upon it, when it attempts to fall back on the operations of sense. In this way it loses the latter without gaining the former, because the senses have *ceased to be the channel of spiritual good...* for the gift being so grand, and an *infused gift,* cannot be received in this scanty and imperfect way" (*The Living Flame of Love,* Stanza III, § 6, pp. 268-9).

4. "... mystical theology, that is, the secret or hidden wisdom of God,... without the sound of words, or the intervention of any bodily or spiritual [imaginative] sense; as it were in silence and in repose, *in the darkness of sense and nature,* teaches the soul— and the soul knows not how—in a most secret and hidden way... [It takes place] in the intellect as it is passive, which, without receiving such forms, receives passively only the substantial intelligence of them *free from all imagery*" (*Spiritual Canticle,* stanza xxxix, p. 208). The saint also excludes imaginative acts, except in the case of distractions, even for the state (night of the senses) which precedes the manifest mystic state (*The Ascent of Mount Carmel,* Book II, ch. xiii, xiv). Also see the whole of ch. xii.

5. After explaining that the imagination counts for nothing in the production of the mystic state he says:

"This explains why some persons, walking in this way, good and timid souls, who, when they would give an account of their interior state to their directors, know not how to do it, neither have they power to do it, and so feel a great repugnance to explain themselves, especially when contemplation is the more simple and with difficulty discernible by them. All they can say is that their soul is satisfied, calm, or contented, that they have a feeling of God, and that all goes well with them, as they think; but they cannot explain their state, except by general expressions like these. But it is a different matter when they have a consciousness of particular things, such as visions, impressions, and the like; these in general are communicated under some *species,* and the senses participate in them; in that case they are able to describe them. But it is not in the nature of pure contemplation that it can be described; for it can scarcely be spoken of in words, and therefore we call it secret" (*The Obscure Night of the Soul,* Book II, ch. xvii, pp. 428-9).

**31** *bis.*—Ven. Bartholomew of the Martyrs, O. P.:

"During the time of our union with God, we must drive far from us all images, even such as are good in themselves, for they introduce something between Him and us. Hence he who, impelled thereto by grace, aims at this ascension towards God, when he feels himself taken possession of by a violent love and drawn upward, should at once retrench all kinds of images; let him run without delay toward the holy of holies, towards that interior silence in which the operation is no more human, but divine" (*Abrégé de la doctrine Mystique,* Part II, ch. xi, quoted by Dr. Meynard, Vol. II, No. 79).

**31** *ter.*—Ven. Blosius:

"When the soul hath thus entered into the vast solitude of the Godhead, it happily loseth itself... although it seeth not God as He is in His glory, nevertheless it learneth by *experimental* knowledge that He infinitely *surpasseth* all things that can be known by the senses, and whatever can be *written, spoken or conceived* by the mind of man. Now doth it understand how far better it is to go forth into God *without any image* in the mind, than to contemplate Him in the noblest and most divine images and likenesses. Lastly, by the intimate embrace and contact of love it knows God better than the eyes of the body know the visible sun" (*Speculum spirituale.* English: *Sanctuary of the Faithful Soul,* ch. xi, § 1. Tr. by Fr. Wilberforce, O.P.).

**32.**—Cardinal Richelieu when enumerating the "different kinds of mental prayer," gives the following definition of the state that he places immediately after meditation:

"Extraordinary prayer or contemplation is that in which man sees and knows God *without using the imagination* and without discursive reasoning" (*Traité de la perfection du chrétien,* ch. xxxi).

### § 2. On Certain Abbreviated Phrases

**33.**—Passages from St. Teresa, showing that she sometimes attributes knowledge to the will, and therefore at times uses the word *will* to mean: the will accompanied by knowledge.

"... *without any labour of the understanding,* the will continues loving, and our Lord is pleased that... she should *understand* that she is conversing with Him, and that she only swallows the milk which His Majesty puts in her mouth,... she *knows* it is Our Lord that is doing her this favour" (*Way of Perfection,* ch. xxxi, p. 96).

"The will here is the captive: who, if she can feel any pain in this condition, it is *to see* that she is to return to her former liberty" (*ibid.,* p. 93).

"His Majesty will teach her [the will] what she is on that occasion to do; which all in a manner consists *in accounting herself unworthy* of so great a favour... " (*Interior Castle,* Fourth Mansion, ch. iii, p. 187. Tr. by Abraham Woodhead).

**34.**—St. Francis of Sales speaks in the same way: "... the will does not even *perceive* the delight and contentment which she receives, enjoying it insensibly, not being *mindful* of herself but of Him whose *presence* gives her this pleasure" (*Treatise on the Love of God,* Book VI, ch. viii, p. 255).

**35.**—Passages from St. Teresa which show that by the phrase "the will *alone* is united," she wishes to say that the attention does not disappear in any enduring way, but that it suffers from a number of little interruptions: "It occasionally happens, even when the will is in union, that they [the memory and understanding] hinder it very much; but then it should *never heed them at all, simply abiding* in its fruition and quiet. For if it tried to make *them* recollected, it would miss its way together with them..." (*Life,* ch. xiv, 4).

"... Certainly to me these powers bring much weariness at times;... Let the will quietly and *wisely* understand that it is not by dint of labour on our part that we can converse to any good purpose with God... " (*Life,* ch. xv, 9).

When describing a state to which I shall have to return again: "It happens at times,... that, the will being in union, the soul should be aware of it, and see that the will is a captive and in joy, that the will *alone* is abiding in great peace,—while,... the understanding and the memory are so free, that they can be employed in affairs... " (*Life,* ch. xvii, 5).

"The will is so enamoured, and fixed upon God, that the restlessness of the understanding displeaseth her exceedingly; therefore she must not heed it" (*Interior Castle,* Fourth Mansion, ch. iii, p. 187. Tr. by Abraham Woodhead).

**36.**—St. Francis of Sales, *Treatise on the Love of God,* Book VI, ch. x, p. 260. Passages in which he adopts the same meaning as that in paragraph 35:

"... the *will* having once tasted the divine *presence* does not cease to relish the sweetness thereof, *though* the understanding or memory should *make an escape* and slip away after foreign and useless thoughts... Indeed, we have seen a soul... who... had her understanding and memory... free from all interior occupation,... [but who] could not answer, or loose herself from God, to whom she was united by the application of her will. This soul, then,... having *only* her will engaged... resembled... the little child, who, while sucking, might see and hear and even move his arms, without quitting the dear breast."

**37.**—Passages in which the saint takes the opposite sense and supposes the absence of distractions:

"Now this repose sometimes goes so deep in its tranquillity, that the whole soul and *all its powers* fall as it were asleep, and make no movement nor *action whatever,* except the will *alone,* and even this does no more than receive the delight and satisfaction which the *presence* of the well-beloved affords" (Book VI, ch. viii, p. 255).

"Now it fares in like manner with the soul who is in rest and quiet before God; for she sucks in a manner insensibly the delights of His *presence,* without any discourse, *operation or motion* of any of her faculties, save *only* the highest part of the will, which she moves softly and almost imperceptibly, as the mouth by which enter the *delight* and insensible satiety she finds in the fruition of the Divine *presence.* But if one trouble this poor little babe, or offer to take from it its treasure because it seems to sleep, it will plainly show then that *though it sleep to all other things* yet not to that; for it perceives the trouble of this separation and grieves over it, showing thereby the pleasure which it took, though *without thinking of it,* in the good which it possessed" (ch. ix, p. 257).

# CHAPTER X

## The Seventh and Eighth Characters of the Mystic Union

**1.—Seventh character.** It consists in this, that these states exhibit continual fluctuations. The mystic union does not continue at the same degree of intensity for five minutes together. The divine ocean, into which we have penetrated some few steps, has waves that advance and retire, an ebb and a flow.

**2.—And this is a source of suffering.** For during the ascending. We hope to rise higher than ever before. But it is not to be; and behold! we begin to descend again.

During the first phase, God is like the mother, showing a sweetness to her child and allowing it to come quite near, and then the sweetness is withdrawn.

And we may wait in this way for years, just as the paralytic man in the Gospels waited by the pond of Bethsaida for the coming of the angel.

Throughout this repeated successions of risings and fallings the mean level may continue about the same for a considerable time.

**3.—The eighth character** consists in this, that the mystic union requires much less *effort* than meditation; and correspondingly less again as the state is a higher one. There is none at all in ecstasy.

These facts are evident from the comparison that St. Teresa makes use of to depict the successive degrees of prayer in the Book of her *Life* (ch. xi). She regards the soul as a gardener, watering his garden with ever less and less labour.

**4.**—In the **prayer of quiet an effort** *is still required.* This does not consist in procuring the substance of the prayer for ourselves (God alone can bestow it), but:

1° In driving away *distractions:* a labour that is never wholly successful. This must be done gently, so that we do not injure the mystic union itself.

2° In producing here and there such *additional acts* as we have an attraction or facility for.

3° In *restraining the weariness* which the semi-aridity causes when the prayer of quiet is experienced in a low degree, and in resisting the temptation to discontinue the prayer.

**5.—Fatigue.** From the moment that labour and renewed effort are required, there is a certain amount of fatigue. We scarcely heed this if the prayer of quiet is intense,* and we continue at prayer without difficulty for three or four hours together. But if the prayer of quiet is weak, fatigue is felt after half an hour or an hour. The state of health is also a factor here.

The fatigue will be still more apparent if we make a retreat of several days in silence, and if during that time the prayer of quiet is nearly always present in a low degree only.

**6.—Other causes of fatigue.** 1° In the case of all mental work, and even of simple reading, a difficulty of application after meals is experienced by those who are not in robust health. The process of digestion concentrates the vital activity upon the stomach at the expense of the brain, and to combat this would entail a considerable tax upon the head. Experience shows that it is generally the same with regard to the prayer of quiet. This kind of union is not yet sufficiently strong to withstand the physiological law.

7.—2° So in the natural life, we find that with many persons *prolonged continuance in an unchanged position* is a cause of anæmia and consequently of fatigue. The unused muscles atrophy, and the respiration and circulation of the blood becomes enfeebled. Doctors combat these effects by contrary causes. They order exercise, either by manual labour or by walking.

Now, the supernatural states do not bring us into a miraculous condition of being. They may lead to fatigue, therefore, by the mere fact of the immobility of the body if we engage almost daily in very long prayers.

This result must be corrected by physical exercise, which restores the natural energy to the circulation and respiration.

**8.—A difficulty.** But whatever the cause of the fatigue, how should we act in the following case? An anæmic person, having plenty of spare time, feels an attraction for very prolonged prayer. He regards this attraction as coming from God, inasmuch as he usually enters to some slight extent into the mystic state at these times. But, on the other hand, he finds that these exercises exhaust him; while external occupations restore his vitality.

**9.—Reply.** Given these *data,* it would seem to me to follow that until he receives some new orders he should give himself to prayer with great moderation, and in such a measure only as not to cause any great fatigue. God

* St. Teresa supposes this case when she says: "The labour is so slight, that prayer, *even if* persevered in for some time, is never wearisome" (*Life*, ch. xiv, 105).

indicates the line of conduct from the moment that He does not give the means of resisting the feeling of exhaustion.*

St. Teresa teaches a similar doctrine. Speaking of inability to meditate, she says: "This comes most frequently from bodily indisposition... Meanwhile, the more *we force the soul* on these occasions, the greater the mischief and the longer it lasts. Some discretion must be used in order to ascertain whether ill-health be the occasion or not. The poor soul must *not be stifled...* and so it is not always right... to torment the soul *to the doing of that which is out of its power.* There are other things then to be done—*exterior works,* as of charity and spiritual readings, though at times the soul will not be able to do them. Take care, then, of the body for the love of God, because at many other times the body must serve soul" (*Life*, ch. x, 23).

In the lives of the saints we often read of exceedingly prolonged prayers, and we are tempted to accuse ourselves of cowardice when we do not try to imitate them. This is an exaggeration if we do more than our strength permits. This aptitude for prolonged prayer is a highly desirable thing (ch. xii, **9**), but it is a special gift; we do not have it merely because we try to produce it.

I said just now that in the case of fatigue we must exercise moderation with regard to prayers that are not of obligation. I did not say that we must discard them altogether. The fatigue is not usually so great as to necessitate such an extreme measure. To say, "I will resume my prayer in better times, when the winds of grace are more favourable," would be a mere pretext. In such a case we should run the risk of waiting for years.

Let us steer a middle course, that of short alternations; taking a quarter or half an hour for prayer and then returning to active life, that is to say; then after a certain time coming back to prayer again, and so on.

Let us not be afraid of asking for this grace—one that is as rare as it is precious:—of being able to remain for a long time in prayer without fatigue and without distractions.

## EXTRACTS

**10.**—St. Teresa on fluctuations in the prayer:

1° "What has often happened to me is this,—I spoke of it before when writing of the previous state of prayer [ecstasy in a weak degree],—the rapture is not

* Speaking more generally, in order to judge whether we have any vocation that is inspired by God, it is not usually sufficient to satisfy ourselves that we have a persistent attraction for it. This mark is not certain unless a natural condition is fulfilled, namely, that we have certain physical, moral, and intellectual qualities also.

continuous, the soul is frequently absorbed, or, to speak more correctly, Our Lord absorbs it in Himself" (*Life,* ch. xx, 25).

Speaking of ecstasy in a weak degree:

2° "... As it seems to me, the period of time, however long it may have been, during which the faculties of the soul were entranced, is very short; if half an hour, that would be a long time. I do not think that I have ever been so long... It is extremely difficult to know how long, because the senses are in suspense; but I think that at any time it cannot be very long before some one of the faculties recovers itself... As the will is calm, *it entrances them again;* they are quiet for another moment, and then they recover themselves once more. *In this way,* some hours may be, and are, passed in prayer... But this state of *complete absorption,* together with the outer rest of the imagination... lasts only for a short time; though the faculties do not so completely recover themselves as not to be for some hours afterwards as if in disorder" (*Life,* ch. xviii, 16, 17).

3° "This [ravishment] lasts for a short space (I mean *in that condition*) [i. e. degree of intensity]; for this great suspension *intermitting* for a while, the body seems in a sort to return to itself, and take breath, that it may afterwards *die again anew...* yet, so this great trance continues not long" (*Interior Castle,* Sixth Mansion, ch. iv, p. 23; Tr. Abraham Woodhead).

4° Speaking of certain transports of love which the soul is not able to produce by herself: "... though it is felt for a long time yet it *comes and goes.* In short, *it is never permanent* and therefore does not wholly inflame the soul, except at times, when, as the soul is ready to take fire, the little spark suddenly dies out, leaving the heart longing to suffer anew the loving pangs it gives" (*Interior Castle,* Sixth Mansion, ch. ii, 6, 7). In another place the saint says, when speaking of the spiritual inebriation of the full union: "Nor does this state ever last more than a very short time. Although the soul may *become absorbed again...*" (*Interior Castle,* Fourth Mansion, ch. iii, 12).

5° With regard to the prayer of quiet, the saint speaks indirectly only of its fluctuations. She refers to those of extraneous thoughts in the intellect and in the imagination. But these variations imply the other fluctuations, and cause them to occur in the very essence of the prayer itself. And further, if ecstasy is subject to the inconvenience of fluctuations, we may thereby conclude *a fortiori* that it is the same in the prayer of quiet.

## CHAPTER XI

### The Ninth Character of the Mystic Union

**1.—The ninth character** of the mystic union is that it is accompanied by sentiments of *love*, of *repose*, of *pleasure*, and often of *suffering*.

**2.—Sentiments of love.** These are always produced by the mystic union. But it sometimes happens that the love is very calm and even almost imperceptible. It then seems no stronger than in ordinary prayer. Take notice, however, that it is a question of love felt, and not of that which shows itself by works. We shall speak of this latter in the ensuing chapter (see also ch. xxiv, 22).

At other times the soul's ardours become very apparent under the influence of the mystic union. They may even be violent (see *Interior Castle,* Sixth Mansion, ch. ii; *Relation I,* addressed to St. Peter of Alcantra, 1560; *Second Letter* to Fr. Rodrigo Alvarez). In the case of St. Stanislaus Kostka, the heat became so burning at times that he used to apply cloth steeped in cold water to his breast, in order to obtain relief.

These great transports probably occur only when the soul has attained to the full union. They are often accompanied by a real anguish, an intense desire to see God (see **12**).

**3.**—Whatever the strength of this love, we feel that it **is produced of itself** without our doing anything to bring it about; we even feel that if we wish to strengthen it (and we secretly desire this) it would be labour lost. We are in the passive state. We can barely accept what we receive.

**4.—Sentiments of pleasure.*** Even with regard to the prayer of quiet St. Teresa often speaks of "the great delights" that are enjoyed. This is so in the case of ecstasy; but with the prayer of quiet, experience shows that many souls enjoyed no such great happiness. On this point the saint was speaking chiefly of herself. She received exceptional favours, probably on account of her great

* The sentiment of repose has already been described (ch. iii, 5).

trials, or the part she played as the Foundress of the Order.* And, further, it is to be believed that when ecstatics receive the inferior graces, it is in a much more perfect manner than others.

There is always pleasure inherent to the prayer of quiet. But at times, and even when it is of considerable strength, we are hardly aware of it. In such a case we should feel more enjoyment, although of another kind, when reading an interesting book or engaging in conversation.

**5.**—At certain moments, however, the prayer of quiet causes sudden and very **ardent spiritual delights.** This probably does not happen with beginners.

It is with this grace as with the spiritual embrace (see ch. vi, 17): it is experienced at first for a few seconds at a time only, by gusts, as it were. The two graces are now separated, now united.

This, doubtless, is the grace that St. Teresa wished to describe when she says that we sometimes inhale, as it were, some delicate perfume (see ch. vi, **56**).

It is important to note that it is then not a mere sweetness, the fragrance produced by the *thought* of God, but it is a way of tasting God Himself.†

Of course, we must not reject this pleasure on pretence of self-mortification. It is sufficient if we see in it a means of uniting ourselves with God, and not an end in itself. The object of mortification is to remove all that imposes any obstacle to the divine union, not that which favours it. We can say the same in the case of other spiritual consolations.

**6.—Spiritual intoxication.** When this delectation is ardent or of long duration, it produces a kind of spiritual intoxication that at times resembles a partial slumber, and at others is full of ardour (see St. Teresa, *Life*, ch. xxvi).

**7.**—We apply the term **jubilation**, to a fervour of love and joy such as the soul could hardly contain. Our utmost efforts are required to hide it from those about us (see ch. xiv, **23** *bis*).

**8.—Extraneous influences.** The pleasure caused by the prayer of quiet is influenced by the dispositions that the soul brings to the prayer. It makes itself more clearly felt if we are passing through a period of peace or joy. And it is the same when these graces have a certain novelty for us. On the other hand, if we are going through a period of sadness, of trial, the pleasure caused by the prayer of quiet may be in part disturbed or veiled.

**9.**—*Apart from the times given to prayer* God sends **numerous crosses** to those whom He grants the favour of the mystic union (see ch. xxiv).

* In granting exceptional and visible favours to Founders or reformers of religious orders, and to certain of their spiritual children, God acts like a King who gives letters of credence to his ambassadors. By these signs He shows that the work is His own. This evidence is very useful to each spiritual family, in order to help sustain its life of self-sacrifice and zeal.

† St. John of the Cross says: "it is God Himself who is then felt and tasted [sentido y gustado] though not *manifestly* and *distinctly*, as it will be in glory... This knowledge savours in some measure of the Divine Essence and of everlasting life" (*Ascent of Mt. Carmel*, Book 2, ch. xxvi, p. 177).

The unlearned in mysticism fancy that the soul enjoys continual consolations, and they sometimes go on to say contemptuously: "Personally, I prefer to be led by a more rugged road, that of the Cross." But God, as they should understand, does not dispense His intimate friends from the Cross; quite the contrary.

**10.**—And, further, the mystic state brings with it **sufferings** which are peculiar to it and which may be felt even *during prayer.* I will enumerate them:

**11.**—1° There are the sufferings of the *beginners* who have not been instructed with regard to these things (see ch. v, **18**).

**12.**—2° One great cause of suffering is the need *to possess God more fully.* The stronger and more exalted God's communications, the more acute becomes the thirst for a still more complete communication. St. Teresa tells us of the martyrdom that she underwent at certain times, and which she describes in her Hymn: "*I die in that I do not die.*" The soul then arrives at the **anguish of love** (see *Interior Castle,* Sixth Mansion, ch. xi, and *Second Letter* to Fr. Rodrigo Alvarez).

Even in the prayer of quiet the suffering is very keen at times. To illustrate the possibility of the statement let us imagine a man who, wishing to hear a magnificent concert, can merely with great difficulty get access to a small crack in a partition, where he would catch fragments only of the harmony. What he hears would obviously cause him pleasure, but, at the same time, all that he misses would be a sorrow to him. It is possible, therefore, to feel both pleasure and grief at the same time, although in proportions that vary according to the circumstances of the particular case.

**13.**—When the sentiments of pleasure and suffering are of almost equal strength and are *both* very ardent, the resulting state takes the name of **wound of love.**

To show that the simultaneity is possible, and that it is so in a strong degree, here is a new simile. Also it will show us the physiognomy of the state. Something of the same kind is experienced in human love when it is violent. A great sweetness is felt, the lover does not wish to quit the thought of his beloved; he enjoys it. But at the same time he feels his heart torn because of his absence from her, or because of the difficulty in conversing with her freely. There is thus a mingling of joy and of sorrow. So, too, it is possible to have delicious experiences of God and of His love, and to feel at the same time the secret anguish which is nothing other than the thirst for God, kindled by Himself. Sometimes the suffering has another cause: we are conscious of the desire to serve God, and at the same time we feel that we are doing almost nothing for Him. It may be also that we cannot say why we suffer.

**14.**—Beginners, perhaps, do not feel the suffering caused by the privation of God, to any great extent. They were overjoyed because they have made a step forward, and they are upheld by the **hope**, often ill-founded, that from to-morrow they will advance still farther and will experience something new. But these illusions fade away at last. The cold reality appears, and if the soul preserves her hopefulness it is by virtue alone. She feels how hard it is always to remain riveted to the same spot, and never to hear the divine concert in all its fullness. What a torture this is!

**15.**—We can therefore understand how some weak souls may suffer from **discouragement**. We are astonished at first when St. Teresa, quoting herself as an example, tells us that certain persons, after attaining to the full union, have abandoned everything and have returned to the frivolities of the world. This grievous fall surprises us less when we see what continued trials have to be resisted.

A person who had arrived at an habitual state of the prayer of quiet told me one day that he often began his prayer with these words: "Oh, my God, I know that I shall suffer during this exercise, and I am happy that it should be so. But while resigning myself joyfully to Thy holy will, I pray Thee that Thou wouldst bring me at last out of this miserable state in which Thy justice hath hitherto detained me."

**16.**—3° When the prayer of quiet is weak there is another kind of suffering, that of **tedium.** God does not send us sufficient material to occupy us fully. We should like to supplement what He gives us by certain exercises, so as to avoid a state of semi-idleness. But we shall see farther on, speaking of the ligature (ch. xiv), that we find a great difficulty in doing so. We are therefore reduced to remaining with very little occupation, restraining our natural activity. It is what we might call a semi-aridity. If this state extends over several weeks the tedium that results becomes extremely painful.

**17.**—Where the temperament suffers from a need for action and variety, the **temptation** to give up the prayer becomes very strong, and the person is ready to persuade himself that he will do more good in exterior work.

**18.**—4° And, finally, the soul suffers because of the *alternations* of grace. There are periods of abundance, but also of dearth, in which the mystic state disappears completely at times, even in the case of an ecstatic. See the example of St. Joseph of Cupertino (ch. xxiv, **99**).

**19.**—**To sum up,** the cause of suffering in the prayer of quiet does not lie in the prayer itself but in that which is lacking in it. In itself it may be the cause of slight pleasure, but not a distaste or lassitude.

This is a surprising fact. For nothing similar occurs in the natural order. If every day, for years together, we were obliged to read the same page exclusively, or to listen to the same melody, our patience would not hold out: we should soon become desperate, and beg for mercy.

Here it is quite the contrary. This monotonous, incomplete occupation, this air, repeated a thousand times, is always enjoyed. What we ask is that the possession of this blessing should become more perfect.

**20.**—We must not count on **outside consolations** amidst the sufferings. Those round about us, having experienced nothing similar, understand nothing of our plaints. It is not their fault.

**21.**—We then begin to wish to **meet with a soul** that has arrived at the same degree. We would confide in it, rejoice together over the same joys, be inspired by the same hopes, warn each other of pitfalls to be avoided. St. Teresa approves of these mutual confidences.*

In fact, when these meetings take place we derive a certain consolation from them, but less than we had hoped. These communications eventually become exhausted, and the friend can finally do but one thing only: show that he understands our painful aspirations and that he sympathises; that he is powerless to satisfy them. He cannot raise the cruel veil that hides God from our eyes.

If he is a saint, however, one resource remains. He can hasten our deliverance by his prayers.

With regard to friends who have not received the mystic graces, there is no reason, as a rule, for giving them our confidences; we must deny ourselves this indulgence, and repress our longing to talk. If we yield to this need we shall often suffer for it. After the first moments of curiosity, your friends' doubts will increase more and more, and they will perhaps end by giving you the reputation of being a visionary.

## EXTRACTS

### On Sentiments of Love

**22.**—St. John of the Cross:

"And as all the natural operations of the soul, which are within its control, depend on the senses only, it follows that God is now working in a special

* "I would advise those who give themselves to prayer, particularly at first, to form friendships and converse familiarly with others who are doing the same thing... I know no reason why it should not be lawful for him who is beginning to love and serve God in earnest to confide to another his joys and sorrows, for they who are given to *prayer* are thoroughly accustomed to both... For if that friendship with God which he desires be real, let him not be afraid of vainglory" (*Life*, ch. vii, 33-4).

Speaking of the encouragement that she had received from St. Peter of Alcantara, she says: "He delighted in conversing with me. To a person whom Our Lord has raised to this state, there is no pleasure or comfort equal to that of meeting another whom Our Lord has begun to raise in the same way" (*Life*, ch. xxx, 5-6). As the saint feared that she might be acting from a natural attachment in a similar case, Our Lord reassured her (*Life*, ch. xl, 24).

manner in this state... that the soul is the recipient on which He distills spiritual blessings by contemplation, the knowledge and love of Himself together; that is, He gives it the loving knowledge without the instrumentality of its discursive acts, because it is no longer able to form them as before" (*Living Flame of Love,* Stanza III, line 3, § 5).

**23.**—Ruysbroeck. The longing to see God:

"When the soul has known the divine touch, there is born in her an incessant hunger that nothing can assuage. It is love, avid and yearning, the aspiration of the created spirit for the uncreated good. God invites the soul, He excites in her *a vehement desire to possess Him;* and she longs to attain to Him. And thence an avidity, a hunger, *a desire* to obtain, that can never be fully satisfied. The men of this kind are the poorest, the most denuded that the world can contain. Always famished and athirst, although they eat and drink from time to time; for the created vessel can never succeed in absorbing the uncreated God. *Desire, ardent* and incessant, ever stretches out its arms towards God. God bestows upon the soul exquisite and varied foods, known only to him who has experience them; but one last element is always lacking: the possession that satisfies. The hunger goes on incessantly increasing in spite of the unimaginable delights that flow into the mouth of the spiritual man by the divine contact. But all this appertains to created things, it is less than God. Though God were to bestow all the gifts that the saints have received, if *He gave not Himself,* the hunger would never be satisfied. This hunger, this thirst, it is the Divine Touch that has produced them, that excites them, that inflames them, and the greater the intensity of the touch, the more terrible is the hunger. Such is the life of love when it mounts up to this perfect degree, surpassing the reason and the intelligence. The reason can no longer calm the fever that produces it, for this love has its source in the love of God Himself" (*Ornement des noces*, Book II, ch. xl).

**24.**—Extract from *La vie de la Mère Françoise Fournier*, an Ursuline of Angers, Paris, 1685 (born at Lude, Anjou, 1592, died in 1675).

"On one occasion, speaking confidentially to a Canon Regular, to whom she revealed the innermost depths of her soul after the death of her brother, Fr. Fournier, she told him that since her profession until the time of her last election as Superior (for the space of over *thirty years,* that is to say), God had kindled in her soul such ardent and violent desires to die, *so that she might see Him* and be perfectly united to Him, that what she suffered during this whole time, in the space of a quarter of an hour, surpassed incomparably the torments of the wheel, the fire, the gibbet, and all the pains that all men have ever felt; but she estimated that all the pangs of the body and of the mind, are but the shadows of those that she has suffered; that she did not believe that the pain of the damned could be greater than that which she endured in being *separated from God;* that her desires to see him were almost continual, that she even felt them sometimes during sleep, so that day and night she suffered a cruel martyrdom. She wept almost continually, and being so hard-pressed by love, she often uttered loud cries, which on several occasions brought the religious who heard her into her room, they at first thinking that she had met with an accident. But they knew that these cries were due to her torments and the strong attraction that she had to see God. Her body suffered such violence in the vehemence of her desires, that her arms and legs became stiff as iron bars; she clenched her teeth and underwent strange convulsions, so that her body, succumbing under them, fell into weaknesses and languors which obliged her to throw herself upon the ground, being then, indeed, in the position to say to her sisters what the Bride in the Canticles said to her companions: 'Stay me up with flowers, compass me about with apples, because I languish with love.' Amidst her most violent desires to see God, she fell into transports that could not be explained, and she made use of exaggerated expressions by which to depict the greatness of her love. But, what is remarkable, is that in the midst of her greatest torments she was always peaceful, resting upon the divine will, and she used to say that if, in order to see God, she need only have passed from one room to the other, she would not have gone one step, because she only desired to see Him at the moment that He should choose.

"Who then could adequately praise this great servant of God, who desiring so vehemently to see and to *contemplate her Bridegroom's Face,* yet for the pain of being deprived of Him with such a perfect submission to His holy will!

"This highly painful state, which began on the day of her profession, became gradually augmented two years afterwards, and went on increasing up to the end of her life. Her pains diminished a little, however, when she felt attractions to rejoice in God's glory and the salvation of souls.

"During all this time she constantly fell into languors, ecstasies and raptures, suffering the alienation of all the sensible faculties and being wholly lost in God. She was consoled by the presence of Our Lord, the Blessed Virgin, angels and saints. These visits which kindled her heart and inflamed her will, certainly lessened her torments in some degree; but the pain was always there, and the consolations were only like those that the souls in Purgatory receive, who when visited by good angels, do not, on that account, cease to be deprived of God."

**25.**—The Ven. Anne Madeleine de Rémuzat:

"I earnestly longed to go out of my flesh in order to be united at length to my God; this longing is so painful, that it *would occasion death* did not God powerfully uphold me" (*Vie,* published by the Visitation of Marseilles, ch. xv, p. 312. Eng.: *The Nun of the Order of the Visitation*, Anne Madeleine de Rémuzat of Marseilles, by Monsigneur Van den Berghe, ch. iv, p. 110).

**26.**—Mother Marie Thérèse Dubouché, Foundress of the Congregation of the Adoration Réparatrice in Paris (1809-63):

"My heart, which was already so powerfully drawn to the Holy Eucharist, was henceforth united, as it were, to the Tabernacle... My prayers were spent in letting myself burn in silence" (*Vie,* Eng. trans. by Mgr. d'Hulet, ch. iv, p. 98).

**27.**—Fr. Lyonnard, S. J. (1819-87):

"Our Lord had told me that the voice of His love would resound in my ears like the voice of thunder. The following night, in fact, what I should describe as a *storm of divine love,* if this word did not signify something tumultuous, burst upon me. Its sudden impetuosity, the all-powerful way in which it took possession of my whole being, the infinitely strong and sweet embrace with which God united the soul to him, cannot be compared with anything that takes place in the other, inferior states of union.

"Inundated on all sides by the infinite Being of God, *in which she feels herself plunged,* the soul implores her God to take pity on her weakness. As I offered this prayer, beseeching His Divine Majesty to deign to consider that there was no proportion between the vehemence of His love and the weakness of my poor heart, I felt within me a new invasion of this love; and out of the heart of these seas of celestial flame that inundated me on all sides, I heard the voice of this great God who, with the accents of an immense love, complained that men did not love Him sufficiently. I understood that it was, so to speak, a solace to His heart to discharge into my heart all this great love for mankind with which He is filled, and which our coldness condemns to do itself a perpetual violence. My God! how terrible will this love be at the Day of Judgement, when breaking the bounds by which the divine mercy restrains it, it will fall upon those mortals who have despised it.

"... Issuing forth from this crucible of the divine love wherein the whole being melts, so to speak, like wax in the fire, how great is the pain to the poor soul when forced to descend once more to the accustomed routine of this miserable life! How great the pain, especially, on seeing this divine and holy action succeeded by the wearing action of the evil one!... Just as the soul has felt herself penetrated in all her being by the intimate operation of God, even so she sees herself exposed in her exterior being to the persecuting attack of her enemy the devil... When subjected to this action we no longer know where to retreat in order to evade his pursuit, which seems momentarily to thrust the soul to the edge of the abyss" (Biographical Notice at the beginning of *L'Apostolat de la souffrance,* by Fr. Lyonnard, § 9).

## CHAPTER XII

### THE TENTH CHARACTER OF THE MYSTIC UNION

**1.**—The **tenth character** consists in this, that the mystic union is accompanied, and this often in a very *visible manner, by an impulsion towards the different virtues.* God does not come empty-handed, so to speak, to the soul, and His sanctifying action is so much the stronger and more sensible as the prayer is higher. St. Teresa tells us this constantly (see Extracts). The soul who permeates herself with God in the mystic union feels that she thus, without knowing exactly how, permeates herself with love, humility, and devotion.

**2.**—To begin with, **divine love** is the natural effect, as it were, of this kind of prayer, and it would of itself suffice to excite the soul to virtue; provided, that is to say, that she had a certain spiritual grounding.*

It gives an inclination for solitude, because God is more easily found there. It shows itself by aversion from sin and detachment from all that is not God; and it thus removes all obstacles to perfection. It teaches humility; for we love to make ourselves of no account before those whom we tenderly love and of whose superiority we are conscious. Finally, it impels to generosity and to the *spirit of sacrifice.* And at the same time God provides occasions for the exercising of these dispositions; He sends trials of all kinds, temptations, sickness, want of success, injustices or contempt. He imposes the most grievous sacrifices.

**3.**—And the remarkable thing is that certain virtues are sometimes given quite **suddenly.** St. Teresa refers to these instantaneous *changes in the soul,* and she symbolises them by the figure of the ugly, crawling worms becomes a beautiful, swift-flying butterfly. Certain faults have always resisted our efforts, our examen of conscience. And then, suddenly, as we passed to more advanced

* St. J. F. de Chantal: "It is not necessary for the practice of the virtues to keep ourselves always actually attentive to them all... We need only maintain ourselves in humility and charity; the one the lowest, the other the highest. The preservation of the whole building depends upon the foundation and upon the roof... These are the mothers of the virtues, which follow after them as the little chicks follow their mother hen" (*Fragments,* Plon edition, Vol. iii, p. 366).

or deeper prayer, we find our faults corrected without any industry of our own (see Extracts, No. 16).

In this way, God wills to show His power to the soul. Speaking of the effects her ecstasies brought upon St. Teresa, it has been truly said: "Both time and effort, these two conditions indispensable to all human operations, are absent here, and yet there is a complete and enduring change. What does this signify? That this transformation has not come about naturally."*

God thus gives us a lesson in humility. He has two opposite ways of teaching us by facts and making us realise clearly that our virtues depend chiefly upon Him: He either seems to abandon us at times to our weakness, or He gives us a sudden increase of virtue that we have not been able to foresee.

**4.**—But, besides this, the mystic state often brings with it a **direct impulsion towards humility** and towards one of its results, the joy caused by humiliations.† If the unlearned in mysticism are unduly alarmed lest the souls that are given to prayer should fall into the sin of pride, it is because they lose sight of the fact that the supernatural virtues possess this character of bringing the virtues in their train, that of humility especially.‡ They cry out: Draw not too nigh to God; but if you do, then beware of pride. It is as though they said: Do not go to drink at the one source of humility; you would imbibe the poison of pride.

A moderate fear is sufficient, one that will serve to keep us on our guard, but not one that makes us shun God as we would dangerous company.

**5.—Possible falls.** We must not think that these greater aids will necessarily hinder the soul from being unfaithful to grace. We must be ever on our guard. Speaking of ecstasy itself, St. Teresa says: "It is clear from this,—and for the love of God, consider it well,—that a soul, though it may receive great graces from God in prayer, must never rely on itself, because it may fall" (*Life,* ch. xix, 20).

**6.—The unreasonable demands of certain directors.** Nor must we exaggerate the influence of the inferior mystic states. Certain directors imagine that the prayer of quiet should so transform the soul that no defects, not even such as are involuntary, should be visible in her anymore; they think an admirable person should shine forth in her every word and action. This prayer *tends,* doubtless, to correct defects and to augment the virtues, but not with the force of the succeeding degrees. It does not imply that the person is already a saint, but it aids him to become one. It may have the effect, for instance, of

* Dr. Goix, *Annales de Philosophie Chrétienne,* June, 1896. Let us add that if certain virtues are born in us without effort, they do not endure long without it.

† Humility has been defined as the courage of truth applied to ourselves in all its rigour and with all its consequences.

‡ "If they [consolations] be from God, there is no cause to fear, because they carry humility along with them" (*Way of Perfection,* ch. xvii, pp. 50—1). This does not do away with the necessity of corresponding to grace by inciting ourselves to the practice of this virtue.

making him bear joyfully with some infirmity or disappointment; this would already be a service not be despised.

Let us also note that amongst natural defects there are some that in no wise hinder attainment to a high state of virtue; to be slow and always behind-hand, for instance, in work, or precipitate and anxious; or, again, to be too silent or over-talkative in conversation, or to show an occasional want of clearness of perception in business, etc. These involuntary defects are often the result of the temperament. They are irritating to other people, but they may be associated with great self-denial, and they do not hinder God from granting the mystic union to the soul, especially if the person strives to enlighten and correct himself. And, for the sake of maintaining him in humility, God may permit him to strive all his life long without much result. The true obstacle lies in a lack of love and generosity.

The director, therefore, should not say: "What! you pretend to have attained to the prayer of quiet? This is an illusion, for you have such and such a defect which offends those about you." That is not the question. The facade of the house may have preserved its very ordinary aspect. But the important thing to know is *whether there is progress within.* Yes or no? Has there been an increase of solid virtue, such as obedience, kindness towards others, a joyful acceptance of contradictions, sickness, or humiliations? The rest will come in due time.

Let us add that exaggerated reports are sometimes carried to a director concerning the person in whom he is interested. How many right actions are ill-interpreted because the hidden motives are unknown! How many excellent souls always fail to understand those who are not of their own particular way of thinking, whose little practices and theories as to the management of affairs differ from their own! The director has to be on his guard.

**7.**—In those who are favoured with the prayer of quiet, humility should produce **three effects** amongst others.

1° Instead of speaking of their happiness to all comers, these souls will carefully hide their graces, except from their directors. As to others, they will only open themselves up to them in a case of real utility (see ch. xi, **21**).

2° Instead of regarding themselves as having entered into a spiritual aristocracy, dispensing the soul from all the obligations that are imposed upon the common herd, they will redouble their zeal in the discharge of the duties of their state; if they are Religious, they will give the example of fidelity to the least observances of the Congregation.

3° Instead of thinking only of enjoying the celestial consolations and forgetting their practical application, they will tell themselves that these joys are, above all, a preparation for sufferings, and particularly for humiliation; they should be ready to be forgotten, counted for naught, put in the lowest place, reprimanded, thwarted, and perhaps calumniated as to their conduct or opinions. We must accept generously in advance these sacrifices of pride; the perfection of our spiritual condition can be gauged by the degree of this acceptation.

**8.**—When God leads the soul on to great sacrifices, we must be on our guard lest we fall into an **excess of zeal.** Let us say a few words about a very popular devotion which may tend to illusions.

In our days the onslaughts of impiety awaken a need of expiation in saintly souls. As with other things, so here also there is eagerness for new practices that profess to surpass all the old ones in efficaciousness. And certain authors have gone to extremes on the subject of self-immolation, and they circulate their ideas abroad in a multitude of little leaflets.*

There are two ways of understanding expiation in the life of a "victim." The first consists in a courageous and even joyful *acceptance* of all *inevitable* sufferings, doing this in the motive of reparation in union with Jesus crucified. A certain number of voluntary acts of penance are also added. All pious persons can aim at this method. We may call it living *in the spirit* of a victim.

The second way goes on to *ask for* sufferings, not to attempt to avoid those that have serious results, to offer even life itself.

The second manner should be regarded as quite exceptional. As a general rule, we should do better not to make these requests; they incline to illusions, and are often the outcome of pride (see Extracts, No. **19**). It is a mistake, especially, to recommend them to everybody indiscriminately, as is the case in the tracts to which we have referred. It is true that persons are advised to consult a director before so offering themselves, but the directors are not informed as to the proper course to follow. They are left to guess at it, and experience shows that the result has not always been successful.

Such exaggerated exhortations have an unsteadying effect upon many minds. These persons talk only of offerings, or vows of self-immolation; instead of setting themselves to bear their daily crosses—which is a very difficult task—they dream of imaginary trials in some distant future. They offer their lives as if it were the simplest thing in the world. It would be more painful and more useful, perhaps, were they to dedicate this life wholly to the defence of the Church in the purification of society. There is every reason to preach prayer and penance in order to save the Church and the Holy Father and the people

* If I were not afraid of delaying too long over this matter, I would show that the vow of immolation, as imagined by Fr. Giraud of la Salette (*De l'Union à Notre-Seigneur Jesus-Christ dans sa Vie de Victim,* ch. xix, 4th ed., p. 286), is open to serious criticism. It is likely, for instance, to promote scruples. And further, the writer has a singular idea of completing this vow by a second; you engage, under pain of sin (sometimes mortal) not to regret the first. So that you are no longer able to ask to be dispensed from it, even for good reasons, such as scruples. For to ask to be released from engagement is to regret it. This is a refinement of which the founders of the Religious Orders never dreamed. To the three vows of religion, they should have added a fourth, that of not regretting the other three! See what we have come to through a desire for innovations in ascetic science which has been fixed for centuries!

led away by anti-religious doctrines and revolutionary ideas. But to move the people is just as necessary and quite as difficult to achieve. These pious little leaflets say little or nothing on the subject.

These rash petitions are sometimes granted; but we must not therefore conclude God's approval. He merely wishes to give a salutary lesson in humility and prudence. We then see these excitable people besieging their directors for consolations. They weary them with their lamentations, regretting that the trial did not take another form. This one has great disadvantages, they say.

But they all have disadvantages! What such persons really want is suffering in appearance only; thorns that have no points. But in that case this parade of generosity should not be made, nor should they offer themselves for all conceivable sufferings: loss of health, that is to say, of interior and exterior tranquillity, reputation, and fortune!

If, however, anyone should have an attraction to the second manner, the director should first satisfy himself that the person is of a well-balanced mind, and that this desire is not the outcome of his sudden enthusiasm produced by a sermon or leaflet on the subject of expiation. And then, as a noviciate is necessary for all laborious and permanent states, he will require a very long noviciate, during which the first way of expiation is to be practised with perfection. This condition will seldom be fulfilled. These solid proofs of generosity and endurance will scarcely be given.

Finally, if the person obtains permission to *ask* for sufferings, they must exclude temptations and interior sufferings, and also such exterior trials as react upon others, such as illnesses that are distressing to nurse. Other people have trials enough of their own.*

The vow of greater perfection should be preceded in the same way by a long noviciate. St. Teresa made it at the age of forty-five. But it had to be restricted in her case, because, in spite of her great lights, scruples resulted (*Life*, by the Carmelite of Caen, etc., ch. xi).†

* See Abbé Sauve's excellent introduction to the abridged *Vie de Mère Veronique*, Foundress of the Saurs Victimes (Casterman, 1905).

† In a letter to her brother Lorenzo, the saint blames him for having made this vow, and yet Lorenzo had already been raised to the mystic state: "Your resolution has given me some uneasiness, though it has somewhat pleased me; but it seems to me dangerous... What I promised was with other additions, but this I should certainly not have presumed to promise, for I think that even the Apostles fell into venial sins. Our Lady alone was preserved from them... It is so easy to fall into venial sin that without our observing it we may commit it. God deliver us from it" (*Letter* of Jan. 2, 1577. *The Letters of St. Teresa*, Dalton, pp. 51-2). The saint's confessor declared that the vow is invalid (*Letter* to the same, Jan. 17, 1577; *ibid.*, p. 164).

The Ven. Mary of the Incarnation, Ursuline, writing to her son, Dom Martin, dissuaded him from the vow of greater perfection, even when restricted, as in St. Teresa's case. She feared that it would only result in disquietudes (*Letter* of Sep. 25, 1670).

**9.**—I have said that the mystic states create a **tendency to recollection** (No. 2), and consequently to solitude; but we must take care not to fall into error by exaggerating this disposition.

Without thinking of profiting by the leisure moments that our occupations fairly leave us, we try to dispense ourselves from all exterior occupations. We murmur against our Superiors when they do not fall in with our plans which we fancied to have come straight from Heaven.

Religious who have been consecrated to the active life has been known to say to themselves: "I have spoiled my life. My attraction shown me that I was made for a purely contemplative state. I should then have found God in prayer, and I should have attained to a close union with Him." And then they give themselves up to regrets, conceive a distaste for their vocation, and take steps to change their occupation or even their Congregation.

The starting-point of these ideas was good and came from God; it was an attraction to recollection. But false notions came and mingled with them and caused the deviation from the right path. The conclusion no longer bears the divine Hall-mark; it is all discontent, disgust, disobedience, unrest, sterile dreamings, or the blind pursuit of a new life, the difficulties of which are ignored and upon which it is now too late to embark. The cockle has grown up alongside of the wheat.

Again, you say: "My attraction shows that I was intended for the purely contemplative life." It may be that it merely shows that you are meant to be recollected amidst the active life, and to be so to a greater extent than such or such another whose attraction is different. The circumstances in which you are placed prove that this last interpretation is, in all probability, the only reasonable one.

You say again: "I should have found God in prayer." Nothing proves it. Everything depends on His good pleasure. How often, when going to your morning prayer or to your annual retreat, have you not thought that the solitude was going to draw God down to you; and yet you have continued in your aridity? Are you sure that it would be otherwise in the new life of which you are dreaming?

It is true that solitude is of itself a preparation for union with God; provided, however, that we do not neglect the duties of our state. But there are other preparations also: namely, self-abnegation, the active life accepted through obedience, etc. And, as a matter of fact, a large number of souls have been known to arrive at the highest contemplation, although they were occupied with the care of the sick, teaching, or an absorbing administrative work. Instead of losing time in dreaming about some other position, they utilised such opportunities as had fallen to their lot. And then God consented to do the rest.

**10.**—Given that we are in possession of the mystic union, can we conclude that we are in a **state of grace?**

If we merely have revelations and visions, the reply would be in the negative. The Holy Scriptures tell of visions that were sent to sinners, such as Balaam, Nabuchodonosor, and Balthasar.

But we are speaking here of the mystic union. This is the answer: Those that receive this union, without any special revelation as to their state of grace, have merely a moral certainty that they are admitted into friendship with God; but it is a much higher certainty than that which the ordinary Christian deduces from the evidence of his dispositions.

We can, in fact, have a moral certainty that our state of prayer is none other than this mystic contemplation, such as the generality of writers understand it. Now 1° this union contains a continuous act of perfect love, and this would be sufficient to place us in a state of grace, even if we were not in it already. The evidence of the mystic union is a positive proof, therefore, of the state of grace. It either supposes it or produces it; 2° it is admitted that this contemplation is brought about by certain gifts of the Holy Ghost which necessarily suppose a state of grace. It is not in the plan of God's Providence to produce the acts of the gifts without the gifts themselves; 3° in this contemplation God manifests His friendship to the soul; what He accords to it is a friend's presence.* We have a moral certainty, then, and the mystic union is thereby rightly regarded as a first development of sanctifying grace, a preparation for the final expansion which will be the beatific vision. "The mystic life, what is it if it be not the life of grace becoming conscious, and as it were experimental?" (Fr. Bainvel, *Nature et surnaturel,* ch. ii, 5).

But a still stronger assurance can be imagined, when given by such a distinct revelation that the mind would be absolutely convinced of its reality.

What has just been said will serve to reassure the mystic souls that are assailed by violent temptations. They often continue in a state of anxiety, fearing to have yielded in greater or less degree. They should say to themselves that, even if their fears as to some great fault were well-founded, they have been restored to the state of grace by the very fact that the mystic union is granted to them once more.

**11.**—The supernatural states of prayer have the effect of inciting the soul to virtue. And does the practice of the solid virtues lead, **in its turn,** to the mystic graces? Not necessarily, but it is the best disposition for inducing God to grant them. What He chiefly desires for us is eternal happiness, and therefore sanctity. This is the "one thing needful." The rest is but a means. If we labour earnestly at our real end, God will show Himself generous to aid us in one way

* Speaking of the prayer of quiet, St. Teresa says: "Those who discern in themselves this grace, must look upon themselves *as such friends,* if they would fulfil the lot which even the honourable friendship of the world respects" (*Life,* ch. xv, 8). See also 16, 3°.

or another. If, on the contrary, we are negligent, He will usually be sparing with His gifts* (See ch. xxviii, **24**).

## EXTRACTS

### § 1. Virtues That Accompany the Mystic Union

**12.**—St. Teresa on the prayer of quiet:

1. "So miserable are we, so inclined to the things of this world, that he can hardly have any real abhorrence of, with great detachment from, all earthly things who does not see that he holds *some pledges for those things that are above...* A man will hardly wish to be held in *contempt and abhorrence,* nor will he seek after the other great virtues to which the perfect attain, if he has not some *pledges of the love* which God bears him, together with a living faith... It is these graces, therefore, that quicken and strengthen our faith. It may well be that I, who am so wicked, measure others by myself, and that others require nothing more than the verities of the faith, in order to render their works most perfect; while I, wretched that I am! have need of everything" (*Life,* ch. x, 8, 9).

2. "I shall now return to that point in my life where I broke off... Hitherto, my life was *my own;* my life, since I began to explain these methods of prayer, is the *life which God lived in me,*—so it seems to me; for I feel it to be *impossible* that I should have escaped in so short a time from ways and works that were so wicked. May Our Lord be praised, who has delivered me from myself!" (*Life,* ch. xxiii, 1).

3. "This water [the prayer of quiet] of grand blessings and graces, which Our Lord now supplies, makes the virtues thrive much more, beyond all comparison, than they did in the previous state of prayer [meditation]" (*Life,* ch. xiv, 6).

4. "The prayer of quiet, then, is a little spark of the true love of Himself, which Our Lord begins to enkindle in the soul...If men do not quench it by their faults, it is the beginning of the great fire, which sends forth—I shall speak of it in the proper place— the flames of that *most vehement love of God* which His Majesty will have perfect souls to possess. This little spark is a sign or pledge which God gives to a soul, in token of His having chosen it for great things, if it

* "And hence we find (says the *Imitation*) but few contemplatives, because there are but few who can wholly disengage themselves from perishable and created things" (Book IV, ch. xxxi, 1).

St. Teresa: "It is folly then to imagine that He admits into friendship with Him, persons living delicately and without troubles... Hence it is that I see few contemplatives but I perceive them courageous and resolved to suffer; for the first thing Our Lord doth, if they be weak, is the infusing courage into them, and making them not to fear afflictions" (*Way of Perfection,* ch. xviii, p. 523).

will prepare to receive them" (*Life,* ch. xv, 6, 7; and the *Way of Perfection,* ch. xxxi).

"For, God having done us this favour, we are to forget all things of the world, inasmuch as the Lord thereof, approaching, casts all forth. I say not, that *all* such as have it [the prayer of quiet] must necessarily be sequestered from all the world; but I would have them... endeavour to go untying themselves from every thought..." (*The Way of Perfection,* ch. xxxi, p. 97).

**13.**—St. Teresa on full union or ecstasy:

1. She compares two sorts of humility, the one laboriously acquired by "the understanding," the other due to ecstasy, which she says is much superior to the former; it is that "gotten... by a clear verity, that comprehends *in a moment* what the imagination with toiling *cannot attain to* in a long time, concerning the very nothing that we are, and the very much that God is" (*The Way of Perfection,* ch. xxxii, p. 102).

2. On the effects of ecstasy: "One [example of it] I remember at present, of a person to whom in three days Our Lord gave such gifts, that, unless experience forced me to believe it,... I should not think it possible... To another, the like in three months; and they were both young; others I have seen, whom Our Lord hath not done this favour to, till after a long time. And what I have said of these two, I could say of some besides" (*Conceptions of the Love of God,* ch. vi, p. 318-9).

3. "It falls out (and this almost usually) when Our Lord raiseth a soul to do her these favours... that the virtues continue so strong, and the love so fervent, that this thing cannot be concealed; because, they always (though without their intending it) benefit some souls..." (ibid., p. 319).

4. On ecstasy: "For my part, I believe that a soul which has reached this state neither speaks nor acts of itself, but rather that the supreme King *takes care of all* it has to do.

O my God, how clear is the meaning of those words, and what good reason the Psalmist had, and all the world will ever have, to pray for the wings of a dove!" (*Life,* ch. xx, 32).

5. On full union: "In *one* of these visits, how brief soever it may be, the Gardener, being who He is... pours the water without stint; and what the poor soul, *with the labour, perhaps, of twenty years* in fatiguing the understanding, could not bring about, that the heavenly Gardener accomplishes in an *instant...* the soul sees itself to be *other than it was, and it knows not how* it is beginning to do great things in the odour which the flowers send forth... " (*Life,* ch. xvii, 3, 4).

6. "Especially, if it be a strong impetuosity, it seems intolerable, unless the soul employ herself in doing something for God" (*Letter* to her brother, Jan., 1577).

**14.**—St. John of the Cross:

"... there is joy in heaven... when He makes it eat... the bread of infused contemplation. This is the first and principal benefit, and from which almost all the others flow. Of these the first is a knowledge of our own selves and our own vileness " (*The Obscure Night of the Soul,* Book I, ch. xii, p. 359-60).

**15.**—The Very Rev. Fr. Aquaviva, General of the Society of Jesus:

"Yet, care must be taken... not to make light of this holy exercise of contemplation, much less forbid the use of it to members of the Society; for in the opinion of many of the holy Fathers, true and perfect contemplation is a *more effectual means* than any other method of prayer to weaken and destroy pride, to stir up the slothful to a more prompt obedience, and to inflame the tepid with an ardent desire for the salvation of souls" (*Letter on prayer,* 1599).

### § 2. How the Virtues Are Sometimes Acquired Without Effort, and Even Suddenly

**16.**—St. Teresa:

1° On the prayer of quiet: "... There is no necessity for going about searching for reasons, on the strength of which we may elicit acts of humility and of shame, because Our Lord *Himself* supplies them in a way *very different* from that by which we could acquire them... In short, not to weary myself, it is *the beginning of all good:* the flowers [of the mystic garden] have so thriven, that they are on the point of budding" (*Life,* ch. xiv 22-3).

2° Other quotations relating to full union: "Now ye know how exceedingly this *living* water cleanseth... For, if but *once* drunk of, I hold for *certain,* it leaves the soul pure, and cleansed of all its faults. For,... God permits no soul to drink of this water (since it depends not on our will, this divine union being a thing very supernatural) save to purify, and leave it clean, and free from the mire and *misery, wherein by its offences it was involved" (The Way of Perfection, ch. xix, p. 58).*

3° "Oh, infinite greatness of God! A few years ago,—nay, perhaps but a few days, —this soul thought of nothing but itself. Who has made it feel such tormenting cares? If we tried for many years to obtain such sorrow by means of meditation, we could not succeed. God help me! If for long days and years I considered how great a wrong it is that God should be offended, how lost souls are His children and my brothers; if I pondered over the dangers of this world, and the blessing it would be to leave this wretched life, would not that suffice? No, my daughters, the pain would not be the same" (*Interior Castle,* Fifth Mansion, ch. ii, 10, 11).

4° "It being Our Lord's will that the flowers should open, in order that the soul may believe itself to be in possession of virtue; though it sees most clearly that it cannot, and never could, acquire them in many years, and that the heavenly Gardener *has given them to it in that instant.* Now, too, the humility of the soul is *much greater* and *deeper* than it was before; because it sees *more clearly* that it did neither much nor little, beyond giving its consent that Our

Lord might work those graces in it, and then accepting them willingly (*Life*, ch. xvii, 4).

**17.**—Blessed Angela of Foligno. Her fears regarding humility: "Again He said unto me: 'My loved one, My spouse, love Me! For thy whole life, thy eating and drinking, thy sleeping, and all thy manner of living, all are pleasing unto Me, if thou lovest Me. Again He said unto me: 'I will work in thee great things in the sight of the people, and I will make Myself known in thee, and I shall be glorified, and My name shall be praised in thee by many people.' These things, and others like unto them, did He say unto me. But I, when I heard these words, reckoned my sins and considered my defects, how I was not worthy of that great love. And at these words I began much to doubt, and my soul said unto Him who spake unto me; 'If Thou wert the Holy Ghost, Thou wouldst not say these things unto me, for they are not becoming; and I am weak, and *may have vainglory from them.* And He answered unto me: 'Now *see and think, whether with regard to all these things thou wilt be able to have vainglory,* so as to be lifted up, and to go out of these words, and to think of other things.' And I tried to wish to have vainglory, that I might prove if that were true that He had said... Moreover... all my sins were brought back unto my memory, and on my own part I saw nothing in me but sins and defects, and I felt in me *more humility than I had ever felt before*" (*Visions and Instructions,* ch. xx, p. 59).

### § 3. It is Necessary to Be Indulgent With Contemplatives

**18.**—St. Teresa:

1. She relates the criticisms to which she was subject when the graces that she was receiving became known:

"Certainly, I see nothing in the world that seems to me good, except this, that it tolerates no faults in good people, and helps them to perfection by dint of complaints against them... *Perfection is not attained to at once,* unless Our Lord grant that grace by a special privilege; yet the world, when it sees any one beginning to travel on that road [of perfection], insists on his becoming *perfect* at once, and a thousand leagues off detects in him a fault, *which after all may be a virtue.* He who finds fault is doing the very same thing,—but in his own case, viciously,—and he pronounces it to be so wrong in the other. He who aims at perfection, then, must neither eat nor sleep, nor, as they say, even breathe... and so... great courage is necessary here; for though the poor soul have not yet begun to walk, *the world will have it fly*" (*Life,* ch. xxxi, 19).

2. The danger of a soul becoming discouraged when it sees that, in spite of supernatural favours, it does not make great progress in virtue:

"And until He, of His goodness, had done all, nothing was done by me... beyond falling and rising again. I wish I knew how to explain it, because many souls [of whom too much is required], I believe, delude themselves in this matter; *they would fly before God gives them wings...* When they see in all the books written on prayer and on contemplation an account of what we have to do in order to attain thereto, but which they cannot accomplish themselves,—they lose heart... Let them not distress themselves; let them trust in Our Lord: what they now desire, His Majesty will enable them to attain to by prayer, and by doing what they can themselves; for it is very necessary for our weak nature that we should have great confidence..." (*ibid.*, 20-1).

3. Speaking of ecstasy and of the confessor so inexperienced that "nothing seems safe to him; he dreads and suspects everything which is not quite commonplace, especially in a soul where he sees *any imperfection,* for he thinks people on whom God bestows such favours *must be angels,* which is impossible in this life" (*Interior Castle,* Sixth Mansion, ch. i, 15).

### § 4. Sufferings Not to Be Asked For

**19.**—St. Teresa:

1. "In order to attain at length to the possession of our divine Crucified Lord, you know we must bear the Cross after Him. It is not, however, necessary, as Fr. Gregory affirms, to *ask God for sufferings;* for He never fails to send them to those that He loves, and to lead them by the same way as His Son" (*Letter* to Mother Mary of St. Joseph, June, 1578).

2. Another letter to her brother who was raised to the prayer of quiet and would have preferred to be led by the way of suffering only:

"It is great stupidity and *little humility* to think of arriving at this degree without prayer... Believe my words, and leave the matter to the Lord of the Vineyard who knows well what everyone stands in need of. *Never asked Him for interior trials,* though He has given me many during my life, and these were very great. Our natural disposition and constitution contribute much to increase these afflictions" (*Letter,* Feb. 20th, 1577. Dalton's trans., pp. 175-6).

3. Letter to Father Gratian: "I smiled when you told me that you are already desiring fresh tribulations. For the love of God let this wish alone, for you cannot bear them by yourself... And as I do not know whether those tribulations are not to fall upon other persons as well as him who is wishing for them, I cannot desire them " (April 21st, 1579).

Ten years earlier, when the saint was writing *The Way of Perfection,* her language was different. In an outburst of generosity she said: "I smile at those persons that dare not beg crosses of Our Lord, as conceiving it follows from this He must send them presently." But she even then prudently added: "I speak not of such as decline them out of humility, as judging themselves unable to bear them" (*Way of Perfection,* ch. xxxii, p. 99).

**20.**—St. Francis of Sales:

1. "... If divine Providence permits afflictions or mortifications to come upon you, you must not refuse them, but accept them courageously, lovingly,

and calmly; if Providence does not send you any, or does not permit them to come to you, then *do not desire them or ask for them*" (*Spiritual Conferences,* vi).

2. "For my part, I think we ought not to *summon* bitternesses into our heart as Our Lord did, for we cannot govern them as He did; *it is enough that we suffer them patiently.* For which reason it is not required that we always go against our inclinations, when they are not bad..." (Letter to Mère Angelique Arnauld, who found his manner of direction too gentle, May 25th, 1619).

**21.**—Life of Blessed Mary of the Incarnation, Carmelite:

1° "It happened one day that a young religious who had not yet been professed three years, told her that she *did not desire any consolations in her devotions,* but rather to walk amidst thorns and desolations, because this was the royal way, divine and highly meritorious. Blessed Mary rebuked her, made her realise her weakness, which was not able to bear up under such privations, and showed her that it is good to have consolations and sensible fervours in order to make us seek God with greater ardour" (*Vie,* by André du Val, Book II, ch. xii).

2° A religious, having said to her that it had occurred to her to ask God to send her purgatory to her in this world, she replied: "Beware of asking such a thing; how do we know if we have the patience to bear so much? We must leave that in God's hands." She added that she had seen a soul who, during her life, had asked the same thing; and being near death, she suffered such strange pains and torments that she was greatly afraid of failing in patience. And this person then said to her: "Oh, how we should beware of asking God what I have asked Him! I see now that I did not know what I was asking. God knows the measure of our strength, and what is necessary in order to raise it to Him." She said this soul was very virtuous and made a good death; but that God wished to show by this how we should humble ourselves and depend on Him in all things; and that if He tempers the bitterness of our affliction with the oil of sensible consolations, we should not refuse them, but on the contrary accept them, leaving it entirely to Him " (*ibid.*).

### § 5. Why God Does Not Give Mystic Graces Oftener

**22.**—Ven. Marina de Escobar:

"Let us now speak of this higher degree of virtue that may be compared to pure gold. This is a very excellent disposition for enabling God to carry out His work of lovingkindness, wisdom and mercy in the soul, that is to say, that He may grant her extraordinary graces, that He may visit her Himself or by His saints, that *He may manifest to her His Being* and the divine secrets; that He may cause her to taste and make experience of the good things that she will possess in Heaven. This is so true, that in my opinion it is absolutely certain that God's goodness *will overlook none of these chosen souls;* but He will give either more or less, according to His good pleasure and His wisdom, or according to the dispositions of each soul. If He acts otherwise, it will be an *exceptional,* extraordinary *case,* due to special reasons. But normally, God acts as I have described; and the more perfect and sublime the soul's virtue, the more familiar, so I think, will be her intercourse with God, and *God's with her,* overwhelming her with His special gifts. If God does not communicate Himself with abundance to any souls, it is, in my opinion, solely *on account of the imperfection* of their virtue" (Vol. I, Book V, ch. xxxiii, § 4).

"God wills to communicate Himself to those who ardently love Him; just as a great king opens his heart and his secrets to his familiar friends. This prince may have two motives: either he wishes to give one of his ministers charge of some important business, of advantage to the state; or he is simply actuated by affection. He keeps none of his thoughts from him, he loves to converse with him, to delight him by this confidence... his happiness is to recompence magnificently all his love and fidelity by opening his heart to him completely. Our great God and Sovereign Lord acts in the same way with regard to those of His servants who love Him with all their hearts " (*ibid.,* § 6). (See ch. xxviii, 26 *bis*).

# CHAPTER XIII

## The Eleventh Character of the Mystic Union

**1.**—The **eleventh character** consists in this, that the union acts upon the body, which in its turn acts upon it again.

**2.**—In the case of **ecstasy,** it is clear that the mystic union acts upon the body. It is from this that the definition of the degree is derived (ch. iii, **8**).

This action is exercised in four ways:

1° *The senses* cease to act, or they convey a confused knowledge only. According as the cessation of action on the part of the senses is complete or *almost* complete, the ecstasy itself is called *complete* or *incomplete.*

2° As a general rule, the *limbs* become immovable, and one can neither speak nor walk nor make any gestures unless God restores this power miraculously. This last state is called *mobile ecstasy.*

Here are some examples of this exception. St. Catherine of Siena, St. Catherine of Ricci, and St. Mary Magdalen of Pazzi spoke during their ecstasies. We thus have accounts of what they saw or heard. St. Mary Magdalen of Pazzi spoke so rapidly at times that six secretaries were required to take down her utterances (*Vie,* by Cepari, ch. vii. Eng. trans., Orat. series, ch. xxviii). She sometimes walked during her ecstasy. On one occasion she even climbed up one of the columns of the church without the aid of a ladder. This occurred frequently with Catherine Emmerich when she was Sacristan and it was necessary to clean or decorate cornices or other places that were, humanly speaking, inaccessible (see M. Ribet, *La mystique divine,* Vol. II, ch. xxxii).

St. Frances of Rome heard her Confessor's questions when she was in an ecstasy, but not those of other persons. She composed verses of hymns at these times, which she sang. She moved and made gestures corresponding to the consoling or sorrowful pictures that were passing before her; she took part in these scenes, getting ready the manger, for instance, which seemed to her to be about to receive Our Blessed Lord upon His Nativity.

3° The *respiration* is almost arrested; sometimes it seems to be completely so. It is the same with the heart-beats, and consequently the pulse. In all these things there are differences of degree, according as the contemplation is more or less deep. Sometimes, at certain moments, there has even been ground for fearing that death has supervened (see Extract, 21).

4° The *vital heat* seems to disappear, a coldness sets in at the extremities of the limbs.

To sum up, everything seems *as if* the soul were losing in vital strength and motive power all that it gains from the side of the divine union. Farther on I shall say a few words as to certain accessory phenomena (No. 11).

**3.—The prayer of quiet.** Since the mystic state has an influence on our organs when it becomes very strong (as in the case of ecstasy), we can imagine that it would also begin to have a certain action in the prayer of quiet, which is only a lesser degree of the same state.

Experience confirms this *a priori* idea. But the degree of influence is not the same with everyone. I think it is more marked in persons with delicate constitutions.

In any case, if this influence is not felt in the prayer of quiet, it will certainly begin to be felt when the union is more profound, although still inferior to ecstasy. Sooner or later it will be experienced. Otherwise there would be no continuity between ecstasy and the state that precedes it: there would be a sudden leap when passing from one kind to another.

**4.**—Let us now enter more into **detail:**

1° *The effect upon the eyes.* This can only be observed properly if, while the body is immovable, the eyes remain wide open and fixed. Several persons have told me that they then only saw the objects about them as though they were veiled by a whitish mist. It is like an evenly dispersed fog, or the smoke of incense. This fog has its fluctuations, like the prayer itself. And with the prayer it increases in strength at times, and then diminishes in the same way.

If the eyes are closed, the influence of the prayer of quiet is less easily shown. The union then has to be very strong. The eyes feel as if they were being darkened; so much so that at certain moments, when the state is at its deepest, it is as though one were in complete darkness. The cause is the same as that given above. The eye partially loses its power of sight. The result just now was that external objects could no longer be seen distinctly; here it is the light through the eyelids that begins to disappear.

On the other hand, certain persons have told me that they do not ever remember to have experienced this impression of a fog. But in the majority of cases their testimony proves nothing either way, for they say that they have never made the experiment. They have always instinctively closed their eyes.

They are right in doing so, for in this way one is more recollected. And if they did not, the sight might be greatly fatigued, as it would remain riveted to one fixed point. And then, further, in the case of the mist just referred to, the eyes would necessarily make an effort to penetrate it, and there would be a second cause of fatigue.

2° The hearing loses its activity less easily than the sight.

3° Certain persons feel that *their limbs* become slightly less mobile. The fingers seem to lose their power of grasp.

4° The *respiration* is influenced to a certain extent. It seems to become feeble at times, and then it has sudden reawakenings. We feel the necessity for obtaining the requisite amount of air by taking a deep breath.

5° Sometimes, when the prayer of quiet becomes stronger, a *slight chilliness* is experienced in the hands and feet.

**5.**—Since the prayer of quiet acts as a check to bodily movements, these **in return** should react so as to impair the prayer of quiet. Experience confirms this expectation in an undeniable manner; but with this restriction, that *very brief movements have but a slight and momentary influence.*

**6.**—Thus, when we **walk,** read, or, more still, look about us, we feel that the divine action is diminishing.

But that the prayer of quiet, if it is frequent, should disappear altogether, we must continue to move about or to divert the attention. When, on the other hand, we only move *momentarily,* to cough, for example, or change our position on our chair, or to give some brief information, the diminution is insignificant, or transient. We return at once to the former state, more especially if the eyes have been closed.

**7.**—St. Teresa blames those who **will not stir at all** for fear of marring the prayer of quiet.* The saint does not go so far as to say that certain prolonged or violent movements would have no result. They would certainly do so. She implies this herself later on, for she adds: "It is good... at the most to let fall *at times some* sweet word, as one that gives a *blast* [*"soufflé leger"* in the French translation] to a candle when he sees it out to kindle it again, which if it be burning serves only to extinguish it (*Way of Perfection*, ch. xxxi, p. 95). The saint then admits, as not being detrimental, acts in which the body participates, provided that it does so in a slight degree only.

**8.**—It follows therefore, that there is **a way of quitting** the prayer of quiet or diminishing it when necessary (see ch. fol., **15**). We begin to walk or to move to and fro.†

**9.**—Let us suppose the case of a person who has voluntarily quitted this supernatural prayer, by moving or attending to some business on account of

* "They would not have the body *move,* because they conceive so they should lose that peace; and therefore they dare not stir... when they find in themselves that joy... They think they can continue it, and so would not even breathe" (*Way of Perfection,* ch. xxxi, p. 93-4). The soul "dares not move nor stir, because it thinks that this blessing it has received must then escape out of its hands; now and then it could wish it did not even breathe" (*Life,* ch. xv, 1).

† When driving or travelling by train, the prayer of quiet is not very easily maintained. We see why this is so. The continual shaking of the vehicle interferes with the state of tranquillity which the body requires.

which he had been disturbed. If after several minutes' interruption he comes back again to his prayer, will the supernatural prayer **return?**

I do not know that we can give any general reply in cases where the prayer of quiet only occurs occasionally. For everything depends upon God's free will; the state may return or it may not.

But if the prayer of quiet is habitual during the times of recollection, the mystic state goes on again as though it had not been interrupted. It does not matter although it is interrupted several times running. It is as if we broke off momentarily from reading a book and then returned to it again. If it were a question of ordinary meditation, it would annoy us to have the threads of our thoughts cut in this way. We should require to pick them up again with an effort. Here we have merely to give our consent; it is instantaneous and without effort.

**10.—Tears.** The mystic state does not produce these necessarily. St. Teresa does not speak of them in her own case except in connection with very sublime contemplations. She says (*Life,* ch. xix, 2) that "in the beginning" she found herself in a flood of tears when she came out of her ecstasy. She attributes them to "an exceeding great tenderness" for God. She gives the same reason in the *Interior Castle* (Fifth Mansion, ch. ii, 6): "It [the soul] is bitterly grieved at seeing them [all men] offend Him." She again alludes to tears in the *Way of Perfection* (ch. xix). Elsewhere she recognises that the temperament is a factor in this matter. "You must also notice that *bodily weakness* may cause such pain, especially with people of sensitive characters who cry for every trifling trouble. Times without number do they imagine they are mourning for God's sake *when they are doing no such thing...* the cause may be an accumulation of humour round the heart, which has a great deal more to do with such tears than has the love of God" (*Interior Castle,* Sixth Mansion, ch. vi, 7). We might translate this sentence into modern phraseology by saying that with certain persons ecstasy may perhaps have, not a moral effect, but a purely physical action upon the lachrymal glands.

**11.—Phenomena that accompany ecstasy. In** the case of ecstatics we meet occasionally with the following phenomena which concern the body:

1° The body rises up into the air. This is what is termed *levitation;*

2° Or it is enveloped in a luminous *aureole;*

3° Or it emits a *fragrance.*

These phenomena are not a necessary *effect* of the mystic union itself, like those that we have just described above (**2.**) They are superadded to it. When God produces these exceptional phenomena, it is usually with the object of giving credit to one of His servants whom He has charged with some important mission: such as the founding of a religious Order or reviving the Faith in any country. On these questions, see M. Ribet, *La mystique divine,* Vol. II; and ch. xxii, **67**, note.

Let us say a few words regarding levitation.

**12.—Levitation.** Here are the **circumstances.** 1° Sometimes the ecstatic develops a *considerable strength* in his ascents. Thus we read in the *Life* of St. Joseph of Cupertino that on three occasions he seized one of his companions and carried him up with him into the air. He was present one day at a ceremony in which ten men were vainly endeavouring to hold up and fix a heavy Cross. He darts forward, flying as though he were a bird, lifts up the Cross like a feather and fixes it in its place (*Vie,* by Mgr. Bernino, chs. x and xii). The same saint, when saying Mass, adopted an attitude which, had it been natural, would have necessitated considerable effort. "At the moment of consecration he raised himself up so that he touched the ground with the tips of his toes only, and remained in this position until after the Communion" (*ibid.,* ch. xxii).

St. Gerard Majella, a Redemptorist lay brother (died 1755), when speaking one day to the Prioress of a Convent, fell into an ecstasy. He seized the parlour *grille,* as if with the object of restraining his fervour. The grating yielded and bent in his hands as though it were soft wax (*La Stigmatisation,* by Dr. Imbert, Vol. II, ch. xxvii, p. 420). St. Michael of the Saints, a Trinitarian (died 1625), being in an ecstasy, ran across the fields at such a pace that eight Religious who were trying to bar the way were unable to stop him (*Vie des Saints,* by Collin de Plancy and Abbé E. Daras, July 5th, p. 255).

2° When the body is lifted up into the air it often becomes as *light as a feather,* so that a breath is enough to set it in motion and to cause it to float like a soap-bubble (see the facts quoted by Dr. Imbert, Vol. II, ch. xviii).

3° At other times the ecstatic's body *cannot be moved.* It is as resistant as a rock (see Dr. Imbert, Vol. II, ch. xviii). We have the instances of Margaret Agullona, a Franciscan Tertiary (died 1600), and of Giles of Santarem, a disciple of St. Dominic. St. Mary Magdalen of Pazzi became sometimes so heavy during her ecstasies that they could not move her. They were not even able to stir her arm or her hand. But "when she had recovered the use of her senses, she felt pain in such of her limbs as had been too roughly handled" (*Vie,* by Cepari, ch. vii).

Generally, with ecstatics, the body is immovable only when lying on the ground.

4° There is no fixed rule with regard to the *height* to which the body ascends. When St. Francis of Assisi had withdrawn to Mount Alverna, his only companion being Brother Leo, his confessor, this latter saw him lifted up sometimes to a man's height from the ground, sometimes above the highest trees, and at others so high that he was no longer visible (*Vie,* by Chalippe, Book IV).

5° *At the conclusion of the ecstasy* the body redescends slowly, without injuring itself.

One day when Blessed Thomas of Cori (died 1729) was giving Communion, he rose up in an ecstasy as high as the vaulting of the church, still holding the Ciborium. He then gently and gradually descended, and went on giving Holy

Communion (*Vie des Saints,* by Collin de Plancy and Abbé E. Daras (Jan. 11th, p. 472).

6° St. Teresa tells us that she was seized with great fear on the first occasion when she felt herself thus lifted up (*Life,* ch. xx, 9).

7° In St. Joseph of Cupertino's numerous ecstasies it was remarked that his *garments* were always harmoniously arranged as though by another hand (*Vie,* ch. xxii).

With regard to the naturalistic explanation of levitation and of the stigmata, see ch. xxxi.

**13.**—At the beginning of this chapter we considered the effects produced upon the body by the mystic union, during the actual time of the prayer. It will be well to ask if it has any after **influence upon the health.** As regards *ecstasy,* let us consult the lives of the saints. St. Teresa states that ecstasy, "however long it may last," has never injured her health. "Nor do I remember, however ill I might have been when Our Lord had mercy upon me in this way, that I ever felt the worse for it; on the contrary, I was *always better afterwards.* But so great a blessing, what harm can it do?... It thus robs us of our bodily powers with so much joy, in order to *leave them greater*" (*Life,* ch. xviii, 15).

The only inconvenience that the saint experienced was fatigue. "If the rapture lasts, the nerves are made to feel it" (*Second Letter* to Fr. Rodrigo Alvarez, *Life,* p. 457). She also says: "Even on the following day, I have a pain in my wrists and over my whole body, as if my bones were out of joint... So then, though I do all I can, my body has *no strength to move* for some time; the soul took it all away. Very often, too, he who was before sickly and full of pain remains healthy, and even stronger" (*Life,* ch. xx, 16, 29). It has been observed that with other persons the ecstasy has produced a considerable degree of physical weakness afterwards. Dr. Imbert cites several examples, such as St. Elizabeth of Hungary (Vol. II, ch. xvii, pp. 273, 274) and Dominic of Jesus-Mary Ruzzola, General of the discalced Carmelites. His is an extreme case. After his ecstasies "he experienced severe pains. His bruised limbs made it impossible for him to stand or move. He even vomited blood."

The Ven. Mary of the Incarnation, Ursuline, speaking of the ecstasies that she had while still in the world, adds: "I came out of this state after an hour or two in profound peace and great sweetness of spirit... As to my body, it emerged from this prayer *more enfeebled* than would have been the case after the most frightful austerities, but, nevertheless, always able to attend to my ordinary occupations" (*Histoire,* by Abbé Chapôt, Part I, ch. iv).

Another striking example is that of Blessed Mary of the Incarnation, Carmelite (Madame Acarie). At the age of twenty-eight, says her biographer, "God's onslaughts took her with yet greater impetuosity and with such a violent trembling that it made her bones crack, and wrung from her piercing cries as if she were being stabbed to the heart... She expected that they would cause her death, so much so that she once told M. Fontaine, her confessor at Pontoise, that on *several hundred occasions* she had gone to bed not expecting to live until the morning" (*Vie*, by André du Val, Book I, ch. v; see also Book II, ch. xiv).

St. John of the Cross, speaking of high raptures, says that they are not "always attended by such terrors and shocks of nature as in the case of those who are entering into the state of illumination and perfection [the mystic union]... and as in this kind of communications, namely, of ecstasies and rapture. For in others [those who have reached the spiritual marriage] they take place with greater sweetness" (*Spiritual Canticle,* Stanza XIV, line 5, p. 84) He had previously dealt with the subject at greater length. Speaking of the "Beloved," he says: "The soul, because of its intense longing after the Divine eyes, that is the Godhead, receives interiorly from the Beloved such communications and knowledge of God as compel it to cry out, 'Turn them away, O my Beloved.' Such is the wretchedness of our mortal nature that we cannot endure—even when it is offered to us—but at the cost of our life, that which is the very life of the soul and the object of its earnest desires, namely the knowledge of the Beloved. Thus the soul is compelled to say, with regard to the eyes so earnestly, so anxiously sought for, and in so many ways—when they become visible— 'Turn them away' " (*ibid.,* Stanza XIII, line I, pp. 68-9).

"So great, at times, is *the suffering* of the soul during these ecstatic visitations — and there is no other pain *which so wrenches the very bones* and which so oppresses our natural forces—that, were it not for the special interference of God, death would ensue... Such graces cannot be perfectly received in the body, because the spirit of man is lifted up to the communion of the Spirit of God, Who visits the soul, and it is therefore of necessity, in some measure, *a stranger to the body.* Hence it is that the *flesh suffers, and consequently the soul in it,* by reason of their union in one person" (*ibid.,* stanza 13, line 1, p. 69). Elsewhere he again says that with the more advanced "ecstasies, raptures, and dislocations of the bones occur at times" (*Obscure Night,* Book II, ch. i, p. 374). Sometimes the weakness comes, not from the ecstasy itself, but from the transports of love that follow it. In her youth, the Ven. Anne of St. Bartholomew, one of St. Teresa's companions, fell ill from this cause, and it was thought that she would die (*Vie,* by Fr. Bouix, 2nd ed., Book II, ch. v).

To sum up, the divine ecstasy is far from being prejudicial to the health; but the limbs may feel a great fatigue from it at times.

Benedict XIV, on the other hand, maintained that this fatigue indicates that the ecstasy is not divine, but purely the result of ill-health. It is not possible to agree with him here. He does not rely upon the lives of the saints, but on the mere statement of the physician Zacchias (*De canon.,* ch. xlix, No. 5).

**14.**—With regard to **the prayer of quiet,** we have seen that if it is greatly prolonged it may be *the indirect* cause of a certain fatigue (ch. x, **5**). As we see that this sometimes happens in the case of ecstasy, it will be well to inquire whether the prayer of quiet produces this fatigue directly.

It is very difficult to decide on this question of fact. For those anæmic persons who receive this prayer, recognise several other causes of their sickly condition. I have never been able to learn that they had come to any conclusion as to whether this supernatural state played an important and particularly a direct part in the matter.

**15.—Stigmata.** Several ecstatics have borne on their feet and hands and side, or upon the brow, the marks of Our Saviour's Passion, accompanied by corresponding and very acute sufferings. These are the visible stigmata. Others have had the sufferings only; these are the *invisible* stigmata (see also ch. xxxi, **8**).

St. Catherine of Siena's stigmata became at once invisible in response to her request. The pain was usually so intolerable that she said that a miracle alone prevented her dying from it (Bolland., April 30th, No. 195).

The existence of the stigmata in the case of many saints is so well-established by historical proofs that, as a general rule, it is no longer disputed by unbelievers. M. Georges Dumas, professor of religious psychology at the Sorbonne, admits it distinctly in his article in the *Revue des deux Mondes* (May, 1907), while seeking for a naturalistic explanation.*

**16.**—The sufferings form the **essential part** of the visible stigmata. The substance of this grace is compassion for Jesus Christ, the participation in His sufferings. There could be no reason for our bearing the symbol without having something of the reality, according to the measure of our moral strength and in conformity with our condition. There would be danger of pride in appearing as though we were honoured with a privilege, and there would not be the merit of a painful ordeal as a compensation. Finally, if the stigmata really comes from God, it is a miracle prolonged for years together; it cannot consist in a mere spectacular effect.

The sufferings of the stigmata occur even where there is no hemorrhage from the wounds.

As a rule, other trials are added to these. "The life of those who bear the stigmata," says Dr. Imbert, "is but a long series of pains which lead up to the divine malady of the stigmata, and then form an escort, as it were, continuing with it up to the hour of death" (*La stigmatisation,* Vol. II, ch. x, p. 126).

**17.**—It seems to be historically proved that all those who received the stigmata were **ecstatics.** As a rule, they had visions in keeping with the part of fellow-sufferers with Jesus Christ: Our Lord showing Himself to them in the bloodstained garments of His Passion.

Amongst apparitions of this kind (and they are numerous) we may cite as very characteristic those that were granted to St. Catherine of Ricci, of the third

* He makes a clear admission that none has yet been found when he says: "At the present moment we are *very near* getting the corroborating evidence of facts."

order, regular, of St. Dominic, near Florence. Her *ecstasies of the Passion* began when she was twenty years old (1542), and for twelve years they were reproduced weekly with minute exactness. The ecstasy lasted exactly twenty-eight hours, from midday on Thursday until four o'clock on Friday afternoon (Bull of canonisation), being interrupted only so that the saint might receive Holy Communion. Catherine conversed aloud with the actors in the various scenes that were present before her; her frame imitated the gestures, attitudes, and various movements of Our Lord's body during His sufferings. The drama was subdivided into scenes, about seventeen in number, which began at a regular hour. On coming out of her ecstasy her limbs were covered with wounds produced by the rods, cords, etc. (*Vie,* by Fr. Bayonne, Vol. I, ch. ix; English: *Life,* by F. M. Capes, ch. vi). For several months the saint, distressed by the celebrity that these ecstasies of the Passion brought her, caused her Religious to pray that she might be delivered from them. This prayer was granted.

We have had facts similar to these, and remarkable for the length of their duration, in the nineteenth century. Maria von Moërl, the ecstatic of Kaltern, in the Tyrol (1812-68), after prolonged sufferings, began at the age of twenty to have ecstasies. A year later she received the stigmata, and during the thirty-five remaining years of her life she had the ecstasy of the Passion regularly every week from Thursday evening until Friday evening. Each scene was reflected in her attitudes (see Dr. Imbert, Vol. I, ch. xxxii; and Léon Boré, *Les extatiques du Tyrol.*)

**18.—The number of those who have received the stigmata.** Dr. Imbert, who has made extensive researches on the subject of stigmatisation, comes to the following conclusions:

1° No stigmatised persons were known before the thirteenth century; the first case of which a description was given being that of St. Francis of Assisi.

2° Since that time this writer reckons 321 cases, with regard to which there is every reason to believe in a divine action as the cause (*Preface,* p. xxi). He thinks that others would be found by searching through the great libraries of Germany, Spain and Italy (*ibid.,* p. xii).

3° In this list 41 are men.

4° There are 62 saints or *Beati* of both sexes (*ibid.,* p. xvi).

5° There are 29 persons who lived in the nineteenth century.

6° There have been false stigmatics. These were finally found to be simulating the stigmata and sanctity, in order to make themselves interesting (Vol. II, p. 1).

# EXTRACTS

## § 1. The Physiological Features of Ecstasy

**19.**—St. Teresa:

1°... "*When the rapture is at its highest,* [the soul] neither sees nor hears, nor perceives" (*Life,* ch. xx, 24). When it diminishes "it is as if the things heard and seen were at a great distance, far away" (*ibid.,* 23). At certain times "I was so much myself as to be able to see that I was being lifted up" (*ibid,* 9).

2° Upon ecstasy in a slight degree: (*a*) "The soul... is, as it were, utterly fainting away in a kind of trance;... it cannot even *move the hands* without great pain,... (*b*) The eyes... if they are open,... are as if they saw nothing; nor is reading possible,—the very letters seem strange and cannot be distinguished,—the *letters indeed are visible,* but as the understanding furnishes no help, all reading is impracticable... (*c*) The *ears hear;* but what is heard is not comprehended... (*d*) It is useless to try to speak,..." (*Life,* ch. xviii, 14). (*e*) "If the soul is making a meditation on any subject, the *memory* of it is lost at once, just as if it had never been thought of. If it reads, what is read is not remembered nor dwelt upon; neither is it otherwise with vocal prayer" (*ibid.,* 19).

3° "It rather seemed as if the doors of the senses were closed against its will, in order that it might have more abundantly the fruition of our Lord. It is abiding alone with Him: What has it to do but to love Him? It *neither sees nor hears,* unless on compulsion" (*Life,* ch. xix, 2).

**20.**—Suarez. He gives as a fact of experience that "ecstatics sometimes seem to have neither pulse *nor heart-beat.* And further it is with difficulty that any remnant of vital heat is detected in them; they have the appearance of death" (*De Orat.,* Book II, ch. xviii, No. 6).

**21.**—Scaramelli. After speaking of the alienation of the five senses and of the absence of movement, he continues:

"Whatever certain people may say about it, the other vital actions do not cease in ecstasy: such as nutrition, the circulation of the blood, the beating of the heart, and respiration; although these operations become very weak and are carried on remarkably slowly. For the *beating of the heart* is very feeble and the respiration is so slight that it is very difficult to distinguish it, as is *clearly* deduced from numerous experiments made with great care upon ecstatic persons" (Tr. 3, No. 181).

When the ecstasy is at its intense period, "the imagination remains drowsy, without calling up any images, and it is the same with the sensitive appetite"; this occurs even in the case of the full union (*ibid.,* No. 182).

### § 2. Sufferings Due to Invisible Stigmata

**22.**—St. Mary Magdalen of Pazzi received the invisible stigmata at nineteen years of age on Monday in Holy Week (1585). "Three days after... on Holy Thursday in the evening... she was again rapt, and remained in rapture for 26 hours successively... witnessing all the Passion, step by step, and enduring most acute pains, not only in mind but also physically, being found worthy to share in soul and body the torments of the holy Passion of Our Lord. This same favour was renewed seven years after on Holy Thursday (1592)... the spectators clearly saw all that they wrote explained and illustrated by all her movements, gestures, words, and actions" (*Vie,* by Cepari, ch. v, English trs., Oratorian Series, ch. xxxv, p. 127).

**23.**—A letter from the Ven. Anne Madeleine de Rémuzat:

"Some days ago, during prayer, Our Lord offered me the choice between these two alternatives: either the marks with which He deigns to honour me should appear outwardly, which would diminish my pains and would lead men to bless Him for His marvels; or these marks, remaining always hidden, the pains would become more violent, by which He would be yet further glorified. I then had no other inclination than that of giving myself up to whatever would most contribute to my Saviour's glory, and I besought Him to choose Himself. He did so, and His choice fell upon the increase of sufferings; but what sufferings! I cannot explain them except by my powerlessness to do so" (*Vie,* published by the Visitation at Marseilles, ch. xv, p. 329).

# CHAPTER XIV

## Twelfth Characteristic of the Mystic Union: the Ligature

### § 1. General Aspect

**1.**—The **twelfth character** consists in this, that the mystic *union impedes, to a greater or lesser degree,* the production of certain *interior acts* which could be produced at will in ordinary prayer. I will go into the matter more fully later on (**12, 24**).

**2.**—This impediment is called the **ligature** of the faculties (Bossuet, *États d'Oraison,* Book VII, No. 21), and, when it is very strong, *the suspension* of the faculties.

This last word does not signify *suppression* (as when we say that a certain action is suspended), but that the faculties are no longer applied to their ordinary object. They are seized upon, *riveted,* by a higher object.

The word *ligature* indicates that the soul is in the condition of a man whose limbs are *bound* more or less tightly by bands, and who can only therefore move with difficulty.

**3.**—**The exigence** of the ligature in ecstasy is as obvious as possible. Save in exceptional cases, one thing only can be done: to *receive* what God gives. We are *bound* with regard to all beside.

Consequently we *foresee* that there will be something analogous in the prayer of quiet, which is a lesser ecstasy; the law of continuity renders this idea *a priori* probable. And the expectation is so fully confirmed by experience that the question is one in which mystics have been most deeply interested. It has, as we shall find, many practical consequences.

**4.**—**In the prayer of quiet** we do not begin to take real notice of this impediment until the day when the mystic grace surprises us during vocal prayer, which it tends to interrupt; or when, not finding sufficient occupation in our prayer, we endeavour to complete it by reflections or vocal prayers. We are then conscious of an obstacle.

**5.—True signification.** In the prayer of quiet, the ligature does not amount to an absolute impossibility. Thus we can *begin* to recite a vocal prayer such as the *Paternoster,* But after two or three words, some unknown and secret force often stops us. We hesitate and stammer. A new effort then enables us to resume, and so it goes on. We should soon be weary if we attempted to continue the struggle. The proper course is to resign ourselves, as I shall say later on.

**6.**—When we are in the degree of meditation we find nothing resembling this obstacle. We may not, perhaps, feel an *inclination* to recite a vocal prayer. But that is an impression of a very different kind; and the effort to begin once made, we can generally continue without difficulty. But the opposite occurs here.

Even the partial powerlessness that occurs in aridity is less marked.

**7.—Intensity.** The ligature is weak when the prayer of quiet is weak. They generally increase together in strength during the course of the same prayer. But, in process of time, the prayer of quiet acts rather less than at the beginning. The impression of repose that accompanies the prayer of quiet equally becomes strengthened as the union itself becomes stronger. It is very likely that this impression is an effect of the ligature.

St. John of the Cross points out that there is a first beginning of the ligature in the state, slightly lower than the prayer of quiet, which he calls the *night of the senses* (see ch. xv).

**8.—What does it affect?** Let us examine in detail the acts with regard to which this impediment is felt. They are those that I have previously called *additional acts* (ch. ix, 13).

Further, it is only a question of *voluntary* acts, such as the recitation of a vocal prayer. But if it is God who is producing these additional acts in the soul, the thought of a Christian truth, for example, no difficulty is experienced. Nor does the ligature, when occurring in a weak degree, oppose any obstacle to another class of involuntary thoughts; namely, distractions. We have seen that these, unhappily, are not always prevented.

And this is a fact worthy of notice: in the prayer of quiet there is one rule of action for voluntary and another for involuntary thoughts. The one (which, however, appear to be useful) are hampered; the others (which are certainly harmful) find no impediment.

**9.**—We can **enunciate** the foregoing principles **under another form by** saying: the mystic state usually has a *tendency* to exclude everything that is foreign to it, especially such things as proceed from our own industry, our own effort.

**10.**—Finally, also, we may give this **definition** of the ligature: it is an impediment experienced with regard to the *voluntary* production of additional acts during the mystic state.

**11.**—The impediment may affect two kinds of additional acts: prayers and reflections. I will examine these facts separately, and afterwards point out the rules that should be followed.

### § 2. Some Facts Concerning Prayer, Whether Interior or Vocal

**12.**—With regard to the prayer of quiet, **four cases** may occur over and above those where it is very weak (**7**). For proofs of their existence, see Extracts.

**13.**—1° If it is a question of *very simple desires,* of *short and wordless petitions,* there is no difficulty as a rule. We can introduce them here and there in our prayer, provided that this is not done too frequently. We can thus send up a crowd of desires to God.

**14.**—2° Let us now consider such petitions or affections as are *purely interior,* but *formulated in words.*

We have almost as much facility here as in the first case, so long as these utterances are *very short* and are repeated *without variation,* such as: "Jesus, mercy." Acts that are not varied adapt themselves well enough to the mystic repose.

**15.**—3° But it is otherwise with regard to *recitations,* properly so called; made, that is to say, *vocally,* although in a low tone of voice; for these suppose *long and varied* phrases. They can only be said conveniently when the prayer of quiet is weak. Also there are times when we are unable to recite the Rosary or the Breviary while standing still. We are obliged to move about; to walk, as has been said elsewhere (ch. xiii, **8**). In this way the prayer of quiet is, as a rule, warded off sufficiently to enable us to perform our exercises.

**16.**—**Exception.** And yet, if there is a great abundance of graces, it is sometimes impossible to regain a full freedom of action, as happens in the case of ecstatics in the intervals between their ecstasies.

St. Catherine of Ricci, having entered her convent at the age of thirteen, was subjected, during two or three years, to great humiliations on account of her extraordinary union with God. She was drawn to Him so powerfully that she seemed like a person half asleep, showing aptitude neither for the Choir nor for manual labour, and appearing stupid at recreation. Nobody suspected the cause of this abstraction; she let herself be accused without making any defence, not knowing that she ought to have opened her heart at least to her Director. So that they treated her as if she were some gentle and harmless idiot who is allowed to be at large (*Vie,* by Fr. Bayonne, Vol. I, chs. iv, vi; English: *Life,* by F. M. Capes, ch. iv, pp. 32-3).

St. Philip Neri was often unable to say his Office unless he took alternate sentences with a companion. "Otherwise," says his historian, "he experienced great difficulty. For the ecstasy seized him, and he lost himself in God"

(Bolland., May 26th, No. 183 of the second *Life.*) St. Joseph of Cupertino could not manage to say his Office.* St. Ignatius was dispensed from it for the same reason.† He was compelled to interrupt his Mass several times, so that it took him at least an hour, in spite of his wish to observe the limit of half an hour which he had fixed for his Religious. In the above instances, the case for dispensation from the Breviary is just as good a one as that arising from a sick headache or any other illness.

**17.**—It is well to be acquainted with the examples of these three saints, for they meet an **objection** that is sometimes heard. "If your prayer thus prevents your performing exercises that are of obligation, it cannot come from God, for if it did He would be contradicting Himself."

The answer is that God is no more contradicting Himself here than when He sends an illness that hinders the hearing of Sunday Mass or keeping the Friday abstinence. When a law of the Church is morally impossible of execution, it ceases to oblige. God would be contradicting Himself only were He still to impose the obligation while taking away the power of fulfilling it.‡

**18.**—4° **Recitations made aloud.** Here the faculty returns in a great measure. Priests generally find no serious difficulty in reciting the prayers of the Mass.§

How can this be, when we said just now that there is a difficulty in the case of vocal prayers recited in a low voice?

The reason is that when these prayers are said aloud there are a great many movements of the chest, throat, etc. In reading, too, the eyes are in motion.

* Sometimes by the evening he had not said his Office, although he had been turning over the leaves of his Breviary all day (*Vie* by Mgr. Bernino, ch. xxii). In the Acts of Canonisation we read: "For more than thirty-five years his superiors were obliged to exclude Brother Joseph from the ceremonies of the choir, from processions, and the refectory, because he upset the exercises by his raptures" (*ibid.*, ch. iv).

"It was a miracle that amidst all his ecstasies the saint should have been able to finish his Mass. As soon as he had done so... he flew rather than walked to his cell. Reaching it he uttered a cry, threw himself upon his knees and fell into an ecstasy" (*ibid.*).

† *Life* of St. Ignatius, by Bartoli, Book IV, ch. xii, translated into French by Fr. Terrien (Paris, Lefort). The same thing is related of St. Ignatius in the *Life* of Fr. Balthasar Alvarez, ch. xli, No. 6: "The day scarcely sufficed him for the fulfilment of this single obligation."

‡ Joseph a Spiritu Sancto occupies eighteen folio pages in the attempt to prove that such a prayer is open to suspicion (*Cursus,* Vol. III, disp. 18, q. 3, No. 151). One of his strongest arguments is drawn from the facts. He says that this condition has never occurred with canonised saints (No. 169). Now I have just given three examples to the contrary. But he recognised that the condition has been found in others than the saints, properly so-called (No. 152), and that various doctors have held wider views than his own (No. 172). Finally, and contrary to expectation, he does not venture to draw any practical conclusions, unless it be that we should suffer this kind of prayer to continue, but with a certain mistrust. And those who have the prayer of quiet ask for nothing else. To be left in peace is all that they want.

§ And yet St. Philip Neri, who experienced the mystic union in a very intense degree, found a difficulty here. In order to repress these transports he was in the habit of turning from right to left and rubbing his head violently with his hand (Bolland., May 26th. 1st *Life,* No. 23). "At other times he made such violent efforts to repress his fervour that his whole body fluttered and made the predellæ of the altar tremble." But the ecstasy frequently overpowered him, and "the server was obliged to pull him by the chasuble and remind him of the epistle or the gospel" (*The Life of St. Philip Neri,* edited by Fr. F. T. Antrobus, Vol. I. p. 145).

This, as we have said, is itself an obstacle to the prayer of quiet in any intense degree.

And, further, in saying Mass there are changes of position between all the prayers. And, finally, the fact of standing erect, often with the arms raised, of itself demands a slight but continuous effort, which is sufficient to prevent a strong absorption in God. And the same man who cannot recite his Rosary during the day without a great effort can say his Mass quite easily.

**19.**—It is the same with **singing the Office in choir.** Wishing to inform myself as to the facts (instead of trusting to *a priori* ideas), I have made various inquiries on this subject in convents of the Contemplative Orders.

The *most usual reply* has been that a slight impediment exists, but is easily overcome; a material recitation of the words can, at any rate, be accomplished, the attention being mainly fixed upon the divine interior action.

Others, but as a rare exception only, have stated that the impediment might be very strong; and others, again, on the contrary, have said that they had never heard of this difficulty.

Further inquiries into this question are very desirable.

**20.**—The first of these replies, then, would seem to give the best representation of the **habitual facts.** These once accepted, it remains to give the reason.

The explanation is the same as above. During the recitation in common, or in singing, the body executes a number of movements; the lungs are actively employed, the eyes are attentive to the text, and are continually in motion. And then the verses of the Psalms are only said alternately. Consequently, the efforts required, instead of being continuous, are made easier by a series of short pauses. The noise going on all around contributes to prevent a very strong union. But it also affords a special facility for recitation, and thus helps the struggle against the ligature. For it is rhythmic, and it therefore carries us along with it and produces a need to imitate it. Physiologists tell us that movements become in this way automatic, because the rhythmic sounds act directly upon our organs. There is no longer any necessity for a great effort of the will, and there is consequently more facility.*

**20** *bis.*—Where a person experiences great difficulty with regard to the recitation in common, we should not **reproach** him, for he does not deserve it. And, further, in the case of certain impressionable souls, this method might have quite the opposite effect to that which was intended; the emotion produced by the fear of fresh rebukes would paralyse them still more, And still less should we persuade them that they have not the vocation to a contemplative Order. We must trust in God and in time to put everything right.

* It is largely for this reason that regiments are obliged to march in step with a band at the head. The instruments produce a physiological effect, even when they are as simple as the drum and fife.

**21.**—**Restrictions that should be noted.** Let us note that the preceding facts would be inaccurately expressed by this simple formula: *the prayer of quiet hinders the saying of vocal prayers.* Broadly speaking, this proposition is true enough; but in order to be quite accurate, I have been obliged to add certain modifications bearing either upon the *intensity* of the prayer of quiet (**12**), or upon the *nature of the prayers,* distinguishing four different cases. The reply varies slightly with each.

I would gladly have avoided this little complication in my explanations. But it does not rest with us to simplify facts.

**22.**—These **hard and fast formulas** have the drawback of provoking reasonable objections. And, further, they lead to chimerical rules of conduct, for these rules then respond to cases of conscience which do not exist in practice.

**23.**—**Praying quietude.** We have seen that, with regard to certain acts, there is more or less *liberty* and no ligature of the faculties. At times we even experience the opposite condition to the ligature; this is the *impulsion* of the faculties. For instance, some request formulates itself almost irresistibly and we have then what may be called the *praying quietude.* This shooting impulse presents a curious contrast to the repose that we continue to feel. One would say that it was the play of a fountain issuing from some tranquil pool.

**23** *bis.*—I said also (ch. xi, 7) that there is a state called jubilation. The soul then feels a need to overflow in ardent colloquies, or even to break out into singing. When this occurs in the prayer of quiet, it is another partial exception to the ligature. We may call this species the **quietude of jubilation.**

St. Teresa points out that a similar case may occur in the full union; we speak, compose verses, etc. (*Life,* ch. xvi, p. 124, on the third state of prayer). See also 63 *bis.*

### § 3. Some Facts Regarding the Thoughts and Reflections

**24.**—Various cases have to be considered. Here again we must carefully avoid such hard and fast propositions as this: the prayer of quiet prevents our thinking of Our Lord, of His mysteries, or of the virtues.

Let us take **four different cases,** still leaving on one side that in which the prayer of quiet is very weak.

**25.**—1° It is generally easy, during the prayer of quiet, to think of Our Lord's *Person,* or of that of a saint, provided that it is done *simply* and without reasonings and that there are interruptions. We can thus produce acts of love towards Our Saviour from time to time.

**26.**—2° With certain persons, or at certain times, it is the same with regard to the *mysteries,* provided that they look at them in a *simple manner,* calling lovingly to mind Our Lord's interior dispositions, for example, or those of the Blessed Virgin upon such or such an occasion.

**27.**—3° The contrary occurs if we wish to turn our attention to any *developments* or to the reviewing of the circumstances of some historic fact. Unless the mind turns as of its own accord to these considerations, we should then find a real resistance.

**28.**—4° When the *period of ecstasy* is reached (sometimes even before this time), a great facility for the contemplation of these mysteries is again experienced. But this depends upon God, whether He sends a special light or no, and not upon the reappearance of the reasoning faculty.

We then see several different things in one and the same ray of light, which is a simple one; our own efforts could not achieve this. In the same way, in Heaven, we shall have several simultaneous kinds of knowledge without any research.

**29.**—**Consequence.** From this last remark it follows that the prayer of quiet should be regarded as a period of transition in which certain exercises become difficult, but only temporarily so. If we mount higher we find them again, and that under a more perfect form.

**30.**—**Accusations of idleness.** This accusation has often been levelled against the prayer of quiet. There is an apparent foundation for this charge. The rather marked absence of images and acts of reasoning seems, at first sight, to leave the soul slightly empty, and the ligature appears to heighten this lack of occupation. And then, too, nothing new is learnt in the way of doctrine.

**31.**—**Reply.** 1° The soul, on the contrary, has a *very perfect occupation:* that of thinking of God, feeling Him present and loving Him; and this without counting all the reflections that come of their own accord to join themselves on to this state. We need only repeat here what has been said concerning the same objection as applied to the prayer of simplicity (ch. ii, **43**).

2° We shall see that *this occupation is the best* that could be desired. People fancy that the practical resolutions will lack force because they are not led up to by numerous reflections. This is an error which has already been refuted in connection with the prayer of simplicity. But it is even more evidently false here. For we have seen that the supernatural degrees of prayer are accompanied by virtues produced without any reflections of our own (ch. xii). We accumulate a reserve of spiritual energy. If the soul seems idle, God is not so.

Let us take another comparison, showing this hidden action. Anæmic subjects often resort to an air-cure as a treatment. They go to the country, or the seaside, or the mountains, and there they simply fill their lungs with pure air. They are apparently idle, but their surroundings exercise a hidden action upon them, which transforms them without their knowing how. And it is the same in the mystic state. We seem sometimes to be doing scarcely anything; but we are plunged in a divine atmosphere, which acts upon us. It is life-giving; and in it the feeble soul recovers her strength. It is warm; and the frozen soul begins to burn with love. It is a treatment that is quite unlike the common way, but none the less good for that. And then, how should it be otherwise? Why should

God depart from His ordinary rules in order to communicate Himself to this soul if it were not to advance her in sanctity?

Is God going to work for the soul's amusement only, without requiring any practical fruit of her? The unlearned need have no anxiety about this so-called idleness. The soul is in good hands. She needs but to correspond to grace.

**32.**—When, after having been Confessor to St. Teresa, Father Balthasar Alvarez became Master of Novices, he had to weather a great storm on the subject of the apparent idleness of the prayer of simplicity and the supernatural states. Some of his brethren denounced him to his General as teaching a profitless kind of prayer.

"They suspected him of despising the method of praying by reasonings and meditations, which is practised in the Society of Jesus and is approved by the saints, and of wishing to conduct our subjects by other strange and dangerous modes of prayer." Father Balthasar Alvarez then drew up a formal apology, a great part of which has been preserved in his *Life* by the Ven. Louis du Pont (ch. xl), and which received the approbation of the General. Let us hope that this refutation, and so many others that have succeeded it, will prevent this discussion being renewed.

### § 4. The Three Rules of Conduct Relating to the Ligature

**33.**—Here are three general rules similar to those that have been given for the prayer of simplicity.

**34.**—**First rule**, concerning those acts which the ligature renders *difficult* in ever so slight a degree during prayer: we must never do violence to ourselves in order to produce them. In a word, we must accept God's action just as it is, instead of resisting it.

**35.**—**Reasons**. Because if we did otherwise, we should be struggling to no purpose. We might succeed for a moment, but not for longer. The only definite result would be that we should have fatigued ourselves and have interrupted the supernatural state. All mystics agree in laying down this rule; there is not one that is more universally accepted.

The action of the will upon the ligature may be compared to its action upon our respiration. We can accelerate or retard it, but only within certain limits, and if we exceed these limits it is only momentarily; it is a struggle, and causes fatigue.

**36.**—If the prayer of quiet is **very weak**, the difficulty arising from the ligature is hardly felt. But in order to apply the third rule, it is enough that we have no taste for certain acts during prayer. For we are then drawing near to the prayer of simplicity, and this broad rule has already been given for it. It applies here even more necessarily.

Scrupulous people will object that their case is often *doubtful.* They do not know whether their want of inclination and facility do not proceed from idleness.

The answer is that, when in doubt, we have the right to do as we like. We may incline without scruple, then, to the side that we prefer. And they will probably prefer the repose. And then, practically, this doubt will not occur if we take a rapid survey of a sufficient number of devotions together.

**37.—Another** very important **reason** for the first rule is sometimes given. It is that conformity to the will of God requires that we should not resist His action.* This argument was already applicable to the prayer of simplicity. For God's will showed itself there by the taste and the facility that were experienced and by the difficulty of changing our methods. But in the prayer of quiet these reasons are even more forcible. God not only gives the attraction, but He introduces a new element; not only have we a leaning towards a discontinuation of all movement, but we feel this to be *inevitable.* If the difficulty arising from the prayer that God sends us were merely an insignificant one, we could more easily suppose that He asks us to surmount it. What makes the divine design so clear is that our only choice lies between leaving our prayer altogether or taking it as it is.

**38.—Consequences** of this rule. 1° With regard to *prayers* that are *not of obligation,* they may be omitted without scruple when a difficulty is experienced. And the same will hold good in all non-essential acts, in examinations of conscience and other exercises. At other times they served to excite devotion, but they may now become an obstacle to a more perfect union. And, again, we are not to force ourselves with regard to readings that fatigue us and for which we no longer feel any inclination.

2° On the other hand, with prayers *that are of obligation,* we shall strive, without any violence, to accomplish them. We shall begin to walk to and fro, for instance.

3° The director should not insist upon *great efforts* being made with the object of producing the acts of ordinary prayer. Those who give such orders do so in good faith, but show their ignorance of mysticism. Or else they think the struggle a very slight one, or that the ligature proceeds from the Devil. These are errors. See St. John of the Cross with regard to directors (*Living Flame,* Stanza III, line 3: especially § 11 and following).

**39.—Second rule,** concerning those acts for which we feel *a facility* when at prayer: it is advisable to accept them. But if we do not do so, our action must, at any rate, not be the result of a preconceived determination, we must not say to

* St. Francis of Sales laid great stress upon this. See the comparison of the statue, for instance (*Treatise on the Love of God,* Book VI, ch. xi).

According to the context, the saint applies it to the prayer of simplicity equally with the true prayer of quiet.

ourselves with pride: The thought of Our Lord or of the virtues is an exercise for beginners; contemplation of the Divine Being alone is henceforth sufficient for me. Or again: The exclusion of any remembrance of Our Lord is the road leading to contemplation; this remembrance would be an obstacle to it.

This was the language of the quietists. They held that souls desirous of attaining to perfection should *a priori* prohibit all *distinct thoughts* and *desires* in their prayer. We have seen that our first rule is based not on this absurd system, but upon the moral impossibility in which we find ourselves of producing these acts. This reason vanishes, therefore, when the impossibility itself disappears. There is then no further reason for remaining inactive.

**40.**—It is advisable, on the contrary, *to add our action to the divine actions, in such a measure as not to hamper it.* This **maxim** sums up the two preceding rules.

Thus, during the prayer of quiet, we shall go forward gently. With regard to distinct affections, we shall be consent to produce those for which we feel an inclination and at such times as we feel it.

**41.**—The quietists spoke with contempt of **Our Lord's Sacred Humanity** and of His mysteries. They wished these subjects of contemplation to be put on one side. This doctrine is contrary to the spirit of the Church, for she invites us throughout the year to celebrate in her Feasts the principal events of Our Lord's life.

It is ingratitude, too, light-heartedly and systematically to forget Him to whom we owe everything, including this supernatural prayer which is so precious for our sanctification.

Finally, the object of supernatural prayer should be to give us a love of suffering. Now, according to the opinions of the masters, the chief means of attaining to this end is by thinking often and with love of Our Saviour's Passion.

Even during St. Teresa's lifetime, the *illuminati* of Spain, the precursors of Falconi and Molinos, were preaching quietism (1575). The Spanish Inquisition brought about their partial disappearance; Fr. Balthasar Alvarez refuted their teachings. Their twelfth proposition recommended that the Sacred Humanity should not be made a subject of meditation.

**42.**—**Breadth of Application.** If, at such or such a time, we find difficulty in thinking of Our Lord, or in praying to Him, we must not be uneasy. All that is asked is:

1° That Our Saviour should play an important part, and the greatest possible part, in our spiritual life *as a whole.* It is not a question of any particular hour;

2° That there should be no obstinate exclusion on our part. Instead of rejoicing in this difficulty, as if it were a perfection, we should regret it as a natural infirmity and look forward to the time when we shall recover our freedom.

**43.**—**St. Teresa** states that she was for some time under a delusion upon this point (*Life,* ch. xxii). She adds that since then certain pious persons had seemed to her to have false ideas also, but that the divergence of opinion between her and them was perhaps apparent only (*Interior Castle,* Sixth Mansion, ch. vii).

When we read her writings upon this subject with care, we see that she did not ask that persons should force themselves in prayer (first rule), but simply that they should observe the other two rules.

**44.**—**Third rule,** which is to be followed when we *are not* at prayer: there are many moments in every day when the ligature is not so strong as to hinder us from praying or thinking of Our Lord and the virtues. We must take advantage of them.

The opportunity will often be afforded by reading, sermons, or the public Offices of the Church.

**45.**—These rules enable us to reconcile (which appears difficult at first) the *powerlessness* caused by the mystic state with the *duty* of honouring and loving Our Lord Jesus Christ.

## § 5. Various Remarks

**46.**—The **anxieties** of beginners. We have seen that when beginners are uninstructed, the mystic state causes them various kinds of anxieties (ch. ii, **48**; v. **18**). The ligature is a new cause of fear to them. "Not only am I idle (they say to themselves), but something hinders my praying. This action can only come from the Devil."

No; prayer does not become open to suspicion because of the ligature. And we may go farther, and say that if it were never felt we should have to admit that, in all probability, we were not in the mystic state, since we should be without one of its most invariable characters. God, however, is of course free to make exceptions here.

**47.**—**The influence of exterior occupations.** These usually hamper the prayer of quiet and cause it to disappear, even when the part taken by the body is very small. This is the case with conversations or reading. But God gives a special grace at times, so that these two very different occupations persist together for a considerable time. St. Teresa is astonished at this, and remarks that one is wholly attentive to neither of the two subjects (see Extracts, No. 63). This mixed state may be called the *acting prayer of quiet.** It is only in a degree bordering upon the *spiritual marriage* that the two operations cease to impede each other.

**48.**—In **Church,** however, the prayer of quiet is not hampered by any well-rendered music which we hear with pleasure. These strains, which indirectly, at any rate, excite to divine love, blend easily with the supernatural action. The two form a soothing whole which leads on to God. This facility forms a contrast

* I have already distinguished three other varieties of the prayer of quiet; the one silent (ch. ix, 24), another praying (ch. xiv, 23) and another, again, of jubilation (ch. xiv, 23 bis).

to the irritation caused at other times by the comings and goings of the faithful, and the scrapings of their chairs on the floor.

If we listen to a preacher, rather more effort is required to follow him. But the difference is not great, for it is still a question of receiving only.

**48** *bis*—Can we say that the ligature exists in the most ordinary form of the prayer of simplicity, that which is not as yet the night of the senses (of which we shall speak later)? I reply that such an expression would be somewhat exaggerated. For, firstly, the constraint experienced affects considerably fewer acts than in the mystic union. No obstacle is felt to vocal prayers, but only to long trains of varied considerations and reasonings. Secondly, it is less intense; there is a lack of relish rather than any great difficulty.

In the first night of the senses we are already approaching more closely to the ligature in its proper sense.

## EXTRACTS

### § 1. On the Difficulty in Reciting Prayers or Making Reflections During the Prayer of Quiet (Description and Rules)

**49.**—St. Teresa describing the prayer of quiet:

1° "For even speaking *wearies* it,—I mean by this, *vocal prayer* and *meditation;* it would do nothing but love" (*Relation VIII,* 4, to Fr. Rodrigo Alvarez, *Life,* p. 456).

2° "In a word, *mental prayer* is not to be abandoned *altogether* now, nor even vocal *prayer,* if *at any time* we wish to, or *can,* make use of either of them; for if the state of quiet be profound, it becomes difficult to speak, and it can be done only *with great pain*" (*Life,* ch. xv, 14).

3° "It is a kind of *mortifying interiorly* and exteriorly, so that the exterior man (I mean the body, that ye may the better understand me) would not stir at all... Speaking *troubles* them [the faculties]: in saying only one *Paternoster* they will sometimes spend an hour" (*The Way of Perfection,* ch. xxxi, p. 93).

4° During the prayer of quiet, "It is good... at the most, to let fall, at times, some sweet word, as one that gives a blast to a candle, when he sees it out, to kindle it again; which if it be burning, serves but only to extinguish it" (*Way of Perfection,* ch. xxxi, p. 95).

5° "In mystical theology—of which I spoke before—the understanding ceases from its acts, *because God suspends it*" (*Life,* ch. xii, 8). It is the prayer of quiet which is spoken of here and of which the saint has said in ch. x, 1: "I believe it was what is called mystical theology."

6° "When God suspends all the powers of the soul,—as we see He does in the states of prayer already described,—it is clear that, whether we wish it or not, *this presence* [the sacred Humanity] is withdrawn. *Be it so, then.* The loss is a blessed one, because it takes place in order that we may have a deeper fruition of what we seem to have lost" (*Life,* ch. xxii, 12).

7° "The method of prayer I observe at present is this: when I am in prayer, it is very rarely that I can use the understanding, because the soul becomes at once recollected, remains in repose, or falls into a trance" (*Relation I,* to St. Peter of Alcantara, in 1560, *Life,* p. 403).

**50.**—St. John of the Cross:

"Whenever God is anointing a soul with the unction of loving knowledge, most delicate, serene, peaceful, lonely, strange to sense and imagination [such a collection of qualities is only found in the mystic state]; whenever He withholds all sweetness from it and *suspends its power of meditation*—because He *reserves it* for this lonely unction, inclined to solitude and quiet—a spiritual director will appear, who, like a rough blacksmith, knows only the use of his hammer, and who, because all his knowledge is limited to the coarser work, will say to it: Come, get rid of this, this is waste of time and idleness: *arise and meditate,* resume thine interior acts, for it is necessary that thou shouldest make diligent efforts of thy own..." (*The Living Flame of Love,* Stanza III, line 3, § 8, p. 273-4).

Second Rule (**39**).

"He [God] produces them [distinct acts] sometimes specifically in the soul, and that for some space of time. And in that case the soul too must be lovingly intent upon God *without specifically eliciting other acts beyond those to which He inclines it;* it must be, as it were, passive, making no efforts of its own, purely, simply, and lovingly intent upon God, as a man who opens his eyes with loving attention" (*Living Flame,* Stanza III, line 3, § 6, p. 269).

**51.**—St. Catherine of Siena. One of her historians says:

"When her soul had made some progress in contemplation, vocal prayers *ceased little by little.* At last her raptures came to such a point that she could not finish the Lord's Prayer without falling into an ecstasy" (Bolland., April 30th, No. 113).

**52.**—Ven. Blosius: conduct to be observed with regard to additional acts:

"Observe well, a soul cannot arrive at this intimate union with God unless it hath become entirely pure and simple, and thus hath a likeness to God... Lastly, every image and thought of perishable things, yea, even a thought about the angels, or even of the passion of Christ, and any intellectual reflection *impedes* a man in this mortal life when he desires to rise to mystical union with God, Who is above all substance and all intellect. *At the moment,* therefore, when God deigns to raise a soul to union with Himself, holy thoughts and images of any kind, *though at other times most useful to be received and entertained,* are to be avoided and left, because they in some degree stand between the soul and God. Wherefore, the spiritual man who desires to attain to this union, directly he feels himself vehemently inflamed and drawn upwards by the love of God, should cast out all images from the mind, and should betake himself to the

Holy of Holies, and to that internal silence in which there is no longer human, but only divine working" (*A Book of Spiritual Instruction,* ch. xii, section iii, No. 1, pp. 104-6).

**52** *bis.*— St. Francis of Sales; first rule (34).

"Wherefore, when you shall find yourself in this simple and pure filial confidence with Our Lord, *stay there,* my dear Theotimus, *without moving yourself* to make sensible acts, either of the understanding or of the will; for this *simple love* of confidence, and this love-sleep of your spirit in the arms of the Saviour contains by excellence all that you go seeking hither and thither to satisfy your taste; it is better to sleep upon this sacred breast than to watch elsewhere, wherever it be" (*Treatise on the Love of God,* Book VI, ch. viii, p. 256).

**53.**—Ven. Bartholomew of the Martyrs (O. P.):

"Many persons have thought that this exceedingly pure union may be disturbed by all kinds of images, even by those that, in themselves, are most useful and had formerly produced excellent dispositions in the soul; such as representations of the mysteries of the Incarnate Word, or the thought of the divine attributes. But we must accept this with discretion, for fear of falling into error. If they mean to say that the soul, resting in and tasting this pure union, should not persist in seeking for them or in retaining them for any length of time, but should rather close the eyes of the spirit to such objects, well, yes, I allow that *this doctrine is generally correct.* But if they go to the length of claiming that these images *always* hamper or impede the vigour and perfection of the union, I think that it is false. In fact, experience shows that often, when the soul goes out to God with fervour, a thought suddenly presents itself to the mind. For example: 'This God became man for me, and was crucified.' Not only does such a thought not hinder the union, but it contributes to strengthen the love and the admiration which enter into the union" (*Abrégé de la doctrine mystique,* ch. xi, § 2; quoted by Fr. Meynard, Vol. II, No. 125).

**54.**—Blessed Mary of the Incarnation, Carmelite (Mme. Acarie): "This attraction, which she had from the age of twenty-two, not only prevented her from reading, but also *from praying vocally,* having so little power in this respect that she could not say more than a single Latin *Ave* without great difficulty. Walking out in the meadows with her, I have seen her begin to recite her Rosary with her eldest daughter, and be unable to say the first *Ave* without at once going out of herself. An interior recollection instantly took possession of her and prevented her continuing. Her daughter was in no way astonished, for she knew that this was habitual with her. She spoke two or three words of what she had to say close to her mother's ear; but upon receiving no reply, she went on with it alone. This is why B. Mary's confessors found it difficult to give her a penance in confession; so much so, that they sometimes, knowing how difficult vocal prayer was to her, imposed these two words only: Jesus, Mary, or some alms, or that she should prostrate herself on the ground. This was one of the causes that deterred her from being professed [as a Carmelite]. For although the lay-sisters, of which she was one, had not much Office to say, they still had too much for her, and it was impossible for her to manage it. She was dispensed from it by her Superiors,... however she never omitted it, and always said all that was enjoined on those of her condition, although she experienced *very great difficulty*" (*Vie*, by André du Val, Book II, ch. xiii).

"When she was young, she was often constrained to shut herself up in her chamber, as much for the sake of hiding the strong attractions that came to her, as to prevent their great impetuosity. *She then began walking rapidly* to and fro, rubbing her hands and arms, or applying herself steadily to some difficult piece of work... Sometimes she took her spinet, which she played very well, not in order to draw down upon herself the divine motion, as we read in the case of certain saints, but rather to prevent it, and to distract herself from it" (*Ibid.*, Book I, ch. iii.)

**55.**—Ven. Mary of the Incarnation, Ursuline:

1° She tells of the mystic states that she experienced before she became a religious:

"I was no longer able to *pray vocally*. If I tried to recite my Rosary, my spirit was at once rapt, and I could no longer *utter a word*. It was the same with the Office. Sometimes, however, the hidden meaning of the Psalms was suddenly communicated to me with an indescribable unction, and I could then recite them. For my reading, my confessor had given me the works of St. Teresa. I sometimes found solace in them; but sometimes, again, reading was *impossible* for me, on account of the great interior recollection of which I have been speaking" (*Histoire*, by the Abbé Chaput, Part I, ch. iv).

2° "No matter what subject of prayer I may take, although I have read it or heard it read with the greatest attention, I forget it. It is not that, at the beginning of my prayer, I do not *consider* the mystery [with a simple regard], for I am powerless to meditate, but I find myself in a moment, and without any reflecting upon it, in my ordinary place, wherein my soul contemplates God, in Whom she is" (Letter of October 8th, 1671, to her son).

**56.**—Bossuet:

1° Mme. de Maisonfort wrote to him: "It would seem that amongst the persons who are in this simple prayer, some have no difficulty with vocal prayers, *others have a great deal*, and some again suffer from a kind of *impossibility*. It is said that Mother Mary of the Incarnation, who established the Carmelites in France, could not say a *Pater* from beginning to end" (Letter I, No. II, Vol. XXVII of the Lachat ed., p. 325). Bossuet replies: "I believe these dispositions to be very real in souls."

2° In the following passage and some others, Bossuet uses a slightly exaggerated expression to describe the ligature. He calls it a *powerlessness*. It is often only a *difficulty*. He, however, modifies his language elsewhere, when he says that this powerlessness "is not always absolute" (*Ibid.*, Letter XII, No. XII,

p. 388). He states, and this is an important point, that the existence of the ligature is admitted by all the mystics:

"This... is what we find with regard to the passive states in the writings of the approved mystics; and I reduce them to six propositions.

"*The first,* that according to them, the passive state is a state of suspension and *ligature* of the powers or intellectual faculties, in which the soul continues *powerless* to produce the *discursive acts.* We must notice this last phrase, for it is not the intention of these doctors to exclude from their prayer the free acts... which might *be formed without any reasoning;* but those acts to which we *incite ourselves* by reasoning or *previous reflection...* And there is a great change here in the soul's manner of operating. For the soul, accustomed to reasoning and to *provoke* her own affections by the *consideration of certain motives,* suddenly, as though impelled by the sovereign hand, not only reasons no longer, but further *cannot* reason; which brings *other kinds of powerlessness* during the time of prayer" (*Instuction sur les états d'oraison,* Book VII, No. 9).*

"God does not stop there, and having once withdrawn the soul from her accustomed manner [of prayer] He does with her as He pleases. Often He wills that she should merely *regard Him* with admiration, and in silence. She knows not where she is; she merely knows that all is well with her; and a peace that nothing can disturb *makes her feel that she is not far from God.* Another time she will make the ordinary acts of a Christian; at this moment she neither will *nor can* make any other act than that of remaining lost in God" (*Ibid.,* No. 11).

**57.**—Blessed Margaret Mary Alacoque:

1. "My good Master, making me feel His *divine presence* sensibly, discovers His beauties to my soul. His love *so binds at the same time all its powers,* that I am unable to say anything to Him to testify the ardour of my love, which is a torment to me, though its sweetness is so great. *I use every effort to escape from this state, but in vain.* God sees with pleasure my vain endeavours, without giving me any help... Such is my ordinary employment in prayer; though it is not what I do, but what God Himself does in me, His wretched creature. Most commonly, I finish it without knowing what I have done in it, and without making *any resolution,* petition, or offering, except that of my Jesus to His Eternal Father, thus: My God, I offer Thee Thy well-beloved Son as my thanksgiving for all the blessings Thou conferest upon me...

"But nature and self-love meanwhile assail me violently. They tell me *that I am losing my time,* and that I am in the way of perdition. This throws me

* It may seem that Bossuet should not thus have classed the ligature as the "first" character of the mystic state. But his object being the refutation of the quietists, it was necessary to begin by following them on this ground, which was their principal tenet. As to the foundation of the mystic states, he defers its study for a while: "This is not the place in which to explain *what it is that occurs* in this excellent prayer... In course of time we shall say what it is that the Holy Spirit teaches those men of God whom He has brought to the practice of this prayer" (*Ibid.,* No. 16). He did not find an opportunity of speaking of it again.

sometimes into such great trouble that I know not to whom to have recourse except to my God. I find Him ever ready to assist me to escape from this disquietude. He allows my soul to enjoy *His divine presence,* and infuses into it a peace which restores me at once to my former tranquillity. 'A child can never perish,' He says to me, 'in the arms of an Almighty Father' " (Vol. I, of the *Life,* published by the Visitation Convent at Paray-le-Monial; 2nd edition, p. 93. The note was written by St.Margaret Mary in 1673, when she was twenty-six years old, three years after she had entered the convent at Paray-le-Monial).

2. She says again, when speaking of Fr. de la Colombière: "When I had told him that my soul was pursued so closely by the Sovereign Goodness, *without regard to time or place,* that I could not pray *vocally* without doing myself *violence* so great that I sometimes remained with my mouth open *unable to pronounce a word,* and that this happened particularly whilst saying the rosary, he told me to make such efforts no more, and to confine myself to my vocal prayers of obligation, adding to them the rosary, *when I could*" (Vol. II, Mémoire addressed to P. Rolin, p. 404. Also quoted in Mgr. Bougaud's *Life* of St. Margaret Mary, ch. x. See also No. 62).

**58.**—Rev. J. B. Rousseau, O. P., on passive prayer:

"The new sufferings that you have made known to me are its marks. You sometimes find yourself so closely united to God that the powers of the soul, you say, are suspended during your prayer; so that, for the time being, *you* not only *cannot reason,* but you even feel some difficulty in turning a simple and loving gaze... upon *the Humanity of Jesus Christ,* or on *some other special object;* and you feel as though in a state of powerlessness to make short *aspirations* towards God. You add that the difficulty, under which you have been for a long period, to perform your accustomed *vocal prayers,* has not yet passed away.

"My dear brother, be not anxious about all this, it is a mark that God is drawing you to a more passive state and to a prayer of more perfect union than that which you have hitherto known" (*États d'Oraison,* letter 13).

### § 2. On the Ligature During the Prayer of Full Union

**59.**—St. Teresa:

1. "... Our Lord may put you into perfect contemplation... suspending his [the contemplative's] understanding, and binding up his thoughts, and, as they say, *taking the word out of his mouth,* that though he would, he cannot speak, but *with much difficulty*" (*Way of Perfection,* ch. xxv, p. 75).

2. "Souls whom God has led by supernatural ways and raised to perfect contemplation are right in saying they cannot practise this kind of meditation. As I said, I do not know why, but as a general rule they are unable to do so" (*Interior Castle,* Sixth Mansion, ch. vii, 14).

3. "Some people,... after Our Lord has once raised them to perfect contemplation, wish to enjoy it continually. This is impossible; still, the grace of

this state remains in their souls in such a way, that they *cannot discourse about the mysteries of the Passion and the Life of Christ* as they did before. I cannot account for this, but it is very usual for the mind thus to remain less apt for meditation" (*Interior Castle,* Sixth Mansion, ch. vii, 9).

### § 3. How There is a Way of Thinking of the Sacred Humanity of Our Lord

**60.**—St. Teresa:

1. "Our good Jesus and His most blessed Mother are too good company to be left... Besides... consolations are not so frequent in prayer, *that we have no time for this as well.* If anyone should tell me she continually enjoys them, I should feel very doubtful about it,—I mean if she is one of those who can *never* meditate on the divine mysteries" (*Interior Castle,* Sixth Mansion, ch. vii, 16).

2. This facility is restored to the soul in a higher state of prayer: "... the more the soul advances, the closer does this good Jesus bear it company" (*Interior Castle,* Sixth Mansion, ch. viii, 1).

3. "... Those whom Our Lord admits into the seventh mansion... are constantly in the company of Christ Our Lord, both in His Humanity and His Divinity" (*Interior Castle,* Sixth Mansion, ch. vii, 11).

4. "Such a soul [one raised to perfect contemplation] comprehends these mysteries [of the life of Our Lord]... in a more perfect way than do other people; so that the *mere sight* of Our Lord... suffices to detain the thoughts, not for an hour alone, but for several days. The soul dwells *in all simplicity* on the thought of Who He is,... I think this is why such souls cannot *reason* much about the Passion, and fancy they are unable to meditate on it. Those who do not *meditate on this subject, had better begin to do so*" (*Interior Castle,* Sixth Mansion, ch. vii, 14-15).

5. What the saint requires is that we should not, of set endeavour, turn our thoughts from the Sacred Humanity: "[It] is a little failure in humility, in that the soul desires to rise of itself *before* Our Lord raises *it,* and is not satisfied with meditation on so excellent a subject,—seeking to be Mary before it has laboured with Martha. If Our Lord will have a soul to be Mary, *even on the first day,* there is nothing to be afraid of; *but we must not be self-invited guests...*" (*Life,* ch. xxii, 13).

**61.**—Ven. Mary of the Incarnation, Ursuline, tells of "the new gift of prayer" that she received when she was twenty-three:

"It was a close union with Our Lord in each one of the Mysteries of His life... from His birth to His death. It was given me in this way to know, by experience, how true it is that Our Lord is the Way, the Truth, and the Life, as He has said of Himself. This divine Saviour henceforth became more and more my life and my sustenance... Not for one moment could I dispense with this celestial food of my Divine Shepherd, who operated within me ceaselessly, by a continual communication of His spirit and His life... Although I considered the Humanity united to the Divinity in this divine Saviour, my imagination had no part in it" (*Histoire*, by Abbé Chaput, Part I, ch. iv).

**62.**—Blessed Margaret Mary:

Before she became a religious, she wrote:

"He then *presented Himself to* me in the mystery in which He would have me consider Him, and He applied my mind so closely to it, holding my soul and all my powers so absorbed in Himself, that I felt no distraction. My heart felt consumed with the desire of loving Him, and this gave me an insatiable desire for Holy Communion and to share His sufferings."

She felt also the effects of the ligature, for she adds: "His goodness kept me so strongly fixed in this manner of prayer, that it took from me all taste for vocal prayers. *I could not make use* any more of vocal prayer before the Blessed Sacrament, where I felt myself so absorbed that I was never tired of being there" (Vol. II, p. 346, Mémoire addressed to P. Rolin).

### § 4. On the Persistence of the Mystic State in the Midst of Exterior Occupations

**63.**—St. Teresa:

1. The case of the prayer of quiet: "In this prayer of quiet, God sometimes doth another favour *very hard to be understood,* unless there be great experience... and I believe God oftentimes doth this favour, *together with* that other... When this quiet is great and for a long time [without any break]... unless the will were attached to something, it could not continue so long in that peace: for it happens that we go a day or two with this satisfaction, and do not understand ourselves: I speak of those that have it. And indeed they see, *they are not entirely taken up in what they do,* but that they want the main, that is the will; which seems to me to be united with God, and leaves the other faculties free that they may attend to things of His service; and for this they have then more ability; but, for treating of matters of the world, they are stupid, and fools as it were sometimes... The will is busy at her work,... and continues in her contemplation; the other two powers [understanding and memory] serve in the office of Martha; so that she and Mary go together" (*Way of Perfection,* ch. xxxi, p. 94).

2. The case of full union: "It happens at times, and indeed very often, that, the will being in union, the soul should be aware of it, and see that the will is a captive and in joy, that the will alone is abiding *in great peace,*—while, on the other hand, the understanding and the memory are so free, that they can be employed in affairs and be occupied in works of charity. I say this that you, my father, may see it is so, and understand the matter when it shall happen to yourself; at least, it carried me out of myself [by surprise], and that is the reason why I speak of it here. It differs from the prayer of quiet... though it does seem as if it were all one with it. In that prayer, the soul... is delighting in the holy repose of Mary; but in this prayer it can be like Martha also... Still, those who

arrive at this state are not *wholly masters of themselves,* and are well aware that the better part of the soul is elsewhere. It is as if we were speaking to one person, and another speaking to us at the same time, while we ourselves *are not perfectly attentive either to the one or the other.* It is a state that is most easily ascertained, and one, when attained to, that ministers great joy and contentment, and that prepares the soul in the highest degree, by observing times of solitude, or of freedom from business, for the attainment of the most tranquil quietude" (*Life,* ch. xvii, 5-6).

The saint returns elsewhere to this dual state, and says that St. Francis Borgia told her that it often happened (*Relation VIII* to Fr. Rodrigo Alvarez, *Life,* p. 456).

3. The saint refers implicitly to this mixed state, when, in her *Life,* ch. xvi, she describes the prayer of full union, and says how she sometimes, when in that state, composed verses.

**63** *bis.*—Ruysbroeck:

"The spiritual inebriation leads to many and unaccustomed actions. Some, in the abundance of happiness, break out into canticles and sing God's praises. Others shed tears of joy. Some feel an eager longing for movement in their limbs, they cannot remain still; they must run, leap, stamp their feet, clap their hands vigorously. Others show their delight by loud cries. Others, again, find all their faculties taken possession of to such an extent that they stand silent, and, as it were, melting with love" (*L'ornement des Noces,* Book II, ch. xx).

# PART III

## A Study of Each of the Degrees of the Mystic Union Separately

## CHAPTER XV

### The Two Nights of the Soul, the Borderland of the Mystic State

**1.**—Having considered the twelve characters of the mystic union, we must now study in detail each of the four stages that constitute it. This task will be performed in the following chapters; but first we must go back a little and describe a state of prayer which forms the extreme borderland separating ordinary prayer from the mystic union, properly so called. We shall even find that it contains, although secretly, something appertaining to this last state.

If I speak of it so tardily, the reason is that we cannot understand its nature properly unless our ideas are perfectly clear with regard to the prayer of quiet. We cannot speak satisfactorily of a frontier without first showing the country that lies beyond it.

**2.**—As **St. John of the Cross** has given us a careful description of this state, and has called it the first of the *two nights of the soul*, we had better explain what it is that he understands by these two nights.

He gives this name to *two successive states of prayer*, or, as he expresses himself, two degrees of the *contemplation* of God.*

* Once only he speaks of a third night, which is none other than the spiritual marriage, and which, like the dawn, precedes, he says, the vision of Heaven (*Ascent of Mount Carmel*, Book I, ch. ii, p. 11; while he alludes to it in Book II, ch. ii). The *active* part of the two first purifications (the strife against the passions and habits, even those good in themselves but which form an obstacle to the mystic union) is found chiefly in the *Ascent of Mount Carmel* (Book I, ch. i, and Book II, ch. ii). The passive part is principally described in the *Obscure Night of the Soul*. The two other treatises, *The Living Flame of Love* and *The Spiritual Canticle*, celebrate the happiness of a soul arrived at the spiritual marriage.

If we wish to avoid misconceptions as to the meaning of certain passages, we must remember that the saint often refers to the spiritual marriage, or perfect union, by the general terms *divine union*, or *union*

These states are the cause of sufferings; but the sufferings are a secondary element only, a *consequence.* People make mistakes about this sometimes, because of the difficulty of defining the exact nature of the principal element, the *contemplation* of God. They prefer only to consider the sufferings, which have nothing mysterious about them (aridity, the sight of our sins, etc.). In a word, instead of endeavouring to penetrate into the saint's real meaning, they are satisfied with adapting his language to ordinary things which are already familiar to them.

I have already alluded to these two nights (ch. iii, **14**). But we must go into the subject more fully.

### § 1. Description of the First Night

**3.—Definition.** If we judge by appearances only, by things that we can observe directly in ourselves, that is to say, the *first night* of St. John of the Cross is a prayer of simplicity, but possessing characters, and two in particular, which constitute it a special kind: 1° it is a state of aridity, either sweet and tranquil, or, more often, bitter and painful; 2° and the simple gaze is directed almost wholly and uninterruptedly towards God.*

The saint has also called this state the *night of the senses.* The first half of this expression shows that the knowledge given by God in this prayer is obscure, and that He deprives us of certain other knowledge that we possessed before; the second indicates that the divine action no longer makes use of the sensible faculties: namely, the imagination, the sensible memory, and the reasoning faculty, which last, using words as it does, employs the two other faculties. The acts that they then produce, proceed from our natural activity only.

In all this, of course, there may be variations of degree.

**4.**—We find in this state **five distinct facts,** which I shall term its elements. Two are perceived in the mind, two in the will, and the fifth is hidden (see St. John of the Cross; especially *Obscure Night,* Book I, chs. viii, ix, x, xi; *Ascent of Mount Carmel,* Book II, chs. xiii, xiv, xv). In each case I shall quote passages from the saint's writings, so that the reader can satisfy himself that I have represented his ideas correctly.

**5.—First element.** This is an *habitual aridity,* of great strength at times. Not only is there no inclination for reasoning, for following up a thought, or applying ourselves to any subject whatsoever, but the mind is powerless to do

*of love,* names which might be applied equally well to other states. The context shows this, as well as the general bearing of the treatises.

* The saint does not speak of affective prayer, or even of the prayer of simplicity in its most usual form. He places the aridity of the night of the senses immediately after ordinary meditation (*Obscure Night,* Book I, chs. viii, ix; *Living Flame,* Stanza III, line 3, § 4, 5, 6, 7).

these things, or at least it cannot *persist* in these acts. The imagination can hardly act at all, unless it be to embarrass us with distractions.*

So far there is nothing extraordinary. Those who are still in discursive prayer pass through *quite similar* periods of dearth. But what follows will be different, and will establish a distinction between the two neighbouring states.

**6.—Second element.** This is a *memory of God,*† *simple, confused,* and general,‡ returning with a singular *persistence* which is *independent of the will.* It alone escapes the powerlessness caused by aridity, and more than this, it obtrudes itself. At one time it triumphs over distractions, at another it is overcome by them. It is a continual alternation of success and failure.

**7.—Explanation.** I said that this memory is **simple.** It cannot be still further reduced. It is a thought similar to that which occurs to us when the Name of God comes up in the course of conversation. The mind does not begin reasoning in order to develop all that this idea contains. It does not enlarge upon God's attributes, His benefits, His rights, etc.; otherwise it would not be in aridity. And, much more, we learn nothing new.

**8.**—I then referred to the singular **persistence** with which this memory returns, in spite of distractions, when we are at prayer. It is the same during the day, notwithstanding exterior occupations, if we try to recollect ourselves.

In this respect the soul may best be compared to the needle of a mariner's compass. In a squall of wind, it seems to offer no resistance. But the storm once over, it returns obstinately to its original position. So, after being carried away by distractions, the mind comes back invariably to its *one and only attraction.*

So too, do the reeds bow before the blast, and then straighten themselves and lift up their heads again to the heavens.

**9.**—Finally, I said that this return often takes place **independently of the will.** For it is not from inclination that we always revert to this arid idea of God which generally has nothing pleasing about it. It recurs independently of us.

* The first sign of this state is when a man "finds that he *cannot meditate* nor exert his *imagination,* nor derive any satisfaction from it as he was wont to do" (*Ascent,* Book II, ch. xiii, p. 102). In the *Obscure Night* this sign is given as the third: "The third sign... is an inability to meditate and make reflections and to excite the *imagination* as before, notwithstanding all the efforts we may make; for God begins now to communicate Himself, no longer through the channel of sense, as He did formerly, in *consecutive reflections,* by which we arranged and divided our knowledge, but in pure spirit, which admits not of successive ideas, and *in an act of pure contemplation,* to which neither the interior nor exterior [imaginative] senses of our lower nature can ascend" (*Obscure Night,* Book I, ch. ix, p. 352). See also *Ascent,* Book II, ch. xiv. "In the purgation of the appetite... the *inability* to make our *meditation* continually grows" (*Obscure Night,* Book I, ch. ix, p. 352).

† "The second sign and condition of this purgation are that the memory *dwells ordinarily* upon God, with a painful anxiety and carefulness" (*Obscure Night,* Book I, ch. ix, p. 349).

‡ "... The third sign whereby we may discern when we are to cease from meditation. That sign is a knowledge of and attention to God, *general* and loving" (*Ascent,* Book II, ch. xiv, p. 106). "... Thus, what the soul elicited before, at intervals, by dint of meditation, in particular acts of knowledge, is now by practice converted into the habit and substance of knowledge, loving, *general,* not distinct or particular as before" (*ibid.,* p. 105).

This point, like those that went before, stands out in all St. John of the Cross's explanations.

**10.**—Here we have facts (the attraction towards an idea that is always the same, for example) that were not met with in the degree of meditation, or even in that of the prayer of simplicity, and they prove that we have travelled away from it. At the same time we find very strong **analogies with the prayer of quiet** from the point of view of what I have called the second element. First it is a *contemplation,* a simple gaze that recurs frequently. Then, as in the prayer of quiet, the proper *object* of this gaze is *one alone:* it is God. Further, and particularly, it is not *freely and by inclination* that we choose this object. It is imposed upon us; while the others are not so; far from it. Here is a beginning of the passive state* (see also Nos. **14** and **15**).

**10** *bis.*—**The degree of clearness** of this special kind of prayer is not always the same. "It is, however, true that in the commencement of this estate this loving knowledge is, as it were, imperceptible, because it is then wont to be, in the first place, most subtile and delicate and, as it were, unfelt; and because, in the second place, the soul, having been accustomed to meditation which is more cognisable by sense, does not perceive and, as it were, does not feel this new condition, not subject to sense, and which is purely spiritual. This is the case especially when, through not understanding his condition, the spiritual man will not allow himself to rest therein, but will strive after that which is cognisable by sense" (*Ascent of Mount Carmel,* Book II, ch. xiii, p. 103).

**11.**—**Third element.** The memory of God is loving. With certain persons it is consoling. There is an attraction for it, but this seems to me to be rare. In general, there is a *painful and persistent need* for a closer union with God.†

In these two instances we are not disposed to procure this union for ourselves by our former devotional exercises; we rather feel a distaste for them, we feel that they are incompetent to bring us to the good that we are seeking.‡

What, then, do we seek? At first, we wished to be inflamed with divine love. But now, on the contrary, the aridity of the mind extends to the will also. We

* For we understand that we receive something and merely give our consent. But there is a great difference between this passivity just begun and that other which is more complete, namely, the mystic state. For in the first we see that with an effort we could produce the state that we receive, but in the second we feel that it is quite out of our power.

† "Sometimes... the soul feels itself touched and inflamed with the love of God, without knowing how or why that feeling arises... The longings of the soul for God are so deep that the very bones seem to dry up in that thirst... This love, in general, is not felt at first, but only the aridity and emptiness of which I am speaking; and then, instead of love, which is afterwards enkindled, what the soul feels amidst its aridities and the emptiness of its faculties is a general painful anxiety about God, and a certain misgiving that it is not serving Him. But a soul anxious and afflicted for His sake is a sacrifice pleasing unto God. Secret contemplation keeps the soul in this state of anxiety" (*Obscure Night,* Book I, ch. xi, pp. 356-7).

‡ "Together with this aridity and emptiness, the soul feels a longing for solitude and repose, being unable to fix the thoughts on anything distinctly, or even to desire to do so" (*Obscure Night,* Book I, ch. ix, p. 351).

are inert all along the line. No soaring flights, no great ardours! And this grieves us; we blame ourselves for this coldness, and are inclined to regard it in the light of a punishment from God. The coldness is not, in reality, as great as it appears; a little spark of divine love remains hidden under the ashes. The proof lies in this persistent longing for God. We see from this that the night of the senses must not be confused with lukewarmness, for the characteristic of that condition is the absence of any want or desire for a more intense spiritual life.

But even if God should satisfy this thirst for divine love, a deeper desire would still remain to torture the soul. To love Him is a beginning only, and it does not suffice. He has made us for something more than this: to possess Him.

**12.**—But to what kind of possession do we aspire in this state? Do we know exactly what it is that we desire?

If we have ever had the prayer of quiet transiently, the **desire becomes defined.** It is this that we long to regain. It is there, as we understand, that we can plunge into the balmy atmosphere, where, untrammelled by methods, we shall breathe the divine love.

**13.**—But if, on the other hand, we have not yet received this mystic grace, the desire is more vague with regard to its object, and the **uneasiness** is only so much the **greater.** We suffer from an unsatisfied longing, without being able to say exactly what it is that we desire. Reading the lives of the saints gives us some inkling as to the object of our search; for we find there, more or less vaguely described, some of the higher states of union with the Divinity. We learn that, over and above the *thought* of God, there is, further, a *possession* of God. We turn our eyes in this direction, but without obtaining any very clear idea of what it is that we are seeking. But God, who gives this blind instinct, knows whither it leads.

The longing by which these two classes of souls are tormented makes us think of the impulse which brings about the migration of the swallows. When the bad weather approaches, they get ready to fly away in search of a better climate. The older birds, those that have made the journey already, remember and know exactly what it is that they want. It is the charming country of which the German ballad sings: there,

> Far away, "is the land where the orange-tree grows,
> Where golden fruits ripen, where blossoms the rose.
> Where the bird is more buoyant, nor tires on the wing,
> Nor the honey-bee ceases from pilfering."

The young birds, who are without this experience, make up for it by the marvellous instinct which suddenly awakens in their breasts. They set out, without knowing why, towards a country that they have never seen.

But, alas! there is a difference between us and the swallows. They depart when they choose. But we, on the contrary, do not change our supernatural country at will. We are caged, held captive by the limitations of our prayer; we beat against the wires, but they resist us. Thou alone, O God, canst unbar the door. In pity, open!

**14.**—I said that we felt no inclination to seek God by the help of our **former devotional exercises;** we only take them up again as a last resource. Those, on the other hand, who are suffering from ordinary aridity have but one desire—to return to meditation.

Whence we see that the *third element,* like the second, is characteristic of a state which must not be confused with the ordinary way.

**15.**—We can **sum up** all this by saying: the night of the senses is 1° a simple gaze; 2° an aridity; 3° with this peculiarity that the soul finds a facility for one *single* memory only, that of God; 4° it has also one *single* desire, that of possessing God more fully; finally, 5° this shaping of the soul's course is not due to her own efforts.

**16.**—**Fourth element.** It affects our natural tastes. It is a persistent action of grace, designed to detach us from all the things of sense, even such as are lawful, and to imbue us with a distaste for them. Nature opposes itself to this action and suffers from it. In this conflict the soul may incline to one side or the other.

When speaking just now of the longing for union with God, I instanced a particular case of the divine action, and I said that we were no longer led to seek this union by way of our former exercises (**14**). These, as a matter of fact, contained a considerable element of the things of sense. It is a question now of a much vaster action. It extends even when we are not at prayer, to all our passions, to all forms of sensible knowledge or inclinations, and seeks to turn our hearts away from them. The mystic state will continue this work later on.

St. John of the Cross describes this inner travail at great length. He occupies the whole of Book I of the *Ascent of Mount Carmel* and the first chapters of the *Obscure Night* in reviewing all our appetites, which he connects with the seven deadly sins. He declares this conflict to be the sign by which we should judge as to the probability of our being really in the night of the senses.*

**17.**—I have called attention to the fact that the **soul may resist** this action of grace. This is because God does not sanctify us in spite of ourselves. If He inspires the inclinations, He leaves nature free to act in opposition to them; we may choose for ourselves. St. John of the Cross admits the existence of this

* Here is this sign: "The first [sign] is when men find no comfort in the things of God and none also in created things" (*Obscure Night*, Book I, ch. ix, p. 348). Speaking of the first night, he says that it is "the privation of and purgation from all sensual desires in all external things; all the pleasures of the flesh and all the satisfactions of the will... which is the privation of all desire wrought by God, a condition which is as night to the soul" (*Ascent of Mount Carmel*, Book I, ch. i, p. 9). "The privation of all pleasure to the desire in all things is here called night... As the faculty of vision is nourished by light and fed by visible objects and ceases to be so fed when the light is withdrawn, so the soul by means of the desire feeds on those things which, corresponding with its powers, give it pleasure; but when the desire is mortified it desires no more pleasure from them, and thus, so far as the desire is concerned, the soul abides in darkness, without occupation" (*Ascent*, Book I, ch. iii, pp. 11, 12).

resistance, for he says that the work of purification may be very prolonged. Otherwise, it would be almost instantaneous.

When the grace of detachment is thus resisted, experience shows that the person may often go on for some time without being aware of it. This occurs with those who are overwhelmed with exterior occupations. Nature inclines them to take pleasure in a distracting activity and to plunge into it to excess, were it only for the sake of escaping the tedium of their interior desert. They only realise their error later on, when a book or a clear-sighted Director leads them to moderate their excesses, to reserve a larger share of their activity for their spiritual life, and not to fly from their inward purgatory.

**18.**—The four elements enumerated above are **things that can be observed;** not that we perceive them distinctly at the end of an hour's prayer, but if we take a general survey, covering several weeks or months, their detection will usually be easy.

Quite a number of persons, after reading the above descriptions, have told me that they had found the exact reproduction of their own experience. It is proved by experience, then, that *the state of prayer there described* exists, and that it is not rare.

We have yet another proof of its existence—namely, the testimony of St. John of the Cross. For the passages that I have quoted show that all the characters of this state have been referred to by him, and that it is to these characters, as a whole, that he has given the name of the night of the senses. If anyone were to deny this last proof because he puts a different interpretation upon the words of St. John of the Cross, the proof of experience would remain in all its force.

Finally, the existence of this state may be foreseen *a priori.* We have only to admit that the prayer of simple regard, directed towards God, may be arid, painful, and persistent. And this fact must, at least, seem probable.

**19.**—**Fifth element.** I will call this the *hidden element.* For we do not perceive it directly, as in the case of the other four. We must *attain to it* by the reason. It consists in this: *God begins to exercise upon the soul the action that characterises the prayer of quiet, but He does this in too slight a degree for us to be conscious of it.*

We may say, then, that the night of the senses is the prayer of quiet in a *latent,* concealed state. It only needs to be strengthened afterwards and to pass on to the visible state.*

**20.**—A comparison will help us to form a **general idea** of the development of the mystic union in the soul (see ch. vii, **3**). It is that of a tree, the seed of which is hidden at first in the earth. The roots that are sent down secretly in the darkness constitute the night of the senses. Then a frail stem is put forth and

* Physics show us that in the same way heat and electricity are sometimes latent. They do not then make their presence known to the sense of touch, although they are really present.

emerges into the light; this is the prayer of quiet. The tree grows, and finally, when it is covered with flowers and fruit, represents the spiritual marriage. This is the final end of its development.*

We see now why I said that the night of the senses is the borderland between ordinary prayer and the mystic union. We must rank it with the first if we depend upon the things that we see, and with the second if we penetrate to those that are hidden. It is an incomplete mystic union.

We can sum up this fact by saying that the night of the senses merits the name of *sub-mystic union.*

**21.—Proofs** of the existence of the fifth element. To establish this thesis we have two kinds of arguments. The first are taken from St. John of the Cross.

1° We can satisfy ourselves at once that he admits the existence of a hidden element since, when speaking of the four visible elements, he is satisfied with calling them "signs," "marks," of the night of the senses. This last is different, then: it is something more than they; it has an underlying part.

2° To the first night he gives the name of infused contemplation (*Obscure Night,* Book I, ch. x, p. 355); and it is on account of this quality, he says, that "it is therefore expedient for the soul which is in this condition not to be troubled because its faculties have become useless" (*ibid.,* p. 355. See also *ibid.,* ch. xii). Otherwise it would be hardly different from those that remain idle. Here it receives something, although this something is visible only in its effects. He also says that in the aridities of the night of the senses, the soul "is conscious of strength and energy to act, because of the substantial nature of its interior food which is the *commencement of contemplation,* obscure and dry to the senses. This contemplation is in general *secret* and *unknown to him who is admitted to it*" (*Obscure Night,* Book I, ch. ix, pp. 350-1).

3° This thesis is implied in several comparisons developed by the saint. When he distinguishes three nights instead of two (see note to No. **2**), he says: "The three nights are *but one* divided into three parts" (*Ascent of Mount Carmel,* Book I, ch. ii, p. 11). Now, the third, with him, is the spiritual marriage, and the second, as will be shown later on, is already the mystic state. The night of the senses itself, then, is mystic in a certain way and in essence; otherwise they would not be parts of one whole; the saint would certainly not have said that the spiritual marriage was one with ordinary prayer.

The same idea is expressed by the simile of the fire that consumes the wood (*Obscure Night,* Book II, ch. x; and *Living Flame,* Stanza I, line 4). He shows us that this fire is *one,* but that it produces successively three different effects: it

* Between ordinary prayer and the prayer of quiet, there can be no other intermediary than the contemplation of the night of the senses. For three cases only can occur. Either there is no mystic union, and it is ordinary prayer; or the union is present in a latent state, and it is the night of the senses; or, finally, it is present in the manifest state, and it is the mystic union in the strict sense of the word.

blackens the wood, it covers the outward surface with flames, it transforms it into itself. The first of these actions symbolises the first night.

Elsewhere he makes a comparison between the night of the senses and the night of the spirit. "*Secret contemplation* keeps the soul in this state of anxiety until, in the course of time, having purged the sensitive nature of man in some degree of its natural forces and affections by means of the aridities it occasions, it shall have kindled within it this Divine love" (*Obscure Night*, Book I, ch. xi, p. 357).

Again, he says: "The purgation of sense is merely the gate and *entrance* [*solo es puerta y principio*] of contemplation" (*ibid.*, Book II, ch. ii, p. 375), which implies that they are of the same inner nature.

He says also that God *ordinarily* **leads** into the second night those who have been **called** in a marked degree into the first night (*Obscure Night,* Book I, ch. xiv, p. 371). We can understand this if we admit that the essential part of the mystic grace has already begun to be received. The seed is sown; it is in the order of nature that it should develop and put forth a stem (see 33).

**22.—The direct** argument in favour of this thesis is that it gives us the obvious explanation of the deep-reaching **analogies** which we have shown to exist between the prayer of quiet and the night of the senses. Otherwise we should see no reason for them. 1° Each is a contemplation, a simple regard, that is to say; 2° their object is the same and is very restricted; 3° they come into being of their own accord without our so much as thinking of them; 4° they exclude the former exercises, the imagination and the reason (each in its turn); 5° finally, when the prayer of quiet is very weak, either in itself or because we are moving about, we find that it scarcely differs to any appreciable extent from the night of the senses. We see that a continuity exists between these two states.

If we do not admit the thesis, not only do we fail to see any reason for these analogies, but this state seems a most fantastic one. What can be God's object in thus imposing one single idea upon us, while so many others are useful to us? Why put so many obstacles in the way of our former devotional exercises, which are excellent, in order to replace them with an inadequate occupation?

Let us note that this assemblage of analogies does not exist with a prayer of simplicity of any kind whatever; which, besides, is not regarded as belonging to the mystic union in its hidden state.

**23.**—I have just represented the night of the senses as *always* containing the hidden element. But, it has been objected, are there not sometimes **exceptions?** May not certain—it may be, rare—souls receive this degree in an *incomplete manner?* They might possess the four elements that can be observed, but not the latent beginnings of God's mystical action.

This opinion is so closely allied to my own that I should hardly dare to condemn those who prefer it. Perhaps St. John of the Cross meant to speak only of what happens almost always. The arguments merely establish a strong probability in favour of the thesis, and do not therefore absolutely exclude all exceptions.

**24.**—**History of this state.** It is clear that before St. John of the Cross's time thousands of souls had passed through this arid contemplation. But no one had taken the trouble to study it; no one had distinguished it either from common aridity or from the neighbouring mystic states. *They did not perceive the hidden element* which gives it all its value, and they consequently attached no importance to it.

St. John of the Cross made this most helpful discovery. We must attribute it both to his own perspicacity and to the assistance of the Holy Spirit. This is the really important discovery that we owe to him.

### § 2. Various Details Regarding the First Night

**25.**—**Sufferings** accompanying this state. St. John of the Cross may well describe the night of the senses as a purgatory. Several kinds of sufferings are to be found there, as follows:

**26.**—1° **Tedium.** It proceeds from the first element, which is aridity. The faculties are restive at being thus kept without employment. They desire movement, variety; but here they are condemned to an incessant absence of movement and a monotonous occupation! And, unhappily, this state is inevitable. We cannot change our prayer at will.

When this trial lasts for several days, even so it is exceedingly wearisome. But it is sometimes prolonged for several years; and it then becomes intolerable, provided, that is to say, that, instead of going in search of outside consolations, we maintain ourselves in recollection.

**27.**—**How may we remedy** this suffering to a certain extent? By making use of a book whilst we are at prayer. When the weariness is excessive, it is a solace only to make some little attempts, although we may have satisfied ourselves that they rarely succeed.

**28.**—2° There is also the torment of **distractions,** which is another consequence of aridity. It is more severe than in the prayer of quiet, because there we have a certain compensation—the possession of God.

**29.**—3° The third element is a source of sufferings; for it is the **thirst** for a closer union with God, and it remains **unsatisfied.** There is something in it that is analogous to the pain of loss that tortures the holy souls before their entry into Heaven.

Those who have never left the ordinary way feel little or nothing of this painful and constantly renewed longing; and they are inclined to be astonished at it. But they ought to admit that God does not give the same attractions to everyone alike. With a loving cruelty He may quite well enkindle a great craving for eternal blessedness, breathing into us a home-sickness for the Divine Essence, that true country of our souls.

Some people go farther than astonishment. They condemn this disposition, and say that the distress is fanciful. "It is simply the work of your imagination," they exclaim contemptuously; "a foolish dream. Think of something else, and you will be cured."* Exactly! But that is just what cannot be done. And we ought to congratulate ourselves that this is so, for if we were to succeed and accomplish the impossible, we should be deprived of a great grace: the loving memory of God.

**30.**—4° The fourth element also brings sufferings, for human nature groans under this conflict with the **sensitive appetite.** "The first night, or purgation, is bitter and terrible to sense... They now find nothing but insipidity and bitterness" (*Obscure Night,* Book I, ch. viii, pp. 346-7).

Those to whom God sends great trials of this kind often feel overpowered with sadness, and they are astonished and say to themselves that this sadness is causeless. But they are mistaken. There is doubtless no special cause such as a reprimand or sickness. But there is a general cause which they have overlooked. It is this: Other souls have a certain inclination for even the humblest of their habitual occupations; they like to exercise their faculties in this way and to escape the tedium of inaction. It is in this manner that persons in the world, even such as are occupied in the most futile fashion, ward off low spirits. So with the workman who takes a pleasure in his work. But suppose that God secretly removes this natural pleasure in all earthly things, without, however, giving us a taste for those of heaven, our faculties are then applied incessantly to subjects that are distasteful to them; and a perpetual atmosphere of sadness results.

**31.**—5° If we have not been instructed as to the existence of this kind of prayer, we have **doubts** as to the goodness of such a way. We say to ourselves: "This state is too vague to deserve the name of a prayer. I must therefore try to find another." Nothing hinders our seeking, but it will generally be in vain; we cannot get out of our *desert.* We must accept this situation generously.

This anxiety is due to a narrow idea as to what prayer should be. It consists essentially in a loving converse with God; now we have that here, painful as it may be; and we draw strength of action from it—if we allow grace to lead us on to generosity.

Or we say, again: "In the time devoted to prayer I do nothing more than when I unite myself to God during the day. Now, this is not enough." I beg your pardon; it is enough for you, and God wills that it should be so; either in order to exercise you in patience, or to lead you to the mystic states.

Nothing is so calculated to quiet these doubts as the knowledge that we are in a state known and approved by the masters of the spiritual life. But for this,

* St. John of the Cross: "Some will be sure to tell him... that his sufferings are the effects of melancholy" (*Ascent of Mount Carmel,* Prologue, p. 5).

instruction is necessary. The remedy would be to comfort our hearts with thoughts of faith.

**32.**—6° **The Devil** often makes the ordeal harder by other sufferings, which, however, are not (as in the case of those that went before) *the natural* consequences, as it were, of this arid contemplation. He torments us with scruples, for instance.

Or again: God allows us to suffer from sickness, the failure of our undertakings, grave temptations, or the worries incidental to our surroundings, etc. (see *Obscure Night,* Book I, ch. xiv).

**33.**—Amidst all these sufferings the superior part of the soul may experience **peace and joy.** This is only the case with fervent and truly mortified souls: the Cross has become their happiness.

St. John of the Cross describes this desirable condition, which, however, so it would seem, is only met with when the soul has reached the mystic state: "The soul *delights to be alone,* waiting lovingly on God, without any particular considerations, in interior peace, quiet, and repose, when the acts and exercises of the intellect, memory, and will, at least discursively—which is the going from one subject to another—have ceased; nothing remains except that *knowledge* and attention, *general* and *loving,* of which I have spoken, without the particular perception of aught else" (*Ascent of Mount Carmel,* Book II, ch. xiii, p. 102).* The saint recognises that this ideal is not realised in the case of those who do not yet understand their state. "This striving, notwithstanding the abundance of loving interior peace, disturbs him in the consciousness and employment of it" (*ibid.,* p. 103). See *ibid.,* chs. xiv, xv, xxxii.

**34.**—**The utility** of these trials is very great. The sufferings experienced here are highly meritorious, and the universal distaste which God inspires in us for all created things is a powerful means to perfection. St. John of the Cross, when eulogising this state, goes as far as to say (he is speaking of beginners): "After all our exertions to mortify ourselves in our actions and passions, our *success will not* be perfect, *or even great,* until God Himself shall do it for us in the purgation of the Obscure Night" (*Obscure Night,* Book I, ch. vii, p. 345).

This statement does not seem, however, to be absolutely in accordance with experience. I think that I have met with souls who have arrived at the mystic state without having passed through the night of the senses but only through other great trials which resulted in detachment. In the period previous to the prayer of quiet they felt a loving attention to God, which, however, had nothing bitter or painful about it.

**35.**—What is **the issue** of these trials? In a word, if we are in the night of the senses, are we sure, sooner or later, to arrive at the mystic state? St. John of the

* It is well, however, to note that this passage allows of two rather different interpretations: we can apply it either to those whose contemplation is naturally sweet and tranquil, or to those with whom it is bitter, but who are generously resigned to it.

Cross distinguishes two cases. If the night of the senses is present occasionally only, and if during the intervals we revert to ordinary meditation, it seems to him that God is probably merely proposing to purify the soul without intending to lead her higher.

In the contrary case, the saint admits that the soul is *generally* destined for the mystic state. The probability is that she will reach it.

The saint adds: "God does not elevate to perfect contemplation everyone that is tried in the spiritual way, and He alone knoweth why" (*Obscure Night,* Book I, ch. ix, p. 353). There is a similar difference with regard to the fate of seeds carried by the wind; some remain on the surface of the ground and die; others penetrate into it and grow.

The fact is still better explained if we admit that in exceptional cases certain souls experience the night of the senses in an incomplete state only (**23**), without the hidden element, that is to say. They would not have received the least germ of the mystic state, and we must not be surprised, therefore, that this state does not come to maturity.

The probability of attaining to the mystic union is greater when the soul has already received it several times before falling for any considerable period into the night of the senses. We can hardly admit that God would have bestowed such a gift in order to withdraw it altogether, unless there had been a grave infidelity to grace.

**36.**—We must cheer ourselves by these thoughts, so as to resist the **temptation to discouragement,** which leads to that of relaxation. Those who, in spite of their aspirations, thus find themselves in a prolonged state of aridity, conclude from this that they are abandoned by God on account of their infidelities, and they carry the absurdity to the point of declaring that this rejection is final. The hope of success would have sustained them in the conflict, but when they believe that they can say: "It is clear that I shall never succeed"; they lose all their courage and abandon themselves easily to frivolities and dissipations. This lack of confidence in the divine goodness, or this relaxation, hinders them from meriting His deliverance; and God is thus obliged to prolong this purgatory. The farther they go, the greater the temptation to despair.

The director should encourage and console those who are thus tried, and should not treat them as if they were tepid or negligent.

**37.**—Can the **duration** of the trial be foreseen? Are there certain Providential laws or signs that permit the prediction of a speedy deliverance?

Alas! no; so says St. John of the Cross: "But how long the soul will continue in this fast and penance of sense *no one can with certainty* tell" (*Obscure Night,* Book I, ch. xiv, p. 371). He adds: "But those souls that are to go forward to so blessed and exalted a state as this of the union of love, however quickly God may lead them, tarry long, in general, amidst aridities, as we see by experience" (*ibid.,* p. 372).

**38.—In order to shorten our time of trial** we must, on the contrary, guard our recollection carefully, and pray insistently for deliverance. We then have a vocation for the mystic state (**21**); and when anyone has a vocation, they ought to pray that it should ripen, and that quickly (see also ch. xxv, **6**). Unhappily, it is found to be very difficult to ask to be cured of aridity, for it paralyses and makes us incapable of every kind of petition. The devil, on his side, also dissuades you from it. He wishes to keep you in this state of suffering and darkness, and also in tepidity and dissipation, if he can do so. He trembles lest you should enter into the mystic union.

**39.—Rules of conduct** for souls in the first night. There are three rules to be followed relatively to prayer. They have been given for the prayer of simplicity (ch. ii, **60**), of which this, if we judge by appearances, is only a special case. The first rule told us not to do violence to ourselves in order to produce acts with regard to which we feel a difficulty or a distaste. Therefore, in the night of the senses, we must learn to content ourselves with our arid contemplation, with the vague and general thought of God, that is to say, with a painful aspiration towards Him.*

Those who are passing through this trial often torment their directors "to teach them how to pray," by which they mean a very full prayer. They inquire after new books, hoping to discover some infallible method.

These temptations are a proof of goodwill, but they will fail. For if they were to succeed they would require the use of the sensible faculties, the paralysing of which is the precise object of the night of the *senses.* The only thing, then, is to resign ourselves to this terrible situation: frankly to accept a prayer the foundation of which is *repose in suffering* (see ch. xxiv **58** *bis*).

It is true that we shall often be assailed by a scruple. This rule, we shall say to ourselves, presupposes powerlessness. But is mine real? Can I not, without putting undue pressure on myself, follow up and develop a point of meditation? You will find that you cannot.

This is the reply that we should make to those directors who, with a considerable show of irritation, say: "What a complicated soul! Please do as everyone else does." The penitent would desire nothing better, but he cannot. Let us accept the divine action, then, as it comes to us.

* St. John of the Cross, speaking of this arid contemplation: "Now if they who are in this state knew how to be quiet, to disregard every interior and exterior work, the accomplishment of which they labour after, and to be without solicitude about everything but the resignation of themselves into the hands of God, and a loving interior obedience to His voice, they would have in this tranquillity a most delicious taste of interior refreshing. This refreshing is so delicate that, in general, it eludes our perceptions if we are in any degree anxious to feel it, for it works in the soul when most tranquil and free" (*Obscure Night,* Book I, ch. ix, p. 351).

### §3. The Second Night of the Soul

**40.—Its nature.** St. John of the Cross gives the name of the *second night* of the soul to all those mystic states that are lower than the spiritual marriage, but held in esteem in so far as they contain obscurity and even sufferings. He also refers to it as the *night of the spirit.* And this is correct, since throughout the whole mystic series the spirit continues in the divine darkness.

Finally, he calls it the *second purgatory.* It is true that in the mystic state there are great joys. But we have seen that they are plentifully mingled with sufferings (ch. xi, **10**).

**41.**—The **interpretation** of the saint's meaning that I have just given has sometimes been disputed. It has been said, for example: the second night consists merely in a penetrating insight into our miseries and our nothingness.

I do not think that it is quite as simple as this; if it were so, the saint could have explained it in a few lines. I shall discuss in another chapter the, as I think, inaccurate way in which the saint's teachings have been summed up by certain writers (ch. xxxi, § 6).

But let us not be surprised at these divergences amongst commentators. The saint has not attempted to proceed rigorously by the help of complete definitions. When a state contains several elements, he points them out sometimes only here and there, and this in some other connection—by associating them with some rule of asceticism, for instance; and he thus makes only imperfect classifications. And so, when quoting from him, I have had to take my passages from various parts of his works. It is easily understood that commentators may thus pass over some essential phrases without noticing their import.

**42.**—Here are a few extracts which justify my way of understanding the second night: 1° "This [second] Obscure Night is a certain inflowing of God into the soul... Contemplatives call it *infused contemplation* or *mystical theology*" (*Obscure Night,* Book II, ch. v, p. 380). This passage alone would serve to prove my thesis.

The saint adds: "God secretly teaches the soul and instructs it in the perfection of love, *without efforts on its own part* beyond loving attention to God, listening to His voice and admitting the light He sends, *without understanding how* this is *infused contemplation...* So when the divine light of contemplation shines into the soul not yet perfectly enlightened, it causes spiritual darkness, because it not only surpasses its strength, but because it obscures it and deprives it of its *natural perceptions.* It is for this reason that St. Dionysius and other mystic theologians call *infused contemplation* a ray of darkness, that is, for the unenlightened and unpurified soul..." (*ibid.,* p. 381).

See also similar passages: *Obscure Night,* Book II, ch. xvii; *Ascent of Mount Carmel,* Book II, ch. viii; *Spiritual Canticle,* Stanzas XXVII, XXIX.

2° "The way of the spirit... is also called the Illuminative Way, or the way of *infused contemplation,* wherein God Himself nourishes and refreshes the soul *without the help of any active efforts* that itself may make" (*Obscure Night,* Book I, ch. xiv, p. 370).

The saint repeats that this night contains a contemplation. Now he shows us what it is that is synonymous in his eyes with this last word: "Mystical theology, which is the *secret* science of God, and which spiritual men call contemplation" (*Spiritual Canticle,* Stanza XXVII, p. 148).

3° When describing the man who has gone through the night of the senses, the saint adds: "... He must change his garments. This *God Himself* will do... He will change them from old into *new* by infusing into the soul a *new understanding of God in God,* the human understanding being set aside, and a new love of God in God..." (*Ascent of Mount Carmel,* Book I, ch. v, p. 21).

4° The soul seems to say: "In poverty, unsupported by any apprehensions, in the obscurity of the intellect, in the conflict of the will, in the affliction and distress of memory... I went forth out of myself [during the first night], out of *my low conceptions and lukewarm love,* out of my scanty and poor sense of God... I went forth out of the scanty intercourse and operations of my own to those of God; that is, my intellect *went* forth out of itself, and from human became Divine... it understands no more within its former limits and narrow bounds... My will went forth out of itself *transformed into the Divine will...* all the energies and affections of the soul are, in this night and purgation of the old man, *renewed into a Divine temper and delight*" (*Obscure Night,* Book II, ch. iv, pp. 379-80).

5° Comparing the two nights, the saint characterises the second as follows: "For this is a certain fire of love in the spirit whereby the soul, in its dark trials, feels itself wounded to the quick by *a certain impression* and foretaste of God, though it understands nothing distinctly because the intellect is in darkness... And inasmuch as this love is infused in a special way, the soul corresponds only *passively* with it, and thus a strong passion of love is begotten within it. This love has in it something of the most perfect union with God [the spiritual marriage], and thus partakes in some measure of its qualities which are *chiefly actions of God,* in the soul rather than of the soul, which is *consenting* unto them in *simplicity* and love" (*Obscure Night,* Book II, ch. xi, p. 406).

6° The saint says that ecstasies belong to this period, and that they definitely diminish towards its close (*Obscure Night,* Book II, ch. i, pp. 374-5).

7° We have proved above that the first night belongs already to the mystic state, although unconsciously (**19**). The second night, being the development of the first, should therefore belong to the mystic state also, and in a higher degree, which can be nothing but the conscious state.

8° When we take a general review of the saint's rules of conduct for the second night, we see that they resolve themselves to this: accept the fact that the *mind* rises to a *new* and higher mode of operation in this prayer. And in the same way, in the first night, they are reduced to this: accept the fact that the *senses,* the sensible faculties, that is, cease to act.

9° Finally, it is clear from the whole of Book II of the *Obscure Night* that the spiritual marriage is the outcome of this second night. Now, this is true of the mystic states only. The same idea is indicated by the title of the first Treatise: *The Ascent of Mount Carmel.* This ascent has the summit for its goal. Now, the saint says that the summit is "the high estate of perfection, called here *union of the soul with God*" (*Ascent of Mount Carmel,* Prologue, p. 1, and Book I, ch. xiii, p. 50, No. 3). See also the summary of the two nights of the soul in *The Living Flame of Love,* Stanza III, line 3, § 5 and § 6, pp. 267, 270, and Stanza I, line 4, p. 227.

### § 4. The Question of Terminology

**43.**—The **signification of the word faith** for St. John of the Cross. The saint constantly says that we attain to the perfect union by the way of faith. Is this to say that mystic contemplation is merely a knowledge by faith? which would seem to suggest that it is not experimental.

All depends upon the wider or narrower sense in which we interpret the word faith. In the broad sense it signifies all supernatural knowledge of a degree lower than the beatific vision. But between faith, taken in a more restricted sense, and the intuitive vision, there is an intermediary; namely, *infused knowledge,* which is also described as *faith illumined* by a gift of the Holy Ghost. Faith, strictly so called, rests solely upon the testimony of another, that is to say, of God. Infused knowledge goes farther; by it we begin to see with more or less clearness. Mystic contemplation is an act of infused knowledge.

Now, St. John of the Cross takes the word faith in the first and wide sense,* and he can therefore say that mystic contemplation is inside the domain and way of faith.

But the usual sense is the second.† It is to be feared, therefore, that readers may interpret in their usual sense things that the saint said in his own. The quietists based their position upon this false interpretation, which seemed to attach importance only to the simplified prayer, which they described as *naked*

* We see this everywhere by the context. Here is one definition amongst others that does not apply to faith taken in the restricted sense: "Rest not therefore, neither wholly nor in part, on what the faculties can embrace; never seek to satisfy thyself with what thou comprehendest in God, but rather with what thou comprehendest not. And do not rest on the love of that which thou canst understand and feel, but rather on that which is beyond thy understanding and feeling: this is *to seek Him by faith*" (*Spiritual Canticle,* Stanza I, line I, p. 19).

† Cardinal Bona takes the word faith in the usual sense when, speaking of sublime contemplation, he says: "This vision is a *mean* between the obscure knowledge that we possess here by *faith* and the clear knowledge that the light of glory gives in our celestial country" (*De discretione Spir.,* ch. xviii, No. 5.)

*faith.** Briefly, they thus strove to confuse mystic contemplation with acquired contemplation, the only one that they held in esteem.

**44.**—Even taking the word faith in this restricted sense, it is still true that, when judged by certain characters, mystic faith and mystic contemplation bear a great mutual resemblance. 1° They proceed from a supernatural illumination; 2° they are above reason; 3° they are obscure; 4° finally, contemplation bears upon matters of faith. It is within the order of faith.

* This expression may have an orthodox meaning. But writers have often forgotten to define it, or, which comes to the same thing, to say with what they contrast it.

# CHAPTER XVI

## Further Details Regarding the Prayer of Quiet (The First Stage of the Mystic Union)

**1.**—Let us recall the **definition.** It is a mystic union in which the divine action is not yet strong enough to hinder distractions (ch. iii, **8**).

It is called by St. Teresa "the *second manner* of drawing the water which the Lord of the vineyard has ordained" (*Life,* ch. xiv, i); the "fourth *mansion of the Interior Castle*" and "the enjoyment of the presence of God" (*Interior Castle,* Fourth Mansion, ch. ii, i°).

I need not describe this state under its general aspects here. This has already been done implicitly, for the various characters that I have previously pointed out in connection with the mystic union, as a whole, apply equally to the prayer of quiet as a particular instance of the union. They are merely less marked than in the higher degrees of prayer. It only remains, therefore, to describe certain details peculiar to this state.

### § 1. Its Successive Phases

**2.**—Here is the **order** that God *usually* appears to adopt for the first mystic graces.*

**3.**—1° **At first** the prayer of quiet is most commonly given from time to time only, and then merely for a few minutes together; the space of an *Ave Maria,* for instance. (It is the same with the full union.) This is what happened to St. Teresa, who was then twenty years of age (*Life,* ch. iv, vi, 9).

This grace comes abruptly, then, and when you are not expecting it. You are suddenly taken possession of by an unaccustomed state of recollection which you cannot help noticing. You are overtaken by a divine wave which penetrates you. You remain motionless under the influence of this sweet impression. And

* Amongst the researches that remain to be made in mysticism, that on the duration and mode of development of the various *stages* fixed by God would be amongst the most interesting.

then it all vanishes with equal suddenness. Beginners feel surprised at this, for they find themselves seized by an action the nature of which they do not entirely understand. But they yield themselves to this inclination because they see at first sight that the occupation is a holy one. They put off to a later date the task of examining it more closely.

With other persons, however, these graces seem to have come gradually, imperceptibly.

**4.**—2° **The time** when this grace first begins to appear. This usually takes place when the soul has already arrived at the neighbouring state of prayer: the prayer of simplicity, or rather to the night of the senses, that is to say; and it is into this last state that she usually falls back when she is not experiencing the prayer of quiet.* It is often at about the period of the first appearance of this grace, sometimes before, sometimes after, that the prayer of simplicity becomes arid† (see ch. ii, **21**).

**5.**—3° **Cessation or diminution**. A degree of prayer is not a definite state, excluding reversions to former states. After bestowing certain mystic graces upon the soul, God sometimes sends a long interruption, lasting several years, it may be. This was so with St. Teresa. She had eighteen or twenty years of almost unbroken interruption (*Life,* chs. viii, 4; xxiii, 13). This is sometimes (but not always) a punishment for our infidelities. If we are to continue to receive these favours, God desires us to renounce our many frivolities and to enter resolutely upon the way of the Cross.

It may be, also, that He wills to put our trust in His goodness to the proof. The devil whispers: "Why should you pray? You are rejected; you will never regain those lost blessings". But God would have us hope, like Abraham, against all hope.

**6.**—4° Finally, a time often comes when the prayer of quiet is not only very frequent, but **habitual.** We then possess it as our state, at will, *as it were.*‡ (See St. John of the Cross, *Ascent of Mount Carmel,* Book II, ch. xv, pp. 112-13.)

In this case it occurs even outside the time of prayer, and *every time that the thought of God presents itself,* in conversation, for instance. Nothing more than this is required in order that we should be seized by the divine action. If this action is strong, then we find our occupation interfered with; but usually it all

* In the same way we may ask what the prayer of ecstatics is, apart from their ecstasies. We lack the information that would make it possible to answer positively.

† Two persons have told me that, previous to their arrival at a state in which they frequently experienced the prayer of quiet, the prayer of simplicity had always been consoling. But one of them, at least, had passed through other severe trials.

‡ I say, "at will, *as it were*" to show that this facility is not in opposition to my definition of the mystic graces (ch. i, 1). In fact, it is still true, even here, that our will does not produce the mystic state *directly;* it is satisfied with making us begin to pray; God does the rest. He is pleased to lay down certain conditions which will be sufficient to cause Him to deign to operate; we confine ourselves to fulfilling these conditions.

disappears rapidly. At other times the divine operation has, as it were, a mute influence which persists in the midst of external affairs.

But even when the soul reaches this point, she is not certain of being called to mount higher.

7.—**Alternations of intensity.** When we have thus reached the *period* when the prayer of quiet is habitual, we are not, however, exempt from interruptions in its abundance. At times the mystic state takes strong possession of us; at others it is weak. So that life is a series of alternations of wealth and semi-poverty.

Here, again, there, are sometimes real retrogressions. The prayer of quiet ceases to be habitual: it once more becomes brief or of rare occurrence.

### § 2. How is the Director to Recognise Whether a Person Has Had the Prayer of Quiet?

**8.**—The director may be led in various ways to **ask himself the following question:** Has such or such an individual received the mystic union? Sometimes the person in question has felt fearful on account of the silence and repose of his prayers, which condition he takes for sloth. And then it is necessary for the director to know whether it is the prayer of quiet or the prayer of simplicity. And then, at times, certain details seem to indicate that something extraordinary has taken place. He feels it himself in a confused way, and wishes to be enlightened on the subject.

**9.**—Given that it has seemed advisable to try to clear up this point, the director must have recourse to **interrogations.** What shall he ask?

The most natural and sensible method is to see if the prayer presents all the characters of the mystic union without any exceptions. These characters have been shown above to amount to twelve (ch. vii, **1**); we need but run through the list, adding to each head some of the additional details belonging to it. We must take care that the question is not put in such a way as to suggest the answer. A bare yes or no should also be mistrusted. These may be easily uttered without reflection.

If we decline to confine ourselves to these interrogations from a list, prepared in advance and carefully drawn up, we run the risk of omissions and, consequently, of an imperfect understanding of the situation. A doctor, in his diagnosis of a case, is not satisfied with two or three questions due to the inspiration of the moment.

**10.**—In this interrogation a **precaution** is to be observed with regard to the two fundamental characters. To begin with, at any rate, we must pass lightly over the first, and not inquire whether the person has *really* felt God's presence. The idea of such a grace appears too presumptuous to a beginner. We should meet with doubts and objections. It is enough to know if he was *thinking* of God and of His presence; if the basis of the occupation was that of being united with

Him, of being recollected. The matter can be gone into more closely at a subsequent date.

So, too, with the second character. We must put our questions in strict conformity to the statement of the thesis (ch. vi, **5**); that is to say, avoiding the terms spiritual senses, spiritual touch, upon which the beginner has not yet reflected sufficiently.

I did not observe these precautions myself when I was explaining the two fundamental characters. And this was because the director's object is completely different from mine. He is not asked, as I am, to state a doctrine precisely, but to utilise certain personal information. He has not to fathom the hidden nature of the mystic state, but to judge of an individual. And for this it is wise, at the beginning, at any rate, to confine ourselves to facts that the person directed can supply with certainty and without hesitation.

**11.**—As to the ten subsidiary characters, they are perfectly evident. However slightly marked his state may have been, the person will **recognise them without difficulty.**

In fact, although these ten characters are supernatural, as to cause, they belong to the common order if they are considered in themselves, and they are therefore more easily perceived by our understanding. They nearly all consist simply in the *exclusion of certain natural acts,* the exclusion of sensible images, for instance, or of physical movements, or discursive acts, or facility in analysing our own state, etc... Acts of this kind being already known to us, their absence is therefore recognised without any effort.

But it is otherwise with regard to the two fundamental characters. It is now no longer a case of something excluded, but of something positively received, and this, too, in the supernatural order. God must give us fresh light if we are to discern them clearly.

**12.**—This method is a **very easy** one for the director, who has not to wander about at random and hew himself a path in an unknown country. And it is easy also for the person directed, for he requires no preparation, no previous examen in order to give clear and accurate replies. But it would be quite otherwise if, instead of asking him for answers to definite questions, we were to call upon him to draw up an account of his spiritual life. He would fatigue himself by searching about for ideas and words, and it would usually end in vague and indefinite phrases.

**13.**—**Objection**. When anybody describes the mystic state, which he believes himself in all good faith to have experienced, and makes use of very accurate expressions, there is always the fear lest he should simply be repeating what he has read in mystical books, repeating them without understanding them?

I reply that no one can repeat so many difficult things without contradicting himself and wandering away from the point. When he has been dealing with anyone (who is in good faith, that is to say) for some considerable time, a skilful director will be perfectly able to judge whether he has experienced what he is relating. There are a thousand shades that cannot be invented. But an ignorant confessor might make mistakes.

The objection would equally argue that doctors could never rely upon their patients' accounts of their symptoms. May they not be repeating phrases that they have read in medical journals or chemists' prospectuses?

**14.**—The particular **case** inquired into by the director will often be **doubtful.*** This is so when the various characters of the mystic union are not very clearly manifested. Or, again, the director has to deal with someone who is not instructed in these matters, able to observe the facts clearly and accurately, and knowing or instinctively selecting the proper terms to be made use of. There is often even a contradiction in terms. In vain do we question such persons in the endeavour to assist them. In their emotion they answer everything at cross purposes or almost at random.

**15.**—In these doubtful cases we must not be too set upon putting these questions, but **wait** quietly, for a long time, it may be. There is only one point that must be decided: has the person in question passed beyond the way of meditation? To know more would be useful, but is not necessary. In fact, if the director undertakes this inquiry, he does so especially for the sake of solving these two practical problems: 1° Should the person be allowed to pursue his way? 2° Should he be allowed to dispense himself from certain devotional exercises?

Now, in order to answer the first question, there is no need to distinguish between the prayer of quiet and the prayer of simplicity. The points with regard to which we have to satisfy ourselves are the same in each case, namely: 1° that the occupation is good and holy in itself; 2° that there is facility or even an attraction with regard to it; 3° that it is profitable (ch. ii, **53**).

**16.**—As to the **second question,** namely, whether such or such a vocal prayer or devotional exercise should be omitted, it is sufficient to ask what is the motive that prompts this desire for its suppression. Is it caprice? a desire for singularity? or is a real difficulty experienced?

In this last case we shall give the rule of not forcing oneself in the matter. And the director will be at particular pains to reassure those souls to whom these new paths are a source of fear.

* The following objection has sometimes been wrongly deduced from this uncertainty, namely, that the characters attributed to the mystic union are not sufficient to differentiate them from ordinary prayer. They are sufficient if we consider them in themselves; for example, perceiving a thing is different from imagining it. But in practice they may be so obscure that we do not distinguish them clearly. This drawback is inevitable, as there is not always a sudden leap between ordinary prayer and the mystic state. We stand hesitating before certain almost imperceptible transitions. So, too, doctors have been able to define the character proper to certain diseases which are thus theoretically and scientifically differentiated from all others. But in practice they are often embarrassed because these characters are scarcely perceptible. We cannot require of medical science that this should be otherwise.

**17.**—By like arguments we should see that if the director, or the person directed, **supposes wrongly** that the prayer has advanced beyond that of simplicity, this illusion has no practical ill-effects. But the contrary is the case with illusions where the person wrongly believes that he has received revelations.

Again, if a man has had an extraordinary prayer and fancies that he has arrived at the full union, when he is merely at the prayer of quiet, it is of small importance.

**18.**—If the director has detected the presence of an extraordinary degree of prayer, should he **conceal his opinion** from the persons concerned, in order to keep them in humility?

He should at least enlighten them sufficiently to enable him to point out the proper course to follow and to dispel their fears. I should even prefer him to act still more frankly, and give them a book in which a good description of their state is to be found. There is a very simple way of maintaining in humility a person who has not gone beyond the prayer of quiet. Instead of trying to persuade him that he has experienced nothing extraordinary (which makes too great calls upon his ingenuousness), it is only necessary to explain that his degree is a very small thing in comparison with those to which other souls have attained. We shall thus be saying nothing but the truth.

**19.**—The person who believes himself to be thus favoured will do well, on his side, to **seek for enlightenment** with regard to his state. This is the way to avoid false rules of conduct and to co-operate with the divine action. But we must avoid too much self-analysis. By over introspection we do not arrive at a clearer view of our state; we only disturb ourselves uselessly.

**20.**—**Degree of certainty.** I will suppose that the person in question is regarded as sufficiently serious-minded to allow of reliance being place in his answers. But if, on the contrary, he were to be of a credulous disposition and badly balanced, the examination would be almost useless. His statements would be of little value. But it is easy to be informed in advance upon this point. Such defects manifest themselves on a hundred occasions.

I will further suppose that the prayer inquired into presents all the above-mentioned characters clearly. I say that *we can then be morally certain that it is the mystic union.*

What might be feared is a counterfeit of the Devil or one proceeding from our own minds. We will show that this double fear would be groundless.

**21.**—And, to begin with, the **Devil** cannot imitate the mystic state. Both St. Teresa and St. John of the Cross hold this doctrine (see Extracts, No. **40**).

In the first place, there is one character that the Devil would be careful not to imitate, at least, sincerely; and this is the impulse towards virtue. And then the actual foundation of this prayer is beyond his powers; while the contrary holds good with regard to revelations and visions, such, at any rate, as are not purely intellectual. For, according to the teaching of the Schools, neither good nor evil angels can act directly upon the intelligence or upon the will. They operate upon our interior faculties only, the imagination and the feelings, and this by the agency of the body alone.* The Devil, like the good angel, may awaken sensible images, as well as pleasure and emotions of the same order. But all mystic writers declare that this disturbance of the lower faculties is powerless to produce the mystical knowledge of God and the union corresponding with it.

**22.**—In the same way there can be no counterfeit proceeding from **our own minds.** The true mystic contemplation has an assemblage of characters that we can never reproduce at will. The imitation will be so gross as to be instantly apparent. And no writer has thought of pointing this out as a possible danger, while quite the opposite is the case where revelations are concerned. And then there is one circumstance that can always reassure the director and the penitent himself: it is this latter's astonishment with regard to his prayer; his objections, his difficulties. His constant attitude of mind may be summed up thus: "I should never have imagined that things would happen like this; a different way would be better." But if this state were a product of his own mind, it would fit in with his preconceived ideas instead of shocking them. He would not be incessantly asking that his prayer should be explained to him. He would find it perfectly intelligible.

**23.**—The **imagination** is especially powerless to imitate the mystic union, because it can represent sensible images only, and this is the exact opposite of the state in question. And, further, those in whom this faculty predominates, have no inclination towards this union. Their attraction is towards apparitions of Our Lord and of the saints, and converse with them. And they feel nothing but weariness in a prayer that is without images and acts of reasoning. In a word, imaginative persons tend, naturally and strongly, to feed the imagination and not to condemn it too fast.

### § 3. Some Other Observed Facts

**24.—Natural sleep** may quite well, alas! overtake us during the prayer of quiet. Some persons who suffer from fatigue are very prone to this infirmity during the morning and evening exercises.

A semi-slumber may also be experienced under the following conditions: Take a man who is subject to insomnia at night, for instance. He is then in a state of drowsiness, midway between the lucidity of the waking state and sleep; now he is more fully awake, now he slumbers, to return once more to a certain degree of consciousness. If he were in the natural state during this time, the

* St. Thomas (1, q. cxi, a. 3, ad. 3) and Suarez (*De Angelis*, Book VI, ch. xvi, Nos. 10, 12) say that in order to insinuate thoughts and sentiments they make use solely "of nervous fluids and humours (*spiritus et humores*)." It is in the same way that angelic spirits perform the inverse operation that consists in reading our thoughts.

imagination would alternately go off upon some capricious *excursion,* and then persistently bring back to him the remembrance of some work with which he had been much engaged. But if he has the prayer of quiet *each time that he thinks about God,* this prayer often replaces, in part, the wanderings of the imagination. It is not a special state of prayer, but the mingling of two states; in one the drowsiness is natural, and the other supernatural.

**25.**—On the other hand, has ecstasy or any one of the neighbouring states sufficient strength to *dispel* sleep completely for several hours at the least? I believe so; but we are reduced here to simple probabilities.

I even think that ecstasy may do more than this, and in a good measure *take the place* of sleep without causing any inconvenience to the body; so that no more fatigue is felt during the day than if the natural rest had been enjoyed at night. This would explain why some saints could pass a great part of their nights in prayer, as St. Francis Xavier did, without becoming worn out. St. Peter of Alcantara, so St. Teresa tells us, went for forty years without sleeping more than an hour and a half each night (*Life,* ch. xxvii, 18).

**26.—Gifts that are added to the prayer of quiet.** I have already pointed out that in this prayer the claspings of the mystic union may become the *spiritual embrace,* and that at certain moments the soul is taken possession of by a *very ardent delight* (ch. xi, 5).

**27.**—A third grace may also supervene: we begin, but in a very low degree, to have **a certain sight of God.** We do not attain to Him by an interior touch only. A new manner of acting seems to be produced in the soul, and it is compared to a look. This look inclines towards something external, subtle, mysterious, immense, something that can be compared to a misty and luminous atmosphere.* But we feel that this is not a material light, that this space is not that in which material bodies exist. If it is weak, we perceive it before us and above us only; otherwise it surrounds us on all sides; it is of uniform appearance in all directions.† In vain should we try to analyse this sensation in order to understand it better; we should discover nothing new.

At the same time it produces great pleasure without our being able to explain why.

It causes scarcely any ligature, and is not affected by walking or external movements. It differs here from the mystical touch.

* This must not be confused with the mist that I spoke of in ch. viii, 4, and which affects the bodily eyes.

† St. Alfonsus Rodriguez was no doubt alluding to this circumstance when he wrote: "The bodily eyes see what is before them, not what is behind, but the eyes of the soul, which is a spirit, see not before only but also behind, to right and to left. Thus the soul that is *enclosed in the midst of God,* possesses God, sees Him and knows Him from all sides by the aid of that bright light that God communicates to her for the purpose of seeing Him and tasting Him. But she does not understand Him, for He alone understands Himself" (*Vie* of the saint, compiled from his Mémoires. Retaux edition, 1890, No. 12).

**28.**—This manifestation is sometimes **still more accentuated.** We are then aware, in this immensity, of a majestic Being who fills us with fear and love. At times we even feel His gaze.

St. Teresa appears to have alluded to these *pre-visions* in ch. xvii, 8 of her *Life.* She speaks of a variety of the mystic union having the two following characteristics: 1° that God "constrains the will and even the understanding, as it seems to me, seeing that it makes no reflections, but is occupied in the fruition of God: like a person who looks on, and sees so many things that he knows not where to look—one object puts another out of sight, and none of them leaves any impression behind." Certain divine attributes, then, are seen; 2° this state, although an absorbing one, is connected with the prayer of quiet. For the saint says that it is inferior to the full union (which she had previously described), and she confirms this estimate by adding that the soul suffers from distractions in it.

**29.**—It has been said (ch. v, **16**) that the prayer of quiet makes God felt as being present in the soul. But in the special case under our notice, God manifests Himself as **present outwardly** at the same time. And further, if this light is strong, if it becomes an abyss of brightness and exercises an attraction over us, then, instead of being led to fall back upon ourselves in order to enjoy God, we wish to precipitate ourselves out of our bodies, to go and lose ourselves in that spiritual cloud and to attain to a fuller possession of Him who conceals Himself therein. In the case of ecstatics, this outward tendency often shows itself unconsciously by their gestures and attitudes: their eyes and arms are raised towards Heaven.

To sum up, the impression of exteriority does not constitute the basis of the prayer of quiet, but is merely added to it at times.

**30.**—This act of sight, all intellectual as it is, does not seem to me to be separated from an **accompanying act of the imagination.** The imagination, which has a need of action, seeks to imitate the intellectual impression by representing a luminous space. It gives a minimum of representation. But this is what proves its presence to me: several persons have said to me: "I see a sort of whitish atmosphere." Now, to speak of colour is to point to an element that belongs to a sensible faculty. And in the same way they spoke of seeing it in front of them. This localisation of the Divine Being implies a co-operation of the imagination.

We must not, however, go so far as to claim that the imagination does everything here, and that it is an illusion to believe in the existence of an intellectual and supernatural sight. The clear proof to the contrary is that no pleasure could be experienced in contemplating such an attenuated and impoverished image, and that no one would try to return to it. Who would resign themselves to gaze for any length of time at a material mist or a sheet of blank paper?

**31.**—At the risk of appearing over subtle, I add a last instruction. As it is not of great importance, the reader need not linger over it if he finds it unintelligible.

It is this. When God sends the intellectual light of which I have spoken, even in a low degree, certain exterior circumstances may affect our **facility for discerning it.** Let us suppose that we are in some lighted place. If the eyes are shut, we might think that it would be more easily distinguished if the eyes were open, for then we could be more readily attentive.

But we find, on the contrary, that the task of discernment is then less easy. The cause must be sought in the imaginative act, which, as I have said, comes to associate itself with the intellectual impression. According as it is itself more or less distinct, it renders this impression more or less apprehensible.

Let us see what occurs with the imaginative act in the two cases referred to. If the eyes are closed, they only see the luminous eyelids, and thus receive the sensation of a white, uniform expanse, without any fixed outlines. The imaginative act, being quite similar, is no longer discernible as distinct from the bodily impression, in spite of the attention brought to bear upon it; and the supernatural vision, which is weak and subtle, suffers from this confusion.

If, on the contrary, the eyes are open, they perceive a multiplicity of objects, of various forms and colours. It then happens, and this is proved, that this variety causes the imaginative act (which, as we have just said, is of a quite contrary kind) to stand out in contrast to it. It becomes more perceptible, and with it the intellectual vision.

**32.**—I described farther back (ch. xi, **10**) the **sufferings** experienced in the prayer of quiet. The same kind of sufferings were found also in the first night of the senses, the painful aspiration, for instance, after a fuller possession of God, and sometimes tedium. This shows us once more that the states of prayer follow each other continuously. There is one difference, however—namely, that in the prayer of quiet you have begun to enter upon this possession.

### § 4. Of an Illusion That is Easily Avoided

**33.**—**Real revelations** are, generally speaking, only received when the period of ecstasy has been reached, or nearly so. Those who have not passed beyond the prayer of quiet, or an infrequent full union, should be on their guard against the idea that they may hear supernatural utterances. Unless the evidence is irresistible, they should attribute them when they occur to the activity of their own imagination.

**34.**—But may not these revelations occur, at least, in diminutive? May we not have **very distinct inspirations** which dictate the proper line of conduct under difficult circumstances when the reason is silent or is even inclined in the opposite direction?

As a general rule, nothing of the kind is received. There is a danger here of illusions, which may be very grave *if we have not been warned,* but which vanishes if we are prepared. Finding herself in a new and extraordinary state, the inexperienced soul is inclined to say: "The whole tenor of my life is now doubtless about to become extraordinary. God, who is doing so much for me, wishes to be my counsellor. There will be no further need for a prudent study of the arguments for and against in important circumstances. An inner voice will point them out to me, and I shall merely have to follow these indications blindly."

Such a contention is exaggerated. God has given you *no undertaking* that He will direct you Himself. You take a great deal upon yourself by attributing such obligations to Him. He has done very much for you already by inclining you strongly to virtue.

If, then, you feel that some idea takes possession of your mind and endeavours to *impose itself upon you,* as though it were a divine inspiration, do not conclude that this is so in reality and that you must follow it. Continue, *like those who are still in ordinary prayer,* to weigh the *pros* and *cons,* and to decide at your *leisure* in accordance with the rules for the discernment of spirits. We shall see farther on (ch. xxiii) that it is necessary to act with the same reserve, even with regard to revelations properly so called.

**35.—It is greatly to the Devil's interest** that you should act in the contrary manner, that you should consider yourself as being inspired, and even a prophet. You will in this way commit great imprudences which will destroy your credit with those about you, so that you will not accomplish the good to which your state of prayer should have led, and you will bring these states into contempt. People will say: "See what they lead to!" They only lead witless or badly instructed people to these lengths; but you will not get your adversaries who are full of prejudices to understand these distinctions. It is a duty here not to compromise your reputation for good sense and prudence. Mysticism would suffer for it.

It is not the prayer of quiet, however, that we must blame for these blunders, but a quite accidental circumstance—namely, the ignorance of those who receive it.

**36.**—The **exaggerated terms** in which certain authors speak of the prayer of quiet, and of the "admirable lights" which, according to them, are received in it, help to foster the above illusion. They speak truly, in the sense that God is felt as being present. But the reader generalises, and believes that *distinct counsels* are constantly received.

Others say: "In the prayer of silence we must listen to God. Speak, Lord, for Thy servant heareth." Some very good authors have made use of these expressions. But they may be wrongly understood. Certain readers will conclude from them that in the prayer of quiet God *really* converses with the soul in supernatural *words,* and not merely by the familiar voice of conscience.

There is not the same drawback when this language is used with reference to ordinary prayer, for it is then evident that the expression, "listening to God," is purely metaphorical.

As an instance of these exaggerations let us quote a seventeenth-century writer who, really little in sympathy with mysticism, shows himself over-enthusiastic in this passage: "The conscience of these souls," he says, "is an *exact and perfect book* The Holy Spirit generally *says* and *does everything,* while these souls *have only to read and look* at what is happening... The Spirit of God in them is a real teacher who instructs them *incessantly.*"

It may, perhaps, be so in the case of certain ecstatics, at certain moments, at least. But it is a wild fantasy to depict the inferior degrees in this fashion.

The saints themselves were not content "to read and to look" in the divine book. We see, for example, that certain great founders of religious Orders—St. Dominic, St. Francis of Assisi, St. Ignatius, and St. Francis of Sales—groped about, as it were, to a large extent before they found the true form of their Institute or of many characteristic rules. It was not sufficient for them, therefore, to turn over the leaves of the divine book.

There is another significant fact: during the great Western Schism the saints were not all of one mind, not even those who had the gift of reading consciences. St. Vincent Ferrer and Blessed Peter of Luxembourg proclaimed the legality of the Avignon Pope; and St. Catherine of Siena, with St. Catherine of Sweden, the daughter of St. Bridget, were on the side of his rival. The Holy Spirit did not choose to intervene, in spite of the great advantages which would have resulted.

Far more, the angels themselves are not always informed of the divine intentions. For Daniel saw the angel of the Jews in conflict with the angel of the Persians. If they had read in the eternal book, the question at issue would have been decided.

**36** *bis.*—I have put souls on their guard against the inspirations or impulsions that they believe themselves to receive relating to their *conduct.* But the contrary attitude should be recommended for things seen suddenly and luminously with the *eye of faith,* and which give a higher comprehension, not of novelties, but of truths held by the Church. Such illuminations can be accompanied by no drawbacks; they are, on the contrary, very precious graces.

**37.**—At times the above illusion occurs in **a modified form.** Here the person does not count on the gift of prophecy, or even on inspirations in cases of difficulty. He merely expects more help than if he had continued in the ordinary way. So far there is nothing that is not quite reasonable. But here is where the illusion begins; he is inclined to say: "I need not exercise such great care over my conduct; God will be responsible for preserving me from all *faults* and all *imprudences.* And, further, He exhibits a special friendship towards me; now friendship knows how to turn its eyes away from seeing slight faults."

This would be a very unsound argument. Here, again, God has never engaged to preserve you from faults, and still less from blunders. You are tempting Him. The Devil is inciting you to an exaggerated confidence, as he did with Our Saviour in the desert, setting Him upon the pinnacle of the Temple and saying to Him: "Cast Thyself down, for it is written that He has given His angels charge over Thee, and in their hands shall they bear Thee up, lest perhaps Thou dash Thy foot against a stone." On the contrary, you must use your wisdom and good sense.

With regard to familiarity with God, there are two kinds of familiarity, as with men. The bad kind consists in no longer attaching any importance to small faults.

**38.**—History shows us by **two celebrated examples,** those of Fr. Falconi and Mme. Guyon, that, in spite of extraordinary graces of prayer, we may fall a victim to *false ideas* which we wrongly attribute to God. They were the great apostles of quietism: the one in the first part of the seventeenth century, and the other towards its close.

Fr. Falconi, of the Order of Mercy, who died in Madrid in 1658, was apparently of a high virtue and possessing great gifts of prayer, so much so that he was raised to the dignity of Venerable.* His *Life,* written by his friends and disciples, equals that of the greatest saints. Nothing is lacking: ecstasies, prophesies, and miracles. Even when rejecting the greater part of these interested eulogies (which Rome does not seem to have taken seriously), it is still probable that Falconi received at any rate, for some time, very great graces. His absurd doctrines rendered them sterile. Three of his works were circulated for a long time before being condemned (see the Bibliographical Index at the end of this volume).

Mme. Guyon offers an analogous case. When we read her *Life,* written by herself, and it appears to be sincere, we are led to regard it as probable that she really had the prayer of quiet in her youth. She then gave admirable examples of patience amidst all the contradictions with which she was surrounded. But she intoxicated herself with quietistic theories, and persuaded herself that she had a vast mission in the Church. She put faith in one of her revelations, according to which, equally with Our Lady, she was pre-eminently the type of the Spouse celebrated by the Canticle of Canticles and the Apocalypse. Her director, who was rather her disciple, the Barnabite Fr. La Combe, encouraged her in these foolish fancies. The fruit of the earlier graces that she had received was lost.

* I do not know if he has retained this title, which in reality is merely provisional. At Rome, a name is quietly removed from the list from time to time. It was in this way that the celebrated Dom Jean de Palafox, Bishop of Osma, the enemy of the Jesuits, was Venerable. Had Falconi and Palafox been beatified, it would have been the glorification of Quietism in the one case and of Jansenism in the other.

Fr. Falconi and Mme. Guyon would seem, then, to have received everything that was necessary for sanctity. In spite of their good faith, they only ended by harming souls and becoming a wound in the Church's side.

**39.—Conclusion.** Those who begin to experience supernatural states of prayer should not exaggerate the confidence that they feel in being the object of a special providence on God's part. God has not promised to perform miracles in order to preserve them from false notions and imprudences of conduct. It is for them to be on their guard and to accept serious direction.

## EXTRACTS

### § 1. The Devil Can Neither Produce the Mystic Union Nor Even Understand It

**40.**—St. John of the Cross:

1° "The reason why the soul is free, *concealed from* the devil and his wiles in the obscurity of contemplation, is, that *infused contemplation,* to which it is now admitted, is passively infused into it, in secret, without the cognisance of the senses, and of the interior and exterior powers of the *sensitive part.* And that, too, is the reason why it escapes... from the evil one who, *were it not for the sensitive faculties,* could never know what is passing in the soul. The more spiritual therefore the communication is, and the farther it is removed beyond the reach of sense, the less able is the devil to perceive it" (*Obscure Night,* Book II, ch. xxiii, p. 446). "*Neither can he know* of those Divine touches in the substance of the soul wrought in loving knowledge by the substance of God" (*Ibid.,* p. 451). See also *ibid.,* ch. xvii.

2° Speaking of the obscure contemplation of the second night: "... Satan himself *cannot penetrate* this secrecy, *nor discover this converse,* nor can any intellect ascertain how it is effected" (*Living Flame of Love,* Stanza IV, line 3, pp. 302-3).

**41.**—St. Teresa on full union:

"... the devil cannot interfere, nor do any harm, for His Majesty is so joined and united with the essence of the soul, that the evil one dare not approach, *nor can he understand this mystery.* This is certain, for the devil does not know our thoughts, much less can he penetrate a secret so profound, that God does not reveal it even to us. Oh, happy state, in which this cursed one cannot injure us!" (*Interior Castle,* Fifth Mansion, ch. i, 6).

The saint speaks in the same way of every grace that is purely intellectual.

### § 2. It is Not Necessary to Conceal From the Soul the Mystic Graces That She Receives

**42.**—St. Teresa:

1. "The knowledge you are not labouring under a delusion will *console you greatly,* in case Our Lord should *ever* grant you any of these favours... People may say such things appear impossible; and it is best not to give scandal to those weak in faith by speaking about them. But it is better the latter should disbelieve us, *than for us to desist from enlightening souls which receive these* graces, that they may rejoice and endeavour to love God better for His favours..." (*Interior Castle,* First Mansion, ch. i. 4, 6).

2. The saint tells how, at the age of twenty, she was sometimes "raised to the prayer of quiet, and now and then to that of [full] union, though I understood not what either the one or the other was, nor the great esteem I ought to have had of them. I believe it would have been *a great blessing to me if I had understood the matter*" (*Life,* ch. iv, 9). Till she was forty years old she "had no master—I mean no confessor—who understood me,... which did me much harm, in that I frequently went backwards..." (*ibid.,* 8).

3. "Therefore, for the love of Our Lord, I implore those souls to whom His Majesty has given so great a grace—the attainment of this state [prayer of quiet]—*to know and make much of themselves,* with a humble and holy presumption, in order that they may never return to the flesh-pots of Egypt" (*Life,* ch. xv, 5).

4. "Our Lord bestows a signal grace on the soul *if it realises* how great is this favour" [the prayer of quiet] (*Interior Castle,* Fourth Mansion, ch. ii, 7). If the person concerned does not receive this knowledge directly it must be given him either by books or in conversation (See ch. xxvi, 16).

5. A false argument drawn from the necessity of humility. The saint, speaking of one who has received the prayer of quiet, says: "Let him not regard certain kinds of humility which exist, and of which I mean to speak. Some think it humility, *not to believe that God is bestowing His gifts upon them.* Let us clearly understand this, and that it is perfectly clear God bestows His gifts *without any merit whatever* on our part; and let us be grateful to His Majesty for them; for if *we do not recognise the gifts* received at His hands, we shall never be moved to love Him... An opposite course tends to *take away all courage;* for we shall think ourselves incapable of great blessings, if we begin to frighten ourselves with the dread of vainglory *when Our Lord begins to show His mercy upon us.* Let us believe that He Who gives these gifts will also, when the devil begins to tempt us herein, *give us the grace to detect him,* and the strength to resist him—that is, He will do so if we walk in simplicity before God, aiming at pleasing Him only, and not men" (*Life,* ch. x, 4, 5).

6. "... because a soul, when Our Lord begins to bestow these graces upon it, does not understand them, and does not know what to do with itself; for if God leads it by the way of fear, as He led me, its trial will be heavy, if there be no one who understands the state it is in; and to see itself as in a picture is a great comfort; and then it sees clearly that it is travelling on that road. The knowledge of what it has to do is a great blessing for it, *so that it may advance forwards* in every one of these degrees of prayer; for I have suffered greatly, and *lost much time,* because I did not know what to do; and I am very sorry for those souls who find themselves alone when they come to this state "(*Life,* ch. xiv, 10).

# CHAPTER XVII

## DETAILS REGARDING THE FULL UNION (THE SECOND STAGE OF THE MYSTIC UNION)

1.—**Definition**. After the prayer of quiet, or incomplete union, comes, as I have already said (ch. iii, **8**), the full union, or semi-ecstasy, which St. Teresa calls the *prayer of union* (*Interior Castle,* Fifth Mansion, ch. ii, 1), or *third water* (*Life,* ch. xvi, 1; xvii, 7), or *fifth mansion* of the interior castle. I have said elsewhere (ch. iii, 15) that Scaramelli and many other writers after him have employed the term *simple union,* which suggests an inaccurate idea.

Let us begin by recalling our definition (ch. iii, **8**): It is a mystic union 1° of such strength that the soul is *fully* occupied with the divine object; in a word, there are no distractions. But 2° the senses continue to act, or partially so, at any rate.* By a greater or less effort, moreover, it is possible fully to re-establish relations with the external world, to move, and thus come out of our prayer.

2.—**Where it differs from the prayer of quiet.** The fundamental difference is that the soul is plunged more deeply in God. The clasping of the mystic union is much stronger. And hence follow several consequences; the first mentioned in my definition is the absence of distractions. The second is that the personal effort is reduced almost to nothing. Finally, the third is that there is a much greater certainty of God's presence in the soul. St. Teresa regards this last character as the surest mark of this prayer (*Interior Castle,* Fifth Mansion, ch. i, 8).

3.—**Discussion.** According to this, there would be nothing really new in the full union. The facts would be the same as in the prayer of quiet, only their intensity would be greater. But is it quite certain that no other important differences exist? I do not think that there are any. †

* St. Alphonsus Liguori gives a similar definition: "In the simple union, the faculties are suspended, but not the bodily senses, although they may be greatly hampered in their operations" (*Homo. Apostol.,* Appendix I, No. 7).

† Here I maintain a very reserved attitude with regard to any positive statement. As to the prayer of quiet, I have a great number of documents, but not many as to the full union. I know a few persons only who have attained to it.

We must turn to St. Teresa for the reply, for she was the first to establish a distinction between this state and the neighbouring prayers; and it was she also who introduced the usage of giving it a special name. Up to then, no one had noticed that there was an important stage between the lower degrees of union, called the prayers of repose, and that of ecstasy (see ch. xxix, **8**).

St. John of the Cross continues to look at things as a whole (ch. iii, 14), and with him the word *union* has a more general sense. And still less must we endeavour to solve the problem by quoting yet earlier writers who employ the word *union*. They also understood it in its wide sense.

This matter settled, St. Teresa proceeds to ask herself, in the *Way of Perfection* (ch. xxxi), in what the *prayer of quiet* differs from that of *union;* these words being, of course, understood in the restricted sense that she had given them. Now, she does not think of indicating any new feature in the second of these states. She refers to two only of the characters of which I have spoken: the absence of distractions, and the almost total disappearance of effort on the part of the soul.

She had already given expression to this last thought in her *Life* by the comparison of watering a garden. Now she compares God, not to a fertilising water, but to a food, to milk or manna.* What she desires to call attention to is the difference in the *effort,* not the difference in the *result,* for this result is the same—namely, to possess in ourselves the divine food.

**4.**—The **old writers** who have followed St. Teresa in describing this state make mention of no other differences. For they merely repeat, with the addition of superlatives, what they have already said of the prayer of quiet.†

A modern writer, however, very reliable on other points, seems to hold (without bringing forward any proofs) that, while this state lasts, it contains a new element— namely, a beginning of the *transforming union.* For he gives this definition: "It is an interior sensation by which the soul is made aware that God is uniting Himself with her and *making her participate in His life.*"

But this transient participation takes place at the most in certain raptures, and this is probably what St. Teresa calls *espousals* (*Interior Castle,* Seventh Mansion, ch. ii, 2). The saint says plainly: "I think the union which takes place in the prayer of [union],‡ though not actually the spiritual espousals, resembles

* Speaking of the prayer of quiet, she says: "... Herein is this prayer distinguished from that wherein the soul is *altogether united* with God; for then the soul receives not this nourishment as here, by swallowing it down; but finds it within herself without perceiving how Our Lord put it there. Here, it seems, He will have the soul take a little pains, though this with *so much ease* that it is scarce felt" (*Way of Perfection,* ch. xxxi, p. 96).

† It will suffice to quote Vallgornera (Part IV, d. 2, a. 16, No. 11) and Scaramelli. The latter, when describing the full union (Tr. 3. chs. xv, xvi, xvii), repeats fundamentally the same explanations which he has already given for the prayer of quiet.

‡ The English rendering gives prayer of *quiet,* but the French is *l'oraison d'union,* and the Spanish *"la* UNION *aun no llega a desposiono espiritual"* (*Translator*).

the preliminaries that take place when two people are contemplating a betrothal." She adds that her future Spouse then visits the soul, as He wishes her to get to know Him better (*ibid.*, Fifth Mansion, ch. iv, 2).

**5.—Objection.** St. Teresa compares the soul in the enjoyment of the full union to the silkworm enveloped in the cocoon that it has spun for itself. And then it comes fresh from this state like "a lovely little white butterfly" (*ibid.*, Fifth Mansion, ch. ii, 5, 6). This comparison seems to imply a transformation, and refers consequently to the spiritual marriage, which is called the transforming union.

**6.—Reply.** You yourself admit that, according to the saint, the soul *does not merit the name of butterfly until she has left* this prayer. During the prayer itself, and each time that she falls back into it, she is merely like the silkworm. It is therefore a question of a *transformation in behaviour,* and not of a new manner of operation *during the continuance* of the mystic state. All the context helps to convince us of this.*

And, further, the saint tells us that the butterfly must undergo a new and final *metamorphosis,* and that it will have to *die* in order to take on the life of Jesus Christ through the transforming union (*Interior Castle,* Sixth Mansion, ch. xi; Seventh Mansion, chs. ii, iii). The transformation does not take place, then, in the full union, nor even in the ecstasy.

**7.—The condition of the sensible faculties.** When the union is strong they begin to be in a dormant state, as it were; all feeling is partially lost, or rather, as St. Teresa seems to say, the soul is too absorbed to notice† them, which is not quite the same thing but rather less pronounced.

**8.—Intensity.** St. Teresa says that this may be either more or less (see Extracts, 8°, 10°). It is an intermediate state between the prayer of quiet and ecstasy, and it is one which may fall at times to the first of these states or rise to the second.‡

At first sight it seems that St. Teresa is contradicting herself when, speaking of the third water (*Life,* ch. xvi, 4), she says "the faculties of the soul now retain only the power of occupying themselves wholly with God," and at the same time she declares that it is possible to compose verses in order to give expression to the soul's joyful intoxication. But she takes it for granted that this last case can only occur at moments when the union is greatly diminished; or, again, it is a question of a derogation of the mystic state such as has been

* Example: "The little butterfly, which is never still, but always fertile, *doing good* both to itself and to *others,* for it can find no true repose" (*Interior Castle,* Fifth Mansion, ch. ix, 1).

† "It is deprived of all feeling whatever" (*Interior Castle,* Fifth Mansion, ch. i, 3). "So completely does this take place [the being deprived of all feeling] that I know not whether the body retains sufficient life to continue breathing;... I believe it does not; *at any rate,* if it still breathes, *it is done unconsciously*" (*ibid.*).

‡ Fr. de Clorivière says: "The prayer of union is the goal and perfecting, as it were, of the prayer of quiet" (*Considerations,* etc., Book II, ch. xxxviii).

referred to elsewhere: God allows us to do two very different things simultaneously in exceptional cases (ch. xiv, 47).

To sum up, the essential character of the mystic union is the absence of distractions. The remainder is merely an accessory, and may simply serve to distinguish the sub-degrees.

**9.—Duration.** According to St. Teresa (*Interior Castle,* Fifth Mansion, ch. ii, 6), the union in its plenitude does not last half an hour. It then falls back into a lower degree —the prayer of quiet; but it may increase again afterwards. It is the culminating state which is of such short duration. We shall see that it is the same in the case of ecstasy (ch. xviii, 8).

**10.**—There is reason to believe that, **apart from the time of prayer,** those who receive the full union frequently feel it, to a certain extent, in all their exterior occupations. They often have a continuous although fainter and more confused sentiment of union with God.

Courbon says that this is so (Part V, ch. i),* and several persons have told me the same thing. If this sentiment were strong, it would usually interfere with their occupations.

## EXTRACTS

**11.**—St. Teresa. In the prayer of full union the faculties are wholly occupied with God:

1. "God then [when He raises it to the union] deprives the soul of all its senses that He may the better imprint in it true wisdom; it neither sees, hears, nor understands anything while this state lasts, which is never more than a very brief time; it appears to the soul to be much shorter than it really is" (*Interior Castle,* Fifth Mansion, ch. i, 8).

2. After giving to distractions the name of "agile little lizards which will try to slip in," and saying that these troublesome animals penetrate into the prayer of quiet, the saint adds: "However active these small lizards may be, they cannot enter the fifth mansion, for *neither the imagination, the understanding, nor the memory,* have power to hinder the graces bestowed in it" (*Interior Castle,* Fifth Mansion, ch. i, 5).

* His testimony carries great weight, for he has known persons who had reached this degree (Part V, ch.iii).

He also endeavours to prove this fact by a passage from St. Teresa's *Life* (ch. xvii). But the argument has little value, because the saint says particularly that she is speaking of *one of the varieties* of the prayer of union only. Is there *always* something similar, although less marked, in the other cases? The saint does not say so.

3. "... The soul is asleep, fast asleep, as regards the world and itself... being unable to think on any subject [save God], even if it would. There is *no need here of any effort* to suspend the thoughts; the soul can only love, if it can do that: it knows not how, nor whom it loves, nor what it desires. In fact, it has died entirely *to this world, to live more truly than ever to God.* This is a delicious death to suffer. The soul is deprived of the faculties it exercised while in the body" (*Interior Castle,* Fifth Mansion, ch. i, 3).

4. "Do not imagine that this state of prayer, like the one preceding it, is a sort of drowsiness (I call it 'drowsiness' because the soul seems to slumber, being neither quite asleep nor wholly awake). In the prayer of union the soul is asleep, *fast asleep,* as regards the world and itself, and in fact, during the short time this state lasts, it is deprived of all feeling whatever, being unable to think on any subject, even if it would" (*Interior Castle,* Fifth Mansion, ch. i, 3).

5. "When *all* the faculties of the soul are in union,... they can then do nothing whatever, because the *understanding* is, as it were, surprised. The *will* loves more than the understanding knows; but the understanding does not know that the will loves, nor what it is doing, so as to be able in any way to speak of it. As to the *memory,* the soul, I think, has none then, nor any power of thinking, nor are the *senses* awake, but rather as lost, so that the soul may be more occupied with the object of its fruition; so it seems to me" (*Relation VIII* (*Second Letter*), to Fr. Rodrigo Alvarez, *Life,* p. 436).

6. "That which torments her here [prayer of quiet] is the understanding, or imagination; which it doth not do when there is a union of all the three powers [memory, understanding, and will], because He that created them *suspends them;* for with the delight which He then gives, He busies them all without their knowing how, or being able to understand it" (*The Way of Perfection,* ch. xxxi, p. 96).

7. Speaking of the *third water:* "The faculties of the soul now retain *only the power* of occupying themselves *wholly* with God; not one of them ventures to stir, neither can we move one of them without making great efforts to distract ourselves—and, indeed, I do not think that we can do it at all at the time" (*Life,* ch. xvi, 4).*

8. "... The *union* of which I am speaking may also be called a trance. The difference between union and trance *is this,* that the latter lasts longer and is more visible outwardly, because the *breathing* gradually diminishes, so that it becomes *impossible to speak* or to open the eyes; and though this very thing occurs when the soul is in union, there is more violence in a trance, for the natural warmth vanishes, I know not how, when the rapture is deep; and in all

* This passage shows that the third water is indeed the prayer of full union, since it agrees with the definition that I have given of this state.

these kinds of prayer there is *more or less* of this" (*Relation VIII* to Fr. Rodrigo Alvarez, *Life*, p. 457).

9. The effects of full union "although they are there [in ecstasy] *of the same nature*, yet in a more advanced state the effects are very much stronger" (*Interior Castle*, Fifth Mansion, ch. ii, 6).

10. There is a greater and a less degree in full union:

"I said 'some,' but in reality there are very *few* of them who never enter these mansions; *some more and some less*, most of them may be said at least to gain admittance into these rooms. I think that several of the graces I am about to describe are bestowed on only a few of the nuns, but if the rest only arrive at the portal of these mansions, they receive a great grace from God, for: 'many are called, but few are chosen.'... My daughters, if you would purchase this treasure of which we are speaking, God would have you keep back *nothing* from Him, *little or great*. He will have it *all*; in proportion to what you know you have given Him, will your *reward be great or small*. There is no more certain sign, whether or no we have reached the prayer of union" (*Interior Castle*, Fifth Mansion, ch. i, 2, 3).

# CHAPTER XVIII

## ECSTASY (THE THIRD STAGE OF THE MYSTIC UNION)

### § 1. DEFINITION AND FIRST SERIES OF FACTS

**1.—Definition**. Let us recall our definition of ecstasy (ch. iii, **8**), but adding to it some supplementary details.

Supernatural ecstasy is a state that, not only at the outset, but during its whole existence, contains two essential elements: the first, which is interior and invisible, is a very intense attention to some religious subject; the second, which is corporeal and visible, is the alienation of the sensible faculties.

This last expression signifies not only that sensations no longer penetrate to the soul, but that it would be extremely difficult to produce them, either if one wished to do so oneself, or if other persons endeavoured to incite the action of the organs of sense.

I have already defined (ch. xiii, **2**) what is understood by complete or incomplete ecstasy.

**2.—Explanation** of the definition. 1° I am only defining supernatural ecstasies here. Farther on (ch. xxxi, § 3) I shall define natural ecstasies and inquire whether any such phenomena have ever existed.

2° The beginning of the definition may be slightly modified by saying that the soul is in a mystic state interiorly. I do not specify exactly whether it is a question here of union with God, of supernatural locutions or the apparition of a saint. We shall see presently whether any ecstasies are produced by one of these apparitions without the accompaniment of the extraordinary union with God as present at *the same time* (ch. xx, **30**).

I shall occupy myself exclusively in this chapter with the ecstasy that includes union with God.

3° I have been careful not to present the alienation of the sensible faculties as being *produced* by the interior state. This would be to prejudge a delicate question of causality which will be studied farther on (ch. xxxi, § 5). It is enough for the moment to know that one element *accompanies* the other, without inquiring into their connection with one another.

I have already dealt with the four physiological facts that characterise ecstasy (ch. xiii, 2).

**3.—Various names.** St. Teresa describes ecstasy under the name of *the fourth water* (*Life,* ch. xviii and fol.), and as the *Sixth Mansion* of the *Interior Castle.*

Several authors have been in error when quoting from this eighteenth chapter of her *Life.* As the saint tries to avoid using the word ecstasy, she often employs the more general term of *union,* and then these passages are wrongly cited as referring to the preceding degree, the full union. The evident proof that it is a question here of ecstasy is that the state described responds to the definition of ecstasy: according to the saint, there is alienation of the sensible faculties. (For a fuller discussion of the subject, see ch. xxix, 6.)

The early writers often give to ecstasy the name of *elevation of the spirit,* or *flight of the spirit* (*excessus mentis*).*

**4.—Various kinds of ecstasy.** It is called:

1° *Simple ecstasy,* if it comes on gently, little by little, or if it is not of great strength. As a rule, it is then thought not to contain any revelations;

2° *Rapture,* when it is sudden and violent;

3° *Flight of the spirit,* when, says St. Teresa, "the soul suddenly feels a rapid sense of motion that *appears* to hurry it away" (*Interior Castle,* Sixth Mansion, ch. v, i). "I cannot say whether the soul dwells in the body meanwhile; I will neither affirm that it does, nor that the body is deprived of the spirit" (*ibid.,* 10). See also the *Second Letter* to Fr. Rodrigo Alvarez).

**5.—Some special features.** 1° These raptures are *"very alarming, especially at first"* (*Interior Castle,* Sixth Mansion, ch. v, i; *Life,* ch. xx, 4).

2° This violent motion cannot, as a rule, be resisted (*ibid.; ibid.*). But in the case of simple ecstasy, resistance is possible, at least, at the outset.

3° The body "continues in the *position* that it was in when the rapture came upon it" (*Life,* ch. xx, 23).

4° God nearly always reveals *secrets* of the supernatural order in raptures, and as a rule it is felt that the understanding has been amplified (**30, 45**).

5° *After* a rapture, there may be a *difficulty in resuming* the ordinary exterior occupations, and this sometimes continues for several days (*Interior Castle,* Sixth Mansion, ch. iv, 18; *Life,,* ch. xx, 29; xl, 11).

6° The memory of what has been seen is retained; but the soul does not usually know how to express this exalted knowledge by means of our human language which is so imperfect, and which is obliged to make use of images (see Benedict XIV, *De canon.,* Book III, ch. xlix, No. 12).

7° When the soul *comes out* of a rapture that has overtaken her in the middle of a conversation or a prayer, it often happens that she continues the phrase

* St. Thomas: "In Greek it is called *extasis,* and in Latin *excessus mentis"* (2, 2, q. 175, a. 2, No. 3; and *De Veritate,* q. 13, a. 2, ad 9).

where it was broken off. St. Francis of Sales was doubtless acquainted with this fact; for one day, when Sister Anne Rosset had fallen into an ecstasy while conversing with him on divine love, he said to the Sisters: "Note carefully what she says when she comes back to herself." And, as a matter of fact, she then went on with the conversation that had been interrupted (*Œuvres de Ste. J. F. de Chantal,* Migne ed., Vol. I, p. 979).

A similar fact is related in the *Life* of the Ven. Jeanne of the Cross, of the Order of Poor Clares of Roveredo, in the seventeenth century. As she was speaking one day to the Sisters on the divine perfections she fell into a rapture that lasted for seven hours. When she came out of it she "took up the thread of her discourse at the point where she had interrupted it" (*Vie,* by Bede Weber ch. xiii).

Dr. Imbert cites similar facts which occurred to St. Thomas of Villanova, Blessed Nicholas Factor, Francis of Cocogliedo, Giles of Santarem, Mary of Maillé, and Paul of Sogliano (Vol. II, ch. xvii, p. 275).

8° Some saints used to utter a *cry* as the rapture seized them: this was the case with St. Peter of Alcantara, for example, and St. Joseph of Cupertino. The latter, when questioned on the subject, declared that his cry was a simple outburst of love (*Vie,* by Bernino, ch. xxii). See Benedict XIV, *De canon.,* Book III, ch. xlix, No. 11.

Towards the end of her raptures St. Frances of Rome often uttered moans. These were caused by the, at times, violent suffering that she experienced when obliged to tear herself from the celestial vision. The saints who appeared to her had to preach resignation to her, and even to reproach her (Bolland., March 9th; see especially Visions, 13, 14, 34, 37).

**6.**—The **age** at which the saints became ecstatics. Dr. Imbert has compiled the following table: "St. Hildegard, Catherine of Racconigi, Dominic of Paradise, St. Catherine of Siena, at the age of 4; St. Peter of Alcantara, Blessed Osanne of Mantua, St. Angela of Brescia, Mother Agnes of Jesus (of Langeac), at 6 years of age; Blaise of Caltanisetta, at 7; Christina of Stommeln, at 11; Agnes of Montepulciano, at 14; Mary of Agreda, at 18; Veronica of Binasco, at 40; and St. Teresa, at 43" (Vol. II, ch. xvii, p. 276).

**7.**—**Duration** of the ecstasies. I am led to believe that it is the exception when they do not last more than half an hour. In the *Lives of the Saints* we have instances of a great number of ecstasies that lasted for several hours. One of the most remarkable is that of St. Thomas of Villanova. When reading the Office for Ascension Day, says the Bull of his canonisation, he was seized by an ecstasy, and remained suspended in the air for twelve hours. There have been ecstasies that lasted for several days; Blessed Angela of Foligno, St. Catherine of Siena, St. Clare of Montefalco, 3 days; Blessed Colomba of Rieti, 5 days; Ven. Marina de Escobar, 6; St. Ignatius, 8; St. Colette, 15; St. Mary Magdalen of Pazzi, 40 (Bolland., 1st *Life,* No. 151).

**8.—Objection.** St. Teresa says that ecstasy lasts "but a short time" (see ch. x, 10). She even speaks of half an hour.

**9.—Reply.** It is not exactly that. The saint is careful to tell us that it is a question not of the ecstasy itself, but of its greatest intensity. In short, the alienation of the sensible faculties does not disappear to be resumed later on. No instance of interruptions of this kind is cited. It is not a descent from the mountain's summit to the plain, but only to a lower ridge, except just at the last. It is a case of oscillation between a maximum and a minimum which is very much above the prayer of quiet.

**10.—Frequency.** This has been very great with several of the saints. With some, their life has been little else than a series of ecstasies. This was so with Blessed Hermann Joseph (of Steinfield), a Premonstratensian Canon of the thirteenth century,* St. Michael of the Saints, St. Catherine of Ricci, and St. Joseph of Cupertino. It was the same with St. Mary Magdalen of Pazzi, excepting during two periods of her life (ch. xxiv, **93**). Blessed Raymond of Capua, who became General of the Dominicans, has written the life of his penitent, St. Catherine of Siena. He states that he has seen her thousands of times in an ecstasy. Much the same thing has been said of St. Colette.

The most astonishing case is that of Maria von Moërl (ch. xiii, 17). During the last thirty-five years of her life her ecstasy was continuous. She only came out of it in obedience to her confessor's orders, which were given either upon the request of a visitor or that she might attend to her daily household affairs. For she continued to manage the housekeeping in her humble family. "She thinks of everything, cares for everything, forestalls the needs of those who are in her care, and owing to her sound common sense everything about her is perfectly organised" (*Goerres,* Book IV, ch. xxi).

**11.—Influence upon the health.** See ch. xiii, **13.**

**12.—The recall.** A certain procedure, which goes by the name of the recall, is often followed with regard to ecstatics. Their Superior or confessor—in a word, someone to whom the Church has given spiritual authority over these persons—gives them the formal *order* to return to the natural state.

This order is sometimes *exterior* and *oral,* uttered aloud, that is to say, so that it reaches the ecstatic; sometimes it is *mental,* or its equivalent, the sound of the voice not reaching the person's ears.

Before describing the results of these recalls, let us put a preliminary question.

* Towards the close of his life, during Mass, towards the offertory, he fell into an ecstasy almost daily. He continued motionless with his eyes open for several hours. Numerous complaints from strangers, the faithful, and from nuns, when he said Mass for them, resulted. Nobody would serve his Mass. They said also that such devotion entailed a needless expense in lights. But it was finally proved that by a miracle the candles were not burnt down more than would have been the case in a Mass of ordinary length (Bolland., April 7th, Life, No. 34,35).

**13.**—Who is it *that really obeys* when an order is thus received during an ecstasy?

In reality, it is God who obeys, notwithstanding appearances. For if the act could be attributed to the ecstatic, 1° he would have to *hear* the order. Now, persons do not usually hear while they are in an ecstasy; 2° even if we suppose this condition to be fulfilled, he must be able to *carry out* the order. Now, no one can come out of an ecstasy at will. With reference to the Superior, then, the ecstatic is in the state of a person who is asleep.

**14.**—It does not follow from this that the Superior cannot issue an order to the ecstatic, but only that he should not do so lightly, from idle curiosity or vanity.

**15.—Results of the mental recall.** Experience shows that it is *sometimes* successful. But more often, according to Scaramelli, it is ineffectual (Tr. 3, No. 192). Fr. Séraphin also speaks of not having succeeded with the mental recall (*Théologie mystique,* No. 194).

The following reason may be given. In consenting to execute the order given, God wishes to glorify the spiritual authority of the Superior. The intervention of this authority should therefore be made openly.

**16.—Results of the exterior recall.** It is regarded as historically proven that this is *invariably* successful, if the ecstasy is of divine origin. No known saint has proved an exception to this rule.

It is not easy to establish this thesis clearly *a priori.* Scaramelli gives this reason only: the person is not withdrawn from the ranks of the living; he therefore remains subject to the authority of the Church. But the same thing can be said when it is a case of natural sleep; and yet the order is then ineffectual.

**17.**—There is a **partial exception** pointed out by Fr. Séraphin . When the ecstatic is ill, he makes a movement like one who is trying to awake. He thus shows his obedience. But for physical reasons that we are ignorant of, he comes to himself with great difficulty only (*Théologie mystique,* No. 197).

**18.**—Experience shows that ecstatics obey a **representative** of the Superior equally with the Superior himself.

**19.**—If, while giving the order *exteriorly,* the Superior has the *interior* will not to be obeyed, the ecstatic remains in the same state.* It is the same if, instead of an **absolute order,** it is given conditionally, or merely in the form of a request.

Finally, the Superior has no right to obedience if he orders a miracle; for instance, if he tells an infirm ecstatic to get up and go into the church.

If the Superior wishes the ecstatic to answer a question without coming out of the ecstasy, I am assured that he is not always obeyed. He has no right to get

* See the experiment of this nature made upon the Ven. Dominic of Jesus-Mary by Philip II, of Spain, to whom had been delegated the powers of the General of the Carmelites (Dr. Imbert, Vol. II. ch. xviii, p. 287).

information by this extraordinary means, even upon spiritual subjects. It is not seemly that God should be interviewed, so to speak.

**20.—And conversely.** If the recall succeeds, are we certain that the ecstasy is divine? No. It being admitted that the Devil is able, strictly speaking, to simulate ecstasy outwardly, he could do the same as to obedience. He would not go so far as to give the interior disposition to this virtue, but he would produce the appearance of it, for the moment, at any rate.

**21.—Does the ecstatic know that he is recalled?** Many ecstatics have answered in the negative (see Dr. Imbert): St. Joseph of Cupertino, for example (*Vie,* ch. xxix); God merely withdraws, the subject not knowing why. But there is an example of the contrary also. Joseph a Spiritu Sancto quotes the case of the Ven. Dominic of Jesus-Mary. If his Superior, even when absent, ordered him to come out of his ecstasy, he heard God say to him: "Resume the use of your faculties and obey the order that I give you by the mouth of your Superior" (Vol. III, disp. 18, q. 3, No. 169). Maria von Moërl was a similar case. *

**22.**—Fr. Séraphin says that he has proved that the recall nearly always **causes great suffering** to the ecstatic. He has met with one exception only, which was when the ecstasy followed closely upon Communion, and the Sacred Species were not yet consumed at the moment of the recall (*Theol. myst.,* No. 194). It is not known whether this is a general law.

Fr. Séraphin concludes from this fact that the recall should be made very seldom and only by necessity.

I know another director who has proved that the recall, if made suddenly, produces a violent and painful shock. To avoid this result, he ordered the person in the rapture to return slowly, progressively, for instance, in the space of a quarter of an hour. If he specified the moment, the rapture ceased exactly at the time fixed.

The Ven. Anne Madeleine de Remuzat's Superior relates that she found her one day in an ecstasy in her room: "I told her to rise up under obedience... At this word 'obedience' she came back to herself, but so exhausted that I had to put her to bed" (*Vie,* ch. xii).

### § 2. What It Is That Takes Place in the Soul During the Ecstasy

**23.—Intellectual visions of the Divinity.** In the preceding degrees God permitted the soul to lose herself in Him more or less deeply. But, ordinarily, He did not allow Himself to be seen. In rapture, the contrary usually happens. Several *attributes* that have been hidden now begin to manifest themselves. One

* It would be incorrect to say that the communication thus established between the ecstatic and his Superior is identical with that existing between the hypnotised subject and the operator. For the superior has had nothing to do with the production of the ecstasy, while the hypnotised person has submitted to an action that concentrated all his faculties upon the operator.

of the sublimest communications which is often referred to by writers, is the intellectual vision of the *Blessed Trinity.* Even if we did not know by the Church's teaching how many Persons there are in God, and how they proceed One from the Other, we should come to know it, and, by way of experience, through seeing it. We shall return to this vision later on (ch. xix, 15).

The Ven. Marina de Escobar relates that she sometimes saw intellectually one of the Divine Persons without the other two: either the Word (Vol. II, Book II, ch. xxxi, No. 1), or, more often, the Holy Ghost (Vol. I, Book II, ch. xxxiii, § 4; xxi, § 3 and 5; xxiv, § 1 and 3; Vol. II, Book I, ch. xlviii, No. 2; Book II, ch. xxx, No. 3).

**24.—Blinding contemplation.** When God thus allows His attributes to be seen, a certain obscurity always remains. It is a singular thing that the stronger the light, the more dazzled, *blinded,* does the soul feel. It is in this way that the sun would blind an owl and cause it suffering. An excess of light produces almost the same result as darkness. It is a mingling of knowledge and of ignorance, the ignorance being what strikes us the most. The attribute of incomprehensibility manifests itself more and more. We bury ourselves in the "divine darkness."

**25.—Incommunicable attributes.** This effect of blindness is produced not merely by the too great strength of the divine light, but by the nature of certain attributes that have been manifested. Some of these attributes are a thousand times more incomprehensible to us than the others. The terrifying obscurity that they produce is called "the *great darkness.*"

These profounder attributes are those that *no creature can possess:* those that are incommunicable. For example: infinity, eternity, the creative power, universal knowledge, immutability, a-se-ity (the absence of an external cause), the absence of any real distinction between the attributes and their fusion in an indefinable and higher good that contains all other goods.*

The divine nature may be compared to the solar sphere. When our eyes contemplate this orb, they at first see the flaming exterior surface only. But through the fissures in this surface astronomers perceive the great semi-obscure

* To give us an idea of this fusion of the divine attributes into one, which is the fulness of being, let us consider what it is that takes place when, holding a glass ball in the hand, we look at it from the outside. We see it limited by a circular outline. If we alter our position, we see another circle, and each time that the point of view varies, there is a fresh circle. But if the eye is inside, the aspect is totally changed. Do we still see circles; yes or no? We can reply in two different ways. We can say: No, we no longer see them. One uniform surface meets the eye on every side and upon this nothing distinct is traced. And yet these circles are there in a certain way which we call visual; by an effort of thought they can be detached from the whole: all that we have to do is to take one portion of the surface only, instead of the whole.

So there are two ways of knowing God. One human, and appertaining to the reason, which is outward. He is then seen under the special aspect of this or that attribute. The other knowledge is divine, it is seen from within, from the centre; God grants it to us by participation in His nature. There is no change now according to the points of view taken. All is blended into one. But by a mental effort the former distinctions can be found again.

central nucleus. So in God there are, as it were, two strata of attributes. Those on the surface can send out their light to creatures and be reflected in them. We already know these attributes in them. For example: beauty, justice, mercy, and intelligence. But above is the semi-obscurity of the central nucleus of the incommunicable attributes. The creature does not receive their radiance. And because our reason has nowhere encountered them, it stands abashed before this unexpected manifestation. And there results for us a special obscurity; the joy of attaining to a new and a marvellous knowledge is mingled with the uneasiness of feeling that we are not fitted to understand them properly.

**26.—Contemplation that is called "by negation."** The greater part of the incommunicable attributes can only be apprehended by our infantine intelligences, or described indirectly, by means of the negation of known things. But they exist in God in the positive state, and it is as positive quantities that infused contemplation attains to them, thus surpassing the reason which confines itself to the negative idea. And so when writers say that the contemplative *proceeds by negation,* they merely intend to allude to the imperfect and negative *language* that he is obliged to make use of, in order to describe what is perceived.

In the ordinary way of prayer there is an *acquired contemplation,* which is also called contemplation "by negation." But this is not a state of prayer. It is rather a way of forming ideas about God, by declaring that such a perfection is not in Him after the same manner as it is in creatures, but that it is present in a higher way. It is a negation followed by an explanatory affirmation. We must not confuse these philosophical mental operations with prayer, and still less with the mystic state.

It is true that many of the early writers speak of it as a kind of prayer. This is, I think, due to an over-literal interpretation of Dionysius the Areopagite. If anyone were to try to uphold this interpretation, I should say to him: "Have you really met with contemplatives who can occupy themselves for an hour together with these negations?"

**27.**—The great darkness is sometimes pierced by the blaze of a rapid *flash* of light which we readily interpret as the light of glory, because it seems to show God as He is.

**28.—Comparison of the beatific vision** with intellectual visions of the divinity. Let us first question the descriptive mystics, and then the theologians who complete what the mystics have begun. The former content themselves, as a rule, with two statements which give the impression that they experience. They say, first, that the knowledge given to them is experimental, and this is an analogy with the vision enjoyed by the blessed in Heaven; they say also that it is never without a certain obscurity; and this is a difference.

Now, in reality the difference goes much deeper. The vision of the mystics is of another nature altogether; it does not manifest God "such as He is in Himself" (see ch. xxxi, § 4).

**29.**—Has it ever happened to certain souls to possess the **beatific vision,** in the strict sense of the word, *transiently?* The question has been argued at great length by theologians, so I will merely refer the reader to their writings. Definite experiences on this point are lacking.

Upon the whole, it is generally admitted that this grace is possible, but excessively rare. The difficulty begins when we wish to decide if the favour has been accorded to this or that saint in particular. We are reduced on this point to reasons of fitness or of sentiment, which do not convince everybody. God is not obliged to do everything that seems suitable to us. Has He done it, yes or no? That is the question; it remains obscure.

**30.**—I said farther back (**5**) that the full plenitude of the understanding is retained during the rapture; it even seems to be enlarged and that there is a growth of activity in the higher faculties. All ecstatics affirm this fact (see Extracts, **68**), which stands out in all that they tell us concerning the mysteries that have been revealed to them. Magnificent sights, profound ideas present themselves to the mind. They are powerless to explain in detail what they have seen, however. This is not because the intelligence has been as it were asleep, but because it has been raised to truths which are beyond the strength of the human understanding, and they have no terms by which to give expression to them. Ask a *scholar* to express the intricacies of the *infinitesimal calculus* in the vocabulary of a child or an agricultural labourer!

As Fr. de Bonniot remarks: "It is not enough to say that the language which is adapted to the ordinary operations of the human mind is necessarily insufficient; *the ideas themselves,* those ideas by which we understand everything, because they are the basis of our judgments, are no longer applicable to the intuitions of ecstasy which are of an infinitely higher order" (*Le miracle et ses contrefaçons,* Part II, ch. vii, § 2).

Certain sceptic philosophers hold, on the contrary, that there is a diminution of the intelligence in ecstasy. For this they are obliged to reject the testimony of ecstatics themselves, the actual *data,* that is to say, upon which our arguments should be based (see ch. xxxi, **48**). This *a priori* rejection is the consequence of their religious system. According to them, there is no such thing as the supernatural. Hence they are obliged to deny all states of soul which are raised too far above those that we see every day. Further, many of these unbelievers are Monists, not admitting any personal God as distinct from the world. Consequently, anyone who claims to rise to the real knowledge of this Being and to gaze into His very depths, is simply suffering from hallucinations: his cause is condemned in advance. He claims to see admirable attributes and perfections. But how can he see them when nothing of the kind exists!

These philosophers, I have said, like to think that not only is the intelligence not amplified, but that it is impaired, and so much the more as the ecstasy is deeper. According to them, the ecstatic has merely freed himself, after a more or less painful struggle, from the multiplicity of ideas and images. He arrives at something subtle at an almost imperceptible "residue," at one single idea (monoideism), which is merely an attenuated image. In high raptures, the soul rises to a yet simpler degree: stultification, which they qualify, through politeness, with other less offensive names, such as loss of consciousness or of personality (see Extracts, **74**).

For the support of this theory they rely upon certain somewhat exaggerated expressions that mystics have sometimes employed, and which are easily explained by the context; as when they say that the understanding has ceased to act (see ch. ix, **15**).

If ecstasy really or even partially extinguished the faculty of knowing and loving, directors of all ages would not have failed to pursue it with their anathemas, as being time ill-spent; but they knew that the contrary was true.

**30** *bis.*—This theory of unconsciousness, then, falsifies facts in a most audacious way and replaces them by fantastic descriptions. Some authors prefer a less drastic system. They adopt the **emotional explanation.** This concedes that the ecstatic is not plunged into a kind of deep sleep. On the contrary, he experiences violent emotions which cause him to lose the use of his senses. Then, as nothing new comes to take their place, it follows that his mind should apply itself solely to some trivial idea; so trivial, indeed, that the writers do not think of paying any attention to it.

This second system is less opposed to recorded facts than the first, since it does not reduce the ecstatic's occupation to zero; but it denies half the facts that are positively affirmed by the mystics; it admits the emotional part of the ecstasy, and rejects *a priori* the intellectual part which belongs to the superior order.

Another objection can be offered to the two preceding theories. Mystics admit that, as a rule, the period of ecstasy is not reached suddenly. It is generally preceded by a series of phenomena on a lesser scale, the least of which St. Teresa has called the prayer of quiet. If any theory explains ecstasy, it ought, in due proportion, to explain its diminutives. But they never attempt this, because they see too plainly that it would not be successful. If ecstasy were a mere state of stupefaction, as the first theory teaches, the state that preceded it should be the beginning of this lamentable condition, but this in no wise corresponds to the classical descriptions. Mystics and their directors would be suspicious of this psychological poverty and would repel it. If, on the contrary, as the second system requires, ecstasy resolves itself into an immense outpouring of love, will they say that this vehemence begins with the prayer of quiet? To do so would be contrary to experience. Do they say, on the other hand, that the person is often very calm and almost cold? But then this lack of warmth in the will would be associated, by supposition, with a trivial idea. In what does such a state deserve to be called mystic? In what does it differ from the most ordinary mental prayer? Why does it cause surprise and even terror in beginners?

The true mystic theory, on the contrary, responds fully to these questions. It tells us that this surprise, this feeling of mystery, arises because a new faculty appears in the soul, giving intellectual perceptions. It matters little that this mode of knowledge is weak in its beginnings; it astonishes and terrifies, as does everything that is new and unexplained. The emotional theory fails completely here.

**31.—Spiritual sufferings during ecstasy** or at its close. We must not think that the only sentiment experienced during or immediately after the ecstasy is one of joy. There are ecstasies, or transports of love, which are more or less painful (see St. Teresa, *Life,* ch. xx; and *Interior Castle,* Sixth Mansion, ch. xi).

This depends upon the attributes that God manifests and the secondary knowledge that He adds to them. If, for instance, we see God's infinite goodness, His holiness and *His hatred of sin,* and if at the same time we are enlightened as to our own unworthiness, the contrast will be so striking that we shall feel a sentiment of self-disgust and horror.

We then understand the saints' utterances, saying that they are great sinners, and even exaggerating this to the point of saying that they are the greatest of sinners. No expression seems to them strong enough to render the *feeling of repulsion* that they experience towards themselves. Hatred leads people to overwhelm their enemies with abuse; and the saint, in the light of God's brightness, has come to hate himself, in so far as he is a sinner.

**32.**—Or, again, God shows **the severity of His judgments** upon the lost, and He makes us see that His judgments are just. Before this angry Father the soul trembles, she feels as though threatened by His wrath. So little more is needed that she should herself become the object of this Divine justice! She ranges herself on the side of this justice and wishes herself the victim of a thousand pangs in order to satisfy it.

**33.**—And even when God manifests the abysses of His love, the inebriation that this sight causes, changes into torture if God shows us that this **love** is **forgotten.** What do I say? Blasphemed, cursed by sinners and the damned. The soul suffers for God, Who is forgotten, and for her fellows, who so madly renounce all these eternal joys. Her zeal for souls and her powerlessness to lead them back to God becomes a martyrdom.

**34.—The sight of God** may also be the cause, after the ecstasy is over, at least, of great suffering; because it is not yet possible for the soul to possess Him completely (St. Teresa, *Life,* ch. xx, and *Interior Castle,* Sixth Mansion, ch. xi).

**35.**—Sufferings of another kind have been sent to the saints during their ecstasies. God causes the **scenes of the Passion** to pass before their eyes. Like the Blessed Virgin on the way to Calvary, or rather throughout her whole life, they participate in all Our Lord's sorrows. Blessed Angela of Foligno gives vigorous expression to this idea when she says that contemplating "that sharp sorrow which was in the soul of Christ... *I was transformed into the sorrow of the*

*Crucified*" (*Visions and Instructions of Blessed Angela of Foligno,* ch. xxxi, pp. 111, 113).

**36.**—Should we be fulfilling the precept as to the **hearing of Sunday Mass** if we had been all the time in an ecstasy?

Theologians who have gone into this question say yes. The Church's intentions have been sufficiently complied with.

**37.—Does the soul acquire merit** while in an ecstasy? Let us consider this question, although it has little practical importance. The essential thing is to know that ecstasy contributes powerfully to sanctification, we need not understand how this takes place. The most general opinion is that the soul does then acquire merit.* St. Teresa gives a reason for this view, based on common sense. She says "that God should do her so great a favour to the end she lose her time, and gain nothing as to meriting in it; this is not credible" (*Conceptions of the Love of God,* ch. vi, p. 375).†

Suarez also thinks that the contrary "is improbable."

This argument is considerably strengthened by the following considerations: 1° that ecstasies have lasted for several hours in the case of many saints, and have been very frequent. How much time would thus have been spent without meriting! It will be objected that these graces gave the saints strength to bear meritorious trials afterwards. But God could accomplish the same result in a few minutes. St. Teresa refers to visions that were only momentary, and which, however, brought her considerable fruit (*Life,* ch. xxviii). 2° And especially there have been long ecstasies at the moment of death. St. Teresa died after an ecstasy of fourteen hours; St. Aloysius Gonzaga under similar conditions; and St. Alphonsus Rodriguez after three days of ecstasy. The Menology of the Society of Jesus states that the Portuguese Fr. Laurence Rebello was in an ecstasy for twelve days before his death (1679). He came out of it only long enough to kiss his Crucifix. Now, this is just the time when it would be regrettable to lose merits by an anticipation of the joys of Heaven which will endure for all eternity.

**38.—Objection.** In order to merit, you must be free. Are you free in ecstasy?

**39.—Reply.** Exactly; with regard to acts of love we hold that this is so in a certain measure.‡ St. Thomas says that the beatific vision is alone capable of compelling the will *absolutely* (1°, 2nd q. 10, a. 2). According to him, when any

* See Suarez (*De oratione,* Book II, ch. xx, No. 6). Philippus a SS. Trinitate (Part II, Tr. 3, a. 4), Antonius a Spiritu Sancto (Tr. IV, No. 505), Joseph a Spiritu Sancto (Vol. III, disp. 18, q. 2, No. 74. The discussion runs to 102 folio columns). Scaramelli (Tr. 2, No. 254), Schram (Vol. II, No. 607 of the 1848 edition and No. 597 of the old edition). He quotes Antonius de Annunciatione and Gravina.

† Scaramelli says: "This is a thing worthy of consideration that so humble, so circumspect a saint when speaking of devotional matters, speaks so resolutely when she is treating of the soul's merit in these ecstatic unions" (Tr. 2, No. 254).

‡ But this knowledge to which we like to cling does not depend upon free-will. And this is enough to make the definition of the mystic states correct (ch. i, 1).

good is offered to us with some admixture of imperfection (and this is the case with contemplation, because of its obscurities), *a certain measure* of liberty always remains with us. We may not perhaps go so far as to hate the object, or to choose a different act, but it rests with us to produce these acts or not, or to produce them with more or less strength or rapidity.*

**40.**—In the lives of several of the saints we see that prayers continued **during sleep.** Examples: St. Alphonsus Rodriguez and St. Vincent Ferrer. St. Teresa received this favour when her ecstasies first began (*Life,* ch. xxix, 9). See ch. xix, **8** *bis.*

It is advisable to ask ourselves by what signs we may distinguish ecstasy from the prayer that continues supernaturally during natural sleep. These two states have, in fact, two resemblances which lead to their being confused: in neither do the senses act, and in both there is union with God. Writers do not say whether there are really any differences and, if so, in what they consist. Is it a simple question of intensity, so that the word ecstasy would only be used when the interior occupation is extremely strong? Is it that the body needs to be extended and supported, as in the case of ordinary sleep, and that there are moments when there is a confused feeling of consciousness? Or, again, is the decision to depend upon some extraneous circumstance, the fact that it is the usual hour for going to sleep, for example? This is a question that should be cleared up.

### § 3. Errors Regarding Ecstasy: How it is Confused With Certain Conditions of Ill-Health

**41.**—In our days doctors have made a careful study of certain states of ill-health which they liken to the ecstasy of the saints. But the majority are careful not to confess that the **resemblance** is merely **external**; it holds good with regard to the bodily phenomena only, which are of no importance. There is, on the contrary, a profound dissimilarity from the point of view of the soul, as I am about to show.†

* In scholastic language it is the distinction between the liberty of *specification* and that of *contradiction* or of *exercise.*

† Upon these questions, consult Fr. de Bonniot's learned work *Le Miracle et les Sciences médicales,* Book II. With regard to ecstasy, he refutes the unproved statements made by Lemoine, Maury, Morel, Lélut, Michéa, Cousin, and Barthélemy St.-Hilaire.

He makes this remark on the subject of the physiological phenomena of ecstasy: "They have as their immediate condition *the organism and its actual dispositions.* The cries, the signs of weakness, the *morbid symptoms,* the tremblings, the immobility, the rigidity, the lowering of the temperature and the blood-spittings can, strictly speaking, be nothing but manifestations of the ecstatic's *temperament...* If simple-minded people think differently, it is due to the fact of their simplicity, and if doctors class theologians with the simple people in this connection, it is an effect of ignorance, which is a form of simplicity" (*Le Miracle,* Book II, ch. i, § 1).

And further, nothing hinders God from giving even supernatural states of prayer to a person having some trying or strange malady, and then the exterior manifestation will be affected by it.

Let us remark in passing that most of the doctors who occupy themselves with religious psychology are mental specialists. Being constantly with persons suffering from hallucinations, they are inclined to identify with them anyone whose state of mind is exceptional. They are fond of busying themselves with mysticism, instead of leaving this study to theologians; they see in it an extension of their own special subject.

**42.**—They have begun by likening ecstasy to **lethargy** and **catalepsy,** which also paralyse the limbs, but there the soul is deprived of knowledge. Just as well might we confound sleep with the ecstasy of the saints. In the latter the soul is filled with light and joy.

**43.**—Then they have gone on to try to identify ecstasy with the hypnotic state. Physically, there is again a certain analogy here with ecstasy. Certain sensations are abolished. And, further, the person can assume the attitudes of prayer by suggestion. And yet, even from the point of view of the body, there are differences at times. For true ecstasy always produces an effect of calm and dignity; at the Salpétrière Hospital, on the contrary, you often see convulsive and repulsive movements. I speak, of course, of cases where these sick persons are left to themselves and to their own natural attacks. If, on the contrary, they act under the influence of a hypnotiser, their state can no longer be compared with that of the saints. A new element comes in. These hypnotisers can order them to assume noble or pious attitudes. The saints have no need of this extraneous influence.

**44.**—But it is from the **point of view of the soul** that the differences are so obvious, whether *during* the ecstasy or *apart* from it.

**45.**—To begin with, **during true** ecstasy the intellectual faculty grows in a surprising way, as we have already said (**30**).

The contrary effect is produced by false ecstasy upon the neuropathic patients in the hospitals. There is a diminution of intelligence to be set against a small display of imagination. A single absolutely insignificant idea, that of a flower or a bird, is sufficient to absorb the attention *profoundly.* Medical men describe this fact by calling it the *narrowing of the field of consciousness* and of knowledge. This is the point of departure for the theories in vogue that are intended to explain the hypnotic ecstasy.

During the attack the sick person is induced to speak, but he merely utters commonplaces.

And then the hallucinations under observation in the hospitals always consist of representations of the imagination. They are visual, aural, or tactile, and are therefore very different from the purely intellectual perceptions that are generally found in the saints. We cannot, therefore, set out from the hypothesis that the two kinds of phenomena are identical.

**46.**—**Outside the ecstasy** the difference is still more easily proved: 1° the patient, upon whom experiments are sometimes publicly made in the hospitals, emerges from them depressed, dull, and stupefied. He usually exhibits an *intelligence* of a very mediocre kind, dominated by the imagination; there is no connection between his ideas; 2° but, above all, his will is very weak. And this, according to many doctors, is the fundamental character of hysteria. They explain the fact of his being unable to resist the suggestion made to him, by this unhealthy weakness. What another person orders firmly, he at once wills, especially if he has acquired the habit of yielding. These poor crazy creatures are barren dreamers, without will, incapables; 3° finally, the *moral sense* is of a very low order, and the same with the reason. We sometimes ask ourselves whether these neurotics have any real conception of duty, and if the idea of morality has any hold on them. In short, from a threefold point of view, we are confronted with a degenerate condition, an impoverished nature.

We find the three diametrically opposite characteristics in the saints who have been favoured with ecstasy, and no one, consequently, has the right to liken them to those who are either mad or half-mad. 1° They are *strong characters,* the originators of projects that are vast and difficult of execution. St. Teresa, St. Ignatius, and many others are the proof of this. They are guided not by imagination, but by reason; 2° their *will* is so strong that they fight against all opposition in order to bring their enterprises to a successful termination; but they fight, above all, against themselves, and the prolonged labour which they have had to undergo in order to practise certain virtues fills us with astonishment. We, who think that we have iron nerves, do not feel ourselves capable of such a succession of efforts;* 3° they all have a very high *moral ideal*

* Fr. Hamon calls attention to the wonderful "attitude of the saints in the face of suffering." "The neurotic man does not know how to bear suffering. When in pain, he is impatient, he murmurs, he pities himself like a baby... The ecstatic suffers, and he not only accepts his pain, but he dominates it, he triumphs over it, he accepts it with enthusiasm. These joyful sentiments are not of the earth... He interests himself, as though he were in complete health, in the joys and sorrows of others" (*Revue pratique d'Apologétique,* Dec. 15, 1906, p. 351). The writer quotes those beautiful words of St.Margaret Mary: "Who, then, is to hinder us from becoming saints, since we have hearts with which to love and bodies with which to suffer? But alas! can we suffer when we love?"

A professor at the Sorbonne has laid down this proposition: "There is no phenomenon by which, when *taken alone,* the presence of hysteria can with certainty be determined."

"From this we may deduce," says M. H. Joly, "that it is not from any one such isolated phenomenon that the character of the whole is to be concluded, but it is from the character of the whole that we must conclude the essential nature of the symptoms. Now in an individual who is struggling against the attacks of a malady that is defined as nervous, where will the dominating characteristic be, where the character of the whole, if it be not in the control which the person is or is not able to exercise over his dispositions, his sentiments, his beliefs, his resolutions?" (*Vie de P. Eudes,* p. 100). At present, however, the doctors' views concerning hysteria change greatly from year to year. See in *La Presse Médicale* of July 25, 1908, the account given of the meetings held in Paris by the *Société de Neurologie,* in May, 1908. They were not able to agree upon a definition of hysteria. Here is the conclusion of the report:

"From the discussions, an important general impression has resulted, namely, that henceforth the word hysteria should no longer be employed except with extreme reserve... Henceforth we can record this important result, namely, that certain facts which yesterday were unreservedly accepted, have been with which they are constantly occupied: the desire to forget self in order to devote themselves to the glory of God and to the temporal or spiritual good of their neighbour. They fly from honours, while often the one desire of hysterical subjects is to play a part before a little circle of spectators. The saint is not a degenerate, but a hero. To use a modern expression, he is a super-man.

Another difference is that, after the ecstasy is over, the saints remember their visions. This is rare with neuropaths.*

**47.**—The ecstatics who have **founded religious Orders** have been very remarkable for their energy and power of organisation.† Even the women have shown themselves superior to many men. They had to find subjects, money, and lands, while fighting against a thousand obstacles.

St. Teresa, at the time of her death, left 16 Convents of women and 14 of men. St. Jane Frances de Chantal left 87 Convents, 12 of which were directly founded by herself. St. Colette founded at least 13 Convents and restored the discipline in a great many more.

Mme. Acarie, one of the foundresses of the French Carmelites, led a very active life, notwithstanding her continual ecstasies. These began soon after her marriage (at fifteen and a half: 1582). Her married life lasted thirty years; she brought up six children and skilfully repaired the fortunes of her family; her correspondence was considerable. She became a Carmelite in the last five years of her life only.

St. Catherine of Siena, who died at the age of thirty-two, played a very considerable part in politics from the time she was eighteen, although she could then neither read nor write. She has been called "a statesman, yea a great statesman" (Emile Gebbart, in the *Revue hebdomadaire* of March 16, 1907).

Other ecstatics have written books that argue an immense work, both of erudition and composition, and, consequently, great strength of will. Denis the Carthusian has left forty folio volumes; St. Thomas Aquinas and St. Alphonsus Liguori were surprisingly prolific writers.

**47** *bis.*—3° An attempt has also been made to liken ecstasy to **natural somnambulism,** with which the "trances" of certain spiritualistic mediums have also been identified.

There are various kinds of somnambulism. Some last a short time only. The person may compose verses or speeches. But it has been shown that the part played by the mind has been exaggerated here. It is not the mind, but the

recognised as open to dispute or even erroneous: certain classical interpretations have lost their character of scientific absolutism."

* Some hours after the hysterical crisis, certain sick persons remember the sequence of their imaginations. Others, the crisis once over, recollect the end of their dream, and by dint of great efforts can retrace their steps little by little. In divine ecstasy these difficulties do not exist.

† M. Murisier makes the following avowal: "Renan has rightly called attention to the fact that with most mystics we find the *powerful organizer* side by side with the strange dreamer" (ch. i, § 3, p. 37).

imagination, and especially the memory, that are at work. We merely obtain a series of reminiscences (see Dr. Surbled, *La Morale,* Vol. IV, Part II, ch. i).

Other somnambulistic sleeps last for days and weeks. But whatever the kind, it cannot be profitably considered until we have described in detail the mental condition of the subject of the attack. I do not think that this has been done. We are thus arguing about a state which is not clearly defined, so much so that it is sometimes difficult to distinguish it from the state called the first or normal state. And yet, without any more information, an attempt is made to compare it with ecstasy.

There is one case of considerable difficulty which it is desirable to examine; it is that of certain somnambulists who, at first sight, seem to differ from the ecstasy of the saints in one point only—namely, that the mind is occupied with secular instead of religious ideas.

The most striking case, after that of certain mediums, is presented by Hélène Smith, of Geneva, which Professor Flournoy has had under his observation for several years, and which he has described in his learned work, entitled *Des Indes a la planète Mars* (Alcan, 1900). During her spontaneous somnambulistic trances she spoke or wrote, and described all that took place in her vision. Sometimes she saw the inhabitants of the planet Mars; now she was living with Arabs or Hindoos in the fourteenth century. Her health was otherwise excellent, and her mind apparently well-balanced!

Now, in reality this kind of vision is profoundly different from that of the saints: 1° The saints remember what they have seen, although they do not always find adequate terms with which to describe it. Hélène Smith, on the contrary, loses all recollection of her visions. 2° The faculties brought into play during the vision are not the same. With the saints, the imagination does not act during the height of the ecstasy, and is never more than an accessory; while the intellect is enormously strengthened, certain of God's transcendent attributes, and even the Blessed Trinity seeming no longer mysterious. With Hélène Smith the imagination alone acts, and this in quite a sordid manner. Not one lofty thought, but only descriptions of houses, animals, and plants, all copied from those on the earth. They are Jules Verne's romances, but much more puerile. These are true psychological, functional differences. But there is also an ethical character which forms a feature of difference between them. The saints' visions show their divine origin because they conduce powerfully to difficult virtues, to a conflict with pride, sensuality, egoism. Hélène Smith's visions have no similar result. She is a worthy young woman, nothing more. Her life is not transformed.

**47** *ter.*—4° Neither must we confuse ecstasy with the disturbing illuminations and reveries produced by **alcohol,** ether, chloroform, haschisch, opium, morphia, or nitrous-oxide.

To begin with: (*a*) the physical state is quite different. For example, no one would confound an ecstatic's noble attitude with that of a drunken man.

(*b*) The kind of knowledge is not the same. If, after taking the above-named drugs, a state of complete unconsciousness has not been arrived at, and the person still has intuitions, they "are characterised by a multiplicity of images which succeed one another without any logical order or real connection one with another; they bear the mark of essential incoherence. The mind has become the sport of whimsical, strange, and unexpected representations which pass before it" (Abbé Michelet, *Revue du Clergé Français,* Jan. 1, 1908, p. 40). With the mystic, all is coherent and exalted.

In his book, *The Subconscious* (translated into French, Alcan, 1908), Professor Joseph Jastrow gives some interesting details with regard to the mental effects of anesthetics, taken in a moderate dose so as not to produce complete loss of consciousness. It is then a kind of semi-dream.

"Opium and haschisch often produce the sense of amplification" (p. 255). All objects are enlarged: houses appear enormous, the time that it takes to wind your watch appears a century; the man feels of athletic proportions and of more than normal importance.

Mescal, a Mexican toxicant, produces the illusion of objects that change incessantly with the most brilliant colours. You see splendid butterflies; "a cigarette-box of violet hue shone like an amethyst." Real objects are transformed by the brilliant surroundings into which they are plunged. The lines of "a white spear of grey stone" "were... covered or hung with clusters of what seemed to be huge precious stones, but uncut, some being more like masses of transparent fruit," and everywhere the "vast pendant masses of emerald-green, ruby-reds, and orange, began to drip a slow rain of colours" (pp. 259, 260).

"Ether seems peculiarly disposed in favourable temperaments—by what affinities we know not—to incite reflective, contemplative, philosophic visions; and with the suspension of all feeling of effort, with the vanishing of the objective world, the seer becomes intimately merged with his thought, has no feeling of reaching his conclusions by transitional steps, but soars in the realms of exalted truth, seemingly momentous, because potent to dissipate his most troubled, most baffling obsessions of doubt" (pp. 503-4).

These effects are still more marked by the inhalation of nitrous-oxide. Professor William James, who has tested it himself, says: "He is overwhelmed by an 'exciting sense of an intense metaphysical illumination. Truth lies open to the view in depth beneath depth of almost blinding evidence' " (*ibid.,* pp. 249-50).

But he found that the phrases by which he translated his fine discoveries were devoid of all significance. Jastrow quotes on this subject a typical account by Dr. Holmes: "The veil of eternity was lifted. The one great truth, that which underlies all human experience and is the key to all the mysteries that philosophy has sought in vain to solve, flashed upon me in a sudden revelation. Henceforth all was clear: a few words had lifted my intelligence to the level of the knowledge of the cherubim. As my natural condition returned, I remembered my resolution, and staggering to my desk, I wrote, in ill-shaped, straggling characters, the *all-embracing truth* still glimmering in my consciousness. The words were these (children may smile, the wise will ponder): 'A strong smell of turpentine prevails throughout' " (*ibid.*, p. 251).

Ecstatics have no need of anesthetics in order to feel the intelligence expanded; and when they return to the normal state they remember the truths that they have contemplated and give proof of their great worth. It is an entirely different psychosis.

(*c*) "When recovered from their intoxication, the alcohol drinker and the opium smoker remain in a stupefied condition... Thought and action are diminished simultaneously. One would call it a wreck after a cataclysm. If the intellectual life has been weakened, the social life is far from being improved. Who ever became humbler, purer, more charitable, after intoxication?" The ecstatic, on the contrary, has become "better, both as to himself and others" (M. Michelet, *loc. cit.*, p. 41).

**48.**—One last question remains. Cannot ecstasy be produced without illness but in a purely natural manner, by an intense concentration of the attention on a religious object? This point will be gone into separately in ch. xxxi, § 3; the reply will be that the possibility must practically be denied.

**48** *bis*.—Those free-thinking, scientific men (see **74**), who confuse the dissimilar states of which we have been speaking, too readily forget their scientific methods when they come to touch upon religion. As long as they are upon professional ground, their prudence, *sincerity in observation,* and distrust of all unproved hypotheses, are admirable. And, besides, if they chanced to depart from these strict rules, their professional brethren would be there to call them to order. But as soon as they leave their own special province, they at once lose their fine scientific demeanour; they no longer verify facts. They make simplistic and *a priori* syntheses. But no matter! Their readers are no sharper than they, and equally *wish* these anti-religious theses to be true. It is really not worth troubling about.

Only it is no longer science: it is imagination.

**49.—Swooning.** The preceding counterfeits of ecstasy imply that the nervous system is profoundly affected. But there is a simpler, less painful counterfeit: this is swooning. It may happen to one who is very anæmic, or exhausted by indiscreet penances. Any moderately strong emotion, if only an ardent movement of divine love, and they succumb. St. Teresa describes this state (*Interior Castle,* Fourth Mansion, ch. iii, n. 12; *Book of Foundations,* ch. vi, p. 91).*

* The saint tells us who the persons are in whom she has seen this fact produced: "Some persons on account of their penances, prayers, and vigils, or even merely because of debility of health, can receive no spiritual consolation without being overcome by it." She points out the proper treatment in consequence. "Let the Superior prevent such a nun from spending more than a very few hours in prayer, and make her eat and sleep well until her usual strength is restored, if she has lost it in this way" (*Interior Castle,* ibid. ). This passage shows us that St. Teresa was well able to distinguish true ecstasy from its counterfeits.

This counterfeit of ecstasy occurs under the following conditions: 1° the person has begun to pray; and then 2° has fallen into this species of sleep, during which *his mind has been entirely inactive;* 3° and, naturally, on coming to himself again *he remembers nothing.*

**50.**—If these persons call this state prayer, it is only because there was prayer at the outset, perhaps even the true prayer of quiet. They argue in this way: "Since a grace of prayer was present at the beginning, it probably continued."

But this is a wholly **gratuitous hypothesis.** Just as a tired person may quite well give way to natural sleep while receiving the prayer of quiet (ch. xvi, **24**), so, with a worn-out constitution, he may fall into a fainting fit. The natural has quite simply succeeded to the supernatural. It is a pathological condition.

**51.**—**Scaramelli,** who describes these states (Tr. 3, No. 82), considers, on the contrary, that this is a special kind of ecstasy. He calls it *spiritual sleep,* taking this word in a sense that is not St. Teresa's. He supposes, at least, that such a state leaves good effects behind it: the soul comes to herself again in a profound peace: the mind remains attached to God and detached from creatures. It is solely because of these effects that he judges the state to have been supernatural.

But this argument is not conclusive. How do you know that these good effects are due to the prayer of any one particular hour, rather than to the spiritual life taken as a whole? You do not know it. You say that in coming out of this kind of sleep the person's soul is calm or full of ardour for action. But natural sleep produces these same restorative effects upon those who have been overcome with fatigue. A "good night" makes them alert and joyous.

**52.**—Let us firmly *maintain this principle,* proved by thousands of examples, that true ecstasies *amplify* the intelligence and the will instead of depressing them, and especially instead of annihilating them.* If anyone tries to make us admit an exception, even a rare one, let us show ourselves very exacting with regard to the proofs. Now, Scaramelli has merely given us hypotheses.

**53.**—I shall explain later on (ch. xxii, **67**) how we may in practice distinguish the divine ecstasy from its diabolic or natural counterfeits.

## EXTRACTS

### § 1. Various Effects of Rapture

**54.**—St. Teresa:

* St. Teresa: "The lesson to be learnt from this is, that whatever moves us in such a way as to make us feel that our reason is not free, should be looked on as suspicious..." (*Foundations*, ch. vi, p. 45).

1° First beginnings of rapture: "A rapture is *absolutely irresistible;* whilst union, inasmuch as we are then on our own ground, may be hindered, though that resistance be *painful and violent;* it is however almost always impossible. But rapture, for the most part, is irresistible... At other times He is pleased to be satisfied when He makes us see that He is ready to give us this grace [of rapture], and that it is not He that withholds it. Then, when we resist it out of humility [in public, for instance], He produces those very effects which would have resulted if we had fully consented to it" (*Life,* ch. xx, 3, 8).

2° After a succession of raptures. "On those days I am almost like one drunk (*como un borracho en parte*); still I am well able to perceive that the soul is in a good state, and thus, as the faculties are not free, it is painful to attend to anything more than to what the soul wishes [the Divine object]. For about a week before these happened, I was in such a state, that often I was not able to have one good thought, but rather was filled with very great aridity" (To Lorenzo de Cepeda, brother of the saint. Date, 1577, *Letters,* p. 166).

3° "There appear to me to be two things in this spiritual state [the longing to see God] which might endanger life—one is what I have just spoken of, which is very perilous, the other is an excessive gladness and delight, which is so extreme that the soul appears to swoon away and seems on the point of leaving the body" (*Interior Castle,* Sixth Mansion, ch. xi, 11).

**55.**—St. Alphonsus Liguori, speaking probably of himself, on the subject of the *flight of the spirit:*

"A person who has received this grace told me that in these elevations of the spirit, it seemed to him that his soul was *torn* from the body and violently lifted up as though she traversed in an instant a thousand miles. And this was a *great terror* to her, for she did not know whither she was going. When she stopped, she was enlightened by some divine secret" (*Homo Apost.,* App. I, No. 17).

### § 2. Visions of the Divinity and of Certain Attributes in Ecstasy

**56.**—St. Teresa: "While the soul is in this ecstasy, Our Lord favours it by discovering to it *secrets* such as heavenly mysteries and imaginary visions... But when the visions are intellectual, they *are not thus easily related,* some of those received at such a time being so sublime, that *it is not fitting for man, while living in the world, to understand them in a way that can be told,* although when the use of the faculties returns, one is able to describe much of what was seen in intellectual vision... Though the recipient is incapable of describing them, they are deeply imprinted in the centre of the soul and are never forgotten... I think that if, at any time, the soul learns no *mysteries* during a rapture, it is no true rapture... In genuine raptures... I think God ravishes the soul wholly into Himself; as one who is His very own and His bride, and He shows her some small part of the kingdom she has won" (*Interior Castle,* Sixth Mansion, ch. iv, 5, 6, 12, 13. See also *Way of Perfection,* ch. xxxiv).

2° "In an instant... [the] mind learns so many things, that if the imagination and intellect spent years in striving to enumerate them, it would be impossible to recall a thousandth part of them... Although no words are pronounced, the spirit is taught many truths; if, for instance, it beholds any of the saints, it knows them at once as well as if acquainted with them for years" (*Interior Castle,* Sixth Mansion, ch. v, 8, 9).

3° "Those who were sent on first to the Land of Promise brought back tokens from it; so here Our Lord seems to have sought to show the soul something of the land to which it is travelling" (*ibid.,* ch. v, 11).

These raptures produce in the soul "the following three graces of a very high order. The first of these is a *perception of the greatness of God,* which becomes clearer to us as we witness more of it. Secondly, we gain self-knowledge and humility... The third grace is a contempt for all earthly things" (*ibid.,* ch. v, 12, 13).

4° Speaking of the visions of the Blessed Trinity, she says: "I see clearly that the Persons are *distinct, as I saw it yesterday,* when you, my father, were talking to the Father Provincial; only I saw nothing and heard nothing... But there is a *strange certainty* about it, though the eyes of the soul see nothing; and when the presence is withdrawn, that withdrawal is felt... Though the Persons are distinct in a strange way, the soul *knows* One only God" (*Second Letter* [Relation VIII] to Fr. Rodrigo Alvarez, *Life,* p. 463).

5° "God is sometimes pleased, while a person is engaged in prayer, and in perfect possession of her senses, to suspend them and to discover *sublime mysteries* to her, which she appears to behold *within God* Himself... This is no imaginary vision, but a highly intellectual one, wherein is manifested how all things are *beheld* in God, and how He *contains them* within Himself. It is of the greatest value, for, although passing in an instant, it remains deeply engraved in the memory" (*Interior Castle,* Sixth Mansion, ch. x, 2).

**57.**—Blessed Angela of Foligno:

"Likewise, when the most high God cometh unto the rational soul, it is *at times* given her to *see Him,* and she seeth Him within her, without any bodily form, and she seeth Him more clearly than one mortal man can see another; for the eyes of the soul behold a fulness, spiritual not bodily, about which I can say nothing at all, for words and imagination fail me. Moreover, in this vision the soul is delighted with unutterable delight, and then she looketh at nothing else save that alone; for this it is that filleth the soul beyond all that can be reckoned" (*Visions and Instructions,* ch. lii, pp. 177-8).

**58.**—The Ven. Anne of Saint-Bartholomew, a companion of St. Teresa, had an ecstasy in her youth in which the eternity of God was shown to her. "This spectacle," she says, "endured only for a moment's space, the time that it takes to open and close the eyes" (*Vie,* by Fr. Bouix, 2nd edition, Book II, ch. iv).

**59.**—St. John of the Cross:

1° Sometimes "the soul here sees that all these things are distinct from God, in that they have a created existence, and understands them in Him in their force, origin, and strength, it knows also that God in His own essence is, in an infinitely preeminent way, all these things, so that it understands them better in Him, their First Cause, than in themselves. This is the great joy of this awakening, namely, to know *creatures in God, and not God in His creatures...* it is as if God drew back some of the many veils and coverings that are before it so that it might see what He is; then indeed,—but still obscurely, because all the veils are not drawn back, *that of faith remaining,*—the Divine face, full of grace, bursts through and shines" (*Living Flame,* Stanza IV, line 1, pp. 298-9).

2° Speaking of "this knowledge [which] relates directly unto God, in the deepest sense of some of His attributes, now of His Omnipotence, now of His Might, and again of His Goodness and Sweetness."... "It is only a soul in union with God that is capable of this profound, loving knowledge, for it is itself that union. This knowledge consists in a certain *contact of the soul with the Divinity,* and *it is God Himself* who is thus felt and tasted, though not manifestly and distinctly, as it will be in glory. But this touch of knowledge and of sweetness is so deep and profound, that it penetrates into the inmost substance of the soul" (*Ascent of Mt. Carmel,* Book II, ch. xxvi, pp. 176-7).

**60.**—St. Alphonsus Rodriguez:

Speaking of himself: "This person placed himself in the presence of God, saying to Him lovingly with heart and mouth: 'Lord, let me know Thee, and let me know myself.' And, at once, he was lifted up above all created things. He found himself as it were in another region, alone with God, who gave him great light concerning the knowledge of God and of self... His knowledge of God which was without intermediary and reasoning and, consequently, his love for God and his intimate familiarity with Him, rose to such a pitch that it seemed as if the Almighty *desired to make Himself known to him as He does to the Blessed in Heaven...* The soul now has but to feed on what she most desires amongst the many divine viands that are served up on the table of the divine perfections, viands that are of an excellent savour, because their *savour is the savour of God Himself.* O heavenly banquet! God invites the soul, and in this banquet of love He giveth Himself! O supreme love! O heavenly love! O precious love! O deep and divine love in which the Master of the feast *gives Himself* as nourishment to the soul... The soul forgets all earthly things and forgets her own self also, because she is solely occupied in loving God who *is* so intimately *present* to her and as *though face to face*" (*Vie,* from his Memoirs, Retaux, 1890 edition, No. 12).

As related by a contemporary: Brother Alphonsus "told me that on one occasion he was rapt in an ecstasy, to which Heaven he knows not; but he remembers, so that he can never forget, how he saw the Divine Essence. The vision took place with certain limitations which he cannot explain, unless it be by a comparison such as this: The Divine Essence was, so to say, hidden by two veils, which must be lifted before it could be seen. He only saw it imperfectly, because one veil alone was removed; but those who are in glory and amongst the Blessed see it without these two intervening veils, and therefore, perfectly. Although he was unable to see it with equal perfection and clearness, yet has he no words or intelligence whereby to describe what he saw, either as to the manner in which he had this vision or the extreme felicity that it gives" (*ibid.*, Appendix after No. 275).

**61.**—St. Joseph of Cupertino. Being asked to make known what he saw in ecstasy: "Sometimes," he replied, "I see God's attributes united in one whole, so that my spirit can neither distinguish nor divide them; at other times I see them separated and distinct. I discover ever new beauties, each part of which, equally with the whole, fills my mind with astonishment" (*Vie,* by Bernino, ch. x).

**62.**—The Ven. Mary of the Incarnation, Ursuline, describes the vision of the Blessed Trinity that was given to her when at the age of twenty-six:

"This impression was without form or figure of any kind, but clearer and more intelligible than the light itself... I saw the divine and mutual intercourse of the three Divine Persons amongst themselves, the mind of the Father, who, contemplating Himself, brings forth His Son, which generation has been, is, and will be from and for all eternity. And then my soul beheld the mutual love of the Father and of the Son, from which, by a reciprocal effusion of love, the Holy Spirit proceeded, and this without mingling or any kind of confusion... I perceived their oneness of essence, as also their operations, the interior no less than the exterior, instantaneously and without any interval of time. By this same impression the most Holy Trinity enlightened my soul concerning His exterior operations, and first with regard to the supreme hierarchy of angels, seraphim, cherubim, thrones, etc., signifying to them directly and without intermediary the requirements of His holy will..." (*Histoire,* by Abbé Chapôt, Part I, ch. vi).

Two years later she had a similar vision, but with this remarkable feature, that the vision of the Word predominated:

"While I was rapt in God by this sublime contemplation, I gradually became entirely absorbed by the ineffable vision of the Divine Word. He caressed my soul as being wholly His... Sometimes a ray of light brought back my thoughts to the Father and the Holy Spirit, and then I felt filled with confusion at having forgotten them, as it were, for a moment... But soon I was again unconsciously rapt and absorbed by the Word, in whom I once more lost myself as before" (*ibid.*, ch. vii).

**63.**—Sister Gojoz:

"Unworthy as I am, for the space of six months I have seen in God an image of the eternal generation of His Word. I have received such sublime knowledge on this subject, that in truth I believed myself to be no longer on earth. My gaze was simple, but it was so riveted and held in the bosom of the Eternal Father, that, day and night, I saw only this adorable object—His only Son, as He was there incessantly engendered... I can add nothing further concerning this marvellous grace... for who can express, in our words and to our human understanding, what it is to *see God in God,* to behold the light in the light, to enjoy an infinite love?... All that I can say regarding this most merciful favour is that the *adorable object that engrossed me was infinite;* what I saw and received of it was incomprehensible... Yes, I admit that I believe myself at times to have enjoyed the sight of the Divine Essence for some minutes only; but this latter grace was the more merciful because it was granted to me in all its strength during eight or ten months... it was a simple and fixed gaze to which no distraction opposed itself. Can we ever adequately describe this sublime grace; to see a little, to understand in a measure; by an infinite grace, an infinite Being; to be known and to know by an infinite knowledge and to feel ourselves closely united to this God who knows and is known in Himself?" (*Vie,* Part III, ch. iv).

She often received a similar knowledge with regard to the Holy Spirit, seeing Him "as it were proceeding incessantly from the bosom of the Father... by the mutual love One for the Other, of the Father and of the Son" (*ibid.,* ch. v).

**63** *bis.*—The intellectual vision of the Blessed Trinity is mentioned in several of the preceding extracts. It has been referred to by many servants of God. Thus St. Ignatius experienced some of these visions at Manresa. He describes them in a little spiritual diary that he had forgotten to burn and which covers four months of his life. At times a symbolic figure, such as that of a sun, accompanied this vision; but it was evidently nothing but an accessory. Sometimes he perceived "not obscurely, but in a vivid and highly luminous brightness, the Divine Being or Divine Substance," "without distinction of persons;" at others, in this vision, he saw the Father alone, "without the other two Persons." "I saw the Father's Being, but in such a manner that I first saw the Being and afterwards the Father, and my devotion attained to the Substance before reaching the Father"; at other times again, he saw how the "Second and the Third Person were in the Father." "My mind," he says, "is so vividly enlightened, that long courses of study, so it seemed to me, could not have taught me as much... I believed that I had *almost nothing more to learn* on the subject of the Most Blessed Trinity" (*Vie,* by Bartoli, Book V, ch. iv).

Here is another example, taken from a modern book, the *Vie de la Mère Suzanne Lévêque,* of Les Filles de Notre-Dame (1695-1760), by Dom Louis Lévêque (Lethielleux, 1893). Mother Suzanne wrote to her confessor: "I am often favoured with a very sublime prayer, in which I see the adorable Trinity by an intellectual vision. *I see* in an inexplicable manner *all that faith teaches us* concerning one God in Three Persons, and my soul is inundated with a torrent of delights, which makes all that is not God contemptible to me... I have *no doubt* that the good that I enjoy is *God Himself.*"

### § 3. That Even Ecstatic Contemplation is a Mixture of Light and Darkness

**64.**—Blessed Angela of Foligno:

1° "On one occasion, however, my soul was lifted up and... when it was in that darkness, wished to return back to itself, and could not, wished to proceed and could not. Then suddenly it was lifted up higher and enlightened, and it saw the unutterable *Power* of God, and it saw the *Will* of God and His *Justice* and *Goodness,* in which I most fully understood all the things about which I had asked [concerning the Fall of man and his Redemption]... And I was so full of charity [*claritatis*] and with such joy did I have understanding of the power and will and justice of God, and not only did I have knowledge of those things about which I had inquired, but I was also satisfied with regard to all things. But this I cannot make known in any words whatsoever; for it is wholly above nature" (*Visions and Instructions,* ch. xxiv, pp. 76-7).

2° The supreme darkness: "Frequently, therefore, do I see God in this way and in this good that cannot outwardly be related, nor even thought of by the heart. Yea, I say, in this most certain and enclosed good which I understand with so much *darkness,* I have all my hope; and in seeing, whatever I wish to have, *I have all;* whatever I wish to know, *I know all,* and in it I see all good... [and the soul] delighteth in an ineffable way in the All-Good, and... because this good is joined with darkness, the *more it is seen in darkness,* the more certain it is, and the more it surpasseth all things... Again, when the soul seeth the power of God, and when it seeth the wisdom of God, and even when it seeth the will of God, all of which I have seen in other wonderful and ineffable ways, all this is less than this most certain good. For this good that I see, is whole; but all other things are [so to say] in part... For in the darkness I see the Holy Trinity, and in the Trinity Itself, which I see in such great darkness, it seemeth unto me that I stand and abide in the midst of It... Again, when I see this good, I do not then, when I am in it, have any thoughts of the Humanity of Christ, or of the God-Man, or of anything which hath form; and yet at such a time I see all things, and see nothing. But when I am separated from this good, of which I have spoken, I see the God-Man, and He draweth my soul with such gentleness as at times to say: 'Thou art I, and I am Thou.' And I see those eyes, and that face, so full of peace that it embraceth and draweth my soul with immense closeness. And then from those eyes and that face there cometh that good of which I have spoken, which I see in the darkness. And this floweth forth and cometh from within, and it is this that delighteth me so, that I cannot express it" (*ibid.,* ch. xxvi, pp. 85-8).

**65.**—Tauler:

1° "The temptations take place in the inferior faculties... But God desires to dwell in the superior faculties—the memory, the intellect, and the will, and to operate in these after a divine manner. This is His true abode, His field of action; it is there that He finds His likeness. It is there that we must seek Him if we desire to find Him, and by the shortest way. Then the spirit is transported high above all the faculties into a void of immense solitude whereof no mortal can adequately speak. It is *the mysterious darkness* wherein is concealed the limitless Good. To such an extent are we admitted and absorbed into something that is one, simple, divine, and inimitable, that we seem no longer distinguishable from it. I speak not of the reality but of the appearance, of the impression that is felt. In this unity, the feeling of multiplicity disappears. When, afterwards, these persons come to themselves again, they find themselves possessed of a distinct knowledge of things, more luminous and more perfect than that of others... This state is called the *ineffable obscurity,* and yet it is the true light of the Divine Essence; it is also called, and with reason, the immense and *incomprehensible* solitude, because in it we find neither pathway nor bridge nor any special manner of being; it is above all these things. I wish to insist still further upon this, so as to be the better understood. This obscurity is a light to which no created intelligence can arrive by its own nature. It is also a solitude, because this state is naturally unattainable... It is here that we drink at the source of the waters of the Divine sweetness that gush forth from the Divine Essence. As with all waters, they are the purest and the coldest at their source. The soul plunges in with her whole being and all her faculties, and would fain drink long draughts of its waters. But this is not possible here below. There are moments when we lose ourselves and disappear into the great deeps of God, even as the water that falls upon the earth is absorbed into it by degrees" (First Sermon for the 2nd Sunday after the Epiphany).

2° The vision that comes like a lightning flash: "Sometimes a supernatural longing for God breaks out in the soul; this grace is so manifest that it is impossible to doubt that *God has actually showed Himself,* as in the instantaneous flash of the lightning. This vision comes and disappears so suddenly that no [distinct] idea of what has been seen is retained. *We cannot understand what it was.* Only we know with certainty that it was something, but we cannot analyse it. And this grace always excites in the soul a violent desire for this good, and a spiritual renewal; otherwise the light would be misleading... This great splendour of light, if we can give it this name, should also be called an *obscurity,* a *darkness,* on account of its incomprehensibility and of our blindness" (*Institutions,* ch. xxii).

**66.**—St. Mary Magdalen of Pazzi. *Dialogue* between the soul and the Heavenly Father.*

"God the Father.—Another fruit of the communication of My Essence, is a kind of disappearance of faith in the soul. †

* These conversations were taken down from her lips during her ecstasies.

† Brother Giles, of Assisi, one of the companions of St. Francis, also said after his ecstasies that faith had been lost and replaced by a better gift. A religious once answered him as follows: "What would you do if you were a priest and had to sing the Credo at High Mass? How could you say I *believe* in *one God?*" For his sole reply Brother Giles, with a joyful air, sang in the tone of the Credo: "*Cognosco* unum deum, Patrem omnipotentem" (I *know* one God, etc.). (Bolland., of April 23; *Life,* Nos. 55, 56.)

"The Soul.—O Eternal Father! How can this be, since without faith we cannot be saved?

"God the Father.—In this way, my child. By the communication of My Essence I instil into you a knowledge of Me which is so profound, so clear and so intimate, that it in a sense compels you to admit that you no longer exercise faith. It is this that I call a disappearance of faith, because the knowledge is so clear that it belongs to sight rather than to faith. This state produces in you a perpetual admiration, from which an intimate and immense love is born. This very faithful infidelity is a nuptial garment of which the soul is justly proud, a garment woven (who could think it?) *of light and of darkness,* similar to that with which I am credited when I am said to be clothed with light as with a garment and to dwell amidst the *thick darkness.* In fact, in proportion as My immensity renders me clear and knowable in Myself, so I become more *incomprehensible* to My creatures, because of their incapacity. And in this I resemble the sun, which is never less visible than when it shines the most brightly; and as you cannot see the sun by any light other than its own, so neither can I be intimately known except by the light that I shed abroad in souls. The garment of the soul deprived thus of faith is then like Mine own, composed of *light and of darkness,* and she glories in it; but how? She glories in this: that she knows not God. This is the *darkness;* and yet she knows Him so well that in a certain sort she loses the faith that she had in Him; this is the *light.* She believes as though she saw; now she who sees, no longer exercises faith, since faith consists in believing that which we see not; and from another side she sees that she knows nothing, considering the immense and infinite abyss of My perfections which she can in no wise fathom. She is then at once *in the light and also in the darkness;* and this is the great faith without faith, of which I have told you.

"The Soul.—O disappearance of faith, how little art thou known!" "(*Œuvres,* Part IV, ch. xvii).

**67.**—Ven. Marina de Escobar. The divine darkness.

1° *The vision of the divine river.* "The angels approached my soul and detached her from the sensible faculties. I found myself before the heavenly Jerusalem which was encircled by an exceedingly vast river, of great beauty and brightness. Its banks were fair and shaded with trees and were all thronged with holy angels singing most wondrously and accompanying themselves upon instruments of music. They sang: Glory to God in the highest! From the river there ran here and there little canals or streams, whereby the heavenly water flowed downwards and *fell upon the earth.* It descended like a dew and its divine influence comforted the souls of the just.

"The vision continued a long time; and then the angels deposited me on the banks of this vast and mysterious river. Suddenly, they plunged me into it to a profound depth, and there was granted to me a great and extraordinary knowledge of God's greatness, His *omnipotence,* His wisdom and *immensity.*

And I heard the angels say to me in a loud voice: 'Hast thou yet attained to the full understanding of God?' My soul was then enlightened by a knowledge that showed her that all that she saw in the divine immensity was very little in comparison with the infinity of things that were still to be known. And, her admiration making her forget what she had just seen, she cried out: 'Still are His mysteries unfathomed!'

"Then the angels plunged me still more deeply into the river, and I received a greater light and a more perfect knowledge regarding *the Essence of God and the divine darkness.* Again the angels repeated their question: 'Hast thou yet attained to the full understanding of God?' And after receiving yet further illumination and knowledge, I again replied: 'Still are His mysteries unfathomed.'

"Yet a third time the angels plunged me to the depths and into the abysses of the mystery, and again inquired of me as before. For the third time my soul, more and more enlightened, and with a further knowledge of the Divine Being, thought only of the infinity of things that still remained unknown, and replied: 'Still are His mysteries unfathomed.'

"And then the angels drew me forth from this deep and mystic sea, and uplifting me thrice to heights that were each time greater than before, they again put to me the mysterious demand. My soul received an ever-growing light and knowledge; she was lost, submerged in the Divine Being, and cried out: 'Ah, a thousand times no. His mysteries are still unfathomed. '

"Finally the angels raised me to I know not what *infinite and incomprehensible* height, to an immensity of good which no tongue can describe. Here it was as a *flash of lightning,* or as though a curtain were drawn aside to allow of a momentary sight of some wonderful treasure, and were then suddenly replaced. God thus showed me the *infinite immensity and incomprehensibility* of His Being, but my small capacity could not bear all that it saw in that instant of time; my strength failed and my whole body began to tremble. And in the twinkling of an eye, the angels laid hold of me, restored me, and brought me back into my cell" (Vol. I, Book III, ch. i, year 1615).

2° *The Divine Ocean.* "The holy angels surrounded me, and preceded by the Lord of all Majesty, they bore me to a very great height, traversing, so to speak, the whole vault of heaven. They placed me on the shore of a kind of immense ocean, which was the vastness of God Himself, His goodness, His wisdom, and His Essence. In the presence of Jesus Christ they cast me suddenly into this vast sea of the divine obscurity and of the essence of the unknown and incomprehensible God. I was submerged in it and lost. No language can describe the secret marvels that are there wrought between God and the soul, or the grandeur of God which is there manifested. No created intelligence can speak of it adequately. If anyone would attempt to do so, I pray that God may give him an experience of this favour; he will then think as I do. The divine assistance was needed to prevent my soul parting from the body, so overpowering was the might of God's operation.

"For a space of time, which seemed to me shorter than it really was, I remained plunged in this ocean. Afterwards the angels carried me back to the shore. By this I mean that they drew me forth from this immensity, and not that there was really a sea, a shore, or any material image.

"I rested a short time on this shore so as to regain my strength. Then the angels cast me in again, with more force than the first time, so that I was submerged and lost in the divine essence more profoundly than before. Again they brought me back to the shore. I was in even greater danger, as it seemed to me, of losing my life, if God had not upheld me. When I had rested for a few minutes they cast me for the third time. By the word cast I would express a certain admirable way employed by God and the angels to bring the soul into the immensity of the divine perfections. There is no question here of anything corporeal.

"How long I remained in this sea I could not judge. But this last submersion was slighter than the two previous ones and so I experienced less fatigue. God then gave me His blessing and the angels bore me back to my cell. When I had come to myself again, I felt great weakness. I was seized with admiration, and while conforming to the will of God, I raised my eyes towards the angels with great grief at finding myself thus in this exile" (Vol. I, Book III, ch. i).

3° *The same subject:* "When, in a deep ecstasy, God unites the soul suddenly to His Essence, and when He fills her with His light, He shows her, in a moment of time, the sublimest mysteries and all His secret things. And the soul sees a certain immensity and an infinite majesty... She knows that all creatures depend upon God's providence and are preserved by Him; she knows *in what manner He is the beatitude of the angels and the elect;* how He is the sole *beginning* and *sole end* of all things, which apart from Him have neither beginning nor end; that He is the *first Cause,* and that He holds the sovereign dominion over all things. The soul is then plunged, as it were into a vast ocean which is God, and again God. She can neither find a foothold nor touch the bottom. *The divine attributes appear to her as summed up in one whole,* so that no one of them can be distinguished separately. Sometimes at the beginning or the end of this rapture, God discovers certain imaginative figures to the soul. But while the soul is plunged in this union, there are neither words nor figures for the interior senses of the imagination to grasp, and still less for the bodily senses. All is intellectual and takes place in the superior part of the soul" (Vol. II, Book II, ch. xxxiv).

4° *The Divine Tower.* "One day when I was overpowered by sickness and affliction, I saw His Divine Majesty Who with sweetness spoke to me, saying: 'Thou art weary; wilt thou come with Me?' Then when the Lord God had accepted my consent, He embraced me in a very close union. And He showed me an immense Tower, strongly built and most beautiful."

(Then God explains to her that this Tower is a symbol of the Divine Essence.)

"The Divine Majesty caused me to enter in and to mount the tower, up and up. I had never been to such a height before. And there He gave me a new knowledge of His perfections, of His *Eternity,* of His *Infinity,* of His wisdom and His other attributes. And this was not by the aid of any imaginative figures, but solely by an intellectual knowledge. I did not think it possible to have a more accurate and a more complete knowledge. Astounded, I cried out: 'Oh, who is like unto this great God? Where is there a like boundless immensity? What infinitude! What wisdom!'

"I was thus absorbed in admiration of these perfections, when the Divine Majesty raised me to another altitude much greater than the first. He then gave me an understanding of the same attributes, but so superior to the first and so much above my capacity, that I was as if lost. The grandeur of the things that I grasped was such that it seemed as though the superior part of the soul were torn violently away. I could only ejaculate this one thing: 'God is more than all this, much, much more.' Yes, I was entirely bewildered.

"When back again in my cell I felt myself wholly changed... It seemed as though my soul were no longer wholly in my body, but that the superior part had remained in those heights, inebriated, plunged in the vision of God's supreme perfections, and that I retained the inferior part, that which gives life to the senses and bodily faculties only" (Vol. II, Book I, ch. xlvii).

5° *The three mountains and the three lightning flashes.*

"The Lord one day said to me: 'Thou art greatly afflicted, come with Me; I will bring thee to My holy mountain, and I will recreate thee in the house of My prayer.' And suddenly I was led in the spirit to a high mountain whence the whole world was visible to me. A heavenly light shone for an instant, like a flash of lightning, and with a majesty that impelled my admiration, I saw thereby the immensity of the Divine Essence. And the Lord said to me: 'Take courage, for thou shalt mount up still higher. That which thou hast seen is but little in comparison with that which still remains.' And I was brought up to another higher mountain. And there, a light, much stronger than the first, shone forth again like a flash of lightning, and revealed to me still more clearly, the same Divine Essence. I saw more things than I had seen before.

"Again the Lord said: 'Courage, for thou must mount still higher.' And instantly I was taken up to a third and yet higher mountain which seemed to reach to the highest summit of Heaven. And a light, a *flash of lightning,* shone out with a brilliancy greater than that with which the others had shone before, and it showed me the Essence of God, His perfections and His *hidden judgments.* I was astounded at the spectacle of this immensity! And further, God, in uniting Himself with me, revealed to me the mystery of the Holy Trinity. And I said *to* myself interiorly: 'Lord, how incomprehensible are Thy judgments! Who shall understand them?' And God answered: 'The little and the humble of heart, those who have left all for Me and who seek only to please Me' " (Vol. I, Book III, ch. ii; year 1618).

She had many other similar visions.

### § 4. The Expansion of the Intelligence During Ecstasy and the Neighbouring States

**68.**—Blessed Angela of Foligno:

"There is nothing then that the soul understandeth or apprehendeth, to be compared with the rapt [rapture] in which she understandeth and apprehendeth nothing save that unto which she can inwardly attain. For when the soul is lifted above herself by the illumination of God's *presence,* and is placed in the bosom of God, and God in her, then she understandeth and taketh delight, and resteth in those good things of God, that she can in nowise describe, for they are above the understanding, and above all manner of speech and above all words. But in these the *soul swimmeth in joy and knowledge*" (*Visions and Instructions,* ch. lvi, pp. 191-2). See also ch. xxvii and Brother Arnold's Second Prologue.

**68** *bis.*—St. Teresa:

"When Our Lord suspends the understanding and makes it cease from its acts, He puts before it that which astonishes and occupies it; so that without making any reflections, it shall comprehend in a moment [*en un credo*] more than we could comprehend in many years with all the efforts in the world" (*Life,* ch. xii, 8).

**69.**—The Ven. Anne-Madeleine de Rémuzat:

"For some little time past... God appears to pour into my heart, and into all the powers of my soul, a divine principle, that concentrates, *elevates,* and *dilates* them, in order to render them capable of receiving the good that He deigns to impart" (*Vie,* by the Visitation at Marseilles, ch. xv, p. 323. English *Life,* by Mgr. van den Berghe, ch. vii, p. 190).

**70.**—St. Gregory the Great relates a vision of St. Benedict. It happened, at least in part, outside the state of ecstasy, since the saint several times called one of his companions to show him the spectacle spread out before his *eyes.* St. Benedict "saw a light which banished away the darkness of the night... Upon this sight a marvellous strange thing followed... the whole world, gathered as it were together under one beam of the sun, was presented before his eyes." St. Gregory adds, for those who might be surprised at such a condensation of knowledge: "Assure yourself... that all creatures be, as it were, nothing, to that soul which beholdeth the Creator; for though it see but a glimpse of that light which is in the Creator, yet very small do all things seem that be created." That was the case with St. Benedict, though he had but a glimpse of Almighty God: "For by means of that supernatural light the *capacity of the inward soul is enlarged...* But albeit we say that the world was gathered together before his eyes, yet were not the Heaven and earth drawn into any lesser room than they be of themselves, but the soul of the beholder was more *enlarged*... and therefore, in that light which appeared to his outward eyes, the inward light, which was in his soul, ravished the mind of the beholder to supernal things" (*Dialogues,* Book II, ch. xxxv, Migne ed., Vol. LXVI, col. 199. English, Fr. Coleridge, Quarterly Series).

**71.**—Vision of B. Hermann Joseph. Contemporary account. "By such graces as these... the Lord comforted the good B. Hermann because he had to eat the daily bread of suffering... we shall hear further how the good God comforted him by means of irrational creatures, so that others who have reason may gain thereby... Once when B. Joseph was buried in these meditations, he stood at night at the window of the sacristy, and gazed at the rising moon and stars. And a great longing seized him that he might see creation as it is in the eyes of God; so he said to the Creator: 'O dear Lord, Thou Creator of all things, although, so long as I remain here in Babylon, I can only see Thee dimly through a glass, yet wilt Thou give me such a knowledge of Thy creation, by which I may know and love Thee better.' And as he stood there praying, he was suddenly raised above himself in such a wonderful manner that he could not afterwards account for it, and the Lord revealed to him the whole beauty and glory of the firmament and of every created thing, so that his longing was fully satisfied. But afterwards, when he came to himself, the Prior could get nothing more out of him than that he had received such unspeakable rapture from his perfect knowledge of the creation, that it was beyond human understanding" (Bolland., April 7, No. 32. English: *Life,* by Wilfred Galway, ch. xxx, p. 77).

**72.**—A vision of St. Ignatius (he is speaking of himself in the third person):

"As he was going to pay his devotions at the Church of St. Paul, about a mile out of the town of Manresa, and was sitting on the banks of the Cardenero, or as some say of the Rubricato, his mind was suddenly filled with a new and strange illumination, so that in one moment, and without any sensible image or appearance, certain things pertaining to the mysteries of the Faith, together with other truths of natural science, were revealed to him, and this so abundantly and so clearly, that he himself said, that if all the spiritual light which his spirit had received from God up to the time when he was more than sixty-two years old, could be collected into one, it seemed to him that all this knowledge would not equal what was at that moment conveyed to his soul" *Vie,* by Ribadeneira; Book I, ch. vii; English *Life,* Oratory Series, ch. vii, pp. 43, 44).

**73.**—A Vision of the Ven. Francis-Xavier-Bianchi, Barnabite:

"One day when Peter Magno, a doctor, *littérateur,* and distinguished philosopher, was delivering himself of an enthusiastic eulogy of these sciences to which he was devoted, Francis, in order to make him appreciate the higher value of the sciences of God, replied: I also, in my youth, ardently pursued these subjects of knowledge, and I even prayed God to help me to attain them in order that I might be more useful to my congregation. After this prayer I once found myself inundated with a vivid light; it seemed to me that a veil was lifted up from before the eyes of the spirit, and all the truths of human sciences, even those that I had not studied, became manifest to me by an infused knowledge, as was once the case with Solomon. This state of intuition lasted for about twenty-four hours, and then, as if the veil had fallen again, I found myself as ignorant as before. At the same time an interior voice said to me: 'Such is human knowledge; of what use is it? It is I, it is My love that must be studied' " (*Vie*, by Fr. Baravelli, ch. iv).

**74.**—We have given the opinions of ecstatics, founded upon observation. On the other hand we will briefly indicate the theory adopted by free-thinkers; a theory deduced solely from their own preconceived ideas and therefore anti-scientific.

1° (The theory of the annihilation of the faculties). M. Murisier has written a book: *Les Maladies du sentiment religieux* (Alcan, 1901). It contains inaccurate descriptions; the title shows a bias, although the author has claimed to the contrary; for he insinuates that the mystic states are maladies. This is what he tells us on the subject of the higher mystic state: "What is this simple idea of the divinity which takes the place of the complex vision and the eliminated association of ideas? At times it is an *abstract idea,* similar to the idea of good, which was Plotinus's supreme object of meditations, or to the law of the causality of suffering, the knowledge of which leads the Buddhist to the repose of Nirvana. More frequently it is a *vague and confused image* derived from former representations, or rather it is a *residue* of these representations, which are blended, *impoverished* and simplified by the gradual effacement of their differences and outlines.* For instance, instead of seeing three divine persons sculptured in a block of marble, God the Father with a long beard... the ecstatic will see only a cloud of resplendent brightness... And yet the single image, the sovereign light, does not fail to fade away in its turn. The memory, the imagination, and even the *understanding* disappear, so the mystics say" (ch. i, § 4, p. 61). "The ecstasy ends in the annihilation of the personality" (*ibid.,* p. 43); "The monoïdeism becomes absolute" (p. 60);† the supreme degree "is the total extinction of consciousness" (p. 67).

In the *Revue philosophique* of November, 1902, M. Leuba mentions two characters of ecstasy which he regards as essentials: 1° Thought is "so *reduced* as to give place to unconsciousness... the mystic favours are not a revelation made to the intellect" (p. 476, 477). In contemplation, "Christ's disciples taste the Buddhist salvation, Nirvana" (p. 470); 2° the ecstatic union with God is "an

* It is very true that the accompanying sensible images disappear more and more as the mystic state grows higher (see ch. ix), what is false is to say that the intellect becomes equally impoverished.

† We might say that there is but one idea (that of God) on condition that we understand that the content of this idea is very full. In the same way, we say that a great general has only one idea: that of conquering the enemy. But how many subsidiary ideas does this one contain! With regard to purely intellectual visions, rationalists, being unable to explain them, prefer to deny their existence, in spite of the universal testimony of ecstatics.

*identification* of the individual with the divine essence" (p. 476). The author gravely declares that all this is written "in the descriptions given by the mystics themselves." But they say precisely the contrary. The second error is actually anti-Catholic; it is pantheistic mysticism. It has been condemned by John XXII in the tenth proposition of Eckhart (1329), whom the Church has never reckoned amongst her orthodox mystics, or even amongst the mystics.

**74** *bis.*—2° (The emotional theory). Some rather more moderate writers say that the ecstatic forms to himself a vague idea of God; and that he loves this representation with an extraordinary intensity, out of all proportion to the idea. This is Cousin's definition, which is quoted with eulogistic comments under the word *Mysticism* in Franck's *Dictionnaire des sciences philosophiques:* "Mysticism suppresses *the reason* in man, and leaves *sentiment* only; or at least it subordinates and sacrifices the reason to sentiment." It is thus that M. Rousselot, in his *Mystiques Espagnols* (Didier, 1867) interprets the supreme union, described by St. John of the Cross.

3° M. Ribot has successively expressed two very opposite ideas: (*a*) he says that mental prayer carried to the point of ecstasy is "a hypertrophy of attention. [It] is an evolution and tends towards *increase;* [hysteria] is a dissolution and tends towards *decrease...*" The positive side of ecstasy is "the *exaltation of intellect...* [It] is a state of intense and circumscribed ideation... the state of ecstasy in every individual may exalt the intelligence to its *highest degree of power...*" (*Psychologie de l'attention,* 2nd edition, pp. 119, 138, 141; English, *Psychology of Attention,* ch. iii, pp. 81, 94, 96).

(*b*) In another place the same writer says just the contrary: "There is a continual progress of intellectual impoverishment and simplification carried to extremes... According to Godfernaux, the moment of true ecstasy is not one of monoïdeism even, but of aïdeism, that is to say, a return to the pure, almost undifferentiated, not known, but only felt affective state" (*La logique des sentiments,* 1st edition, 1905, Alcan, p. 171, ch. iv, No. 3).

### § 5. The Manner in Which, According to Certain Mystics, God is Seen

**75.**—Blessed Angela of Foligno, speaking of raptures:

"And this manifestation of God I have had more than a thousand times, and each time in a new and other and different manner from the time before... It was also said unto me that the aforesaid unutterable manifestation of God *is the same good which the saints possess in life eternal,—nor is this good other than the aforesaid,* but there it is another kind of experience and only different from the aforesaid that the least saint who possesses least thereof in life eternal hath more than can be given unto any soul in this present life, before the death of the body" (*Visions and Instructions,* ch. xxvii, pp. 98-100). See also ch. xxi.

**76.**—St. Catherine of Siena, repeating in her ecstasy the words whereby God describes it to her:

"Passing suddenly... by the narrow door of the Word, she reaches me, the Sea Pacific. For sea and door are united together. I and the Truth, My only-begotten Son, being one and the same thing. What joy such a soul receives who sees herself so sweetly arrived at this pass, for in Truth she tastes *the happiness of the angelic nature!...*" (*Dialogue of St. Catherine of Siena,* p. 261. Eng. trans. by A. Thorold).

**77.**—The Ven. Marina de Escobar:

The Ven. Louis du Pont, her confessor, who collected her revelations, writes thus: "She told me that she had seen clearly the divine Essence and the face of God, One in Three Persons, as well as the beatitude of the saints, and *the manner in which it takes place.* I asked her what kind of clearness she was speaking of; was it that of the Blessed and that which St. Paul is said to have had in his rapture? Or was it a clearness of a lesser kind, although still considerable, such as is usually granted to us in this mortal life? This is what she answered me in writing: 'The light that my soul received for the understanding of these mysteries, was as great as is possible during this life; but with this characteristic: that the knowledge was extremely *clear and distinct.* I know with certainty that I see exactly *the same object* as the inhabitants of the heavenly Jerusalem, but the revelation has not told me whether it is with the same force and in the same manner. However, here is one fact: I have seen the interior beatitude of several saints, and *how God brings it about.* And I have compared it with what I experience when the Divine Majesty manifests to me the greatness of His Essence, and it has seemed to me that these divers manifestations were absolutely identical. I even believe that on one or two occasions I have not been far from that clearness of vision of which you speak and with regard to which you quote St. Paul's example to me.' I told her that if she had an opportunity, she would do well to question her angels on this subject. But she never found that it would be opportune. For it is not in her power to put any questions that she pleases to the angels. It is possible that God may not wish us to know more on the subject that we are now considering" (Vol. I, Book, III, ch. ii, § 4).

**78.**—Alvarez de Paz, describing the highest contemplation:

In this degree, which is the highest, "*eyes are given unto the soul* by which she may see God... God manifests Himself to the soul by an image that represents Him very perfectly. The sensible faculties neither receive it nor give it, it is not composed of forms that are already in our possession, but it is a new infusion made to the mind... Thus furnished and strengthened by the highest help, the *mind sees God.* It does not accomplish this by *denying* or withdrawing anything from Him, as when we say: God is not limited, not finite. Neither is it *by affirming* something of Him, attributing it to Him, as when we say: God is good and wise. But it is by *regarding* the divine greatness without any admixture of anything else, in the tranquillity of a calm day. Certainly, oh reader, when you see the light with the bodily eyes, you do not arrive thereat by a comparison of ideas, as when we say: 'Light is not darkness,' or 'it is a quality.' You simply see the light. In the same way the soul, in this degree of contemplation, affirms nothing, denies nothing, attributes nothing, avoids nothing, but in complete repose *she sees God.* It will be said: This is astonishing, or rather unbelievable. For we take it as indisputable, that God is not seen here intuitively. If then the soul does not see God, how can we say, nevertheless, that she sees Him; and if she sees Him, in what sense is it that she does not see Him? I admit that it is astonishing. The fact, however, is very certain...

"In this supernatural manner the soul knows God in the depths of her being, and *she sees Him,* so to say, more clearly than she sees the material light with the eyes of the body. She sees God as being One in three Persons, and she sees how the Father engenders the Son eternally and without change. She sees that the Holy Spirit proceeds from the Father and from the Son as from one sole principle; she sees how these Persons are one sole nature and one sole substance, and that they are infinitely alike and equal; and how these persons dwell in the soul... We see all these things and many others in God, simultaneously, in one glance, just as you, reader, see instantaneously a friend's face as a whole, and at the same time you see his eyes and cheeks, his mouth and forehead. This sight [of God] inflames the soul with a very ardent love... neither the senses, nor the imagination, have the least part in this vision; all takes place in the summit of the spirit" (Book V, Part III, ch. xiv).

# CHAPTER XIX

## The Spiritual Marriage (Fourth and Last Stage of the Mystic Union)

**1.—Definition**. The supreme goal of all the mystic unions is called the soul's *spiritual marriage* with God, the *transforming* union, the *consummated* union, *deification.* St. Teresa also calls it the *seventh mansion* of the interior *Castle.* She speaks of it only in this last treatise, which she composed five years before her death. When she wrote her other works, she had not yet been raised to this degree (see ch. xx, **16**).

Of these various expressions, that of *transforming union* is the most accurate, and it indicates the inner nature of this grace better than the others. The words *spiritual marriage* are constantly employed. But we should note that, taken alone, their sense is vague. And then various significations have been given to them in religious literature; they sometimes mean all union with God by love, or even by grace.

And hence arises a great difficulty in knowing what we are intended to understand when pious souls tell us, without any explanations, that they have arrived at the spiritual marriage.

Question them as we may, we cannot discover the sense in which they use these words. Perhaps they merely wish to express that they feel closely united to God, that they have a very ardent love for Him. Gently, and little by little, we shall be able to correct their ingenuous ideas by showing them, for instance, to what a very ordinary level of virtue they have attained.

**2.**—The transforming union is a mystic state containing **three principal elements.**

1° A union that is almost *permanent,* persisting even amidst exterior occupations, and this in such a manner that the two different operations do not interfere with one another.

2° A *transformation* of the higher faculties as to their manner of operation (hence the name of transforming union).

3° Generally a permanent *intellectual vision* of the Blessed Trinity or of some divine attribute.

Let us enter more into detail.

**3.—First element:** an *almost permanent union.* "Unless she [the soul, entered into the seventh mansion] first deserts God, I believe He will never fail to make her sensible of His presence" (*Interior Castle,* Seventh Mansion, ch. i, 11).

**4.**—I have said "almost permanent," because here and there it may undergo an **eclipse.** "This mansion differs from the rest in that, as I said, the dryness and disturbance felt in all the rest, at times, *scarcely ever* enters here..." (*Interior Castle,* Seventh Mansion, ch. iii, 8). If there are intervals at times, "yet such intervals are very short" (*ibid.,* 9). "... Our Lord occasionally leaves such persons to the weakness of their nature. The venomous creatures from the moat round the castle, and the other mansions, at once join together to revenge themselves for the time when they were deprived of their power. True, this lasts but a short time—a day perhaps, or a little longer..." (*Interior Castle,* Seventh Mansion, ch. iv, 1, 2).

We see that when the mystic union attains to a higher level, it also often increases in frequency. At the outset (the prayer of quiet) it was brief and transient; then it came to be habitual in prayer (ch. xvi, 6). Finally, it is no more subject to interruptions.

**5.**—I have said that this union persists amidst exterior occupations. The result is that there are then two simultaneous operations of a very different kind; we express this fact by saying that the soul **appears divided.** In this state, says St. Teresa, "she seemed divided from her own soul... She complained of her soul as Martha did of Mary, saying that it always enjoyed solitary peace while leaving her so full of troubles and occupations that she could not keep it company. This may seem extravagant to you, my daughters, for though the soul is known to be undivided, this is fact and no fancy, and often happens" (*Interior Castle,* Seventh Mansion, ch. i, 14, 15).

St. John of the Cross speaks of this division of the soul even with regard to states lower than that of spiritual marriage: "When these favours are shown to the soul... in the spirit only, the higher and lower portions of the soul seem to it—it knows not how—to be so far apart that it recognises *two divisions in itself,* each so *distinct from the other,* that neither seems to have *anything in common* with the other, being in appearance so separated and distinct. And, in reality, this is in a certain manner true, for in its present condition, which is *wholly spiritual,* it has no commerce with the sensitive part" (*Obscure Night,* Book II, ch. xxiii, p. 452).

Ven. Mary of the Incarnation, Ursuline, is a striking example of this double state of soul. Her exterior activity was remarkable, and she showed great talents for "the mechanical arts, embroidery, and painting." Now (so her son tells us), "it seemed, according to the Jesuit Fathers, her directors, as if she had *two souls,* one of which was as much united to God as though she had nothing else to do but to engage in contemplation, and the other as much attached to exterior things as if she had been *entirely* occupied in them" (*Vie* by an Ursuline of Nantes, ch. xx).

**6.**—We had a **transient** instance of this division, only to a **lesser extent,** in the state that I described under the name of the acting prayer of quiet (ch. xiv, **47**. See also ch. xvii, **10**).

**7.**—This union does not completely exclude **temptations** or interior sufferings. It is not easy to define those that may supervene.

St. John of the Cross seems to say that such things no longer occur. "... The sensitive part, except in the state of the spiritual matrimony, never loses all its imperfect habits, and its powers are never wholly subdued. It has to... endure trouble and affliction in the lower part, and at the hands of the devil. But all this *ceases* in the state of spiritual marriage" (*Spiritual Canticle,* Stanza XV, p. 89). But farther on (Stanza XX) he allows certain occasional exceptions.

St. Teresa seems to admit the existence of trials, but considers that they are of rare occurrence. She deals with this point in a general way only. "It is not intended that the powers, senses, and passions should continually enjoy this peace. The soul does so indeed" (*Interior Castle,* Seventh Mansion, ch. ii, 14). Other writings show that these sufferings may be violent at times. These trials of the soul or of the body heighten the feeling of division of which I was speaking just now. A person that I had to examine once wrote to me: "I have this feeling very vividly. There is an inferior part of me that lives on earth, that *works, suffers,* and *is tempted;* then there is another, that lives above, far off, in an unchangeable peace, and contemplates the lower part with astonishment and compassion. In the same way the inmate of a fortress sees the enemies in the plain, but feels almost entirely secure."

St. Alphonsus Liguori employs another comparison: In this state, "when the passions appear, the soul sees them without being either saddened or tormented by them, even as a man above the clouds would see the storm raging below him without being touched by it" (*Homo. apost.,* Appendix 1, No. 18). The soul's centre might also be compared to the depths of the ocean, which continue motionless while the waves rage furiously on the surface. See two other comparisons given by St. Teresa (*Interior Castle,* Seventh Mansion, ch. ii, 15).

**8.**—**And conversely,** if the soul experiences the mystic union with God in a permanent manner, should we conclude that she has attained to the spiritual marriage?

No; for St. Teresa received the grace of continued union towards her forty-fifth year, at the same time as the visions of Our Lord—that is to say, twelve years before the spiritual marriage; "When they had begun to insist upon my putting my visions to a test like this, and resisting them, the graces I received were multiplied more and more. I tried to distract myself; I *never ceased* to be in prayer: even during sleep my prayer seemed to be *continual*... Neither was it in my power—though I desired and, more than that, even strove—to give up thinking of Him" (*Life,* ch. xxix, 9). See also the case of St. Gertrude (ch. v, **45**) and that of the Ven. Mary of the Incarnation, Ursuline, in the Extracts at the end of the chapter.

This uninterrupted union does not, then, fulfil all the conditions necessary to the spiritual marriage. But it is a nearly allied state (see also ch. xvii, **10**). The life is lived in common with God, without, however, the intimacy reaching its greatest degree: the fusion of two lives.

**8** *bis.*—I have been speaking of the union with God that is felt **during sleep.** St. Teresa is not the only one to have received this favour. St. Margaret Mary often had it, and it was the same with St. Alphonsus Rodriguez (*Vie,* No. 145). Mother Veronica of the Heart of Jesus (1825-83), the Foundress of the Soeurs Victimes of the Sacred Heart, often passed the whole morning in ecstasy, notwithstanding her arduous labours; at night she scarcely slept, and "her heart continued to watch, remaining united to the Heavenly Bridegroom... It was the same amidst the day's most absorbing occupations" (*Vie,* by Fr. Prévot, ch. xviii). See ch. xviii, **40.**

**9.**—The union of the spiritual marriage does not *of itself* bring about the alienation of the sensible faculties; or, since this state is continuous, the person would then always be in ecstasy. But at times it may be *accompanied* by ecstasies.

As a rule, these **ecstasies** are **rarer** than in the preceding degrees. St. Teresa observed this fact in herself. "I, too, am astonished at seeing that, when the soul arrives at this state, it *does not go into ecstasies, except perhaps on rare occasions;* even then they are not like the former trances and the flight of the spirit..." (*Interior Castle,* Seventh Mansion, ch. iii, 10).

This fact might well exhibit a certain number of exceptions. For with several saints, ecstasies have not seemed to diminish at the end of their life, and yet we may admit the probability of their having arrived at the supreme union.

**10.**—This habitual liberty which is left to the faculties, notwithstanding the interior contemplation, is a foretaste of life in Heaven. The angels and the elect, although plunged in the beatific vision, can converse with one another; and after the resurrection this vision will not be the cause of any alienation of the faculties. So, too, upon earth Our Lord had the full use of His human faculties, although beholding His Father face to face.

**11.**—**Second element.** The spiritual marriage may be thus defined: It is a state in which the soul is habitually conscious of the divine co-operation in all her higher operations and in the depths of her being. No union of a more intimate kind can be imagined. This grace can be considered under another aspect, which gives a still higher idea of it: in concurring in our supernatural acts God makes them His own; He renders them divine and shows that He does so. There is therefore a **transformation** of the higher faculties with regard to their manner of operation. The soul is aware that in the supernatural acts of her intellect, her love or her will, she *participates in the divine life, in those* *analogous acts that are in God.* This is the essential part of the spiritual marriage.

**12.**—To **explain the meaning** of this sentence, let us remember that in Heaven we shall rejoice in the vision of God, but that we shall further feel that we *participate in His nature.*

And, indeed, all good qualities that exist in the creature deserve to be called a participation in the divine nature. But it is a question here of a supreme degree, carried to such a height that, as far as is possible, man becomes *like unto God.* He is *deified: dii estis.*

We get some idea of this transformation by the comparison of iron, which, when plunged into the fire, becomes *like it;* in a way it has *become fire,* without, however, losing its own nature. These expressions could not be employed in the case of boiling water. It has a certain participation in the nature of fire, but insufficiently. The natural qualities of the creature bear but this distant resemblance to the divine attributes.

When theologians try to make the word *participation* still clearer, they are obliged to relinquish the attempt, and to declare that this grace is so much above all human conceptions that it must be regarded as a mystery. We shall not be able to form a correct idea of its meaning until we ourselves experience it. Is it even possible to find an accurate comparison by which to describe it? No; all comparisons are necessarily below the reality; for they are borrowed from created things. Nothing really resembling it can be found. Otherwise it would no longer be a mystery, but merely a difficult question.

**13.—Baptism and** sanctifying grace already give us this participation in the divine nature, but it is in an unconscious state. It is otherwise in the spiritual marriage. We are then *conscious* of the communication of the divine life. God is no longer merely the *object* of the supernatural operations of the mind and will, as in the preceding degrees. He shows Himself as being the joint cause of these operations, the *aid* which we make use of in order to produce them. Our acts appear to us as being, after a certain fashion, divine. Our faculties are the branches in which we feel the circulation of the divine sap. We think that we feel God within us, living both for us and for Him. We live in Him, by Him, and *through* Him. No creature can manifest himself to us in this manner.

In Heaven the mechanism of grace will appear in all its clearness; we shall thus see unveiled the "marriage" of two operations, the divine and the human, and even the predominance of the former, our "divinisation," that is to say. The fourth and last degree of prayer is the anticipation, the *more or less marked* foretaste of this experimental knowledge. In the lower degrees the transformation has begun, but we know it only by faith.

**14.**—The mystics have fallen at times into **exaggerations** of speech by reason of their inability to describe all the sublimity of this participation. They speak of thinking by the eternal thought of God, loving by His infinite love, willing by His will. They seem to confuse the two natures, the divine and the human. They thus describe what *we believe* ourselves to feel; like the astronomers, they speak the language of appearances (see note to No. 29). As a rule, they finish by correcting any such exaggerations of language into which they have fallen.

So, too, they sometimes go as far as to say that they not only feel *union* with God in this state, but that there is *oneness with Him.* This is only a manner of speaking. St. Alphonsus Liguori sums up this language by saying: "In the spiritual marriage, the soul is transformed into God and becomes *one* with Him, just as a vessel of water, when poured into the sea, is then *one* with it" (*Homo. apost.*, Appendix I, No. 18).

**15.—Third element.** In this degree, certain persons have a continual vision of the Blessed Trinity. St. Teresa even says that it is always so. This does not seem to be the case, however, with all who have come to experience the transformation in God, and who thenceforward possess that condition which constitutes the foundation of the spiritual marriage. I think that I know two such cases. One has had the vision of the Blessed Trinity a very few times only. The other told me that it is possible never to have had this vision. It is replaced by another that shows God ceaselessly without any distinction of attributes, or, again, it shows one amongst them in a brighter light than the others.

Neither does St. John of the Cross speak of the visions of the Blessed Trinity as being connected with the transforming union. And yet he has written two treatises which turn almost wholly upon this degree (*A Spiritual Canticle; The Living Flame of Love*). He contents himself with referring to a very sublime contemplation of the divine attributes.

**16.**—According to St. Teresa, this vision varies in clearness. "Although, however, it ['this presence'] *is not always seen by so clear a light,* yet *whenever she reflects on it* she feels the companionship of the Blessed Trinity" (*Interior Castle,* Seventh Mansion, ch. i, 12).

**17.—Conversely,** if the vision of the Blessed Trinity becomes habitual, has the soul attained to the transforming union?

No; for St. Teresa, after having described this continual vision in the first chapter of the Seventh Mansion, begins the next chapter thus: "We *now* come to speak of divine and spiritual nuptials." She had also said (ch. i, 3): "... He, *before* consummating the celestial marriage, brings her into this His mansion or presence-chamber" (into this contemplation, that is to say). Thus the habitual vision of the Blessed Trinity is not necessarily completed by the transformation; and as long as it is not so, we are but *on the threshold* of the seventh mansion."

**18.—The part played by the Divine Persons.** According to what has been said, the transforming union is a relation with God, of *nature with nature** since

* "Then the two natures are so united, what is divine is so communicated to what is human, that, without undergoing any essential change, each seems to be God—yet not perfectly so in this life, though still in a manner which can neither be described nor conceived" (*A Spiritual Canticle,* Stanza XXII, p. 120).

it is a union of minds and of wills between them, and it is thus a marriage with *God.* But have the mystics stopped there? and do they not think of the marriage as contracted more especially with one of the Divine Persons, and as being thus a relation not only of nature with nature, but of person with person?

I have not been able to arrive at anything conclusive upon this question. Several mystics, indeed, speak of a special union with the Word; but they give so few explanations that we do not know if it is a question of the essential part of the spiritual marriage or of something that their piety likes to superadd to it.*

The Ven. Marina de Escobar went through ceremonies of marriage first with the Word (Vol. I, Book I, ch. xx, § 1; in 1598, at the age of forty-seven; § 2, in 1611, at the age of sixty; Book II, ch. xxi, § 4; in 1617), then with the Holy Spirit (Vol. I, Book II, ch. xxiii, §§ 2, 3, 4; in 1622). One of these revelations made known to her that the second of these marriages was the chief one.

Perhaps the differences are not great. The transforming union establishes with the divine nature a relation that may very probably *manifest itself separately* as union with the Father, or with the Son, or with the Holy Ghost.

**19.—The part played by Our Lord**, as Man. It is, perhaps, simply that of one who introduces to the union, as happened in the case of St. Teresa: "*The first time* God bestows this grace, He, by an imaginary *vision of His most Sacred Humanity,* reveals Himself to the soul... He may manifest Himself in a different way to other people" (*Interior Castle,* Seventh Mansion, ch. ii, 1). In the lives of the saints it is true that they speak of marriage with Jesus Christ. But this may be quite another union than that with which we are now dealing. The word marriage contains a metaphor which may easily be applied to different unions (see No. 1).

To solve such questions with any certainty, we should have to be acquainted with several persons who had received this grace.

**20.—Objection.** It seems as if the union were contracted with Jesus Christ, since theologians tell us that He is the *Bridegroom* of souls and of the Church.

**21.—Reply.** This is, perhaps, in a very different sense. For the reasons that they bring are derived from the fact of the Incarnation. They are applicable, then, to all Christians. Since they are not deduced from the special characters of the transforming union, it could not be concluded that this latter has as its effect a special union with the Word-Incarnate.

* In his preface to the *Opera* of the Ven. Marina de Escobar, Fr. Tanner says: "When God wills to espouse a man, He takes the feminine character of Mercy or Wisdom, as was the case with St. John the Almoner, St. Laurence Justinian, Blessed Henry Suso, and others" (See also (*Œuvres* of B. Henry Suso, translated into French by P. Thiriot, ch. iv). The examples quoted seem, however, to be too few to enable us to state that the fact is universal.

**22.**—It may happen that the spiritual marriage begins with a **ceremony** and rejoicings. But these are passing facts that must not be confounded with the marriage itself, which is a permanent state.

For example, in certain *Lives* of the saints we read of the interchange of rings, of angelic chants, etc. These circumstances are not necessary; and, further, they may just as well symbolise simple espousals or other unions.*

**23.—Confusions to be avoided.** From what has been said, we see that we must not suppose that the spiritual marriage consists in a perfect conformity to the will of God. This would be to confuse a state of prayer, a special mode of divine communication, that is to say, with a virtue, which is something very different. This virtue, however, is *one of the consequences* of the transformation.

So, too, it is too vague to say, as has been done: It is a union with God by love. The same can be said of all the mystic states, and even of the entire spiritual life.

**24.**—Effect upon the **virtues.** "Besides, this company it enjoys gives it *far greater strength* than ever before. If, as David says, 'With the holy thou shalt be holy,' doubtless by its *becoming one* with the Almighty, by the union of spirit with spirit, the soul must gather strength, as we know the saints did, to suffer and to die..." (*Interior Castle,* Seventh Mansion, ch. iv, 15).

**25.—Assurance of salvation.** St. John of the Cross says that in this degree the soul is confirmed in grace (see Extracts). Scaramelli also allows this, and St. Laurence Justinian (Tr. 2, No. 259). St. Teresa is not so positive. She merely says that imperfections only or indeliberate venial sins are committed here: "Wilfully they do not commit them [venial sins]...; as far as they are aware, they are free from mortal sins" (*Interior Castle,* Seventh Mansion, ch. iv, 3). But this does not make the future absolutely sure. The saint remarks this, saying that the soul is not therefore "certain to be saved and cannot fall again... Whenever I say that the soul seems in security, I must be understood to imply, for as long as His Majesty thus holds it in His care, and it does not offend Him" (*Interior Castle,* Seventh Mansion, ch. ii, 13).

Whatever opinion may be adopted, this, at least, is the case, that it *seems* to the soul that she can no longer sin, so fully does she feel herself to be participating in the life of God. This does not prevent her seeing very clearly at the same time that of herself she is capable of all kinds of sins. She sees the abyss into which she may fall, and the powerful Hand that sustains her.

**26.**—The **espousals** are the formal promise of spiritual marriage. St. Teresa even seems to say that they are a *passing* possession of the transformation. She says that the espousals take place during rapture (see Extracts, No. 27). The full

* Dr. Imbert gives a list of seventy-seven persons who have had the mystic marriage, or, more exactly, who have been admitted to a spiritual *feast,* symbolising a marriage; but there is nothing in these feasts to tell us if it is a question here of the transforming union. Our Lord gave rings to fifty-five persons, forty-three of whom had the stigmata. There have sometimes been other wedding gifts (Vol. II, ch. viii).

union does not rise to such heights (see ch. xvii, **4**). The saint calls it a simple *interview* of the future spouses (*Interior Castle,* Fifth Mansion, ch. iv, 2).

In the *Ascent of Mount Carmel* and the *Obscure Night,* St. John of the Cross seems, by the whole trend of his writings, to suggest that the transformation takes place by imperceptible degrees, at least from a certain period in the mystic life. He does not say this explicitly, however.

In the *Spiritual Canticle,* on the contrary, he says clearly that the transformation is only reached by the way of ecstasy: "The *spiritual flight* signifies a certain high estate and union of love, whereunto, after many spiritual exercises, God is wont to elevate the soul: it is called the Spiritual Espousals of the Word, the Son of God... The first time that God so elevates the soul, He reveals to it great things of Himself" (*A Spiritual Canticle,* Stanza XIV, p. 74).

## EXTRACTS

**27.**—St Teresa on the spiritual espousals:

1° When these take place. "You will learn how His Majesty ratifies these espousals; probably this is done when He ravishes the soul by ecstasies, so depriving it of its faculties; if the use of these were retained, I think the sight of its close vicinity to so mighty a sovereign would probably deprive the body of life" (*Interior Castle,* Sixth Mansion, ch. iv, 1).

2° They are probably the transitory possession of the transforming union, for the only difference between them which the saint points out is that of their duration:

"There is the *same distinction* between spiritual espousals and spiritual marriage as there is between people who are only betrothed, and others who are united *for ever* in holy matrimony... Thus He has... bound Himself to her as inseparably as two human beings are joined in wedlock. Spiritual espousals are different, and like the grace of union are often dissolved... This is not so in spiritual marriage with Our Lord, where God *always remains* in the centre of the soul. Union may be symbolised by two wax candles, the tips of which touch each other so closely, that the wick, the wax, and the light become one, but the one candle *can again be separated* from the other..." (*Interior Castle,* Seventh Mansion, ch. ii, 2, 3, 4).

3° The raptures of the sixth mansion border on those of the seventh: "... this [sixth mansion] and the following mansion... may be treated as one, the door leading from one to the other being wide open" (*Interior Castle,* Sixth Mansion, ch. iv, 4).

**28.**—St. Teresa. On the second element in the spiritual marriage, the *transformation:*

1° "The *spirit's* being lodged in this centre of our soul is so difficult to express, and even to believe..." (*Interior Castle,* Seventh Mansion, ch. ii, p. 274, Tr. Abraham Woodhead).

2° "This is *mysterious and hidden;* the favour is sublime, that God thus bestows in an instant on the soul, which feels a supreme delight, only to be described by saying that Our Lord vouchsafes for the moment to reveal to it His own heavenly glory... I can only say that *as far as one can understand,* the soul, I mean the spirit of this soul, is made *one with God...*" (*Interior Castle,* Seventh Mansion, ch. ii, 3).

3° "Spiritual espousals... like the grace of union are often dissolved... But spiritual marriage is like rain falling from the sky into a river or stream, becoming *one and the same* liquid, so that the river water and the rain cannot be divided; or it resembles a streamlet flowing into the ocean, which cannot afterwards be dissevered from it. This marriage may also be likened to a room into which a bright light enters through two windows,—though it passes through the two, *the light is one...* Now the little butterfly I spoke of *dies* with supreme joy, for Christ *is her life.* This becomes more manifest as time goes on, for the soul learns that *God is this 'life,'* by *certain secret intuitions* often too strong to be misunderstood... These produce such overmastering feelings that the person experiencing them cannot refrain from amorous exclamations, such as: 'O Life of my life, and Power which doth uphold me!' with other aspirations of the same kind... A person who was unexpectedly plunged into water could not fail to be aware of it; the case is the same, but even more evident, in what I am speaking of. A quantity of water could not fall on us, unless it came from some source,—so the soul feels certain there must be *someone within it* who launches forth these darts and *vivifies its own life.* The mind is convinced there is a sun whence this brilliant light streams forth *from the interior of the spirit to its faculties...* She is like a tree grafted on a stock growing near a stream, which makes it greener and more fruitful. Why marvel at the longings of this soul, whose spirit has indeed *become one with the celestial water* I described?" (*Interior Castle,* Seventh Mansion, ch. ii, 4, 5, 6, 7, 8, 13).

**29.**—St. John of the Cross. The same subject:

1° "The soul then by resigning itself... becomes immediately enlightened by, and *transformed in,* God; because He communicates His own supernatural *Being* in such a way that the soul *seems to be God Himself* and to possess the things of God. Such an union is then wrought when God bestows on the soul that supreme grace which makes the things of God and the soul *one* by the transformation which renders the one a partaker of the other. The soul seems *to be God rather than itself,* and indeed is God by participation, though in reality preserving its own natural substance as distinct from God as it did before, although transformed in Him, as the window preserves its own substance distinct from that of the rays of the sun shining through it and making it light" (*Ascent of Mount Carmel,* Book II, ch. v, p. 69).

2° "This [the spiritual marriage] is, beyond all comparison, a far higher state than that of *espousals,* because it is a complete *transformation* into the Beloved; and because each of them *surrenders* to the other the entire possession of themselves in the perfect union of love, wherein the soul becomes *Divine,* and, *by participation, God,* so far as it is possible in this life. I believe that no soul ever attains to this state *without being confirmed in grace in it,* for the faith of both is confirmed; that of God being confirmed in the soul" (*Spiritual Canticle,* Stanza XXII, line 1, p. 119).

"[The soul] reposes between the arms of such a Bridegroom, whose spiritual embraces are so real that it now, through them, *lives the life* of God" (*ibid.,* line 2, p. 121).

3° In Heaven "I shall then love God even as I am loved by Him. For as the *understanding of the soul will then be the understanding of God, and its will the will of God, so its love will also be His love.** Though in Heaven the will of the soul is not destroyed, it is *so intimately united with the power of the will of God,* Who loves it, that it loves Him *as strongly* and *as perfectly* as it is loved of Him; both wills being united *in one sole will and in one sole love of God.* Thus the soul loves God with the will and strength of God Himself, being made one with that very strength of love wherewith itself is loved of God... In the perfect transformation, also, of the estate of spiritual marriage, such as is possible on earth, in which the soul is all clothed in grace, the soul loves in a certain way in the Holy Ghost, Who is given to it in that transformation. We are to observe here that the bride does not say, There wilt Thou give me Thy love, though that be true —for that means only *that God will love her*—but that He will there show her *how she is to love Him* with that perfection at which she aims, because there He will give her His love, and at the same time show her how to love Him *as He loves her...* He also enables it to love Him *with that strength* with which He loves the soul, transforming it in His love, wherein He *bestows upon the soul His own power,* so that it may love Him... The soul is not satisfied until it reaches this point... And as I have said of the state of spiritual matrimony of which I am speaking, there is now, at this time, though it cannot be that perfect love in glory, a *certain vivid vision and likeness* of that perfection, which is *wholly indescribable*" (*Spiritual Canticle,* Stanza XXXVIII, line 1, p. 197).

4° After having explained (Stanza XXXVIII) that a line of the *Canticle* refers to the Beatific Vision by the relative pronoun: "What":

"... The soul, in the state of Spiritual Matrimony... cannot but *know something* of this 'What,' seeing that because of its transformation in God something of that 'what' must be experienced by it, it will not omit to say something on the subject... The soul refers... [first to] the aspiration of the Holy Spirit of God after it, and its own aspiration after God... This [compared to a breath of air] is a

* The saint is here using the language of appearances.

certain faculty which God will there bestow upon the soul in the communication of the Holy Ghost..." (*Spiritual Canticle,* Stanza XXXIX, p. 202).

5° "For granting that God has bestowed upon it so great a favour as to unite it to the most Holy Trinity, whereby it becomes *like unto God, and God by participation,* is it altogether incredible that it should exercise the *faculties of its intellect,* perform its *acts of knowledge and of love,* or, to speak more accurately, should *have it all done* in the Holy Trinity together with It, as the Holy Trinity Itself?" (*ibid.,* line 1, pp. 203-4).

6° "... All I say falls far short of that which passes in this intimate union of the soul with God... The soul—and this is the subject of these stanzas—when *transformed,* and *glowing* interiorly in the fire of love, is not only united with the Divine fire, but becomes a living flame, and itself conscious of it" (Prologue, *Living Flame of Love,* pp. 217-8).

7° "The soul now *being one* with God *is itself God* by participation... It loves God *by means of* God. This is an admirable perfection..." (*The Living Flame of Love,* Stanza II, line 6, pp. 293-5).

8° "[The Bride feels that] as she is so vehemently *transformed* in God, so profoundly possessed by Him, so richly adorned with gifts and graces, she is *near unto bliss,* and that a slender veil only separates her from it" (*ibid.,* Stanza I, Explanation, pp. 219-20).

9°. Variations in intensity in this union:

"He [the Beloved] is there as it were *asleep* in the embraces of the soul, and the soul is, in general, conscious of His presence, and, in general, has the fruition of it most deeply. If He were always *awake* in the soul, the communications of knowledge and love would be unceasing, and that would be a state of glory" (*The Living Flame of Love,* Stanza IV, line 3, p. 303).

**30.**—Ven. Mary of the Incarnation, Ursuline, began, a little before she was twenty-one,* to enjoy an almost permanent union with God, which continued to increase for fifty-two years until her death. Although she had the intellectual vision of the Blessed Trinity from the beginning and called her state the spiritual marriage, there is reason to think that her words should not be understood in their strict sense. For until she was forty-eight years old the union suffered long interruptions (see ch. xxiv, 98); this, according to the common opinion of spiritual writers, does not occur in the transforming union. She called this union "her vested and permanent state." "In this state, she says, one can talk on any subject, one can read, write, work, and do what one wills and yet this fundamental occupation ever remains, and the soul does not cease being united to God whose greatness, even, does not distract it... The storms of

* For, in the September of 1670, two years before her death, she wrote to her son that this state had continued for about fifty years. She became a widow at twenty and joined the Ursulines at Tours when she was thirty-one (1631). Eight years later she went to Canada (1639).

temptation do not reach thither, and nothing can draw the soul from her blessed abode" (*Vie*, by Cl. Martin; ch. xxviii, add.; Abbé Chapôt, Part I, ch. viii).

**31.**—Ven. Anne Madeleine de Rémuzat.

1° The sister here relates her experiences dating from the time of a Retreat in 1723, seven years before her death (she was twenty-six): "I found myself all at once in the presence of the Three adorable Persons of the Trinity... I understood that Our Lord wished to give me an infinitely purer knowledge of His Father and of Himself than all that I had known until that day... How admirable were the secrets that it was given to me to know in and by this adorable bosom!... My God, Thou hast willed to *divinise my soul*, so to say, *by transforming it into Thyself*, after having destroyed its individual form..." (*The Nun of the Order of the Visitation*—Anne-Madeleine de Rémuzat, of Marseilles, by Monseigneur Van den Berghe, ch. vii, p. 181-2).

"God has deigned to introduce this criminal nothingness into His adorable bosom in order that by this sort of *divinisation* a proportionate glory might be formed in me... Whereas before, the light seemed to produce darkness in my soul, on account of its weakness, and that it still needed to be purified; the soul is now, on the contrary, able to sustain in some measure the weight of the majesty of God, and the splendour of His glory, no longer by the lights of faith but by a clearness of vision which has given it a kind of foretaste of the beatific vision more fitted for heaven than for earth..." (*ibid.*, ch. vii, p. 190).

"I was, as it were, surrounded and penetrated with the glory of God, who has made me participate in the *knowledge whereby He knows Himself*, and in *the love wherewith He loves Himself*. I have understood, but in a way that is beyond all expression, that the Three adorable Persons of the Trinity have operated new things in me, and have contracted with me an *alliance* of love and of mercy. I do not know how it is that these views and impressions have lasted; all that I know is that the senses have had no part therein... God has made me see and taste... His divine perfections. It is an abyss of delight which is all the greater and more excellent, in that it is contained in the *simple* view... of the essence of God"* (*ibid.*, ch. vii, p. 192).

"Having thus *become*, as it were, *one thing* with my God... I was, as it were, filled with the knowledge of God *in His own knowledge*. I saw Him as a Being infinitely perfect, solely occupied with Himself and His adorable perfections, finding in Himself the sole source of His felicity, and unable to receive any perfect homage from His creature save only that which He renders to Himself in her. This homage appeared to be formed in me in a manner worthy of Him, and without my having contributed to it in the least degree. Do not ask me what

* It was at the same period that she wrote: "My state is a mingling of suffering and of joy; while the soul's exterior is given over to sorrow and depression, the central part is always united to God by God's own operation" (*ibid.*).

took place; it was neither light, nor taste, nor a suffering, nor a full joy; but *God Himself,* such as He is, and in so far as He can be received in a vile creature" (*ibid.,* ch. iv, p. 112).

"That which astonishes me beyond measure is, that the depth of my soul is occupied with God in such a manner as not to be hindered in the least by the impressions from without. So completely is my soul thus occupied and filled, that it has no longer any eyes or room for anything external. God makes Himself understood no longer by words that seem to flow from Him, but by a knowledge drawn from His bosom, and *that is Himself* as He is. The light that He sends in words shows His will in a manner worthy of Him" (*ibid.,* ch. vii, p. 191).

2° On permanent union. In 1728, two years before her death, Anne-Madeleine was appointed to the post of *econome,* so distracting for others. She writes: "My taste and my strength were not considered, but I regarded neither the one nor the other... The Spirit of God supplied all without any care on my part... *My interior occupation is always the same;* it *even seems to gain strength* in the dissipation inseparable from such an employment. God communicates Himself, and permits *that He should be found everywhere...* In my greatest occupations, I feel *neither any difficulty nor any pain,* and I am as much *occupied with God as in the time of prayer.* I never have the slightest doubt as to what I ought to do or to leave undone. The Spirit of God deigns to prompt me in all my duties, and He enables me to fulfil them so perfectly that there is no room for fear... The body is strengthened... in a way that I do not fear to term miraculous... I suffer more than ever, but all the same I continue my way... Concerning the body, nothing is more astonishing than the way in which God comes to its assistance. If I have any hard work to do that requires strength, that strength is given to me, but only for the time in which it is required, and afterwards I fall back into my previous state of weakness and languor. This experience, many times repeated, has emboldened me to take nearly everything upon myself, or rather upon the strength that God has given me, without fear, and without having recourse to the assistance of anyone" (*ibid.,* ch. vii, pp. 183, 184).

**32.**—Mother Veronica of the Heart of Jesus (see 8 *bis*):

"The most perfect form of her union was a sort of compenetration of her whole self by the Divinity, so that she felt God Himself think, speak, and act in her and become the cause of all her movements.

"This state lasted for the two years following her profession. During all this time she took no food with the exception of a little *pain bénit* on Sunday and one glass of water a week "(*Vie,* by Fr. Prevot, ch. xviii). It is supposed that this state still continued after these two years. But there are no documents to prove it.

# PART IV

## REVELATIONS AND VISIONS

## CHAPTER XX

### ON REVELATIONS AND VISIONS (OF CREATED THINGS)
### DESCRIPTIVE PART

**1.**—From the point of view of sanctification, these graces are of much **less importance** than the mystic union.

Many Christians think otherwise. They are misled by the preponderating part given to revelations in the majority of the *Lives* of the saints. They imagine that these graces occupied as large a place in the existence as in the accounts of their lives.

The compilers of these books have been led to treat facts in this way because the mystic union is so simple and intangible that ten lines have often contained all that a saint has been able to say on the subject, while visions lend themselves to long narrations. Also the writer understands them better. And, finally, he knows that by appealing to their imagination he will please his readers more.

#### § 1. DIVERS KINDS OF REVELATIONS

**2.**—There are **three kinds** of supernatural **locutions,** or words, corresponding in order of superiority to the faculties that come into play: the bodily hearing, the imagination, and the intelligence.

**3.**—1° The **exterior** or *auricular* locutions are heard by the ear, as is the case with natural speech. Sounds are received, but they are produced supernaturally.

**4.**—2° **Imaginative locutions*** are also composed of words like the foregoing; foregoing; but they are received directly without the assistance of the ear. They

* In French [as in English] it is the custom to say imaginary locutions and visions, following the Latin. If I make this change it is because in our language the word imaginary nearly always means a flight of the imagination; it applies to things that are entirely non-existent, while imaginative means an act of the

can be said to be received by the imaginative sense. They, with those that come after them, are included in the term interior locutions.

**5.**—3° **Intellectual locutions.** This is a simple communication of thought without words, and consequently without the use of any definite language. "It is our Lord's will" (says St. Teresa) "... that the soul should have some knowledge of what passes in Heaven and I think that, as the blessed there without speech understand one another... so it is here" (*Life*, ch. xxvii, 12).

The human mind itself sometimes dispenses with words. For when we are writing it often happens that we say: I cannot find words that express my thought exactly.

Both good and bad angels can speak to us intellectually, but on condition that God intervenes to give us, momentarily, at any rate, the faculty to understand them. Otherwise they can only, in this world, act upon our bodies or imaginations.

The same thing must be said with regard to intellectual visions of angels.

**6.**—St. John of the Cross makes use of an expression that I shall not employ, because it seems to me to be too obscure. He gives the name of intellectual **"successive locutions"** to speech that would be designated with greater clearness as apparent speech. It is that which is produced by the mind, either by its own activity alone or with a real foundation, defining and *arranging* certain truths that God has revealed to us or other seeming truths presented to us by the devil. In reality, God says nothing, but this is how the illusion arises: In certain cases the mind "puts words and reasonings together so much to the purpose, and with such facility and clearness discovers by reflection things it knew not before [or that it had forgotten], that it seems to itself as if it was not itself which did so, but some third person which addressed it interiorly, reasoning, answering, and informing... Thus the mind addresses itself to itself as if to some other person" (*Ascent of Mount Carmel,* ch. xxix, p. 189).

Since these are not true words, I prefer to designate them accordingly. And, further, the word *successive* suggests that the true intellectual words never deserve this name. Now, the saint says the contrary in the following chapter. "Sometimes it is one word, at another two or more, and occasionally *successive words,* as in the former case; for they *continue* in the way of instruction to the soul" (*ibid.,* ch. xxx, p. 196).

See in No. **25** two other expressions employed by the saint.

**7.**—The **visions** also are of **three kinds.**

imagination, but one that is not inordinate. The word *imaginary* is often wrongly understood by the uninstructed in these matters, because they take it in the everyday sense.

**8.**—1° **Exterior visions,** also called *ocular* and *corporeal,** are visions perceived by the bodily eyes. A material being is formed, or seems to be formed, outside of us, and we perceive it like anything else that is round about us.

**9.**—2° **Imaginative visions** are visions of material objects, seen without the assistance of the eyes. They are perceived by the imaginative sense.

**10.**—3° **Intellectual visions** are visions perceived by the mind alone without any interior image. We may thus see God or the angels, and even material objects, but in the same way as one would see angels intellectually, without any form, that is to say. These visions may be either confused or distinct (see Extracts, **49**).

**11.**—The visions that occur during **ecstasy** or in a dream, belong (save in the case of a miraculous exception) to one of the two last categories, for, normally, the action of the eyes is suspended during the ecstasy.

Some of the states that the Holy Scriptures call prophetic sleep may perhaps in reality have been ecstasies.

**12.**—When either good or evil **angels** appear in a corporeal or imaginative vision, what we see is not really them, because they have no bodies. It is a borrowed form. And, in the same way, when we see another man, we do not really see his soul in his face.

When the devil appears under a bodily form, there is nothing to prevent him from giving himself the same charm, the same air of holiness, as a good angel. If the vision is intellectual, the mask falls off, except perhaps when the vision is very obscure.

St. Bridget says that if we were to see an angel quite clearly we should die of pleasure, and that if it were a demon we should die with fright and horror (Book II, ch. xviii).

**13.**—It is possible also to have an **intellectual view of our own soul.** In the natural state we are conscious only of our mental activities, and we thence *conclude* the existence of our faculties. But God can raise us supernaturally to a higher knowledge, and show us our nature such as it actually is, and can even cause us to see our state of grace, etc. In Heaven we shall have all these kinds of knowledge.

**14.**—St. Alphonsus Ligouri truly remarks that "the revelations of secret or of future things, such as the mysteries of the Faith, the reading of consciences, the predestination of certain persons, their death, their elevation to some dignity, and other similar things, may occur in three ways: by visions, by locutions, and by a simple apprehending of the truth" (*Homo. apost.,* Appendix 1, No. 22).

**15.**—History proves that visions or exterior locutions have often been received, transiently, at any rate, by persons who were still in the way of

* Taken alone this last word is ambiguous. It might only mean to signify that the *object* of the vision is corporeal. But it is also intended to point to the exterior *mode* of vision, to the exclusion of the two following modes.

ordinary prayer. The apparition to the children at *La Salette* would seem to be a case of this kind. But visions and supernatural locutions of a higher order are not *usually* granted, with any frequency, at least, until **the period of ecstasy** is almost reached.

St. Teresa heard words before she had visions. Here is a summary of her graces and the order in which she received them:

**16.—The progress of mystic graces with St. Teresa:**

1° At the age of twenty (1535) she passed a year in a state of recollection and received the *prayer of quiet* or *full union* from time to time for "the space of an Ave Maria" on each occasion (*Life*, ch. iv, 9).

2° She afterwards relaxes in fervour, recovers it at the age of forty (1555), and is again favoured with the *mystic union* (*Life*, ch. xxiii, 2). Two years later St. Francis Borgia reassures her with regard to her way of prayer (*Life*, ch. xxiv, 4). Some time before this she had made the Exercises of St. Ignatius under the direction of Fr. Juan de Padranos.

3° At the age of forty-three (1558) she places herself under the direction of Fr. Balthasar Alvarez, who was twenty-five years of age, and she had her first *ecstasy* while she was imploring Our Lord to set her free from certain too natural friendships, with regard to which her Confessor expostulated with her (*Life*, ch. xxv, 6). She then begins to hear interior locutions (*Life*, ch. xxv), which raises a great storm against her. Her confessors order her to reject these locutions. She continues in a great agony of mind for two years. Her friends pray that she may be led by a way less open to suspicion. She tries vainly to desire this herself (*Life*, ch. xxvii).

4° About two years later, at the age of forty-five, she is favoured with *visions* of Our Lord (*Life*, ch. xxvi, 6). These visions were at first *intellectual* (*Life*, ch. xxvii), and lasted continually for two years and a half* (*Life*, ch. xxix, 2). She saw Our Saviour at her right hand and continually at her side, and walking with her† (*Life*, ch. xxvii, 3), and St. Peter and St. Paul on her left hand (*Life*, ch. xxix, 6). St. Peter of Alcantara reassured her with regard to these favours towards the

* At this period Fr. Balthasar Alvarez was her confessor. He continued to act in this capacity for seven years, but he was only raised to mystic contemplation later, in 1567, a year after his departure from Avila, when he was thirty-four years of age and had just been professed (*Life* by the Ven. L. du Pont, ch. xiii). The result was that while at Avila he did not completely understand the saint's state, and he became doubtful when he found that everyone was condemning her visions. She says: "This great humility of his brought me into serious trouble, for though he was a man much given to prayer, and learned, he never trusted his own judgment, because *Our Lord was not leading him by this way*" (*Life*, ch. xxviii, 20). Later on, ten years after he had received the grace of contemplation (1577), he was obliged to defend his method of prayer against some violent attacks made against it (see ch. xiv. 32).

St. Teresa gives a list of her principal directors in her *First Letter* to Fr. Rodrigo Alvarez (1576) (*Relation*, VII, *Life*, p. 446).

† The Ven. Mary of the Incarnation, Ursuline, at the age of fifty-two was favoured for some considerable time with an intellectual vision of the Blessed Virgin. She was thus assisted during the construction of her Convent at Quebec (*Vie*, by an Ursuline of Nantes, ch. xv).

year 1560, and he thus put an end to her anguish and her resistance to them (*Life*, ch. xxx, 5).

5° Some time after the first of these visions she had some *imaginative* visions. On the first occasion she saw Our Saviour's Hands only (*Life*, ch. xxviii, 2); a few days later His divine Face; and finally she saw His whole Person. She saw Him almost always as He was after the Resurrection, in His glorified Body (*Life*, ch. xxix, 4). She never had any *exterior* visions (*Life*, ch. xxviii, 5; xxx, 5; *Interior Castle*, Sixth Mansion, ch. ix, 3), nor heard auricular words (*Relation* VII, 4, made for Fr. Rodrigo Alvarez, S.J., *Life*, p. 445). God the Father spoke to her at times, the Holy Ghost never, the Word very often, but always by His Sacred Humanity (*Relation* VIII, 20, 21, to Fr. Rodrigo Alvarez, *Life*, p. 463).

6° At the age of fifty-one (about 1566) she concludes the *Book of her Life* and composes the *Way of Perfection*. After her raptures were over she was seized by a most grievous pain, the yearning to see God. "This is my present state... It is a communication made, not to console, but to show the reason why the soul must be weary: because it is far away from the Good which in itself comprehends all good" (*Life*, ch. XX, 11, 12). "The sufferer gives vent to loud cries, which she cannot stifle... there is great danger of death in this state. Short as is the time during which it lasts [in its greatest intensity], it leaves the limbs all disjointed..." (*Interior Castle*, Sixth Mansion, ch. xi, 3, 4).

7° At the age of fifty-seven (the end of 1572) she is raised to the *spiritual marriage*. This was fourteen years after her first ecstasy and ten before her death. She died at the age of sixty-seven (1582). She had composed the *Interior Castle* five years earlier.

### § 2. Descriptive Details Concerning Interior Locutions

**17.**—We shall occupy ourselves principally with *imaginative* words. I shall follow St. Teresa (*Life*, chs. xxv, xxvi, xxvii; *Interior Castle*, Sixth Mansion, chs. iii, iv). It is solely a question of true words.

**18.**—1° **When do they occur?** Often outside the ecstasy; and then it is frequently unexpectedly and when the mind is occupied with other things. "It may occur, too, when the understanding and the soul are so troubled and distracted that they cannot form one sentence correctly" (*Life*, ch. xxv, 6).

So, too, when the locutions are intellectual it happens that "generally—so I think— the senses are not taken away, and the faculties are not suspended: they preserve their ordinary state" (*Life*, ch. xxvii, 9).

"... If we see *visions* and hear *words*, it never is as at the time when the soul is in union *in the very rapture itself*... The soul is then wholly in the power of another... but when this instant is passed, the soul continuing still entranced, then is the time of which I am speaking; for the faculties, though not completely suspended, are so disposed that they are scarcely active, being, as it were, absorbed and incapable of making any reflections" (*Life*, ch. xxv, 7).

**19.**—2° **Clearness.** The interior words "are very distinctly formed... they are, however, *much more clearly understood* than they would be if they were heard by the ear" (*Life*, ch. xxv, 2). "The divine locution is a voice so clear that not a syllable of its utterance is lost" (*ibid.*, 6). As a rule, the words that are counterfeited by the imagination are undecided, without consistency; the phrase hesitates and is left unfinished.

**20.**—3° **Strength.** "... There is no escape, for, in spite of ourselves, we must listen; and the understanding must apply itself so thoroughly to the comprehension of that which God wills we should hear, that it is nothing to the purpose whether we will it or not... My resistance lasted nearly two years [at the age of forty-two and forty-three] because of the great fear I was in: and even now I resist occasionally; but it is of no use" (*Life*, ch. xxv, 2). "The soul is like a person whose hearing was good, and who is not suffered to stop his ears, while people standing *close beside him* speak to him with *a loud voice*. He may be unwilling to hear, yet hear he must" (*Life*, ch. xxvii, 10). "Those Our Lord does not lead by this path may suppose that the soul can avoid listening to these locutions, and that even if they be interior it is at least possible to distract the mind from them, and so escape such dangers. This cannot be done" (*Interior Castle*, Sixth Mansion, ch. iii, 27).

**21.**—4° **Certainty.** "*The words*, their effects, and the assurance they carried with them *convinced the soul at the moment* that they came from God. That time, however, is now past: doubts afterwards arise whether the locutions come from the devil or from the imagination, although while hearing them, the person had no doubt of their truth, which she would have died to defend" (*Interior Castle*, Sixth Mansion, ch. iii, 12).

It is only afterwards that doubts may arise (*Life*, ch. xxv, 10).

**22.**—5° **What feelings,** what emotional states, do these words produce? "The second sign is a great calm [after the first moment, that is to say] and a devout and peaceful recollection which dwell in the soul, together with a desire to praise God... If these locutions proceed from the imagination, they show no such signs, bringing neither conviction, nor peace, nor interior joy with them.*... But Satan could never counterfeit the effects spoken of; he leaves no peace nor light in the soul, only anxiety and confusion" (*Interior Castle*, Sixth Mansion, ch. iii, 10, 16, 24). The saint also speaks of "the great aridity which remains in the soul after these evil locutions... yet this disquiet is such that I know not whence it comes" (*Life*, ch. xxv, 13).

**23.**—6° The **majesty** of these words. "As to the divine locution, we listen to that as we do to a person of great holiness, learning, or authority... for these locutions proceed occasionally in such great majesty that, without our

* Neuropathic patients in the hospitals who think they hear voices do not generally feel this joy. The words are disagreeable, aggressive, and usually take the form of an obsession. Further, these persons have not the feeling of conviction, for by their very nature they are doubters.

recollecting who it is that utters them, they make us tremble if they be words of reproof, and die of love if words of love" (*Life*, ch. xxv, 9).

**24.**—7° **Instantaneous knowledge.** "The divine locutions instruct us without loss of time, and we understand matters which seem to require a month on our part to arrange" (*Life*, ch. xxv, 12).* The meaning of these locutions is therefore fuller than that of our own words.

**25.**—8° The **effects upon the conduct.** There is one case in which these are very evident; it is when the divine locutions counsel or command an *interior disposition;* for instance, if they bid the soul be at peace or correct some defect, they produce this change *suddenly* in the soul. "When Our Lord speaks, it is at once word and work" (*Life*, ch. xxv, 5), like the Word by which the world was created.

St. Teresa says that this is the most decisive test of all, as proving that a locution is from God. On the other hand, "the words formed by the understanding effect nothing" (*Life*, ch. xxv, 5; *Interior Castle*, Sixth Mansion, ch. iii).

Locutions of this nature might be styled *operative* locutions. St. John of the Cross applies the name *substantial* to them, which does not suggest clearly the work that they perform (*Ascent of Mount Carmel,* Book II, ch. xxxi, p. 200). "The soul is not called upon to do or attempt anything with regard to these locutions, but to be resigned and humble." He adds that neither the intellect nor the evil spirit can imitate this action (*ibid.*). This is easily understood, because the devil cannot seek to produce a real transformation of the will, in a good sense; and the intellect cannot accomplish it without the help of some previous considerations.

The saint says that there exist, on the contrary, cases where, although the locutions are divine "and render it [the soul] ready to accomplish what is commanded" (*ibid.*, ch. xxx, p. 196), yet the effect on the mind is not great, which doubtless means that the efficacy depends upon our free-will, which may resist it.† He gives as an example the divine command that Moses received to go and speak to Pharao. Moses angered God by his resistance.

Words sent chiefly to enlighten the mind, such as prophetic warnings, or even commands to execute some exterior work, are generally of this number.

**26.**—9° **Persistence in the memory.** "The third proof is that these words do not pass from the memory, but remain there for a very long time; *sometimes* they are never forgotten" (*Interior Castle,* Sixth Mansion, ch. iii, 11).

* The same fact is related with regard to St. Bridget by one of her secretaries (*Prologue*, by Alphonsus de Vadatera, ch. iv). He affirms that she received the whole of the fifth book of her revelations instantaneously, with the Rule of her Order, which occupies forty folio columns (Roman ed., 1628). St. Hildegard says that everything that she learnt with regard to human affairs was always given "as though instantaneously" (Migne ed. col. 18 A).

† He gives them the name of *Formal Words,* which in no way suggests the quality he attributes to them by definition, that of effecting little without the active participation of the mind.

"The divine locution is a work done; and though some of it may be forgotten, and time have lapsed, yet it is not so wholly forgotten that the memory loses all traces of what was once spoken—unless, indeed, after a very long time, or unless the locution were words of grace or of instruction. But as to prophetic words, they are never forgotten in my opinion" (*Life*, ch. xxv, 10).

**26** *bis.*—10° **Whence** do these locutions **proceed?** "Sometimes," says Alvarez de Paz, "they seem to descend from the sky, sometimes to be uttered near by or at a distance, sometimes to rise up from the heart's profoundest depths" (*De Inquis. pacis,* Book V, Part III, ch. vi).*

### § 3. Details Regarding Visions (Of Created Things) Especially the Imaginative Vision

**27.**—I will speak of those of Our Lord, following St. Teresa (*Interior Castle,* Sixth Mansion, chs. viii, ix; *Life,* ch. xxviii and following). We take it for granted that it is a question of visions that are really divine.

**28.**—1° **Their object.** "... When Our Lord is pleased to caress the soul, He shows it in vision His most sacred Humanity, *under whatever form He chooses;* either as He was during His life on earth, or after His resurrection" (*Interior Castle,* Sixth Mansion, ch. ix, 2).

**29.**—2° **At what times do they come?** Sometimes it is outside the time of the ecstasy, and they are then unexpected. Sometimes "a person is not thinking of seeing anything, nor has any such idea crossed the mind, when suddenly the vision is revealed in its entirely, causing within the powers and senses of the soul a fright and confusion which soon afterwards change into a blissful peace" (*Interior Castle,* Sixth Mansion, ch. ix, 7).

At other times the imaginative vision occurs during the ecstasy, or even produces it. "The former vision, which, as I said, represented God without any likeness of Him, is of a higher kind... These two... visions come almost always together, and they do so come; for we behold the excellency and beauty and glory of the most Holy Humanity with the eyes of the soul. And in the other way I have spoken of—that of intellectual vision—we learn how He is God, is mighty, can do all things, commands all things, governs all things, and fills all things with His love" (*Life,* ch. xxviii, 14).

* With regard to the words that are heard, as it were, within our own breast, the writer supposes that there is a sound perceived by the imaginative faculty. We must not confuse this case with that which is observed in certain hospitals. There is no sound, but only the movement of an interior organ, which has the same result. The sick person experiences involuntary movements of the tongue, or the larynx, the throat or the lungs, identical with those that would take place if he pronounced the words aloud. These motor perceptions suggest to him (with the help, perhaps, of arbitrary interpretations) corresponding ideas, as would be the case with words either heard or real. Consequently the sick man wrongly imagines himself to be entering into conversation with a mysterious being, whether a friend or an enemy. This is what is called kinesthetic language, in contradistinction to audible and visual.

"... So exceedingly great is the power of this vision, when Our Lord shows the soul much of His grandeur and majesty, that it is impossible, in my opinion, for any soul to endure it, if Our Lord did not succour it in a most supernatural way, by throwing it into a trance or ecstasy, whereby the vision of the divine presence is lost in the fruition thereof" (*Life*, ch. xxviii, 14).

**30.**—If the imaginative vision occurs when there is no ecstasy, does it always **produce** it? No. There is no necessity that the one should bring about, the other. For St. John of the Cross speaks of these visions as "... that supernatural light, wherein he beholds what God wills, most easily and most distinctly, whether they be things of heaven or of earth; neither is their presence nor absence any impediment to the vision" (*Ascent of Mount Carmel,* Book II, ch. xxiv, p. 171). It should be so more especially when the apparition only lasts a moment (**33**). St. Teresa merely says, when speaking of imaginative visions of Our Lord, that the ecstasy "*almost* always" follows (see Extracts, **37**).

St. Thomas, on the other hand, seems to say that there is necessarily a certain alienation of one of the sensible faculties—that of sight. Otherwise, he says, "we should confuse the subject of the vision with other bodies" situated in the same direction (2, 2, q. 173, a. 3, c.). But to this we can reply that to obviate this drawback all that is necessary is to keep the eyes closed. As the holy Doctor must have foreseen such a simple answer, we must believe that he does not take the word *alienation* in its strict sense of a failure of the power of sight, but that he has stretched it so as to include any hindrance to its action proceeding from an external cause.

But even if the eyes are open, God has two very simple means of preventing this unfortunate confusion of two different impressions. The first consists in the brilliancy of the vision. It will then eclipse the rival sensation, just as the sun's splendour prevents our seeing the stars during the daytime, although our eyes still receive their rays. So, too, when the light of a lamp shines strongly in our eyes it prevents our distinguishing the objects in a dimly lighted room. We can imagine that it would be the same in the contest between two visual objects—one interior, the other exterior.

There is a second way also. When I fix my eyes upon some neighbouring object, even when such an object is transparent, the things that are beyond it or on this side of it seem merely a confused mass that hardly distracts my attention. This is due to what is called the mechanism of adjustment of the eyes to different distances (by a convergence of the optical axes and a change in the curvature of the crystalline lens). During an interior vision the open eyes may, therefore, by the act of adjustment, interrupt their connection with any distant objects that would be a hindrance to them; and as this adjustment is habitual to them, it may readily be believed that they will perform it easily and suddenly. In this way God would not need to suspend any natural law.

**31.**—Inversely, when an imaginative vision produces alienation of the sensible faculties, does this state always contain the mystic union **over and**

**above the vision,** and while the vision lasts? This is a question that no writer has ever set himself to solve, and it is one that is not cleared up by anything that we read in the saints' lives.

The question comes back to this: Are supernatural ecstasies *always* of the type described in ch. xvii—that is to say, having the mystic union as their foundation? We do not know.

**32.**—3° **Reality** of imaginative visions. "Now and then it seemed to me that what I saw was an image; but *most frequently* it was not so. I thought it was Christ *Himself,* judging by the brightness in which He was pleased to show Himself. Sometimes the vision was so indistinct, that I thought it was an image, but still not like a picture, however well painted... If what I saw was an image, it was a living image—not a dead man, but the *living* Christ: and He makes me see that He is *God and Man*... as He was when He had... risen from the dead... No one can have any doubt that it is Our Lord Himself, especially after Communion: we know that He is then present, for faith says so" (*Life*, ch. xxviii, 11, 12).

**33.**—4° **Duration.** According to St. Teresa, "the vision of Him passes so quickly that it may be compared to a flash of lightning" (*Interior Castle,* Sixth Mansion, ch. ix, and the *First Letter* (*Relation* VII, 4) to Fr. Rodrigo Alvarez, *Life,* p. 445).

"When anyone can *contemplate* this sight of Our Lord *for a long time*, I do not believe it is a vision, but rather some overmastering idea" (*Interior Castle*, Sixth Mansion, ch. ix, 5).

"God puts it [this light] before us so instantaneously, that we could not open our eyes in time to see it, if it were necessary for us to open them at all. But whether our eyes be open or shut, it makes no difference whatever" (*Life*, ch. xxviii, 8).

St. John of the Cross speaks of imaginative visions in the same way: "When these visions occur, it is as if a door were opened into a most marvellous light, whereby the soul sees, as men do when the lightning suddenly *flashes* in a dark night. The lightning makes surrounding objects visible for an instant, and then leaves them in obscurity, though the forms of them remain in the fancy [i. e. the imagination]" (*Ascent of Mount Carmel*, Book II, ch. xxiv, p. 171).

We may ask ourselves, however, whether this impermanence is a general law. For the lives of the saints rarely exhibit this circumstance, and, on the contrary, they often seem to describe a persistence of these visions. And, further, in those cases where a picture of some historic fact, such as the Passion, passes before the eyes of the person in the ecstasy, it is certain that the scene takes some considerable length of time to unfold.

In the same way I have heard from several favoured persons that their imaginative visions were prolonged, for some minutes, at least, especially when Our Lord spoke to them. One says that these apparitions (sometimes vague, sometimes very distinct) at times produced a fairly deep absorption, but this without, as a rule, hindering him from going and coming and carrying on his occupations (see **30**). He adds that this state is not accompanied by the mystic union (see **31**).

In the life of Sister Gojoz, of the Order of the Visitation, in the seventeenth century, it is said that she had a vision of Our Blessed Lord's Sacred Humanity that lasted for three years consecutively. He kept at her side. This vision was not exterior, however, for we are told that it was perceived by the "eye of the soul." It appears to have been imaginative and not intellectual, for it revealed "traits of the rarest beauty" and garments that did not bear the tint of any earthly colourings. "The most cloudless sun seemed obscure after the light that surrounded my Lord Jesus" (*Vie*, by Mère de Provane, Part II, ch. viii).

**34.**—"This vision [St. Teresa is speaking of intellectual visions]... unlike an imaginary one, does not pass away quickly, but lasts for several days, and even sometimes for a year... a most tender love for Him results from being constantly in His company... Our Lord makes the soul conscious that He is close at hand" (*Interior Castle*, Sixth Mansion, ch. viii, 3, 6).

We have seen (**16**) that St. Teresa had intellectual visions of the Sacred Humanity before she had imaginative visions. I know a person whose case is the same. This may cause surprise, for the intellectual visions are of a higher order. But, on the other hand, they are less distinct. There has been progress, therefore, in the sense of distinctness. What confirms this idea is that the same process of gradual development was followed in the case of St. Teresa's imaginative visions. First she saw only Our Lord's Hands, then His Face, and finally the whole Body (*Life*, ch. xxviii).

**34** *bis.*—5° These visions possess **great beauty** and perfection. "So beautiful are glorified bodies, that the glory which surrounds them renders those who see that which is so supernatural and beautiful beside themselves... If I were to spend many years in devising how to picture to myself anything so beautiful, I should never be able, nor even know how, to do it; for it is beyond the reach of any possible imagination here below: the whiteness and brilliancy alone are inconceivable" (*Life*, ch. xxviii, 3, 7).

The vividness of her visions contrasts with the difficulty that she had in her ordinary state, in picturing Our Lord to herself.

**35.**—Although certain details are shown with clearness, the imaginative visions are sometimes **incomplete** in certain respects, and we cannot make them more perfect. "As to the vision of which I am speaking, there are no means of bringing it about; only we must behold it *when* Our Lord is pleased to present it before us, *as He wills* and what He wills; and there is no possibility of taking anything away from it, or of adding anything to it; nor is there any way of effecting it, whatever we may do, nor of seeing it when we like, nor of abstaining from seeing; if we try to gaze upon it—part of the vision in particular—the vision of Christ is lost at once... I was extremely desirous to behold the colour of His eyes, or the form of them, so that I might be able to describe them, yet I never attained to the sight of them, and I could do nothing for that end; on the contrary, I lost the vision altogether" (*Life,* ch. xxix, 1, 2).

In the imaginative vision "it is no more possible to *continue looking* at it [the vision of Our Lord's Humanity], than to gaze for a long time on the sun" (*Interior Castle,* Sixth Mansion, ch. ix, 2).

So, too, intellectual visions may be very clear or partially obscure. St. Teresa speaks of the first only. Our Lord, she says, "renders Himself present to the soul by a certain knowledge of Himself which is more clear than the sun" (*Life,* ch. xxvii, 5). Alvarez de Paz describes the obscure kind of vision (see Extracts, **49**).

**36.**—6° **Certainty.** 'The soul *for some time afterwards* possesses such certainty that this grace comes from God, that, whatever people may say to the contrary, it cannot fear a delusion. Later on, when her confessor suggests doubts to her, God may allow such a person to waver in her belief for a time, and to feel misgivings, lest, in punishment for her sins, she may possibly have been left to go astray. However, she does not give way to these apprehensions, but (as I said in speaking of other matters) they only affect her in the same way as the temptations of the devil against faith, which may disturb the mind, but do not shake the firmness of belief. In fact, the more the evil one assails her with fears, the more certain does she feel that he could never have produced the great benefits she is conscious of having received, because he *exercises no such power over the interior of the soul.* He may present a false apparition, but it does not possess the *truth, operations,* and *efficacy* of the one she has seen" (*Interior Castle,* Sixth Mansion, ch. ix, 8).

**37.**—7° **What are the sentiments** produced by these visions? The divine Master causes "within the powers and senses of the soul a fright and confusion which soon afterwards change into a blissful peace. Thus, after St. Paul was thrown prostrate on the ground, a great tempest and noise followed from Heaven; so, in the interior world of the soul, there is a violent tumult, followed instantly, as I have said, by perfect calm" (*ibid.,* 7).

"The soul to whom God grants this vision almost always falls into an ecstasy, nature being too weak to bear so *dread* a sight. I say 'dread,' although this apparition is more *lovely* and *delightful* than anything that could be imagined, even though one lived a thousand years, and spent all that time in trying to picture it, for it far surpasses the limits of our imagination and understanding; yet the presence of such surpassing majesty inspires the soul with *great fear*" (*ibid.,* 3).

St. John of the Cross says: "The effects of these (imaginative) visions in the soul are quietness, enlightenment, *joy* like glory, *sweetness,* pureness, love, humility, inclination or *elevation of the mind to God,* sometimes more, sometimes less, sometimes more of one, sometimes more of another, according to the disposition of the soul and the will of God... those of Satan result in *dryness of spirit,* in a tendency to self-esteem... and in no degree whatever do they produce the *gentleness* of humility and love of God... [They are] remembered... with great *dryness of spirit,* and without the fruit of humility and love which issue out of the good visions whenever they recur to the memory" (*Ascent of Mount Carmel,* Book II, ch. xxiv, pp. 171--2).

**38.**—8° *Observance of* **propriety** *in the visions.* "There never was anything in any of these spiritual visitations that was not wholly pure and clean, nor does she think it can be otherwise if the spirit be good and the visitations supernatural" (*Relation* VII, 23, *Life,* p. 453).

"The raiment worn by the Person seen, looks like fine linen" (*Interior Castle,* Sixth Mansion, ch. ix, 3).

"These satanic visions are very different things... the joy which Satan ministers must be, I think, very different—it shows *no traces* of *pure* and *holy* love" (*Life,* ch. xxviii, 15). See ch. xxii, 34.

**39.**—9° **A wide range of knowledge.** "Certain sublime truths have been so impressed upon the mind that it needs no other Master" (*Interior Castle,* Sixth Mansion, ch. ix, 7). The saint explains elsewhere (*Life,* ch. xxvi, 6) how Our Lord became a "living book" to her by these visions.

In the visions many kinds of knowledge may be simultaneously received. St. Alphonsus Rodriguez relates that, being transported to Heaven in an ecstasy, "he saw and knew *all* the Blessed together, and each one of them separately, as if he had passed his *whole life* with them" (*Vie,* from his Memoirs, Appendix No. 275).

And the same thing happened with regard to the angels (No. 6; see also 52, 148). It is related of St. Bridget that she often, in one single instant of time, saw all the inhabitants of Heaven, earth, and Hell, and perceived what each was saying to the other (*Revelations, Prologue,* by Alphonsus de Vadatera, ch. iv).

With regard to the variety of the knowledge acquired by means of visions, we may cite St. Lidwine. Nearly every night for twenty-eight years she had an ecstasy, lasting an hour, during which time she was conveyed to Heaven, to Purgatory, to Hell, or to a great variety of places, such as the Holy Land, Rome, etc., where she venerated the relics of the saints; and also to a great many churches and monasteries, the situations of which she knew and the names of the inhabitants (Bolland., April 14, ch. v).

The counterfeits of the imagination have no power to increase our knowledge in this way.

**40.**—10° **Effects upon the conduct.** "... For as there were most holy persons in the place... whom God did not lead by this way, they [Fr. Balthasar Alvarez and those whom he told her to consult] were at once filled with fear; they thought it all came through my sins. And so my state was talked about and came to the knowledge of many... I said to them once... [that] all who knew me saw clearly that *my soul was changed*—and so my confessor said; for the *difference* was *very great* in every way—not a pretence, but such as all might most clearly observe. As I was formerly so wicked, I said, I could not believe that Satan, if he wished to deceive me and take me down to Hell, would have recourse to means so adverse to his purpose as this of *rooting out my faults*, implanting *virtues and spiritual strength*; for I saw clearly that I had become *at once* another person through the instrumentality of these visions" (*Life*, ch. xxviii, 18, 19).

"And it is from this it comes to pass that he in whom God works these graces [visions of Our Lord] despises himself, and becomes *more humble* than he was ever before, for he sees that this is a gift of God, and that he can neither add to it nor take from it. The love and the desire become greater of serving Our Lord..." (*Relation* VII, 26, made for Fr. Rodrigo Alvarez, *Life*, pp. 454--5).

**41.**—11° **Persistent memory.** "... This most glorious picture makes an impression on the imagination, that I believe can never be effaced until the soul at last sees Christ, to enjoy Him for ever." While, on the other hand, illusory visions "pass from the memory more quickly than do dreams" (*Interior Castle*, Sixth Mansion, ch. ix, 2, 6).

### § 4. Various Questions

**42.**—Let us speak first of the nature of exterior or corporeal visions (whether of divine or diabolic origin). They may be produced in **four different ways:**

*First manner*, which is objective. The body is really that of the person appearing; it is *its substance* that acts upon our eyes.

This case cannot occur with angels and disembodied spirits, as they have no bodies. But we can conceive of this mode as possible for Our Lord and the Blessed Virgin, whose bodies and souls are in Heaven, and also for a living man who might appear to us.

In such a circumstance, the body, although real, may not retain its natural appearance. It was thus that Our Lord showed Himself to St. Mary Magdalen, after His Resurrection, in the likeness of a gardener, and to the disciples at Emmaus as a traveller. And yet it was His real Body that was perceived. Only His garments may have lacked actuality. Even in His appearances to the apostles, Christ did not allow all the splendour and beauty of His glorified Body to appear.

*Second manner*, which is also objective. A body exists materially, but it is a borrowed body, and it is then admittedly formed by the ministry of angels. God thus makes use of secondary causes for works which they are capable of executing.

*Third manner*, which may be called semi-objective. There is no longer any true body, but there is still something material outside the person who sees it, namely, luminous rays, similar to those that a body would have been capable of emitting. The angels produce these undulations as they would produce sound waves, and they cause them to travel from the place that the object is supposed to occupy. At times it would even be sufficient for them to utilise, by diverting them, the diffused rays of the surrounding light. And as the eye of the person who sees the vision will then receive the light in a natural way, as occurred in the above-mentioned cases, the pupil will be lit up as it would be before any brilliant object, and will reflect the picture before it. The bystanders might be able to see the reflection, which has the appearance of a finely wrought cameo. I know two ecstatics in whose cases this phenomena has often been verified.

*Fourth manner,* which is purely subjective. The angels imprint the image of the object directly upon the retina.

St. Thomas (3, q. 76, a. 8, c.) describes these different manners with the exception of the third. He could not imagine this one on account of the theories current in his day on the subject of light. It was not then understood to be a vibration, something that propagates itself, and of which the movement may be brought about artificially, without the qualities of a real body.

**43.**—St. Thomas admits that the last manner is rather **less probable** when *all* who are present see the apparition. The other means seem to give the simplest explanation of the phenomenon.

When, however, the seer of the vision is the only one to perceive the apparition, St. Thomas is inclined to think that the vision is purely subjective. The following explanation may be given: if the luminous rays existed (and this would be the case in the three first modes), God would have to prevent their reaching the other persons who are present. This would seem to be multiplying miracles without necessity.

But for many visions we are reduced to mere conjectures. At Lourdes, for instance, Bernadette was the only one to see and hear the Blessed Virgin. It cannot be decided with any certainty which of the four above-mentioned modes was employed.

**44.—Actual personal presence in corporeal apparitions.** Theologians have discussed the question as to whether, since His Ascension, or at least since His appearance to St. Paul on the way to Damascus, Christ has shown Himself in the first manner—that is to say, with the substance of His Body. It would take too long to go into all the conflicting opinions and the reasons of congruity that have been brought forward to support them. M. Ribet has carried out this task (Vol. II, ch. vi). Like Suarez (*De incarn.*, disp. 51, a. 4, sect. iv), he is inclined to admit that this kind of vision may have occurred. He adds: "St. Teresa seems to favour the contrary opinion (*Additions* to her *Life*); but she relies less on the revelations that she had received than on the conclusions that she drew from them." And these conclusions may have been influenced by the theological opinions of her directors.

**45.**—There is a **point** the decision of which is much **more important.** Whether it is or is not the actual Flesh of the Sacred Humanity that we see, is for us a question of but secondary importance. But have we *really* to do with His *Person,* or only with one of His envoys? This is what is meant when we inquire whether the apparition is personal. It is this, above all, that we wish to know.

There is no difficulty if Our Lord shows Himself in close proximity to the Sacred Host. But in other cases there are two opinions. According to the first, there is a purely moral presence only, that of the King who is represented by his ambassador. Briefly, the apparition would merely be produced upon an order given to an angel by Our Lord, the Blessed Virgin, or a saint, and there would be no further link than this between them and the seer of the vision.

It is further added that the reverence and love shown towards the image are legitimate. For these sentiments merely pass through the image, so to speak, and go to the person whom it represents.

The contrary opinion holds that something more than this is present, and that it can be called a real presence, although it is not possible to state its nature exactly. We should *really enter into relation* with the saint who appeared: just as when we come in contact with the sun's rays we really enter into relation with the sun; but it is far otherwise when we look at a picture representing it.

This doctrine of a *personal action* is the only one that seems probable to me. It is held by all the saints who have seen corporeal apparitions. They have never imagined that they had before them, or that they held in their arms, a mere statue, only differing from others by the perfection of colour or movement. This is evident from their accounts of what had passed and from their actions. For example: St. Anthony of Padua covered the Infant Jesus with his kisses. It was certainly a question here of a corporeal apparition, for he touched the Holy Child, and the scene was witnessed by the owner of the house where the saint lodged. St. Peter, at the gate of Rome, threw himself at the feet of the apparition (which argues that it was corporeal), saying the well-known words: "Lord, whither goest Thou?" This phrase would have had no meaning if he had thought that he was speaking to a mere image.

Finally, it has often happened that the saints have been confirmed in this conviction by the language uttered by the apparition. It said: "I am such or such a saint," not "I represent such or such a saint." None but Jesus Christ could reply to St. Peter: "I go to be crucified in Rome."

St. Thomas admits the same opinion by implication. For he asks (*loc. cit.*) if God does not deceive the seer of the vision when He gives a borrowed body to a saint, since the appearance is so perfect that it cannot be distinguished from the reality. But he replies to this difficulty in the negative only when it is a question of Christ and of an apparition in close proximity to the Sacred Host. For, according to him, the borrowed form then exhibits a reality, an actual presence. Such a reply implies that if there were not always a certain presence of Christ or of the saint, the seer of the vision would be misled by God.

**46.**—In the lives of several saints we see that they received graces which are, as it were, lesser examples of revelations properly so called, the **infused knowledge,** that is to say, of certain religious questions, the meaning of passages in the Bible, for instance. St. Teresa says that she received them at times (*Life*, ch. xv, 12).

What is the exact nature of this gift? I am inclined to think that, in general, it is not a question of really scientific knowledge, or historical information fitted to dispel the uncertainties of exegesis, or of new dogmatic views. For we do not find that the greater number of these communications have been transmitted to scholars, in the strict sense of the word. God's aim is a more practical one. He gives thoughts conducive to piety, analogies that elevate the soul; and in order to do this, in the case of the Holy Scriptures, all that is necessary, is to reveal some appropriate meaning.

**47.**—Many saints, such as St. Catherine of Siena, the Ven. Ursula Benincasa, St. Catherine of Ricci (*Vie*, by Fr. Bayonne, Vol. I, ch. viii), have received a grace that is called **change of heart.** We do not know its nature. Something takes place in the material heart. Is it a real modification or a simple impression? The saints have not explained this point. It is always the symbol of a new life for the soul, or even, perhaps, for the body.

And, equally, other saints have spoken of entering **into the Heart of Jesus,** or into the Wound in His Sacred Side. Are these metaphorical expressions to indicate the contemplation of His love, of His sufferings, or even of His Divinity? Or is it a mysterious grace, of a kind apart? We have no material by which to decide this question either.

## EXTRACTS

### Description and Object of Intellectual Visions

**48.**—St. Teresa:

1° Speaking of herself: "She sees nothing either outwardly or inwardly... but without seeing anything, she *understands what* it is, and *where* it is, *more clearly than if she saw it,* only nothing in particular presents itself to her. She is like a person who *feels* that another is close beside her; but because she is *in the dark* she sees him not... without a word, inward or outward, the soul *clearly* perceives who it is, where he is and occasionally what he means. Why or how she perceives it, she knoweth not; but so it is" (*Relation* VII, 26, to Fr. Rodrigo Alvarez, *Life,* p. 454). See also the simile of the diamond in the closed casket (*Interior Castle,* Sixth Mansion, ch. ix, 1). In the imaginative vision the casket is open.

2° Still speaking of herself: "Her confessor... asked her how, if she saw nothing, she knew that Our Lord was near her, and bade her describe His appearance. She said she was unable to, for she could not see His face, nor could she tell more than she had already said, but that she was sure she was right, and that it was He who spoke to her... You will ask: 'If we see no one, how can we know whether it is Christ, or His most glorious Mother, or a saint?' One cannot answer this question, or *know* how one distinguishes them, but the fact remains *undoubted*" (*Interior Castle*, Sixth Mansion, ch. viii, 3. 8).

3° "Jesus Christ seemed to be by my side continually, and as the vision was not imaginary, *I saw no form*" (*Life*, ch. xxvii, 3).

4° "She was conscious of His being at her right hand, although not in the way we know an ordinary person to be beside us, but in a more sublime manner which I cannot describe. This Presence is, however, quite as evident and certain, and indeed far more so, than the ordinary presence of other people. About this we may be deceived, but not in that" (*Interior Castle*, Sixth Mansion, ch. viii, 4).

5° "It is very rarely that I saw Satan assume a bodily form; I know of his presence through the vision I have spoken of before, the vision wherein no form is seen" (*Life*, ch. xxxi, 10).

6° "Multitudes of angels seemed to me to be above the canopies of the stalls... but I saw no bodily forms, for the vision was intellectual" (Relation III, 16. *Life*, p. 429).

7° When one of the cherubim "his face burning," pierced the saint's heart with "a long spear of gold, and at the iron's point there seemed to be a little fire," she saw him on her "left side, in bodily form." The vision was an imaginative one. For intellectually we cannot see a body that does not really exist, and we have said (**16**, 5°) that the saint never saw visions with her bodily eyes. And further, she particularly says that this was so, for she adds when speaking of the borrowed form that was thus represented to her: "This [the bodily form] I am not accustomed to see, unless very rarely. Though I have visions of angels frequently, yet I see them *only by an intellectual vision*, such as I have spoken of before" (*Life*, ch. xxix, 16, 17).

**49.**—Alvarez de Paz.

He says that with intellectual visions some are very distinct, and others, on the contrary, are confused. If we see Jesus Christ or the Blessed Virgin in the second manner, "we see nothing formed, with regard either to the face or the body, and yet we know more certainly than by the evidence of the eyes that the person in question is either at your right hand or in your heart... It is as though you were suddenly, *in the darkness,* to feel that someone is beside you, and to know that goodwill and not enmity is felt towards you; but you are quite ignorant as to whether it is a man or a woman, whether young or old, good-looking or no, and whether standing or sitting."* The writer adds: "Perhaps you would like to know

* Here is an example of the obscure intellectual vision,—one, that is to say, giving a very incomplete manifestation of the qualities of the object seen. A person wrote to me as follows: "I had a sister who lived at a great distance from me and who died very young, after a short illness. The day of her death, of which I was wholly unaware, I suddenly began to tremble. I experienced in a quite indefinable manner the impression that someone, some soul, was gazing at my soul. I had not the impression that the soul was suffering, but on the contrary it appeared to me to be wholly filled with joy and all enflamed with love. Not knowing that manifestations of this nature were possible, I tried to reject this impression. But it

whether we see the person who appears thus intellectually, as he really is? I reply that with regard to the angels, they show themselves present really and by their substance." As for Our Lord's body, in order to be seen close to us intellectually, there is no need for Him to leave Heaven, for "a sound philosophy teaches us that God can, in the absence of an object, represent it to us just as it would appear if it were present" (*De inquisitione pacis*, Book V, Part III, ch. xii).

persisted all the afternoon, although less distinctly. I felt that this someone remained in my company, on my left hand and a little in front of me. For the next two or three days the impression was still weaker. And then it suddenly seemed to me that this invisible being was leaving me in order to ascend to Heaven, there to obtain the graces that I was beginning to receive. Who was it? I was only able to guess at the answer later, when learning the coincidence of the death and of my impression."

# CHAPTER XXI

## Revelations and Visions (*continued*)
## Illusions to Be Avoided

**1.**—We distinguish **two kinds** of revelations. The one, called *universal,* are contained in the Bible or in the deposit of the apostolic tradition, and are transmitted by the organ of the Church. They came to an end with the preaching of the apostles, and are matters of faith for everyone. The others are called *special* or *private.* These have always occurred amongst Christians. I need only concern myself with this latter kind.

**2.**—With regard to the special revelations that have been made to the saints, **belief** in them is **not required** by the Church even when she approves them. By this approbation she only intends to declare that nothing is to be found in them contrary to faith or morals, and that they can be accepted without danger and even with advantage. "It matters little" (says Melchior Cano) "whether or no one believes in St. Bridget's revelations or those of other saints, these things have nothing to do with faith" (*De locis theologicis,* Book XII, ch. iii).

Benedict XIV is quite clear with regard to this question. "What is to be said of those private revelations which the Apostolic See has *approved* of, those of the Blessed Hildegard [which were approved in part by Eugene III], of St. Bridget [by Boniface IX], and of St. Catherine of Siena [by Gregory XI]? We have already said that those revelations, although approved of, ought not to, and cannot, receive from us any assent of Catholic, but only of human faith, according to the rules of prudence, according to which the aforesaid revelations are probable, and piously to be believed [*probabiles et pie credibiles,*]" (*De canon.,* Book III, ch. liii, No. 15; Book II, ch. xxxii, No. 11. Eng. trans.: *Benedict XIV on Heroic Virtue,* Vol. III, ch. xiv).

Cardinal Pitra says the same: "Everyone knows that we are fully at liberty to believe or not to believe in private revelations, even those most worthy of credence. Even when the Church *approves* them, they are merely received as *probable,* and not as indubitable. They are not to be used as *deciding questions* of history, natural philosophy, philosophy, or theology which are matters of controversy between the Doctors. It is quite permissible to differ from these revelations, even when approved, if we are relying upon solid reasons, and especially if the contrary doctrine is proved by unimpeachable documents and definite experience" (Book on St. Hildegard, p. xvi).

The Bollandists lay down the same principles (May 25, p. 243, No. 246, and *Parergon*, p. 246, No. 1).

Granted that the Church assumes no further responsibility, a question then arises: "What is the last word regarding the actual authority of private revelations?—They have the value of the testimony of the person who witnesses to having received them, neither more nor less. Now, this person is never infallible: it is evident, then, that the points vouched for are never absolutely certain—except in the sole case where a miracle is worked directly in favour of the attestation. In a word, private revelations have only a purely human or probable authority" (Fr. Toulemont on *Private revelations* in the Review, *Les Etudes,* 1866, p. 61).

**3.**—After perusing these passages, the reader will be less astonished when we say that even the revelations of the saints may contain errors occasionally.

I will now endeavour to classify the different kinds of illusions that are to be feared. But first I must warn the reader against two **exaggerated** conclusions that he might be inclined to draw from the pages about to follow:

1° Seeing that the causes of illusion are numerous and difficult to avoid completely, he will perhaps conclude that all revelations should be rejected without examination. No; wisdom lies in the middle course: we should neither believe nor reject unless we have sufficient proofs: lacking such, we must not pronounce any opinion;

2° As examples of these illusions I will choose, by preference, those of the saints or other pious persons.* It must not be concluded that the saints are always or even often mistaken. The instances of errors are not frequent; and where they occur they are not of any great importance.

And further, if one of their revelations be false, it does not follow that it should be the same with their ecstasies, for ecstasy is much less subject to illusion.

In making this selection, I have not acted in any captious spirit and with the object of diminishing the respect that we owe to the saints, but for a grave

* The servants of God of whom I shall speak, trying sometimes to find a favourable explanation of the facts related, number thirty-two. I give them in alphabetical order: Blessed Alain de la Roche, Blessed Amadeus, Sister Andriveau, Blessed Bonomi, St. Bridget, St. Catherine of Bologna, St. Catherine of Ricci, St. Catherine of Siena, Catherine Emmerich, St. Colette, St. Elizabeth of Schoenau, St. Frances of Rome, St. Gertrude, Sister Gojoz, Blessed Hermann Joseph, St. Hildegard, Ven. Holzhauser, Blessed Joan of Arc, the Prophet Jonas, Blessed Jordan of Saxony, Sister Laboure, Marie Lataste, Ven. Mary of Agreda, Ven. Marina de Escobar, St. Mechtildis, Melanie of La Salette, St. Monica, St. Norbert, St. Peter, Blessed Veronica of Binasco, St. Vincent Ferrer, Ven. Anna-Maria Taïgi.

reason of utility.* It is the best way of persuading certain pious persons to mistrust their own revelations, and of persuading their directors to do the same. If I were to quote cases of none but quite ordinary souls, people would say: "Yes, certainly illusions are to be feared; but for ignorant people and beginners. As for the instructed and clear-sighted, they escape, especially when they are pious and of more than ordinary virtue (we always rank ourselves amongst the select few). If this were otherwise, God, who is so good, would be betraying the trust that we put in Him." But if this argument were applicable in our own case, it would be much more necessarily so still where the saints are in question. They were far more enlightened than ourselves and were the object of a much closer protection on God's part. And yet they have sometimes been mistaken. The facts are before us.

But by this method there is no possible point of escape. All must frankly apply to themselves the rules of prudence to be given further on. We can no longer listen to the self-love that whispers: "These rules are excellent, but they are not meant for you. You are not like other men."

Practically, in the case of those who have not attained to high sanctity, we can admit that at least three-quarters of their revelations are illusions.

3 *bis.*—I am led to believe that illusion is easier in the case of interior locutions (intellectual or imaginative) than with imaginative visions. They are much more nearly allied to the ordinary operations of the human mind in which ideas and phrases arise perpetually. If these are clear and sudden, an inexperienced person will conclude that he cannot have produced them himself. The illusion is due principally to an interpretation based on insufficient facts. There has been no fundamentally new act. On the contrary, the interior visual illusions are very superior, both with regard to accuracy and intensity, to the current representations of the imagination. It is then more difficult, so it seems, to mistake one for the other.

These considerations also explain why certain persons, like St. Teresa (ch. xx, **16**), begin to hear divine locutions in the waking state, before being favoured with any frequency, at least, with imaginative visions. It is that the first-named, as we have just said, are more closely allied to our own nature. God thus avoids too sudden transitions.

3 *ter.*—It is clear that revelations and visions are without danger and **very useful** if they are divine, for grace operates only for our welfare; and when it is likewise of such an extraordinary order it cannot be destined for a merely ordinary good. Holy Scripture is filled with facts of this nature which have

* Let us not say: "Out of respect for the saints, it is better to conceal the few illusions from which they may have suffered." Leo XIII, on the contrary, was not afraid to remind historians of Cicero's motto: "Speak nothing that is false; be silent regarding nothing that is true" (*ne quid falsi dicere audeat; ne quid veri non audeat.* Brief *Sæpè numero,* August 18, 1883).

rendered great spiritual service. St. Teresa often explains that this has been so in her case. I give no example, the thesis being so evident.

The revelations that are due to Satan, on the other hand, always tend to produce evil or to hinder good. And, further, those produced by our own imagination are usually useless or dangerous.

It is very important, therefore, in such a matter to learn to distinguish the true and the certain from the false or the doubtful, This will be the object of this chapter and the two succeeding ones.

### § 1. Five Causes of Error That May Have Had an Influence Upon True Revelations, or Revelations Regarded as Such, at Certain Periods and in Certain Countries.*

**4.**—These **five causes** of error are: 1° faulty interpretations of revelations or visions; 2° ignorance of the fact that historic events are often given with approximate truth only; 3° the mingling of human activity with supernatural action during the revelation; 4° the subsequent, but involuntary, modifications made by the person who receives the revelation; and, finally, 5° embellishments by secretaries or compilers of the Life.

**5.**—*First cause of error.* A divine **revelation** may at times be **interpreted wrongly** by the person who receives it.

**6.**—This may be due primarily to the **obscurity** of the revelation. God at times gives only a **partial comprehension** of its import. His communication has a deep meaning that is not understood; it is taken in the everyday sense.

St. John of the Cross says on this subject: "... many prophecies and Divine locutions disappointed, in their fulfilment, the expectations of many of the ancient people, because they understood them *too much according to the letter* in their own way... This is the way in which many souls deceive themselves in the matter of revelations and Divine locutions. They understand them *in the letter according to their apparent meaning.* For, as I have said, the *chief purpose* of God in sending visions is to express and communicate the Spirit which is hidden within them, and which is very hard to be understood. This is much more abundant than the letter, more extraordinary, and surpasses the limits thereof" (*Ascent of Mount Carmel,* Book II, ch. xix, pp. 133-6).

Like St. John of the Cross, Scaramelli cites various examples drawn from ancient history (Tr. 4, ch. xviii). To give a more recent instance, let us take the words heard by **St. Joan of Arc** in prison. She says in her examination: "I inquired of my voices whether I should be burned; and they answered me that I

* I need not enter carefully here into the question of what should be thought of certain books of revelations, taken as a whole, that have had a great reputation, such as those of Mary of Agreda, Catherine Emmerich, etc. A treatise on mysticism should keep to general principles, illustrated by certain examples. Their application to a whole book is a subject for a special treatise.

should trust in Our Lord, and that *He would aid me...* St. Catherine told me that I should *receive succour.*" Joan states that she interprets this utterance as indicating her deliverance. She adds: "As a rule, the voices tell me that I shall be *delivered by a great victory.* And afterwards they say: 'Fear not because of thy *martyrdom.* It will bring thee at last to Paradise.'" These predictions were quite accurate. But Joan did not see their real significance. She thought, as she herself explains, that the word martyrdom meant "the great pains and adversity that she suffered in prison"; and the "deliverance by a great victory" caused her to think of something quite different to her death.*

7.—We have an example of an interpretation that seems to be inaccurate, in one of **St. Mechtildis's** revelations. Her pupil, St. Gertrude, had asked her to pray that she might obtain "the virtues of docility and patience that she thought herself to need." St. Mechtildis related Our Lord's utterances to her on the subject, saying that Gertrude already possessed these virtues, and adding words of encouragement that concluded thus: "The patience (*patientia*) that pleases Me in her, derives its name from *pax* and *scientia* (peace and knowledge). She must so apply herself to patience as never to lose *peace* of heart in adversity, and have the *knowledge* that consists in knowing why she suffers: it is through love and as a mark of inviolable fidelity" (*Le Hérant de l'amour divin,* Book I, ch. xvi). The saint would have been right if she had understood these words as signifying that St. Gertrude's patience *had its source* in peace and knowledge, or again, that the word patience ought to remind her of two others; but the ambiguous words, "Patience *derives* its name..." seem rather to suggest that the saint understood it to be a question of the actual etymology, a historic connection between these different words. If she accepted them in this sense, as Amort believes her to have done (Part II, ch. viii, § 3), she was mistaken. For philologists know that the root of *patientia* has no relation to the word *pax.* Our Lord did not wish to give her a lesson in philology, but to remind her of a useful counsel.

So, too, **St. Gertrude** relates that on Easter Day Our Lord said to her, when speaking of the word *Alleluia*: "Observe that all the vowels, except the *o*, which signifies grief, are found in this word; and that, instead of this *o*, the *a* is repeated twice." And then follows a description of the joys of the risen Christ that the saint could associate with each vowel (Book IV, ch. xxvii). The revelation may be a true one, if it is a question of a conventional signification given to the letter o. But *by itself,* as Amort remarks, this vowel serves as well to express pleasure as grief (Part II, ch. viii, § 10); and the others express grief equally with pleasure. However, it may have been otherwise in the language that

* See *La Vraie Jeanne d'Arc,* by P. Ayrolles, Vol. II, ch. v, No. 4. p. 161; or the *Proces de Jeanne d'Arc,* by Jules Quicherat, Vol. I, March 14.

the saint herself spoke. But even so, we must not turn what is simply a pious expedient for fixing the attention, into a philological decision.

**8.**—We have seen that there is sometimes only a partial understanding of a divine revelation; but cases may be quoted where it is even less than this. God does not make the meaning of the vision appear at all at first. Thus Pharaoh and his two servants had to have recourse to Joseph to interpret their prophetic dreams. Nabuchodonosor could not even recall the dream of the statue with the feet of clay. Daniel was obliged to repeat all the details to him; he did this, pointing out that such a supernatural knowledge was the sign of the truth of his interpretation. Daniel was equally the only one to understand the king's other dream: that of the tree which was cut down and of which the stump alone was left, and the vision of Baltasar's feast.

These visions were sent by God to men who were sinners, and those of the saints have sometimes been as unintelligible to them for a time. When **St. Peter** had the vision of the linen sheet containing all manner of beasts, a voice said to him thrice: "Arise, Peter; kill and eat." He thought the words referred to his food, all the more because the ecstasy came upon him when he was hungry and a meal was being prepared for him (Acts x. 10). He did not see the true meaning, which was symbolic; namely, the command to baptize the Gentiles without first laying upon them the ordinances enjoined by the Mosaic Law. He strove vainly to understand (*dum intra se haesitaret*, x, 17). The significance only came to him two days later, when called to Cesarea to the Centurion Cornelius, who wished to become a Christian (x, 28).

**9.**—Or, again, false interpretations may arise, not from the obscurity of the revelation, but because, unknown to the person receiving it, it contains **conditions that are understood** but not expressed. It is wrong to take it unconditionally.

It was thus that Jonas, when preaching the destruction of Ninive after forty days, was persuaded that it would be destroyed even if the inhabitants repented. God had decided otherwise, without acquainting him of the fact. On seeing that repentant Ninive stood and was spared, he "was exceedingly troubled and was angry," and he prayed that he might die (*Jonas*, iv, 1).

Perhaps a false prophecy made by **St. Norbert,** founder of the Premonstratensians, may be explained in the same way. Here is St. Bernard's account of the circumstance (Migne ed., *Letter* 56; written about 1128): "I asked him what he knew about Antichrist. He declared that he knew by revelation and in a *very certain* way that he would come in this generation. As I did not share this belief, I asked him his reasons. His reply did not satisfy me. He tried at least to persuade me that he would not die without having seen a general persecution in the Church."

St. Vincent Ferrer **offers us a yet more striking instance of conditions that must** be understood, although they are not expressed in the prophecy. He spent the last twenty-one years of his life (1398-1419) announcing that the Last

Judgment was *at hand,* in the everyday sense of the word. He had learnt this by a very clear and unconditional vision,* the truth of which he proved by his numberless miracles. These had amounted, by his own showing, to more than three thousand when he came to preach at Salamanca (1412); it was here that he worked the most famous of all these prodigies in support of his preaching, bringing to life for the space of fifteen minutes a woman who was being carried to the cemetery, and who confirmed his predictions. And yet this prophecy has not been fulfilled. This fact is accounted for by saying that it was conditional. The time of the great Western Schism truly merited the end of the world as a chastisement. But this misfortune was averted by the wholesale conversions wrought throughout Europe amongst Catholics, heretics, Jews, and Moslems by the saint's threats and miracles.†

**10.**—We may believe that all **prophecies** of punishments to come are conditional; and it is the same with those **promising special favours**. As an example, we may give the promise concerning the Scapular. The Blessed Virgin appeared to St. Simon Stock, the sixth General of the Carmelites in 1251, at Cambridge, and said: "Whosoever shall die clothed in this Habit shall not suffer the eternal fires." Theologians hold that this phrase, though at first sight unconditional, is not to be interpreted too rigidly. It is true that very great graces are attached to the wearing of the Scapular, and that we thereby create a kind of right to the special protection of the Queen of Heaven. But if anyone were to reject the aids of religion on his death-bed, it is clear that he would not merit this protection and that he would be lost. It would be the same if a man relied upon this promise in order to plunge more completely into vice (see Fr. Terrien, *Marie, mère des hommes,* Book X, ch. i). Also, speaking of this revelation, Benedict XIV says: "She does not say that those who have worn the Scapular will be preserved from eternal fire *by this means alone*, without having done anything else. Good works and perseverance in well-doing are necessary to eternal salvation" (*De festis,* Part II, No. 96). He points out, with Cardinal Bellarmine, that Holy Scripture sometimes promises salvation in connection with practices that cannot *suffice by themselves*, such as faith, hope, almsgiving, Holy Communion.

So, too, many divine promises made to the religious Orders or to Confraternities suppose a co-operation, but this co-operation will be brought about by the great graces bestowed.

* He supplemented this revelation by his own reasonings, with which he did not confuse it. "I have formed an opinion and a belief of *great probability* in my own mind, but *without sufficient certainty* to preach it, that Anti-christ was born nine years ago."

† See *Histoire* of the saint by Fr. Pages, O.P. (Paris: Picard. 1901.) It contains many references and facts. The author sums up his discussion on the prophecy of the Last Judgment in these words: "The preaching of Jonas saved Ninive, that of Vincent Ferrer saved the world."

**11.**—*Second cause of error.* When visions represent **historic scenes,** those of the Life or Death of Our Lord, for instance, they often have an **approximate** and probable likeness only, although no intimation of this circumstance is given. It is a mistake to attribute an absolute accuracy to them.

This is a very natural mistake. For, at first sight, it seems that, as the visions are divine, all their details should be the faithful reproduction of the event, as to scenery, dress, the words and gestures, etc. Many saints have, in fact, believed that the event depicted took place exactly as they saw it.

But God does not deceive us when He modifies certain details. If He tied Himself down to absolute accuracy in these matters, we should soon be seeking to satisfy in visions an idle desire for erudition in history or archeology. He has a nobler aim, that of the soul's sanctification, and to arouse in her a love of Jesus suffering. He is like a painter who, in order to excite our piety, is content to paint scenes in his own manner, but without departing too far from the truth.* What would be the use of seeing the exact costume that the various persons were wearing on that particular day? whether their garments were red or blue?

We have positive proof of these partial modifications. For some saints, beholding Jesus on the Cross, perceived that there were three nails only; others saw four. Consequently, it is clear that God has not chosen to decide this controverted question by a revelation. †

**12.**—God has another reason for modifying certain **details.** Sometimes He adds them to a historical scene in order to bring out the secret meaning of the mystery. The actual spectators saw nothing similar.

* This argument cannot be applied to the historical books of the Bible. For God has proposed to preserve certain facts of religious history for our instruction there. But we have no proof that He had a similar aim in the visions of the ecstatics. Their contradictory statements actually prove the contrary in many cases.

† In the first category were St. Mary Magdalen of Pazzi, Blessed Varani, Blessed Gerardesca of Pisa, and Catherine Emmerich. St. Clare of Montefalcot and St. Veronica Giuliani had the three nails imprinted on their hearts. The second category is represented by St. Bridget. There is even a difference with regard to the form of the Cross, and whether it was set up before or after the Crucifixion (see the Bollandists, May 25, p. 246; *Parergon,* No. 2).

Certain stigmatics have had the wound on the shoulder; but with some it has been on the right, and with others on the left. And the same with the wound in the side (Dr. Imbert, Vol. II, ch. vi, p. 77).

There are other historical contradictions occurring in well-known visions, which I still avoid discussing as a whole. Catherine Emmerich says that Our Lady died thirteen years after her Son (*Life* of the Blessed Virgin, Part II, ch. xii). Sister Gojoz gives the same figures (Vie, by Mère de Provane, Part III, ch. viii); Mary of Agreda reckons twenty-one years, four months, and nineteen days (*Cité mystique,* Part III, Book VIII, ch. xix); St. Bridget, fifteen years (Book VII, ch. xxvi.); St. Elizabeth of Schoenau, a year and a half (Bolland., June 18, No. 110). The third said that Mary was raised from the dead three days after her death (*ibid.,* ch. xxi); the fourth, fifteen days; the fifth, forty days; Blessed Bonomi says three days.

St. Bridget (Book VII, ch. xxi) and Mary of Agreda (Part II, Nos. 479, 481) contradict each other with regard to the Nativity at Bethlehem. There and elsewhere they both enter into details that are quite useless and which pious souls could no longer tolerate.

Catherine Emmerich believed Mary of Agreda to have taken literally a large number of pictures which she she should have understood allegorically and spiritually (*Vie de Jesus Christ,* by Catherine Emmerich, Vol. I, Preface by Brentano, ch. ix).

**13.**—So, too, in visions of Paradise, Purgatory, or Hell, God only shows in part that reality which is so far beyond our powers of understanding. He adapts Himself to our nature by making use of **symbols.** The saints and angels show themselves to us with bodies, which they do not in reality possess; they are clothed in rich garments, and take part in processions or ceremonies. Heaven becomes a banquet or an exquisite garden. These pictures appear in accordance with the ideas of the person who sees them, or those of the painters of his day. We have an example of this in St. Lidwine's vision (see *Vie*, by Huysman, ch. viii), and in that of the Apocalypse of the four living creatures round about the Throne. St. John borrowed its chief features from Ezekiel, who himself took the imagery from the gigantic bas-relief of the Assyrian palaces which the Jews had ever before their eyes during the Babylonian captivity.

All this should be understood in a spiritual sense.

**14.**—These considerations will enable us to understand how Amort, who has made a deep study of these questions, was able to say: "The revelations of persons whose sanctity and doctrine have been approved by the doctors and heads of the Church, **contradict each other;** for example, those of St. Bridget, St. Gertrude, St. Catherine of Siena" (Part I, ch. xxii, § 1, No. 24). He quotes Baronius, as saying that St. Mechtildis and St. Bridget also contradict one another (Part I, ch. viii, No, 12).

**15.**—We see, therefore, that it is imprudent to seek to **remake history** by the help of the saints' revelations. Blessed Veronica of Binasco saw Our Lord's whole life pass before her eyes, as did also St. Frances of Rome and Catherine Emmerich. The Bollandists have reproduced her accounts of these visions (January, 13), but they warn us in the preface (No. 4) that "learned men" consider that they contain many historical errors. The visions of St. Frances of Rome have been still more explicitly criticised. In the life written by Maria Anguillara, who succeeded the saint in the government of her Congregation of the Oblates in Rome, the authoress expresses herself with the following reserve: "*Many* of the things that she saw when in ecstasy must be considered as being merely *pious meditiations* and contemplations *due to her own action,* especially those that concern Our Saviour's Life and Passion; this is easily apparent in reading them. We cannot, however, deny that true revelations may be mingled with them. Leaving the task of discrimination to the pious reader and to Superiors, I will, without distinction, transcribe all that the ancient manuscript contains" (Bolland., March 9, 1st *Life* of the saint; Preface, No. 10). The third cause of error would also apply here.

**16.**—*Third cause of error.* It may happen that during a vision the human mind retains the power of **mingling its notion with the divine action** in a certain measure. We make a mistake, then, in attributing *purely* to God the information that is thus obtained. At times it is the memory that supplies its recollections; at others the inventive faculty that is at work.*

Various authors think that this danger is much to be feared when the person speaks during the ecstasy. For if he speaks, his sensible faculties have not completely lost their activity. They may then have a share in the revelation.

Amort considers this a proof that St. Frances of Rome was a factor in her own visions (see preceding number), for she was neither silent nor motionless in her ecstasies (see ch. xiii, 2).

**17.**—There is a danger of confounding the divine action with our own, even in non-ecstatic prayer, when God seems to send us a somewhat strong **inspiration.** No matter how brief and almost instantaneous it may be, we like to think that it is longer, and the illusion is easy, for we do not know the precise moment when the divine influence ends and ours begins. When a stone is thrown into a calm lake, the shock only lasts for a moment, but the water does not immediately resume its former immobility. A series of ripples continues to rise from the spot, as if fresh stones were falling there. So in the soul, a movement once produced does not come suddenly to an end with the action that caused it. It seems as if we were continuing to receive something; but the notion is purely human.

**18.**—Further, those who often have true revelations may **become negligent** about discerning their origin, and they then prophesy falsely.

Sister Labouré, a Sister of Charity, who in November, 1830, received the revelation of the Miraculous Medal, foretold several events correctly (for instance, she announced forty years in advance, and with their exact date, the massacres of the Commune of 1870); but other predictions were not fulfilled. In such a case, so her biographer, M. Chevalier, tells us, she quietly acknowledged her mistake and would say: "Well, I have been mistaken; I thought that I was telling you correctly. I am very glad that the truth should be known."

**19.**—What **kind of** personal **ideas** are we specially inclined to attribute wrongly to the divine influence, either during ecstasy or when in close union with God?

They consist of two kinds:

**20.**—1° The ideas that **appeal to our own desires**. If we have a project greatly at heart, and still more if we are moved by the imprudent desire to see it encouraged by a revelation, it will easily seem to us that God is speaking in order to advise or command its execution.

* Fr. Seraphin has written a volume in vindication of Mary of Agreda. The force of his argument loses considerably from the fact that, *without being aware of it,* he bases it upon the false principle that a non-diabolic revelation is *entirely* divine or *entirely* human. He also believes that the mind can contribute nothing to intellectual visions (p. 173), which is not always true (See 37).

**21.**—2° **Preconceived ideas** in matters of *doctrine* or *history;* and also the recollection of anything that has struck us vividly in reading or conversation. Thus, when the person belongs to a religious congregation, his revelations are often coloured by its doctrines. This is due to the ideas with which his mind is occupied, and also to the opinions of his Confessors. These latter act upon him unconsciously by their *repeated* instructions and by their manner of putting their questions, which lead naturally to certain answers, and sometimes more openly, by allowing it to be seen how much they desire that a revelation should come to stamp their ideas with approval.

The *Life* of St. Colette presents an example of the influence of these preconceived ideas. In accordance with the belief of her directors, she began by holding that St. Anne had been married three times and had had several daughters. She believed that she saw St. Anne appear to her with all her supposed family (Bolland., May 25, p. 247, *Parergon,* No. 8).

Certain facts related in these disputed revelations are but reproductions of incidents belonging to the apocryphal gospels or legends of a later date. At the end of the Middle Ages and at the time of the Renaissance they were popularised by such books as Jacque de Voragine's *Golden Legend.*

The errors that we have just enumerated have sometimes gone so far that it has been difficult to know how much value to attach to certain revelations made to the saints. Fr. Lancisius, quoted by Benedict XIV (*De Canon.,* Book III, ch. liii, No. 17; English trans., *Heroic Virtue,* Vol. III, ch. xiv, p. 404), says: "The revelations of some holy women [ecstatics] canonised by the Apostolic See, whose sayings and writings in rapture, and derived from rapture are *filled with errors,* and therefore are not allowed to be published."

**22.**—As one of the principal causes of error is due **to the mental activity** of the person who has the revelation, it is as well to quote some examples of these cases.

**23.**—Let us begin with **St. Elizabeth,** the Benedictine Abbess of **Schoenau,** near Trèves, and a friend of St. Hildegard (1129-65). She had many revelations on historical subjects, notably the martyrdom of St. Ursula and her companions, whose bones had just been discovered (1156). When these relics were brought to her she thought she knew supernaturally the names and the lives of those to whom they had belonged. To obtain more information, she plied her Guardian-Angel and the saints with questions. At first she did not venture to do this; but her directors unfortunately encouraged her in this dangerous curiosity. And, further, the revelations having ceased, she caused the community to pray urgently for seventeen days that they might be continued (Bolland., June 18; *Life,* No. 102).

These were just the dispositions for being led astray. But the saint was persuaded, on the contrary, that all her revelations were the pure truth. She maintained this even on her death-bed, and was greatly astonished at encountering any opposition. She even went so far as to demand that they should be officially published during her lifetime. "I had just written the book of my revelations," she says, "when, on the Feast of St. Peter and St. Paul, my Guardian-Angel appeared to me and dictated these words for the Bishop of Trèves, Cologne, and Mayence: 'Be it known from the great and terrible God and from me, the Angel of this book, that you are *to make known to the Holy Roman Church and to all the people* the words that are to be found in this work. Think not that they are women's tales! Almighty God is their author. What I say to you I say for all " (*ibid.*, No. 106).

Posterity has not endorsed the saint's opinions. Amort proves that these visions are full of historical errors, and he attributes the greater part, at any rate, to imagination. The Bollandists have accepted his conclusions (October 21, Prologue to the *Life of St. Ursula,* § 5).

**24.**—The Bollandists regard the revelations of Blessed Hermann Joseph, concerning St. Ursula, in the same light (ibid., § 7). But they do not for this reason dispute the other graces received by these two saints. They admit that Blessed Hermann prophesied truly and worked miracles.

**25.**—The study of the books written by St. Hildegard also shows us how human action can join itself to the divine action without our being aware of it. This saint must have received exceptional graces of infused knowledge and prophecy, otherwise we could not explain her influence upon her contemporaries.* She herself recognised, indeed, that this knowledge was not complete (see her works, published by Cardinal Pitra, p. 333). But she was convinced that she had added nothing of her own to it. This is what she wrote at the age of seventy: "I am *ignorant* of all that I do not see in my vision, for I am illiterate; and when I write by virtue of this light, I set down *no other words* than those that I have heard" (Migne ed., col. 18, A; Card. Pitra, p. 333).

* She never learnt to read or to write, and neither music nor Latin. She acquired all those things miraculously; and she also understood the meaning of the Bible and the writings of the "philosopher-saints" (Migne ed., col. 104, A.). Another proof of a supernatural intervention regarding her knowledge of Latin is that she grasped, as a whole, the sense of the passages that she was reading, without being able to separate the different words or parse the cases and tenses (Migne, col. 384, A). She needed a secretary to correct what she dictated in this language. She had no ecstasies (Dom Pitra, loc. cit.). She derived her knowledge from a divine light which she received uninterruptedly from the age of three, and this when she was awake (Migne, col. 384, A; 13, D). She called it the shadow of the living light. From time to time she received a still higher knowledge, that of God; and she called this, by contrast, the living light (Migne, col. 18, A). Mary of Agreda gives us a similar description of her knowledge (*Cité mystique,* Part I, Book I, ch. ii). This enlightenment with regard to created things and events had a special character in the case of Ven. Anne-Maria Taïgi (1769-1837). For forty-seven years she saw close to her a symbolic sun which seemed to be as large as the natural sun. When she looked at it (she did not allow herself to do so without a motive) she saw many things that were useful for souls. These were often arranged around the sun, as though in some living picture. She was thus enabled to answer questions promptly and accurately, and almost without giving time to have the subject explained to her. Is this to say that she never made a mistake? The process of her beatification will show us. She predicted a great temporal triumph for the Church in terms that led her friends, and Pius IX himself, to believe that it would be realised under this Pontiff. Nothing of the sort occurred.

And yet it is impossible to admit that all that this saint wrote came from God. For her works are full of scientific errors, and exactly those errors that were prevalent in the twelfth century. *

**26.**—We may then be allowed to think that God was content to **quicken her intelligence** and her imagination. In this state she was able to learn, to imagine, to remember in a far greater degree than would be possible in the normal state. But, unknown to her, much of her knowledge really proceeded from her frequent conversations with the theologians and learned men of her day, from tools that she had read, or the sermons that she had heard.

It is very fortunate, let us add, that she was not in advance of the science of her time. If she had known the truths that have since been discovered in astronomy, physiology, and in physics, scientific men, instead of admiring, would have persecuted her, as has been the case with so many pioneers, and she would thus have lost a great part of her religious influence (see Biographical Index, No. 125, on Fr. Séraphin ).

**27.**—In order to explain in a favourable light St. Hildegard's illusions on scientific subjects, we may admit the following **hypothesis:**

God, it seems, may supernaturally convey into a person's mind a portion of the knowledge of the day, such as it is found in existing books or in the minds of contemporaneous scientists; whilst giving in some way a general warning that He does not guarantee the contents of this whole, and that it is therefore to be accepted only at the receiver's risk.

Such a gift, although imperfect as regards certainty, would still be a magnificent one. Those amongst us who have toiled over our books during our whole lives, and who forget incessantly what we have learned, would be enchanted to possess such an expeditious process of learning and remembering.

The important point to remark is that God does not deceive the soul here, since, by our hypothesis, He has warned her in one way or another. God is satisfied with teaching supernaturally those things that the soul would have learnt naturally. As regards certainty, she is no worse off than ordinary learned men. Notwithstanding their confidence in their teachers, they admit that all science is subject to error, and that alongside of the solid and positive portions

* One of her writings in particular is full of errors. This is *The Book of the Subtilties of Nature,* a treatise on physics and medicine, in nine books and 534 chapters (Migne, col. 1126), where the qualities of physical bodies are explained after the ancient methods, by the (purely fanciful) proportions in which they contain dryness and humidity, heat and cold. See especially the chapters on the air, the sapphire, the lodestone, eggs, the mandrake, the basilisk, the elephant, the lion, the dragon (which she believes in and describes without any hesitation), the unicorn, the griffin, etc. See also the *Liber divinorum operum,* visions 3 and 4, where the saint shows in 124 chapters the relation that appears to her to exist between the spiritual world and those of astronomy and physiology. She also attributed to a supernatural source the music that she composed, and the new and strange language, a dictionary of which she compiled. No one has been able to discover its utility; which proves that it was probably merely the product of her own imagination. She seems to have had exceptional graces and great illusions.

we find also some that are provisional and other that are falling into disrepute. If men fail to understand it aright, they have only their own want of cleverness, their mental inferiority, or their hastiness to blame.

**28.**—We will continue to give some examples, in spite of a very natural repugnance to discover either historic or scientific errors in saints whom we have delighted in regarding as infallible. But we must never be afraid of the truth. And, besides, the proofs that we give are useful: they justify the strict rules that we shall have to lay down later on upon the subject of revelations.

In St. Frances of Rome's time they believed in a sky composed of crystal. Imbued with this idea, she declares that she has seen it, seen it distinctly, in the numerous visions in which she visited the firmament. It is situated between the sky in which the stars are to be found and the empyrean. She compares these three skies as to light and beauty; her confessor having asked their relative distances one from the other, she said they were further one from another than the earth from the nearest sky. Not knowing that the blue of the sky is merely that of the atmosphere, she attributes it to the sky in which the stars were supposed to be, and which would consequently be a solid body (Bolland., March 9, 1st *Life,* No. 30).

**29.**—**St. Catharine of Ricci** was perhaps also influenced by preconceived ideas. All her life she had a great devotion for Savonarola, who was a friend of the family. She wished to rehabilitate the memory of the fiery tribune who strove to transform all Florence into a cloister, who plunged into political struggles and died at the stake in 1498. She strove to make him an object of public veneration as a prophet and martyr. He often appeared to her surrounded with glory and followed by his companions on the scaffold; he twice cured her suddenly of a serious illness. These appearances seemed an obstacle at first to Catharine's beatification. The *Promotor fidei** the future Pope Pope Benedict XIV, opposed it on this ground, declaring that the Sister had sinned in invoking a man whom the Church had handed over to the secular arm (*De Canon.,* Book III, ch. xxv, Nos. 17-20. English translation: Benedict XIV *On Heroic Virtue,* Vol. I, ch. v, Nos. 17-20). This point was easily solved. But one more delicate still remained. To beatify Catharine, was not this to proclaim that these visions were divine? Now, according to these visions, Savonarola was a saint in the eyes of God, if not in those of men. A burning and controverted question had thus been decided by divine authority. Benedict XIII brought the discussion to a close by ordering Catharine's devotion to Brother Jerome, and consequently the apparitions which caused it, to be left out of the question (*ibid.,* and *Vie,* by P. Bayonne, Vol. II, ch. xvii. English *Life,* by F. M. Capes, pp. 270-1). This separating of the saint's virtues from visions amounted

* Popularly known as the Devil's Advocate [Translator].

to a declaration of this principle: when a servant of God is canonised, it is his virtue that is canonised, and not his visions.

**30.**—Whatever opinion we may form as to **Mary of Agreda's** revelations, taken as a whole, we are obliged to admit that they contain some errors. Thus she fancied that she knew by revelation of the existence of a crystal sky (Part II, No. 17); that it was divided up into eleven portions at the moment of the Incarnation (ibid., No. 128): this passage is omitted in the French translation. She learnt that the six days of the Creation were each of twenty-four hours' duration*; that from the Fall to Our Lord's coming, there were 5199 years to a day. With regard to space, she says that the earth's radius is 1251 miles (Spanish). Amort has shown that these figures are false (*Observations,* prop. 2), like many others relating to dates and distances. He quotes twenty-one points on which she contradicts other revelations. Finally, she considers that it is a sin not to believe her (see ch. xxii, 27). Now, this is a gross error. For the Church alone, and not any private revelation, has a right to impose belief on the faithful at large; and she imposes only such as are contained in Holy Scripture and tradition.

Theologians have pointed out other descriptions as being probably the result of illusion. They are chiefly attributable to the desire to fill the Blessed Virgin's life with innumerable prodigies, showing a singular contrast to the simplicity of the gospels. We find in them all the pomp and splendour of the Spanish Court (see in the *Theologic mystique,* by Mgr. Chaillot, the censures passed upon this book at the Sorbonne and by Rome).

Let us not, however, conclude from this that Mary of Agreda deceived herself also as to her purely intellectual visions of the Divinity (*Cité mystique,* Part I, Book I, ch. ii). Amort, who has criticised her a great deal, begins by saying that, without doubt, "her virtues were heroic." "This stands out clearly," he says, "from her process of beatification which I read in Rome." He adds: "I unhesitatingly admit that she received wonderful lights from God; it is not likely that in her frequent raptures† so virtuous a person, whose death was

* She even lays down that the Angels were created on the first day. "which answers to the Sunday"; they were cast out of Heaven on Monday morning and conspired until Thursday morning (Part I, No. 122); Adam was created very early on Friday morning, March 25 (Part II, No. 138).

† These ecstasies presented some extraordinary characteristics: 1° She came out of them immediately when one of her Superiors gave her the order mentally and from a distance; 2° she was usually raised above the ground. Her fellow Religious yielded at last to the curiosity displayed by strangers, and after the Communion they opened the Choir grate so that she could be easily seen; "They removed the veil that covered her face, so that her extraordinary beauty could be seen, and these lay persons used to make the experiment of seeing her move by merely blowing on her from outside the grate... They advised that nothing of this should be told the servant of God" (*Life* by Samaniego, ch. xiii). But, finally, at the end of three or four years she came to know of it by chance. She tried to avoid this publicity by going to make her thanksgiving in a room, the key of which she turned in the door. But the nuns removed some of the planks of a partition; they conveyed her through the opening, "carrying her easily as though she were a feather" (*ibid.*). The pious sister was finally told about this; seized with horror, she prayed that God

without any features that could shock us, should have been constantly deceived by the Devil. But did not her imagination lead her astray, reproducing what she had read or heard about the Blessed Virgin, or what she had seen in theatrical performances? I leave the Church to be the judge on this matter" (Part II, No. XIII, prelude).

The eulogy just quoted will not appear exaggerated to those who read the life of the servant of God by Samaniego. It is very beautiful, and gives the impression of great sanctity and a high degree of union with God.

With regard to her revelations, Amort remains doubtful. This seems the wisest attitude. For if many learned men, especially amongst the saint's fellow-countrymen, have been enthusiastic with regard to the *Mystical City,* others, no less numerous and learned, have refused it credence. They explain this book by the pious Sister's readings, combined with an exceptional power of invention, such as the great novelists have given us examples of (see Bossuet, *Remarques sur la mystique Cité,* at the end of Vol. XX, Lachat ed.). The psychology of Mary of Agreda, like that of St. Hildegard, is an enigma that we have not by any means completely solved. Clement XIV, of the Order of St. Francis, also showed that he regards her revelations as, to say the least, doubtful, since in his Decree of March 12, 1771, he forbids her Beatification to be proceeded with "on account of the book" (see Mgr. Chaillot; conclusion).

Once more, it is a question only of Sister Mary's revelations. Let us beware of thinking that, if they are false, it is the same with her sanctity and her extraordinary union with God.

**30** *bis.*—**Alain de la Roche,** a Breton Dominican (1428-75), is honoured in his Order on September 8 with the title of Blessed. After teaching theology, he spent the last five years of his life in successfully instituting and propagating Confraternities of the Rosary in the north of France and in the Low Countries. He is not said to have had ecstasies, but he believed himself to have received many revelations, particularly of an historical kind. They served as the theme of his preachings upon the Rosary. Shortly after his death, the Carthusians of Gripsholm, in Sweden, published the manuscript containing the chief of these discourses (*Sponsus novellus Beatissimae Virginis Mariae,* 1498). After protestations from Frs. Quétif and Echard (*Scriptores ordinis praedictatorum,* Vol. I, p. 851) and from the Bollandist, Cuper (1733), the majority of writers, even those of the Order of St. Dominic, agreed in regarding these revelations as being of no value. "He was undoubtedly a religious of sincere piety, but one who was led by a feverish imagination to strange hallucinations" (*Analecta*

would take away everything that was visible outwardly. She was then twenty-two years of age. Her prayer was granted. For the remaining forty years of her life her interior graces had no further effect upon her body. The other Sisters were dissatisfied at first by this change, and their explanations were of an unfavourable nature. But four years later they elected her Abbess. It was during this hidden time that she had her revelations on the Blessed Virgin's life.

*Bollandiana,* 1903, p. 219). Alain believed firmly in his revelations: "All these things," he said, "I affirm them and bear witness to them on oath, by my faith in the Blessed Trinity. May I be accursed if I have departed from the way of truth!"

**31.**—*Fourth cause of error.* A true revelation may **subsequently** be **altered** involuntarily by the person who receives it.

This danger is to be feared with intellectual locutions. After receiving them, the temptation to translate them into words cannot be resisted; but there is the risk of slightly modifying the meaning of the thought, and particularly of giving it a definiteness that it lacked. Suppose that someone speaks to you simply by signs—by a movement of the eye, for instance—you would understand. But if you try to translate the intention by words, you risk adding shades of your own invention.

Thus when praying for one who is sick, you may receive an assurance of a cure; but God leaves you in ignorance as to whether it will be total or partial, sudden or slow, soon or late, or even physical or moral. It is difficult to translate this communication without making it more definite than it was originally.

**32.**—The danger is also great when the written **revelation** is very long and yet has been received almost **instantaneously.** It is not rash to believe that not all the words used were supplied by the revelation, and that the thoughts were not given in detail. They were developed later by the person who received them.

St. Bridget recognises that this is sometimes so in her own case. In fact, in one of her visions Our Lord, without blaming her, remarks that she retouches her revelations, through not having understood them properly, or not knowing how to express them exactly (nunc volvis et *revolvis* in animo tuo, nunc scribis et *rescribis* ea, donec veneris ad proprium sensum verborum meorum. *Revelationes Extravagantes,* ch. xlix); and, further, He approves the saint's secretaries who in translating from Swedish into Latin add "colour and ornamentation."

**33.**—*Fifth cause of error.* I have just referred to **secretaries**. They may easily alter the text without any wrong intention. For their own personality intervenes in the choice of expressions. They sometimes, with a certain amount of good faith, think that they can add whole sentences under pretext of making the thought clearer. "We know (they say to themselves) that this is what the saint *wished* to say." The account gains, perhaps, in clearness; but only half of it is revelation.

We have examples of these cases where the accuracy of the text is disputed: those of Mary of Agreda, Catherine Emmerich, and Mary Lataste. We may read them for edification, but we do not know exactly in what measure their revelations, even supposing them to have been true originally, have been retouched.* Many persons believe these writings to be a mixture. There would have been three concurrent actions: the divine revelation, the seer's own activity (which has interpreted or invented and perhaps supplied a good half of the results); finally, the embellishments made by secretaries and friends.

Benedict XIV (*De Canon.*, Book III, ch. liii, No. 16; English: *On Heroic Virtue*, Vol. III, ch. ix, No. 16) examines one of St. Catherine of Siena's celebrated revelations (ecstasy of 1377), in which the Blessed Virgin would practically have told her that she was not immaculate. He quotes several authors who, for the sake of the saint's reputation, prefer to sacrifice that of her directors or editors, who are thus accused of falsification. He afterwards gives us Fr. Lancisius' opinion, admitting the possibility of the saint having deceived herself as a result of preconceived ideas (ibid., No. 17; Lancisius, opusc., *De praxi divinae praesentiae*, ch. xiii).†

**34.—Compilers,** like secretaries, have sometimes modified revelations. Thus, in the first German edition of Catherine Emmerich's works, it was said that St. James the greater was present at the Blessed Virgin's death. It was afterwards seen that this statement was incompatible with the chronology of events in the *Acts of the Apostles*. In the recent Ratisbon edition the erroneous phrase has simply been effaced. This method is deplorable, for it robs the serious reader of a means of forming his opinions. The sentence should have been retained, adding a note saying: the Sister was mistaken here. Are they afraid lest this avowal should interfere with the sale of the book?

Fr. Croset, who translated Mary of Agreda in the seventeenth century, softened down certain passages. I am told that in an edition that appeared at the end of the nineteenth century the style of this translation has again been retouched, making fresh suppressions.

### § 2. Five Causes of Absolutely False Revelations

**35.**—These five causes are: 1° Simulation; 2° an over-lively mind or imagination; 3° an illusion of the memory that consists in believing that we recall certain facts which never happened; 4° the Devil's action; 5° the inventions of falsifiers.

* When Marie Lataste's *Works* appeared, the theologians, who had admired certain passages, ended by proving that they had been translated word for word from St. Thomas' *Summa*. They counted thirty-two passages of this nature. This objection was conveyed to the person who was supposed to have collected the revelations. He did not deny the fact, but replied majestically that, as Our Lord had inspired St. Thomas to write these pages, He could repeat them to Marie Lataste! Circumstances pointed, however, to a simpler explanation, which subsequent events tended to confirm.

Catherine Emmerich had a symbolic vision showing that Mary of Agreda's *Works* had been recast and amplified (Preface by Brentano, already quoted). Who is right in this disagreement?

† In the archives of the Generals of the Dominican Order there is a manuscript dating from 1398 which contains this relation (Book of Prayers, prayer 16).

**36.**—*First cause of falseness.* To begin with, it may happen that the persons who claim to have received these revelations are **untruthful** and in bad faith. One of the best known examples is Magdalen of the Cross, a Franciscan of Cordova, who lived at the beginning of the sixteenth century.

She was born in 1487, entered the Convent at the age of seventeen, in 1504, and was three times Abbess of her Monastery. From the age of five the Devil appeared to her under the form of different saints, and inspired her with a strong desire to pass as a saint herself. She was thirteen when he considered that her soul was sufficiently possessed by the spirits of vanity, pride, and sensuality; he plainly declared his identity to her, and promised that if she would enter into an agreement with him, he would spread abroad her reputation for sanctity and would procure her, for thirty years at the least, all the pleasures that she desired. She agreed, and Satan became her councillor, although there were days when she would gladly have driven him away, so terrified was she at the fearful shapes that he took. Thanks to his aid, she realised all the outward appearance of divine marvels: ecstasies, levitation, predictions that were often fulfilled. She made herself the stigmatic wounds, and for eleven years persuaded others that she lived without taking any food; while procuring it for herself secretly. For thirty-eight years, up to 1543, she succeeded in deliberately deceiving the greatest theologians in Spain, the Bishops, Cardinals, Inquisitors, and great nobles about the Court. People came from all sides to consult her, and alms were showered upon her. Having been at death's door, she confessed everything publicly, and then regretted her avowals. Exorcism had to be resorted to before the Devil lost his hold over her will. Finally, she was condemned to be confined in another Convent of her Order (Amort, Book II, ch. iii; Gorres, Vol. V. ch. xi; Bizouard, Vol. II, Book X, ch. iv; Dr. Imbert, Vol. II, p. 1).

**36** *bis.*—Mgr. Dupanloup, Bishop of Orleans, in a letter to one of his clergy, March 23, 1874, says: "Cardinal Albitius, who wrote about the middle of the seventeenth century, enumerates in his great work *de Inconstantia in fide* more than twenty condemnations pronounced in his time" by the Holy Office against simulators. He adds that in 1747 a professed religious of the monastery of St. Clare, at Chieri, was condemned for the same reason; also, under Pius VII, one named Jeanne Marella (simulated stigmata); and in 1857, a certain Catherine Finelli (Letter published in *Le Correspondant*, March 25, 1874, p. 1105).

**37.**—*Second cause of falseness.* We will now suppose a person who is in good faith. He may perhaps be deceived by his **imagination** or his **mind,** that are **over lively.** It was said above (**16**) that our faculties sometimes mingle their own action with the divine revelation. But, when the temperament is badly balanced or overexcited, they may do still more: they construct an altogether false revelation. Thanks to their feverish imaginations, such persons, during the most ordinary prayer, can pronounce interior words with such clearness that they seem to be said by someone else.

Or, again, on particular days they have an extraordinary power of visual representation. A picture offers itself to their interior eyes with very vivid colours, almost equal to those shown by real objects. If a scene of Our Lord's life is in question, or some future event in which they are interested, they willingly believe that the picture is supernatural.

There are even cases where the illusion may take the form of thinking that an intellectual vision of a saint has been seen. This is when it is obscure. For instance, you imagine, without any sufficient reason, that you feel the saint near you. It is necessary to be much more exacting as regards proof here than when it is a question of the presence of God. With regard to God, the error does not go to the lengths of affirming a presence that does not exist—He is there; the question is simply that of knowing it He makes Himself felt. It is quite otherwise with the saints.

The same must be said with regard to intellectual locutions. This is how St. John of the Cross speaks of them: "There are some men whose intellect is so quick and penetrating that their conceptions, when they are self-recollected, naturally proceed with great facility, and form themselves into these locutions and reasonings so clearly [it is a question of intellectual locutions, as was stated in a preceding chapter, the twenty-third] as to make them think that God is speaking. But it is not so. All this is the work of the intellect, somewhat disengaged *from the operations of sense*; for it may do this and even more *without any supernatural help whatever,* by its own natural light. This is a state of things of frequent occurrence, and many delude themselves into the belief that... God converses with them: they write down, or cause others to write for them, what they have experienced. And, after all, it is nothing" (*Ascent of Mount Carmel,* Book II, ch. xxix, p. 192).

St. Teresa, it is true, says that when a person has had true visions or true locutions they can no longer be confused with the feeble imitations of the imagination. But for those who have never had experience of these divine favours the difficulty continues undiminished.*

**38.**—It may happen that this imaginative power has an accidental cause. Cardinal Bona says that hallucinations may at times result from excessive abstinences, **fasts** and vigils; this excess enfeebles the muscular system and the faculties; they cause a predominance of the nervous system (*De discret. spir.,* ch.

* St. Teresa: "Not three or four only, but a large number of people have spoken to me on the subject, and therefore *I know by experience* that there are souls which, either because they possess vivid imaginations or active minds, are so wrapt up in their own ideas as to feel certain they see whatever their fancy imagines. *If they had ever beheld a genuine vision,* they would recognise the deception *at once.* They themselves fabricate, piece by piece, what they fancy they see:—*no after-effects are produced* on the mind, which is left *less moved to devotion* than by the sight of a sacred picture" (*Interior Castle,* Sixth Mansion, ch. ix, 6). The saint reverts to the same idea, *ibid.,* 6, ch. iii, and three times in ch. xxv of her *Life.*

xx, No. 3). Benedict XIV adopts this view (*De Canon.*, Book III, ch. 1, No. 1; *On Heroic Virtue,* Vol. III, ch. xii, No. 1).

**39.**—*Third cause of falseness.* This is an **illusion** or special disease of **the memory,** which consists in thinking that certain facts are remembered, although they never existed.

This illusion would seem impossible, and yet it is seen even outside mystic things: certain minds *invent* stories and sincerely persuade themselves that the incidents occurred. These are *inventors in good faith.* This case must not be confused with the preceding, where the imagination conjures up a picture, nor with another, much more common, that of romancers who relate imaginary anecdotes, *as a joke,* and finish by being half persuaded of their historic origin. Those that I am now speaking of are earnest persons who invent right and left, but *who believe what they say,* and this from the first moment of saying it.

Some will relate their journeys in distant countries where their friends know quite well that they have never been. They describe the least details, which are always picturesque. Others believe that they have visited Kings, Bishops or other prominent personages, who have confided to them secrets or important opinions, or who have encouraged them warmly. Finally, others describe the fearful dangers that they have escaped, or the unworthy persecutions of which they have been the object.* We are disposed to believe them, for their tone is one of such conviction; and then they enter into details with regard to time and locality and the conversations that took place, until we say to ourselves: It is impossible that the foundation of all this should not be true. And yet all is invented.

These people are not mad; in all other things they are reasonable and intelligent, although usually in a state of agitation and ebullition. How are we to explain their aberration? We do not know. But there is a strange confusion between the *imagination,* which constructs a scene, and the *memory,* which affirms that it took place. The reason no longer distinguishes between these two very different operations. They probably begin by thinking of the anecdote as possible in itself, then as possible for themselves, then as likely, then as probable, then as certain. It is after this unconscious elaboration, and when the illusion has come to its full maturity, that they relate the history to us.

Let us not endeavour to explain this illusion, which is fairly common. Let us simply apply it to our subject.

* At times their faculty for invention will have more unfortunate results: they will carry their calumnies to the point of denunciation. The Law Courts have had to decide cases where serious accusations have been brought, *with full conviction* and all the appearances of probability, against doctors or priest; and the *impossibility* of the facts alleged have been proved. If I leave the subject of mysticism for a moment in order to speak of this tendency, it is for the sake of putting people on their guard against certain accusations. It is necessary to acquaint ourselves not only with the story, but with the narrator.

We will then suppose certain persons leading a very retired life and having the unfortunate turn of mind which I have just described. They will not be inclined to lay claim to long voyages, or dinners with political or literary celebrities. This would be too much; they have still enough good sense to understand that people would laugh in their faces. They will rather invent facts that cannot be disproved. An exalted piety will sometimes incline them to the side of revelations. They relate that they were visited by the Court of Heaven, and that Our Lady herself gave them her salutary counsels. If they have the "passion for persecutions," they invent or exaggerate those which they suffer from men or devils.

The director will always find that his advice has little effect; which will be a first means of unmasking the illusion. There is yet another: that of informing himself as to these persons' lives as a whole. If they have the defect of romancing, they would show it in many other circumstances. It will occasionally take some time to arrive at a clear view of the situation. But where is the need of hurry?

**40.**—*Fourth cause of falseness.* The Devil may give false revelations or visions. His action may *sometimes* be recognised by the circumstances of the vision (see the following chapter).

He can also produce alienation of the sensible faculties, trying to counterfeit the divine ecstasy. This case must be extremely rare, for hardly any undoubted examples are quoted. I have cited (**36**) that of Magdalen of the Cross; but here it was a purely exterior imitation, and made in complicity with the person involved.

In the seventeenth century there was an example of the Devil's action upon a young woman, Nicole of Reims, who seems to have been in good faith. André du Val gives her story at great length in Mme. Acarie's *Life* (Book I, ch. vi). Nicole appeared to possess the most extraordinary graces; she was approved and consulted by a number of pious persons; she even seemed to labour for the conversion of souls; she organised public prayers and processions. Mme. Acarie was alone in affirming that it was all due to the Devil. At last one day the young woman reverted to her natural state so completely "that she no longer had this sublime turn of mind, these beautiful discourses... nor the appearance of these great virtues. She was very coarse, rough, and imperfect... She married, and was on the point of becoming a Huguenot."

**41.**—*Fifth cause of falseness.* The inventions of falsifiers.
Political prophecies have often been their handiwork. They were inspired by motives of political or pecuniary interest, or by the desire to mystify the public.

We find an instance of the first motive at the time of the taking of Constantinople by the Turks (1453). The future schismatic Patriarch, Georges Scholarios, who was secretly on their side, through hatred of the Latins, wished to dishearten the defenders of the city. With this object, and he afterwards admitted this himself, he composed false prophecies, upon which the people fed eagerly. One of these predictions announced that the assailants would begin by entering the city, but would suddenly be miraculously routed.

At other times the authors simply wished to amuse themselves at the expense of credulous persons. A prophecy made by Cazotte, on the subject of the French Revolution, has often been reprinted. But now it is thought to have been composed after the event by La Harpe. It may have had a historical foundation, but a less marvellous one than it was made out to be. Suppose that the death of Louis XVI and the French Revolution were really foretold. These events were decided beforehand by secret societies; Cazotte, who was a high dignitary amongst the German *illuminati*, knew these projects and could easily foretell their fulfilment.

Another famous prophecy is that of Orval; it was made in 1839 and was supposed to have been found in a book printed in the fifteenth century. It contains minute details relating to events of a date previous to the year of its publication. The rest is obscure. The Bishop of Verdun, in a circular letter of February 6, 1849, declares that the author was a priest of his diocese. "In the beginning," the Bishop says, "he had no object in this fraud other than an aimless amusement; but when time brought the fulfilment of some of his predictions, vanity on the one hand, and false shame on the other, caused him to persevere in a course of action from which he was afterwards glad to escape." (This letter is quoted intact at the end of Fr. Pouplard's book, *Un mot sur les visions).*

Later writers, such as the Abbé Curicque (*Voix prophetiques*), have disputed the genuineness of the foregoing confession, saying that it was wrung from him by intimidation, and they quote witnesses who stated that they had read a *similar* prophecy at the time of the Revolution. As no authentic copy of such a prophecy has been preserved, no one can say how far this resemblance goes. But even if the editor of 1839 embellished an ancient document, it is none the less true that he was a falsifier of facts.

**42.**—The different causes of falseness just enumerated have often been combined with the object of giving publicity to false prophecies of a political nature. These abound particularly at times of great **political or religious disturbance,** the popular imagination being then over-excited.

In the thirteenth century St. Bonaventure complained of hearing to "satiety" prophecies dealing with the Church's troubles and the end of the world (*De profectu religiosorum*, Book III, ch. lxxvi).

At the end of the fourteenth century, during the great Western Schism, "seers arose on all sides, and their visions gained such an influence and a circulation as had been unknown before... In some of the gravest sermons reliance was put upon these baseless predictions" (Salambier, *The Great Schism of the West,* ch. vi, § 4). Gerson, who took part in the Council of Constance, at which the Great Schism and the struggle between the rival Popes was put an end to, says that there were then an incredible number of *holy and mortified* men who had false revelations at this period, and that he has this information from credible witnesses. He adds: "Many believed that they had learnt by revelation and with certainty that they would themselves be the future Pope" (*De distinctione verarum visionum*).

At the beginning of the sixteenth century Italy experienced a regular epidemic of politico-religious prophecies. This effervescence began with those made by Savonarola in Florence. Religious and hermits swarmed over the country, and while commenting upon the Apocalypse, they announced from the pulpit or in public places revolutions in the temporal and spiritual governments, to be followed by the end of the world. Peasants and young girls alike fell to prophesying.

In the fifth Lateran Council, in 1516, Leo X was obliged to publish a Bull by which public prophecies by preachers were prohibited (Pastor, *History of the Popes*, edited by Fr. Antrobus, Vol. V, end of *Introduction;* also Mansi, Collection of Councils).

Let us now come to the eighteenth century. There were "prophecies springing up constantly during the French Revolution, prophecies that were clear and full of detail with regard to past events, vaguer as to future occurrences and often refuted by facts when they thought fit to be definite; promising a deliverer who did not appear, and soon substituting another prediction, which was put forward in the character of an infallible utterance" (Abbé Sicard, *L'ancien Clerge de France*, Vol. III, Book III, ch. vi, p. 153).

In the nineteenth century we have also epidemics of prophesyings: they announced the Comte de Chambord's reign, or that of the Naundorff. They took their inspiration from doubtful prophecies regarding "the great Pope and the great King," which the Ven. Holzhauser had inserted in his *Commentary on the Apocalypse* in the seventeenth century. It is to be regretted that religious journals should so often have collected and spread abroad these absurdities which bring religion into discredit.

In a letter already quoted (**36** *bis*), Mgr. Dupanloup laments the great number of prophecies "that are hawked about on all sides by the enterprise of booksellers." "I have now," he says, "more than *twenty* volumes before me, from Belgium and France in particular" (p. 1108). He recalls the words of Pius IX in his allocution of April 9, 1872: "I do not give much credit to prophecies, because those especially that have recently appeared do not merit the honour of being read"; and this other, of July 5, 1872: "A large number of prophecies are in circulation; but I think that they are the fruit of the imagination."

The twentieth century is in no wise behind its predecessors. When, in 1901, the French Chambers were discussing at great length the laws that were destined to destroy the Religious Orders, prophetic imaginations came into play. Certain visionaries felt themselves impelled to go to the Holy Father to confide to him their predictions and secrets. One of their directors told me that on arriving in Rome his penitent was much surprised to find ten other persons who had come with the same intention. A cardinal listened to them very patiently, but audience with the Holy Father was refused to them.

I have it from a reliable source that one of the present claimants to the French throne constantly receives letters from prophets and prophetesses who foretell his destinies and give him advice, professedly in God's name. He is weary of them.

**43.**—Nothing is easier than to invent **political prophecies** in this way. It is only necessary to announce the advent of great misfortunes to be followed by extraordinary deliverances. These statements can be put about without fear, for no one can prove the contrary.

A suspicious character in *modern* political prophecies is the fact that they never lead us to withstand wicked men, and never suggest any serious manner of resisting them. Some even predict that the world is to change suddenly, *by a miracle.* "A new era" is on the point of appearing; everyone will become holy in an instant. The conclusion drawn from such predictions is that we should fold our arms and wait. Since God is to do everything, and makes a point of proclaiming it in advance, it would be an indiscretion and foolishness on our part to wish to help Him and to anticipate His appointed hour. Let us, then, go on doing nothing! This is a convenient doctrine.

I was objecting to one of these false prophetesses, one day, that the world seems, on the contrary, to become more and more wicked, and that we were proceeding in the opposite direction to the great renovation that she was announcing. She replied: "It is a good sign. God will not intervene until the evil is at its height." This answer teaches us nothing. When can anyone say that the evil is at its height? And, further, you declare that this maximum will he reached soon, and not in two thousand years. How do you know this?

### § 3. The Security of the Mystic Union, as Compared With revelations

**44.**—We have just seen that **revelations** are subject to many illusions. Our own action, especially, may counterfeit the divine action, or mingle with it. This first drawback brings with it others still more grave. In fact, the revelations do not generally aim at being useful to the seer's own soul only; they lead to exterior acts, such as the teaching of a doctrine, the propagation of a devotion, prophesying, or embarking on some enterprise that requires considerable expense. If these impulses came from God, and from Him alone, no evil results could be feared. But in the contrary case, which is much more frequent and difficult to discover, the soul begins to tread in perilous paths. Hence it follows that revelations are usually a source of danger.

**45.**—On the other hand, with the **mystic union** there is nothing to fear. We will put things at their worst, and suppose that the state of prayer is nothing but a pure imitation. From the moment that this prayer claims resemblance with the mystic state and cannot be distinguished from it with any certainty, it is that it presents the same characteristics and, in particular, that it inclines the soul to divine love and the practice of the virtues. This result is excellent. Further, it does not lead to the exterior acts enumerated above, otherwise it would degenerate into revelation, which is contrary to the hypothesis. And thus it is *completely inoffensive.* And, moreover, I have made too great a concession. I have supposed that the mystic state could be counterfeited by the human mind or by the Devil. I have shown the contrary elsewhere (ch. xvi, **21**). Therefore a state of prayer, which in all seriousness presents the general aspects of the mystic state, comes from God, and cannot thus be other than advantageous.

**46.**—Mysticism is so little studied, even in many religious Houses, that numbers of pious persons confound revelations with the mystic union, or are, at least, unaware that these should be **appreciated differently.** They accordingly fall into one of the two following exaggerations:

1° If they are acquainted with *the danger of revelations,* they extend their adverse judgment to the mystic union and turn certain souls away from an excellent path.

2° If, on the contrary, they are persuaded, and rightly so, of the *security and utility of the mystic union*, they wrongly include revelations in this favourable verdict, and urge certain souls into a dangerous way.

# CHAPTER XXII

## Revelations and Visions (*continued*)
## Course to Be Followed in Our Judgments With Regard to Them

### § 1. Of the Degree of Probability or Certainty That Can Be Arrived at

**1.**—Let us first consider this question: Can we ever be **morally certain** that a revelation is *purely* divine?

Yes; although when we think of all the causes of error that have been enumerated it would not appear to be so.

**2.**—And first, when He so wills, God can give a complete certainty, while the revelation lasts, at any rate, to the person **receiving it.** The light and the *evidence* are of such strength that any kind of doubt is impossible.

A similar fact occurs in the natural order. Our senses are subject to many illusions. But it is none the less true that in a multitude of cases we feel that we cannot have been mistaken.

**3.**—Can we ever be certain that a **revelation made to another person** is purely divine?

Yes. For the Old Testament prophets furnished *indubitable* signs of their mission. Otherwise they would not have been believed, and, further, it would not have been right to believe them. For there were always false prophets who obtained a hearing from a section of the people and led them astray. Holy Scripture enjoined discernment in the matter.

By what means can this result be obtained? That is the important but difficult question with which we shall deal in this chapter.

**4.**—When a **miracle*** is performed, and it is stated that it is worked with this intention, or when circumstances show this to be the case, it is an undeniable

* A miracle came thus to encourage St. Teresa at the beginning of her reform which she had been commanded to undertake by revelations. While secretly building her future Convent at Avila she

proof of the divine nature of the revelation. A prophecy fulfilled, will be the equivalent of a miracle if it was couched in definite language and could not have been the result of chance or a conjecture of the Devil.

Apart from these rather rare means of forming an opinion, there is another which is slower and more delicate: the *discussion* of reasons for and against.

**5.**—This inquiry, in practice, usually gives nothing more than a greater or a lesser **probability.** And when this is so we must not be afraid to own it.

Authors are often satisfied with vague utterances on these questions. They certainly speak of *signs* of discernment; but they forget to point out that, taken separately, these signs do not furnish a complete certainty and that their existence is not always easily detected.

In the same way they speak of the divine action, but they do not always ask themselves whether it is absolutely without any admixture of another element. And yet this is an important point also.

**6.**—The **right course to adopt**, when judging of revelations or visions, can be summed up in the three following steps which I am about to examine separately: 1° To obtain detailed information regarding **the person** who thinks himself thus favoured; 2° and also as to the actual facts of the revelation; 3° these data once obtained, to draw the *conclusions* that they admit of.

In order to show that a revelation is divine, *the process of exclusion* is also resorted to at times. This consists in proving that neither the Devil nor the individual mind can have added their own activity to God's action, and that no one retouched the revelation afterwards. But this process differs from the preceding one only by the manner of classifying the information and drawing the conclusions. Practically the same inquiries have to be made, but in a less natural order.

**6** *bis.*—Theologians, as such, have the following **problem** only to solve with regard to visions and revelations: *is this state purely divine, or is it not?* It is only indirectly, and as a means of solution, that they will ask themselves this other, slightly different question: *is this state purely natural, or is it not?*

This second problem is often as difficult as the first. Psychology cannot yet furnish definite replies concerning certain supernormal operations of the human mind, such as those observed in hypnotism, somnambulism, telepathy, thought-reading, experiments with mediums, etc. With regard to these obscure facts we must maintain a very reserved attitude. In such matters we should

arranged that her sister, Juana de Ahumada, and her brother-in-law, Juan de Ovalle, should live there; they thus seemed to be building a house for themselves, and in this way the opponents of her scheme suspected nothing. Going one day to inspect the works, the saint brought to life again her five-year-old nephew, Gonsalvo, who had been struck down by the fall of a wall and had lain lifeless for several hours (1561). Taking into account the circumstances of time and place, this miracle was the sign of God's approbation of the enterprise and of the idea that had inspired it.

pronounce in favour of the existence of the supernatural in simple and evident cases only.

### § 2. Seven Kinds of Inquiries to Be Made Regarding the Person Who Believes Himself to Be Thus Favoured

**7.**—Before examining the text or the circumstances of a revelation, we must know **with whom we have to deal.** There is a series of questions for this purpose which I am about to enumerate. They show us the person from the triple standpoints of the *natural, the ascetic, and the mystic.* When it is a question of a canonised saint, this inquiry has already been made by the Church.

**8.**—1° What are this person's **natural qualities,** or what, on the other hand, are his natural defects, whether *physical, intellectual,* and, above all, *moral*?

Amongst those who have known him at different times in his life, has he been regarded as sincere, cool-headed, and of sound judgment, being guided by reason and not by impressions? Briefly, is his mental equilibrium perfect? Or, on the contrary, are his descriptions of fact exaggerated, or are they even fabrications? Is his mind weakened by ill-health, vigils, fasts, etc.?

If the results are favourable, they prove, with a certain amount of probability, that the chief causes of error enumerated in the last chapter are not to be feared. For such a person's habitual tendencies are calculated to save him from these dangers; but an accidental lapse is possible.

**9.**—2° There is an inquiry that relates to the intellectual qualities. It is well to know the **degree of education** that the person has received, what books he has read, and what information he may have acquired by frequenting the society of learned men.

This will sometimes show us that certain revelations are less marvellous than they appear. We were inclined to call them supernatural, because of their erudition or a sublimity for which no other explanation could be found. But we must satisfy ourselves that this knowledge has not been derived from books or the conversation of theologians. We saw the case of St. Hildegard further back (ch. xxi, **26**).

**10.**—*Another application.* In order to prove that **Mary of Agreda's** revelations were divine, she has been described as being, as she herself says, an ignorant girl. But she could read. She was well acquainted with the Bible, which she quotes continually and comments upon. Cardinal Gotti, O.P. (+1742), has also shown that several of her revelations were borrowed from an apocryphal (or re-written) book of the fifteenth century, the *Raptures of* **Blessed**

**Amadeus,*** and another, the treatise *On the Nativity of the Blessed Virgin,* falsely attributed to St. Jerome.

Her biographer tells us "that having collected *various treatises* on this devotion [to Mary], she one night conceived a vehement desire to compose one herself" (ch. xix). She confesses to the assistance of theologians. "I have recourse to my director and to my spiritual father in the most delicate and difficult matters" (Part I, No. 24). When she wrote her book for the second time, she made use of fragments that had been collected by her second Confessor, "who conferred with her regarding the matters found therein" (*Vie*, ch. xxii).

The upshot of all this is that she had other than supernatural aid in her work. She exaggerates when she says: "No human mind could have imagined this work" (Part III, No. 789).

**10** *bis.*—Another example. I have spoken elsewhere (ch. xviii, 47 *bis*) of **Hélène Smith,** of Geneva, and of her somnambulistic states. The spiritualists were greatly impressed by the things that she related during her trances, and considered this sudden facility of speech an evident proof of the influence of another spirit. With remarkable patience and sagacity, M. Flournoy has shown that the majority of these accounts were simply the reproduction of certain books, of which the subject remembered nothing in the normal state.†

We know already that in the somnambulistic state the memory undergoes a prodigious development at times. In the case of Hélène Smith, the imagination was equally powerful; during her crises she had created a new language, of 160 words, which she spoke fluently, but which she did not understand when she was not in a trance. She claimed that this was the language in use in the planet Mars. It has been proved to be an adaptation of known languages. Before believing that a medium is inspired, spiritualists should inquire carefully into his or her antecedents.

**11.**—In cases where the seer is educated, and his unaided **account** of the vision shows a talent for composition superior to that which he ordinarily displays, is there not at least some probability that he was subject to a supernatural action?

* A Franciscan, confessor to Sixtus IV. Skies of crystal occur here. Sister Mary especially takes from him the idea of Our Lord's Body being formed out of three drops of blood from Our Lady's heart. I will merely point out two physiological errors in such a doctrine. To begin with, it implies the circulation of the blood, the discovery of which was quite recent (1628), to have been still unknown at Agreda. Since all the blood passes through the heart, no special privilege can be attached to it, and there is no further reason for presenting it as a marvellous symbol of Mary's sentiments. And, further, there is an error with regard to the function of the blood. It is as powerless as milk to create tissue or to dispose it after a given plan; it serves to nourish the already existing tissues. God can gain nothing by thus changing the course of nature.

† M. Flournoy has given the name cryptomnesia to this fact, that certain forgotten items of knowledge reappear without being recognised by the subject, who henceforth regards them as something new.

Yes. But we cannot find a proof in this circumstance. The higher literary level reached in these pages may simply be due to the excitement that accompanies or follows a true supernatural grace. St. Teresa, describing the intoxication into which the full union threw her, says of herself: "I know one who... composed, without any preparation, certain stanzas, full of feeling, most expressive of her pain: they were not the work of her own understanding, but, in order to have a greater fruition of that bliss which so sweet a pain occasioned her, she complained of it in that way to God" (*Life,* ch. xvi, 6). The saint has the wisdom not to claim that God dictates her verses; it is her own pious intoxication. Thus the talent displayed in the composition of certain passages is not a clear proof that God revealed them to her.

**12.**—3° What **virtues** does this person possess? What has been his general level from the standpoint of perfection, whether *before* the revelation or *afterwards*?

If **before** the revelation he was vicious, and particularly if of scandalous conduct, it is not likely that God has chosen him as the recipient of His favours, except for the purposes of his conversion. On the other hand, experience seems to prove that God has at times manifested Himself to simple souls of quite ordinary virtue, in order to found a pilgrimage or to suggest some useful undertaking. Thus at the beginnings of certain special revelations, it may be that an ordinary piety is sufficient.

**13.**—The important point is to know whether there has been much progress **after** the revelations. Have these states created a centre of moral energy?

If a great advance in sanctification has been noticed, and if, further, this can be attributed to the revelations and not simply to other graces, there is a strong probability in their favour. It is not a certainty, because, as we have already seen, canonised saints have been mistaken at times.

If, on the contrary, the seer of the vision has remained at an ordinary level of virtue, his visions must be regarded with suspicion. Such extraordinary means are not made to lead to a merely ordinary state of self-sacrifice.

Lopez de Ezquerra says, with regard to this subject: "*All* passive and extraordinary communications proceeding from the good spirit... produce an efficacious excitation to good works... and the soul feels that this movement comes, not from herself, but from the divine virtue. She is conscious of an overflowing life, as it were, in her faculties, turning her away from created things and towards God and great actions. This motion, excitation, impulsion, is called the gift of excitation. To a greater or lesser degree it accompanies *all* supernatural favours and infused movements; *and this without any exceptions.* The Devil, on the other hand, produces no vision or illusion that does not end in a strong inclination to evil. This may not be perceived at once; but he soon shows himself openly by his results" (*Lucerna*, Tr. 4, No. 178).

**14.**—The author here quoted has told us that evil tendencies coming from the Devil may not show themselves at the outset. What the Devil cannot do is to incline the soul towards the solid virtues in a **real and durable manner.** But he can, by a ruse, feign to encourage them for a time for the sake of landing his victim in exaggerations and oddities. Provided that the end is evil, the road leading up to it matters little to him.

Under his influence bodily penances will be pushed to the length of ruining the health*; they will be accompanied by disobedience, and will lead to disgust or will make the person ridiculous. Purity of conscience will degenerate into scrupulousness, humility into sloth or discouragement; while zeal will become indiscretion.

In the saints' lives we see that Satan, on more than one occasion, has given exalted ideas of the active live to contemplatives in order to turn them aside from the state that they had embraced and in which they were being sanctified. His object was to engage them in profitless undertakings. On the other hand, he will represent the joys of solitude to those who are successful teachers or sick nurses. He tries to make them change their vocation at an age when it cannot be done. In all these cases the tree is known, sooner or later, by its fruits.

**15.**—We have an **instance** of one of these ruses of Satan in the life of Blessed **Jordan of Saxony,** second General of the Dominicans. When crossing the Alps he was taken with a high fever. He was accompanied by a certain Prior, skilled in medicine, under whose obedience he had put himself in these matters, and who had ordered him to sleep on a feather-bed. The Devil, who wished to increase his illness so that he might not be able to preach, appeared to him during the night under the form of an angel, and, rebuking him severely for his self-indulgence, made him decide to lie on the ground. The next day the doctor renewed his orders. That night there was another apparition of the angel. The sick man again yielded to his injunctions. A third time the doctor repeated his order. Again the angel returned. But by this time Blessed Jordan had realised that obedience was the only safe path. He spat in the apparition's face, and it took to flight (Bolland., Feb. 13, *Vie*, by Cantimpré, No. 5, and Amort, Book I, ch. viii, after Castaldo, O.P.).

**16.**—Amongst those virtues that a revelation should bring in its train, one that should shine forth most brilliantly, and regarding which it is of paramount importance to be informed, is **humility**. It is the one most opposed to our nature and of which Satan has the greatest horror.

If this virtue is real, it can proceed only from God, and is a very favourable sign. It is this that has led Gerson, rather exaggerating the value of the sign

* In the *Lives* of the Saints, in that of the Blessed Cure d'Ars, for instance, we read of fasts and vigils which would be indiscreet for many of us. They would reduce our strength and, more serious still, would weaken our faculties. We have even known cases of saints who have gone without food for several weeks. Whence is this different standard of conduct for them and us? It is that God aids them miraculously, and they *are aware* of this fact. They know that they can go to such or such lengths, *physically* and *morally;* either because they have received an extraordinary light, or because they have made a series of attempts, as St. Ignatius advises in his *Rules for Temperance* (Rule 4).

when taken alone, to say: "This is the first and the principal sign by which to decide the value of the spiritual coin: whatever may be in question, whether interior warnings, overpowering instincts, ecstatic love, contemplations, raptures; if humility precedes, accompanies, and follows it without any contrary element, you may be sure that the work comes from God or from the good angel [in part, at least]" (*De distinct. ver. vision.*, sign. 4).

Pride, on the contrary, is a mark of diabolic illusion or imposture.* It shows itself by contempt for our neighbour, an independent spirit with regard to Superiors and directors, by obstinacy in our opinions, by the refusal to submit to the necessary examination and by anger.

It is a sign of pride, and therefore of illusion, to have a craving to divulge the graces that we believe ourselves to have received. Humility leads to their concealment, except in the somewhat rare cases of real utility (see ch. xi, **21**).

**17.**—4° What extraordinary graces of **union** with God does the person believe himself to have received previously, and what has been the verdict regarding them?

If he has merely had strong sentiments of love of God, or even the prayer of quiet, it is best to reserve judgment regarding the revelations and visions, especially if they are of frequent occurrence. It is only in exceptional cases that these graces are granted, unless the soul is much further advanced in prayer. †

If, on the contrary, the person has reached the period of ecstasy, there is a probability in favour of the revelation, but nothing more, since the ecstatic saints have sometimes suffered from illusions, and their imagination came into action either during or after the divine visitation.

**18.**—5° And, moreover, what **revelations** or visions has he previously believed himself to have received, and what was thought about them? Has he made **predictions?** Were they quite clearly expressed and clearly fulfilled, without its being necessary to resort to subtleties of interpretation?

**19.**—When an isolated *prediction* has *come true*, there is sometimes only a probability of its being divine, even where it is a question of human actions that are dependent upon free-will. For it may have been uttered at hazard and fulfilled by chance. And then the Devil conjectures many future events, because he knows the habitual trend of both the divine and the human will under similar circumstances. He is especially likely to be correct when it is a question of the populace, who often let themselves be carried away by unreasoning instincts which can be foreseen. Finally, the Devil, after announcing some

* St. Teresa: If "the soul receives favours and caresses from Our Lord, let it examine carefully whether it therefore rates itself more highly; if self-abasement does not increase with God's expressions of love, certainly they do not come from the Holy Spirit" (*Interior Castle,* Sixth Mansion, ch. iii, 2).

† I have been told of two persons who for a long time have been having visions and locutions of Our Lord, and who yet have never, it appears, experienced the mystic union with God or with the Sacred Humanity.

unwelcome event, can assist in its realisation (see St. John of the Cross, *Ascent of Mount Carmel*, Book II, ch. xxi).

**20.**—We have an instance of a prophecy true in part, but which by its **false elements** had disastrous consequences at the close of the Great Western Schism. Benedict XIII, the last of the Avignon Popes, escaped to Spain by sea.* P. Nider, O.P., relates how, in a town on the sea-coast, the Abbot of a monastery warned the inhabitants to be ready to receive the Pope. They laughed at such an unlikely prediction. But the wind, changing suddenly, carried the Pope's ship six miles back upon its course, and obliged it to enter the port in question. Benedict asked the Abbot how he had known of his arrival beforehand. He replied that he had read this prophecy recently in a book, which further said that the same Pope would triumph over all opposition, would return to Rome, and would rule there in peace as before. Seeing that the first part of the prediction was fulfilled, Benedict believed in it, rejected the citation sent by the Council of Constance, was deposed and excommunicated, and died in exile in the island of Peniscola (1422) (quoted by Amort, Part II, preface).

**21.**—Let us now suppose that the predictions made are not fulfilled, and that there is no serious reason for supposing them to be conditional; it is then to be believed that they are not of divine origin.

**False prophets** do not allow themselves to be easily discouraged by their repeated failures. They always find some good reason to explain them away, or they pretend that the event is only delayed! When necessary, they proceed to confirm their first utterance by some new revelation.

**22.**—6° Has this person suffered great **trials** before or after the revelations: sicknesses, contradictions, want of success, or delay in certain enterprises that he had at heart, etc.?

The saints' lives are full of these trials. It is scarcely possible that crosses should not accompany extraordinary graces. For both alike are a mark of God's friendship, and each is a preparation for the other. If, then, a person who was supposed to be in the way of revelations had no crosses, the way would be open to suspicion.

**23.**—There is one trial in particular that necessarily, as it were, accompanies these extraordinary ways. Those who know the secrets of these paths, and more certainly still the public, will be inclined to show themselves **sceptical or hostile** when they hear them spoken of. "Why, they will say, do these things happen to this person rather than to others who are of greater virtue? It is all due to his imagination! We have no wish to be troubled with these difficult and perhaps unanswerable questions." These criticisms and doubts are an excellent touchstone by which to test the person's humility, patience, and trust in God. If a novice in these virtues, he will meet opposition with words of irritation or discouragement; but if otherwise, he will not be astonished at the divine tarryings, and will continue, in perfect peace, to hope that God's designs will sooner or later be accomplished.

* It was probably the first voyage (1408). The Pope went from Italy to Port-Vendres, which, like Roussillon, belonged at that time to Spain.

**24.**—We have a fine **example** of this **patience** in Blessed Juliana, a Cistercian prioress of Mont Cornillon, near Liège (1192-1258). She was chosen by God to institute in the Church the Feast of the Blessed Sacrament. She can be said to have passed her whole life awaiting God's appointed time without ever seeing the realisation of her hopes. Her visions on the subject began two years after her entry into the noviciate. She was then only sixteen (1208). Not until twenty-two years later (towards 1230) does she venture to submit her project to a group of learned theologians. They approved it; but her enemies avenged themselves for her reforms by bringing about the pillaging of her Convent by the populace. Sixteen years later (1246) success seems at last about to arrive; for the Bishop of Liège institutes the Feast in his Diocese. But he dies the same year, and one church alone, the collegiate Church of St. Martin, pays any heed to his order. The convent is again pillaged. Blessed Juliana, being calumniated, is forced to leave it. She wanders from place to place during the last twenty years of her life, and dies at the age of sixty-six, after a fruitless wait of fifty years' duration. All seemed lost; but an aged Archdeacon of Liège, who had formerly been one of the group of theologians mentioned above, became Pope under the title of Urban IV. Six years after Blessed Juliana's death, in the Bull of 1264, he instituted the Feast of Corpus Christi for all Christendom, and caused St. Thomas Aquinas to compose the proper Office. But all was not yet completed. For the wars that disturbed Italy caused this Bull to be long forgotten. Finally, in 1316, John XXII celebrated the feast with all solemnity. More than a century had elapsed since the beginning of the revelations! (See *Vie*, by Le Pas; Desclee, 1893.)

**24** *bis.*—**St. Louis Grignon de Montfort,** the celebrated missionary in Brittany and La Vendée in the eighteenth century, also showed an heroic trust in God. He had known for some time that he was destined to form two new congregations: that of the *Filles de la Sagesse,* for hospitals and the instruction of poor children, and the *Compagnie de Marie,* composed of missionaries. It was only a year before his death that he was able to inaugurate these two foundations, and he only succeeded in getting together four Sisters on the one hand, and two priests, with a few lay-brothers, on the other. The work appeared therefore to be a failure. But St. Louis Grignon knew that the tree would grow. And, in fact, at the beginning of the twentieth century the Sisters of *La Sagesse* numbered 5000, with 44 houses.

**25.**—The holy souls to whom God commits a mission of utility to the Church are not all thus obliged to submit to the long **martyrdom of hope deferred.** But they have other trials.

As an example of rapid success, we may quote the case of St. Catherine Labouré, of the Sisters of Charity. She saw in 1832 the striking of the *Miraculous Medal* that had been the subject of her visions only two years before (November, 1830); and she took part in its distribution for forty-four years (1876) without, however, being known to the world.

It was the same with Sister Apolline Andriveau, also a Sister of Charity. In 1846 she received the revelation of the Scapular of the Passion. In the following year Pius IX instituted this devotion. The Sister did not die until forty-seven years later (1894).

**26.**-7° Has the person taken **three precautions** that are regarded as indispensable for the avoidance of illusions: (*a*) fearing to be deceived; (*b*) perfect frankness with directors; and (*c*) abstaining from desiring these revelations?

**27.**—(*a*) It is clear, first of all, that to believe oneself to be **safe from illusions** is an excellent disposition for suffering from them. The soul is then like a city that takes no precautions against the enemy by which she is invested.

Mary of Agreda does not seem to have been penetrated with this fear. On the contrary, she expected that not even her least revelations should be questioned. She declared that God said to her: "I desire that these revelations should be regarded not as opinions, or simple visions, but as *certain truths*" (Part I, No. 10). The Blessed Virgin is quoted as speaking in the same sense: "There is nothing of yours in this history, and you can no more attribute it to yourself than *to the pen with which you write it.* You are but the instrument in the Lord's hand... If anyone fails to believe in what you have written, he will not injure you; *the outrage* will be to me and to my words" (Part III, No. 621; in the French translation, No. 619; and *Lettre a ses religieuses,* No. 9). Thus Sister Mary considers herself securely protected from all error, and that it is a sin not to share her conviction!

**28.**—(*b*) **Manifestation of the conscience** is necessary. In such difficult matters we must not be both judge and one of the parties concerned. The Devil dissuades us from this sincerity, for, says St. Ignatius, he is afraid to see his wiles unmasked (*Rules for Discernment of Spirits,* 1st Week, 13), and he abhors such an act of humility.

In revenge he leads us to unbosom ourselves without any reflection to friends who have no authority over us, which enables us to put their advice aside, if it does not please us.

On the other hand, humble souls avoid publicity as much as possible.

**29.**—(*c*) **The desire for revelations** also exposes the soul to deception. It causes us to find a thousand subtleties by which to substantiate the visions that we believe ourselves to have had, and it excites the imagination to invent new ones.

St. Augustine relates that his mother, **St. Monica,** only just escaped falling into illusion by this means. As she was striving to convert him and bring about his marriage, she wished to know by revelation the issue of her endeavours. False visions were the result. Happily she had previously enjoyed true visions; she perceived that these differed from the others, "by I know not what kind of relish which she knew not how to express," and she was able to reject these empty appearances (*Confessions,* Book VI, ch. xiii).

**30.**—It therefore follows that a revelation should generally be regarded as doubtful if it has been desired. I say: generally; for in exceptional cases it may happen that this desire has been inspired by the Holy Spirit and is clearly recognised as being from Him.

**31.**—**Mary of Agreda's** desire to know by revelation the events that she describes is regarded as an unfavourable sign. "This is so sometimes," says Cardinal Gotti, "even in questions of pure curiosity, which in no way help to perfection" (2nd *Censure*, presented to Clement XII; quoted by Mgr. Chaillot). Further examples occur in *La Cité mystique*, Part I, Nos. 4, 33, 52 (where she is occupied with a scholastic question: the order of the divine decrees), 73, 242, 353 (where she wishes to know if in her infancy Our Lady was hungry, how she asked for food, if she wore swaddling-clothes, if she cried, if she was treated like a great personage!); Part II, Nos. 298, 647.

Far from reproving her, her confessors sometimes ordered her to make these indiscreet requests: Part II, Nos. 138 (they wish to know if the Roman Martyrology is correct); 477 (to obtain certain details regarding Our Blessed Lord's birth); 211 (to find the site of St. Elizabeth's house).

### § 3. Nine Points Upon Which Information Should Be Obtained, Either With Regard to the Revelation, Considered in Itself, Or the Circumstances That Accompanied It

**32.**—1° Is there an absolutely **authentic** text? Have not certain expressions been *corrected* as inexact or obscure, or have not certain other passages been actually *suppressed*? These things would be allowable if the edification of the public were the only object. But it is otherwise from the critic's point of view; it means that we are depriving ourselves of very important data.

Instead of curtailments, have there, on the contrary, been *additions* to the revelation? for the sake of accrediting certain doctrines, for instance? This would be a real falsification.

**33.**—2° Is the revelation in full accord with the **dogmas and** teachings of the Church, and also with the undoubted pronouncements of history and science?

With regard to dogma, if one sure point alone be contradicted, as has happened many times in supernatural communications, it is sufficient to allow us to affirm that the speaker is not one of God's envoys.

If, on the contrary, a revelation contains no error, a conclusion cannot yet be drawn from this fact alone. The human mind may confine itself prudently within the limits of received truths. The Devil can restrain himself for a time, can give himself the appearance of truth as of holiness, so as to inspire confidence. He resembles those gamblers who intend to cheat; they begin by making their opponents win, that they may afterwards make them lose ten times as much again. It does not hurt him to make some concessions to truth for the sake of insinuating an error. Thus, in communications from spirits you sometimes find pages that are quite correct and (although more rarely) of a high tone of thought; but a dogma will be denied in them. If this snare is successful, the Devil will go further and will teach other errors.

**34.**—3° Does the revelation contain no teaching, or is it accompanied by no action that is contrary to decency and **morals?**

In all divine visions there is a perfect propriety of bearing, gestures, and words (ch. xx, **38**).

The aberrations at which certain badly balanced persons have arrived through ignorance of this rule, and their absurd way of understanding what familiarity with Our Lord means, are hardly believable.

If, for example, as has sometimes happened, an apparition professing to be Jesus Christ were to appear without clothing, we might be sure that it was not divine. On this subject see St. Bonaventure (*De profectu religiosorum,* Book II, ch. lxxvi, *alias* lxxv). More obviously still, the instrumentality of the Devil is plain in the case of words or actions that are a clear offence against chastity. God's commandments bind all men without distinction. He dispenses no one under the pretext of friendship. On the contrary, the objects of His visit is to lead us further and further away from the life of the senses.

**35.**—Certain writers, such as Schram (old edition, No. 549; edition of 1848, No. 559), look with suspicion upon a **supernatural revelation** of other people's **vices** and sins, because of the temptation to a lack of charity and an exhibition of contempt or repugnance for certain persons. But this is a matter that depends upon the circumstances of the individual case.

St. John of the Cross says that this knowledge of vices is to be attributed either to God or to the Devil, according to the case in question. "God sometimes represents to holy souls the necessities of their neighbours, *that they may pray for them or relieve them.*"

This utility is a favourable sign, and it is clearly perceived in the numerous saints who possessed the knowledge of the secrets of hearts. By its means they help in the reformation of souls. St. Joseph of Cupertino, St. Catherine of Siena, St. Mary Magdalen of Pazzi, enjoyed this favour so habitually that persons were often unwilling to encounter them without having first cleansed their consciences (Scaramelli, *Tr. du discern.,* No. 28). St. Bridget saw the damnation of several persons. She drew a lesson from this knowledge for others.

On the other hand, says St. John of the Cross again, "He [the Devil] is wont occasionally to reveal, falsely, but with great distinctness, the sins of others, evil consciences, and corrupt souls, with a view to detraction" (*Ascent of Mount Carmel,* Book II, ch. xxvi, p. 183).

**36.**—This knowledge of other people's sins is also often a mere illusion of the imagination. I have known two cases of women who saw visions and who were thus haunted by the rooted idea of the relaxation of **religious Houses,** or the **clergy.** They delighted in discussing these matters, in order, as they said, to bring about a reform. One at least of them has turned out ill. They had no other evidence by which to prove their facts than their revelations, which were sufficiently explained by the propensity of poor human nature to occupy itself with unbecoming subjects. Owing to a perversion of piety, these delirious imaginations finished by yielding to their natural cravings.

In the middle of the nineteenth century another visionary, Cantianille by name, won the confidence of a pious but imprudent Bishop who issued an official publication of the text of her revelation, which was a horrible picture of the morals of the clergy in his diocese. He was obliged to resign. Satan obtained the result that he sought.

It is true that St. Catherine of Siena in her *Revelations* speaks openly and forcibly of the vices of the clergy. But this was in the troublous days of the Great Schism, when the relaxation of the clergy was a matter of common knowledge.

*Les Secret de Mélanie of la Salette* is thought by certain persons to have been modified by the imagination of the person who had the vision. One of the reasons relied on is that the text contains very harsh and unqualified accusations regarding the morals of the clergy and the religious communities from 1846 to 1865. History speaks quite differently, and indicates a period of fervour and apostolic zeal. It was the time of Pius IX, of Dom Bosco, the Cure d'Ars, etc., and of the spread of Christian teaching throughout France.

**37.**—4° Is the information received **useful** for our eternal salvation? We can be sure that revelations are not divine when their subject is simply the acquisition of ordinary matters that are of no utility to souls. God does not go out of His way merely to satisfy curiosity.

It is with revelations as with miracles: they do not occur without a serious motive. They are the works not only of God's power, but of His wisdom.

**38.**—We see, then, what is to be thought of those prophetesses who pretend to speak in the name of an angel or of a saint, and who at all hours and to all comers give audiences, during which inquiries are made regarding births, marriages, legal proceedings, diseases, the outcome of political events, etc. In spite of the religious *mise en scene,* they are simply fortune-tellers. Nothing is lacking but the conventional pack of cards or coffee-grounds. God does not stoop to run an Inquiry Office.

Their clients (although deeply sceptical in many ways) are inspired with confidence by the fact that they are often fortunate in their predictions, and this without either the Devil's aid or being endowed with specially brilliant perceptions. The fact is that they know their trade. A glance enables them to seize the least indication of what they should say, or how they should correct what they have already said. They can even be successful only by replying yes and no at random. For when you play heads and tails, tails have as many chances as heads. They may be right, on an average, five times out of ten in this game. The idle inquirers forget the five unsuccessful cases; they only remember the others, and so sing the prophet's praises.

**39.**—In **spiritualist** meetings the spirits are often occupied with mere **trifles.** They condescend to reply to idle questions or to provide a drawing-room game.

They push furniture about, cause vibrations in musical instruments, and introduce small objects from outside. The medium will amuse you in this way for a whole evening, just as conjurors will do at a fair. Would spirits who have our eternal welfare at heart consent to lend themselves to such childish things. How far removed is all this from the office attributed by theology to our Guardian Angel!

These puerilities become still more distressing when the spirits pose as being our deceased relations, or great philosophers. For if they endeavour to be serious, it is to dictate an appalling tirade of platitudes. Such are the high thoughts that occupy these beings immersed in the light of eternity!

When these spirits claim to be those who were great *savants* on earth, we find that their intellect has become singularly enfeebled in their new life. They are no longer up to date in any subject. It has been proved that spiritualistic communications have not advanced science by a single step. No obscure point of history has been cleared up. No mathematical problem has been solved; no chemical formula or theory of physics has been revealed.

Once only Aksakof and other spiritualists thought that they had found an exception. The spirits seemed to have explained a phenomenon that had resisted all the wisdom of men of science. It was a question of the retrograde movement of the satellites of the planet Uranus. But an astronomer, M. Flammarion, went to the root of this assertion and proved that the spirits' explanation was absolutely false (*Las Forces naturelles inconnues*, ch. iii).

**40.**—A revelation is equally to be regarded with suspicion when its only object is the solving of some **question** that is in **dispute,** whether theological, historical or astronomic, etc. God leaves these discussions to the human intellect because we do not need them for our sanctification. Let us understand that eternal salvation is the only thing of any importance with God. For all else, says St. John of the Cross, it is "always His will that we should make use of our natural endowments" (*Ascent of Mount Carmel*, Book II, ch. xxii, p. 163).

**41.**—The revelation is also to be mistrusted if, although good from the spiritual point of view, it is a *truism,* occurring in all ascetic writings. God would not employ such great means for such a small result. It is rather probable that the person is thus unconsciously repeating things that he has learnt from books. Or, again, the Devil is amusing him with trifles until the day when having allayed his suspicions, he can become bolder.

**42.**—If the **revelations** or visions are **very numerous,** this circumstance, *taken alone*, does not constitute an unfavourable sign.

In fact, no substantial reason can be brought *a priori* for the contrary opinion. And, further, it would be to condemn a number of saints; they have had revelations in very great abundance. Examples: St. Bridget, St. Gertrude, St. Frances of Rome, St. Catherine of Siena, St. Margaret Mary, Ven. Agnes of Langeac, Ven. Marina de Escobar, St. Ignatius, etc. Many have left us enormous volumes, in which, however, everything that they wrote is not included. The opponents of these revelations have never thought of finding fault with this abundance, and no apologist has supposed that objections would be made on this point.

It is true that a letter of St. Francis of Sales (Migne ed., Vol. V, col. 1448) is quoted, which seems to condemn a nun because she had so many visions. But the context shows that the saint was not considering this circumstance alone; it is also stated that these revelations had no practical utility; they were mere words.

**43.**—We see here how we can **turn** these numerous visions to **account** *indirectly*. We can generally see clearly whether or no they have served any purpose. In the case of an isolated vision the answer might be doubtful.

If the revelations are long or numerous, and if they contain nothing false, indecent, or futile, we may conclude with probability that they do not emanate from the Devil. For if this were so, he would fail in his object. As Samaniego remarks (*Prologue* to the *Works* of Mary of Agreda, No. 26), it is not possible that he should always continue hidden.

**44.**—5° If we examine all the **detailed circumstances** that accompany the vision, the attitudes, gestures, words, etc., do we find the **dignity,** the **gravity,** in keeping with the Divine Majesty? Or, on the contrary, do we not perceive oddities, a grotesque deportment, convulsions, or a lack of restraint that are unworthy even of people who are merely rational and well brought up?

(*a*) This alone should have sufficed to condemn the extraordinary events that took place towards the middle of the eighteenth century at the Saint-Médard cemetery, at the tomb of the deacon Paris. The so-called inspired discourses were extravagant and accompanied by contortions and convulsions; the blows which these persons caused to be inflicted, and their accompanying insensibility to pain, passed as miracles, but they were simply insensate practices, for they did no one any good. I do not speak of the acts opposed to morality that were subsequently added to these hideous scenes. Many Jansenists, however, saw in these things God's manifestations in favour of their teaching.

(*b*) In spiritualistic communications we often find vulgar modes of speech that would offend us in good society. Great historic personages talk a Billingsgate language, and if the audience is in sympathy they soon descend to obscenities.

Certain spiritualists are embarrassed by these facts, but they will not on that account admit the instrumentality of the Devil.* They prefer to believe that the

* Spiritualists lay it down as a principle that spirits holding communication with them are the spirits of the dead only, or, to use their language, disembodied spirits. In order to be sure that such or such a spirit is one of their own relations or friends, they have one proof only, namely, that the spirit in question should acquaint them with a secret known only to themselves and the dead. But the answer is that this reason is not sufficient. For they admit that during our lives we are surrounded by spirits that know all our secrets. One of these may therefore act the part of a dead relative and mystify us.

souls of the dead carry their vices into the other world, and that the offensive replies are given by the dead, who are still liars, or libertines, triflers, hoaxers, etc.

(*c*) In Protestant countries gatherings, called "revivals," are organised from time to time. Crowds weep over their sins, but with a strange exaggeration, a kind of intoxication. We have here, let us not forget it, an excellent principle: ardent sentiments of the love of God and of repentance. But another element which has nothing divine about it, a neurotic exaltation which is contagious, mingles with it. Sometimes imitations of foreign languages, consisting really in a succession of sounds which of themselves have no meaning, are spoken.

**45.**—When the angels or the saints assume an apparent body in order to manifest themselves, this body never exhibits **deformed limbs** or an animal aspect. It would be unworthy of them. Forms of animals are only met with in very different cases, in symbolic visions, such as Ezekiel's, or St. John the Evangelist's four living creatures. Perfectly rational allegorical explanations have been given of these forms.

On the other hand, when the Devil appears to those who invoke him, he delights in taking repulsive shapes; he blends the human form with those of the vilest animals. Suarez regards it as being proved "by the admissions of sorcerers themselves," that Satan never reveals himself to them in a completely human shape; there is always a suggestion of something monstrous, such as the feet (*De angelis,* Book IV, ch. xxxv, No. 5).

This idea of Suarez has sometimes been made light of, it being said that he included in this proposition all apparitions of the Devil, not excepting those which Satan wished to pass off as divine. But Suarez does not say a word implying this doctrine; and, indeed, it is not in accordance with facts.

As de la Reguera (*Theol. myst.,* Vol. II, p. 666, No. 534) and Schram (first edition, No. 507; or No. 517 in the edition of 1848) remark, if the deformity of the apparition were visible, the ruse would be immediately apparent, and the Devil would exhibit a childish want of skill; if it were invisible, hidden either by garments or clouds, the Devil would be ill advised to give himself so much useless trouble making limbs which would not be seen; and, besides, what actual proof would there be of his doing so?

**46.**—Many authors have repeated, without discussing it, a statement of two seventeenth-century writers (F.F. Thyrœus, 1600, and Del Rio, 1600). According to them, the Devil is never permitted to take the form of a **dove** or of a **lamb** in his apparitions, because these are symbols of the Holy Spirit and of Christ (Schram, *ibid.*).

But this twofold assertion is contradicted by facts, as we see in the life of St. Frances of Rome. For six devils presented themselves to her one day under the form of six beautiful doves. The saint saw through the deception, and they then changed into crows and tried to injure her* (Bolland., March 9; 1st *Life,* Book **III**, No. 37).

So much for the doves. But there were lambs also. One day the Devil took the form of a lamb that came and lay gently down at the saint's feet. She recognised him, and he became a furious wolf (*ibid.*, No. 23). Another time seven devils appeared to her as white lambs of an engaging appearance, declaring that they symbolised the seven gifts of the Holy Ghost. She again recognised them, and they changed into wolves and tried to attack her (*ibid.*, No. 33).

Another example: The celebrated Magdalen of the Cross, who worked wonders by the Devil's power (ch. xxi, **36**), had an apparition of the Devil one day publicly, under the form of a dove. She claimed that it was the Holy Spirit (Görres, Book VII, ch. xi).

Finally, if the Devil were forbidden to simulate these symbols, he would *a fortiori* be forbidden to represent Christ Himself, which he has sometimes, however, done. If he does not make use of these figures, or does so but rarely, we may attribute it to a much simpler reason: when he tries to entangle us in an illusion he must adopt means that are really powerful, such as the representation of a saint. The person seeing it will at once feel drawn to him by an impulse of devotion. But the sight of a symbolic animal, on the contrary, produces an impression of expectation; it allows time to reflect and to ask ourselves what fruit we can derive from this vision.

In resorting but seldom to these symbols, Satan shows his practical sense. That is all.

If he risked using these unsatisfactory methods with St. Frances, it was for a special reason. The saint often saw symbolic doves or lambs in her visions. There was reason to hope that she would rely on the likeness and accept it from force of habit.

Hitherto it has been a question of *apparitions* of the Devil, wishing to produce an illusion. But there is another very different case, which people forget to distinguish from the preceding: that of the Devil *speaking* during the exorcisms. He then sometimes takes the name of an animal symbolising a vice (see ch. xxiv, **63**). Now, he has often stated that God does not permit him to apply to this vile purpose a symbol employed by the Church for holy things. He has declared that he cannot take the name of a dove, a lamb, or of a fish (the symbol of Christ in the Catacombs, because of the Greek word *ichthys*).

**47.**—Scaramelli seems over-severe in the following case. A person who was by way of seeing frequent visions of the Infant Jesus believed that he had one on Good Friday during a sermon on the Passion. This writer considers it unseemly

* Instead of the word crow, which is in the Italian tent, the Bollandists say deer; this is a printer's error. An "e" has been substituted for an "o," *cervorum* for *corvorum* (this was remarked by Dom Rabory, author of a *Life* of the saint).

that on such a day and at such a moment we should fix our thoughts on Our Lord's Infancy. He concludes it to be an illusion (*Traité du discern.*, No. 87).

But this line of reasoning proves too much. It amounts to the general admission that if on some Feast Day, and during a sermon, a spiritual consolation of a different kind takes possession of our souls, we should repulse it. No; there is no sort of obligation to do this. On the contrary, the thought of one mystery of Our Lord's life can throw light upon the others. This author adds that "other reasons had since been found to prove that this person's visions were false." That may be so, but the foregoing reason was worthless.

**48.**—6° What **sentiments of peace**, or, on the other hand, of **disquiet**, has the person experienced during the revelation, or subsequently?

St. Ignatius, like St. Catherine of Siena (*Dialogues*, ch. lxxi, English, p. 223), attaches great importance to this means of discernment.

When it is a question of passing inspirations, it may happen that these sentiments are hardly perceptible; but it can scarcely be so in the case of such an extraordinary action as a revelation or a vision, unless, however, it proceeds, not from another spirit, but from our own activity.

**49.**—This is the **rule** that can be laid down: *With those who are in good faith* (we need speak of no others) **the action of the good spirit** (God or one of His angels) *is characterised by the gift of peace, joy, assurance, and courage, save perhaps at the first moment.*

Let us note this last restriction. At the first moment not astonishment only may be felt, but also anxiety, disquietude, and even fear. But a fuller survey restores the peace of mind. It was thus that the Blessed Virgin was momentarily troubled by the Angel Gabriel's salutation (Luc. i, 29). But her calm returned directly, and Mary listened to the message. Holy Scripture refers to the agitation that Abraham experienced, although transiently, in one of his visions (Gen. xv, 12); to that of Zachary, when the Angel Gabriel announced to him that he would be the father of St. John the Baptist (Luc. i, 12); of the shepherds at Bethlehem when the angels announced Our Saviour's birth (Luc. ii, 10); of the holy women, at the tomb where the angel was keeping guard (Mark xvi, 6, 8); of the apostles when the risen Lord appeared amongst them, and calmed their fears by these words: Peace be to you (John xx, 19, 26).

The first agitation may also be due to the fact that sensuality or pride rebel against the sacrifice demanded of them. But only the inferior portion of the soul is thus affected.

When he thus gives peace, the good spirit does not act only upon the will, by inclining it gently to good, but upon the intelligence also: the idea seems natural to us, wise, and in conformity with what God would expect of us. Whether as light or as an impulse, God takes possession of the soul without any shock. St. Ignatius gives us a rapid picture of this way of acting by saying that "the good angel comes with sweetness, peace, suavity, like a drop of water falling on a sponge" (*Rules for the discernment of spirits*, II, 7).

**50.—The Devil's action** has diametrically opposite effects: *when he acts upon these who are of good-will, he produces, except it may be at the first instant, uneasiness, sadness, discouragement, agitation, and darkness.* St. Teresa adds that we often experience these feelings without discovering their cause (*Life*, see especially ch. xxv).

At the first moment there may be a feeling of joy; if we search into the real cause we shall see that the Devil is suggesting some ideas that appeal to our passions or to some earthly tendencies, the desire for honours or sensible pleasures. But at the last his light, like the light of a storm, is scanty, shifting, interspersed with darkness. His impulsion is enervating, often contradictory, ending in disgust, discouragement. This action, says St. Ignatius, is "like rain in a storm, beating on a rock" (*ibid.*). In short, Satan's inspiration encounters a mysterious resistance in souls of good-will.

St. Teresa, like St. John of the Cross, often describes the character of the infernal action.* The saint explains it thus: "I am thinking whether this may not be so because one spirit is conscious of the presence of another" (*Life*, ch. xxv, 13).

**51.**—From what has been said, it would seem that when one of these sentiments is well marked, the inference to be deduced from the resulting peace or disquiet affords a sure means of discerning true revelations from the false; because each of the two contrary spirits acts steadily in a contrary way.

When these conditions as to clearness are fulfilled, there would be a moral certainty if we had to decide only between the good spirit and the diabolic spirit. But there is a third action, that of **the human mind.** For example, it will frequently happen that the revelation comes while we are in a state of deep recollection. This state of union will exhibit the character of the divine influence, namely, peace, which may quite well not be disturbed by the natural activity of our own mind even if it comes to the point of simulating supernatural words. It is not from this source that the feeling of peace proceeds,

* Speaking of intellectual visions of Our Lord: "She was conscious of His being at her right hand, although not in the way we know an ordinary person to be beside us, but in a more sublime manner, which I cannot describe... It brings with it such *graces* and effects as could not come from melancholia nor from the Devil. If they did, the soul would not be so filled with *peace* and a constant desire to please God, with an utter contempt of all that does not lead to Him. Consequently, my friend recognised this to be no work of the evil one, as Our Lord showed her more and more clearly... This favour brings with it an overwhelming sense of self-abasement and *humility;* the *reverse* would be the case did it come from Satan... I believe it to be impossible for the Devil to produce an illusion lasting so long, nor could he benefit the soul so greatly, nor give rise to *such interior peace.* It is not his way, nor, *if he would, could* such an evil creature bring about so much good... The mind's continual keeping in the presence of God and the concentration of its thoughts on Him would so enrage the fiend that, though he might try the experiment once, he would not often repeat it" (*Interior Castle,* Sixth Mansion, ch. viii, 4, 5, 9).

and consequently the peace is not *of itself* sufficient to prove that these words are divine. It only gives a probability to this effect.*

And, further, in practice it may be feared lest the person should be under a delusion with regard to the strength and persistence of the sentiment of tranquil joy that has been experienced, for: 1° Has the examination of his interior state been sufficiently exact and complete? 2° Was there not a secret desire to obtain such a counsel, such a reply from God? What he felt would then be a purely natural joy at seeing his ideas approved.

**52.**—Desiring to punish a presumptuous feeling in **St. Catherine of Bologna** (Poor Clare) at the outset of her religious life, God permitted that she should not detect the diabolic action for some length of time, in spite of the disquiet that accompanied it. Feeling herself favoured with great graces, she had said audaciously to the Devil: "Know that you could send me no temptation without my perceiving it?" After this imprudent challenge she had false apparitions of Our Lord and the Blessed Virgin for five years. They reproached her with a lack of abnegation and obedience to her Superior; but she could not find out what it was that they required of her; then, as she afterwards endured violent temptations against these two virtues, she took the temptations for sins. All this threw her into a state of anguish. At the same time she fell into a dreadful aridity. What saved her from despair was the opening of her conscience to her Superior. God finally enlightened her completely with regard to this temptation (Bolland., March 9, 2nd *Life,* No. 10 and fol.).

**53.**—7° It often happens that a revelation leads to the execution of some bold **enterprise**; the establishing of a new devotion, for instance, the foundation of a religious Congregation or pious Association, the remodelling of the constitutions of another, the correction of the relaxed state of a certain group of persons, the building of a Church, the inauguration of some work for which the available resources are insufficient, the preaching of a more refined spirituality which God is supposed to have reserved for our time (as being less gross, they say, than those that went before, etc.).

In this case it is necessary to see if the work is: (*a*) *good* in itself and in conformity with the spirit of the Church; (*b*) *useful,* and of a utility that explains such an exceptional means as a revelation; (*c*) *opportune,* if it responds to a new need; (*d*) if it injures any similar work which it would be better to support. (For the rest of the practical conduct of the matter, see ch. xxiii.)

**54.**—Amort says that the revelations of women are probably false when they lead to a wish to direct **clergy and princes** and to teach them, speaking with an air of authority. For this is not the part that women should play in the Church—at least, not as a regular practice (*Sommaire des Règles,* § 3, rule 30).

* Suarez: "This sign gives a strong probability, but does not amount to infallibility" (*De Relig.,* Tr. X, Book IX, ch. x, No. 37).

He instances this prudent trait in the Ven. Louis du Pont. He was director to the Ven. Marina de Escobar, and approved of her revelations as a whole, and was afterwards their editor. But he would never believe in those that she often thought she received from her Guardian-Angel, indicating various counsels that she was to transmit to the King regarding the management of his Court (Part I, ch. viii, Rule 24).

**55.**—**Mary of Agreda,** on the contrary, kept up a correspondence with Philip IV of Spain for twenty years. The King divided each sheet of his letters into two columns, and wrote upon the first only. The Sister replied upon the other. M. Germond de Lavigne has published a French translation of forty of these double letters. They are quite commonplace, and consist in general advice that anyone could have given. It is strange, too, that this Sister, who was so in the habit of receiving revelations, had none regarding the King's relaxed morality and his culpable carelessness concerning affairs for which he was responsible. And yet she was in a position to exercise a great influence over her correspondent. Many of the letters amount to nothing more than the vague declaration that she is interested in the preoccupations made known to her by the King; 614 other letters have been published in Spain.

**56.**—8° Have the revelations stood the test of **time** and **scrutiny**?

Without this condition, the favourable judgments that may have been passed upon them are not a sufficient guarantee. Amort thinks that it is only in exceptional cases that a revelation can be regarded as assured until after the death of the person who received it (Part I, ch. iv).

In any case, when the revelations form *a series,* having a fixed object, such as the inauguration of a pilgrimage, we must allow events to unfold themselves and wait to pronounce an opinion until the vision has announced that the series has come to an end.

If during this long period of waiting the revelation withstands all attacks, there is a great probability of its truth.

**57.**—9° If the object of the revelation was to institute a new devotion, have subsequent events clearly shown that God favoured this work in a special manner? For example, has it produced **great** fruits of grace on all sides? Have the Sovereign Pontiffs, the Bishops, favoured its progress? This character is found in a marked degree in the Scapular of Mount Carmel, the devotion to the Sacred Heart and the Miraculous Medal.

### § 4.—Conclusions to Be Drawn From the Preceding Data

**58.**—In enumerating the points upon which it is necessary to inform ourselves, we have seen that a certain number of characters belong peculiarly to true revelations and visions, and others to those that are false.

When we have to prove that the action comes from the Devil, one of these signs alone is so clear at times that there is no room for doubt. But this is not so when it is a case of proving that the action is from God with no admixture of another action; we have seen that *no one character,* **taken alone**, then *leads to certainty.*

Is the problem insoluble, then, when there is no miracle to confirm the revelation? Must we always resign ourselves to possessing a slight probability only? In a word, will the conditions that are regarded as necessary never be sufficient? Here is the reply.

**59.—Principle.** *Given that we desire to judge of the truth of one or more revelations, at least when taken as a whole, we may regard it as very probable, sometimes even as morally certain, that the conditions are* SUFFICIENT, *if those that are commonly regarded as* NECESSARY *are all verified, and in an unmistakable way.*—The assurance is so much the stronger as the characters are more striking.

**60.**—In order to prove this proposition, we can begin by bringing an **argument based on authority**. Gerson, who has made a special study of these questions, formulates the principle under an equivalent form.

"We may," he says, "be mistaken if we consult one sign only or a few; we must group a number of them together (*plura in unum conglobentur*)" (*De probatione spirituum,* Consid. 6). Schram adds: "The more numerous these favourable signs, the greater will our assurance be. From this assemblage (*ex horum signorum collatione*) we shall with prudence deduce, according to the particular case, a more or less strict *certainty* or a strong or medium or weak *probability,* or a favourable *conjecture,* or, on the contrary, an uncertainty which will cause us to suspend our judgment" (Old edition, No. 572; 1848 edition, No. 582).

Amort (Part I, ch. vi, Rule 22) adopts a like attitude.

It may be said that, although the above principle has not been laid down by the majority of writers, the universal practice in all times and in all places has implicitly taken it for granted. We find that all authors, having to discuss the value of a revelation, content themselves with reviewing characters that, taken alone, are not a sufficient proof that the revelation is divine. If, however, the signs are favourable, they consider themselves justified in concluding it to be so, without any other explanation. They therefore admit by implication that these necessary characters are sufficient when they are found together.

**61.—Arguments based on reason.** 1° No other principle except this one has ever been formulated in order to establish the fact that a revelation is very probable or morally certain. If we refuse, then, to accept it, we have to say that the Church should have maintained a strictly reserved attitude regarding numberless revelations that have been made to the saints in the last 2000 years. It would have been a mistake to think it possible ever to depart from this expectant attitude.

2° It has always been admitted as a law of Divine Providence that God never permits evil to have *all* the characters of good. What will be the signs that can warn souls of goodwill? We cannot say beforehand, but they will be there. The wisdom and goodness of God require that this should be so. Therefore, if the examination of a revelation has been conscientious, if the man has done all that he could for his enlightenment, and if God has allowed no signs of falsity to appear, we can conclude from this assemblage of circumstances that God wishes us to regard it as probable, and sometimes even as morally certain.

**62.**—**Objection**. In these researches must one *always* be afraid of having overlooked a circumstance that would have aroused serious doubts?

**63.**—**Reply**. No; not always, for these problems have been put so often that the conditions "commonly received" practically include all that can be said in the matter.

The same objection could be made in all the problems of the moral order: for instance, You have come to regard such a man as honest, thanks to your long relations with him and the general opinion regarding him. Who knows whether you have observed him sufficiently? Or again: The critics admire the high literary excellence of such and such a work; all the rules seem to be in its favour. But perhaps there is one that has been forgotten, and which would be sufficient to change the verdict? And yet in these questions everyone allows that we can *sometimes* arrive at a certainty.

**64.**—The real **drawback** to the above method is that it requires much time and labour. But we must resign ourselves to this. It would certainly be much more convenient to have to verify two or three obvious characters only, furnishing evidence beyond dispute. In the same way, in deciding whether a book is a masterpiece, one would like to be able to settle the matter by putting a few short questions; and so also when forming an opinion concerning a man's honesty. But this ideal cannot be realised in things that relate to the moral order.

**65.**—According to the above pronouncement, a revelation may possess divine characters as a whole without this being so with regard to all the details. In fact, the reasons that prove the worth of the complete revelation are not always sufficient to justify all the elements of which it is composed.

**66.**—Short of positive proof to the contrary, however, the details have the benefit of the verdict pronounced upon the whole. The presumption is in their favour.

**67.**—In order to judge whether **ecstasies** are divine, we shall act upon the same principles as in the case of revelations, after having inquired into the person's character.

The two chief points of evidence are as follows: 1° How has the soul been occupied while thus deprived of the use of the sensible faculties? Was she taken captive by intellectual knowledge of the higher order, carried away by an immense love? 2° What was her degree of virtue before attaining to this state, and what great progress has resulted from it afterwards?

If the replies are favourable, the probabilities are on the side of the divine ecstasy. Neither the Devil nor disease can carry imitation to this point.

As to the physiological effects, no conclusions can be drawn from them, as a rule. The alienation of the sensible faculties can quite well present the same appearances in a divine ecstasy and in its counterfeits.

There may, however, be added certain phenomena that dispose of the hypothesis of disease and reveal a supernatural cause, whether divine or no: levitation, for example.*

**68.**—With certain persons, in very close union with God, the slow study of the various signs has sometimes been aided, or even replaced, by a **supernatural intuition**. This is what is called the *infused* gift of the discernment of spirits; the other is termed *acquired.*

Scaramelli defines this infused gift as "an instinct or a light given by the Holy Spirit to discern correctly, in oneself or in others, the principle from which the soul's interior movements proceed; whether it is good or bad" (*Discern.,* No. 21).

**69.**—In some pious persons' lives we find that they have not only asked God in a general way to **confirm** such and such a project or revelation by a sign; but they themselves fixed the sign, and especially its value as a mark of certainty saying: If such an event takes place, I shall regard it as indicating that God desires such and such a thing. Can we rely on this sign?

We will leave out of the question the exceptional cases where the request is prompted by an inspiration of the Holy Spirit. By this fact in itself we possess the certainty that God will reply by means of the event.

Let us suppose the contrary case. If a true and personal miracle has been asked for and it has taken place, God thus gives His approval.† But more often

* I do not speak of aureoles. For we may ask ourselves whether they have not a natural foundation. In fact, Dr. C. Feré states that he observed the head and hands of two hysterical patients to become luminous, of an orange colour, during their attacks. With the first, the light extended to a distance of seventy centimetres from the head (*Revue de Médecine,* April 10, 1905, Alcan). It is regrettable that no photograph was taken of this phenomenon, which might be disputed on account of its extreme rarity. In such a case we might ask ourselves whether the observations were carried out with all desirable precautions.

In the same way, many saints have emitted agreeable odours during their lifetime or at death. These odours were various; they resembled those of the violet or the rose, orange blossom, cinnamon, musk, benjamin, etc. We can no longer admit that this was a miracle *in itself,* but only in virtue of the circumstances (which should be examined in each concrete case). In fact, doctors have observed, although rarely, a certain number of maladies in which the above-named odours are produced. In diabetic persons, in particular, suffering from acetonemia, we find an odour closely resembling that of a russet apple. In a normal state, the derivatives of alcohol (aldehydes and acetones) resulting from digestion are oxydised; but in certain troubles of the nervous system and of the interior nutrition of the tissues these bodies, perspiration, etc., escape by the breath (see Dr. G. Dumas' article in the *Revue de Paris* of Dec. 1, 1907).

† We may regard as almost miraculous the sign that Rev. Mother Marie de la Providence, foundress of the Helpers of the Holy Souls, asked for; but she only made the request by obedience to her director, F. Aussant, O.P. The circumstances seem to prove that he had received a true revelation. The newly formed community were contemplating leaving a cramped and insanitary dwelling-place and buying a house. The Director said: "Since you have such trust in Providence, pray that God will lead you whither He

He will not hear our request, it being an indiscretion to make it. This was why the Curé of Lourdes did not obtain the sign that he desired. He said to Bernadette: "Ask the Lady, in proof of the holiness of her apparitions, that the wild mountain-rose, now all shrivelled from the winter cold, shall blossom in this month of February." The wild rose did not blossom, but God worked a much more useful miracle: a spring gushed forth.

Blessed Angela of Foligno asked Our Lord, as a proof of the divine nature of His apparitions, to give her a precious stone or to light the taper that she had in her hand. Our Lord refused to give her this miraculous sign: "That which thou askest is a sign which would give unto thee joy only when thou shouldst touch it, but it would not draw thee out of doubt, and in such a sign thou mightest be deceived. But I will give unto thee a sign, better than that thou askest; and this sign shall be continually with thee, inwardly in thy soul, and thou shalt always feel it. Moreover, this shall be the sign: thou shalt ever be fervent in love, and in the love of God, and enlightened by the knowledge of God within thee. And let this be a most certain sign unto thee, that it is I, because none can make this sign, save I alone. And this is the sign that I place inwardly in thy soul, and that is better than the other that thou didst ask. I place in thee a love of Me, by which thy soul will become inebriated, and fervent, and constantly glowing by reason of Me, so that thou wilt desire to suffer tribulations for the love of Me. And if anyone shall say or do unto thee evil, thou wilt take it for a favour, and wilt cry out that than art unworthy of such a favour" (*Visions and Instructions of Blessed Angela of Foligno,* ch. xxix, pp. 104-5).

**70.**—We will now suppose that the event asked as a sign is **not miraculous**. If it takes place, the circumstances accompanying it can, with all probability, show the will of God, provided that all human means of information have previously been resorted to.

This last precaution appears in the life of the Rev. Mother Marie de la Providence. Before taking an important decision she frequently fixed upon a sign and was heard on account of her immense confidence in the divine goodness. But she acted thus after much prayer and having realised the expediency of the decision. The fresh sign that she sought was only the final confirmation of several others, showing that it was time to act. Sometimes this sign was the sudden arrival of the sum of money or other aid that was necessary for the enterprise, and then it was more than a sign—it was also the means of realising the project. If the event asked for does not take place, or if, on the

wills. Then pass down the Rue de Sèvres, the Rue de Vaugirard, and the Rue du Cherche-Midi; but do not trouble to read the notice-boards, because it will be in one of the *cross streets running* into these that you will find the home destined for you. Go straight on, therefore, and when you hear in your heart something that says 'Turn,' you will turn." The Mother carried out the order, and felt the interior movement at the corner of the Rue de la Barouillere. Here she found a house for sale, and heard an interior locution which assured her that this would be the Mother-House. This did not prevent her making use of human methods, such as visiting and inspecting the house (*Notice* on her Life).

contrary, it occurs without having been preceded by the precautions already indicated, we can draw no conclusions. God will often allow the operation of secondary causes, while He stands, as it were, apart. You have had the temerity to impose conditions upon Him without observing the requisite forms; you have limited Him to the summary alternative of a throw of the dice, which you consider as the equivalent of a revelation. He may refrain from intervening.

St. Ignatius, at the beginning of his conversion, exposed himself in this way to making a deplorable choice in a serious matter. He was travelling with a Mussulman who blasphemed against the Blessed Virgin. The saint, who was still full of the maxims of Chivalry, asked himself if he ought not to avenge the honour of the Mother of God with the miscreant's blood. The Devil would naturally encourage St. Ignatius in an illusion which would have resulted in his conviction for homicide. Finally, he decided that, according as his horse should turn to the right or the left at the next crossways, he would attack his enemy or not. God was not obliged to fall in with this contrivance; but as He had designs with regard to St. Ignatius, He protected him. The horse turned to the left, although there were obstacles in the way. Later on, when he was better instructed in the spiritual life, he pointed out less expeditious but surer methods of discovering God's will.

**70** *bis.*—**The gift of tears.** I have spoken elsewhere of tears shed during ecstasy (ch. viii, **10**). Let us now treat a more general question. It is said that a person has the gift of tears when certain pious thoughts cause him to weep often and abundantly, and when this facility can only be attributed to the divine action. This has been the case with many saints.

The restriction that concludes the definition is an important one. Tears may, in fact, come from other causes than the divine action. The Devil can produce them, either to enfeeble the health or to give rise to pride (see **71**, 3°). Much more frequently they may be the result either of an over-sensitive nature, which often happens with women, or persons of a neurotic condition. In the present stage of knowledge it is difficult to define the exact part played by the temperament.

**70** *ter.*—**Line of conduct** to be followed by the director. It would be too difficult for him to seek to distinguish clearly between God's action and that of the Devil. It is sufficient that he should inform himself on two practical points:

1° What is the *immediate origin* of these tears? Are they solely emotions produced by a religious thought: love, joy, sorrow for sins, gratitude, compassion for Our Lord's sufferings, etc.? It is this that gives the value to tears; without this circumstance they would be an unimportant physiological phenomenon.

2° *Are* the tears detrimental to the health?

If the replies to these two questions are favourable, there is a greater or lesser probability that the action is divine; at any rate, there is nothing blameable. The soul, then, will be left in tranquillity, but she should be warned to be on her guard. In the contrary case, he will not go so far as to forbid the tears, for their suppression is not directly in the penitent's power. But he will employ indirect means: (*a*) he will try to direct the thoughts to less moving subjects; (*b*) and develop the conviction that the phenomenon, being physical, has no value.

## EXTRACTS

### How the Devil Sometimes Inclines Us to Certain Virtues. Signs of His Action

**71.**—St. Teresa:

1° "I told you elsewhere how the devil frequently fills our thoughts with great schemes, so that instead of putting our hands to what work we can do to serve our Lord, we may rest satisfied with working to perform impossibilities" (*Interior Castle,* Seventh Mansion, ch. iv, 21).

2° Another "sign of the devil's presence" [is that] "the soul is thrown into a state of disgust, and is troubled... for if it conceives good desires, they are not strong; its humility is fictitious, disturbed and without sweetness" (*Life,* ch. xxv, 17). In short, this action weakens and distresses. The divine action, on the contrary, strengthens and brings peace.

3° "Some persons seem as if they could never stop crying: believing that tears are beneficial, they do not try to check them nor to distract their minds from the subject, but encourage them as much as possible. The devil seizes this opportunity to weaken them so that they become unable to pray or to keep the Rule" (*Interior Castle*, Sixth Mansion, ch. vi, 7).

4° Describing how she at times felt such an extreme horror of her sins as almost led her to despair: "This is but a false humility, and Satan invented it for the purpose of disquieting me and trying whether he could thereby drive my soul to despair... That it is his work is clear from the restlessness and discomfort with which it begins, and the trouble it causes in the soul while it lasts; from the obscurity and distress, the aridity and *indisposition for prayer and for every good work,* which it produces. It seems to stifle the soul and trammel the body, so *as to make them good for nothing.* Now though the soul acknowledges itself to be miserable, and though it is painful to us to see ourselves as we are, and though we have most deep convictions of our own wickedness... yet true humility is not attended with trouble; it does not disturb the soul" (*Life,* ch. xxs, 10, 11).

72.—St. Ignatius:

"As soon as the devil sees us to be humble, he strives to inspire us with a false humility, that is to say, an excessive and vicious humility" (First Letter to Sister Rejadella).

# CHAPTER XXIII

## Revelations and Visions (*continued*)
## Rules of Conduct

### § 1. Seven Rules for the Director

**1.**—*First rule.* To resign himself to a slow progress. We have seen that much time and labour are required before we can pronounce an opinion concerning the truth of revelations. Instead of pressing forward, the director must know how to rest content with provisional judgments. He will have to be on his guard against his own precipitation and that of his penitent. This latter will be questioning him incessantly, and saying: "Tell me whether these extraordinary things really come from God, or if you attribute a part, at any rate, to the imagination," etc. In such cases we may reply: "These delays are inevitable. While the full light is not granted, to give a definite approval to your visions and projects would be an imprudence. It may be your own fault that the light continues insufficient. It is for you, by your prayers and sacrifices, to obtain that some more certain signs be given to us."

Often, too, the director will be urged on to a premature decision by people who are well-intentioned, but who have no idea of the precautions with which we have to surround ourselves. "What is the use," they will say, "of suspending judgment in this fashion? Take the simplest, and usually the safest way, and declare that God is not the author of these extraordinary occurrences." But we should thus be exposing ourselves to illusions. For, as Scaramelli tells us, quite as many err in taking God's favours for diabolic works as by doing the reverse (*Discern.*, No. 213).

**2.**—*Second rule.* **Not** to display **admiration** for these visions, even if they *appear to him to be real.* On the contrary, he will prove that they are less estimable than the mystic union, and particularly than the practice of the virtues. In this way he will be keeping to the truth, and, at the same time, will have the advantage of being protected from endless and insignificant details.

**3.**—*Third rule.* To be **gentle** in his treatment of the person. *If the visions appear to him suspicious,* not to show his distrust harshly. He will only intimidate penitents, which would lead to their hiding important details. While admitting his doubts, he can show a kindness that will set them at their ease. It may not be a person's own fault, if he is himself deceived. St. Teresa and St. John of the Cross both advise this gentleness (see Extracts, No. **39**). Let him strive with prudence, however, to enlighten them with regard to these illusions. This is the way to cure them. But they will be confirmed in them if the visions are rejected without any explanation. They will fancy themselves the victim of prejudice. Knowing that true revelations are accompanied by trials, they will falsely persuade themselves that the trials suffice to prove the truth of their revelations.

To sum up, let the director's language be neither harsh nor ironical.

**4.**—*Fourth rule.* To bear in mind the **end** to which the visions, and especially the revelations, tend. He must exhibit a proportionately stronger **mistrust** if it is a question of a matter having consequences of greater magnitude.

**5.**—**Three cases** may present themselves:

(*a*) This end may be *solely* to augment the love of God, of Our Lord, the Blessed Virgin, and the saints in the seer of the vision. Such an end is good. Nothing then hinders our regarding these visions or even these revelations *provisionally* as divine, and accepting them after an earnest examination; but we must be on our guard, and satisfy ourselves from time to time that this continues to be the sole end.

Thus we need not interfere with a person who, without being very far advanced in other ways, believes himself often to enjoy the intellectual presence of Our Lord; but without revelations.

(*b*) The object may be to *instruct* the person who sees the vision. More precautions are needed here. Such an instruction should be watched (see **24**).

And it is the same if there are predictions. We must have very strong proof of their divine origin to allow of their being communicated to others than the director or Superiors.

(*c*) Finally, the revelation may urge some enterprise.

It is here especially that great caution is necessary. The mere affirmation, even of one who is closely united to God, is never sufficient. We have seen, on the contrary (ch. xxii, **53**), how the matter must be examined by the sober light of reason and submitted to *prudent* and *learned* men. In this way, if the advice received by the revelation is followed, and if, later on, this revelation should be recognised as false, there will be no reason for regretting the work that has been undertaken. All that the revelation will have done will be to have *suggested* an idea; it will have been accepted, as would have been the case if it had come from a person endowed neither with authority nor any special guarantees. It is merely the *occasion* of any decisions that are taken.*

**6.**—As a matter of fact, the Church has not proceeded otherwise in instituting certain **Feasts or devotions** which have had their origin in a revelation. The revelation itself continues on the footing of a pious opinion, having nothing obligatory about it. But its results are of service to souls; this is what the Church looks to.

**7.**—This **reserve on the Church's part** appears in the institution of the Feast of Corpus Christi. Urban IV sets forth the reasons in a special Bull, and it is only at the end that he makes a vague and very brief allusion to the revelations that had asked for the institution of this Feast (see ch. xxii, **24**). They only occur as accessories.

The public cultus rendered to the Sacred Heart was brought about by revelations to St. Margaret Mary. But it contained in itself all that was necessary for approval; so that the revelations merely suggested the idea. They are not even mentioned in the Mass for the Feast.

In 1832 the Miraculous Medal was circulated everywhere, following upon St. Catherine Labouré's visions, but leaving the verdict regarding these visions on one side. It was merely stated that this devotion was good in itself. And it was the same in 1846 with the Scapular of the Passion, due to the revelations made to Sister Andriveau (ch. xxii, **25**). Pius IX approved it at once, without insisting upon any official inquiry into its origin.

When in June, 1899, Leo XIII publicly dedicated the whole world to the Sacred Heart, it was after requests had been addressed to him by Mother Mary of the Divine Heart, Superior of the Order of the Good Shepherd at Oporto. But he would not allow his decision to be based on Mother Mary's revelations. Cardinal Mazzella and the Sacred Congregation of Rites relied solely upon the theological reasons.†

**8.**—Sister Andriveau's life furnishes us with an interesting **confirmation** of the motives by which the Church acts. She had presented another proposition that had not been listened to, although she believed it to be founded upon a revelation like the other (Letter of April 25, 1849). But the idea did not appear to be a wise one. According to the Sister, Our Lord wished Pius IX to establish a Feast of the Passion during Easter-week. There were serious reasons for seeing an illusion here, for it is in the spirit of the Church to preserve the distinctive characters of penance or of joy to certain seasons of the year. At Easter time we

* Speaking of intellectual locutions, St. John of the Cross says: "The real and secure teaching on the subject is, *not to give heed to them,* however plausible they may be, but to be governed in all *by Reason,* and by what the Church has taught and teaches us every day" (*Ascent of Mount Carmel,* Book II, ch. xxx, p. 198).

† Leo XIII said on this occasion that he often received letters of this nature, written, usually, by enthusiasts (*Vie,* by Mgr. de T'Serclaes, Vol. III).

rejoice in the Resurrection; it would have necessitated a sudden return to sentiments of penitence and compassion; and this when we have been devoting to them all Lent and Holy Week. This illusion, moreover, is explained by the special devotion to the Passion that dominated Sister Andriveau's life.

**9.**—This same way of acting on the Church's part shows itself also with regard to certain **pilgrimages** which have for their origin a fact that is regarded as historic; those, for instance, of Lourdes, la Salette, Pontmain, Loreto, or the apparition of St. Michael at Monte Gargano, etc.

In these cases the Pope approves or encourages the pilgrimage, but without guaranteeing the historic fact by his infallibility. Also belief in it is not obligatory. The fact is regarded as resting upon a human testimony having as great a probability as a host of others. Criticism can be applied to it. What the Church gives as the object of the devotion of the pilgrimage is the saint himself, who is honoured there. This homage and these prayers are not exposed to any illusion.

**9** *bis.*—These invariable rules of the Church appear in the question of the pilgrimage to Notre-Dame de **Pellevoisin**, founded in 1876 after a revelation. By a decree of April 4, 1900, the Sacred Congregation of Rites had approved the pictures and statues, but with this noteworthy restriction, that they insisted on an alteration of certain details, which, however, were signified in the vision, and also of the title taken by Our Lady on the occasion. They had acted in the same way with regard to the Scapular and the corresponding Arch confraternity. Many persons concluded from these approbations that Rome recognised the truth of the apparitions whence these devotions proceeded. The diocese of Bourges became the theatre of violent discussions on this subject, and the Archbishop, who was considered overcautious, was attacked. Then, by a decree of September 8, 1904, the Holy Office informed this prelate that the above-named apparitions implied "no approbation, whether direct or indirect, of no matter what apparitions, revelations, graces of healing and other similar facts which might be related concerning the said Scapular or the said pious confraternity."

**10.**—Many **religious congregations** have been founded after revelations. But these have been only an accessory, a spur to undertake a work that, considered on its own merits, was judged worthy of performance, and which responded to some fresh need.

**11.**—**St. Teresa**, under circumstances of grave importance, wished that her advisers should not be influenced in their decision by her revelations. It was a question of an important stroke of policy, of breaking with her old Convent at Avila and founding a rival House in the same town, where the reform would be inaugurated. The saint wished to have the advice of a learned Dominican, Fr. Ybanez. He began by thinking this idea a piece of folly, but soon became its supporter. "She made known to him the motives that had decided her to engage in this enterprise; without speaking, however, of the order that she had received from Our Lord, or of her revelations or other supernatural favours" (*Histoire*, by a Carmelite of Caen, Vol. I, ch. xii).

A modern hagiographer is astonished that in this conjuncture, and for a considerable time, Fr. Balthasar Alvarez, the saint's Confessor, should not have ventured to take any decision either on one side or the other. But besides the fact that his Superior prevented him at that time from compromising himself in a very critical enterprise, he had not made up his mind about all the graces of which his penitent spoke to him. Now that St. Teresa is canonised, it is easy to pronounce against those who thwarted her. But she was then only Sister Teresa. They felt misgivings concerning the extraordinary way in which she was led, and with the more reason that in Spain they were suffering, according to La Fuente's expression, "from an epidemic of pious fanatics, the victims of hallucinations" (*facsimile* of the manuscript of the *Life*, ch. xxiii). What should we do nowadays under similar circumstances?

**12.**—As a contrast with the prudence displayed by St. Teresa and her directors, let us recall the deplorable facility with which **Mme. Guyon** believed in her own revelations and in her divine mission, as she claimed it to be; a facility imitated by Fr. La Combe and Fénelon, who became her directors, or rather her associates and her disciples. The consequences that resulted were disastrous to them.

Fr. La Combe, who had impregnated himself with Molinos' ideas in Rome, could not fail to be filled with Mme. Guyon's quietist notions. They both believed themselves to be called to an extraordinary apostolate (1681). "I felt my soul sealed (she says) for a mission similar to that of the Apostles when they received the Holy Ghost" (*Vie*, by herself, Vol. II, p. 16). For seven years they set themselves to preach quietism on all sides, in Switzerland, at Turin, at Grenoble (where Mme. Guyon tried in vain to win over the Carthusians, who, however, consented to hear her), at Verceil, Marseilles, and Paris. Their connection ceased in 1688 when, by the King's orders, Fr. La Combe was confined in the Bastille and underwent a series of trials that drove him out of his mind.

About a year after this separation, Mme. Guyon obtained a rapid ascendency over Fénelon's mind.* She made his acquaintance at the house of Mme. de Béthune, on the outskirts of Versailles. "I was suddenly, with extreme force and sweetness, interested [in] him. It seemed to me Our Lord *united him to me very intimately,* more so than anyone else. My consent was asked for. I gave it. Then it appeared to me that, as it were, a *spiritual filiation* took place between him

* M. Maurice Masson, Professor at the Fribourg University, has published a very instructive book: *Fénelon et Mme. Guyon* (Paris, Hachette, 1907). It is a collection of letters, covering a period of about a year (1689), at the beginning of the relations between the two correspondents. I summarise here the psychological study which this book furnishes; the facts are typical, and may serve for our instruction.

and me" (*Autobiography of Mme. Guyon,* Vol. II, Part III, p. 218, translated by T. T. Allen). *

**12** *bis.*—It is surprising to see such an intelligent man as Fénelon allow himself to be so quickly won over and directed by a woman of no culture. Thirty-seven years of age, and director of the fashionable world, he was in no wise led by an earthly passion, for the lady had reached forty and was disfigured by the smallpox. But he felt a curiosity, a need to meet a saint who should reveal to him the secrets of Heaven, and he ignored the precautions that should be taken with prophetesses who wish to take possession of an influential person. "He saw her," said Saint-Simon, "their minds were pleasing one to the other and their sublimity mingled. I do not know whether they clearly understood one another, but they persuaded themselves that this was so." At the outset Fénelon's letters show that he is suspicious, and still regards himself as a spiritual master who is to command; but at the close he is a submissive disciple. He follows the counsels of the seer of visions, repeating after her: It is necessary to become a little child (that is to say, *her* obedient child), to be guided by the "not seeing" and the "not knowing." He accepts, for the future, the subordinate part that Mme. Guyon had ordained for him after one of her revelations: "*You shall be my tongue,* you shall speak my very language, and together we shall accomplish all justice." The most absolute obedience is imposed upon him: "Your littleness must extend itself to the point of *believing* and practising what God *causes to be said* to you by me" (*Letter* 108). "Acquiesce by *littleness* in that which I say to you, even if you should not yet know that I speak the truth to you" (*Letter* 75). Fénelon submitted to this oracle who declares herself infallible: "I am persuaded that God admonishes me by you, and gives me by you my daily bread. It is a state of complete *infancy*" (*Letter* 93). He puts his resolutions into bad verse:

> "I have a taste for *infancy*:
> With my coral content,
> Weakness and *obedience*
> Of me a little child have made.
> Oh! Doctors, let me live
> Far from you, *from self afar;*
> Leave me, for I will follow
> The *blind law* of infancy" (p. 354).†

The lady makes this clever man share her belief in her revelations the more easily because she brings the most seductive promises. She assures him that a

* See all the details of these fantasies in Maurice Masson's book, p. 4 and following.

† J'ai le goût de *l'enfance*
De mon hochet content
La faiblesse et *l 'obeissance*
De moi font un petit enfant.
Docteurs, laissez-moi vivre
Loin de vous, *loin do moi;*
Laissez-moi, car je veux suivre
De l'enfance *l'aveugle loi.*

great providential mission awaits him. Fénelon will be "the general" of a great army of mystics, soldiers of St. Michael, or "Michelins," who will renew the world and establish the reign of true prayer.* God promised him, as He did Abraham, that he should be the father of a great people: "God's designs upon you are great; you are the bright and shining lamp that will give light to the Church." As for Mme. Guyon, she is to content herself, as she says, with remaining in the shade, with being "the eternal victim, burning before God"!

For some time success seemed to confirm these fine predictions. Mme. de Maintenon and a number of great ladies, notably the three duchesses, Colbert's daughters, doted on the doctrine of the *Moyen Court,* and Fénelon, the fashionable director, was admitted to expound these subtle novelties to the ladies of Saint-Cyr. This *elite* founded *"la Petite Église."* Twenty-two years later (1711) hope rose to the point of exaltation. The prophetess had already announced that a child would aid in the triumph, and then she further explained that the Duke of Burgundy was referred to; he would become the chief of the Michelins. And so, when the grand-dauphin died, believers were persuaded that the throne was assured to Fénelon's pupil and that he would become his Richelieu. But the prince died a year later, and fortune returned no more to the Archbishop of Cambrai. Notwithstanding these successive deceptions, he never seems to have cured himself of his ingenuous hopes. This talented man, then, spent a great part of his activity in what was pure loss.

From this saddening story of the power of a woman, "half saint, half lunatic," we may derive a lesson for those who think that they can yield themselves up blindly to a visionary, and allow themselves to be guided by his or her revelations.

**13.—The pretensions** *of certain seers of visions.* They often decline to admit the need of any proofs other than their own personal conviction or the tone of piety prevailing in their revelations. At times even, in despair of otherwise vanquishing our blindness, as they call it, they bring us some fresh revelation that threatens us with the divine anger. But this one is no more proven than those that went before.

Finding myself exposed one day to this class of menace, I quietly replied: "Such words are a sign that your revelations are not from Heaven. The spirit who speaks to you does not know my interior dispositions. He is not aware that I *sincerely* wish to obey God, and that if I am exacting with regard to proofs it is *from a sense of duty,* in order to avoid illusions. God cannot threaten a man who acts from such motives; He ought to do so, on the contrary, if I committed

* Mme. Guyon had decided the offices of this order. Besides the general, there would be two assistants, a secretary, an almoner, a novice master, a *jailer,* a *street porter,* a *flower-woman,* a portress, a female sacristan, a superintendent of recreations, and other officers, male and female, of less importance. Amidst these fantasies Mme. Guyon retained sufficient practical sense to marry her daughter, aged thirteen, into the world of duchesses.

the imprudence of believing you on your word alone. And, further, it is you that He should blame, for if I am without proofs, it is because you do not furnish me with that of sanctity."

The spirit responsible for the revelation (if there was one) felt that he had been unskilful. For in the next communication he took my side, declared that I was more than right, and that I was indeed a saint. He promised to supply, but *at a later date,* proofs that would be *irresistible.* I am still awaiting them; and yet the seer has left this world!

When a seer wishes to be believed on his bare word, we can generally get rid of him by saying: "You assure me that God speaks by your mouth. I have no right to believe you unless you prove it. What sign do you bring?" In his ingenuousness he has not expected this question, and retires abashed.

**14.—Another example.** I have heard of three persons living in our own time who have seen visions and who, each in her own Convent, had succeeded in getting her so-called revelations accepted without attempting to bring any valid proofs. People were simple enough to consult them about everything; so that they had practically taken over the management of their respective Houses. And thence arose disorders and indiscretions.

How ignorant one must be of true mysticism to be willing to consent to this form of government *by oracles* who tolerate no objections to their pronouncements!

**15.**—*Fifth rule:* to strive after **supernatural aims.** Let the director be occupied in working for his penitent's sanctification. Let him always come back to this question: What profit have you derived from the words that you think you have heard?

Even when he has not made up his mind regarding the nature of the revelations, he will thus, at least, have attained a very practical and important end; and in this way he remains on solid ground.

Seers of spurious visions are often not at all in sympathy with this kind of advice. They even end by going in search of another director, who shall be more credulous and less concerned about their sanctity. So much the better! We shall be spared much waste of time.

**16.**—*Sixth rule:* to avoid certain **dangers.** *The first* is that of allowing **oneself to be dominated** by another person. Let the director be on his guard against certain prophetesses who, dreaming of some great enterprise and seeing their own powerlessness, form the idea of **entering into partnership with their director.** They tell him that Heaven has chosen him; which is very flattering. They skilfully reserve the divine communications to themselves, as more in keeping, so they say, with the obscurity in which a woman should remain enshrouded; the priest will have the publicity of the exterior work, all the heavier tasks. In reality, they leave the priest the inferior position; *he has only to obey.* The visionary herself prefers to command, while protesting how greatly it distresses her to do so, and explaining that it is not to her, but to God, that one is subject.* And, further, she often ends by compromising the priest in this way.

The suspicious thing here is not the fact that use is made of another person's prayers and actions; for many of the saints have felt the need of such a co-operation. It is the spirit of domination, the director being reduced to a state of servitude; his being asked to abdicate his reason in order to bow down before the authoritative revelations of another person, and this sometimes an ignorant one.

**17.**—*Second danger.* He must also beware lest the seer carry him away into sentimentality, into **romance**. There are persons who are tormented with the need of affection. Finding no outlet in the natural order, or not allowing themselves to seek for it there, they turn instinctively to the supernatural side. They dream of I know not what "unions of souls," declaring them to be inspired by God, while really they are merely ridiculous and *lead to nothing.* They claim to draw two souls mutually to the summits of divine love. But the end is often a human love; or, rather, from the beginning it was this earthly, violent, and blind tendency that sought so skilfully to satisfy itself. It concealed itself behind a mask; it was not recognisable. Let us mistrust all sentimentality, no matter what its pretext.

St. Bonaventure describes in very forcible language the danger of familiarities that had their rise in "charity and devotion" (*De profectu religiosorum,* Book II, ch. v; quoted also by Scaramelli, *Discernment,* No. 248). See also Blessed Angela of Foligno, ch. lxiv.

**17** *bis.*—*Seventh rule.* To pray much and to make the person directed pray, in order to obtain the necessary illumination. God cannot fail to reveal the true way to those who ask it of Him humbly. If, on the contrary, we rely only on our natural prudence, we expose ourselves to being punished for our self-sufficiency.

### § 2. Seven Rules for Those Who Believe Themselves to Receive Revelations and Visions

**18.**—In order to discern *the source* of these revelations, see the preceding chapter. Here are some other practical rules:

* I have seen several examples of attempts of this nature. One of these persons assured me that I had a magnificent mission. Providence would take me to Jerusalem, and there (with her aid, be it well understood) I was to bring the Jews throughout the world back to the one true religion. What an attractive offer! To be charged with the task of renewing the world and putting an end to all the conflicts of anti-semiticism! Only I had to resign myself for a long time to receive the divine commands solely through this new Egeria. In fact, I was to *begin by obeying,* and let myself be led like a child; then later on, much later on, I was to receive my reward. It was a fool's bargain.

Another that I was told of, had invented a "maternity of souls," which permitted her to busy herself in all the trifling affairs of those whom she described as her children. See above (12), the similar case of Mme. Guyon.

**19.**—*First rule.* Submit everything to a good **director** (see Ch. xxvi). St. Ignatius compares Satan to a seducer who wishes to keep his advances secret, and who loses courage if they are known (*Rules for the discernment of spirits,* 1, 13). See also St. John of the Cross, on the necessity of overcoming a reluctance to disclose the state of the conscience (*Ascent of Mount Carmel,* Book II, ch. xxii).

St. Teresa, however, gives a direction allowing greater latitude in a case where it is a question of intellectual visions and not of revelations; and when, further, this way has been examined and approved, and nothing new occurs. "It would be as well at first to tell your case, under the seal of confession, to an extremely learned priest... or to some highly spiritual person... When you have conferred with these persons, be at peace; trouble yourself no more about the matter, for sometimes... the demon gives rise to such immoderate scruples, that the soul cannot be satisfied with consulting her confessor only once on the subject" (*Interior Castle,* Sixth Mansion, ch. viii, 10, 11).

Eleven years before, in the Book of her *Life,* the saint would seem to give a contrary direction. But the contradiction is merely an apparent one. For it was then a question of interior locutions, that is to say, of revelations; and it was the time when, far from approving her new way, the learned were nearly all in accord in condemning it. "One of my confessors," says St. Teresa, "to whom I went in the beginning, advised me once, now that my spiritual state was known to be the work of God, to keep silence, and not speak of these things to anyone, on the ground that it was safer to keep these graces secret." Our Lord told the saint that she "had been ill-advised by that confessor," and that by acting thus she "might at any time fall into delusions" (*Life,* ch. xxvi, 5). See ch. xxvi, on directors.

**20.**—*Second rule.* To **mistrust** revelations, in general, and to remember that this way is very subject to illusions of the imagination or of the Devil. Even if the vision appears to be divine, to mistrust the *interpretation* that is given; to fear lest personal ideas should have *mingled* with it (see St. John of the Cross, *Ascent of Mount Carmel,* Book II, the end of ch. xxix).

**21.**—An **example** of wise distrust. Blessed Margaret of Ravenna and her companion, Blessed Gentilis (sixteenth century), had numerous revelations; but they protested that they attached no importance to them, and that credence must only be given to such things in them as were already known by means of the Church's teachings (for the first, see Bolland., January 23, first *Life,* No. 9; for the second, January 28, 1st *Life,* No. 16). And yet the Holy Spirit's action showed itself in them by predictions that were fulfilled, and by miracles.

**22.**—*Third rule.* **Not to ask or desire** this kind of grace,* and still for this reason, that it is very conducive to illusions. "No soul who does not deal with them [interior locutions] as with an enemy," says St. John of the Cross, "can possibly escape delusions in a greater or less degree in many of them" (*Ascent of Mount Carmel*, Book II, ch. xxx, p. 198).

**23.**—Some over-enthusiastic persons forget this rule when they are acquainted with an ecstatic (see ch. xxii, **31**) or anyone who is by way of receiving extraordinary lights at times. They are not satisfied with asking the assistance of their prayers, or with appealing to their human wisdom and experience, so as to obtain their advice. What they ask for are real revelations: "When you are in an ecstasy, inquire as to what will occur in this circumstance, or what decision I ought to come to." These **consultations** are **imprudent**. They expose the asker to erroneous replies, due to the imagination of the ecstatic.

Let us be content to express a desire to be enlightened from Heaven, and by the means that God selects. God alone can judge if a revelation is useful; if it is His good pleasure, He will make it. And, again, it must be accepted only at our own risk. The confidence placed in it may be greater if the seer has given many proofs that he is inspired by God.

It was in this way that numerous persons were able to make prudent inquiries of the Cure d'Ars. Long experience showed that his replies could be trusted. And then he was not asked bluntly for revelations, but for *direction,* which might be human to an extent that is hard to define.

It was thus also that in the seventeenth century St. John Eudes, Fr. de Condren, M. Olier, and the founders of Saint-Sulpice, sought after interviews with Marie Rousseau, a very holy woman, the widow of a Paris wine-merchant. "Although this poor woman," says M. Olier, "is of lowly birth, she is nevertheless the light and the councillor of the most illustrious Parisians by birth, and the most exalted in graces and virtues" (*Vie de M. Olier,* by M. Faillon, Vol. I, 4th ed., Part I, Book VIII, No. 17, p. 340). "I shall not describe the effect of her words... When she is consulted, she replies in the simplest manner without explaining things, or enlarging on the exterior reasons which might serve to persuade people. She says simply: God wills that one should act in such a way. She has, sometimes, given advice contrary to that of the most enlightened persons, without being able to furnish any other explanation of the reasons of her replies, and *experience* has always shown that, after considering

* Spiritualists have a diametrically opposite practice. If they invoke the souls of the dead, it is in order to ask them for *information* or advice. However, their curiosity is rarely satisfied. The replies generally teach nothing that was not already known, or they make statements of unverifiable facts. Often, again, when it is a question of difficult problems in science or philosophy, they are vague or contradictory. The spirits (if so be that the medium alone is not responsible) have convenient ways of escape; when they confine themselves to stating that these mysteries surpass our human understanding, for example. This is a poor result.

the matter well at their leisure, these persons found themselves obliged to return to her way of thinking" (*ibid.*, Book VIII, note 10, p. 369).

This last sentence shows that they tested Marie Rousseau's sayings instead of believing in them blindly; and, consequently, that they placed confidence in her only by degrees. M. Olier's biographer proves this, moreover, by facts (*ibid.*, Book X, No. 3, p. 438). Marie Rousseau herself was very reserved. Knowing prophetically that a group of priests were destined to found the work of the Great Seminaries and to reform the parish of Saint-Sulpice, she refused to associate herself with this enterprise for the space of ten years, although God urged it on her. Her resistance persisted until her director, Fr. Armand, S.J., made her give her consent in writing (*ibid.*, Book VII, No. 22, p. 302).

**24.**—*Fourth rule.* In the beginning, at any rate, gently to do our utmost to **repel the revelations** and to turn the thoughts away from them. (As to visions without revelations, see **5**.) I say "gently"; for we must not go the lengths of causing a loss of the soul's peace and disturbing our prayer. It we cannot do more, we should keep this rule by inclining always in this direction.

I also say: "in the beginning, at any rate" (see an extract from St. Teresa, **36**, 1°); that is to say, as long as a prudent and learned director has not decided that a certain reliance may be placed in them. And it has been explained above (**5**) that he can show this confidence provisionally, without much delay, if these extraordinary facts aim *solely* at inciting the soul to the love of God, to mortification, and the other virtues. He will proceed more slowly if there are any instructions, predictions, and especially works that are difficult of achievement.

If prophetic visions occur from time to time, he may cease to repel them when it has been proved that they come exactly true and are free from other disadvantages. He must continue to be on his guard, however. Illusions are easy.

Even with these restrictions, the preceding rule may seem severe. It is, however, strongly enjoined by several saints, such as St. Ignatius (Bolland., July 31, Prelimin., No. 614), St. Philip Neri (Bolland., May 26, 2nd *Life,* No. 375), St. John of the Cross (*Ascent of Mount Carmel,* Book II, chs. xi, xvi, xvii, xxiv), St. Teresa (see Extracts), and St. Alphonsus Liguori (*Homo. apost.,* Appendix I, No. 23). The principal reason is that which is predominant in the whole matter: the danger of illusion. "The devil," says St. John of the Cross, "greatly rejoices when a soul seeks after revelations and *is ready to accept them;* for such conduct furnishes him with many opportunities of insinuating delusions and derogating from faith as much as he possibly can; for such a soul becomes rough and rude, and falls frequently into many temptations and unseemly habits" (*Ascent of Mount Carmel,* Book II, ch. xi, p. 95).

The saint adds two other reasons: the first, which, in reality, derives its value from the one that went before, is that "we are thereby delivered from the risk and labour of discerning between good and bad visions," which "is rather waste of time, an occasion of many imperfections and delay on the spiritual road" (*ibid.*, ch. xvii, 127.) The contrary method "is not the way to direct a soul in matters which are of real importance, nor to relieve it of the vexation of trifles which are involved in particular apprehensions and perceptions..." (*ibid.*).

The other reason applies to communications that are not purely intellectual, because "they are hindrances in the way of the spirit if they are not rejected; for the soul rests upon them, and does not regard the invisible" (*ibid.*, ch. xi, p. 92).*

St. John of the Cross is doubly severe when it is a question of visions or locutions affecting the bodily senses. "We must fly from them," he says, "without examining whether they be good or evil" (*ibid.*, Book II, ch. xi, p. 89).

When we strive in this way to repel a revelation, all that is implied is that we are not certain of its truth; we do not declare it to be false, or even partly so, and consequently there is no need to distress ourselves and to think that we have merited an illusion as a chastisement from Heaven. We must not take such a gloomy view of the situation. It merely resolves itself into a prudent precaution, without prejudging the rights and wrongs of the question.

**25.—First objection**. If the revelation comes from God, He will be angry if we repulse it. It is a want of respect.

**26.—Reply**. St. Philip Neri and St. John of the Cross affirm the contrary. This conduct is inspired, not by contempt, but by prudence (*ibid.*, ch. xi, regarding exterior visions). And, more than that, this refusal is a source of graces: "When the soul is resigned and not attached to such visions, the devil retires, seeing that he cannot injure us then; and, on the other hand, God *multiplies His graces* in the humble and detached soul, placing it over many things... The soul that is faithful amid these visitations God will not leave, till He shall raise it up, step by step, to the Divine union and transformation" (*ibid.*, pp. 93-4).

* "The soul can never attain to the height of the Divine union, so far as it is possible in this life, through the medium of any forms or figures... In the high estate of the union of love, God does not communicate Himself to the soul under the disguise of imaginary visions, similitudes or figures, neither is there place for such, but mouth to mouth [as to Moses]; that is, it is in the pure and naked Essence of God, which is as it were the mouth of God in love, that He communicates Himself to the pure and naked essence of the soul, through the will which is the mouth of the soul in the love of God.

"The soul, therefore, that will ascend to this perfect union with God, must be careful not to lean upon imaginary visions, forms, figures, and *particular intelligible objects*; yea, rather they are an obstacle in the way, and to be *guarded against and rejected*' (*ibid.*, ch. xvi, pp. 117, 118). "The objects of sense and the knowledge which results from them are the occupations of a child. That soul which ever clings to these, and which never detaches itself from them, will never cease to be a child... relying in the outward veil of the senses which is childish, it will never attain to the Substance of the Spirit... These things the soul must not regard; yea rather it must renounce them wholly, having its eyes fixed on that spiritual good alone which they effect... and we shall [in this way] also *pass by* that which He too would have passed by, if we could without it have received the blessings He intends to confer, namely the usage and appliance of sense" (*ibid.*, ch. xvii, pp. 126-128).

**27.**—**Second objection**. If we reject a vision, we deprive ourselves of the interior fruit that it should have brought us; and, further, when it orders us to perform an exterior work, the good that ought to result does not take place.

**28.**—**Reply**. As to the interior fruit, St. John of the Cross assures us that it will never be lost, for "all corporeal visions, emotions of the senses—the same is true of all other interior communications—if from God, effect their chief object at the moment of their presence, before the soul has time to deliberate whether it shall entertain or reject them." It is the same even with exterior visions, if they are from God. "Even if the soul wills it not, they produce their effects, chiefly and specially in the soul rather than in the body" (*ibid.*, p. 91, and chs. xvi, xvii).

If the object of the revelation is to instruct us, God has many other means by which to make His thoughts known to us.

**29.**—With regard to **external actions** that we are advised to perform by a revelation, when we say that the revelation itself is to be rejected, it is not suggested that these projects must be given up. It is enough that there should be other good reasons for undertaking them.

**30.**—There are merely **two precautions** to be taken: (*a*) to let ourselves be decided, at any rate chiefly, by the value of these reasons (**4**), and entirely so, if the revelation does not seem very certain; (*b*) to imitate St. Teresa (**37**), in not bringing forward the revelation as a reason to other people. In this way we shall avoid the temptation to take a tone of command, as though we were speaking in God's name. And, further, we thus augment our chances of success. For our hearers would be afraid lest we should first ask for their belief in the vision; they would very wisely require us to begin by justifying this claim, which is almost always impossible. Finally, the person who has had the vision will avoid a great source of trouble, namely, bitter or violent discussions, with those who dispute his inspiration; and objectors will always be numerous.

**31.**—Let us also note that the rejection of visions should not apply to those that are **deific** (*indeiques*), those of the Divinity. For these are merely a kind of mystic union. It is a question of *ex-deific* visions, those of created things. St. John of the Cross, although so rigid with regard to visions, notes this exception expressly: "This knowledge relates directly unto God, in the deepest sense of some of His Attributes... this becomes pure contemplation... It is only a soul in union with God that is capable of this profound, loving knowledge, for *it is itself that union*... it is God Himself Who is then felt and tasted... I do not say that the soul is to conduct itself negatively here, as in the case of the other apprehensions; because the Divine touches are a part of the Union to which I would direct the soul, and for attaining unto which I teach it to withdraw and detach itself from all besides" (*Ascent of Mount Carmel*, ch. xxvi, pp. 176-8).

**32.**—*Fifth rule.* If we believe a corporeal apparition of Our Lord or of the saints to be due to the Devil, not to go to the length of insulting it or **treating it with contempt**, any more than we should do towards a sacred picture that had been painted by a scoundrel (see Scaramelli, Tr. 4, Nos. 56, 68; and St. Teresa, *Book of Foundations,* ch. viii; *Interior Castle,* Sixth Mansion, ch. ix).

St. Philip Neri, however, held and followed the contrary doctrine (Bolland., May 26, 2nd *Life,* No. 374 and fol.). But on one of the two occasions when he ordered the person who saw the vision to spit in the apparition's face, he seems to have known by a revelation that it was a diabolic apparition. So the case is no longer the same as where there is a doubt.

**33.**—What is to be done **if the director orders** these contemptuous gestures? Here there are two opinions. According to the first, you must obey. For we should always do so where there is no sin; which is the case here, since in the intention of the seer of the vision the mark of contempt is not addressed to the saint or his likeness, but to the Devil, who is suspected of being present. St. Teresa submitted to her director in this way, and Our Lord said to her that she "did well to obey" (*Life,* ch. xxix, 7). The Blessed Virgin used the same language to Blessed Francis Ferrari, a disciple of St. Philip Neri.

In spite of the encouragement that she had received from Heaven, St. Teresa, at the end of her life, adopted the contrary opinion, namely, that it is permissible, and more seemly not to obey. "My advice is, if you are given such an order, that, humbly alleging the reasons I have set before you, you should not carry it out" (*Interior Castle,* Sixth Mansion, ch. ix, 11).

**34.**—*Sixth rule.* If, in spite of yourself, you have visions, to be chiefly concerned in making them serve your **progress** *in virtue.* For if they come from God you will thus have attained the sole end that He desired. In the contrary case they cannot harm you.

St. Teresa says: "The good or the evil is not in the vision, but in him to whom it is given, and who does not profit by it in humility; for if he is humble, the vision, even if it came from Satan, *can do him no harm,* and if he is not humble it *will do him no good,* even if it comes from God" (*Book of Foundations,* ch. viii, p. 56).

The Ven. Louis du Pont relates that when Fr. Jean del Campo was in the noviciate, he received visions. One day, in anguish, he asked himself if he was not the sport of his own imagination. He then heard Our Saviour address these words to him: "When thou art hungry, if thou art given a branch of a tree loaded with fruit, what dost thou do?" "I eat the fruit and cast the branch away," he replied. "Even so," Our Saviour continued, "act in the same way with regard to the visions. Eat the fruits thereof, humility, patience, and the other virtues; and whatever the vision may be, be not troubled any more" (*Menology* of Aug. 11).

**35.**—*Seventh rule.* Display much calmness and **patience** if Superiors will not permit the execution of enterprises that you think have been inspired by Heaven or revealed. He who, in the face of opposition, is angry or discouraged, shows that he has small confidence in God's power and little conformity to His will; he will do well to attribute his want of success to these bad dispositions.

If God wills the project to succeed, He will be able to make the obstacles vanish suddenly at the time that He has appointed. This time is perhaps far distant; your scheme may even be realised only by your successors. What matter, provided that the good is achieved? You will, at least, have contributed to if by your efforts and your prayers, and your intentions will receive an eternal reward.

## EXTRACTS

### § 1. How We Should Do Our Utmost to Ward Off Revelations, at Any Rate, at the Outset

**36.**—St. Teresa: "There is need for caution... until it is certain from what spirit these things proceed. I maintain that, *in the beginning*, it is always *wiser to resist* these communications; if they come from God this is the best way to receive more of them, for they increase when discouraged" (*Interior Castle*, Sixth Mansion, ch. iii, 3).

2° "Nor have I heard where the earthly paradise is... as for asking His Majesty to reveal anything to me, that is what I have never done. In that case I should immediately think I was *imagining* things, and that I must be in a delusion of Satan" (Relation VIII, addressed to Fr. Rodrigo Alvarez, *Life*, pp. 463-4).

Regarding apparitions of our Lord: "I most earnestly advise you, when you hear of God bestowing these graces on others, that you never *pray* nor *desire* to be led by this way yourself, though it may appear to you to be very good; indeed it ought to be highly esteemed and reverenced, yet no one should seek to go by it for several reasons" (*Interior Castle*, Sixth Mansion, ch. ix, 13).

Two notable reasons given by the saint are as follows:

(*a*) "Such a one is certain to be deceived, or at least is in great danger of delusion, for a door is thus left open to the devil" (*ibid.*, 14).

(*b*) "When people strongly desire a thing, the imagination makes them *fancy they see or hear it*, just as when one's mind is set on a subject all day, one dreams of it at night" (*ibid.*, 15). And then to meet an objection, the saint adds: "Our Lord [by depriving us of these apparitions] does not deprive us of anything that can gain us more merit, for this rests in our own hands; thus there are many saints who never knew what it was to receive such favours, while others, who received them, are not saints at all" (*ibid.*, 19).

### § 2. How We Should Regulate Our Actions Not by Revelations, but by Sound Reasons

**37.**—St. Teresa:

1° Speaking of herself: "She *never undertook anything* merely because it came to her in prayer; on the contrary, when her confessors bade her do the reverse, she *did so* without being the least troubled thereat, and she always told them everything" (Relation VII, addressed to Fr. Rodrigo Alvarez, *Life*, p. 450).

2° Letter to Fr. Suarez, Provincial of the Society of Jesus, who had reproached the saint with having counselled a grave step on the strength of a revelation (February, 1578).

"Even supposing I myself had this revelation, which you call 'dreaming,' I could not be so imprudent as to wish him to make so important a change, *through any such cause*... for, thank God, I have many good friends who teach me what credit is to be given to such revelations" (St. Teresa's *Letters*, p. 115, 1902 ed.).

3° Speaking of locutions: "If they treat of some weighty matter in which we are called upon to act, or if they concern any third person, we should consult some confessor who is both *learned* and a servant of God before attempting or thinking of acting on them, although we may *feel more and more convinced of their truth and of their divine origin*... Our Lord will reassure our confessor, whom, when He so chooses, He will inspire with faith that these locutions are from the Holy Ghost. Unless He does so, we are under no further obligations in the matter. It would, I think, be very dangerous to act against our confessor's advice, and to prefer our own opinions in such a matter. Therefore, my sisters, I *admonish you*, in the name of our Lord, never to do anything of the sort" (*Interior Castle*, Sixth Mansion, ch. iii, 18).

4° "When [however] they only *console* you, or *warn you of your faults, it matters not from whom they come*, or *whether they are only fancy*" (*ibid.*, 4).

**38.**—Fr. Balthasar Alvarez, speaking of consolations: "It is not by these motions and consolations that a soul must regulate and direct herself, but by the doctrine of the Church... it would be a mistake to regard them as an *infallible proof* that God *wills this*, and does *not will that*... They should consult enlightened directors, and confine themselves to what they prescribe" (*Life* by du Pont. Vol. II, ch. xxxiii, § 3).

### § 3. That the Director Should Deal Gently With Those Who Believe Themselves to Have Revelations

**39.**—St. John of the Cross:

"But remember, though I say that these communications are to be set aside... it is not right for spiritual directors to show themselves severe in the matter, nor betray any *contempt* or *aversion*; lest their penitents should shrink within themselves, and be afraid to reveal their condition, and so fall into many inconveniences... rather, they must treat them with *gentleness* and *calmness*, encouraging their penitents, and giving them every opportunity to explain them. And, if it be necessary, they must enjoin upon them this manifestation, for at times, everything is necessary in the difficulty which penitents experience when they have to reveal their state" (*Ascent of Mount Carmel*, Book II, ch. xxii, p. 166).

**40.**—St. Teresa:

1° On the fear of being deceived in our prayer: "And certainly the affliction to be borne is great, and caution is necessary, particularly in the case of women—for our weakness is great—and *much evil may be the result* of telling them very distinctly that the devil is busy with them... Women should be directed with much discretion; their directors should encourage them, and bide the time when our Lord will help them" (*Life*, ch. xxiii, 14, 15).

2° On supernatural locutions. "At times, indeed, very often this [voice] may be nothing but a fancy, especially with persons of a lively imagination or who are afflicted with melancholy to any marked extent. I think no attention should be paid to such people when they say they see, hear, or learn anything supernaturally. *Do not disturb their minds* by telling them it comes from the devil, but *listen* to them as if they were sick persons. Let the Prioress or confessor to whom they tell their story, bid them *think no more of it*, for such matters do not conduce to the service of God: the devil has deceived many Christians thus, although perhaps it is not so in their case; therefore they *need not trouble* themselves about it. Thus we must accommodate ourselves to their humour; if we tell them their fancies *proceed from melancholia* [their nervous temperament, we should say], they *will never believe us*, but will persist in maintaining they have seen and heard these things, for so it seems to them. The truth is, care should be taken to keep such people from too much prayer, and to persuade them, as far as possible, to take no notice of their fancies" (*Interior Castle*, Sixth Mansion, ch. iii, 2, 3).

# PART V

## The Trials That Are Sent to Comtemplative Souls

## CHAPTER XXIV

### § 1. General Survey

**1.**—With the exception of St. John of the Cross' first *night* of the soul and certain obsessions, none of the trials of which I am about to speak are confined to those who are in the mystic way or destined to it; but with those persons they sometimes reach an **exceptional degree** of acuteness. That is what obliges me to speak of them instead of referring my readers to the ascetic writers.

**2.**—It is a **fact proved by experience** that God always sends trials to the souls that are aiming at perfection, and this sometimes during their entire lives. All the biographies of the saints witness to this; the masters of the spiritual life agree in proving it.

This general law applies more particularly to souls that are much given to prayer, especially if they are favoured with mystic graces.

And as persons who are leading the purely contemplative life are not obliged to undergo the arduous labours which the active life entails, God sends them interior crosses by way of compensation. And then they also feel these crosses more keenly, being more thrown back on themselves. "If ever," says Scaramelli, "my book should fall into the hands of one who aspires after infused contemplation from vain motives, I beg him to reflect upon the severe sufferings to which you must pass, and upon the wine-press of those innumerable sorrows under which you must grown before attaining to it. It may be that all frivolous desire for these favours will then die out of his heart" (Tr. 5, No. 41). This thought of the trials to be endured is useful for the purifying of any overly-human element that may be mingled in the desire for divine favours.

**3.**—God has five principal motives for thus sending us numerous crosses.

1° He wishes to make us expiate our sins and infidelities and to punish our negligences. Just as it is necessary to be purified by the sufferings of Purgatory in order to enter Heaven, so, in order to attain to a state of familiarity with God here below, and to enjoy His favours, we must pass through the fire of tribulation. If we would enter into Christ's kingdom, we must first drink of His chalice (Matt. xx, 22). We shall therefore enter into God's designs by accepting our sufferings in the spirit of penitence.

2° In order to attain to the mystic union, it is necessary to detach ourselves from all that is not God. Now, every trial, borne with resignation, serves to weaken some natural attachment; attachment to health, to the joys of the senses, to the world's esteem, and fortune, to certain friendships or occupations, to tranquillity, etc. God only gives us extraordinary favours to aid us to attain to an extraordinary renunciation.

3° Even if we are not called to the mystic life, God wishes to sanctify us, whether by making us practise the virtues—especially patience and trust, the humble recognition of our weakness and dependence—or by combating our defects; or, again, by giving us an antidote against pride. For the avoidance of this sin, it is desirable that great graces should be compensated for by great humiliations. Hence St. Paul's words: "And lest the greatness of the revelations should exalt me, there was given me... an angel of Satan to buffet me" (2 Cor. xii, 7).

In order to co-operate in the divine action, (*a*) we should, at least, attain to a state of simple resignation and calm; and (*b*) make an effort to rise to a higher degree, that of joyful resignation. We must feed on the thought that suffering is a good gift of God, we must offer Him our grateful thanks for it, and never cease to stimulate the love of the Cross within our hearts. Let us not forget that each act of resignation obtains for us a new degree of sanctifying grace and happiness in Heaven. The total at the close of each day may be enormous. We thus amass incalculable riches. The way of consolation would perhaps have been much less advantageous to us. God takes care of our true interests, those of eternity. The day will come when we esteem no others than these.

Unhappily, trials have a quite opposite effect upon souls that are lacking in generosity. When confronted with suffering, Satan tempts them and leads them to impatience, to discouragement, to a want of trust in the divine goodness. Crosses for them are no longer a help and a remedy, but an obstacle and a danger.

4° God thus provides our directors and ourselves with the means of *judging* as to our *degree of virtue*. For instance our way of bearing interior sorrows shows whether our love for God is sincere, if we are striving for His glory and our eternal happiness, and not in order to obtain temporal favours or immediate spiritual rewards. While we are enjoying consolations, we cannot know certainly what is the motive that impels us to self-sacrifice, nor its degree of solidity. It is quite otherwise when we persevere in prayer, notwithstanding tedium, or continue to mortify ourselves, regardless of the sadness into which we are thrown by the divine abandonment.

5° We can also derive other fruits from our trials; making use of them, for example, in order to obtain a more vivid conception of the pains of Hell or of Purgatory. I can scarcely endure this illness, or that arid prayer; what, then, would it be if I were condemned to it for all eternity, or even for a hundred years?

**4.**—With certain persons, their trials continue without intermission for a considerable time. But more usually life is a succession of **alternations** of joys and sufferings. In the same way, in nature, sunshiny days alternate with rain and storm; springtime, with winter.

The soul's alternations have also been compared to those that we find in seaports. Sometimes there is a low tide, nothing to be seen but muddy and repulsive sands and boats lying motionless upon their sides. The high tide returns, bringing with it gaiety and movement.

**5.—The error made by beginners.** They often imagine that after their first sacrifice, after their entry into the novitiate, for example, their path will be strewn with roses. No more temptations! they think, since they have left the world that offered them daily occasions of temptation. But they have not succeeded in flying from themselves, or from their passions, which get incensed at the prospect of the sacrifices that are to be made. In the same way, no more difficulties, nor bitterness in prayer! because they have given themselves wholly to God, and in fairness, so they think, He should reward them immediately. But they forget that the real payment will take place in the next life. Here on earth we must acquire merit, and consequently we must suffer.

Let us face things as they really are when we enter God's service. Let us not imagine that our existence will be passed in the delights of divine love and without the onslaughts of temptation. It is only in the poet's legends that we find the Golden Age, when it is always spring. The Holy Spirit tells us to the contrary. "The life of man upon earth is a warfare" (Job vii, 1). If we form a false conception of life, the cold reality will drive us to the opposite extreme. Disillusioned of an impossible ideal, we shall fall into disgust and discouragement.

Thus, instead of wondering because we find ourselves confronted with trials, let us rather be astonished if we are without them.

**6.**—There is **another error**, a frequent one amongst those whose sufferings are very prolonged and without any admixture of spiritual consolations. They are hunted by the false idea that such trials cannot overtake souls that are pleasing in God's sight. They conclude that God is angry with them on account of their sins, and that their crosses are purely chastisement. And as, on the other hand, they vainly examine themselves in order to find what important reformation they could make in their lives, they sink into discouragement and hopelessness. Of what use is it, they say, to go on imposing upon myself so many sacrifices, since God makes it clear that I am not one of those to whom

He wills to show His friendship? Let me be satisfied with ensuring my salvation by a merely average virtue.

It is necessary to repeat to these persons that they are mistaken in thus seeing nothing but a punishment in their tribulations. We have said that God may have quite other motives for crucifying us; and when it is a question of the soul with a sincere desire for sanctification, it is probable that these motives are the principal ones. When we are not suffering, this truth will seem trite to us; but as soon as we are in affliction the mind becomes clouded.*

God said to Blessed Varani: "While I was afflicting thee, I showed thee more love than in the moments when I clasped thee lovingly in My paternal arms" (*Vie*, ch. vi).

**7.**—When spiritual writers attribute trials to the **Devil**, they do not mean to say that he is always the sole, or even the principal, cause. They merely claim that he has a share in them, as in all that is harmful to us; but at times he merely reinforces our natural tendencies.

It follows, therefore, that the remedies to be applied need not always be exclusively supernatural. We must see whether there are no human means with which we can combine them.

Thus certain interior sufferings, such as scruples or other ideas that take firm hold of us, may become very strong without any supernatural action on the Devil's part. It suffices that he should operate in a slight degree upon a *temperament* predisposed to fear, sadness, or uneasiness. It would be well then to resort to some way of calming and diverting the mind. When these states continue for any length of time, a physician who has studied them should be consulted.

**8.**—Trials may be divided into **four groups**, which we will examine in succession.

(*a*) Sickness; (*b*) persecutions from our fellow-men; (*c*) interior sufferings; (*d*) visible assaults of demons—that is to say, possession and obsession.

I will subdivide the interior sufferings into fourteen kinds: 1° temptations; 2° an apparent inability to do right; 3° the searching spectacle of our sins and

* Speaking of the soul that "God leads... along the highest road of obscure contemplation and aridity," St. John of the Cross says: "Some confessors and spiritual directors, because they have no perception or experience of these ways, are a hindrance and an evil, rather than a help to such souls... It is a hard and miserable thing for souls when they cannot comprehend their own state, nor meet with anyone who can... And in this darkness and affliction, temptation and distress, some will be sure to tell him, like the comforters of Job (iv, 7), that his sufferings are the effects of melancholy, or disordered health, or of natural temperament, or it may be *of some secret sin* for which God has abandoned him. Yea, they will decide that *he is, or that he has been, exceedingly wicked,* seeing that he is thus afflicted. Some also will say that he *is going backwards,* because he finds no consolation or pleasure, as before, in the things of God. Thus they multiply the sorrows of this poor soul, for his greatest trial is the knowledge of his own misery... his grief and misery are infinitely increased and rendered more bitter than death... They do not understand that... they ought to leave him alone, comforting him, indeed, and encouraging him to bear his trials patiently" (*Ascent of Mount Carmel*, Prologue, pp. 4—6).

natural defects; 4° the lively sense of moral isolation in which we live amongst those who are round about us, but who have other ideas and other tastes; 5° inability to do good to others; 6° tedium and sadness; 7° doubt with regards to graces received; 8° an ardent thirst after God; 9° the poignant impression of being forsaken of God; 10° or even of being hated by Him and being destined to perdition; 11° involuntary sentiments of hatred for God and the impulse to blasphemy; 12° distractions; 13° scruples; 14° aridity.*

**9.—Different paths.** Scaramelli bids us remark that these different pains are not all imposed upon every soul given to prayer, nor is it with the same rigour nor with the same duration (Tr. 5, No. 5). I will also add: nor at the same periods of the spiritual life. For some examples drawn from the lives of the saints, see § 3 and § 8. From these we deduced the irresistible conclusion that certain writers have been mistaken in supposing that the great crises of interior sufferings always occur before the stages of ecstasy, or a long time before death.

**10.**—The various interior sufferings just enumerated (**8**) are also included under the name of spiritual **desolation**; the distaste or difficulty experienced in attaining to a loving union with God, in praying or in practising the virtues, being thus described. Spiritual consolation, on the contrary, is the taste and facility for the same acts.

**Consolation** of the higher order (also called substantial) is that affecting the higher faculties, the intelligence, and the will. This is what is asked for in the prayer *En ego,* usually recited after communion. "With the most fervent desire of my soul, I pray and beseech Thee, that Thou wouldst impress upon my heart *lively sentiments of faith, hope, and charity,* with true repentance for my sins and a firm desire of amendment."

The great danger attending desolation is that it leads to discouragement. Everything seems difficult, and we grow disgusted with the strife, the result of which appears doubtful. In consolation, on the other hand, says St. Ignatius, God makes everything look easy to us (*Rules for the Discernment of Spirits,* I, No. 2). This discouragement is strengthened by two prejudices that I have explained elsewhere (**6, 22**).

**11.**—The expression **sensible consolation** and its synonyms, *sensible devotion, sensible tastes,* do not signify a consolation that is felt, for all consolation is more or less felt. It refers to a consolation of the lower order, that which has its beginning in the senses or sensible faculties. We must not despise it on this account, because it leads us finally to good.†

* What grief for a director to see the souls in whom he is interested suffering thus, and so often to feel himself powerless to save them from their pain!

† St. Alphonsus Liguori says: "Spiritual consolations are gifts which are much more precious than all the riches and honours of this world. And if the sensibility itself is aroused, this completes our devotion, for then our whole being is united to God and tastes God. The sensibility is to be dreaded when it takes us away from God, but it is very well ordered when it unites us to God" (*Love for Jesus Christ,* ch. xvii. See also Suarez, *De Orat.,* Book II, ch. xviii, n. 1, 4).

When the saints lift up their hearts to God by contemplating the beauties of nature, this was sensible devotion. The Church also makes use of sensible means when she captivates our ears with her chants, or our eyes with noble architecture, pictures, statues, or the pomp of her ceremonial. Protestantism was wrong in rejecting nearly all of these aids, wishing to address itself to man's highest faculties only. His whole nature should be appealed to.

St. John of the Cross is not speaking to all Christians indiscriminately when he counsels the rejection of sensible consolations. He is only concerned with those who are beginning to enjoy the mystic state, and he simply asks them to give the preference when it encounters any obstacle and devotions of the sensible order and the pleasure felt in them.* When no such conflict occurs, we must resort to all the means that can lead us towards God.

12.—**Sensible desolation** is the opposite of sensible consolation. It may co-exist with consolation of a higher kind, just as in the natural order we can feel sufferings in the body and joy in the soul at one and the same time.

13.—With regards to interior griefs, there is a supernatural means by which they may often be diminished or made to disappear, namely, **asking** God to **deliver us** from them. In many cases this request takes effect, too, in a natural manner. For it implies a desire, a will. Now, whether in physical or moral maladies, a vigorous desire for a cure and a firm conviction that it is at hand, contribute largely and naturally to its realisation or some approach to it. Doctors are acquainted with this treatment by persuasion, and many make a successful use of it; this is what is called of the *moral treatment,* or psychotherapeutics.

If, on the contrary, we keep our souls in the condition of soft wax, indifferent to all events, no appeal is made to our latent vital forces, and the sick person goes on getting worse rather than better. Stagnant water in a boat becomes more and more filled with unhealthy germs; while running waters have the secret of throwing off their impurities on their banks or in the atmosphere.

It therefore follows that the director wishing to cure his penitent will do well to arouse in him a similar exercise of will and hope. He is doubtless right to

* Here is one passage out of many: "He [Satan] labours, therefore when the soul has entered into those deep solitudes, wherein the delicate unctions of the Holy Ghost are infused... to throw over the soul's detachment and estrangement from the world, certain cataracts of *knowledge,* and the darkness of *sensible sweetness, sometimes good,* the more to entice the soul, and to draw it back to the way of sense. He would have it fix its eyes on this, and make use of it with the view of drawing near to God, relying on this kind of knowledge and *sensible sweetness"* (*Living Flame,* Stanza III, § 14, p. 284). "He deludes the soul and feeds the senses... The soul... accepts the suggestions of the evil one gladly, for it thinks that God has come to visit it; consequently it omits to enter into the inner chamber of the Bridegroom, and stands at the door to see what is passing without in the *sensitive part* of itself' (*ibid.*, p. 285). "O souls, *now that God shows you mercies so great,* leading you into solitude and recollection, *withdrawing you from the labours of sense,* do not you return thereto. If your own exertions were *once* profitable, enabling you to deny the world and your own selves when you were but *beginners,* cease from them now when *God* of his mercy *has begun to work in you,* for now they will only embarrass you" (*ibid.*, § 15, p. 286).

show patience when called upon to listen incessantly to the same complaints; but this compassion is not enough. He must know how the penitent can react, and must instigate this reaction.

When we have thus done our utmost to deliver ourselves of these interior trials, it remains only to resign ourselves generously to the divine will. Like Noe in the ark, we find ourselves assailed by the impetuous fury of the deluge. What are we to do? Should we torment ourselves by seeking a thousand new means of repelling the waters? It would be a useless labour. God alone can make the floods to cease. Let us continue praying in our securely closed ark, patiently awaiting the apparition of the olive branch.

### § 2. Of the Two First Kinds of Trials

**14.**—*First kind.* **Sickness** and physical infirmities. It would take too long to enumerate all those that the saints have had to bear. God sends these crosses less frequently to those whom He destines to great exterior labours.

It is for the doctors to decide whether the cause is natural or not. They will form an opinion of greater or lesser probability, according to the circumstances regarded as a whole. With respect to the Devil's intervention, a middle course should be followed: not to show oneself too ready or too reluctant to admit of it. Thanks to the progress of medical science, our conclusions may in these days, and in certain obscure cases, be very different from those of two or three centuries ago. Specialists have discovered and classified many maladies which formerly were not properly understood.

And, further, from the point of view of the sanctification of the servants of God, it matters little whether a malady has one cause or another. The same virtues can be exercised in either case.

**15.**—*Second kind:* **persecutions**, contradictions, injustices, calumnies; and we will add, the deprivation of other blessings than those of the body; the loss of relations and friends, a fortune, etc.

The saints' lives are full of the conflicts that they had to sustain in order that the projects which God had inspired them to undertake might be brought to a successful issue. What a blending of failures and successes, especially at the outset! Calumny has not spared the greatest among them: St. Francis of Assisi (accused by Brother Elias), Blessed Henry Suso, St. Anthony of Padua, Saint Philip Neri, St. Teresa, St. Francis Regis. Some, like St. Ignatius and St. John of the Cross, has been cast into prison. The latter was confined by his rivals for nine months in a dark cell, subsisting upon bread and water and a few small fishes.

St. Thomas Aquinas was still in the novitiate when his relations, wishing to hinder his vocation, caused him to be seized and confined for two years in the castle of Rocca-Sicca. Blessed Crescenita Hoss, a Franciscan nun of the seventeenth century in Bavaria, entered the novitiate at the age of twenty-one, and was subjected to the most cruel trials for the space of four years: false accusations, unheard-of persecutions on the part of the Superior who was afterwards deposed, the condemnation of her spiritual path by unskilled theologians, material molestations of demons, scruples and aridities (*Vie*, by Fr. Jeiler, Book I, chs. vi, vii). This period began and ended abruptly with a vision.

**16.**—There is nothing to which we are more strongly attached by our natural instincts than the **desire to be esteemed,** the care for our honour and reputation. Bodily mortifications are disagreeable enough to human nature, but contempt and injustice are still more painful to us and kindle our indignation. God's usual way of rooting up this instinctive pride, and showing us how little humility we possess, is to reduce us by contempt, faultfinding, and insults (see St. Teresa, *Interior Castle*, Sixth Mansion, ch. i; and Scaramelli, Tr. 5, No. 136).

These contradictions do not proceed only from the hatred of the wicked who wish to put themselves in opposition to the divine operations. The prejudices of good people often produce the same results. St. Peter of Alcantara, wishing to console St. Teresa from the opposition of virtuous people, told her that what he had suffered from most in this world were trials of this nature (*Life,* ch. xxx, 6).

When we feel that we possess certain talents, we are displeased and surprised that Providence does not give us the opportunity of utilising them. We wish to exercise influence by this means; and we cannot therefore understand why God allows us to be treated as incompetent persons and kept in situations that a child could fill.

In giving us talents that are not recognised, God has not, however, performed a useless work. They serve solely to make us produce acts of resignation, and consequently to acquire much merit.

Our Lord at Nazareth has given us an example of this obscure life, voluntarily accepted. He was endowed with all the qualities adapted for with the world. He preferred to plane wood, to sleep, to draw water, the meanest of occupations, in which any child would have been successful.

**16** *bis.*—Another trial, which at first sight would seem a slight one, but which becomes very wearing, is to live with an **irritable person**, one who finds fault with everything, never speaks a pleasant word, when we have exerted ourselves to please him. These difficult characters often have the reputation of being very amiable abroad, because they are full of attention for those whom they need, or those would not allow themselves to be bullied.

These nervous natures may be likened to torpedoes, on account of the charges that they let fly at those who approach them. It is impossible to arrange any matter with them, clearly and quietly. Above all, let no one try to excuse himself when they accuse him of anything, and prove to them that they are mistaken. If the orders received from them have been wrongly carried out, do not show them that they were vague or contradictory. The volcano will then be in full eruption. Such minds will never be in the wrong; they alone are endowed with sound judgement.

This behaviour shows, in itself, a grave lack of charity. In a community, characters of this nature make life very difficult for others, and are sometimes the cause of the abandonment of vocations. It is a grave responsibility.

I have seen very religious persons try to cure themselves of this irritability. They have been unable to succeed. They were doubtless lacking in the prolonged effort and the humility that were necessary. I think that a miracle is required to overcome these temperaments. St. Francis of Sales, who was naturally rather fiery, ended by being a model of gentleness. But he was a saint.

### § 3. Interior Sufferings. The Twelve First Kinds

**17.**—*First kind* (**8**): **temptations**. We find them in great violence in the saints' lives. St. Mary of Egypt, speaking to a solitary who came to visit her, told him that she had endured seventeen years of terrible conflicts with the Devil in her desert, but that for the last thirty years she had enjoyed profound peace.

Eight years before his death, St. Alphonsus Liguori, then eighty-three years of age, was assailed by scruples and temptations against the faith, with such violence that when he called upon God for succour his cries were heard all over the house.

St. Benedict Joseph Labre and St. Frances of Rome suffered great temptations against chastity. With St. Alphonsus Rodriguez (see § 8) these lasted seven years; and with Ven. Caesar de Bus twenty-five years.

St. Teresa and St. Rose of Lima, on the other hand, had no temptations of this nature. It was the same with St. Mary Magdalene of Pazzi, with the exception of nine days only (*Vie*, ch. xxvi), and with St. Margaret Mary, with the exception of some hours (*Vie*, by herself, Paray edition, Vol. I, p. 136). "The Devil," she says, "made me feel a ravenous hunger, and then he pictured to me everything that is capable of gratifying the palate, and this during the hours of my spiritual exercises, which was a strange torment to me. In this hunger lasted until I entered the Refectory to take my refection, and there I at once felt such a strong aversion that I had to do great violence to myself to force myself to take some little nourishment. And as soon as I had quitted the table my hunger began again, more violently than before" (*ibid.*, Vol. I, p. 410).

**18.**—In thus permitting temptations, God's **object** is not only to compel us to bear the Cross, but to make us progress in the various virtues and to establish us in them. In fact, the ordinary way of attaining this end is not to receive them suddenly from Heaven, but to produce many other acts; for we do this every time we fight against the contrary vices;* We also feel a greater detestation for the vices which cause such a painful conflict.

* St. Ignatius says, "God renders us stronger in the virtues against which we have been most violently tempted" (*Bartoli*, Book IV, ch. xvi). "If you will consider your part attentively, you will find that when you fall into most offences and were least desirous of serving Our Lord, you were neither *tempted* so

In order to perfect us in the virtue of faith, God will therefore permit us to be tempted by distressing doubts. For hope, we shall have to endure without flinching attacks of discouragement, to repel the thought that we cannot arrive at anything like perfection, and that the graces accorded to so many others are not made for us. Charity will be developed by spurning the attractions of created things and sentiments of rebellion against God, who seems dead to our prayers, and it will be the same with regard to the various moral virtues.

Temptations, then, to the saints, have been a powerful means of sanctification. They have also been the means by which God has made this holiness manifest.

**19.**—Before being tempted regarding any virtue, many souls suffer from the **illusion** that they possess it. They take the desire to possess the virtue, for the virtue itself. But when the temptation comes to shake them, they pass from an excess of confidence to an excess of mistrust. There is no further illusion, but only discouragement in finding themselves so frail.

True humility preserves a middle course. It does not hide our weakness from us, but at the same time it shows us God's power, to Whom we ascribe the victory. It takes advantage of the unpleasing spectacle unfolded before our eyes to imbue us with self-contempt.

**20.**—Some souls, after entering violent temptations, find their **minds so obscured** that they are no longer sure, so they say, that they have not yielded in certain particulars. In this there is a torture to them. As to scruples, we shall see that we ought not to dwell on such thoughts.

These persons confuse two very different things: the sin, which is an evil, and the temptation, which is a source of merit; or again, the pleasure which attracts us in spite of ourselves, and the consent which depends upon us, and which we have refused to give.

An early writer explains this illusion of the memory as follows: During the temptation the attraction to the evil has arrested our attention forcibly, and so we retain a lively recollection of it. But our acts of faith, hope, and charity, however real, have remained almost imperceptible; we have forgotten them, and the Devil has succeeded in strengthening the oblivion. Just in the same way, says this writer, "in a picture, certain persons can be hidden from view without

much nor *troubled* so much by the serpent, which always tries to causes pain. It is that then your manner of life pleased him, and that he now cannot endure what he sees in you" (*Letter VIII,* to Sister Rejadella).

Father Surin: "Who seeing plate rubbed with ashes, would not say that it was done on purpose to dirty it more? Yet it is but in order to make it more clean. Who would not think that a soul filled with abominable thoughts... must resemble the evil spirit who inspires them? Yet this very thing serves to purify her" (*Fondements de la vie spirituelle,* Book IV, ch. viii. English: *Foundations of the Spiritual Life,* translated by E. B. Pusey, Book IV, ch. viii, p. 168).

St. Teresa: "And as my experience here is large, I will say by way of caution to you, my father, do not think —though it may seem so—that a virtue is acquired when we have not tested it by its opposing vice" (*Life,* ch. xxxi, 21).

hiding the others...; if, in a picture of angels intermingled with devils, all the angels had been hidden, one would only see the devils" (*Vie* of Mother Catherine of St. Augustine, Nun Hospitaller of Quebec, 1671, Book III, ch. xii by Fr. Ragueaneau).

He adds another comparison. If a little wine of a deep hue is added to a glass of water, the water seems wholly changed into wine; the water is no longer visible. In the same way the soul remembers the temptation, but it no longer perceives all the resistance that accompanied it.

**21.**—*Second kind of suffering:* the **apparent powerlessness** for virtue. The soul here is no longer a vessel battling with the storms of temptation; but she feels herself paralysed by a dead calm. She had formed great projects for God's service, some of them chimerical, it may be; and now she has neither the opportunity nor the strength to perform anything. And she groans over this inertia.

There is often a great deal of illusion in this trial. People forget that much merit can be acquired daily by practising the ordinary virtues of their state and occupation. But the imagination does not find these merits sufficiently brilliant; it dreams of virtues of a more dazzling kind.

But (they object) if I had these virtues, I should feel them; now I feel, on the contrary, nothing but repugnance, and I see thousands of little faults that my good resolutions have not been able to prevent. I am very far, therefore, from sanctity, and I have good grounds for being afflicted.

I replied that people often possess virtues without feeling them. We are ignorant of our own degree of faith, hope, and even of charity.* We can only form an opinion at the moment when occasions for exercising these virtues offer themselves. An electric machine may be charged, but the electric field is not visible. But if we approach it, we get proofs of its existence by a sharp shock. Repugnances prove nothing. St. Paul himself groaned over the many inward obstacles to that good which he desired (Rom. vii. 18).

**22.**—The foregoing remarks apply particularly to **divine love**.

Many souls given to prayer are needlessly disquieted; they imagine that they do not love God because they have no vivid sentiment of this love. Others, on the contrary, think that they love much because they recite numerous prayers, that their hearts are inflamed, or that they suffer from a holy intoxication. Both of these views are exaggerated. The love of God should not be estimated by the

* We read in the *Life* of St. Jane Frances de Chantal, by the Rev. Mother de Chaugy: "She was wont to say, weeping most bitterly, that she saw herself without faith, hope, or charity... Our blessed Father said to her, 'It is a real insensibility which deprives you of the enjoyment of all the virtues, which you, nevertheless, possess, and in good measure too; but you do not enjoy them; you are like a child under a guardian who deprives him of the use of his property, so that while everything is his, yet he has no control, and does not seem to possess anything... It is not the will of God that you should have the management of your faith, your hope, your charity, and your other virtues, except in order to live interiorly, and to use them in occasions of pure necessity' " (Part III, ch. xvi, p. 174).

sentiments of this love that we believe ourselves to feel, and still less by the sentiment's reaction upon the body. This last effect, which is purely physiological, depends largely upon the temperament, and has no moral value in itself. These effects are good, but in no way necessary to the love of God.

We love God strongly by the sole fact that we will to love Him, and that this will translates itself into acts when the occasion offers. And this is so even although we fancy ourselves to be as cold as ice. We also love when we suffer at the thought that we do not love. Hence the words that Pascal puts into Our Lord's mouth: "Be comforted: thou wouldst not seek Me if thou hadst not found Me."

When we merely look at red-hot iron, without touching it, we imagine it to be less hot, less active than the fire made of straw which crackles noisily. It is nothing of the kind. We are inclined to think that great heat must manifest itself by tongues of flame and noise.

When you make a study of souls and of their degree of devotion, we find an evident proof of the foregoing principle. The devout woman piously recites a number of prayers and piles of devotion upon devotion. But do not ask her to give herself to apostolic work, or to submit to reprimand; her sloth or her pride would rebel. For her, love of God consists solely in effusions of the heart. It is a very imperfect love.

On the other hand, here is a person who suffers incessantly, but who is always smiling, sincerely glad to be able to bear her Cross, delighted to be put out of her way, reprimanded, to have her tastes thwarted, to be misunderstood, and so on. Is not her love evidently much greater than the other? And yet there are no affective fireworks here, but a calm, energetic, and constant will.

Even with human love, we judge things the same way. It is true that we do not despise effusions of tenderness; but we feel something more to be required, and that they do not constitute the essential part of friendship. They merely supplement. So too, the blossoms of the orange tree complete the tree and make it more beautiful. But the tree can exist without them, and render service by its shade.

**22** *bis.*—The prejudice that I have been combating often arises in connection with **Holy Communion**. We wish to experience emotions; and if we remain cold, we think of relinquishing this holy Sacrament as being useless. This is a great error. The essential fruit of Communion is an increase of sanctifying grace. But this is invisible. The acquisition of such a blessing is more than sufficient motive for communicating.

**23.**—*Third kind of suffering:* the penetrating spectacle of **our sins**, of our spiritual poverty, and even of our **natural defects**. When we see other people's faults, we are sometimes annoyed and disgusted. We cannot resist blaming them loudly, declaring that their conduct is either odious or absurd. With ourselves we are much more indulgent. When the divine light is very vivid, however, we can no longer try to deceive ourselves. Such or such an act in our lives astounds us, so great is the malice or the folly that we see in it. If memories of this nature are intense and frequent, it is a true torment, a slight image of one of those that overwhelm the lost; their life lies open to them like some vast picture; they see the disorder of all their actions, and the spectacle is a source of horror to them, just as an artist is horrified at the sight of a work in which every principle of art is violated. This disgust is accompanied by a sentiment of confusion; we shall all experience it at the hour of judgement.

When the soul is really humble, the spectacle is at once a suffering and a joy: suffering from the point of view of nature; but supernatural joy to know oneself as one is, to estimate oneself according to righteousness, and conformably with God's estimate of us; it is joy also thus to find a remedy available against pride. The remedy is bitter, but we prove how powerful it is.

**24.**—*Fourth kind of suffering:* the vivid and painful feeling of our **moral isolation** amongst those round about us, whose ideas and tastes are different from our own.* When you are dominated by any idea or project whatever, when you are endeavouring to walk in a difficult path, such as that of the extraordinary graces, you are possessed by a strong desire to find souls who will take an interest in even the smallest of your confidences, or who, at the very least, understand what it is that you are undergoing. This desire pursues you in even the most engrossing occupations. It is one of the forms of the need for friendship.

Now, it is rarely that mystic souls meet with this warm affection and real comprehension of their state. They even encounter an unreasoning opposition, beating faintly against a world of ideas absolutely different from their own; it is a source of suffering to find oneself a stranger to others, and unlike persons who are excellent in other ways.

God wills to be these souls' only good, their one friend. It would seem that such a noble prospect would be very easy of acceptance, but in practise we succeed only by dint of conflicts and tears; and we strive with all our skill to escape the prison-cell in which God has confined us. Nature has a horror of this isolation.

If, then, you find interest taken in other people's pious ideas, while yours are considered ridiculous and tiresome, accept the fact cheerfully and do not persist. And act in the same way if your state of soul fails to be understood; be very brief speaking of it, for the result will be no better for heaping explanation on explanation; you will only seem importunate; and what will be gained?

**25.**—*Fifth kind of suffering:* **inability to do good for others.** A zealous soul forms projects for her neighbour's good; she wishes to convert one, to teach the

* "My soul," says St. Catherine of Genoa, "is as it were besieged in such a manner that all spiritual or bodily refreshments are gradually cut off; and when they have been cut off, the soul, although it knows well how it could have been fed and comforted by them, looks at them with feelings of hatred and abhorrence" (*Treatise on Purgatory,* ch. xvii).

secrets of the spiritual life to another, to organise some useful work, etc. God sometimes permits such a one to go on wrestling with material impossibilities for years together, or to be unable to make her intentions understood by those upon whom she depends. She remains condemned to inaction while feeling herself, or believing herself to be, full of resources. And hence a continual suffering.

**26.**—*Sixth kind of suffering:* **tedium and sadness.**

This sadness is very often not produced by any unpleasant incident; it is then **physical**, in its source, at any rate, and is due to the influence exercised upon our nerves and moods by various causes. Some are interior, such as an indisposition, the derangement of the stomach, biliousness, fatigue, and overwork; the others exterior: the action of the atmosphere, cold, rain, or storms. Spleen is more frequent in countries where the sky is more overcast. This is the influence that we wish to express what we described the grey sky by saying that the weather is dull.

The sadness which is physical in origin can often be cured by medical treatment or by occupations which distract the attention from it. It becomes stronger if the person gives way to it by dwelling upon it incessantly. If the state is intense, a doctor should be consulted (see 7).

The Devil can also act on the body, producing the same results as the causes referred to above, and the man is then sad without knowing why.

**27.**—At other times the tedium and sadness have **moral causes**; for instance, a solitary life, want of employment, differences of opinion with those around us, loss of affection, uncongenial occupations, being disenchanted of one of our cherished dreams.

If we feel tedium in prayer, it is usually because we require a variety in our acts. Thus we prefer even a commonplace walk to inaction, or we stand watching the passers-by. The objects that we then perceive are perhaps devoid of all interest, but, at any rate, they change from moment to moment; this satisfies us, for want of something better (see ch. ii, **21**).

**27** *bis.*—In the case of souls that are very zealous after perfection, sadness often results from their not progressing as fast as they desire. Let us arm ourselves with patience in the face of these over-eager desires. It is no small merit to know how to bear with them. It is good to have a high ideal, but on condition that we do not lose peace of mind if it is far from being realised, which is usually the case.

This sadness results from a false conception of perfection. We regard it as a fixed and well-defined goal to which we must attain under pain of having lost our time, and not as an endless road along which we continue to advance.* By

* The early writers often employ this expression, *"perfect souls,"* which suggests the idea of a completed work. By saying, as does St. J. B. de la Salle (ch. ii, 25), the *"more advanced souls,"* the fact that they are still on the way, is better expressed. And further, this title of "perfect" is so laudatory, that no

the sole fact that you daily produce a series of acts of love for God and abnegation, you increase in sanctifying grace, you add thousands of merits to those that you already possessed; you are not stationary in perfection, as you suggest (see 3).

**28.**—I have referred elsewhere (ch. xv, 13) to the sadness which seems causeless, in which is due to God's giving us a distaste for all created things.

There is another, which is highly supernatural, in which consists in participating in an incomprehensible manner in the bitterness of **Our Blessed Lord's Agony,** and does not even hinder the soul's close union with God. There is a summit of the soul, as it were, which remains above the flood of bitterness. The suffering is terrible, but the soul loves it.

Blessed Margaret Mary speaks of the state (vision of 1673). "On every Thursday night," Our Blessed Lord said to her, "I will make thee participate in that mortal sadness which it was My will to suffer in the Garden of Olives. By this sadness thou wilt be reduced, without knowing how, to an agony more insupportable than death." (*Vie*, Vol. I, p. 84).

**29.**—The tedium and sadness are a source of **temptations**. Some are led in this way to a distaste for their vocation; others, at least, to giving up prayer. If they were more mortified, they would endure their suffering in prayer patiently, knowing that it does not hinder the exercise from being profitable to them.

Sometimes the temptation becomes still sharper. St. Elizabeth of Schoenau suffered on several occasions from tedium and weariness of life to such an extent that she thought of committing suicide (Bolland., June 18, *Life,* No. 14).

Even when the sadness is slight, we must resist it. For it makes the soul powerless for good. And, on the other hand, joy and peace are counted amongst the fruits of the Holy Spirit, as giving an impetus towards virtue.

When St. Mary Magdalene of Pazzi "perceived that one of her companions was sad, she said to her, in accents of the tenderest affection: 'Calm your heart, my dear Sister, for God does not shed His graces on sad souls'" (*Vie*, by Cepari, ch. v).

**29** *bis.*—**Remedies** for sadness: to drive away depressing thoughts and to pray for spiritual joy.

**30.**—*Seventh kind:* **doubts** as to the genuineness of **graces** received. This trial is so universal, at any rate at the beginning of the mystic way, that we should be surprised if the soul were not to experience it. The fact is usually due to natural causes, such as the feeling of our own unworthiness, ignorance regarding the true nature of these extraordinary graces (see ch. v, 18), and absence of spiritual direction.

one would dare to class himself in this category, nor consequently, apply to himself the counsels that concern it. We should be afraid to say to anyone: "You are in the requisite conditions for practising the prayer of perfect souls."

**31.**—*Eighth and ninth kinds:* an **ardent thirst** for God, the poignant impression of being **abandoned** by Him. In the mystic way, the soul often suffers from this thirst for God; there is a painful need of a clearer and stronger possession of Him. But there are moments or periods, such as the first night of the soul (ch. xv), when God hides Himself more effectually from us, without ceasing to be Himself desired. We then feel ourselves drawn continually towards God and invited to seek Him; but when we go out towards Him we find only emptiness and silence. We struggled vainly in the darkness.

It is then that the soul experiences a bitter feeling of abandonment. The *Imitation* calls the state "desolation of heart" (Book II, ch. ix, 1). See St. John of the Cross (*Obscure Night,* Book II, ch. vi).

Some souls feel their relations with God constrained when they have committed quite slight faults. They fancy, without any proof, that the sentiment proceeds from God, who wishes to show His displeasure. Not daring to appear before Him, they abandon for several days a part of such of their spiritual exercises as are not of obligation.

This last effect shows that it is simply an illusion of the Devil. He is the author of the constraint that we feel. When we have resisted grace, God asks, not that we should go afar off from Him, but that we should repent and throw ourselves trustingly into His arms.

**32.**—*Tenth kind:* the rooted conviction that we are the **object of God's hatred** and are destined to be lost. It is no longer the feeling, as was the case just now, of being far away from God, but of being rejected. It is a temptation against one of the theological virtues, that of hope; and consequently we must multiply acts of this virtue.

Many saints have had this trial to a terrible degree and for some length of time. With St. Francis of Sales it lasted a month, while he was a student. St. Philip Benizi, of the Order of the Servites, was tempted to despair for three hours only, but this was at the time of his death. St. Hildegard and St. Margaret Mary suffered severely from this trial; and so did the Ven. Perboyre two years before his martyrdom. Blessed Suso relates that he experienced the suffering for ten years. For more than nine years he had temptations against faith, and an inordinate sadness for eight years (*Autobiography,* ch. 23).

M. Olier, at the age of thirty-two, was harassed by interior sufferings for two years, being convinced in particular that he was lost. Some people have to bear this trial all their lives.

**33.**—**Causes**. This idea is not a real conviction, but a strong impression that cannot be shaken off. It may proceed in a certain measure from the vivid spectacle of our sins and malice. If this spectacle came entirely from God, it would, however, bring peace and not despair. It may be Satan, acting directly upon the imagination and the sensibility. If this state is much prolonged, it is probable that the temperament is largely responsible, and recourse should be had to physical treatment (see 7).

Another proof that this absorbing idea comes from Satan is that it is contrary to reason. It is not the result of any convincing argument. It is even contradicted by evident proofs; for it sometimes occurs almost simultaneously with the mystic union; so that in the course of the same day a man may feel closely united to God and loved by Him, and afterwards believed himself to be detested. This illogical behaviour is very noticeable in the lives of certain saints.

Now this is a certain proof of some morbid or diabolic activity going on outside of us and obscuring our faculties. The Devil is not concerned to know whether a feeling is logical or not. As soon as he obtains permission to suggest it, he goes to work. Let us not try to connect these impressions with a syllogism. We should see in them an unreasonable emotion, and respond with the opposite tendencies: love and filial trust.

**34.**—When haunted with the idea of damnation, we are naturally tempted to give ourselves up to **discouragement**: "Since I am destined for Hell, why lead a life of self-sacrifice? As well enjoy myself!"

The saints, with an outburst of generosity, have often replied: If I must hate God and be hated by Him for all eternity, I will, at least, love Him on earth and labour for His glory here below.

This answer, if taken literally, would imply an impossible supposition, but it expresses the soul's need of giving her utmost to God. There is another reply: that no one is damned without the will to be damned. Now the horror that this thought of damnation causes us is the proof that we do not will it. Let us refuse to admit to the enemy that this woe will overtake us.

**35.**—*Eleventh kind:* sentiments of **hatred for God** and the temptation to **blasphemy**. This inclination is sometimes only a consequence of the one that went before. The Devil, after persuading us that God hates us and does so unjustly, by caprice, makes us rebel against this blind and pitiless treatment; he leads us to repay hatred with hatred.

But he can also excite the sentiment of hatred without a motive. He then merely communicates to us the impression with which he is penetrated, but which, in his case, is founded on fact. He makes the soul vibrate in unison with his own rage, and under the same continual ravings. Do not ask the soul the reason: she does not know it. She has become an echo, and the sound that the echo repeats is a blasphemy.

We have a singular example of this temptation in St. Hugh, Bishop of Grenoble (1053-1132), who was associated with St. Bruno in founding the Grande-Chartreuse. God wished to recall him to humility amidst the heroic actions and prodigies that brought him so much applause. To this end he was pursued for fifty-two years by a temptation to blasphemy.

**36.**—Courbon bids us notice that these sentiments of aversion for God are sometimes directed against those who serve Him or **sacred things** (Part III, ch. ix). With regard to blasphemies uttered aloud by persons who are dedicated to God, he thinks that "God does not usually permit them to fall into these excesses in public, but only secretly, or in presence of trustworthy persons who are not disedified, knowing the cause of these horrible words" (*ibid.*).

37.—*Twelfth kind of suffering:* **distractions** during prayer. We have already spoken of them in connection with the prayer of simplicity and the prayer of quiet.

Canon Lejeune says truly that this trial would often be lessened if we took the trouble to pray about it. "When (he says) shall we understand that the success of our prayers, the triumph over distractions, the inclination and facility for converse with God, depend first and foremost upon the *frequency* and *fervour* of our petitions? I wish that this simple question could be put to all who bewail their incessant distractions during prayer: 'How many times a day do you ask God to free you from your distractions?' Would not many persons be constrained to confess that they have never thought of making this request to God? And they are astonished that attention, recollection, and fervour do not descend upon them suddenly as soon as they begin to pray" (*L'Oraison rendue facile,* Part III, ch. iii, p. 280. See also the excellent chapters vi, vii, and viii of the same volume).

### §4. Scruples

**38.—Definition**. A scruple is an ill-founded and disturbing fear of having sinned. If there were no disturbance, it would not be a scruple, properly so-called, but merely the error of an ill-trained conscience. In reality, the man who, when disquieted by a scruple, yields to an impression in spite of reason, is a coward. He is as inconsistent as a child who does not dare enter a dark room in the evening because he says burglars may be there. To convince them of the contrary he is taken into the room with a light, and made to look into all the corners. When he comes out again he admits that no burglars are there. "Very well, then," they say; "now go in alone." "No," he answers, "perhaps there may be some."

**39.**—This is not to say that the scrupulous person shows himself scrupulous in all his actions. He is fearful and hedged about with difficulties only on certain points; but is sometimes **too easy** on others.

**40.**—Many saints have passed through a **period** of scruples. St. Ignatius was of the number, and he declares that if *this trial lasts a short time only,* it is very helpful to the soul, purifying it and estranging it from even the appearance of sin (*Rule 3 on Scruples*).

People readily fall into scruples of the time of their conversion, because they have then a greater dread of offending God. They are therefore led to call into question decisions which they have hitherto regarded as good.

**41.**—If the scruple **continues**, it becomes a dangerous moral malady for the soul.* For, in encouraging it, Satan not only proposes to torture us, but, what is more important, he hopes that this torture will become so insupportable that we shall lose patience. Instead of coming back to a sensible middle course, which seems difficult, the soul allows herself to fall into relaxation or despair. There will often be a hatred for the Sacraments or for our vocation, and they will begin to be regarded as mere instruments of torture. Luther began by being scrupulous.

For, in Satan's designs, the scrupulous person must not always continue so. There would be no advantage in thus heightening the delicacy of his conscience. He must be led by weariness and by way of reaction to the diametrically opposite state: complete carelessness; or again, a distaste for life (St. Ignatius, *Rule 4, concerning Scruples*). It is a real duty, therefore, to seek to cure oneself. Many timorous souls seem to have no idea of this. They ought to become scrupulous about attending to the scruples.

**41** *bis.*—I have just considered the scruple from a psychological point of view. Doctors admit that, if prolonged, it has an organic basis (7). Habitually scrupulous persons are afflicted with neurosis. They come within the category of the **sick persons** who are styled *phobits,* that is to say, those possessed of an instinctive, erroneous, and unreasonable fear, which continues and imposes itself, although the person wishes to overcome it. It is a true obsession, a trouble of the emotional life.

The science of to-day does not know the exact organic cause of phobia. But it, at least, knows that hygienic and medical treatment can combat the evil. Doctors will prescribe sedatives for the nervous system; they will strengthen the muscles and correct digestive errors which produce gloomy thoughts.

I shall concern myself only with remedies of the moral order.

**42.**—To cure ourselves of scruples, the first spiritual **remedy** that we should apply is obedience to our director. Since, like children, we are incapable of guiding ourselves in deciding between good and evil in certain matters, we must resign ourselves to be led by another. The director, on his side, should be very positive in his advice, while being very gentle and encouraging (Aquaviva, *Industries pour guérir les maladies de l'âme,* ch. xviii).

Unfortunately, scrupulous persons sometimes change their confessor, whether involuntarily or voluntarily; and then they cannot resist the wish to recommence their long-drawn-out histories. "I shall be easier," they say to themselves, "if my new confessor thinks the same as the others." They deceive themselves in this, for it is not in their nature ever to feel at ease. Or, again, they say: If such or such an order was given me, it was probably because I failed to

* St. Margaret Mary: "There is nothing in which the devil is more powerful or where he gained so much, as with the soul that is in distress and anxiety; he makes it his plaything and renders it incapable of any good" (*Vie,* by herself, Paray Edition, Vol. II, p. 430).

make myself properly understood. I explain things so badly! But this time I will go into everything in such detail that I shall be definitely enlightened. Another error! This "last word" in the matter will never be more than the last but one. This confession, which will have wasted a great deal of the director's time, will be as hazy as those that went before. We cannot be eternally questioning the same things and propounding the same problems. We must resign ourselves to a frank obedience.

**43.**—A **second remedy** is to become better informed. It is not a question of studying the whole theory of morals, like a Confessor, but merely of getting to know some of the ordinary principles that respond to certain difficulties, always the same ones, that we encounter.

As an example, I will now take three cases that are of frequent occurrence. **44.**—The first two cases of difficulty occur in **confession**. Scrupulous persons ask themselves anxiously: 1° if they must tell such and such a thing, and how they are to say it; or, more specially, 2° if it is necessary to go back on a previous confession. They weigh, they sift. Their minds grow more and more confused; and the only outcome of such an examen is an ever-increasing obscurity and uneasiness. This is not what Jesus Christ intended in instituting confession: quite the contrary.

To quiet these souls, we must first forbid all research into the past, proving to them that it is labour wasted. They wish to get a clear view of their soul. It is always the opposite that happens.* Then we must teach them that the Church, Jesus Christ's interpreter, declares that we are not obliged to accuse ourselves of: 1° venial sins; nor even 2° mortal sins when these are not certain.†

And it is the same with confessions that people wish to make all over again. We are only bound to allow this when we are certain that the former confessions were not properly made. The foregoing principle restores peace to the soul. The truth is that you are troubled because you *do not see clearly* whether you have sinned, whether you had a wrong intention or not, etc., and therefore you do not know exactly whether you are obliged to accuse yourself. This is the case of the *doubtful sin*. Instead of indefinitely discussing the arguments for and against, and making useless calls upon your memory, say: "It

* St. Alphonsus Liguori (in an excellent treatise on scruples, that forms chapter xviii, section 2, 10, of *The True Spouse of Christ*), says: "Scruples are, as it were, a species of pitch, which the more it is handled the more it adheres; the more you reflect on them the more they will fill your mind with darkness" (No. 10). And in the same way, the more we stir the bottom of the pond in order to find any object, the more the water loses its transparency. If these mental ruminations are frequent, they increase the malady more and more.

† See on the subject an excellent little book, *L'ange conducteur des âmes scrupulouses*, by P. DuBois, S.J. (Lille, Desclée).

is doubtful; then I am not bound to mention it or think of it again." You will thus recover your peace of mind.*

**45.—Objection**. But we then hear the scrupulous person saying: "That may be so. I now see clearly what my rights in the matter are. But I shall never have the courage to take advantage of them. Well! so much the worse for me. I shall be apprehensive. It is stronger than I am: I shall examine myself to excess, and I shall accuse myself. In order to be the more certain of having omitted nothing, I shall even exaggerate my culpability."

**46.—Reply**. This is a deplorable weakness of will, and it is a point upon which you should conquer yourself. This weakness ought even to be described as culpable if the judgement were not obscured by fear.

When one is sure of the principle, one must have the strength of character to act up to one's conviction. You are sure *that you are not obliged* to accuse yourself of certain actions; then do not accuse yourself of them.

**47.—Another case**. In his last Rule concerning scruples, St. Ignatius examines a temptation often met with in fervent persons. At the moment of forming a project for some good and useful action, they are suddenly arrested by the fear of falling into pride, vanity, or sensuality. Should they go on with it? The saint answers with this principle of sound common sense: "Reject this inordinate sentiment, but act!" Otherwise one would never act at all.

This temptation leads to a truceless self-analysis; to sifting the grounds of all one's intentions, a course that ends in anxiety and inaction. These continual examinations must be prohibited.

### § 5. Aridity

**48.**—In ch. xv, concerning the first night of the soul, I considered one special kind of aridity. It is as well to deal with the subject in a more general manner.

**49.—Definition**. Aridity is desolation during prayer. It is a state in which, notwithstanding our efforts, we are unable to produce either pious thoughts or right sentiments. In consequence of this condition we experienced tedium and disgust. The trial is sometimes due only to natural causes, in which case it is in our power to avoid or diminish:

1° *A dissipated life* which fills the imagination with frivolities. These distracting memories besiege us at the time of prayer;

* St. Alphonsus Liguori: "A soul tortured by scruples is, according to the divines, not obliged to confess a past sin unless he can swear that it was certainly a mortal sin, and that it was never told in any confession... Scrupulous persons should understand that a general confession is useful for others, but very dangerous and injurious to them. Hence good directors do not permit scrupulous persons to speak of past sins. The remedy for them is, not to explain, but to be silent and obey" (*ibid.*, 12). "The spiritual father who is indulgent in hearing the doubts of scrupulous souls, falls into a great error; for by scrutinising their consciences, they generally become disquieted, and are rendered more incapable of advancing in the way of God" (ibid., No. 16).

2° *The lack of any direct preparation for prayer;*

3° *Fatigue,* proceeding either from ill-health or too many occupations. In this case it is sometimes advisable to change the time for prayer, or to divide it into short portions (see St. Teresa, *Life,* ch. xi).

**50.**—Aridity, like all trials, has both advantages and drawbacks. These two effects may be regarded as compensating one another only in the case where we react seriously against this condition and where it is not prolonged by our own fault.

For a generous soul, the **advantages** are that the dryness affords ample matter for self-mortifications; it can also provide material for humility, by making us realise our own impotence.* The danger is that of falling into discouragement and negligence.

**51.**—Desolation, and aridity in particular, has great **drawbacks** if it is prolonged and if we do not combated vigorously.

1° *On account of the Devil's action.* St. Ignatius says that in desolation it is Satan who has a predominant influence over us. He acts upon the *intellect,* to obscure it and to insinuate evil counsels; on the *will,* to make it regard self-denial with abhorrence; on the *imagination* and the *temperament,* in order to awaken the passions. Such conduct cannot fail, in the long run, to exercise fatal results upon our weakness. The supply of strength that we have absorbed in consolation is soon exhausted.

2° If we consider the desolation *in itself,* leaving the Devil's influence out of the question, we see that it is a *malady of the soul.*† It produces a gradual weakness, like a decline or a deleterious atmosphere. It can also be compared to the slow action of cold upon the body. In a glacial temperature the limbs become first numbed, then paralysed; and unless there is a violent reaction death ensues. Even plant-life cannot, as a rule, develop in cold and darkness.

**52.**—We thus see how important it is to **pray to be delivered** from this trial, for we should not otherwise be making use of *all the means* within our power. The one that we neglect—prayer, is precisely the most powerful among them; still more, without it all the other remedies will generally be inefficacious, for

* Bousset: "A tree, in winter, produces nothing, it is covered with snow; so much the better! The frosts, the winds, the hoar-frost, all protect it. You suppose, then, that it is idle while it is quite dried up outwardly? The root extends itself and derives strength and warmth even from the snow, and when its roots have spread themselves abroad, it is in a condition to produce more excellent fruits in due season. The soul, when dry and desolate, arid and anguished before God, thinks herself inactive; but she is grounding herself in humility and losing herself in her own nothingness; then she sends down deep roots for the bringing forth of the fruits of virtue and all kinds of good works, pleasing to God" (*Opuscule: Questions et résponses,* § 2, Lachat edition, Vol. VIII, p. 491).

† Fr. Aquaviva is right when he gives this named to aridity (*Industries pour guérir le maladies de l'âme,* ch. iii). Molinos, on the contrary, said: "The distaste for spiritual things *is good,* for it purges us of self-love" (Prop. 28).

On this question see Canon Lejeune's excellent treatise, *L'Oraison rendue facile* (Lethielleux, 1904), part III, ch. viii.

consolation and success in prayer are graces. Now, God has ordained that prayer should be the almost necessary means of obtaining all graces (see 13 and 37).

According to St. Philip Neri, "the best remedy against aridity and the torpor which paralyses the soul, is to present ourselves before God and the saints like a poor beggar, who asks with great humility for their spiritual alms" (Bolland., May 26, second *Life,* No. 189).

This prayer for deliverance should, of course, be accompanied, like all others, by a complete abandonment to the divine will. While waiting to be heard, we must continue in a state of joyful resignation.*

There are two opposite extremes to be avoided here: one, to desire so fervently that we lose our peace and conformity to God's will; the other, to be so resigned that we no longer do anything ourselves or unite our own action to that of divine grace.

**53.**—St. Teresa advise us to cling to the **hope** of being delivered, sooner or later, notwithstanding God's silence. "This cross... [distractions and aridity] is a very great one; yet I know that Our Lord leaves us not so abandoned that, if we with humility approach to beg it of Him, *He will not accompany us;* and if we cannot obtain it in one year, be it in many, let us not grudge spending time on a thing whereon it is so well employed" (*Way of Perfection,* ch. xxvi, p. 77).†

According to these words, there is reason to believe that certain aridities would last a shorter time if we were to ask to be delivered from them.

**54.**—On several occasions I have met with persons who would have desired to escape from the state of desolation, but felt fettered, as it were, by a **scruple**. They said to themselves: "It may be contrary to perfection to pray that my trials to be put an end to."

But if it is contrary to perfection to ask for the cure of the soul's maladies, it would be the same with those of the body; we should have to say that even our great places of pilgrimage are only frequented by the imperfect.

"Nobody (says Canon Lejeune) would dare to claim that the sick who crowded about Our Saviour's path during His mortal life committed imperfection in thus doing, and that they would have been better had they

* St. Teresa says: "The soul which begins to walk in the way of mental prayer with resolution, and is determined not to care much, neither to *rejoice* nor to be *greatly afflicted* whether sweetness and tenderness fail it or Our Lord grants them, has already travelled a great part of the road" (*Life,* ch. XI, 20).

† Fr. Rigoleuc: "Hope for great and signal favours from God, and this with a generous confidence worthy of a child of God and an heir to the merits of the God-Man. Persuade yourself, on the one hand, that all the treasures of grace are open to you, not only by the merits of Jesus Christ's death, but also by God's infinite desire to communicate Himself; and on the other, that the low and debased conception that we usually have of God and the love that He bears us, remove us from Him no less than do our pride and presumption" (Tr. 3, ch. ii).

resigned themselves without a word of prayer or a gesture of supplication to the Divine good-pleasure" (*L'Oraison rendue facile*, Part II, ch. viii).

Such an error proceeds fundamentally from the false belief that petitions cannot be reconciled with resignation (see ch. xvii, 25). Were this so, they would be an imperfection.

Others say: "I quite admit that aridity is generally harmful; but *it may be* that for me personally it is more profitable than being able to succeed in prayer. And because of this uncertainty I make no attempt to escape." His one: When you are sick, do you take remedies without expecting a revelation from Heaven? Yes. Well, according to your principles, you should not do so. For *it may be* that the sickness is more profitable for you than health.

**55.—St. Ignatius** was more practical. In his *Exercises* he incessantly makes suggestions of desires that we should stimulate in our souls. He does not wish us to remain inactive while expecting the arrival of such graces of interior prayer as are necessary or useful. Inertia is not this man of action's ideal. Thus he prescribes beginning each meditation with a definite petition. He has the patience to repeat this petition to satiety after one of the preludes. What he makes us ask for is success, and he himself defines the kind of success that is to be. Notice that the formula that he has adopted does not make use of vague or modified expressions, such as "I would desire, I would wish." It is positive. "The second prelude," he says, "consists in asking for the grace that I desire." It is categorical.

One of his chapters is headed "Additions... which will assist us in... obtaining from God what we ask of Him (see the details in Additions, 4, 7; and notes, 1, 3).

This, again, is what he has written in the Rules of his Order: "All must employ their time in spiritual things, and *apply themselves earnestly to the attainment of devotion,* according to the measure of God's grace imparted to them" (Rule 21).

Let us add that Innocent XI has condemned one of Molinos' propositions which discouraged any seeking after devotion. And yet it was only a question of sensible devotion, of consolation of the lower order, that is to say. "He who desires sensible devotion and attaches himself thereto, seeks and desires, not God, but himself. *He who is advancing in the interior way* asks wrongly in desiring and *making efforts to obtain it,* both in holy places and on feast-days" (Prop. 27).

The Church does not approve of this icy constraint before our Heavenly Father. Her language is quite different. In the majority of her prayers she makes us ask for an increase of light, facility for good, a taste for heavenly things; that is to say, for consolation in the noblest sense of the word. She invokes the Holy Spirit as the Paraclete, which is to say the Comforter; and with her we ask that we "may ever rejoice in His consolation" and His gifts (*Veni Sancte Spiritus*).

**56.**—Let us not therefore be afraid to **ask for advancement in prayer,** for an *attraction* to spiritual exercises and facility performing them aright (see 13).

I intentionally do not say: "Ask for consolations," because this phrase lends itself to an unfortunate interpretation. It suggests that we seek for success in prayer chiefly for the pleasure that we are eager to find therein, and not for the very real utility to the spiritual life that we should derive from it.

**57.**—With certain souls it is **pride**, as Fr. Aquaviva remarks, that hinders them from paying too much heed to aridity. They say to themselves: "I am reaching virtues and have no need of anything" (*Apoc.,* iii, 17). "God treats me, not as an infant, that has need of the milk of consolations, but as a grown man." Let us have the humility, then, to recognise that we are poor creatures to whom the graces of prayer are very necessary; and let us know how to stretch out our hands to obtain this alms from God.

**58.**—Here is a way which, with certain persons, is successful in partly overcoming the aridity. It is to bind ourselves after each exercise to note some **thought** that has struck us and given us an inclination towards good. This obligation, that we have imposed on ourselves, acts silently upon the prayer itself; it arouses the drowsy mind and incites it to produce something.

**58** *bis.*—With many persons, **aridity persists** in spite of the means that they employ to guard against it. They are troubled because all their prayer passes in distraction, without their being able to fix their attention with relish continuously on any good thought. They say: "It is time lost; it would be better to give up this exercise." What most often restrains them is that a rule obliges them to continue.

Their directors must reassure these souls, explaining to them that this prayer is very meritorious, because of the tedium that is undergone. It will by this very reason draw down upon them the graces that they need for their guidance, and that they hoped to procure by learned considerations. This exercise is thus at the same time both meritorious and also profitable for their spiritual progress.

Let the director also combat the depressing idea that such a state is necessarily a punishment from God, and this for faults of which we are not ourselves conscious. It is very often devoid of any foundation (see **6**).

### § 6. Diabolic Possession

**59.**—In the trials that we have considered hitherto, the Devil played at times an important part. But he was partially hidden. There are yet more terrible onslaughts in which he shows himself more openly. These trials are called **possession** and **obsession**.

The Roman ritual does not distinguish between these two terms. Nor does St. Alphonsus Liguori in his *Praxis Confessarii* (No. 110 and *seq.*). Many theologians, however, make a distinction between them. This varies slightly with one and the other, but the object is always the same: to divide the diabolic attacks into two categories presenting notable differences.

**60.—Definition.** We shall say, in the strict sense of the word, that a person is **possessed** by the Devil when at particular moments the Devil makes him lose consciousness and seems to take *the place of the soul* in his body; making use, apparently at least, of his eyes in order to see, of his ears to hear, or his mouth to speak, whether to those who are looking on or to his own companions. It is the Devil who suffers, as though from a burn, if any object that has been blessed is brought into contact with the skin. In a word, the Devil seems to be incarnate in the man.

We shall say that a person is **obsessed** when the Devil does not make him lose consciousness, but when, notwithstanding, he torments him in such a way that his action is recognisable; inflicting blows, for instance. The word obsession in Latin means the siege of the stronghold. In possession, the place is captured; however, this is so in appearance only with regard to the citadel itself, where the higher faculties, the intelligence, and the will are to be found. The Devil can never enter without our consent.

**61.**—These two states are often distinguished one from the other by saying: With possessed persons the Devil acts upon the body from **within**, while with the obsessed it is from **without**. This summary description is excellent, provided that people take the trouble to define these terms. Those who find them clear as they stand alone, have the wrong conception of the angels. They believe them to be localised as to their substance, like material things. They think of them as though they were air, that can only be inside or outside of our lungs. But this is not correct. The angelic spirit is independent of space (see St. Thomas, 1, q. 52, a. 1). It is only its *operation* upon matter that is localised; strictly speaking, therefore, we should say that it is *in* a human body only by the fact that it acts upon this body.

That is why I have distinguished possession from obsession in my definition, by the *mode of operation,* which is really different, and not by the place occupied by the operator, because this would be a mere manner of speaking.

**62.—Who are the persons that suffer from these trials**? Some writers of weight are of the opinion that possession (this word being taken in its strict sense) does not befall those who are striving earnestly after perfection, except in very rare and transient cases (Scaramelli, Tr. 5, No. 71; Schram, old edition, No. 208; 1848 edition, No. 217).* They regard this fact as being proved by experience. They explain it by saying that God does not permit diabolic persecutions except in order to enable these souls to acquire great merit. But for

* Scaramelli says again: "*My opinion* is that the Devil never succeeds in acquiring such an ascendancy over a person as to enable him to take possession of his body and his soul, or to fetter the actions of his limbs, especially if it occurs frequently, unless such a person *concurs by some consent* and some co-operation" (Tr. 3, No. 186).

this the use of their reason and their liberty are necessary, and these are often diminished or suspended in the case of diabolic possession. It is necessary, therefore, that these deprivations should not take place, or that they should be of rare occurrence or of brief duration. This reasoning does not seem very conclusive, for if merit is not acquired during the attack itself, the trial can be the occasion of great merit before or afterwards.

Fr. Meynard, quoting an ancient writer (*Viguier,* O.P.), concludes, like the authors mentioned above, "that it is exceedingly rare for possession to occur in the case of souls that are called to contemplation and a close union with God; it is rather a punishment than a purifying trial" (Vol. II, No. 139).

On the other hand, it has quite frequently befallen fervent persons to suffer from *obsession.*

**63.—Some descriptive details.**

1° In exorcisms the devils have often declared that a *large number* of them unite together in possessing one person: they divide themselves into groups, each having a leader;

2° They assume *names.* If it is that of an animal, they indicate its identity by its peculiar cry, or by gestures. The ritual compels them to make this declaration, doubtless in order that they may be recognised each time that they appear before the exorcist. The formula of the ritual is as follows: "I command thee to give thy name and the day and hour of thy departure."

3° Because they take the names of historic characters, such as Judas, Nero, etc., it does not follow that these persons really have any part in the possession. It is pure symbolism—showing, doubtless, the *function* that each demon has chosen, inciting to such and such a vice. The names of animals or fabulous personages would show the same intention. Or, again, these historic names would indicate those of the lost for whose destruction the devil then speaking has laboured, what he regards as one of his masterpieces, and of whom he is proud.

4° According to the demons again, each one of them affects some special part of the body. They are, as it were, *housed* there permanently, their presence being concealed except during the attacks. At these times they issue forth from this hiding-place in order to evade a larger portion of the organism, or to answer the exorcist.

5° The *deliverance* of the possessed person is a difficult task, sometimes requiring efforts of several months' or even years' duration. During this period the sufferer at least obtains some relief. The exorcist's prayers seem to act on the evil spirit like blows inflicted on an adversary; they injure and also weaken him. The demon holds out as long as he can, sometimes lamenting that his leaders threatened him with chastisements if he has not the courage to continue the struggle. The demon recovers his strength again after the previous exorcism if the person has committed sins which he has not yet confessed.

6° With possessed persons, *loss of consciousness* usually takes place during the exorcism. The state begins with the preliminary prayers. The patient who a moment before was talking quite naturally, falls suddenly into a kind of sleep, or, on the contrary, he struggles and writhes; his eyes become fixed and haggard. Another spirit has taken possession of his organism. And this one will reply to questions, will receive the onslaughts of the prayers and endeavour to defy them. Just so a general hastens to the ramparts with his troops, sending those who not do not carry arms to the rear. The battle often lasts for as many hours as the exorcist chooses. As soon as he announces that he ceases fighting, the afflicted person returns as if out of a sleep, the awakening being sometimes quiet, and at other times accompanied by convulsive movements; he does not know what has occurred, and, although fatigued, can resume a natural conversation. Holy water contributes largely to cause the fatigue to disappear.

In the exorcisms at which I have been present all these circumstances were reproduced.

7° When the person attacked looses consciousness, the demon usually speaks *in his own name* and consequently does not attempt to conceal himself. But at other times he suddenly, during a conversation, takes the place of the sufferer's own spirit, leaving it to be supposed that the latter is still speaking and in his normal state. We realise the contrary, at any rate when too late, by certain circumstances; either the things said are the absolute opposite of what, knowing his character and antecedents, we should expect from him, or he awakens afterwards as though from a sleep, having no recollection of the conversation; or the demon owns that he has resorted to strategy and boasts of it.

8° In the case of those who are striving after perfection, the devils take possession of them under compulsion only. They stated this at Loudun, being furious because Fr. Surin was not content merely with exorcising Mother Jeanne of the Angels, but actually made her progress in sanctity. They exclaimed: "The greatest misfortune that can happen to us on earth is to possess a person who is mortified in his passions. We should do better to be in Hell than to remain in one who is really detached from self and from all created things" (*Vie du P. Surin*, by Boudon, Part III, ch. vii, Migne ed., col. 222). They would have liked to come out of her, but were doubtless detained by their leaders or by the hope of some future success.

**64.—Exorcisms** may be either **solemn** or private. The first are performed publicly in church and in sacred vestments. Priests alone can undertake them; the permission of the Bishop is generally required. Private exorcisms are always permitted, even to the laity (see Ballerini's and Lehmkuhl's *Theologia moralis*), but they should speak in their own name, and not in that of the Church. There is no longer any authorised form for this purpose.

Certain confessors employ a hurried formula of abjuration when they find a penitent in bad dispositions or attacked by severe temptations. As God's ministers, they order the devil to withdraw.

We should act in this way when a person presents only doubtful symptoms of possession. But it is better to make the exorcism without his knowledge, so as to avoid any suggestion which would render the question more obscure. Nothing, for instance, hinders our saying that we are reciting a Latin prayer against diseases.

**65.**—The ritual requires the exorcist to be on his guard against the various artifices of the devil: *exorcista cautus esse debet.* At the outset he is advised **not to be very ready to think** that anyone is obsessed: *ne facile credat aliquem a daemonio obessum esse;* and not to confuse the diabolic attack with certain maladies. St. Philip Neri, who had great power over demons, was extremely slow to believe in the reality of a possession (Bolland., May 26; 2nd *Life,* No. 100).

**66.**—The exorcist will be acting prudently, therefore, in obtaining the assistance, at any rate at first, of a Christian **doctor**, who is well-versed in nervous pathology. In these days there are several strange diseases, bearing a resemblance to possession. The priest has scarcely ever made the studies necessary in order to distinguish the one from the other. The doctor alone can determine the real importance of certain physiological phenomena which, to the unlearned in these matters, seem supernatural. For example, if at the close of the interview, certain marks appear on the skin, he will examine whether it is not simply dermatographic (ch. xxxi, 10), and produced by pressure applied to the limbs during the convulsions. He will know how to devise experiments in order to convince himself in the matter. He will also see whether certain pains cannot be explained by auto-suggestion. Finally, if the person is feigning, he will be quicker to detect the fraud than anyone else, and will contrive a trap for his exposure. Even if a possession is real, it may be associated with certain nervous maladies that help to keep it alive, as it were.* The doctor will then have a curative part to play; as soon as he has reduced the disease, he will help to restrain the diabolical action.

**67.**—In particular countries or convents, **epidemics** of possession have occurred, such as at Loudun, in the seventeenth century. Without wishing to deny that the diabolic attack at Loudun was genuine, in the case of this or that particular person, it is admitted that in several instances it was merely a nervous

* This pathological basis seems evident enough in Mother Jeanne of the Angels, Superior of Loudun, who was exorcised by Fr. Surin. Many of the phenomena presented by her were no different from those at the Salpêtière Hospital. Two of Charcot's disciples, Drs. Gabriel Legué and Giles de la Tourette, have studied, from a medical point of view, her state, and that, nearly as strange, of Fr. Surin, in the *Autobiographie inédite de Jeanne des Anges* (Charpentier, in 8mo, 1886). But they wrote under the indulgence of a violent anti-religious passion, denying, a priori, everything supernatural. It would be desirable to undertake the study again, in a scientific and impartial spirit, and to see what pathological explanations may prudently be accepted.

Dr. Legue has published a book: *Urbain Grandier et les possedés de Loudun*, 3rd ed., Charpentier, in 12, 1884, and a more complete edition, Baschet, 1880.

condition, acquired just as contagious maladies are acquired. Experience has shown us that, as in these other cases, a sure and speedy way of effecting a cure is to disperse the affected persons and change their surroundings.

Fr. Debreyne, who was a doctor of medicine, a priest, and religious of La Trappe, tells us in detail how he had to attend a community of women "whose condition showed a great resemblance to that of the Ursulines of Loudun." For example, with one bound they clear the enclosure wall, etc... He cured them, gradually, by purely natural means, hygienic and ethical, such "as steady and varied manual labour" (*Essai de théologie morale*, ch. iv, Dr. Ferrand's revised edition; Poussielgue, 1884, Part IV, ch. iii, § 2).

If exorcisms are performed, it is well to avoid publicity; for this is an exciting cause both to the nerves and the imagination.*

**68.**—The ritual forbids exorcists to engage in "idle talking and **curious interrogations**, especially with regard to future or hidden things." The sole legitimate end of the exorcism is to drive out the demon. It would be very absurd to believe that this applying and malevolent spirit would put himself humbly at our service by supplying us with true or useful information having no relation to the deliverance of the possessed person. Apart from what the Church authorises, we shall only be mocked in his replies. It would be equally improper to engage in a joking conversation with them; it would be playing with an enemy who is cleverer than ourselves.

According to the ritual, the exorcism should always be couched in an imperative form. We are not expressing a wish to the Devil, but addressing a command.

**69.**—The ritual gives the **signs** of the Devil's action on a person who either is or is not conscious of his acts. They come under three principal heads; the two first are of the moral order. "They are, it says, the following: uttering long sentences [not learned by heart] in an unknown tongue, or understanding those who speak this language, revealing future or hidden things [especially having a clear knowledge of the future or of various sciences], displaying powers beyond one's age or condition, and other similar things; when *several of the signs are combined,* the indications are more conclusive."

Let us note the moderation of this last sentence. The ritual does not claim to decide controverted questions of science; it does not state that the above signs always give a complete certainty, especially if they occur separately. These signs are often not clearly apparent.

There are two signs in particular that need to be examined very narrowly. The first is "that of abnormal strength." In certain maladies, the patient gowns and displays a degree of strength that would never have been expected, but which, however, is purely of the natural order.

* At Loudun the exorcism sometimes took place in the presence of over three thousand people, all vibrating with excitement. And the sisters went to the church in solemn procession!

So, too, with regard to the knowledge of distant things; we must not take the expression in the strict sense of meaning a knowledge superior to that obtained from the *habitual* use of our faculties. In certain supra-normal states, such as somnambulism, something of this kind, which is not supernatural, may exist. The sight suffers from suppression, as it were, with regard to certain objects, and hyperæsthesia with regard to others. The tactile nerves of certain animals enable them to feel electric effluvia which the normal man does not perceive, but which can doubtless convey obscure warnings to him when particular nerves are more than ordinarily excited.

Cases exist where it is admitted that the Devil's presence cannot reasonably be disputed, for instance when the exorcist puts a series of questions in Latin to a person ignorant of this language, and he invariably replies with answers showing that the inquiry has been correctly understood.* The proof is still stronger if the reply is contrary to what the exorcist desired.

Those who have performed many exorcisms, often have an argument of probability, which is very strong. They find that persons who are unknown to each other and who have received very different educations, speak the same language during these crises and behave in the same way. This uniformity of manners can only be explained by admitting that the hidden agent in all these cases is one and the same. It is a question of a moral appreciation; it is easier to feel than to explain it to other people. We all form these intuitive judgements which are difficult to account for fully, as when we form an estimate of a man's character by his physiognomy, voice, and gestures.

Can the Devil's presence be certainly inferred by the sole fact that the subject of the attack speaks or acts as we should expect the Devil to do? If he blasphemes, for instance, or thrusts blessed objects away from him?

This circumstance, if standing alone, is not sufficient. For the hospitals afford opportunities of studying diseases that present the same character; hysterical patients who have been hypnotised, and consequently deprived of consciousness, pass (but at the operator's orders) into dreaming states in which they speak. They thus assume the characters of certain persons, just as an actor would do. The suggestion is made that they are a soldier, and orator, or some historic personage; and immediately they assume the corresponding language and attitudes.

Doctors generally considered that these facts are purely natural. It is not very certain that this is so. In order to prove it, it would be necessary to contrive certain experiments, such as the application of blessed objects to the persons in

* It is vain to try to explain this fact by the thought-transference with which some hypnotists are credited. For 1° the hypnotist is a specialist, chosen among the thousands; while the exorcist may be any priest whatever; 2° the first has induced the attack by his will and his actions; the second has done nothing of the kind; 3° the one has endeavoured by a strong effort of his will to communicate his inner thought; the other has had quite the opposite wish.

question, etc. But however this may be, it at least furnishes us with the reason for not being too ready to believe in the Devil's presence when hearing the language used by certain subjects.

Theologians do not regard morbid facts, such as convulsions, sudden paralysis, movements, hoarse or inarticulate cries, a terrible facial expression, grinding of the teeth, transient deafness, etc., as signs of possession. At most these phenomenon may suggest the idea of possession. Charcot and Richer in their book *Des demoniaques dans l'art*, have been entirely mistaken in this respect. They have presented as necessary signs of possession, phenomena that were purely accessory, and have passed over in complete silence precisely those characters which the Roman ritual indicates as necessary. And further, they confuse sorcery and possession (see Dr. Goix's article on *La Folie religiesue et la possession diabolique*, in the *Annales de philosophie chrétienne*, of 1891).

Cardinal Bona describes as almost conclusive, two signs which would no longer be accepted in our day, because similar facts are known to occur in certain nervous maladies, namely, that the person has no longer any recollection of what he has said during his attack, nor of his refusal to recite the Apostles' Creed, or to ask pardon for his sins (*De discret. spir.*, ch. ix, No. 14).

Possessed persons exhibit an important point of difference to those that are hypnotised. During the attack the possessed man is in a continual state of revolt against the exorcist, and against the orders that he gives. They hypnotised subject, on the contrary, has no will but that of the operator. At most he resists the very exceptional cases where he is (apparently) ordered to perform criminal acts, such as an assassination. Further, if in the last case the hypnotist persists in his order, the subject, worn out with the struggle, falls into a fit of hysterics.

No matter how terrible the contest may be with the person who is really possessed, it never has this effect. This can be explained; it is not he who is bearing the brunt of the fight.

**70.**—These extraordinary sufferings, such as possession and obsession, are, like revelations, open to **illusions**; it is clear that we must never desire them; we must merely accept them, in spite of ourselves, as it were.

If we desire to suffer, we have the means of doing so by mortifying our pride and sensuality. In this way we avoid plunging into hazards that we are powerless to control, and of which we do not know the issue. But our imagination delights in the marvellous; it requires those romantic virtues that take the public eye.

What does not lead to illusion is to practise the duties of our state, and joyfully to accept all those sufferings that are independent of our own will. But a leap in the dark is considered more impressive (see ch. xii, **8**).

And further; trials such as possession and obsession are a serious source of embarrassment, not only to the person involved, but to directors and the whole community where he or she resides. Charity forbids us to desire this particular kind of suffering. And much the same thing may be said with regard to stigmata. I have heard of persons who, without asking for the ordeal of possession, have at least persuaded themselves that God called them to it as victims; they felt a secret satisfaction in being chosen for this exceptional part and having sufferings that belong to the extraordinary order. I think this state of mind one of the most dangerous; it would be enough to produce, by means of auto-suggestion, nervous diseases counterfeiting possession, or grave temptations.

### § 7. Diabolic Obsessions*

**71.**—From the lives of the **saints**, it would seem that if they suffer from strong obsessions, this usually occurs when they have reached the period of ecstasy or simply revelations and divine visions. These graces may then continue or may be suspended for a time.

The extraordinary action of God, and especially that of the angels and saints, is balanced, therefore, against the extraordinary action of the devils (see St. John of the Cross, *Obscure Night,* Book II, ch. xiii). The earth is a battlefield, where the two conflicting armies of good and evil angels are closely intermingled and contend for the same souls. If we saw the one army only, without the other, we should not have a proper appreciation of this battle, this conflict. It is natural that the knowledge of these two things should not be separated, since they are of the same nature and are component parts of one and the same drama—that of the Church militant. In the lower degrees of prayer, this parallelism has already been remarked. On one side there were the inspirations, the hidden influences, that is to say, of good spirits; and corresponding with them, the temptations or hidden actions of evil spirits. As we rise higher, the light begins to shine upon the two influences simultaneously.

**71** *bis.*—In the cases about to follow, we must apply what has already been said (7), namely, that everything is not to be attributed to the Devil. It is necessary to consult physicians. They are now acquainted with other obsessions which are purely matters of ill-health, and for which treatment can be attempted.

**72.**—Facts relating to the diabolic obsession may be divided into four kinds:

*First kind:* action upon the **speech** or the **gestures**. The person does not lose consciousness (otherwise it would be possession), but the Devil acts upon the tongue or the limbs, either 1° to *prevent* an act that is displeasing to him, such as a vocal prayer, confession, or the sign of the Cross; or 2° in order *to bring*

* I need not concern myself purely natural obsessions, such as spasms, agoraphobia, the imperative impulse to repeat certain unimportant actions several times consecutively and without any reasonable motive, etc. See *Les obsessions et la psychasténie,* by Pierre Janet (Alcan, 1903). This writer admits that the *aboulique* state (the notable diminution of the will) is the starting-point of all obsessions. See also his shorter book: *Les Névroses* (Flammarion, 1909).

*about* materially and without the person's consent, an irregular act, such as the blasphemous utterance or a gesture of contempt for some holy picture or other sacred object. In all these cases, the person keeps his interior but not his exterior freedom; his body is no longer in complete subjection to him.

These involuntary blasphemies are described in the life of Fr. John of Castille, S. J.* The Devil also made use of this holy priest's hands in order to burn or strike in the face, pictures of the Blessed Virgin (Scaramelli, Tr. 5, No. 115).

St. Teresa experienced this harassing by the Devil. "On another occasion," she says, "I was tortured for five hours with such terrible pains, such inward and outward sufferings, that it seemed to me as if I could not bear them... My body, head, and arms were violently shaken; *I could not help myself*" (*Life,* ch. xxxi, 3).

Blessed Margaret Mary sometimes became dumb when she went in search of her Superior in order to tell her of the spiteful tricks that the Devil played on her. He opposed this act, "because obedience broke down and dissipated his strength" (*Vie,* Paray edition, p. 137).

Fr. Surin describes this exterior thraldom in a letter to Fr. d'Attichy (1635). "The spirit unites himself with me without depriving me either of my consciousness or of my liberty. He is there as though it were another self. It is then as if I had two souls, one of which is deprived of the use of its bodily organs and remains, as it were, afar off, contemplating the other's actions... I am simultaneously filled with joy and overwhelmed with a sadness that finds a vent in lamentations and cries according to the demon's caprice... This stranger-soul, which seems to be mine, is penetrated with despair, as though by arrows, while the other, full of faith, despises these impressions... If, at the invitation of one of these souls, I wish to make the sign of the Cross upon my lips, the other soul forcibly withdraws my arm" (Quoted by M. Ribet, Vol. III, ch. x, § 10).

**73.**—The Devil's action upon the limbs has sometimes been carried to this point—that pious souls of not only thought of **committing suicide,** but had begun to put the intention into execution. Scaramelli speaks of having known several persons in such a case (Tr. 5, Nos. 112, 113). But he adds, "These persons never accomplish the desperate acts by which they had set out to kill or do themselves some other serious injury. No; even in the middle of the act itself, *they wake as though from a deep sleep,* enter into themselves, desist from the evil that they have begun, and remain penetrated with grief and scruples regarding these frenzied transports."† Lopez de Ezquerra states that he had the same experience (Tr. 6, No. 31).

* Details regarding this Father's trials and those of Fr. John Sebastian del Campo, his fellow-worker and contemporary (sixteenth century), occur in the Bollandists, June 22 (Prologue to the *Life* of Christina of Stommeln).

† This fact is not peculiar to the saints. Pierre Janet says that two-thirds of the neurotic persons who have violent impulses toward suicide or homicide, never carry out the act (*Les obsessions,* Vol. I, Part I, ch. i, § 2, p. 78).

This state, composed of a blending of automatism and consciousness, may, when natural, be called a semi-somnambulism.

During one of her great trials, St. Mary Magdalene of Pazzi left the choir and ran to the refectory for a knife with which to take her own life. Another time she made her companions tie her down, fearing to be carried away by a similar impulse.

It must therefore be accepted as a real though very rare fact, that violent crises of obsession (demoniac, or simply from ill-health) may occur, during which crises certain acts, bad in themselves, are automatically performed. The subject would not then be responsible for them. At other times he is in a closely allied state; he is not in possession of his full free-will. His will is sufficiently paralysed to prevent him from having sinned mortally.*

**74.**—These various cases of obsession may easily become a subsequent source of **scruples** for the person whose body is thus tyrannised over. He asks himself if he has not given some consent, at any rate, to these disordered acts, which, taking them as a whole, he has performed in spite of himself (Scaramelli, Tr. 5, Nos. 118, 122; Lopez de Ezquerra, Tr. 6, No. 29). Authors say, with reason, that these doubts are to be rejected, for they are merely doubts. Further, it is better to believe that instead of sinning even venially, the person has acquired merit. For it is not believable that God would permit such exceptional trials with any other design (Scaramelli, *ibid.*, No. 125). And further, if the person who is thus tormented saw that his Confessor considered him really culpable, he would be exposed to the risk of falling into despair, and thence into sin, as Satan desires (Scaramelli, No. 123; St. Alphonsus Liguori, *Homo. apost.*, Appendix I, No. 10; Phillipus a SS. Trinitate, Part I, Tr. III, disc. 2, art. 1).

The Confessor can safely conclude that the person suffering from the obsession is not guilty 1° when he (the latter) is convinced of his innocence, or doubtful about it; 2° when further, in the normal state, he is very fervent and feels deep horror for such an action (see Ribet, Vol. III, ch. ix, No. 6).

**75.**—Certain writers, such as Schram (No. 227, 1848 edition; 218, of the old ed.) have inquired if the state that I have just described under the name of obsession (first kind) should not rather be styled possession, since it is the Devil who sets our faculties in motion.

All depends upon the wider or narrower definition that we prefer to give to this word possession. With the one that I have adopted, a man must not be

* This opinion should not be restricted to those sinful acts for which we feel a natural repugnance, such as blasphemy or preparation for suicide. St. Alphonsus Liguori agrees with Gravina that the power of the obsession may go still further, and he bases his opinion upon this ground: *Si daemon potest alicujus commovere linguam ut invitus proferat obscœna verba aut blasphemias contra Deum, quidni manus ut turpia patrentur?* (*Praxis confess.*, ch. vii, § 7, No. 111). The saint afterwards refutes those who would confuse his teaching with that of Molinos'. The latter taught that when we are in the full enjoyment of our free-will, we may yield to temptations in order to avoid disturbing the soul's peace. There is a difference, therefore, both as to the preliminary hypothesis and as to motive.

called possessed because he strikes himself or blasphemes, if he is aware of his action and protests interiorly. But it is a state closely bordering on possession.

The opposite system would have a drawback, namely, that several saints would have to be classed as possessed and thus confused with persons in whom much more serious attacks occur.

**76.**—The *second kind* of obsession affects the **organs of** sense, and this sometimes to a terrible degree. Let us consider the five senses successively, and describe what many of the saints have experienced.*

**77.**—1° The **sight** suffered at times from representations in which the devil appeared under terrifying forms: armed men, negroes, terrible or repulsive animals, lions, tigers, wolves, wild boars, mastiffs, serpents, toads, spiders, etc. Some of these creatures seemed on the point of springing upon their victims, to bite or devour them. Examples: St. Antony, St. Guthlake (a Saxon hermit of the eighth century), St. Mary Magdalene of Pazzi, St. Colette, St. Philip Neri, St. Margaret of Cortona, the Ven. Grace of Valencia (sixteenth century), Blessed John the Good, hermit (thirteenth century), etc.

At other times the representations were impure, as happened to St. Alphonsus Rodriguez (see No. **94**).

**78.**—2° The **hearing** had to endure the noise of cries, whistlings, all kind of uproar and blasphemies or obscene words. Examples: St. Antony, St. Hilarion, Mme. Acarie, the Blessed Curé d'Ars.

St. Mary Magdalene of Pazzi was sometimes scarcely able to say the Divine Office amidst all this noise. Cassian says the same of certain monks in the desert. To enable them to sleep in peace during the night, several of their number were obliged to continue in prayer so as to keep the enemy at bay.

With some people, these visions and voices may be simple hallucinations produced by illness (Schram, No. 228 of the 1848 edition; 219 of the old). The trial is nonetheless great. But the fact is often a real one, for the noise is heard by those who are round about.

**79.**—With regard to the **sense of taste,** examples are rare. We have that of Sister Veronica, a Capuchin nun (Scaramelli, Tr. 5, No. 88). The devils defiled in a horrible way everything that she proposed to eat.

**80.**—4° The **sense of smell.** The demons caused St. Frances of Rome to smell fetid orders. They once brought a corpse in a state of full decomposition and applied it to her face. Her garments remain impregnated with the stench; it did not even disappear when they have been washed several times (*Vie,* by Dom Rabory, Book I, ch. 6).

**81**—5° the **sense of touch** seems to be the one most usually affected. Many Saints have been unmercifully beaten or bitten. This occurred to St. Antony and St. Germanus, Bishop of Paris. These onslaughts are referred to in the Bulls of

* Many historical details be found in *La Mystique*, by M. Ribet, Vol. II, ch. xi.

canonisation of St. Catherine of Siena, St. Francis Xavier, and St. Frances of Rome. The life of this last was one of the most characteristic of this respect. We possess circumstantial details concerning the last thirteen years of her life, dating from the age of forty-three (1427), that is to say. During this time heavenly ecstasies alternated with fiendish apparitions. The demons scourged her cruelly, but fled immediately when the servants of the house, attracted by the noise, hurried into the room.

**82.**—These attacks cause only **transient pain** as a rule. St. Catherine of Siena was thrown into the fire by the demon on several occasions, but she always emerged without being hurt.

For four years before her profession, the Ven. Agnes of Langeac was beaten twice a week (*Vie,* by de Lantages, Part 1, ch. vii).

St. Mary Magdalene of Pazzi was precipitated down a flight of twenty-five steps without receiving any serious injury. St. Margaret Mary suffered no hurt under a similar circumstance (*Vie,*, Paray edition, Vol. I, p. 138). When seated at recreation beside her companions, it happened on several occasions that the invisible hand pulled away her chair, so that she fell to the ground (*Vie,* Vol. I, p. 292). At other times the demon caused everything that she took in her hands to fall and break (*ibid.,* Vol. I, p. 137).

**83.**—At times, also, **severe injuries** have resulted. St. Teresa, at the age of sixty-two, was hurled one day down the choir steps by an invisible force. Her left arm was broken, and as the surgeon was unable to come until three months later, she suffered a real martyrdom during that time (Bolland, No. 786, and *Vie,* by a Carmelite of Caen, Vol. II, ch. xxvii).

Scaramelli relates that Sister Mary a Crucifixo (Satellico) was dragged over rocky ground so that her face was cut and remained disfigured (Tr. 5, Nos. 90, 91).

St. Nicholas of Tolentino, Augustinian of the thirteenth century, suffered such usage that he was often left half dead. On one occasion he was so ill-treated that he was lame to the end of his life. St. Theodore of Alexandria (fifth century) was covered with wounds. I will not go into the assaults of another kind that the Devil can inflict upon the body, I mean those that concern chastity (see Schram, No. 223 of the 1848 ed., No. 224 of the old; and St. Alphonsus Liguori, *Praxis,* No. 111).

**84.**—When anyone assures us in good faith that blows, bites, or wounds are due to the action of demons, we must find out whether he suffers from nervous attacks, during which he loses consciousness, or sleep in which dreams or somnambulism occur. For in these states persons are in the habit of striking, pinching, or biting themselves without being aware of it.

**85.**—*Third kind of obsession:* strange **maladies**, unlike anything that medical science is acquainted with.

The three kinds of obsession that we have just considered are of the physical order. The next one is of the moral order, it manifests itself in morbid thoughts and ideas.

**86.**—*Fourth kind:* **Temptations** of exceptional violence that you and passions are powerless to explain. The sufferer may feel himself at the end of his moral forces. He says: "It is all up to me. I shall be defeated." And the Devil craftily suggests this thought, "If I have to succumb finally, I may as well do so at once. I shall then at any rate be at peace again."

**87.**—The soul can **derive advantage** from obsessions. She conceives an ever-growing horror of him who thus torments her, and for all that he suggests. She throws herself all the more vehemently into God's arms, like a child, says St. Chrysostom, that takes refuge by its mother when it finds itself threatened by some horrible thing (*Ad Stagyrium,* Book I, No. 4).

**88.**—Spiritual **remedies** against obsession, when of diabolic origin; 1° The person must strive by prayer, by the Sacraments, by the sign of the Cross and holy water;

2° Instead of manifesting discouragement, he must show contempt for the demons. This is what St. Anthony did, saying to them: "You must be very weak, to have come in such numbers to attack one man." St. Frances of Rome used the same language. But we should attribute the victory to the Divine protection, not to ourselves. If the arch-enemy were entirely uncontrolled we could not resist him;

3° Either the person suffering from obsession, or a priest, may employ the formula of exorcism. It has been questioned (Schram, No. 234, 1848 ed.; 225 of the first) whether the efficacy of these prayers is not restricted to true possession. But the reply is in the negative; for the ritual does not make these distinctions; now it could not fail to do so if the object of the exorcism were so restricted. And far more, it explicitly implies at times that the exhortation is addressed to a person who is fully conscious, which is obsession, properly so-called; for it recommends that they should be made to pray during the ceremony.

Another reason is that the question resolves itself to this: what power is given to the Church to expel the demon? Now this is of the fullest. In fact, the Church causes certain places or objects to be blessed, ordering Satan to withdraw and not to attack those who approach them. And it is not even a question here of true possession;

4° We must answer Satan's solicitations with propositions that are distasteful to him. St. Alphonsus Liguori had the following method of driving away the devils who were tempting him; it succeeded, at any rate in ordinary cases. In a tone of authority, "and making a great sign of the Cross, he ordered them to prostrate themselves and to adore the Cross... He added: In the name of Jesus every knee should bow, of those that are in Heaven, on earth, and under the earth (Phil. ii, 10). Afterwards he commanded them to make acts of contrition and to ask pardon of God for their offences." The saint declared "that the devils have not the patience to endure such words and take flight" (*Vie,* No. 174).

**89.**—The obsession of blasphemy may sometimes have a purely natural cause: **the fear** of blasphemy. Let us imagine a pious and impressionable young girl. She hears God cursed, and is completely upset by it. The memory of it returns to her vividly again and again. If she has a timorous conscience, she trembles lest these words should pass her lips. Her imagination is more and more taken possession of, she often finds herself beginning to speak the words, just as others are haunted with an air which has taken their fancy; they sing it to themselves involuntarily.

It may be regarded as likely that other obsessions have, in part in any rate, the same cause; that of fear of offending.

This is the remedy: first, to assure this pious soul, convince her that she is committing no sin, and so quiet her conscience. Then impress upon her that this impulse is not worth thinking about, that it will gradually disappear of itself, just as happens with the musical haunting of which we spoke just now. One rooted idea is thus combatted with another. I would add that many temptations vanish if we attach no importance to them.

### § 8. Examples of Trials of Long Duration

**90.**—Blessed **Angela of Foligno.** Trials that she underwent for more than two years, shortly after her conversion (Extracts from her *Book of Visions and Instructions,* dictated by herself, ch. xix).

"Lest, however, the magnitude and multitude of the revelations and visions should exalt me, and the delights of these things lift me up above what I am, there was given unto me a tempter, who afflicted me by manifold temptation and affliction. For I am afflicted thereby both in body and soul" (p. 39).

1° *The body.* "I can hardly believe that the sufferings and infirmities of my body could be written, for there remaineth not in me one of my members that doth not suffer horribly" (p. 39-40).

2° *Vices.* "Moreover, the torment and sufferings of my soul (which without comparison I say are more bitter and in greater number than those of the body), I suffer as it were continually at the hands of the demons themselves... I see that I am delivered over to many demons, who cause the vices at which I shudder, and which were dead, to come to life again, and they had other vices also, which have never existed... And there is a certain vice permitted by God to come upon me, which was never in me [that of impurity]; but openly and clearly do I know that it is permitted by God to come upon me. And the aforesaid vice is so great that it surpasses all other vices. And there is a certain virtue, which was clearly given me by God in opposition to the aforesaid vice, and by that virtue I am powerfully delivered by God. If I had no certain faith with regard to God, in that one thing alone and not for any other reason I would have faith, and in that one thing my faith would be certain and secure, nor could I doubt about it. And the virtue prevaileth ever, and the vice decayeth and the virtue holdeth me and suffers me not to fall into the vice... So great indeed is the vice that when the aforesaid virtue is hidden from me, and it seemeth unto me that it hath left me, there is nothing with regard to either shame or punishment that could keep me from at once falling into sin. Yet then it is that the virtue of which I have spoken cometh upon me and powerfully freeth me, so that I could not sin for all the good things or evils of this world" (pp. 40-4).

3° *Despair.* "And sometimes I am plunged into the darkness of the demons, in which all hope of good seemeth unto me to be wanting, and this darkness is most horrible... And then I say unto God, 'Lord, if Thou must send me to Hell, delay not, but do it at once, and since Thou hast forsaken me, O do Thou finish with me, and plunge me into the abyss..."

"And afterwards, still being in the same abyss, I turned me to those my brothers, who are called my children, and said unto them, 'Do not believe me for the future. Do ye not see that I am possessed of the devil? Oh, ye who are called my children, ask of the justice of God that the demons may go out of my soul, and make known my most wicked works, so that through me God may be no longer blamed... Know then that I am sunk in such despair as I have never in any way experienced before, and that I have wholly despaired of God and of all His good things, and I have made a written agreement between myself and Him. And therefore am I certain that there is not a person in the world so full of all malice and damnable as I am; because whatever God hath granted unto being given, He has permitted it unto my greater despair and damnation" (pp. 42, 47-9).

"At times, also, such great anger cometh upon me that I can scarcely hold myself from tearing myself all to pieces. At other times I can hardly keep from striking myself horribly; and sometimes when I have struck myself I have caused my head and other members to become swollen" (p. 41).

4° *False humility.* "I see that I have fallen away from every good, and then beyond the reach of all virtue and all grace, and I see in myself so great a multitude of sins and defects that I cannot think that God will for the future have mercy upon me. And I perceive that I am the house of the devil, and that I give credit to demons and do their works, and am their daughter; and I see myself beyond the reach of all righteousness and all truth, and worthy of the lowest and last depths of hell. And the aforesaid humility is not that humility which at times I have, and which maketh my soul contemptible and causes it to arrive at the thought of the goodness of God; for the aforesaid humility bringeth nothing but innumerable evils" (p. 45).

It appears from another passage (ch. xxvi, pp. 86-7) that after these two years the demons continued a part of their attacks upon the body and the soul, but in the latter the superior part enjoyed a sublime contemplation. "Unto this... most high and altogether ineffable manner of seeing God in such great darkness and over-wonderful grace of vision, my mind was only thrice lifted up, although many and numberless times have I seen this All-Good joined always with darkness, but not in the aforesaid most high manner, nor with such great darkness. And whensoever on one side my body is wasted by infirmities, and the world with its thorns and bitternesses is driving me out of it, and the demons with much insistence are afflicting me and infesting me with almost continual persecution;... then, on the other side, God draws me towards Himself in that good which I see in darkness."

Later on she at times felt herself again as though abandoned by God and unable to pray. One of these trials lasted a month. "It seems unto to me that for the space of a month I had no feeling of God... But this at least of God seemed to remain to me, that I was not so greatly troubled as I ought to be, on account of my having wilfully forsaken God through sin" (ch. i, p. 165). At last she heard a voice speaking these words: "When it seemeth unto thee that thou art the more forsaken, then art thou the more beloved and nearer unto God" (p. 166).

At the moment of her death she said to her spiritual children:

"Of a truth, until God permit a person to be all twisted up and trampled on, and trodden underfoot, He suffereth not sometimes temptations and tempests to end; and this He doth chiefly to His true children" (ch. lxx, p. 346).

**91.**—Blessed Baptiste **Varani**, Abbess of the Poor Clares of Camerino (1458-1527), began at thirty years of age to suffer two nearly consecutive trials, each of two years' duration. At the beginning she says: "God showed me in a dream all the labours, all the afflictions that awaited me... And then the depths of the abyss, which had been closed for ten years, opened, and was more terrifying than ever. The dragon came forth from it, roaring against me, and assailed me with such fury that he seemed to wish to devour me alive" (*Vie*, ch. v).

She describes one of her temptations: "I rebelled against God imputing to Him my faults, my sins, and my errors. I dared call Him to account for His conduct. I accused Him of falsehood in several things that He had said to me, or that I found in His writings... I had many other bad thoughts, the recollection of which fills me with horror" (ch. vi). She wrongly considered herself to be culpable here.

**92.**—The Ven. **Anne of Saint-Bartholomew,** a companion of St. Teresa; died at Anvers, at the age of seventy-six.

Some days after her entry into the Novitiate at Avila, at the age of fourteen, the very extraordinary graces that she had hitherto received, disappeared, and gave place to a year of darkness. She said with great simplicity to Our Lord: "What is it? Why have You abandoned me? If I did not know You I should think that You had deceived me, and if I had known that You were to go away, I should not have come to the convent" (*Vie*, by Fr. Boix, second ed., Book II, ch. ii).

Towards the end of her life, she had two or three years of interior sufferings. "They are so great," she wrote, "that if I had not known and tasted the goodness of God, I might lose confidence. But He has left me this grace, that however overwhelmed I may be, I am always resigned to His will... My soul saw a kind of cloud darker than the darkest night, that burst upon her suddenly" (*ibid.*, Book IV, ch. xi).

**93.—St. Mary Magdalene of Pazzi** (1566-1607).

From her entrance into religion, at the age of sixteen and a half, her life quickly became a series of continual ecstasies. But there were two trials, each of five years' duration, in which these favours were reduced to very little.

The first of these, that she called the den of lions, overtook her at the age of nineteen (1585). It was preceded by an eight days' ecstasy, from which she only came out for two hours a day (*Vie*, by Cepari, ch. vi, English Trans. Oratiorian series, ch. xxxix, p. 153). The revelations that she received during this week were so numerous, that, when collected, they form a good-sized volume.

It was in one of these ecstasies that Our Lord foretold her great trials, saying to her: "Know... that for five years I will deprive thee of every feeling of grace, but not of grace itself, which shall ever abide in thee... I will, moreover, act towards thee as a valiant chief who repeatedly tries a soldier before he promotes him to high honor" (*ibid.*, p. 154).

The trial began. It consisted in apparitions of the Devil, and temptations against faith and obedience. "To this aridity of spirit all the exercises of the community wearied her, so that she could not attend to the observances in the choir, the refectory, or anywhere else" (ibid., pp. 155-6).

Finally, she became inclined to gluttony and to despair. At long intervals God solaced her by some spiritual consolation; there was notably one ecstasy lasting a week.

The second trial occurred during the five last years of her life (beginning 1602; she was then thirty-six). She suffered from very severe illnesses, and great spiritual aridities, interspersed here and there with raptures (V, ch. xxxvi; English translation, ch. lxii). She had asked God for "a life of pure suffering."

**94.—St. Alphonsus Rodriguez.**

He passed through three periods of great interior sufferings.

1° Towards the middle of his life, he had eight or ten years of scruples which "plunged him into sadness and anguish."

2° Being then about fifty years of age, and having already received many extraordinary graces, he had to undergo terrible and very perilous onslaughts against chastity for a space of seven years. He was attacked not only by violent temptations, but by diabolic apparitions. Speaking of himself, he says: "Sometimes this person was oppressed and pursued so closely that his suffering was indescribable. At times he was quite weak and panting, as it were; at others, desolate and deprived of all consolation, human and divine. It then seemed to him as though for him there was no God, but only demons who surrounded him, appearing to him under various shapes, inviting him to evil and cursing him because he would not consent to what they proposed. At times he was present during their infernal conversations and heard them blaspheme God; or he was on the verge of death by choking, because they squeezed his throat... They only left him in order to confer together about him, for he then saw how in the depths of Hell they took counsel and consulted a vast number of devils... As a rule they came towards midnight. Finding him asleep, they entered with great clamour in order to terrify him; he woke at the noise. At once they assailed him with temptation... leaving him nothing but a refusal of his consent. In spite of the cold, he was all perspiring, so hot and painful was the conflict that he had to sustain. I only relate a small part of all that I remember." Once, in particular, "Some laid hold of him... without his being able to free himself; he was near dying by suffocation, so furious was the rage towards him. During this trial he was consumed with sadness; if he sought some consolation for the alleviation of his suffering, he found none. He cried to Our Lady, and found her not; he called on the saints and they were dead to his cries... A sadness during these horrible persecutions became so overwhelming that he pined away." "After these conflicts with demons, God consoled him interiorly in such a manner the flesh was at times too weak to bear the abundance of these consolations" (*Vie,* No. 18).

3° During his last illness, he had a period of trial by doubt, aridity, and scruples, lasting five months. Peace was restored to him suddenly, following upon an apparition of Jesus and Mary (*Bull of Canonisation*).

**95.—St. Rose of Lima** (1586-1617).

She had a trial of a quite distinct kind. One of her biographers says "that she was tormented by the devil for an hour and a half a day for fifteen years; and this to such an extent that she suffered in some sort the same pains as the souls in Purgatory. During this violent tempest, she could no longer think of God, she experienced insupportable desolations, abandonments, and aridities, and the spirits of darkness filled her imagination with such horrible spectres that when she felt the hour of her penance approaching, her whole body trembled and she implored her beloved Bridegroom to is one drinking this cup... It is true that after this torment was over, she received great interior consolations."

"There is scarcely any malady with which she is not tormented: quinsy, asthma, chest and stomach troubles and sciatic-gout are those that troubled her the most" (*Les petits bollandistes*, by Mgr. Guerin, Aug. 30).

**96.—St. Jane Frances de Chantal** suffered great temptations and spiritual distresses, even up to the end of her life. The last seven or eight years, says Mgr. Bougaud (ch. xxxii), passed in an uninterrupted moral agony that only ceased a month before her death; aridities, doubts concerning the mysteries of religion, impulses to blasphemy, the feeling that God hated her, abominable judgements passed upon her neighbour and scruples. She never, however, had any thoughts contrary to purity. The year of her death (at the age of seventy) she confided to one of her spiritual daughters that she had been pursued by temptations for forty-one years. Towards the same period she also said: "By the continual violence of my mental temptations and trials, I am now reduced to such a point, that nothing in this world can give me any comfort, save only death" (*Vie,* by Mère de Chaugy, Book III, ch. xxvii).

**97.**—In the life of **Fr. Rigoleuc**, a Breton missionary of the seventeenth century, we have another example of this, as it were, simultaneous presence of the mystic state, together with great interior trials. A violent temptation to despair tormented him for fifty-six years. He was convinced of his eternal damnation. Now previously, at the age of thirty-eight, he had obtained "this gift of infused prayer and the supernatural presence of God that he had so desired" (*Vie,* by Fr. Champion, ch. viii, § 3).*

His biographer adds that "he never lost it from that time onward, even during his great trial, in which it was his chief support." But it is clear that these two states did not occur at the same hour.

**98.**—The Ven. **Mary of the Incarnation,** Ursuline, went through three periods of abandonment, each more severe and of greater duration than its predecessor.

1° The first, which lasted some months, came upon her towards her twenty-fifth year, while she was still living in the world. For nearly five years she had enjoyed a permanent state of union with God. Her mind then became filled with darkness and her will seemed enfeebled. "I saw myself, she says, descend into an abyss. All consolation was taken from me; even the memory of the graces that I had received redoubled my sufferings, being as it were convinced that they were not true graces but a loss of time in which I had been amusing myself... Great efforts were required for continuing my penances... As to my neighbours, I thought everything [disagreeable] that was said to me, I was forced to watch myself continually that I may keep a gentle disposition of mind" (*Vie,* by an Ursuline of Nantes, ch. iv).

At the conclusion of this trial, she received much greater favours than before; notably, the intellectual vision of the Blessed Trinity and, a little later on, an infused knowledge of Latin and of the Scriptures.

Two years before the period of desolation described above, she had gone upon wrong lines in her prayer for want of a director. "Some spiritual books fell into her hands; they taught a way of mental prayer by fixed methods, with preludes, divisions and points, and laid down the danger of following special ways [differing from this one]. Our young widow tried to conform to these rules when meditating upon Our Lord's mysteries, resisting with all her strength the supernatural attraction that usually made her consider her subject all in one glance, as she used to say, and held her passive afterwards under her

* On more than one occasion he was seen in an ecstasy. "At the end of his life the onslaughts of divine love weakened him so that he could not stand upright" (*ibid.*).

Master's action. She applied herself daily to the task; but the strain was such that she contracted violent headaches, from which she suffered for two years. St. Francis of Sales' *Introduction to the Devout Life*, which then became popular, to the great advantage of piety generally, gave her a little more liberty. Finally, God sent her the guide who was to lead her." He made her resume the manner of prayer that suited her. He was a monk of the Order of St. Bernard (*Vie*, by an Ursuline of Nantes, ch. iv).

2° The second period of trials began three or four months after her entry into the convent, and lasted two years with intervals of extraordinary graces. She was then thirty-one years of age.

This trial was made up as follows:

(*a*) Inability to pray. "At prayer, my first thoughts were the recapitulation of my crosses, and this went on from the beginning to the end."

(*b*) The imagination was "assailed by all kind of abominations. The things that I had never loved in the world filled my mind. I had blasphemous thoughts, doubts against faith, strange cowardices when it was a question of certain penances." Pride, vanity, hatred of her neighbour and disobedience seemed to force an entry into her heart. "I feared lest God should have abandoned me on account of all this malice. My past life seemed to be nothing but an uninterrupted series of miseries, and all the gifts of prayer with which I had been favoured appeared as the effects of a deplorable illusion. I began to fall into the imperfections which had disedified me in spiritual people, and this humiliated me all the more because I had always found it difficult to understand how these defects could be allied with a solid virtue; I was never better punished."

(*c*) Tedium and a distaste for holy things oppressed her soul. "The solitude that I was so fond of before, became a purgatory to me. It was insupportable to me to be in my cell all day, seeing no one. My work inspired me with such repugnance that I had to do great violence to myself in order to force myself to it. And I also felt such great fatigue exteriorly that I could hardly bear it."

Her torments inclined her to despair. "This was carried one day to such a point, that finding myself near a window, I had the frightful temptation to throw myself out of it; for my understanding was wholly obscured."

(*d*) In order to detach His servant from all human support, God permitted that the holy religious who had directed her for the last twelve years, and who had her entire confidence, should leave the town when her trials were at their height. He was replaced by one who instead of encouraging her, only treated her harshly; scoffing at her, he declared that the graces of which she told him were pure illusion, and her sufferings the result of not mortifying herself more. So she came to see nothing "but malice and hypocrisy" in herself (see *Vie*, by an Ursuline of Nantes, ch. vi; *Histoire*, by the Abbé Chapôt, Part II, ch. iii).

3° At the age of forty, being then habituated to the highest graces, she embarked for Canada. She then entered into a period of eight years of interior trials, of which the three first were the most agonising (*Histoire,* by the Abbé Chapôt, Part IV, ch. i). This is the summary of them.

(*a*) She felt aversion and mistrust of everyone that approached her.

(*b*) The reverse also occurred. "God also permitted that they should continually feel aversion for me, as they have since admitted to me."

(*c*) "I regarded myself as the basest, the most degraded of creatures and the most deserving of contempt in the whole world... I scarcely dared to raise my eyes; to such an extent that I feel myself *bowed down by a profound humiliation,* that I made it my endeavour, in consequence, to perform the lowest and vilest tasks, not finding myself worthy of any others."

(*d*) "I thought that this great wretchedness had *completely estranged me from God,* and deprived me of all His graces and of His signal mercies. I saw myself, as it were, plunged into a Hell *full of grief* and mortal bitterness that proceeded from *a fearful temptation to despair,* which was as though born in these darknesses, without my knowing the cause... I was at times arrested suddenly on my road by a sudden *vision,* in which *I saw Hell* open under my feet; and it seemed to me that out of this abyss there leapt up flames that were about to absorb and consume me."

(*e*) "At the same time I felt impelled in myself by a frightful interior disposition *to precipitate myself into it through hatred of God."* Once especially during the voyage, this strange temptation to suicide was "so strong and violent, that if I had not happened opportunely upon a bulwark which was beside me, and to which I clung, I should have fallen."

(*f*) "Sometimes, however, during these depressing darknesses a divine ray shone in my soul and enlightened her, kindling in her a love that threw her into an extraordinary transport, so that after such agonies I seemed to be in Paradise. I then enjoyed a very intimate converse with God, who caressed me with His embraces. But that was soon over. This light was like those luminous rays that pierce the clouds unexpectedly on a gloomy day and then promptly vanish... I then passed from an abyss of light and love into an abyss of obscurities and dolorous darkness."

She was at last delivered by Our Lady's intercession (*ibid.,* ch. ii): "I represented to her that she knew my weakness well, and that the spiritual sufferings were opposed to the state of peace which the Divine Majesty wished to establish in my soul's centre... I saw plainly that it was the Spirit of God Himself who made me speak in this way to our Blessed Mother. And at that same moment I felt my prayer granted, and the sensation as though I were relieved of some heavy garment." God made her understand that not only had she lost nothing during these years of trials and temptations, but "that she had on the contrary, amassed a wealth of ineffable treasures."

**99.—St. Joseph of Cupertino,** who had ecstasies from his infancy, was, when about forty years of age, deprived of all his extraordinary graces for the space of two years. At the same time he was assailed by violent temptations. "Grief," says his biographer, "brought on an attack of ophthalmia, that made him unable to raise his eyes" (*Vie,* by Bernino, ch. ix).

**100.**—Blessed **Mary of the Angels**, a Carmelite nun of Turin (died 1717). She had made her profession at the age of seventeen. Seven years later the trials began: 1° for eight months apparitions of demons, who beat her severely. Violent temptations against chastity, faith, and hope. One day the Devil said to her in a compassionate tone: "Believe me, it is better to consent frankly once, then to be always tormented in this way, all the more because I shall end by vanquishing you." And again: "What is the use of serving God? You are damned. Repentances and tears are only so much suffering thrown away, for your sentence of damnation is already pronounced. Why then make yourself two Hells? It is much better to take your life and finish with it altogether." 2° After this period (Blessed Mary was then twenty-four years of age) there came another, extending over a period of five and a half years, and which was still more distressing: abandonment and the temptation to despair. "My life is a mortal agony from the continual fear that I am in of offending God. And, on the other hand, I feel myself carried away by so brutal an anger, hate, and rage that I seem in truth to be rather a demon that a human creature. When I am in these agonies, the only thing remaining for me (this is the impression that I receive) is to cast myself into Hell." Our Lord had warned her of this tribulation, by showing her a Cross from which His figure was absent. It was the symbol of the suffering that is endured alone, believing oneself to be disgraced, hated, damned. "It is a sign that from this day onward you will not feel the sweetness of My presence. You will think yourself abandoned. Your temptations will go on augmenting more and more; you will feel all the force of passions that have hitherto been asleep, and they will torment you like savage dogs. Finally, your greatest affliction will be that you will believe yourself to have incurred My displeasure. But continue unshaken in My love, be humble of heart and submissive to your Superiors. I promise you My succour."

From time to time, however, some great grace made her take fresh courage. When the trial was over, ecstasies became numerous and of almost daily occurrence. She lived for another twenty-seven years (see *Vie,* by Fr. Sernin of Saint-Andre).

**101.**—In the *Life* of the Ven. Anne-Madeleine de **Rémuzat** we read that "during the last six years of her life, she needed supernatural strength in order to endure her excessive afflictions. Associated as she was with Our Lord's Passion, she felt her soul filled with mortal grief and her body with inexpressible sufferings. It is true that the superior part of her spirit tasted the pure delights of the knowledge of God and intimate friendship with Him; still her suffering was excessive, and the natural life would have succumbed if the divine virtue had not sustained it (*Vie,* published by the Visitation at Marseilles, ch. xv, p. 230).

**102.**—**Fr. Lyonnard**, S. J., author of *L'Apostolat de la souffrance*, underwent alternations of sorrows and joys of exceptional persistence and intensity. During the last forty-four years of his life (1842-1886), he passed abruptly from mystic graces to very severe interior sufferings: temptations, scruples, darknesses, physical and moral exhaustion, isolation of soul. He has said that on several occasions it was revealed to him that his martyrdom would entirely supply the place of Purgatory for him (*Biographical notice* at the beginning of his book, ch. x).

**103.**—We have a remarkable example of the **slowness of God's operations** in the life of a French Carmelite who died the beginning of the present century. She entered into religion at the age of thirty, and for forty-two years continued to writhe under the severest interior trials, fighting on without any remission, without any alleviations, living by a blind and naked faith. Suddenly, at the age of seventy-two, she was raised to extraordinary graces; she found Heaven on this earth, and said: "I no longer believe, I see." It was thus up to the time of her death, which took place eleven years later.

## EXTRACTS

### On the Sufferings of Contemplatives

**104.**—St. Teresa:

1° "Ye would wonder at the ways and manner whereby God crosseth them. I know.. that the afflictions God lays on the contemplative are *intolerable;* and of such a kind that unless He gave them this repast of gusts [of interior delights], they could not be endured... They have need that His Majesty should afford them some refreshment, and this not of water, but wine; that so, inebriated with this celestial wine, they may not consider that they suffer and may be able to endure it. Hence it is, that I see few contemplatives, but I perceive them courageous and resolved to suffer... I believe those of the active way, seeing how for a little while they are caressed, think that there is nothing else but those consolations; but I tell you, that perhaps ye could not endure one day what they do" (*Way of Perfection,* ch. xviii, pp. 52-3).

2° "The labour is greatest at first... They who are in the beginning, the middle, and the end, have *their crosses to carry;* the crosses, however, are different" (*Life,* ch. xi, 8).

3° "In one way or another, we must carry the cross all our lives. If people told me that, *ever since* attaining to the prayer of union, they had enjoyed constant peace and happiness, I should reply that they could never have reached that state" (*Interior Castle,* Fifth Mansion, ch. ii, 8).

4° "O my God, how many troubles both interior and exterior must one suffer before entering the seventh mansion. Sometimes, while pondering over this, I fear that were they known beforehand, human infirmity could scarcely bear them, or could resolve to encounter them, however great might appear the gain... [In this state] Our Lord now usually sends severe bodily infirmity... The soul, in its anguish, knows not what to do with itself... I knew someone who, from the time when, forty years ago, Our Lord began to bestow on her the favour I have described, could not affirm, with any truth, that she had been a single day without pain and other kinds of suffering. I am speaking of bodily infirmities" (*Interior Castle,* Sixth Mansion, ch. i, 3, 13, 14).

5° "It doth not trouble me when I see a soul in very sore temptation; because if there be a love and fear of Our Lord, she will come off with much gain... But if I see anyone go on always quiet, and without all kind of war (for I have met with some, who though I saw them not offend the Lord, always kept me in fear), I never am secure" (*Conceptions of the Love of God,* ch. ii, p. 298).

6° "His Majesty can bestow no greater favour on us than to give us a life such as was led by His beloved Son" (*Interior Castle,* Seventh Mansion, ch. iv, 6).

**105.**—Tauler:

1° "When our Heavenly Father has decreed to adorn the soul by exalted gifts, and to transform it after a sublime manner, He is accustomed, not to cleanse it gently, but to bathe it in a sea of bitterness, to plunge it, to drown it, as He did the prophet Jonas" (*Institutions,* ch. xi).

2° Of the calm to be preserved in interior sufferings:

"The man who seeks after God, finds himself sometimes assailed by anguish and heaviness of heart; he fears that he has not had God purely in view and that his works may thus have been useless. Such a fear robs him of his peace and plunges him into grief and anxiety. This sadness is sometimes the result of an enfeebled constitution or of atmospheric influences, or, again, of the evil spirit who seeks to disturb him by his impressions. He must sweetly repel this bad disposition, and quietly preserve his peace of mind. There is no better remedy. On the other hand, it is a mistake to drive his anguish away with violence and anger. These shocks only tire the mind. It is the same if we run in an agitated way after doctors and servants of God, to ask their advice and help, for no one can save us from this trial. We will conclude: When this sadness and storm arise in our souls, let us behave as we do when it rains hard or hails. We hurriedly take refuge under cover until the rain and tempest have passed over. In the same way, if we feel that we desire only God, and the anguish still takes possession of us, let us quietly flee from the storm until the fine weather returns; let us bear it patiently, waiting on God with calm and cheerfulness... Let us continue quietly under the shelter of the Divine good pleasure" (First Sermon for Whit Sunday).

**106.**—Ven. Mary of the Incarnation, Ursuline, speaking of the mystic way:

"I repeat, we must pass through great interior and exterior labours which would appal a soul if they were shown to her before she made trial of them, and might even make her relinquish the design of still going forward when she comes to experience them, did not a secret and deeply rooted virtue sustain her" (quoted by Fr. de Charlevoix in his Vie de la Vble. Marie de l'Incarnation, Book VI).

# PART VI

## Mysticism: Some Supplementary Questions

## CHAPTER XXV

### On the Desire for the Mystic Union

**1.—The complex nature of the question.** If the supernatural states of prayer were merely means of sanctification, graces of sanctity, the question of desiring them would present no difficulty. But they are extraordinary graces, privileges, divine familiarities, bringing with them marvels of condescension on God's part and elevating the soul to heights that are regarded without exception by ordinary people as sublime. Thence arises the question of knowing whether desires and requests relating to such an object do not constitute presumption, an insane forgetfulness of the distance between God and His sinful creature; a seeking after distinctions which is incompatible with Christian humility. The question arises all the more because the prospective view of these states flatters our vanity, leads the imagination astray and nourishes a dreamy sentimentality. In abandoning ourselves to these desires and hopes the danger to be feared is that of feeding our self-love, exchanging the substance for the shadow, and leaving the sphere in which we are striving seriously after our sanctification in order to wander in a world of chimeras.

2.—The question being one of such complexity, the **appearance of disagreement** existing between various writers* or various directors of souls is explained; some looking chiefly at the thesis in itself, others being more concerned with its effects upon conduct and its bearing upon practical life.

To get a correct and complete idea of the subject we must examine its various aspects in turn. Let us first consider the desire *regarded in itself.*

* Fr. Meynard says: "May we desire the extraordinary, perfect contemplation that is derived from the gifts of the Holy Ghost? Writers seem divided upon this point; some, and we think the *greater number, relying upon St. Thomas' teaching,* declare that this desire is quite legitimate; others see presumption in it. This divergence of opinion is *more apparent than real*" (*Traité de la Vie Intérieure,* Vol. II, No. 75).

**3.**—**An important distinction.** To begin with, we must recall the distinction between the mystic union and *ex-deific* (*exdéiques*) favours (revelations, visions of created things). For the first, we shall see that it is perfectly *legitimate and conformed to perfection* to desire and to ask for them. For revelations and visions the contrary is the case. I have shown the dangers attending these favours in a former chapter (ch. xxi). The saints advise us to avoid them to the utmost when they occur spontaneously. Much more, then, they are not to be desired. This would be to expose ourselves to all kinds of illusion (see Extracts, ch. xxiii).

**4.**—We must not say, therefore, in a general way that it is permissible to desire *extraordinary graces.* This phrase is ambiguous; it does not take the foregoing distinction into account. It is true with regard to contemplation; false for the rest.

**5.**—Let us then concern ourselves solely here with **the desire for the mystic union.** There are two cases to be considered.

**6.**—The **first case** is that of souls that already have *a first beginning* of mystic graces. It has always been admitted that they may desire to advance in this way. For God has deposited a seed in their souls in order that it may fructify. To desire this is *to conform our will to God's will.*

St. Teresa often expresses the desire not only to maintain herself in the mystic way, but to advance in it,* when once it has been entered upon.

**7.**—What we have just said applies even to those who are in the **first night** of the soul. For this prayer is ordinary in appearance only. In reality it is an entrance into the mystic way.

**8.**—The **second case** is that of souls who are in *the ordinary way.* They may also desire and ask for the mystic union. But, as in the case of all requests, they

* Example: "With what a thirst is this thirst [for the mystic union] desired!... it is a thirst very painful; it afflicts yet carries with it a satisfaction, wherewith our former thirst is allayed; so that it is a thirst which *only* extinguishes thirst in respect of earthly things; else it satiates so, that *when God satisfies it, one of the greater favours* that He can do the soul is, to leave her in this necessity, which continues always greater to drink again of this water" (*The Way of Perfection*, ch. xix, pp. 56-7).

Speaking of the feelings experienced by those who have, at least, arrived at the full union, she expresses the desire for the spiritual marriage, which is the goal of this way, in eight different passages (*Interior Castle*, Fifth, Sixth, and Seventh Mansions).

Speaking of the soul that is already far advanced, St. John of the Cross says: "*She is not content* with that knowledge of God once granted to Moses—the knowledge of Him by His works—for she prays to see the face of God, which is the essential communication of His Divinity to the soul, without any intervening medium, by a certain knowledge thereof in the Divinity... inasmuch as it is the contact of pure substances, that is, of the soul and the Divinity... 'Do not tell it,' as before when Thy converse with me was known to the outward senses, for it was once such as to be comprehended by them; it was not so profound but they could fathom it. Now let Thy converse with me be *so deep and so substantial*, and so interior, as to be beyond the capacity of the senses... The soul *prays*... that the depth of the secret of the spiritual union may be such as to escape the notice of the senses, like the secret which St. Paul heard, and which is not granted to man to utter" (*Spiritual Canticle*, Stanza 19, p. 106).

should exhibit a joyful resignation to everything that God ordains. They will thus feel no bitterness if their demands are not granted.

And further, it is well understood that they will desire these favours, not from the foolish ambition of being raised above others, or as an agreeable distraction or by any other puerile motive, but because they see here a powerful means for a speedier and fuller sanctification. Otherwise they would be wishing for the means without desiring the end assigned to it by God.*

**9.—This doctrine is based** upon the fact that in itself the mystic union possesses no drawbacks and immense advantages (ch. xxi, **45** and ch. xxii). We are not so exacting with regard to conditions, when it is a question of our other desires, as Fr. Sandaeus bids us notice. "Even if pure contemplation," he says, "were not absolutely good in itself, even if it were only a goodness mingled with imperfections, it would none the less be superior to a multitude of natural blessings affecting the soul or the body, such as a keen intellect, a tenacious memory, artistic talent, knowledge, health, physical strength, good-nature, and a thousand other similar things. Now it is permissible to ask for all these things" (*Theol. myst.*, p. 198; *Commentatio de contempl. pura,* ex. 5, disq. 15).

And further, why should not a man in one degree of prayer desire the succeeding degree? There is no good reason to offer. The nature of things and consequently the divine plan, allow him to seek to perfect himself more and more.

Another reason: We have seen (ch. vi, **19**) that the mystic graces are a part of the gifts of the Holy Ghost. Now the Church sets us the example of asking for the seven gifts. She has never dreamed of excluding any one of them.

**10.**—Finally, this doctrine is, as we may say, **the common doctrine amongst mystics.** A few of them, only, restrict it, but without discussing the question, some to the case where the person feels himself urged thereto by an inspiration of the Holy Ghost (Scaramelli, Tr. 3, ch. xxxii); others to that in which some mystic grace has already been received (St. Alphonsus Liguori, *Homo. Apost.* Append. I, No. 23). If certain others seem not to approve of this desire, it is that they have in view, not the grace of mystic union in itself but its extraordinary accessories (revelations or ecstasies in public. See note to No. 35), or they are concerned with certain practical conditions which I will enumerate in a few words.

**11.**—1° **Bearing in mind the ordinary tendency of humility.** Humility is the usual condition for the bestowal of God's great graces. An increase of humility

* St. Teresa: "It would be well to tell you, sisters, the *reason* why God bestows such favours on souls in this world, although you must have learned this by the effects produced... None of you may think it is only for the sake of the pleasure such persons feel, which would be a great mistake on your part, for His Majesty can bestow no greater favour on us than to give us a life such as was led by His beloved Son as I have often told you. Therefore, I feel certain that these graces are sent to strengthen our weakness, that we may imitate Him by *suffering much.*" (*Interior Castle,* Seventh Mansion, ch. iv, 6).

is one of the most common results, and consequently is one of the surest signs of the divine action in a soul. Humility, in fact, should have a place in all our relations with God, and should, as it were, strike the key-note for them. The reasons are easily given. We have only to verify this fact in the lives of all the saints. The more they advance in the knowledge and love of God, as in the knowledge of themselves, the more they see the infinite distance that lies between God and His poor sinful creatures. If God seems to forget these distances in descending to them lovingly, they are only so much the more faithful in remembering them. If God raises them, so to say, up to Him, they plunge deeper into the thought of their nothingness and unworthiness.

And hence, as it were, a wonderful conflict between God's condescension and the humility of the saints. Hence with the latter an even clearer and more pervading realisation of their nothingness in the presence of the Divine Majesty, as God gives and shows Himself the more to them. This realisation of the dividing distances and this humility show themselves especially in the desire for the graces of interior prayer. These graces appear, doubtless, as sovereignly desirable, and he who has tasted of them thirsts after them with an ardent thirst; but at the same time the soul feels that in her they are, so to speak, sovereignly misplaced; and she realises how utterly unworthy of them she is. Thence a double action: the desire for so great a blessing and the recognition of her own unworthiness. *At times the desire predominates,* but without excluding a humble self-distrust; and the soul cries: "Let Him kiss me with the kiss of His mouth!" *At times humility predominates,* but without stifling the desire; and the soul exclaims with the centurion: "Lord, I am not worthy!" or with St. Peter: "Depart from me, for I am a sinful man, O Lord!" It is this alternating pulsation of desire and of humility that delights the heart of God.

Other considerations of the same kind may also, I will not say limit the desire for the mystic graces, but may repress their flights and *moderate their expression:* the thought, for instance, of the responsibilities that they bring in their train, and the humble fear, tempered by trust, of not corresponding to them aright.

**12.—2° Bearing in mind the dangers of illusion.** I have already, in the preface, referred to these dangers, and there is no need to insist upon them at great length, although they are not chimerical. All that is required is to be acquainted with human nature and to have some experience with souls.

Those who have no knowledge of the mystic graces are more exposed to these dangers. But we are not safe because we have already received some taste of these favours.

The illusions are of three kinds. The illusion of thinking that we have already entered into these states; the illusion of thinking that we are quite near to them, when we are a long way off; the illusion, finally, and whether we are near or not, of neglecting the duties of our state: personal effort and the practice of ordinary virtues, or, as St. Francis of Sales said, of the small virtues, under pretext of extraordinary prayer and of the passive states. These dangers and other similar ones are described by the mystics themselves. Those who would walk in the right path should read one of the works of the most popular of mystics, St. Teresa's *Way of Perfection*.

**13.—Objection**. Is not this illusion of neglecting the present duty generally a consequence of the desire for supernatural graces? When the heart is elsewhere can we have any inclination for perfecting ourselves in our state?

**14.—Reply**. This neglect can only be found in the case of persons who are very ignorant in the spiritual life. The others will understand that in order to obtain fresh gifts from God they must begin by sanctifying themselves as far as possible in the path in which their feet are actually set. Their wish for closer relations with their sovereign Master will be a spur to generosity and not an obstacle. I have known souls whose desire in this respect has never been granted, and yet it has been of great assistance to them.

It is the same with worldly persons. They show greater zeal for their employment when they hope to gain advancement, as they call it, thereby (see Extracts **17**, 3° and **27**).

**15.**—A **love for the Cross** should be asked for at the same time as the mystic union. This will enable us to put the necessary detachment into the latter request, and to prepare ourselves for the trials which will not fail to accompany the extraordinary graces.

**16.**—We have just considered the legitimacy of the desire. With regard to its **efficacy**, see ch. xxviii, **24**.

## EXTRACTS

### The Desire for the Mystic Union That May Be Felt by Those Who Are in the Ordinary Way.

**17.**—St. Teresa. *First series* of Extracts.*

1° "I counsel you, daughters, ever, with the Spouse, *to beg* this so delicious peace;... Certainly these things cannot come from us, but only the *requesting* and *desiring* that He would do us this favour; and even this too by His

* Certain passages of St. Teresa's *Works* have appeared to be opposed to this desire, because they have been misinterpreted. She sometimes wishes to console those souls that do not arrive at the mystic state, and she shows them this very true principle, that it is simply a *means* of attaining to sanctity, and that if they obtain this sanctity by another way, they ought to be satisfied. There is no question of blaming those who desire the extraordinary union. See especially those places where she explains herself on this point. The *Way of Perfection,* the last lines of ch. xx, quoted further on (19, 20), and the first lines of ch. xxi.

assistance. For as to the rest, what can a poor worm do, when as sin makes it so cowardly and miserable that we measure all the virtues exactly according to our mean capacity. Now what remedy of this, daughters? To *desire* with the Spouse that Our Lord kiss me, etc." (*Conceptions of the Love of God,* ch. iii, p. 307). The saint also says that this desire is only fully satisfied by the spiritual marriage (*Interior Castle,* Seventh Mansion, ch. iii).

2° Speaking of the prayer of quiet: "You are *longing,* my daughters, to enter into this state of prayer at once, and *you are right,* for, as I said, the soul cannot understand the value of the graces bestowed by God on it there, nor the love which draws Him ever closer to it: certainly we should *desire to learn how to obtain* this favour: I will tell you what I know about it... Practise... then—humility, humility! for God lets Himself be vanquished by this, and grants *all we ask*" (*Interior Castle,* Fourth Mansion, ch. ii, 7, 8).

3° "Do you think it little concerns the devil to raise these fears? No; but much... one [mischief is] that he intimidates those that hear it from approaching unto prayer... the other, that many would much more apply themselves to God, by seeing Him so good... that it is possible to communicate Himself now also so highly to sinners. This causeth in them a great *desire after the like;* and they do well: for I know some persons, who, *encouraged by this,* have begun prayer, and in a short time have become true contemplatives, Our Lord doing them great favours" (*Way of Perfection,* ch. xl, p. 127).

4° "But because I have much to say hereafter of this sweetness, which Our Lord gives to those who persevere in prayer, I do not speak of it here; only this will I say: prayer is the door to those great graces which *Our Lord bestowed upon me...* His will is, that such a soul should be lonely and pure, *with a great desire to receive His graces*" (*Life,* ch. viii, 13).

5° Speaking of the full union: "Our holy Fathers of Mount Carmel *sought* in solitude and utter contempt of the world for this treasure, this precious pearl of which we speak, and we are their descendants... Therefore, my sisters, rouse yourselves, and since *some foretaste of Heaven may be had on this earth,* beg Our Lord to give us His grace that we may not miss it through our own fault... Ask Him to give us strength of soul to search until we *find this hidden treasure,* which lies buried within our hearts" (*Interior Castle,* Fifth Mansion, ch. i, 2).

6° The desire for the full union is also referred to in the *Interior Castle* (Fifth Mansion, ch. ii, 5). "Forward, then, my daughters! hasten over your work and *build this little cocoon.* Renounce self-love and self-will... Die! die! as the silkworm does... and *you will see God* and will be immersed in His greatness... Understand that when I say: 'You will see God,' I mean in the manner described, in which He manifests Himself in this kind of union."

7° The desire for ecstasy. "Blessed, then, is that soul which Our Lord draws on [by ecstasy] to the understanding of the truth! Oh, what a state for kings! How much better it would be for them if they *strove for this,* rather than for great dominions!" (*Life,* ch. xxi, 2).

8° The desire for ecstasy: authentic summary of a chapter of her *Life*. "Fourth degree of prayer [ecstasy]. The excellent dignity conferred by God upon the soul that He raises to it. Persons given to prayer should therefore *incite themselves* to make efforts to arrive at so sublime a state" (*Life,* ch. xviii).

9° Speaking of the benefits of ecstasy: "O my God, how dear is the meaning of those words, and what *good reason* the Psalmist had, and *all* the world will ever have, to *pray* for the wings of a dove... If I could *purchase* with money the blessings which I possess, I should make much of it " (*Life,* ch. xx, 32, 34).

10° Speaking of ecstasy: "My object in writing—the first is to obey—is to inspire souls with *a longing after so high a good*" (*Life,* ch. xviii, 10).

11° On raptures: "If we hope some day to enjoy this favour, even *during our mortal life,* what are we doing?... What can repay the loss of time of a 'memento' in *searching* for this Lord, *like the Spouse,* through the streets and the squares" (*Interior Castle,* Sixth Mansion, ch. iv, 14).

12° On the "excessive jubilation" felt at times by ecstatics: "May His Majesty *often grant us* this kind of prayer, which is safe from all danger and most beneficial; we cannot acquire it for ourselves, as it is quite supernatural" (*Interior Castle,* Sixth Mansion, ch. vi, 15).

13° The desire for the spiritual marriage. Speaking of the souls belonging to the *Third Mansion,* that is to say of those who, being still in the ordinary way, lead a fervent life: "This is certainly to be desired, and there appears no reason to forbid them entrance to the *last* mansions; nor will Our Lord deny it them *if they desire* it, for this is the right disposition for receiving all His favours. Oh Jesus! can any tell us that they *do not desire this great blessing...?* No, no one can. We all say we desire it, but there is need of more than that, for the Lord to take entire possession of the soul. It is not enough to say so, any more than it was enough for the young man, when Our Lord told him what he must do if he desired to be perfect" (*Interior Castle,* Third Mansion, ch. i, 8-9).

14° On the spiritual marriage. The saint compares it to Noah's ark, wherein the dove, escaping from the flood and tempests, finds peace symbolised by the olive branch. "Since, O my God, Thou dost see of what grave import is this peace to us, do Thou incite Christians to *strive to gain it!* In Thy mercy do not deprive those of it on whom Thou hast bestowed it!" (*Interior Castle,* Seventh Mansion, ch. iii, 12).

**18.**—St. Teresa. *Second series* of Extracts. The saint interprets the *Paternoster* as *asking for* the mystic states.

1° "I am astonished to see all *contemplation* and perfection comprised and couched in so few words... For herein already hitherto Our Lord hath *taught us all the way of prayer* and of high contemplation, from the first beginners proceeding to mental prayer; and that of *quiet* and of *union...* I have sometimes thought why His Majesty did not declare Himself more in things so high and obscure... and it seemed to me that... He left it thus indefinite, that so the contemplative, who seek not after any earthly things... may *ask* heavenly favours" (*Way of Perfection,* ch. xxxvii, pp. 116-7).

2° According to the saint, it is the prayer of quiet that we *ask for* in saying: Thy kingdom come:

"... It seems to me that Our Lord begins [in the prayer of quiet] to make known that He hath *heard our request,* and begins already to *give us His kingdom* here, that we may really praise and *sanctify Him*" (*ibid.,* ch. xxxi, pp. 92-3).

3° "That... we may understand this which *we ask,* and how much it concerns us to *be importunate for it,* and to do all we can to please Him that is to give us it; I will here tell you what I understand" (*ibid.,* ch. xxx, p. 91).

4° "There are seasons wherein Our Lord puts such as are weary of travelling, in a tranquillity of the powers and a quietude of soul; wherein He, as it were by signs, makes them clearly understand how that relishes which Our Lord gives to those whom He brings to His kingdom, and on those whom it is here given to as we desire Him He bestows certain pawns [pledges] that by them they may conceive great hope of going to enjoy eternally what He here lets them *but sip of*" (*ibid.,* p. 91-2).

5° "The soul being arrived to this degree of prayer [prayer of quiet], it now seems that the Eternal Father hath granted her *request,* to wit, of giving her His *kingdom.* O blessed *petition,* wherein, without our understanding it, we *crave so great a good.* O blessed way of *requesting!*" (*ibid.,* ch. xxxi, p. 97).

**19.**—St. Teresa. *Third series* of Extracts. The saint explains that the water which the Samaritan woman *asked for,* symbolises the mystic union.

1° After having incited us to seek in prayer "the fountain of *living water,* that Our Lord spoke of to the Samaritan woman, which whoever drinks of, shall not thirst" (*Way of Perfection,* ch. xix, p. 56), the saint explains what kind of prayer she is symbolising by this water. It is not *ordinary prayer.* "It depends not on our own will, *this divine union* being a thing very supernatural... Other consolations that come by the intervening of the understanding [meditation] how much soever they effect, they draw the water drilling along the ground, they drink it not at the *very spring;* now in this its course, there never want dirty things to stick upon, and so it *runs not so pure* and clean. *I do not call this prayer* (which, as I say, goes discoursing with the understanding) *living water...* for that, how much soever we may labour, there always sticks to our soul... somewhat by the way of that which we would not have" (*ibid.,* ch. xix, p. 58). In this chapter the saint develops three analogies between the prayer of union and the living water: it *extinguishes* the fire of earthly affections, it *purifies* the soul, it satisfies our *thirst* for God.

2° This chapter concludes thus:

"Consider that Our Lord *invites* all [to the prayer of union]; He being truth itself, there is no cause to doubt. *Were not this banquet universal,* Our Lord would not call us all; and though He did, would not tell us: I will give you drink.

He might say: Come ye all; for, in the end, ye shall lose nothing by it; and *to those that I think* fit, I will give drink. But, He speaking to all without this restriction, I hold for *certain* that all those who loiter not by the way *shall not fail of this living water.* Our Lord, who *promiseth* it, give us, for His own sake, the grace to *seek* it, as it should be sought" (p. 61-2).

3° The saint instances her own case as an example in speaking of the transports of love that followed her raptures: "The [holy] desires instantly are on fire... It is like those little wells I have seen flowing, wherein the upheaving of the sand never ceases. This illustration and comparison seem to me to be a true description of those souls who attain to this state... I call to remembrance—oh, how often!—that *living water* of which Our Lord spoke to the Samaritan woman. That gospel has a great attraction for me; and indeed so it had even *when I was a little child,* though I did not understand it then *as I do now. I used to pray much* to Our Lord for that living water; and I had always a picture of it, representing Our Lord at the well, with this inscription: *Domine, da mihi aquam*" (*Life,* ch. xxx, 23-4).

4° After saying that in the battle of prayer, resolution is necessary "as knowing that, come what can come, he must not turn back," the saint continues thus: "Fear not that Our Lord will let you die of thirst, who *invites* us to drink of His fountain. This hath been said already, and I would say it often, because it much debaseth [depresses] such as yet know not by experience the goodness of God, though *by faith they know it.* But it is a great matter to have *experienced* the friendship and caresses [that] He expresses to such as go by this way... And I *wonder not* that those, who *never tried this,* desire the security of *some interest.* Now ye know that there is a *hundred* for one, even in this life, and that Our Lord saith: *Ask, and it shall be given you.* If ye believe not His Majesty in several places of His Gospel, assuring thus much, it avails little, Sisters, that I should break my brains about persuading it "(*Way of Perfection,* ch. xxiii, pp. 72-3).

**20.**—St. John of the Cross:

1° "The desire for God is a disposition for union with Him" (*Living Flame,* Stanza III, line 3, § 3, p. 265).

After having said that by *beginners,* he understands those who still practise meditation, he adds:

"It is necessary to touch upon certain characteristics of beginners, that they may perceive the weakness of their state, *take courage and desire* to be led of God into this night, where the soul is established in virtue and prepared for the inestimable delights of His love" (*Obscure Night,* Book I, ch. i, p. 327).

3° After speaking of favours due to the ministry of angels, he comes to those that God only can bestow, that is to say, the mystic union, and describes the desire to attain to it.

"These communications, because the work of Our Lord Himself, are wholly Divine and supreme, certain substantial touches of the Divine union between Himself and the soul;... These are those touches for which the Bride *prayed,* saying 'Let Him kiss me with the kiss of His mouth.' This being a thing that so intimately relates to God, the soul, anxious to approach Him, values and *desires* one touch of the Divinity more than all the other graces which He bestows upon it. Hence the Bride in the Canticle, after the many graces there described, *is not satisfied, but prays for* these divine touches: 'Who shall give Thee to me for my brother,... that I may find Thee without, and kiss Thee' with the mouth of my soul she means that communication which God makes alone, without, and secret from all creatures" (*Obscure Night,* Book II, ch. xxiii, p. 451).

**21.**—Dionysius the Areopagite:

"We pray to enter within the super-bright gloom, and through not seeing and not knowing, to see and to know that the not to see nor to know is itself the above sight and knowledge" (*Dionysius the Areopagite* on Mystic Theology,* Part I, ch. ii, sec. 1, trans. by J. Parker).

**22.**—St. Peter Damian:

"Jacob did not work, even for a day, with the object of obtaining Lia. It was wholly for Rachel that he resigned himself to serve for two hebdomad of years. And yet more, he only put up with Lia on Rachel's account. In the same way, if we yield ourselves to God, it is not for the sake of finding fatigues, griefs, and the assault of temptations. He who seeks for God has but one aim, one hope: to attain at length to repose, *to plunge into the joy of high contemplation,* like Jacob into Rachel's arms,... But it is necessary to labour in divers combats before attaining to the sweetness of interior repose. We must humble ourselves to serve, that we may afterwards have the right to be raised to perfect liberty" (*De la perfection monastique,* ch. viii; Migne ed., Vol. II, col. 304).

**23.**—Richard of Saint-Victor. In his treatise entitled *De Gratia contemplationis,* or *Benjamin major,* he discusses, in Book IV, the two degrees of contemplation that are outside of the ordinary way. Chapter x has as a title: "With what *avidity* spiritual men *ought to aspire* to these degrees and *are accustomed to do* so."

"The two cherubim of the Ark of the Covenant spread their wings unceasingly above the mercy seat. This is symbolic of those who in all places and at all times aspire after divine contemplation, and are persistent in thinking of it and *desiring* it. When birds wish to fly, they spread their wings. In the same way, we, by *desire,* should spread the wings of our heart, and await hourly, nay, rather momentarily, the coming of the divine revelation. So that when the breath of the divine inspiration comes to disperse the clouds of our spirit, and replaces the shadow with the rays of the true sun, we shall only have to set the wings of contemplation in motion. Our spirit will take flight, and will soar into those heights whence this eternal splendour proceeds. With eyes fixed thereon and impetuous as the eagle, we shall traverse, we shall leave behind the sombre

* With regard to the identification of Dionysius the Areopagite, see Biographical Index, No. 2 [Translator].

and restless clouds of this world... We should keep our spirit hovering over the subjects of divine contemplation, whether those which may be given to us here below, or those that we hope for in the other life; and we should sigh after them ardently. For if God gives us the enjoyment of the first of these graces and knowledge of the second, it is in order to incite us to seek them diligently and to *desire* them" (Book VI, ch. x; Migne ed., col. 145, A).

See another Extract, ch. v, 43.

**24.**—St. Bernard (On the *Canticle of Canticles*):

1° "If, then, any of us finds it, with the Psalmist, good for him to draw near to God (Ps. lxxii, 28) and to speak more plainly, if any among us is so filled with an earnest longing, that he desires to be dissolved and be with Christ, but desires it vehemently, thirsts for it ardently and without ceasing, dwells upon the hope of it; he shall without doubt, receive the Word, and in no other form than that of the Bridegroom in the time of visitation; that is to say, in the hour when he shall feel himself *inwardly embraced, as it were by the arms* of wisdom, and shall receive a sweet inpouring of the Divine Love.

"For the desire of his heart shall be granted unto him, though he is still in the body as a place of pilgrimage, and though only in part for a time, and that for a short time. For when *the Lord has been sought* in watching and prayers, with strenuous effort, with showers of tears, He will at length present Himself to the soul; but suddenly when it has gained His Presence He will glide away. Again, He comes to the soul that follows after Him with tears; He allows Himself to be regained, but not to be retained, and, anon, He passes away out of its very hands... [He] will not return unless He be *sought again with the whole desire of the heart.* Thus, then, even in this body the joy of the *Presence* of the Bridegroom is frequently felt, but not the fulness of His Presence, because though His appearance renders the heart glad, the alternation of His absence affects it with sadness. And this the beloved must of necessity endure, until, having laid down the burden of an earthly body, she shall be borne up upon the pinions, so to speak, of her earnest desires and fly away, passing freely over the plains of contemplation as a bird through the air, and following in spirit her Beloved, whithersoever He goeth, without anything to hinder or retard" (*Serm.* XXXII, 2; English: *Cantica Canticorum,* p. 208, translated by S. J. Eales).

2° In his sermon IX, 2, on the Canticles, he supposes that the Bridegroom's friends come to visit the Bride. They find her lamenting and overwhelmed with heaviness. In a long dialogue they inquire the reason, and continue thus:

" 'Come, then, say in what way we can satisfy your need.' 'I shall not be at rest,' she replies, 'unless He complete His goodness to me. I am thankful that I have been permitted to kiss His Feet; it is still more a cause of gratitude to me to kiss His Hand;* but if He has any care for me at all, let Him grant unto me the

* By these three kisses, St. Bernard designates three *kinds* of dispositions and the corresponding *exercises* of prayer. The first symbolises repentance, which causes us to throw ourselves at the feet of Him

third and crowning grace... Do not, I entreat, complain of my presumption, which is but the effect of my ardent love. It is true that shame would withhold me, but love overcomes shame. I am not unmindful that *the King's honour loveth judgment* (Ps. xcix, 4), but the violence of love does not wait for judgment; it is not moderated by advice, nor restrained by shame, nor controlled by reason'" (*ibid.*, p. 44).

The saint then applies this symbol to his monks.

"I remember that many of you also were accustomed in their private confessions to complain of a similar languor and dryness of soul, and of a kind of heaviness and stupor of mind which rendered them incapable of entering into high or refined thoughts, so that they felt little sweetness of spirit or none at all. What do those souls yearn for, if not for this [the kiss of His mouth]? Yes, they *long and sigh* for the Spirit of wisdom and of understanding; of understanding that they may reach knowledge; of wisdom that they may love and take delight in that which they grasp with the understanding. I suppose that the Psalmist was referring to this disposition of mind when he uttered the prayer: *Let my soul be satisfied as with marrow and fatness, and my mouth shall praise Thee with joyful lips* (Ps. lxii, 6). He sought certainly for this mystical kiss, which, after having spread upon his lips the unction of special grace, should be followed by the effect which in another prayer he asks for: *Let my mouth be filled with Thy praise, that I may sing of Thy glory and honour all the day long* (Ps. lxx, 8). Lastly, when he has tasted that heavenly sweetness, he bursts forth: Oh, how great is Thy goodness, O Lord, which Thou hast laid up for them that fear Thee!" (Ps. xxx, 20) (*ibid.*, 3, p. 45).

3° Elsewhere the saint answers an objection (Serm. LXXXIV, 6):

"What? When thou art fit only to hide thyself, dost thou seek the light, and though more deserving of correction than favour, dare to run unto the Bridegroom? Wonderful it will be if you do not find a Judge to condemn you instead of a husband to receive you. Happy is he who shall hear his soul replying to these reproaches: 'I do not fear because I love, and also I am loved; nor could I have loved unless He had first loved me. Let those fear who have no love; but for the soul that loves there is nothing to be feared. How can those who have no love do otherwise than be under constant apprehension of injury? But because I love, I no more doubt that I am loved than I doubt of my own love; nor can I possibly fear His countenance, whose affection for me I have assuredly felt... Not only has He sought me, unhappy as I am, but has caused me

whom we have offended. This is the purgative life. The second is the illuminative way, the striving after virtue. "We seek His helping Hand to lift us up, and to strengthen our feeble knees that we may stand upright. When we have, with *many prayers* and tears, obtained these two former graces, then at length we perhaps venture to lift our eyes to that Countenance full of glory and majesty, for the purpose not only to adore, but (I say it with fear and trembling) to kiss" (Serm. III, on the Canticles, No. 5). This is the unitive way. The saint even supposes that it is that of high contemplation, "the hidden manna" (*ibid.*, 1).

to seek Him... He sought me when I contemned Him, why should He contemn when I seek Him?" (*ibid.,* p. 514).

4° "If you plead your necessities with frequent sighs and groans too deep for utterance and entreat earnestly... [for] compassion; if, I say, you act thus, I have full confidence in Him who said: *Ask, and ye shall receive....* If you persevere in knocking... you shall not go away empty... You will be able to declare with truth: *The King hath brought me into His banqueting house*'" (Serm. xlix, 3, p. 298).

**25.**—St. Bonaventure:

1° Speaking of the obscure knowledge described by Dionysius the Areopagite:

"The affections are enkindled in a wonderful manner. We see the proof of this in those who have these mystical transports [ecstasy] from time to time. I think that every just man here below *should aspire* to this manner of knowing God" (*Sentences,* ii, dist. 23, a. 2, q. 3, ad. 6).

2° In the *Itinerarium* (ch. vii) he is treating of the mystic union, and he says of St. Francis:

"He passed into God by way of ecstasy, and was thus the model of perfect contemplation, as he formerly had been of the active life... and thus by his example, more than by his words, he *invites* all truly spiritual persons to this passage to that ecstasy... This is a mystic and very hidden operation; only those know it who receive it; those *only receive it who desire it.*"

See again *De Septem itineribus æternitatis,* Itin., 6, dist. 7; this chapter has for its title, "How the mind is *invited* to penetrate by experience into the secret things of God."

**26.**—Blessed Albert the Great (*De adhœrendo Deo*): "And this must be the intention, *scope, and end* of a spiritual man, that he may in this corruptible body deserve to possess an image of the future bliss, and begin even in this world as it were to have a foretaste of the pledge of that heavenly felicity, and of that conversation of glory" (ch. xiii).

"Wherefore *never give over, and never rest you,* until you taste of some pledge (as I may say) and experience of that future fulness, and by some poor principles (as I may also term them) have your part in the pleasure of the sweetness of God, and cease not, in the odour of the sweetness of Him, to run after Him, until you see the God of Gods in Sion" (*ibid.,* ch. vii. Eng. trans.: *The Paradise of the Soule,* including *"Of the Union with God"* by a Jesuit, 1617).

**27.**—St. Gertrude:

"When our Divine Lord revealed to the saint that it was His will she should commit her revelations to writing, her humility was exceedingly amazed." The Saviour said to her: "The *desire* of obtaining the same favours as those which they shall see you have obtained from Me, will produce devotion in the hearts of those who, considering the effusion of My grace and the excess of My mercy, shall endeavour to change their present life for one more perfect" (*Le Héraut de l'amour divin,* Book I, ch. xv. English: *Life and Revelations of St. Gertrude,* by Sister M. Frances Clare, ch. iii, pp. 23-4).

**28.**—Blessed Angela of Foligno:

1° "I desire then, my son, that thou shouldst not fill thy heart save with this Uncreated God, and with His knowledge and love, and that in thy soul there may be no other fulness save that of the Uncreated God. But if thou canst not have this, keep at least and hold fast the knowledge I have spoken of above, that is to say of the sorrow-stricken crucified God-Man, and if each of these be taken from thee, *rest not, my son, until thou shall find it again,* and shalt hold fast one of these two kinds of fulnesses, which truly fill and satisfy the heart and soul...

"The wise soul not only careth to know God in appearance, by a certain superficial consideration, but striveth to know Him in truth, and to learn His goodness and worth, and to such a soul He is not only good, but the Highest Good. And thus knowing Him she wholly loveth Him for the sake of His goodness, and loving Him *she desireth to possess Him.* And then He, the Highest Good, giveth Himself unto her, and the soul feeleth Him, and tasteth His sweetness, and enjoyeth Him with exceeding great delight. Then, too, the soul being made partaker of the Highest, since He is the Highest Love, is affected by this Highest love, and becometh enamoured of this her Beloved One, and desireth to hold Him fast and *embraceth Him and presseth Him to her,* and joineth herself with God. And God draweth her to Himself with exceeding great sweetness of love, and the power of love transformeth the lover into the loved, and the loved into the lover... the soul that is united to God by the perfect grace of the love of God, is made as it were all divine, and is transformed into God, not changed indeed in her own substance, but wholly transformed in her life by the love of God, and is made as it were all divine... But the soul cannot have this knowledge of itself, neither by Scripture, nor by learning, nor by any created thing, although these may help and dispose thereto; but only by the light and grace of God. Moreover, I believe that the soul cannot find this knowledge, nor obtain it from the Most High God, who is the Highest Good and the Highest Light, and possess it for her own *more quickly or more easily* than by devout, pure, continual, humble, and *violent prayer,* not only of the lips, but of the soul and heart and of all the powers of the soul and senses of the body, by asking and seeking for it with *exceeding great desire*" (*Visions and Instructions,* ch. lvii, pp. 203-7).

2° "And afterwards He spoke some words to show His tender love, and He said: 'If a man desired to feel Me in his soul, I would not take Myself away from Him, and whosoever desired to see Me, to him, with great complacency would I give a vision of Myself, and whosoever desired to speak with Me, with exceeding great complacency would I speak with him'" (*ibid.,* ch. xxxiii, p. 118).

**29.**—Ruysbroeck:

1° "Those who flow by desire into the boundless sea, feel the hunger, feel the thirst, and taste unity. But a *moderate* desire insufficient to *suspend the soul to the Divine Essence* is a sad hindrance. The men of moderate desire do not receive the ray; they are not *touched* by the sublime ignorance which knows no human measure. They exist in themselves, and are not swallowed up here below by the gulf of beatitude" (*Livre des Amants de Dieu,* ch. xxx, English: *Reflections from the Mirror of a Mystic,* ch. viii, p. 57, translation by Earle Baillie).

2° The parable of Zaccheus. "When the soul has arrived at true life, and all her actions are referred to the glory of God, she feels herself suddenly *stirred by a desire to see* what her Spouse is like, asking Who and What is He who has become Man for her sake? He who has died to save her, and has given Himself to her? This Jesus Who on leaving the earth has left her His Sacraments and promised her His Kingdom; this Jesus, ever ready to provide for the needs of the body and the consolation of the soul, What is He like? And the soul, full of questions, feels the *desire of seeing* her Spouse increase within her; the longing to know what He is like, *what He is in Himself*; for the knowledge, such as it is, which she gathers from creatures does not content her.

"Then the soul does like Zaccheus the publican, who wanted to see; she goes on in front, far from the crowd, from the multitude of creatures, which keep us low, and prevent the getting the sight of Christ. She mounts the tree of faith which has its root in God, and spreads into twelve branches [the twelve articles of the Creed]. The lower extend towards the Humanity of Jesus, and the world's salvation; the upper tell of the Divinity, the Trinity, the Unity.—The soul mounts like Zaccheus to the top of the tree; for Christ is going to pass by with all His gifts. Reaching the summit she sees the Son of Man; but the light says to her, 'Behold the Divinity, infinite, incomprehensible, inaccessible'; and all created light stops short. This is the Abyss!—and the soul reaches the highest knowledge of God which can be procured here below; viz. ignorance and the confession that she understands not" (*L'ornement des noces,* Book I, ch. xxxvi; English: *Reflections from the Mirror of a Mystic,* ch. i, pp. 17-8).

**30.**—*The Imitation of Christ:*

"Oh, when shall it be fully granted to me to be still, and see how sweet Thou art, O Lord my God? When shall my mind be wholly absorbed in Thee, so that for love of Thee I may not feel myself, but only Thee, *above all feeling and measure, in a manner not known to all*' (Book IV, ch. xxi, 3).

**30** *bis.*—Dom Garcia de Cisneros, Abbot of Monserrat. He enumerates many motives for giving ourselves to prayer, and concludes thus:

"Finally, if you wish to rise to the heights of contemplation and to enjoy the embraces of your Divine Bridegroom, be men of prayer" (*Exercitatorium,* published in 1500, ch. ix).

**31.**—The Carthusian Jean Lansperge:

"My daughter, says Jesus Christ to the soul, hear My voice at all times and in all places. This is that mystic theology which My Father has hidden from the wise of this age, and which He reveals to the babes. It is I, the supreme teacher who cause it to penetrate into hearts when they are detached from the world, from themselves, and from all creatures. My daughter, *lift up thy voice unceasingly* with lamentation to obtain it, *desire it* with a profound humility and wait in peace and in silence with confidence and longanimity" (*Alloquiorum,* Book I, ch. xvi).

**32.**—Ven. Blosius (*Institutio Spiritualis*):

1° The title of chapter i: "*All men* ought properly to aspire after Perfection and Union with God." It is a question of the mystic union, for the writer adds the following explanation to his description:

"For if man attained to this union he would truly find, by intimate experience within his own soul, Him Who by His joyful *presence* would make all want to vanish clean away, would enrich him with treasures the most solid in value, and would fill him with unspeakable joy. From that moment would man be unable to wander forth in search of spurious delight derived from created things, for all would be insipid and bitter which was not God" (A *Book of Spiritual Instruction,* ch. i, No. 1. Trans. from the Latin by Fr. Wilberforce, O. P.).

"Truly, we should feel much compassion for those who, given to things of sense and content with external exercises only, neglect throughout their life to enter into the secret sanctuary of their own soul, and there to cultivate the blessed union they might have with God... Outward exercises are good and pleasing to Our Lord; I mean such things as to sing the praises of God, to say many vocal prayers, to genuflect, to worship God with sensible devotion, to fast, to watch and suchlike things; but the inward exercise by which the soul stretches forth with *ardent desire* towards God in order to be united to Him, not indeed by sensible images, but in a certain supernatural way, is incomparably better and superior. They who adhere to external exercises only, with some self-love and according to their own judgment, and do not endeavour to mortify themselves and to join themselves in spirit to God, will, without doubt, after a life spent in such imperfection, have to pay in purgatory a penalty grievous in proportion to the degree in which they sought themselves. The merciful God does not reject such souls, but, desiring to work in them, He waits to see if, perchance, He may find them fit for His divine operations and free from impediments. He leaves to them their own exercises and ideas, for He never forces anyone. But His desire is *to lead all* to the knowledge of Himself, and to unite them to Himself, if only they would remove the obstacles that stand in the way. It *grieves* His divine Spirit to see us content with the lowest things, when He is ready to bestow on us the highest, for *He desires to give Himself to us in the most excellent way*" (*ibid.,* ch. v, Nos. 2, 3).

"Blessed is he who, even after many years of continual labour and constant digging, at last deserves to find the spring of living waters in the secret essence of his soul. Surely it is no wonder if a man must keep a long watch outside the presence-chamber of the Eternal King; he cannot complain if he has to *knock often* and wait long before he can be admitted within. *May God,* the uncreated abyss, deign to call to Himself our spirit, the created abyss, and to unite it to Himself, in order that our soul, absorbed into the most deep sea of the

Godhead, may happily lose itself in the Spirit of God. In this union the object and end of all spiritual exercises of all the sacred writings and of all instructions will be reached and obtained" (*ibid.*, ch. xii, § 4, No. 4).

4° A prayer of Blosius:

"O my beloved, my beloved, my beloved! O dearest of all friends, O my one love! O spouse of my soul, flower of love! Spouse of my soul, sweeter than honey in the honey-comb! Ah, sweetness, sweetness, sweetness of my heart, life of my soul! O calm light of my inmost soul! O Lord, my God! O most holy Trinity, one God, brighter than light, giving all delight, feed me, feed me; feed my soul with Thy inflowing grace. I adore Thee; I praise Thee; I glorify Thee; for praise and honour are Thy due for ever and ever. O my God and my all! O abyss most sweet, most worthy of love! O good, most simple and most joyful, my true and unchangeable good, fill me with Thyself. O my tenderly beloved, *draw me into the most secret sanctuary of my soul,* that I *may find Thee there, and dwell with Thee, my Creator;* that thou mayest find Thy delight in me. Oh when, when will the happy day come, in which I shall perfectly *find Thee?* When shall I love Thee with ardent affection? When shall I *be closely united to Thee?* Oh when, when wilt Thou *carry me away utterly into Thyself?* When wilt Thou completely absorb me into Thyself? When wilt Thou *unite me to Thyself in intimate union, without any medium between me and Thee?* Remove, I beseech Thee, all hindrances, and make me one spirit with Thee, for the glory of Thy name. Hear me, O Lord; hear me; hear my prayer, not to gratify my will, but for Thy own good pleasure. Teach me, I beseech Thee; enlighten, direct, and help me in all things, that I may do nothing, speak nothing, think nothing, will nothing, except what will be pleasing in Thine eyes" (*ibid.*, Appendix II, *Aspirations of Union*).

**33.**—St. Ignatius. *Letter* to St. Francis Borgia (Rome, 1548); to moderate his excessive penances:

"Instead of striving to draw a little blood, *seek* our divine Master Himself in a more direct way, I mean *His very holy gifts,* such, for instance, as the gift of tears, which causes you to weep, now for your own sins and those of your neighbour, now at the spectacle of Our Lord's mysteries, whether in this life or in the next, now with love for the Divine Persons"; or again: "The intensity of faith, hope, and charity, *joy and spiritual repose,* intense *consolations,* the *flight of the spirit,* impressions and divine illuminations and all other spiritual tastes and feelings relating to such gifts, like humility... All these very holy gifts should *be preferred* to all corporal acts [of mortification], which are only good *in so far* as they serve to acquire these gifts, either wholly or in part. By this I do not mean to say that we should seek them *solely* for the pleasure and delectation that we find in them; certainly not. But recognising that, without these gifts, all our thoughts, words, and works are imperfect, cold, and tarnished, *we should desire these gifts* in order that they may thereby become righteous, ardent, and bright, for God's greater service. It therefore follows that *we should desire* these most precious gifts, either wholly or in part, and these spiritual graces in so far as we can by their aid procure greater glory to God."

**34.**—Fr. Alvarez de Paz. After speaking of the desire for acquired contemplation, and then saying that we ought not to desire revelations and visions of created things, and yet more, that we should not be guilty of the folly of making efforts to obtain them, he goes on thus:

"But there is another supernatural contemplation, that which is simple, without argument, that which, by the gift of wisdom, produces in the soul elevation, suspension, admiration, and ardent love. The souls that are called to perfection and are well practised in virtue, may *desire it ardently* and *ask for* it with humility. Why not, if it is useful to them? And it is so; it is a very efficacious means of arriving at perfection. If we have the right to desire some end, would it be forbidden to desire the means that lead to it?*... If, then, O man of God, Thou hast disposed thyself thereto as much as human frailty permits, if thou dost feel thyself urged by the spur of divine love, then by night and by day let thy tears flow in torrents for the obtaining of this gift. Do not cease. Thou art little, indeed! But little things are made to become great. If it were only a question of an earthly republic, to canvass for the highest places and dignities would argue pride; but in God's house, to aspire after a higher seat and sanctity shows greatness of soul... Be bold then, and say to God: 'If I have found grace in Thy sight, show me Thy face by means of perfect contemplation...' If thy prayer is not granted, continue calm and content" (*De natura contemplationis,* Vol. III, Book V, Part II, ch. xiii).

**35.**—The Ven. Louis Du Pont. 1° He admits the legitimacy of the desire in the *Life of Fr. Balthasar Alvarez:*

"While *waiting for this grace,* they acquire very great benefits, by acknowledging themselves unworthy of it, by labouring to purify themselves more and more and by multiplying their holy *desires,* biding God's time with as much patience as confidence..." (ch. xiv, p. 164).

2° He next quotes the exhortation to perseverance in desiring this grace, addressed by Fr. Balthasar *to his novices:*

"Let us not be tired, my brethren, of going to the gates of God, which are always open, or which will certainly open immediately when we knock... and persevere in knocking... even if an icy cold should seize us. At the moment when we least think of it, Assuerus will open the door to Mardocheus, and admit him into his presence. Then his happiness will make him quickly forget

* Let us not make the objection that we should limit ourselves to *necessary* means when it is a question of perfection. The objection does not hold good. For the religious life is not necessary to perfection, and demands a special vocation. Everyone, however, agrees that it is allowable to desire it, and to pray God to call us to it. We can, in the same way, desire the mystic union under the conditions laid down by Alvarez de Paz.

the miserable days, passed at the gate of this great king. In confirmation of this doctrine he cited to us his own example" (*ibid.*).

3° Fr. du Pont in speaking of ecstasies (ch. xiv, p. 160) says that "These things being very dangerous, we must neither desire nor seek after them." But the proof that he is not speaking of their interior side* is that, when speaking afterwards of sublime contemplation (ch. xv, p. 169) he expresses himself thus without any restrictions: We will give his [Fr. Balthasar's] own teaching on the point: "If God," he says, "takes from a soul the faculty of reasoning in prayer, it is a sign that He wishes to be in a special manner her Master... Now none but God alone can penetrate into the interior of the soul, when the doors are closed. Neither the good nor the *bad angels* have this power; this sign is therefore very certain and *free from illusion.*" See also *Le guide spirituel,* Tr. 3, ch. vi, § 1, and *ibid,* ch. ii, § 1.

**36.**—Fr. Louis Lallemant:

"Nowadays, if anyone aspires after some *gift of prayer* a little above the common order, he is plainly told that such things are extraordinary gifts which God gives only when He will and to whom He will, and that we must *not desire them nor ask for them:* thus *the door* of these gifts is for ever *shut* against him. *This is a great abuse*" (*Doctrine spir.,* princ. 7, ch. i, a. 3, § 2; English translation by F. W. Faber, d. d., p. 302).

**37.**—Joseph a Spiritu Sancto puts forward the argument that infused contemplation is an act of the gifts of the Holy Ghost. Now we can desire the *act* of a *habitus* that is given to us for our spiritual good, to make us acquire merit, that is to say. For this end is not attained by the *habitus* itself; but by its act (Vol. II, disp. 11, No. 28). See also *ibid.,* No. 23; then Vol. IV, disp. 23, No. 100; Vol. III, disp. 7, No. 100.

**38.**—Other writers to be consulted: 1° Philippus a SS. Trinitate (Part II, Tr. 3, d. 1, a. 4); 2° de Vallgornera (q. 3, d. 3, a. iii, No. 604, and q. 4, d. 1, a. xii, No. 927; Antonius a Spiritu Sancto (Tr. 4, No. 42, Tr. 3, No. 229); the three last writers lay down one identical thesis which is much more advanced than my own. Each has two chapters, the respective titles of which are as follows: "All souls *should* aspire to supernatural contemplation; all souls, and especially those

* Certain writers, like Alvarez de Paz, say of ecstasies, as of revelations, that we should not desire them. There is a misunderstanding here that should be avoided. They speak of ecstasy in so far as it displays very strong exterior manifestations, of such a nature that they cannot be hidden. If this were not so, they would be contradicting themselves, as Canon Lejeune bids us remark (*Introduction à la vie mystique,* ch. i, No. 2). Joseph a Spiritu Sancto defines this distinction clearly. "There are, he says, two things in rapture: the alienation of the sensible faculties and its cause. It is not the first that enriches the soul, otherwise those who sleep would be enriched. But with regard to the cause of this state, *spiritual persons wish not to be deprived of it;* still more, *they desire it with all their strength* and fully. *Illam totam suis viribus concupiscunt*" (Vol. III, disp. 17, No. 110, p. 293).

Finally, it is clear that in desiring the mystic union, it is not the physical side that we should desire; to show oneself in an ecstasy to the general public is not what is wanted.

that are dedicated to God, *should* aspire to the actual fruitive union with God, and should aim at it"; 4° Courbon (Part IV, instruct. 3); 5° Brancati (op. 8, ch. ix; op. 6, ch. xi); 6° Fr. Meynard (third ed., 1899, Vol. II, No. 75); 7° Fr. Jeiler, in the *Kirchenlexicon* under the word *Contemplation* (Beschauung), p. 513; 8° Canon Lejeune (*Introduction à la Vie mystique,* ch. 1, No. 2); 9° Abbé Saudreau, (with reference to the prayer of quiet: *passim*); 10° Dom Vital (Part III, ch. xiii); 11° Fr. Vermeersch (*Quæstiones morales,* Vol.I, No. 73).

Total: 31 authors.

# CHAPTER XXVI

## Qualities Necessary for a Director

**1.**—It is a question here of a director who can guide souls in the **mystic way,** and not only in the acquisition of the virtues.

**2.**—St. Teresa says that he should have **four qualities**. Here are the three first. They refer to the light that he should possess.

1° "It is of great consequence that the director should be *prudent*—I mean of sound understanding" (*Life,* ch. xiii, 24).

2° He should be *pious,* a man of prayer, striving after his own perfection; and consequently should have a personal and practical acquaintance with the spiritual life—at least with regard to ordinary cases. By this means he will have a certain aptitude in guiding others in it. (*ibid.*).

It will be still better that he should himself have experienced the mystic states.*

3° He should be *learned* in theology, particularly ascetic theology, so that the fundamental theories of direction shall be familiar to him.

The saint will have none "of those *timid,* half-instructed people, whose *ignorance* has cost me very dear" (*Interior Castle,* Fifth Mansion, ch. i, 7). "I know by experience that it is better, if the confessors are good men and of holy lives, that they should have no learning at all than *a little;* for such confessors never trust themselves without consulting those who are learned—nor would I trust them myself" (*Life,* ch. v, 6).

**3.**—Thus if the **third quality**, theological learning, should be absent, it is only a partial evil; it can be made up for by consulting other directors: "If these *three* qualities cannot be had *together,* the *first two* are the most important, because

* "They are not many, I believe, who know by experience so many things [raptures], and without experience it is useless to treat a soul at all. For nothing will come of it, save only *trouble* and *distress*" (*Life,* ch. xl, 12). Canon Lejeune says: "A priest who professes a jesting scepticism with reference to these special states of prayer, or who continues in a state of systematic ignorance with regard to them, would be rather a harmful than a useful guide" (*Oraison,* Part II, ch. x).

learned men may be found with whom we can communicate when it is necessary. I mean that *for beginners* learned men are of little use if they are not men of prayer. I do not say that they are to have nothing to do with learned men... I have conversed with many;... I have always been fond of them" (*Life*, ch. xiii, 24, 26).

**4.—Another case**. Let us suppose that "these three qualities cannot be had together." "If he be a person living in the world, let him praise God for the power he has of choosing whom he will obey, and let him not lose so excellent a liberty; yea, rather let him be without a director till he finds him—for Our Lord will give him one if he is really humble, and has a *desire* to meet with the right person" (*ibid.*, 29). See also St. John of the Cross, *Ascent of Mount Carmel*, Book II, end of ch. xxx.

**5.**—We must not be in haste to choose. "A person who shall resign his soul to be wholly subject to one director will make a great mistake, if he is in religion, unless he finds a director of this kind" (St. Teresa, *ibid.*, 28).

**6.—Effects of a bad direction.** St. John of the Cross inveighs against directors who turn souls away from the mystic union to which God is calling them. "Some confessors and spiritual directors, because they have no perception or experience of these ways, are a hindrance and an evil rather than a help to such souls" (*Ascent of Mount Carmel*, Prologue, p. 4). He returns to this subject in *The Living Flame of Love*, Stanza III, line 3, St. Teresa speaks to the same effect (*Life*, ch. xiii).

These two saints not only say that such directors destroy their penitents' peace of mind, and "afflict them soul and body," but that they "hinder their progress" (St. Teresa, *Life*, ch. xiii, 21), and "cause them the loss of inestimable blessings" (St. John of the Cross, *Living Flame*, Stanza III, line 3, § 11, p. 280).

Would it then be true to say that the director can go so far as actually to oppose an obstacle to divine action? that he can prevent progress, or even be responsible for a retrogression?

He may do so, but only indirectly; for as I have said with regard to the prayer of simplicity (ch. ii, **32**), he causes the soul to follow false rules of conduct. By persuading her that her state of prayer is worthless, he robs her of a powerful motive for showing herself generous towards God, and does not himself dream of encouraging her in this. He allows her to retain defects that are harmful to union with God, and "the little foxes that destroy the vines are not driven away" (*Living Flame*, Stanza III, line 3, § 11, p. 280).

We must not therefore say, "*If God pleases* to give these graces, no one can prevent His doing so." Yes; but it is precisely this, that *it does not please Him* to give them unless certain conditions are fulfilled and bad direction often hinders their fulfilment. If the soul, in spite of her ignorance, were to do all that she was capable of, if she responded to the utmost to grace, God would preserve her from the untoward effects of which we are speaking. But we are often very far from doing our utmost.

To sum up; the director may be the indirect cause of the evil; *the soul's faults are always the direct cause.*

**7.**—**The absence of any direction** is no less harmful than bad direction. We must not say, as is so often heard: "God who is operating in the soul, will be able to compensate for the absence of direction." By a similar principle it might be proved that God usually compensates for the absence of missionaries amongst the heathen, and that it is therefore unnecessary to concern ourselves as to their conversion.

**8.**—St. Teresa refers elsewhere to a fourth quality that a director ought to have for guiding a soul through the trials of the mystic way. This is **kindness** (ch. xxiii, **40**). He can doubtless require great sacrifices of the soul in order to lead her to conquer her defects. But this does not prevent his showing his interest and trust, and consoling the suffering soul.

To begin with, the precept of charity requires it. Then if souls should be helped to mortify pride and sensuality, they none the less need to be preserved from sadness and discouragement.

By the rules for the discernment of spirits, we know the kind of action appertaining to good and evil spirits respectively. One consoles and fortifies, the other afflicts, agitates, and depresses. The director, who is a coadjutor of the guardian-angel, should take this action and not that of the adversary as his model. He is also the assistant of the Holy Spirit, whose consoling influence is so well described in the prose *Veni Sancte Spiritus.* The director, then, should be the staff upon which we lean, not that which smites us. He should resemble the angel of the Garden of Gethsemane, who ministered to Jesus Christ in His agony, or St. Veronica or Simon the Cyrenean. Let him leave to others the part of the Jews who crucified Our Lord. Lastly, he has the example of Our Lord after His resurrection, of whom St. Ignatius says: "Consider the office of *comforter,* which Christ Our Lord exercises, comparing it with the manner in which friends are wont to *console* one another."

If the director is obliged to administer rebukes, let him mingle marks of sympathy with his severity. When at each slight lapse, he says angrily: "You are always the same; you lack good-will," the soul is depressed and becomes embittered. She loses all hope of making any lasting progress. She adopts the demeanour of a beaten dog before the director. This is not the way of really forming a soul in virtue.

**9.**—Nor is it from motives of charity only that the director should be kind and compassionate. An argument may be found in the **tacit contract** that exists between him and the person directed. If this latter does not guide himself unassisted, which would be much more convenient, it is that he cannot. He is often ignorant of theology, and always so of the subterfuges of his own heart. We are bad judges of our own affairs, especially when we have to fight against our passions. But in submitting to this necessity, the penitent has not professed to go beyond. He asks for enlightenment, as he would do under other circumstances from a doctor or a lawyer.* He wishes for a pilot, not an executioner. He is ready to be enlightened, but not to be bullied.

**10.—The saints observe these rules.** They know how to measure out to the individual soul the trials that they impose, because they have suffered much themselves, which makes them compassionate, and also because they have first tested the burden with their own shoulders; this is the only way of properly appreciating its weight.

St. Teresa remembered with gratitude the charity shown to her by Fr. Balthasar Alvarez at the critical period of her life. While testing her severely with regard to self-sacrifice, he spent three years (*Life,* ch. xxviii, 21) in supporting her against the world and herself. "My confessor... *always comforted* me and he alone did so... He bade me *pray much* to God; *he himself* and all his penitents, and many others *did so earnestly;* I too, with all my might, and as many as I knew to be servants of God, prayed that His Majesty would be pleased to lead me by another way" (*Life,* ch. xxv, 20).

St. Teresa also retained great feelings of gratitude towards St. Peter of Alcantara (*Life,* ch. xxx, 20-24).

Speaking of directors, St. Francis of Sales says: He must be *filled with charity,* knowledge, and discretion (*Devout Life,* Part I, ch. vi). See 20, extracts from the writings of St. Jane Frances de Chantal.

**11.—Exception.**—There are cases, however, in which the director may *seemingly* depart from the kindness of which we have been speaking. This is when he wishes to judge of the degree of patience and humility to which his penitent has attained and when he has *no other easy way* of testing him. He may then feign anger, mistrust, and contempt.

But, that the precept of charity may be safeguarded, this probation must be not only *necessary* but of *brief duration.* For the attainment of its object this experiment hardly ever requires to be prolonged. Even in these passing trials it is necessary to show tact and moderation, so as not to defeat our own ends by throwing the soul into a state of discouragement.

**12.—The novice-master.** His rights are more extensive. For he is charged by his congregation, not only with the task of *forming an opinion* of the subjects who offer themselves, but of *exercising* them in the practice of the solid virtues with an eye to the future. He may therefore give them occasions of practising blind obedience, a love for humiliations, contempt for natural repugnances, candour, etc...

* This comparison refutes the rationalists who, seeing that the mystics seek advice, conclude therefore that they are robbed of their own will, that they are *abouliques* and consequently sick persons. Like the rest of us, they seek direction simply with the object of supplying the lack of the special studies which they themselves have not made. This explains why in the saints' lives we find directors playing a less important part or one of lesser duration with men than is the case with women. It is because, thanks to his theological studies, the priest succeeds in finding the solution of the majority of his difficulties himself.

**13.—Motives for obeying the director.** 1° He has devoted himself to theological and sometimes to ascetic studies, which his penitent usually has not done; 2° even in temporal affairs it is prudent not to trust to our own prudence; 3° God blesses obedience and the humility from which it proceeds. "Daily experience (says St. John of the Cross), teaches us the same truth; for these humble souls to whom these visitations are made, attain to renewed satisfaction, strength, enlightenment, and security as soon as they have revealed them to the rightful person. Yea, such is the fruit of this submission, that some who, until they have revealed them, thought they had received them not, and that they were not theirs, after revealing them receive them as it were anew" (*Ascent of Mount Carmel,* Book II, ch. xxii, p. 165); finally there is a higher reason, relating to the way in which Our Lord Jesus Christ instituted His Church.

The director represents Him if he acts according to His principles, and he receives a special grace from this fact.

But it would be an exaggeration to credit the director with true *inspirations,* to think of him as a prophet, by whom God pledges Himself to speak. Far more, we must not think that the Holy Spirit ordinarily refuses His touches to the penitent, reserving them for the director. Ordinarily it is the contrary: God acts principally upon the penitent. The director's part is a simple one; he prevents swervings aside from the right path and applies certain principles of conduct.

**14.**—Should the director's orders or advice **be followed exactly?**

The reply is often given in the affirmative, without distinctions. And yet there is a difficulty; in the seventeenth and eighteenth century there was a great risk of meeting a director who was a Jansenist, a Quietist, or a Gallican, without being aware of his opinions. In our own days we have seen priests imbued with new and strange forms of spirituality. There can be no obligation to listen *blindly* to such directors; quite the contrary.

**15.—Solution**. I will distinguish two cases. If the director is *given to us* by a competent authority, we must obey him in all that is not opposed to the Church's teaching. God will sooner or later correct any defects in our direction if we take the two following precautions: if we *pray* to be directed aright, and *if we do not remain merely passive* in the hands of our director. It is not contrary to obedience to take the initiative, to point out our attractions to him and to make respectful objections.

When we have *chosen* the director *of our own free will,* we should add two other conditions if we wish to be able to count lawfully upon God's assistance: that of having done all that was *in reason possible* to make a good choice; and being ready to change our director if it becomes *evident* that he is inspired by *general principles* that are contrary to the traditions of the ascetic or mystic writers. If the question is doubtful, the presumption remains in his favour.

**16.**—Should directors permit **the reading of mystic works** by their penitents?*

This question has always been a subject of heated controversy. I adopt the moderate solution: that we may sanction the reading of good mystic works *to all sensible people.* It is even advisable to suggest some of these writings to those who have entered upon the prayer of simplicity.

The danger to be feared is that the reader should fancy himself to have heard interior locutions or to have been visited by some saint. But if the mystic book is well done, it will put people on their guard against all these revelations instead of encouraging them. The best preservative is, not ignorance of these questions, but being persuaded that a thousand illusions are to be feared. As far as I am concerned, I cannot be accused of having concealed these dangers (ch. xxi).

Rigorists who would reserve mystic writings for the chosen few, for confessors and superiors, that is to say, allow, in practice, lives of saints which have just the drawbacks that they are afraid of. They are full of apparitions, revelations, and prophecies. Certain hot-headed persons pay more attention to these extraordinary facts than to the saints' virtues. "There are some persons (says St. Francis of Sales) who force themselves to meditate upon the lives of St. Catherine of Siena and St. Catherine of Genoa, thinking thus to become St. Catherines by imitation" (*Spiritual Conferences,* IX, Annecy ed., Vol. VI, p. 139).

**17.**—For those who come to the prayer of simplicity, and, more still, the night of the senses or the mystic state, we have seen (ch. ii, **48**; ch. v, **18**) that books are usually necessary.

This is in fact a dark and painful period, during which they need to reassure themselves by seeing the description of their state, and by the adoption of rules of conduct at which they can scarcely guess for themselves. They are like a man walking upon solid ground, who finds himself, he knows not how, transported alone into mid-ocean, in a boat, the management of which he does not understand, and which is drifting away from the shore. He trembles and is all astray in his attempts to handle the boat. An apprenticeship is necessary.

It is not enough to tell them to get their instruction from their director; for often he has not studied these matters, or even may be scarcely aware of the very existence of mysticism. And then, according to the saints, a director must be chosen with care; but in order to choose well, it is necessary to be versed in spiritual knowledge; which is not the case with beginners. They require books, therefore (see Extracts, ch. xvi, **42**).

**18.**—**St. Teresa's** works, although eminently mystic, have always been recommended to the faithful. St. Jane Frances de Chantal recommended them

* Read Scaramelli, ch. i.

to her spiritual daughters, with the Ven. Louis du Pont's Life of Fr. Balthasar Alvarez (*Conseils à une supérieure,* Vol. III, Plon ed., p. 338; *Réponses sur le Coutumier,* art. 24, Migne ed., Vol. II, p. 228).

The Church also inclines Christians to this kind of reading. For in her prayer on St. Teresa's Feast, she desires that "we may be nourished with the food of her heavenly doctrine." Now for this, it is not enough to hear it vaguely spoken of; we must read it.

Leo XIII is very explicit in the Brief addressed to Fr. Bouix, March 17, 1883. "There is, in St. Teresa's writings, a certain power that is more celestial than human, *marvellously efficacious* to the reform of a life, so that they may truly *be read with profit,* not only by those engaged in the direction of souls, or who aspire to an eminent holiness of life, but also *by everyone* who thinks seriously of the duties and virtues of a Christian, that is to say of *the salvation of his soul.*"

See in the Bollandists, for October 15, No. 1617, the indulgences granted by various Bishops to readers of St. Teresa's works.

## EXTRACTS

### § 1. The Breadth of Mind Necessary for the Director

**19.**—St. John of the Cross:

1° "... it is of the greatest importance to the soul desirous of perfection... to consider well into whose hands it resigns itself... for a director must be *learned, prudent,* and *experienced...* If *experience* of the higher ways *be wanting,* there are no means of guiding a soul therein when God is showing the way, and inexperienced directors will therefore inflict great evil on their penitents. Such directors, not understanding these ways of the Spirit, will very frequently be the cause of souls losing the unction of the delicate ointments, by means of which the Holy Ghost is preparing the soul for Himself; for they will guide them by other means of which they have read, but which are adapted only for beginners. These directors knowing how to guide beginners only—and God grant they may know that—will not suffer their penitents to advance though it be the will of God, beyond the mere rudiments, acts of reflection, and imagination, whereby their profit is extremely little" (*Living Flame,* Stanza III, line 3, § 4, pp. 266-7).

2° [The spiritual directors'] "object therefore should be, not to guide souls by a way of their own, suitable to themselves, but to ascertain, if they can, the way by which God Himself is guiding them. If they cannot ascertain it, let them *leave these souls alone* and *not disquiet them*" (*ibid.,* § 9, p. 274).

3° Regarding directors who hinder the divine action by urging the "application of sense or desire to any particular knowledge": "Though this evil be so great that it cannot be exaggerated, it is still so common that there is scarcely one spiritual director who does not inflict it upon souls whom God has begun to lead by this way to contemplation" (*ibid.*, § 8, p. 274). See also § 11 and following.

### § 2. On the Gentleness That a Director Should Display

**20.**—St. Jane Frances de Chantal. She is speaking of superiors, but her remarks apply also to directors. The reasons are the same.

1° "The further I go, the more I find that gentleness is required in order to enter into and keep a place in hearts, and to make them do their duty *without tyranny.* For, our sisters, indeed, are Our Lord's sheep; in leading them, it is allowable to touch them with the crook, but not to *bruise* them, this is for the Master alone, etc." (*Conseils à une supérieure,* Plon ed., Vol. III, p. 328).

2° "Our blessed Father used to say that we should listen patiently to the sisters' troubles and objections... Believe me, said the blessed Father, that superiors perform a great act of charity in giving the sisters time to tell them everything that troubles them, *without hurrying them or showing any weariness* at their prolixity, although sometimes it should be nothing but little trifles; for this solaces them and disposes them to receive profitably the advice that may be given them afterwards. Small things weigh as heavily on the weak as large troubles on great souls. Briefly, you should, by the best means at your disposal, keep your daughters closely united to you, by a union of pure charity, and *not a human love* that becomes attached. Should it happen that any one does this, you should lead her *unconsciously* to denudation and to esteem for that happiness of the soul which relies only upon God. For to think to heal such ills by coldness or rebuffs would be to lead to aversions and inquietudes which would be followed by some derangement of mind, particularly in weak-minded persons."

Have a "general love for all, loving them equally, without any special affections, for I say that if a sister is not of a very high perfection, however good she may be below that level, she will not be content *if she does not believe that her superior loves her* and has a good opinion of her" (*ibid.*, pp. 327-8).

"When you have to correct... *you must avoid bitter and hard words* which only wound the heart, vex it, make it slacker in the practice of virtue and diminish the trust and esteem that they ought to feel for the superior. Our blessed Father said that a superior should never be surprised or troubled at any defect that may be committed by the sisters collectively or separately; she should regard them and bear with them gently, and apply to them in *the spirit of repose* such remedies as are possible for her; nor should she frighten those who commit them, but with a sweet charity lead them to know their falls in order that they may profit by them. Believe me, we should not be... so sensible to the sisters' shortcomings and unwilling to tolerate amongst us troublesome and bad-tempered subjects. When they are bound by solemn vows, the shortest way is to bear with them gently. For do what we may, there will always be found in communities, however small they may be, minds that will give trouble to others. God permits this to exercise the superior's and the sisters' virtue" (*ibid.*, p. 328).

"... Neither must we evince... any despair of their amendment, oh no, never; this will cast them down and arrest them altogether" (*ibid.*, p. 332).

"... Live and converse with all, so that each thinks privately that it is she whom you love best" (*ibid.*, p. 333).

**21.**—St. Sophie Barat. When, with Fr. Varin, she founded the Society of the Sacred-Heart, the Father gave her this maxim upon which she ever based her rule: "Firmness at the proper time, *harshness never;* gentleness and charity always." He at the same time laid down this line of conduct for her: "In making a reform, we need more patience than ardour, more prudence than zeal. We must always *go forward slowly* and gain all hearts; the rest comes afterwards and in detail, without clamour and noise" (*Histoire* of Blessed Mère Barat, by Mgr. Baunard, Book II, ch. i).

§ 3. ON THE NECESSITY FOR A GOOD DIRECTOR.

**21** *bis.*—Fr. Godinez says on this subject, but with a certain exaggeration:

"Of a thousand persons whom God calls to perfection, scarcely ten correspond, and of a hundred whom God calls to contemplation, ninety-nine fail to respond. This is why I say: many are called but few are chosen. Instead of exaggerating the difficulties of this enterprise and magnifying human weakness, we ought to recognise the fact that one of the chief causes is the lack of spiritual masters. Woe to the communities in which these masters are wanting, or which, possessing them, know neither how to recognise them nor esteem them!... In the Church triumphant, certain angels instruct the others; in the same way God wills that, in the Church militant, certain men instruct the others, without these latter having recourse to the miraculous ministry of the angels" (*Theol. myst.*, Book VII, ch. i, quoted by Ribet, *Ascétique,* ch. xxxiv, No. 9).

God however aids those fervent souls who have done their utmost.

**21** *ter.*—St. Teresa:

"For the love of God I entreat her who shall be superioress, always to procure of the Bishop or Provincial this holy liberty, that, besides the usual confessors, she and the rest sometimes may confer and communicate their souls to learned persons; especially if their confessors be not such, how good soever they be... [even] though the confessor have all this, yet what I mentioned, must sometimes be done..." (*Way of Perfection,* ch. v, pp. 16-7).

# CHAPTER XXVII

## On Quietism

### § 1. General Survey

**1.—Definition.** Quietism (from the word *quies,* repose) is the error of those who guide themselves by the following maxim: All our efforts after perfection consist in suppressing *as many* of our acts *as possible,* save in the case of a manifest intervention on God's part. The *minimum of personal action* thus becomes the ideal of sanctity.

**2.**—The principal **excuse** for this suppression is that of allowing God to act, of being docile to His grace. But this is an exaggeration. The obstacle to grace does not lie in our own activity; this, on the contrary, is necessary; for God will not act alone, but only in order *to aid* our action. The obstacle lies in an excess or in an insufficiency of this activity.

There is a wide difference between the maxim: Suppress all your acts; and this other which is orthodox: Suppress all that is defective in your acts.

**3.**—This suppression is the basis of quietism. But there are many different **shades** amongst the supporters of this doctrine. The reason is that they do not all apply their common principles to the same kinds of acts, or they do not all venture to carry this process to its logical conclusion.

And further, certain writers are not always consistent in their statements. False doctrines are very unstable. They retreat when they are attacked, and afterwards forget the restrictions which they have been forced to accept.

**4.**—We may give the name of **mitigated quietists** to those who, without being apologists for inaction in theory, are in sympathy with it in practice. They do not proclaim it as a general principle of perfection; but they are in favour of it in *each particular case* where any action is required. Round about every doctrinal error we thus find what is called its spirit. It is the same thing in a lesser degree, but extremely active and formed of its instinctive tendencies and prejudices. It is no longer a question of formulated errors, in a general way at least, but of something intangible; an unhealthy atmosphere that we breathe, instead of drinking a cup of poison. Thus is it with error in a diluted form. The effect upon the conduct is about the same, in the long run, as in the case of explicit error.

**5.—History**. These doctrines are generally traced to the end of the thirteenth century. Sects of deluded devotees, called *Brethren of the Free Spirit,* or *Beghards** spread over Italy, France, Germany, and Bohemia. They were condemned in 1311, at the General Council of Vienna (see Denzinger's *Enchiridion);* but they were still in existence in the fifteenth century. They taught that perfect souls had no further need of prayer or good works, or of the restriction of any laws. All these things, according to them, were detrimental to the liberty of the children of God, and "would have robbed their contemplation of its purity and loftiness" (Prop. 8).

In 1329 John XXII condemned the propositions put forward by Master Eckhart of Cologne. Quietism was confuted shortly afterwards by Ruysbroeck and Tauler, who described it clearly (see Extracts, **48**).

In 1575, some fanatics in Andalusia assumed the name of *Illuminati.* The Spanish Inquisition did not succeed in extinguishing this sect, for it reappeared in 1623. Several of the thirty-five propositions of these heretics are quietistic in teaching, with this modification, that instead of exaggerating the direct advantages of inaction, they exaggerate those of mental prayer; but the conclusions are the same. "By mental prayer all our duties are fulfilled" (Prop. 1). It dispenses from all other spiritual exercises, from distinct acts of virtue, and from God's commandments. By it we become impeccable; we may yield to our passions, which become of no importance. The same ideas were already to be found in the Beghards' eight propositions which were condemned in 1311, with this difference, that they hardly mention mental prayer (Prop. 8), but only "spiritual perfection."

Fr. Balthasar Alvarez published a refutation of the Andalusian *Illuminati.* It occurs in his *Life,* by the Ven. Louis du Pont, ch. xxxiii.

Finally, in the seventeenth century, quietism passed over from Spain into Italy and France. In 1635, Fr. Joseph of Tremblay, a Capuchin, prevailed on his friend, Cardinal Richelieu, to throw into the Bastille three religious who were making thousands of converts to the new doctrines. Their teaching spread widely during the last half of the seventeenth century, becoming at the same time more formulated and more general. The Holy See, beginning in 1687, was obliged to intervene by condemning more than eighty works containing these errors (for some of these see the Biographical Index). Lastly, it condemned Fénelon's *Maxims of the Saints* (1699).

* A diversity of opinion exists with regard to the etymology of this word and of its old synonyms *Béguins* and *Béguines*. Some attribute it to the old German word *beggen*, to ask with importunity, or to beg; others to the name of Lambert of Bègue, a priest of Lièges, who founded Béguinages at the end of the twelfth century. Others finally rely on the fact that the Fraticelli who were condemned, in 1300, were called Beghards (in Italian *bizocchi* or beggars); the word would thus mean beggars.

It is probable that this great growth of quietistic ideas in the seventeenth century, proceeds partially from the Protestant principle that since the fall of Adam, human nature is fundamentally and *totally* evil.* There would thus be no difference between a good and a bad nature; all would be bad. The effects of grace would not then be to *complete* and *to raise* human nature, which would be to imply that something of good still remains to it, but rather to destroy it. Such a theory is contrary to the Church's teaching. The quietists of the seventeenth century did not formulate it explicitly, being less daring in this matter than were the Jansenists; but Protestantism had by this time popularised it; it was in the air. The quietists suffered, at any rate unconsciously, from this pessimistic tendency. They were satisfied with watering it down, saying, not that every operation of man is always a sin, but that it is at least an obstacle to God's operation and therefore to perfection.

**6.—The quietists' cleverness.** In order to spread their errors abroad, many innovators have taken pains to let it be believed that they held the doctrines of the saints, only *better understood* than is the case with ordinary men. Wolves always need a clothing of sheep-skins. Mme. Guyon, in particular, showed wonderful skill in this regard. She may not have been aware of it; her judgment may have been so warped that she did not perceive her own falsifications. But we then have to admit that she was aided by a marvellous instinct which prevented her overstepping the mark. She justified all her ideas by using words that were held in greatest honour in the Church: *abnegation* and all its synonyms: *renunciation, detachment, mortification, love of the Cross, death unto self,* the *destruction of self-love* (which she called *ownership, propriety*), etc. She composed a dictionary in two volumes, in which she explains the terms of ascetic and mystic writers. But they are all understood in the quietistic sense.

The initiated had the key to this change of meaning. Thus *abnegation* and its synonyms no longer signified the destruction of vices, but of all kinds of acts, those of the virtues included. It was the renunciation not only of bad actions but of all action. The word *self-love* no longer meant an *inordinate* love of self, but *all* love of self, that by which we desire eternal happiness included. "*Leave God to act*" signified: "Leave God to do *everything.*"

The majority of readers did not perceive this. They understood the words in their old sense, and exclaimed: "What a heavenly doctrine; what wonderful detachment!" In our days, also, I have seen clever men allow themselves to be thus caught napping and to approve of dangerous books.

* Some of Luther's propositions, condemned by Leo X, in 1516. "The just man sins in every good work" (Prop. 31); "Every good work, perfectly performed, is a venial sin" (Prop. 32); "From the time of the Fall, free-will is but an empty word; even when it does its utmost, it produces a mortal sin" (Prop. 36).

In 1619 St. Francis of Sales waged war with a very similar rigorist prejudice in Mother Angelica Arnauld's mind (letter of May 25, Migne ed.). She imagined that all inclinations that are agreeable to us are displeasing to God. She would not be convinced to the contrary.

In the seventeenth century some souls embraced these ideas from a sincere love of abnegation* and in reaction against the relaxation which, under Louis XIV, was paving the way for the unhappy eighteenth century. Others went in for this austerity through a desire to be in the fashion, because the Jansenists had made it the proper thing in the *salons*. Others, doubtless, by pure hypocrisy, in order to wear the mask of sanctity. When, certain clearer-sighted minds, like Bossuet, showed themselves intractable, Mme. Guyon was astounded; she was merely speaking, she said, the language of the Gospels and of the saints; she was only holding their maxims! Yes, but the interpretation was exaggerated.

She was careful, too, to give none but approved names to her prayer: *acquired contemplation, prayer of simple regard*; but the ideal degree of these states was that there should be no acts of any kind; this simple regard was so simple that there was no longer any regard at all. She spoke of *deification*, like the true mystics; but with her it was the *total* substitution of God for man.

All this was so well wrapped up, her confused mind or her natural subtlety brought so much obscurity into the discussions, that the cleverest doctors of divinity, such as Bossuet, could make nothing of them. She conceded everything, and she conceded nothing.

As an example of the shifting manner in which she put forth her ideas, see chapter xv of her *Moyen Court et très facile de faire Oraison* (*Short and Easy Method of Prayer*). In order to decide in what measure the task of self-examination before confession should be carried out, she makes use alternately of contradictory expressions. Here she declares that God undertakes everything; there, that we must, however, make certain little efforts for ourselves (see **11**, note). When writers contradict themselves in this way without perceiving it, it is very difficult to convict them of error. To each sentence that you find fault with, they oppose another that is in conformity with your ideas.

**7.**—The quietists have often claimed to base their erroneous doctrines upon the **mystics**. But they suppress the wise restrictions that these latter laid down when counselling repose in prayer. When the mystics said: Refrain from inciting yourselves to the performance of certain acts, 1° they were not speaking to all Christians. They assumed that the persons addressed were in the mystic state; 2° they thereby admitted that these persons did not place themselves in a state of inaction, but that they submitted to it; in a word, that the ligature hindered the production of certain acts (ch. xiv, § 4); 3° they did not attribute the happy results of the mystic state to the inaction which of itself is neither

* It was in this way that the austere Mme. de Maintenon was won over for a time. In one of her letters, speaking of Mme. Guyon's *Moyen court de faire Oraison*, she says: "I read it to the King, who told me that it was all fantasy. He is not yet sufficiently advanced in piety to taste of this perfection" (Guerrier, p. 186). It was a good thing that the King refused to accept it; he afterwards prevented the error from spreading.

good nor bad, but to God's mysterious possession, which is the essential basis of this prayer. Now this possession does not in any wise depend upon our own effort. The quietists claim to dispense with it, and they thus parted company with the mystics and admitted a new principle which might be summed up thus: "By the sole fact that you empty a glass of its contents, the surrounding air fills it. In the same way, *cease to act; and immediately God will act.* It is you who arrest His action by your ridiculous activity. You fill the glass instead of emptying it." Make way for God! But no; these things happen otherwise. God does not mean to replace us as the air replaces the water in the glass. He wishes us to work with Him. The comparison is only true with regard to sins and vices.

### § 2. Some Points of Quietistic Doctrine

**8.—Awaiting the divine action.** We have seen that the quietistic ideal is to display the minimum of activity. And yet he is obliged to recognise that in a number of cases action is necessary. What general rule is he to adopt for deciding whether to act or not to act in each individual case?

This is the principle that stands out from the writings of this sect. Given that some practical resolution is to be made, *action will be taken solely when we are urged thereto by God.* As long as the Holy Spirit has not set the soul in motion, she will wait without doing anything whatever.

This is what Bossuet calls "an idle waiting for grace, until it declares itself" (*Préface sur l'instruction pastorale,* ch. lviii, Lachat ed., Vol. XIX, p. 223).

He thus describes the aim which the quietists propose to themselves: put yourself in "a state in which we do nothing but wait, momentarily *expecting* God to set us in motion" (*États d'Oraison,* Book VII, No. 28). Speaking of the *Maxims of the Saints,* he says again: "Throughout the book, souls are habituated to act by *impulsion* in an entire state, that is to say by fancy, and a fanatical impression" (Preface quoted in ch. lx. See other Extracts 52).

**9.**—With certain quietists, such as Mme. Guyon, the ideal is that we should not deliberate, and that action should take place **automatically** (See Extracts **31**, 7°, **37**, 2°). They are logical; for to *feel* the divine action is to perform an act, which, according to them, is not divine. It is a remnant of imperfection, therefore. A puppet that felt its wires being manipulated, would not have the maximum of passiveness and dependence with regard to the operator. This latter would not be doing everything, but the puppet would at least be in the right way.

**10.**—The majority of quietists are more moderate. They take it for granted that people are not acting blindly, but know what they are doing. What they are expecting, therefore, is the impulse **that is felt,** for they admit that the divine action is recognised, which is the same thing as to feel it.

But we see that such a doctrine is very different to that which was universally applied for centuries in the Church. We no longer fatigue ourselves by an examination as to whether the proposed action is good in itself, useful and opportune. The question will resolve itself into knowing whether we feel an impulsion, and whether we believe that we feel it to be divine.

The man's action will thus be reduced nearly to the minimum. Let us note that if the innovators had been satisfied with saying that when there is a divine impulsion it should be followed (being always on our guard against counterfeits), they would then have been in agreement with the orthodox writers. But they go further than this: they say that we must remain inactive as long as this impulsion is not felt.

In the same way, to be slow in making important decisions, to await an attraction, an interior encouragement, would not be quietism. For we do not then lay down this general and *a priori* principle that an impulsion should *always* be waited for. And further, we do not regard this impulsion as dispensing us from weighing motives; it is rather their complement; and in practice, the chief object of these delays is the maturing of thought.

**11.—The absurdity of this principle.** 1° The quietists forget, and certain of them reject, an essential restriction, namely, that their principle cannot be applicable to actions that are matters of precept. Thus, I am bound to hear Mass on Sunday. I have no right to wait until I have received the divine call to take action. The same must be said of the obligation to produce acts of faith, hope, and charity from time to time.

So, too, before going to confession, I am obliged to examine my conscience. I should be tempting God if I claimed that He would suddenly make me remember my sins at the moment of beginning to accuse myself. Mme. Guyon was not of this opinion;* she wished people to continue in quiet without reflecting.

**12.**—There is a precept which many quietists have sacrificed to their doctrine: that of resisting **temptations**. For them, resistance is an imperfection if no such impulsion is felt, for it is to *act* of one's own accord and to place oneself in opposition to a state that they regard as being willed by God. On the other hand, to yield to these temptations is an admirable example of abandonment. With these principles one might commit all kinds of sins.

* She had full confidence in the success of her method. Its adepts had but "to *expose* themselves to God, who *will not fail* to enlighten them and to make known to them the nature of their faults... When we remain *exposed* to the searching gaze of God [in voluntary immobility] that Divine Sun brings to light even the smallest atoms" (*Moyen Court*, ch. xv, 1, English trans. by Marston, ch. xii, p. 39). After this gratuitous declaration, which is disproved by experience, she herself contradicts it by declaring that "we often forget our faults and find it difficult to remember them. But this must not trouble us... this very forgetfulness is a proof that the sin has been atoned for" (*ibid.*, 4. English, p. 41). The authoress gives us the strange reason, namely: "This forgetfulness is a mark of purification from the fault" (*ibid.*). Whence it follows that sins may be regarded as forgiven by the sole fact that we no longer remember them! One is dismayed when one sees how in the seventeenth century so many absurdities could be accepted and admired by theologians and clever men. Later on, will not some of our infatuations be a source of astonishment?

The majority of quietists did not venture to proclaim this theory. Molinos, however, did not recoil from putting it into practice, as his process shows. He was logical (Terzago, *Diss,* 2, § 2, pp. 14, 15).

**13.**—2° Admitting that the principle of the divine impulsion is restricted to **non-obligatory actions**, it still has absurd consequences.* It consists, says Bossuet, "in awaiting the motion of the actual grace, indicating the divine good-pleasure. Consequently there is no need to *consider the dictates of prudence* before deciding upon either thanksgiving, or pious readings or preachings, which, however, are so necessary amidst life's dangers, or, especially the practice of the virtues. In all these cases which form the principal part of the Christian life, we are guided, *not by reason and prudence,* but by instinct and sudden impulses, which leads to fanaticism" (*Mystici in tuto,* No. 141).

Thus, when a sick person is in need of your assistance, when a poor man stretches out his hand to you, do not be in a hurry; you may perhaps lack the impulsion! Await it tranquilly! It will be the same for a thousand daily actions. Inaction! and then again, inaction!

This rule of the quietists leads them, therefore, to perform but few good works. If any such are performed, it is by expecting God to give them a series of inspirations, nearly related to revelations. This is contrary to the order of Providence. The true rule is to do what the divine law, what the gospel spirit, what Christian prudence teach. If there is an inspiration, it is an additional grace that is given to us.

The above rule would perhaps be acceptable if God did not give us His grace each time that the opportunity for a good work offers itself, or if He deferred it. We might then say, "I do not know whether this act is done under the impulsion of grace, and consequently whether it is meritorious. I prefer to wait." But this is to suppose a hypothesis that is contrary to the Church's teaching. God always offers us grace to do right. The grace never comes too late, it is simultaneous with the thought of the act to be performed.† Our initiative is apparent only.

The quietists have sometimes attempted to water down their principle so as to diminish its absurdity. They have said, for instance, with Fénelon: What we reject are merely the efforts of nature. But Bossuet answered him: We blame you for this, that under the pretext of destroying natural efforts, you at the same time destroy all effort. For those that are natural cannot be distinguished from the others" (*Mystici in tuto,* No. 139).

* See a brilliant refutation in La Bruyère's *Dialogues,* particularly Dialogues 1 and 4.

† It is true that orthodox writers say that we should not anticipate grace, or God's call. This is an equivocal phrase, which simply means to say: In important matters, such as the choice of a state in life, do not be precipitate; examine, pray, take advice.

**13** *bis.*—The principle of awaiting the divine motion has not only the drawback of hindering action when it is necessary; it leads to action when it is undesirable. For this doctrine implies that we must yield to the motion that we believe to emanate from God, that is to say, to an emotional state, without examining into the reasons that justify the action. We may thus commit a thousand follies, while attributing them to the Holy Spirit; it is pure illuminism.

**14.**—Certain modern writers have retained something of the preceding doctrine by giving too much importance to the **attraction**. They seem to make it the *general and only rule* of conduct, instead of an aid, excellent, doubtless, but not the only one. Life would, in that case, be made up, not of acts of voluntary choice, but of evident vocations; in this way we are taught to dread taking the initiative.

**15.**—Quietistic ideas regarding **desires and petitions.** They were obliged to see imperfections here, even when it was a question of a supernatural blessing, since these are acts. The great virtue was conformity to the divine will, *abandonment,* exaggerated to the point of reducing oneself to a passive state of expectation. It would seem that we should adopt as our motto: "Do not help yourself; heaven will help you."

In this way *desires* and *abandonment* were falsely considered as two dispositions incompatible with one another; Molinos claimed this to be so in his Proposition 14, which has been condemned.*

The truth is that filial *abandonment* is quite reconcilable with the formulation of *desires* and petitions. Our Lord manifested these two kinds of dispositions simultaneously in the Garden of Gethsemane. He implores His Father to remove the chalice from Him, and at once adds that He submits wholly to His decision.

In the same way, in a family, the most submissive child is not afraid to express his wishes to his father, and yet more, a wife acts in the same way with her husband. Let us not think of God as a jealous, intractable, sullen king who will not tolerate any initiative and who wishes to reduce us to a slave's mute obedience. He has willed us to be His sons, His friends. He is the Bridegroom of our souls. How many persons there are who estrange us from God by the narrowness of their ideas, not showing Him to us as He really is!

He carries this condescension to the lengths of leaving many acts to our own choice; at times the vocation itself is merely suggested. Speaking of the perfect

* Here is the text: "When the man is *resigned to the divine will* he should *ask nothing* of God; for *to ask is an imperfection.* It is an act of self-will; it is to will that the divine Will should conform itself to ours, and not ours to the divine Will. The words of the Gospel: 'Ask, and you shall receive,' *were not spoken for interior souls,* for these desire to have no will. Far more, these souls have arrived at the point of being unable to ask *anything whatsoever* of God." Mgr. Terzago describes this proposition as "rash, scandalous, impious, blasphemous, erroneous, and heretical" (*Theol. historico-mystica,* pp. 91 and 13).

life, to the young man of the Gospels, Our Lord said: "*If thou wilt* be perfect," etc. He laid no obligation upon him.

**16.**—But, objected the quietists, **St. Francis of Sales** has summed up all perfection in this maxim: "Desire nothing, refuse nothing."

This maxim occurs in the last and in the sixth of St. Francis of Sales' *Spiritual Conferences,* but with restrictions that pious books often forget to recall; otherwise the saint would have taught a proposition that is contrary to the precept of prayer, and is condemned. He declares that he speaks only "of earthly things," of those that are not useful for our sanctification.* He is only repeating, therefore, the doctrine of all ages concerning detachment, as Bossuet says (*États d'Oraison,* Tr. 1, Book VIII, No. 1).† The quietists' exaggeration has consisted in converting this maxim into a universal principle.

And further, Bossuet bids us remark that when St. Francis of Sales seems to condemn certain desires, he only wishes to moderate them sufficiently to enable the soul to preserve her peace: "It is one thing to strip oneself of care, *of anxiety and distress of mind,* and another to strip oneself of desire" (*ibid.,* Book IX, No. 8).

**17.**—The quietists' ideas on **mental prayer** have already been explained (ch. iv, 10). In virtue of their theory regarding acts, they only admit one kind of prayer as being perfect, that in which action is reduced to a minimum.

They call this *acquired contemplation,*‡ wishing thereby to indicate that we may *acquire* this state by our own exertions. It would thus resolve itself into a confused idea of God as being present everywhere, the thought of any other divine attribute being excluded; otherwise, they say, there would be too many different acts. Besides (so they add, without any proofs), this act is *an eminent act,* one, that is to say, comprising in a more perfect degree all those that we might perform (Bossuet, *Instruction sur les États d'Oraison,* Book III, No. 3. La Bruyere, *Dialogue,* 2).

And then, as far as possible, it should be one prolonged act rather than a repetition of acts; and always for the sake of arriving at the minimum of activity. Malaval considers that he is showing great consideration for his

* It is even probable that he wishes, above all, to keep his spiritual daughters from those requests which imperfect religious might address to their superior: excessive indulgences, permission to leave a house that is distasteful to them, to discontinue a tedious employment, to be rid of an uncongenial companion, etc. This is why he immediately adds that obedience must be followed.

† He adds: "St. Francis of Sales is not acquainted with these superbly and aridly disinterested ways which would make perfection to consist *in asking nothing for ourselves.* If I were to quote the passages in which he makes petitions to God and recommends them to perfect souls, I should have to transcribe quite half of his letters" (*ibid.,* No. 2).

‡ They call it also the prayer of *pure faith* and *passive* prayer. This last name was very inaccurate, for they seemed thus to confuse this prayer with infused contemplation, from which, however, they distinguished it clearly (Molinos, Prop. 23; Mme. Guyon, *Moyen court,* ch. xv). But by this exaggerated term they wished to indicate their erroneous idea that in this state man does nothing; it is God who does everything.

disciples in allowing them to repeat their act during the first three or four days which they devote to mental prayer: "so that at first you should have something to rest on... I do not require that you should plunge at once into deep water" (Part I, No. 14).

**18.**—By virtue of the same principles, the quietists dissuaded people from **vocal prayers,** the recitation of the Divine Office or the Rosary. Instead of saying wisely, like the Church: "Do not be satisfied with a purely material recitation; animate it by the inward spirit"; some added that "perfect souls" could dispense with bodily penances, even those that are of obligation, such as the abstinence and fast. Contemplation would supply the place of all these things.

**19.**—The **exterior practices** of devotion were also condemned by many quietists: the sign of the Cross, spiritual reading, sermons, invocations of the saints, honour paid to sacred pictures and also the religious vows.

**20.**—The **mania for exclusions** recurs also in many other false doctrines. Instead of saying with moderation: "such a practice is good, at least in certain cases," they inveigh against all rival methods. Whether it is a question of prayer, or any action whatever, they recognise but one path, outside of which there is no salvation. One so exalts docility to the Holy Spirit, that he practically rejects all tradition and all method. Another, on the other hand, thinks of nothing but of imprisoning himself in methods, without admitting any direct action on the part of the Holy Spirit. A third allows only such and such a motive for our actions. Others discover a so-called modern spirituality that exalts the unitive way, while depreciating the purgative and illuminative ways; they wish to give themselves up to exercises of divine love without first or at the same time practising those which make us fight against our defects and for the painful acquisition of solid virtues. They reject, as old fashioned, the spirituality of self-conquest, which is much less agreeable. They seek to erect the summit of the building without thinking of the necessary although less brilliant foundations. With these exclusions they practise an imaginary and fanciful asceticism.

**21.—Summary**. Let us now return to the quietists. While the *Perfect life* resolved itself into one single exercise, repose in abandonment, *perfect prayer* lent itself to the same simplification. It was truly ingenious.

Let us note that this perfection and these practices no longer differed from those of the Buddhists, all of whose efforts are directed towards arriving at nothingness under the name of Nirvana. So that, by the long road round of Christianity, we find our way back to one of the greatest errors known in history, the one which has over-run Eastern Asia for so many centuries. The motives, however, are different.

**22.**—Result. These **methods** seemed so **easy**, so simple to the quietists, that they declared them to be within the reach of all souls of good-will and wished to preach them to everyone, indiscriminately, even to children and labourers (*Moyen Court,* ch. xxiii, No. 1). Fr. La Combe asserted that this prayer should be explained to children of four years of age (Bossuet, *États d'Oraison,* Book VII, No. 28).

**23.**—**Fénelon's** false doctrines. It is usual to include them all under the general designation of quietism. But this is simplification at the expense of accuracy. The Archbishop of Cambrai's principal ideas resolve themselves into two. The first, indeed, is quietist, it is awaiting the divine action (see above, **8**, Bossuet's pronouncement). The other is of quite a different kind: the exaggerated idea of perfect charity, or "pure love." With him this love excludes fear, hope, and all thought of self-advantage (Prop. 1, 2, 4, 5, 6, etc.). Perfection requires that we should act *solely* through disinterested love. The disinterestedness should even be carried as far as indifference with regard to our eternal salvation (Prop. 7, 8, 10, 12). This part of Fénelon's system differs from the immobility of the quietists. It is another kind of exclusion: it is excluding, not action, but certain supernatural motives of action.

Generous souls may be tempted in this direction, and they must be on their guard against it. They think they are yielding to "self-love" if they take pleasure in the thought of paradise, and even if they are concerned with the correction of their defects. There is nothing too highly refined for them with regard to divine love. These doctrines are condemned. With him who aims at perfection *love should be predominant;* that is true, but *it must not stand alone.* St. Ignatius understood this double truth thoroughly when he wrote in his Rules: "Let all endeavour to have a right intention, not only as to their state of life, but also in all particulars, always sincerely seeking in them to serve and please the Divine *goodness for Itself,* and for the charity and *singular benefits* wherewith It has prevented us, rather than for *fear* of punishment or *hope* of rewards (*though they should be helped by these motives also*)." See also the last of the Rules *"Ad sentiendum cum Ecclesia."*

Love is like a melody that should sing on in our souls; but a melody requires an accompaniment. This will consist in sentiments of fear and hope. These three notes will not clash; they produce, not a painful discord, but a perfect harmony.

One of the practical drawbacks of Fénelon's doctrine for souls athirst for perfection, is that it tends to lead them to a **refining of the motives** of their actions, to an incessant self-analysis in order to determine whether these motives are sufficiently high. It is the way to end in anxiety and scruples. When we thus attempt to examine everything under the microscope, we discover microbes in the most limpid waters.

**24.**—With reference to pure love, there is a question that must not be confused with the foregoing. We said that disinterested love *does not exclude* other motives based on self-interest; all these sentiments may exist simultaneously and should habitually do so. But it may be asked whether they are, although united, really independent one of the other; briefly, is the **disinterested love**, disinterested in appearance only? Does it always contain a certain love of self, although in its hidden state? If the answer were in the affirmative, would the name belong to it only because it contains a *minimum of self-seeking* which would not be apparent at first sight?

This is a matter of controversy. On the affirmative side, the facts of the natural order, which for all time have been regarded as acts of disinterested love, may be quoted; that, for instance, of the man who sacrifices his time, his health or his life for a friend, his country, or for an idea. If we analyse the state of soul of one who devotes himself thus, we arrive at the following definition: the love that is called disinterested, consists in finding our own happiness in that of another (if it is a question of an idea, it is the triumph of this which makes our happiness). There are therefore two influences here: the one is the *hidden motive* which makes us seek our own happiness; the other the *visible motive* which is the search after a blessing that we do not possess.

St. Thomas implicitly admits this view of the matter when he says: "If, which is impossible, God were not man's good, man would have no reason for loving Him" (2, 2, q. 26, art. 13, ad. 3). He would be satisfied with esteeming him. He says again: "All friendship contains the desire of possessing, and adds something to it" (Tr. 3, dist. 27, q. 2, a. 1, ad. 1).

St. Francis of Sales develops the same doctrine: "But if, by imagination of a thing impossible, there were an infinite goodness on which we had no dependence whatever, and with which we could have no kind of *union* or *communication,* we should indeed esteem it more than ourselves;... yet, properly speaking, we should not love it, since love aims at union; and much less could we have charity towards it, since charity is a friendship, and *friendship cannot be unless it be reciprocal,* having for its *groundwork* communication, and for its *end* union. I speak thus for the benefit of certain fantastic and empty spirits, who very often on baseless imaginations revolve morbid thoughts to their own great affliction" (*Treatise on the Love of God,* Book X, ch. x, p. 439).

Commenting on this passage, Fr. Massoulié inquires who are these "empty spirits" of which the saint speaks. "It is difficult, he says, to penetrate into his meaning. It is nevertheless probable that he intends to speak of those devout persons who, having conceived a false idea of the love of God, and thinking to love God with a disinterested love, scorn to produce the familiar acts of religion, and even reject the consolations that God offers them, for fear, they say, of self-seeking. Hence it follows that *desiring nothing* and receiving nothing to sustain and strengthen them in the path of virtue, they experience a frightful state of dryness, which soon merges into chagrin and melancholy; and thereupon they come to fancy that they are in a mystical abandonment, and that God wishes to crucify them, instead of its being they themselves *that cling obstinately to a false Cross*" (*Traité de l'amour de Dieu,* by Fr. Massoulié, Part I, ch. iii).

### § 3. The Exaggerations of Orthodox Writers Concerning Abandonment

**25.**—The expressions *abandonment* to the divine will, *leaving all to God,* have an orthodox meaning. But they have often been wrongly understood; we have already shown that this is so. The **exaggeration** consists in believing that the *abandonment should exclude desire* (**15**) and personal effort; and that *leaving all to God,* means leaving all *wholly* to God, taking no thought for any thing, and not merely accepting the ills that we cannot prevent.

Devout persons often approve of these exaggerations, either because these tendencies to self-despoliation respond to their immense need for generosity, or because this kind of virtue is represented to them as being a rapid means of arriving at perfection; or, finally, because, disheartened at the spectacle of their persistent misery, they see in an exaggerated abandonment the sole means of tolerating themselves; it is the proper opiate for calming the desires that cause their fever.

**26.**—Those who condemn these ill-judged devotions may seem to fail in a proper esteem for conformity to the divine will. This is a **mistake.*** As far as I know, nobody has ever questioned such a necessary virtue in itself, but only the exaggerations that we derive from the quietists, and of which our century is not yet entirely free.

It will be well to throw some light on this point, and to show that even orthodox writers have often been responsible for a wrong interpretation. This has been so in two ways; by their silence and by inaccurate expressions.

**27.**—First by their **silence**. The task of supplying the proper corrections should not be left to the readers, who are often very insufficiently instructed. When interpreting the words, *abandonment, leaving all to God,* simple souls allow themselves to follow the ordinary sense of the word in its current use and in things of the natural order.

So then these words signify: *doing nothing,* showing no initiative, no resistance, not even such as is permitted. For example: we say that people *abandon* themselves to their grief, or to their passions, or to the chances of fortune. We mean to say that they are inert, waiting upon events, instead of influencing them. So too, when a man is the victim of an injustice, or has to undergo some painful ordeal of the body or of the soul, we say to him: *Submit;* that is to say, do not struggle. In all these cases we imply inaction. Now if these words conjure up such ideas in the natural order, it is inevitable that it should

*Bossuet himself was obliged to defend himself with regard to this: "The act of abandonment," he wrote, "is excellent, but I have my reasons for asking you in what manner you make it, not from any distrust of you, but with reference to other people who *do it very ill,* and in a way which tends to tempting God" (Letter of Aug. 12, 1694 to Mme. d'Albert).

be the same when we apply them to the spiritual life, unless the reader be warned against this interpretation.

We may say as much regarding the word *self-love.* Many persons, thinking only of the etymology, fancy that this expression applies to all love of self, which is thus condemned wholesale. For the same reason they believe that by *self-will* we should understand all willing that is in accordance, no matter how slightly, with our tastes; and this is what leads to their blaming it.

Some quite sound writers do not think of warning us against these misunderstandings. They may say: "I have laid down no error." It may be so; but they have set up no barrier to the errors that would occur of themselves. The length of their treatises, the incessant repetition of the same strict counsels, also help to suggest the wrong meaning. When for three hundred pages (and sometimes twice this number) we hear it said repeatedly: "Abandon yourself. Mistrust your own activity," we end by no longer daring to act at all. We have breathed an atmosphere charged with chloroform. The author has not intended it, but the effect is produced.

In the same way, by employing certain comparisons without any restrictions, there is an unconscious exaggeration. Thus they tell you that the soul should be a musical instrument, passive in the hands of the musician, who draws from it, without its assent, all the melodies that he pleases; or like the flowers of a garden that the gardener carries here and there as he chooses. These comparisons are acceptable if we make it plain that they are not to be taken literally. But we must not, by multiplying them, leave the reader under the false and rigid impression that God wishes to treat us as we treat inanimate objects.

Let us take, for example, two small modern books. One is *Le Vœ d'abandon,* by a Franciscan Father, published by the *(Œuvre de St. Paul* (Paris, 6 Rue Cassette, 1889). The *Revue Franciscaine,* of June, 1893, published a letter on this subject from the most Reverend Father-General of the Franciscans, to the Rev. Father Thomas, Provincial Minister. He ordered him to "stop its circulation,* and to forbid the practice of the things contained therein." And yet he knew that two theologians of the Order and another, a Dominican, who examined this work, had "found that it did not contain any errors." They, nevertheless, decided that it was "dangerous." If this work does not formulate incorrect ideas, at least it gives rise to them.

The other booklet is *La Retraite de dix jour sur l'abandon et l'Un nécessaire,* by Mother Mary of the Conception, a Carmelite of Aix (Paris, Mignard, second ed., 1897). It consists of forty-three meditations and twenty letters, all on the same idea! With the exception of some exaggerated expressions, it contains no errors. But never a word is spoken to raise up the soul, crushed under the weight of her duties, or to approve any one of her aspirations. This work, which

* The book is still sold, however. I was told that the lady who paid for the printing, and who regards herself as owning the edition, refused to submit to this order.

would be excellent if it were modified here and there, is absolutely depressing. You end by attributing all desire to "self-love"—God's rival. On the other hand, I am glad to add that I greatly admire another book by the same writer: *La Maîtresse des Novices.* With regard to renunciation, the manner of presentment is perfect, and the analyses of soul show a remarkable penetration.

To sum up, there are things which our minds find it difficult to reconcile; as, for instance, *abandonment and initiative,* predestination and human liberty, or again those two qualities which the Gospel requires, the prudence of the serpent and the simplicity of the dove. If we insistently praise one of these things without thinking of alluding to the other, the reader will be led to take what was merely a *forgetfulness* for a deliberate *exclusion.**

**28.**—Thus it is that some writers involve us in error by their silence. I said that their **works** further contain some **greatly exaggerated phrases.** Fr. Ramière, who published Fr. de Caussade's manuscript (re-touched by him after having already undergone this process in the eighteenth century), admits this accusation with reference to this work in the preface to the large edition. "*Learned* men, who had been consulted *on several occasions*" had found passages "which seemed to them *inaccurate and dangerous for the ordinary reader*" (p. 8). He has made some corrections, he says, but has left *many* passages intact, which had thus, "and *not without reason,* been charged with inaccuracy." He hopes that the reader will himself supply the necessary corrections (p. 13). I admit that this may be done in the case of theologians. They unconsciously correct and mentally complete certain phrases. More than once they have been known to praise books that have since been condemned. They had read them in the light of their own kindly corrections. But it is far from being the case that everyone can do as much.†

I admit that where the majority of the laity are concerned, these exaggerations have very few ill-consequences; because they take in but a small percentage of all that may be said to them on the subject of abnegation. Many devout or religious people, however, act otherwise, as I have proved. They wish to sanctify themselves at all costs, and take literally the rules that are given to them as necessary.

**29.**—There is often another kind of exaggeration in these books that I have not yet spoken of. It consists in making **too fair promises.** They announce that

* St. Ignatius puts us on our guard against these omissions in his Rule 14, on orthodoxy, in connection with predestination.

† Certain letters of direction contained in this work show that the persons to whom they were addressed were falling into a kind of despair. This can be understood. They were told to satiety that they must wage war against their nature, without first teaching them to distinguish between the good and the bad; that "all natural aids" must be removed. These persons then endeavoured to repel all their natural aspirations, even those which are willed by God and which may be supernaturalised. In this dreadful strife, which could not be successful, how could anyone fail to lose his peace of mind?

abandonment is the simplest, the quickest and the most powerful of methods.* They seem to guarantee sanctity in three lessons. This path would indeed be one of great simplicity if it dispensed us from studying the other virtues separately and at great length, and then from practising them during our whole lives. It would be an economy both of mind and will. But it is chiefly a contrivance for grouping these virtues together, in theory and in practice; it is a point of view from which to contemplate them; you mark out a main line of conduct which might just as well be that of divine love or of humility, and to this you attach a hundred other practices, like the surveyor, who attaches all the parts of a vast territory to an arbitrary point. But as regards simplicity and rapidity, the advance is but a modest one. It is primarily an orderly arrangement.

Still more is it necessary to warn the reader against the illusion that this central point is a substitute for everything else: briefly, that in the practice of the spiritual life maxims of rigorously universal application are to be found which are all sufficient. At times, on the other hand, they seem to promise that in saying *Fiat* we shall have escaped the thousand daily difficulties that hinder our sanctification.† This would be so were God to tell us openly, and moment by moment, what He requires of us. It would then be enough to reply like Mary: *"Fiat mihi secundum verbum tuum."* But this is not the usual case in the decisions that have to be made. It is necessary to dispense with the direct revelation, to weigh the *pros* and *cons.* The *fiat,* the *leave all to God,* no longer suffices.‡ To be content with it is to run counter to the divine plan, and consequently to fail in conformity to God's will. It must be retained only as a general disposition with regard to particular events.

In conclusion, it is incorrect to hold that the doctrine of abandonment replaces everything and suffices for everything.

We have seen, therefore, that when the thoughts are centred too exclusively upon one single virtue, there is a great risk of exaggeration, both as to theory and practice. To guard this virtue from excess, to hold the balance even, it is necessary to appeal to other principles and to combine them all with discretion.

* It is noticeable that several quietists were so occupied with this thesis that they even referred to it in the titles of their books. Mme. Guyon calls her first book "A *short* and *very easy* method of prayer"; Malaval, "An *easy* manner of raising the soul to contemplation." Benedict of Canfeld, "Rule of perfection, *reducing* the spiritual life *to one point only,* the will of God." In itself it is not a bad thing to strive after simplicity. But something more than an apparent success is needed.

† One of the earliest works of Fr. Piny, O.P., bears this very characteristic title: *The State of Pure Love, or A Way of Attaining Quickly to Perfection by means of the Fiat alone, said and repeated on all occasions,* Paris, 1682. In his treatise entitled, *The Greatest Perfection* (*Le Plus Parfait*), he thus styles his chapter v: *That the way of abandonment to the divine will is of all interior ways the surest and the least subject to illusion.* The history of quietism showed, not many later years, what should be thought of this promise.

‡ Fr. Surin: "What! is it not right to leave all to God? Yes, certainly, when He wills to act and when it is His part to act. But when the soul ought to act, if she indiscreetly ceases to do so, it is the that the Devil acts" (*Catech. Spir.* Part v, ch. iii).

The quietists were preoccupied, exclusively, with submission to the divine action; they ended in inertia. So, too, Mother Angelica Arnauld was suddenly enamoured of regularity and mortification; but she did not understand that it was necessary to be penetrated at the same time with gentleness and kindness, as St. Francis of Sales so urgently besought of her. And so her piety degenerated little by little into an atrocious hardness towards herself, and especially towards others.*

**29** *bis.*—The **rationalists** have accused the great ecstatics, and St. John of the Cross in particular, of arriving at such a state of passivity that it merits the name of automatism. "God does, or appears to do, everything within them; they no longer do anything. In this way they arrive at the point to which the quietists attain by their system of the 'divine motion.' "

Nothing could be more false. The state that would lend itself especially to this exaggerated interpretation is the spiritual marriage. Now on reading St. Teresa, we see that in this supreme state there is no more automatism than between a bride and bride-groom who, through love, consult each other ceaselessly and who regard it as a happiness to be of one mind. The saint maintains the full exercise of her judgement, she does not act without examining motives. She works with God instead of leaving it to God to act alone. It is just the opposite of Mme. Guyon's state and doctrines. Their language, also, is quite different.

Certain pages of St. John of the Cross' writings have been misunderstood upon this point. If we took what he says in Book III of *The Ascent of Mount Carmel,* literally, it would seem as if the use of the memory and the imagination were completely lost at the summit of the mystic states. God would undertake to supplement this great deficiency whenever it is needed; every minute, that is to say. But it would then follow that when the saint, having reached this degree, wrote his description of it at great length in two treatises, all the words of his native tongue would have been forgotten and restored by God, singly. Neither he nor his commentators believed in this transcendent mechanism. Nor was his imagination dead. His last books contain a quite tropical wealth of imagery. He employs as symbols shepherds, forests, and groves, caves, fountains, pomegranates, turtle-doves, stags, the spreading boughs of the cedar trees, wine, perfumes, etc. His writing in no wise seems like matter dictated to him; and he no more attributes this wealth of words to the Holy Spirit than his very free interpretations of Holy Scripture. With regard to St. John of the Cross, then, the suppression of the memory and the imagination applies, not to every-day actions, but to times of sublime contemplation and to special moments. This is not the automatism, the universal passivity of Mme. Guyon.

* This psychological process is analysed with great delicacy of perception in her *Life*, published by Monlaur (Plon, 1901).

# EXTRACTS

## § 1. Quietist Passages Illustrating Their Fundamental Principle: the Search After the Minimum of Activity

**30.**—Propositions by Molinos:

"Man must *annihilate* his powers; this is the interior way"* (Prop. 1). "To wish to be active is to offend God who desires to be the *sole agent*. This is why we must abandon ourselves *totally* to Him, and live henceforth like *a body without a soul*" (Prop. 2)... "God wills to act in us *without* our aid" (Prop. 3).

**31.**—Mme. Guyon:

1° "So the soul does not trouble itself to seek anything or *to do anything*... It remains as it is. But what does it do? *Nothing—always nothing*... It has, as it were, passed into a state of nature; and yet how different from those altogether without God! The difference is, that it is compelled to action by God *without being conscious of it*, whereas formerly it was nature that acted" (*Les Torrents*, Part I, chap. ix, No. 9. English trans.: *A Short Method of Prayer* and *Spiritual Torrents*, by A. W. Marston, ch. ix, pp. 198-9).

2° "This impurity, so opposed to union, is appropriation and activity... Activity, because God being in an infinite repose, in order that the soul may be united to Him, it must participate in His repose, without which there can be no union, because of the dissemblance" (*Moyen Court*, ch. xxiv, No. 3. *Short Method*, ch. xix, p. 79).

3° "Jesus Christ in the Holy Sacrament of the altar is the model of the mystic state. As soon as He descends there by the words spoken by the priest, the *substance* of the bread must *make way for Him*, the simple accidents only remaining. In the same manner we must *yield our being* to that of Jesus Christ... Now this will never be accomplished save by *annihilation*" (*Moyen Court*, ch. xx, No. 3).†

4° "The soul suffers itself to be *destroyed* and *annihilated* to render homage to the sovereignty of God... And the *destruction* of our own being confesses the sovereign being of God... *Nothingness* is true prayer, which renders to God, 'honour and glory, and power, for ever and ever' " (Moyen Court, ch. xx. No. 3).*

5° "We must second the designs of God, which are to strip the soul of all its works, to substitute His in their place" [Make way for Him] (Short Method, ch. xvii).*

* According to him, the "only" *way* should be substituted for the three ways—the purgative, the illuminative, and the unitive—which he declares to be "the most absurd" of ideas (Prop. 26).

† Omitted in the English translation [Translator].

Bossuet adds: "Making way in this language is to do nothing, to desire nothing, to ask nothing of our own accord, and to wait for God to do everything" (États d'Orai*son,* Book III, No. 4).

6° "Abandonment is the casting off of *all care* of ourselves, leaving ourselves to be entirely guided by God... Practically it should be a continual losing of our own will in the will of God, a renunciation of *all* natural inclinations however good they may appear," [directly we are aware of them].* Bossuet adds: "We must renounce them [the acts] directly we are aware of them. Which means nothing less than the entire extinction of every act of piety, the least beginning, the slightest spark and mere thought of which might arise in our minds. If we should renounce them when they appear, we ought still more to hinder their production" (*États d'Oraison,* Book III, No. 10).

7° The ideal is to arrive at acting automatically. "Who can say to what lengths this abandonment should lead, following the grace that granted, so that we become a child, or holily foolish, with regard to all things; so that we act *without knowledge,* without resistance, without repugnances... and without limitations, *like one who is no more,* and who can no more trouble himself of his own accord than if he did not exist. We are not trusting wholly in God if we fall short of this; it is rather *wishing to share His sovereignty with Him,* reserving to ourselves the domain of our own guidance in something" (*Regle des associes a l'enfance de Jesus,* § 9, No. 5). Mme. Guyon afterwards develops the absurd idea that those who practise this kind of blind abandonment cannot be deceived, since it is God who leads them. But that God leads them is exactly what we deny.

8° Mme. Guyon, however, makes a slight concession in the case of beginners; she allows them a certain number of acts: "We do not say, then, as some assert, that there must be *no action;* since, on the contrary, this is the door; but only that *we must not remain in it"* (*Moyen Court,* ch. xxiv, No. 9; *Short Method,* ch. xix, p. 83). Her concession, however, does not extend very far (*Moyen Court,* No. 8, and ch. xxii). She forbade many excellent acts from the outset, pretending that grace has no part in them.

§ 2.—APPLICATION. THE SUPPRESSION OF THOUGHTS.

**32.**—Fr. Falconi. On mental prayer:

"Abstain from thinking voluntarily of *anything, however good* and however sublime it may be; hold only to abiding in the pure faith in God in general and in your resignation to His Holy Will" (*Lettre a une fille spirituelle,* No. 2). "You thus practise almost all the virtues... I have no words in which to express the great good that is contained in this humble, pure and true manner of praying in silence and abandonment" (No. 3). "In doing what I have advised you, be careful, then, to avoid considering that God is present in your soul and in your heart. For although it be a good thing... it is not simply believing... Nor should you trouble yourself to know... whether your prayer goes well or ill. Do not amuse yourself... with thinking whether or no you are practising the *virtues* that I have pointed out to you, or other similar things. To do this would be to occupy your mind with these *small considerations* and to break the thread of perfect prayer" (No. 6). "When Gregory Lopez had arrived at this *spiritual act* of faith, abandonment and love, he allowed himself *neither aspiration nor ejaculatory prayer,* nor anything whatever that pertained to the sensible faculties. It is to this, my daughter, that I wish to see you speedily attain" (No. 11).

**33.**—Malaval:

"*For as long a time as possible* we must *think nothing* and desire nothing" (Part I, p. 8). A blank page—this is the true description of his system.

**34.**—Abbe d'Estival:

"We must continue in the simple regard as long as possible, without thinking of anything or desiring anything, since possessing God, we possess everything" (*Conferences mystiques,* p. 41).—In this way we possess God after the manner of inanimate creatures, but not of reasonable ones.

**35.**—Molinos:

1° "When in doubt as to whether we are in the right or the wrong way, we *must not reflect* upon it" (Prop. 11). "During prayer, *we must* abide in an obscure and general faith,... but without producing any acts, for *God does not like them*" (Prop. 21). "This knowledge by faith is not an act *produced by the creature,* but it is a knowledge *given* by God to the creature. This latter *knows not that it possesses it,* and afterwards knows not that it has had it. It is the same with love" (Prop. 22).

2° "There are three kinds of silences; the first is of words, the second of desires, and the third of thoughts. The first is perfect, the second more perfect; and the third most perfect... By not speaking, *not desiring, and not thinking* [of anything whatsoever], the true and perfect mystical silence is reached" (*Guide Spirituel,* Book I, ch. xvii, No. 128, 129. English: *Spiritual Guide,* trans. by K. Lyttelton, Book I, ch. xvii, p. 116, 128). Thus we may take as a maxim: Do not think! We should have to suppress the use of our faculties, and not only their possible abuse.

3° "Lastly, *consider nothing,* desire nothing, will nothing, *endeavour after nothing;* and then in everything, thy soul will live reposed with quiet and enjoyment" (*ibid.,* ch. xx, No. 202. *Spiritual Guide,* p. 198).

"We arrest the celestial graces by any desire for action" (*ibid.)}*

4° "This annihilation, if it is to be perfect in the soul, must exist in a man's own judgment, in his will, in his works, inclinations, desires, *thoughts,* and in the very soul herself" (*ibid.,* Book II, ch. xix, No. 193. *Spiritual Guide,* pp. 194-5). "This is a great deal," Bossuet remarks, "and we do not know what would be left to a Christian" (*États d'Oraison,* Book III, No. 2).

5° "One reflection upon her actions on the soul's part, hinders her from receiving the true light and making one step towards perfection" (*Guide,* Book I, ch. v, No. 45).*

**36.**—The Italian quietists (from the *Circular* of the Holy Office, in 1687):

"Contemplation, or the prayer of quiet, consists in placing ourselves in God's presence by an obscure, pure, and loving act of faith; and then *remaining idle,* without going any further, without dwelling upon any reasoning, any image, *any thought.* For it is contrary to the respect due to God to repeat the first act, and further, this act is of such great merit and worth that it includes, eminently and in a more perfect degree the acts of *all the virtues.* This act endures *for the whole of life,* provided that it is not retracted by a contrary act" (Prop. 1). (Quoted by Bossuet in Vol. XVIII of the Lachat ed., p. 677.)

**37.**—Mme. Guyon:

1° "This divine life becomes quite natural to it [the soul]. As it *no longer feels itself,* sees itself, or knows itself, so it no longer sees or *understands* or distinguishes anything of God as distinct or outside of itself. It is no longer conscious† of *love,* or light, or knowledge; it only knows that God is, and that it no longer lives except in God" (*Les Torrents,* Part I, ch. ix, No. 6. English, *Short Method of Prayer and Spiritual Torrents,* ch. ix, p. 197).

2° "When the soul has arrived at the supreme union, *all reflection* is banished, and the soul would find a difficulty in indulging in it, even if it desired to do so. But as by an effort it might accomplish it, this habit should be scrupulously avoided" (*Les Torrents,* Part II, ch. iv. No. 3. English, pp. 239-40).

3° "To be willing to be nothing *in the sight of God,* to live in an entire abandonment, *in utter self-despair,* to give themselves to Him when they are the most discouraged, *to leave themselves* in His hands, and not to look at self *when they are on the very edge of the abyss;* it is this that is so rare, and it is this which constitutes perfect abandonment" (*Les Torrents,* Part II, ch. i, No. 10. English, Part II, ch. i, pp. 219-20).

4° "If we tell them [those who practise complete abandonment] to go to confession, they do so, for they are very submissive; but they speak with their mouths *what they are made to say,* like a little child to whom one should say: You must confess that. He tells it *without knowing* what he says, *without knowing whether it is true or not*" (*Les Torrents,* Part II, ch. ii, No. 3). "These souls of whom I speak, can *scarcely ever* make their confession" (*ibid.*)‡

* Not in the English translation [Translator].

† In the French, "*There is no more* love or light or knowledge" (*Il n'y a plus*) [Translator].

‡ Omitted in the English translation [Translator].

### § 3. Application to Desires, Petitions and Exterior Exercises of Piety.

**38.**—Eckhart's proposition, condemned in 1329 by John XXII. "He who asks in prayer for a particular and specified thing, asks for evil and asks amiss" (Prop. 7).

**39.**—Molinos. See ch. xxiv, 55, his proposition 27, against the desire for sensible devotion; and ch. xxvii, 15, his proposition 14: "Even as the soul should make *no demand* of God, so also she should not thank Him for anything, the one and the other being an act of self-will" (Prop. 15).—He pretends that it would not be the work of grace.

**40.**—The *Pater* of abandonment (exaggerated); an ironical imitation of quietist proceedings, by La Bruyere.

"*The Penitent.*—I will own that I was inwardly engaged with the Lord's Prayer *after our manner;* I mean by adjusting it to our principles and to our doctrine.

"*The Director.*—Proceed, my daughter. The project is a praiseworthy one.

"*The Penitent.*—Listen to my composition.

"*The Director.*—I am listening.

"*The Penitent.*—God who art no more in Heaven than upon earth or in Hell, who art present everywhere—I neither will nor desire that Thy name be hallowed. Thou knowest what is expedient for us. If Thou desirest it, it will be so, without my wishing or desiring it.—Whether Thy kingdom come or no is a matter of indifference to me.— Neither do I ask that Thy will be done on earth as it is in Heaven. It will be so without my wishing it. My place is to resign myself. Give us all our daily bread, which is Thy grace, or do not give it to us; I wish neither to have it nor to be deprived of it. So too, if Thou dost forgive me my trespasses as I forgive those that trespass against me, so much the better. If, on the contrary, thou dost punish me for them with damnation, so much the better still, since it is Thy good pleasure.—Finally, oh my God, I am too wholly abandoned to Thy will to pray that Thou wilt deliver me from temptation and from sin!

"*The Director.*—I assure you, madam, that it is not at all amiss. The *paternoster thus reformed* will doubtless edify all *perfectly abandoned* souls, and I should like to send it to our new churches" (*Dialogues,* Fifth Dial.).

In practice, the quietists had a more expeditious manner of treating the *Pater.* They found that it contained too many petitions, were scandalised at it, and liked to reduce it to this single sentence: Thy will be done. They praised to the skies a Mexican solitary who lived at the end of the sixteenth century, Gregory Lopez, who confined himself always to this simplification. We may ask why he did not content himself with the word *Amen,* which would have expressed the same idea with even greater brevity? According to this, all the Church prayers should be replaced by this one word.

Regarding this question Bossuet says: "To wish to suppress all petitions on the pretext that they seem to be included in one, is the same as to say that we should not develop the branches, leaves, and fruit of a tree, under the pretext that the root or even the seed contains them virtually" *États d'Oraison,* Book III, No. 21).

**41.**—Fr. Massoulie, O. P., refuting a faulty indifference:

"The Fathers and Masters of the spiritual life... have taught that a soul, desiring to labour sincerely after sanctification should attain to a complete indifference with regard to all those things *that are apart from God,* considering His glory and His will alone But this indifference should be solely regarding things that are indifferent by their nature, those *that do not lead the soul to God and that are not God Himself.* God alone is sufficient for a soul, all the rest should be a matter of indifference..."

"But these followers of the new spirituality [the quietists] wish this indifference to be *general and even regarding those things that concern eternal salvation.* Indifference with regard to consolations and *aridities;* indifference with regard to the *acquisition of the virtues,* or their loss, and, which is a strange thing, indifference as to being deprived of God; that is to say indifference regarding our eternal salvation or eternal damnation, because, they say, we should in all things consider only God's glory and the accomplishment of His will, which is to be found equally in the salvation and the loss of souls. Who could believe that anyone could ever have arrived at this excess of blindness?" (*Traité de la veritable oraison,* Part I, ch. xviii).

Now "It is an error to contend that, because we should seek God's glory alone, we must become indifferent as to our eternal happiness, which consists in beholding God and all His perfections. This is how we are obliged to reason: We must seek God's glory only. Now this glory *can only be found in the knowledge of His perfections and in the praises that accompany this knowledge.* The desire, then, that we ought to feel, of rendering to God all the glory of which we are capable, necessarily obliges us to desire *to see Him and possess Him,* and in seeing Him to love Him, and in loving Him to praise Him" (*ibid.,* Part I, ch. xix).

**42.**—Bossuet: Upon certain equivocal phrases where the possession of God and the possession of His gifts are represented as two incompatible things, between which perfection obliges us to choose.*

* Mme. Guyon did not fail to deduce an argument in favour of her exaggerated "disappropriations": "The enjoyment of God constitutes our beatitude. I say of God Himself, and *not of His gifts,* which could never make the essential beatitude, nor be capable of giving full contentment to the soul. For the soul is so noble and so great that all the gifts of God, *even the greatest,* could not render it happy if God did not give Himself unto it" *Moyen Court,* ch. xxiv, No. 12, English, p. 146).

But the Beatific Vision is a gift; consequently there are gifts which can give "full contentment to the soul."

"These disappropriations of God's gifts are simply hair-splittings. I know that spiritual writers of the last centuries made use of these terms; but *if we do not understand them* after a sound manner we shall fall into great errors. It is an invariable truth that we *are united to God only by His gifts.* Holiness, justice, and grace are God's gifts; they *are the means by which we possess Him.* To dream of detaching ourselves from them is to dream of detaching ourselves from God Himself. I say the same with regard to faith, hope, and charity. We can be acceptable to God only by our virtues, *which are so many gifts from God.*

"These *direct* unions with God, so much extolled by many mystics, even by the soundest, are an illusion if *we understand them wrongly.* The only way of understanding them aright, and not disappropriating God's gifts to ourselves, is by avoiding, as the rock on which our piety may make shipwreck, their attribution to ourselves. But if we take them as coming from the Father of Lights, we are sufficiently disappropriated.

"We can also detach ourselves from them in another manner: which is not to seek them for the pleasure that we derive from them, but for *their property of uniting us to God Himself,* since He unites Himself to us only by His gifts. Again, there is a celestial and victorious and well-grounded delight in which grace and charity consist; and to detach ourselves from this, is to detach ourselves from charity and from grace, that is to say from God Himself. Believe me, my child, that any other doctrine is only illusion. We must always come back to the simple ideas which are those of Holy Scripture" (*Letter* XII to Mme. de Maisonfort, Lachat ed., Vol. XXVII, p. 384).

We may also say: when speaking in a general way of gifts, writers have intended to speak of *certain* gifts, those of which the utility might be doubtful. All these equivocal phases should henceforth be avoided.

**43.**—La Bruyere, putting these words into the mouth of a quietist lady (on pious exercises):

"Ah, my brother, if you knew, if you could once experience what a fervent soul is, when lifted up by *acquired contemplation* to the confused and indistinct sight of God's Essence, if you understood the pleasure that this soul feels in *renunciations of her own action,* in her plungings into the ocean of the divine will! What peace, what repose, what resplendent darkness for this soul, seeing henceforth nothing more in herself but an entire denudation *of all operation,* so that henceforth she may be subject to no action but God's! How frivolous and ill-judged does the distinction of days [by the Feasts of the saints] then appear to her!... What insipidity she would find in the recitation of the Psalms, what uselessness in sermons, both for those who preach them and those who listen! What coldness, and often what indifference with regard to a Parish Mass! What dryness for her when she meditates upon the justice of God or upon His mercies. Ah, my brother! God present everywhere!" (*Dialogue* IV).—We see here how the quietists pervert the teaching of the true mystics: they declare obligatory, and for all those who aim at perfection, exclusions that can only be accepted by certain souls and this merely at those times when they cannot act otherwise. This false coin is not to be confused with the true.

### § 4. Application to the Pursuit of Virtue and Resistance to Temptations

**44.**—A proposition by Eckhart:

"The good man should so perfectly conform his will to God's will, that he wills all that God wills, and says: Since God has in some manner willed that I should sin, *I would not have not sinned*" (Prop. 14).—This was a gross confusion between the things that *God permits* while detesting them, and those that He wills as good.

**45.**—Molinos:

"He who has given his free-will to God, should have no further concern for anything, neither Hell nor Paradise: he should have *no desire for his own perfection,* nor for the *virtues,* nor for his sanctification, nor for his salvation, the hope of which he ought to lose" (Prop. 12). "It does not become the souls that are in the interior way to make *even virtuous* acts by their choice and their own activity; or to produce acts of love towards the Blessed Virgin, the saints and Our Lord's Sacred Humanity; because these objects being of the sensible order, our love for them is of the same nature"; that is to say, equally low (Prop. 35). "When Satan uses violence to make us produce acts that are culpable in themselves, we must *let him do so* without opposing any labour or any effort... Above all, we must not confess it..." (Prop. 47).

**46.**—Mme. Guyon:

1° "Hitherto she [the soul] has been despoiled of gifts, graces, and favours [*facility for good*]: she has lost all good works, such as *outward charity,** *care for the poor, readiness to help others,* but she has not lost the divine virtues. Here, however, these too *must be lost,* so far as their practice is concerned" (*Les Torrents,* Part I, ch. vii, No. 25. English, p. 169).

2° "If it [the perfect soul] sought to humble itself, it would be astonished, as though it were guilty of unfaithfulness, and would even find it impossible, because the state of annihilation, through which it has passed, has placed it below all humiliation; for in order to be humbled, we must be *something,* and nothingness cannot be brought lower; its present state has placed it above all humility and all virtue by its transformation into God" (*Les Torrents,* Part II, ch. i, No. 4. English, p. 215).

3° Speaking of souls who practise "the short method," that is to say, systematic inaction: "There are none who practise virtue more constantly than those who acquire it in this way, though virtue is not a distinct subject of their

* In the French *les austérités* [Translator].

thought" (*Moyen Court,* ch. ix, 1. English, ch. viii, p. 25). Thus the less we think of it, the more we succeed!

4° Speaking of souls which have arrived at perfect abandonment: "Nothing can harm them, because there is no longer anything hurtful for them, by reason of their union with God, which, in associating with sinners, *contracts no defilement,* because of its essential purity. This is more real than I can express" (*Les Torrents,* Part II, ch. ii. No. 1. English, p. 232).

Thus we do not sin by encouraging others to sin. "[He] who no longer is, can no longer sin" (*Les Torrents, ibid.,* No. 3).

5° "An entire and total abandonment excepts nothing, keeps back nothing, neither death, nor life, *nor perfection, nor salvation, nor heaven, nor hell...* What do you fear, trembling heart? You fear to lose yourself? Alas! for all that you are worth, what would that matter?" (*Les Torrents,* Part II, ch. i, 9. English, Part II, ch. i, p. 218).

6° "You must *drop* [put aside] your defects, when they are pointed out to you, *without departing from your firmly established immobility,* even by a disavowal. What I say is bold; it is however your state. God *never* shows you a past fault to lead you to remedy it; but he acts in the same way as a skilful gardener who shows his child the weeds, without allowing him to pull them up; He wishes to do so himself" (*Letter* to Fénelon, Masson collection, No. 49. See also *Letters,* 92, 109).

**47.**—Propositions by some Italian quietists quoted in the *Circular* of the Holy Office, in 1687:

"Contemplatives should be so stripped of affection for all things, that they reject and despise *even God's gifts and favours,* and go as far as to lose the *love of the virtues* themselves, etc." (Prop. 18). "If during the contemplation, earthly and animal thoughts should supervene, we must be *at no pains* to drive them away, or to have recourse to any good thought, but on the contrary, take pleasure in this torment" (Prop. 15) (document quoted in Bossuet, Lachat ed., Vol. XVIII, p. 679).

### § 5. On Awaiting the Divine Motion

48.—Tauler, describing the quietists of the fourteenth century: "There are false contemplatives. Their characteristic is that the interior repose to which they abandon themselves is purely natural; it is true sloth. They imagine themselves to be exempt from sin, united directly to God, set free from all laws, both divine and human, dispensed from all good works. Their erroneous principle is that this void is so noble and perfect that they must, at all costs, prevent anything coming to disturb it. They therefore reject all that could fetter them in any way, and will not engage in any work either high or low. Just as a tool waits passive until the master makes use of it, so *they await the divine operation in a state of inaction. They believe that this operation would be impeded by any action of theirs.* They remain motionless, without practising any virtue. Would you know the sum total of their conduct? Here it is in two words: They will neither thank God nor praise Him, neither experience nor know anything, neither love nor ask nor desire. All this, they say, is hurtful or culpable. All that they could ask for, they believe that they already possess. They claim to have attained to poverty of spirit, because, so they believe, they have no self-will and have renounced all personal choice" (Second Sermon for the first Sunday in Lent). This passage is taken nearly literally from Ruysbroeck's *Ornement des noces,* Book II, ch. lxxvi.

49.—The Italian quietists (from the *Circular* already quoted):

"No act or interior affection although produced *with reflection* and by faith, can be agreeable to God, because they proceed from self-love, unless they are inspired by the Holy Spirit *before there is any application or endeavour on our part.* This is why, in contemplation or in affective prayer we should *remain idle, awaiting* the miraculous breathing of the Holy Spirit" (Prop. 16).

50.—Molinos:

"If, at communion, sentiments of humility, or petitions or thanksgivings should arise in the soul, they must be repressed every time when we do not see that they come from *God's special impulsion;* otherwise these are the impulses of a nature which is not yet dead" (Prop. 32).

51.—Mme. Guyon:

1° "St. Paul desires that we should *be led* by the Spirit of God... the soul should *suffer itself to be moved* and guided by the living Spirit who is in it, following His direction, and *no other*" (*Moyen Court,* ch. xxi, No. 1. *Short Method of Prayer,* ch. xvi, p. 52). "A statue, *if it could move,* would by its movement prevent the sculptor's perfecting it. *Every* movement of our own hinders the work of the Heavenly Sculptor, and produces false strokes.* We must then remain silent, and only move *as He moves us...* The spirit of the *divine motion* is the spirit of the Church... Now the spirit of the Church cannot be other in her members than it is in herself. To be in the spirit of the Church, her members, then, must be in the *spirit of the divine motion*" (*ibid.,* No. 5).†

"Actions committed by a divine principle are divine actions, whereas the actions of the creature, *however good they may appear,* are human actions,‡ or at best they are virtuous actions, if they are done with the help of grace... We must then give place to this life (the life of Jesus Christ), that it may flow in us, which can only be done by evacuation, and the loss of the life of Adam and of

* No. If there are movements that hinder the divine action, there are others that favour it.

† Omitted in the English translation [Translator].

‡ This passage is nonsense. Divine actions are, at the same time, human, and "good" and "virtuous" actions are divine. What she wishes is that we should perform actions that are purely divine, which is impossible.

our own action" (*ibid.*, No. 6. *Short Method,* ch. xxvi, p. 56. See also 7, 9, and 10).

2° This soul "would have *nothing to ask* [of God], *nothing to desire, unless He Himself should give the impulse;* not that she despises or rejects... the divine consolations...; but these kinds of graces are no longer seasonable for a soul *as annihilated* as she is, and so established in the happiness of the soul's centre (*jouissance de centre*), and [who] having lost all will in God's will *"can no longer will anything"* (*Sur le Cantique,* ch. viii, v, 14).

3° Praise of automatic action: "You may ask one in this condition (of self-abandonment), 'Who leads you to do such and such a thing? is it God who has told you to do it, or has made known to you His will concerning it?' He will reply, *'I know nothing,* and I do not think of knowing anything.'... 'But why should you do this rather than that?' —'*I do not know;* I let myself be guided by Him who draws me... Neither am I capable of *giving any reason for my conduct...* yet I act infallibly so long as I have no other principle than that of the Infallible One' " (*Les Torrents,* Part II, ch. ii, No. 7. English, p. 225).

52.—Bossuet:

1° "The new mystics often tell you that they offer petitions,... that they have special devotions to Our Lord's mysteries, such as His Cross or His Infancy; but this is to say nothing, because they mean that they make such acts, being impelled thereto by an *extraordinary inspiration peculiar to certain states,* and also that, to produce them, *they always await this inspiration...* Instead of saying, as they do: If the Holy Spirit acts in us, we have but to *let Him act;* we should, on the contrary, say: If He acts in us, if He prompts us to make holy groanings, we must *act with Him, groan with Him, with Him* stimulate ourselves and make *pious efforts* to bring forth the spirit of salvation" (*États d'Oraison,* Book III, Nos. 11, 12).

2° It is wrong to believe ourselves to be "given over to grace when we are in a state of *pure expectation,* without wishing to act of ourselves, or to *stimulate* ourselves to act.

"To remain in the expectation of an *extraordinary disposition* is to tempt God... By these waitings we wish to have a proof that God moves us by some extraordinary thing, as if we belonged to a special class, and the commandment given to all the faithful was not sufficient for us. To seek this singularity and to wish to have *special impulsions,* without which we will do nothing, is to reinstate our pride on its throne" (*Letters* to Mme. de Maisonfort, 17 and 24; Lachat ed., Vol. XXVII, pp. 327, 346. See also *États d'Oraison,* Book III, No. 9, p. 433).

3° "One of the reasons that people give is that we should not *prevent* God, since it is God who prevents us; but only *follow* Him and second Him, otherwise We should be acting on our own initiative. But this is to condemn souls to inaction, to idleness, to a mortal lethargy. It is true that God prevents us by His inspiration; but as we do not know when this divine breathing may come, *we must act without hesitation, as though of ourselves,* when the precept or the occasion determines us to do so, in the firm belief that grace is not lacking... We should always *Strive, always urge ourselves on, always incite ourselves to action;...* and with all this believe that when we strive and when we urge ourselves on, grace has prevented our efforts" (*États d'Oraison,* Tr. I, Book X, No. 24).

4° "Every Christian who acts rightly... is incited and incites himself; he is urged and he urges himself, he is moved by God and he moves of himself... In order to act we are not allowed to wait until God acts in us and impels us [until we feel Him do this, that is to say]; but we must act as much, *incite ourselves as much,* move ourselves as much, as if we had to act alone, with a firm faith, however, that it is God who begins, achieves, and continues in us all our good works" (*Letter* I, to Mme. de Maisonport, 53; Lachat ed., Vol. XXVII, p. 346).

# CHAPTER XXVIII

## Rarity Or Frequency of the Mystic States

### § 1. Various Cases to Be Examined

**1.**—This problem is often discussed: Are the mystic states rare or frequent? There applies as a rule are either vague or contradictory, which is due to the fact that people do not begin by defining clearly what they mean by *being frequent*. Here are **two significations** which I will now examine. What we wish to know is: 1° If there are confessors still living who have encountered several persons having attained to the mystic state; 2° if these persons are to be found in most large towns or religious congregations, or in many convents?

**2.**—Let us speak first of the **confessors**. Many of these testify that in the course of their ministry they have met with souls favoured with extraordinary gifts; this is what they mean to say when assuring us that these gifts are not rare.

Others dispute this conclusion. "For (they say) I have preached many retreats; I have heard a great many confessions in convents, and I have found nothing of the sort; therefore nothing of the sort existed." We may reply that cases were perhaps not lacking, but that various circumstances prevented their being made known to the speaker. As a rule, these favoured souls find it useless to consult a passing confessor. Some, already sure of their path, do not wish to reopen the question; others suffer from a want of light, but they have been perturbed by so many examinations that they are afraid to begin again, or at any rate not without proof that they will be understood and kindly received.

But then how do these confessors manage to succeed in loosening their tongues? To begin with, something has to be left to chance, or, rather, to the secret and merciful leadings of Providence. Then they may have heard this particular director favourably spoken of with regard to the subject of interior prayer. It may also happen that someone whom he has helped before puts him in touch with others. Finally the men who have studied mysticism read such souls at times from very slight indications. Some vague words are spoken which might be taken as pointing, at any rate, to the prayer of simplicity. They take notice of them and ask for a fuller explanation. The penitent, seeing that he is understood, and interest taken in him, gathers courage to add the details that he was not thinking of giving, or even had made up his mind not to mention. Little by little a complete understanding is established.

**3.**—Let us pass on to the second *point of view:* Are these favoured persons to be met with in **such or such particular surroundings?**

To begin with, I think that they are to be found in the majority of large towns amongst those who have given themselves up seriously to piety, and who aim at perfection; even when they are persons living in the world.*

These states are more frequent in religious communities and especially in the enclosed Orders. It is clear that a life of recollection would be favourable to the graces of interior prayer.

**4.**—According to St. Teresa, they are much more frequently met with amongst **women** then amongst men. St. Peter of Alcantara, she tells us, "gave excellent reasons for his opinion, all in favour of women" (*Life,* ch. xl, 12).† These reasons are perhaps that men are less loving, less humble, and that they despise these kinds of graces.

However, we often exaggerate the rarity of these favours amongst men. They hide them with much greater ease, either because they have less need of direction, or because those about them have fewer opportunities of observing them.

Fr. Tanner, in his *Preface* to the *Works* of the Ven. Marina de Escobar (Latin ed.), goes further still. He maintains that men receive as many extraordinary graces as women, but that these graces are less talked about because they are of the more intellectual kind that does not lend itself to descriptions.

There is an intermediary option between these two. It consists in saying that women receive the lower degrees of the mystic union more frequently; but that more men attain to ecstasy. Dr. Imbert gives two proofs of this. "I have taken the trouble (he says) to count in Arturus' *Franciscan Mythology,* in Hueber's *Menology,* and Mazzara's *Leggendario Francescano,* all of the ecstatics of the Order there mentioned; they number 500, of which 400 are men and 100 women" (Vol. II, ch. xxv, p. 435). He adds this other argument. "It is sufficient to read the alphabetical list of saints at the end of the Roman Martyrology to

* Scaramelli, who lived in the first half of the eighteenth century, begins his book by apologising for writing about mysticism, he who had been occupied in giving missions for the last thirty years. "Mysticism," he says, "does not seem a suitable subject of study for one who spends the greater part of the year amongst crowds, and in the turmoil of popular gatherings, wholly occupied in drawing sinful souls out of the mire of vice. And yet the wish to aid contemplative souls has come to me even in the thick of these missions. There are two things that I have understood, and put my finger on, as it were, in the exercise of my ministry. The first is that *in nearly every place* some soul is encountered whom God is leading by these extraordinary paths to a high state of perfection. The second is that there is a great dearth of experienced confessors who thoroughly understand God's dealing with these souls. And, as a rule, these directors are with good reason afraid of taking charge of them, or else they undertake it rashly" (Tr. 1, Nos. 1, 2).

† Scaramelli only accepts these favourable reasons with certain small restrictions (Tr. 4, No. 262).

prove that the masculine sex predominates; there are at least six times as many men as women." It may perhaps be admitted that the relative proportion of ecstatics scarcely differs from that of the saints.

**5.**—These, I think, are the **general replies** that may be given. To say more, actual statistics would be required; these are wholly lacking.

**6.**—We have, further, some information concerning **certain groups of persons at specified periods.** It is in this way that St. Teresa says that the mystic state is frequent. She is speaking particularly of her spiritual daughters.*

In the history of the Dominicans of Unterlinden, at Colmar, we find, in the space of a hundred years, 44 religious favoured with the highest gifts. The writers add that there were many others of whom the chroniclers have omitted to speak (De Bussières, *Les Mystiques d'Unterlinden*).

The next section will treat a special group: the canonised saints.

**6** *bis.*—In what I have just said, I have concerned only with the mystic state, properly so-called. With regard to the night of the senses, St. John thinks that it "is common, and the lot of many." He adds: "Recollected persons entered the Obscure Night sooner than others, after they had begun their spiritual course;... In general, there lapses no great length of time... before they enter into the night of sense" (*Obscure Night,* Book I ch. i, pp. 346, 347). See also *Living Flame,* Stanza III, line 3, § 5, pp. 267-8.

The frequency is still greater with the prayer of affection or of simplicity. "In general, says Fr. Balthasar Alvarez [the way of praying by affection, and *discoursing little*] is that of the majority. The highest point of perfection in this way of prayer [the mystic state, that is to say] is that of the minority, seeing that the perfect are always few" (*Vie*, ch. xli, seventh difficulty).

* Four or five years after her first Foundation, she writes: "*For many* are the souls who attain to the state, and few are they who go farther; and I know not who is at fault; most certainly it is not God; for when His Majesty shows mercy unto a soul, so that it advances so far, I believe that He will not fail to be more merciful still, if there be no shortcomings on our part... It is a great sorrow to me; because, as I said before, *I know* that *many* souls come thus far, and that those who go farther, as they ought to go, are so few, that I am ashamed to say it. I do not mean that they are absolutely few; there must be many, because God is patient with us... I speak of *what I have* seen" (*Life,* ch. xv, 3, 7).

About seven years afterwards the saint utters some more still consoling words: "The graces wrought by Our Lord in these houses are so great that if there be in them *one* sister whom Our Lord is leading by the way of meditation, *all the rest* are advancing by the way of perfect contemplation [full union]; some have gone so far as to have had raptures" (*Foundations,* ch. iv, p. 28).

Four years later the saint confirms what she has already said: "Send me, O my Lord, light from heaven to enable me to speak on the subject to these Thy servants, some of whom Thou art pleased should often enjoy these delights [full union]... I said 'some,' but in reality there are *very few* of them would never enter these mansions; some more and some less, but *most of them* may be said at least to *gain admittance* into these rooms" (*Interior Castle,* Fifth Mansion, ch. i, 1, 2).

It would be interesting to know what was the total number of Carmelites at that time. Perhaps a hundred or a hundred and fifty.

### § 2. Did All the Saints Possess the Mystic State?

**7.**—The question that I put here is a **purely historical** one. I do not ask if the mystic state is indispensable in order to arrive at a high state of perfection. The reply would be the negative. The mystic graces are one means only, and God may employ others. It is a question simply of knowing whether, as a fact, He has ordinarily made use of this means.

**8.**—Let us begin by making a **distinction**. The word *sanctity* is often taken in a wide sense. It refers to a very high state of virtue, insufficient, however, for any idea of canonisation. In its strict sense, that of the Church's official acts, it is a question of the resplendent virtue, that of canonised saints. It is the highest degree.

**9.**—If it is a question of sanctity understood in the **widest sense**, the answer to the question is evident, without any research into historic documents. We have all known some of these chosen souls were the admiration of those about them, but without any expectation of ever seeing them raised to the Church's altars. But they did not seem to possess the mystic states.* God had not furnished them with these aids, but He granted them other gifts of the ordinary supernatural order in a high degree.

I will go further still. It may be that a person of this kind is far higher, in point of virtue, then another who has received the prayer of quiet. This may be partly due to the fact that this latter is but poorly endowed either mentally, or with regard to character, direction, etc.

Let us not, however, conclude that the second will not have profited greatly by being raised to the mystic union. For without this gift he would have remained at a far lower level.

**10.**—Let us speak now of **great sanctity**, that which leads openly to canonisation. is it to be met without the mystic graces?

It will, of course, be understood that we must study it solely in the cases of those who were not martyrs and whose interior lives are known in some detail. For with regard to the martyrs, their death sufficed for the canonisation without any heroic virtues having been previously exhibited. As to saints who do not fulfil the second condition, the question remains doubtful.

**11.**—This historic examination will lead us to the following conclusion: *nearly all the canonised saints* have had the mystic union; and this usually abundantly.

* St. John of the Cross: "God does not elevate to perfect contemplation everyone that is tried in the spiritual way, and He alone knoweth why" (*Obscure Night,* Book I, ch. ix, p. 535). It follows from this that if we do not attain to the mystic union, or do not get beyond one of the lower degrees, it cannot be said with certainty whether the fault lies with us or with our director. It may be that the vocation was a different one (see 26 *bis.*).

Benedict XIV lays down a similar principle. "And we read that almost all the saints, especially the founders of Orders, were endowed with visions and revelations... Without doubt, then, God speaks familiarly with His friends, and especially favours those whom He chooses for great things" (*De Canon.*, Book III, ch. lii, No. 3. Eng.: *Heroic Virtue*, Vol. III, p. 351). Fr. de Maumigny space also admits our thesis (Vol. II, Book V, ch. i).

St. Francis of Sales is not really of the contrary opinion when he says: "There are many saints in heaven who were never in ecstasy or rapture of contemplation. For how many *martyrs* and great saints do we see *in history* never to have had other privilege in prayer than that of devotion and fervour" (*Treatise on the Love of God*, Book VII, ch. viii, p. 302).

We see that the holy Doctor is speaking in the first place of those who *are in Heaven*, without defining their degree of sanctity. Now, to reach Heaven, it is sufficient to die in the state of grace; while we are only speaking here of canonised saints, those of heroic virtue, that is to say. And then, amongst those who are canonised, he is including the martyrs. Their number being several millions, they should not be included in the same pronouncement as the contemplative saints. They belong to categories that differ too widely.

**12.**—Before examining this thesis, it will be well to settle a preliminary **difficulty**. This doctrine, it will be said, tends to discourage people. If almost all the saints (other than the martyrs) have received extraordinary graces, they will always be persuaded that an almost necessary relationship exists between these graces and sanctity. And they will say to themselves: Not having the one, I am morally certain of not attaining to the other.

**13.—Reply.**—No. The evidence of history does not prove extraordinary graces to be necessary to sanctity, but simply that God, in His generosity, is pleased to bestow upon the canonised saints a measure of grace far in excess of what is necessary for them. Has He done as much for other saints whom He has chosen to leave unknown? And will He continue to do this habitually in the future for those whom He wills to enlighten? We do not know.

But admitting for a minute that the supreme goal of sanctity can scarcely be attained without the aid of the mystic graces, no discouraging conclusions could be drawn from this fact.

If you were but a few steps from this goal, I could partly understand your sadness. They would be so little of the road left to traverse, and God would be refusing you the indispensable assistance! But you are perhaps a long way off. You have all the graces necessary for accomplishing the greater part of the distance. Show that you are ready to begin to help yourself, and believe that God will do the rest. It lies with us to begin. In the life of several saints, we see, it is true, that God prevented them. From their childhood, even before the age of reason, they were loaded with exceptional graces; St. John the Baptist, sanctified in his mother's womb, for instance. God can show generosity to whom He will, and He wills to remind us of this from time to time. But many saints have not been prevented by grace in this way. Instead of being born rich in spiritual things, they have been children of their own endeavour, so to speak. These have often been converts, like St. Mary Magdalene, St. Augustine, St. Francis of Assisi, St. Ignatius, St. Francis Xavier, etc. They began by performing heroic acts, and when God saw that they had advanced very far, He showed Himself generous towards them. Your conditions are no more unfavourable; you have no cause, therefore, to despair.

**14.**—The historic thesis cannot, then, cause any disquiet to souls. On the other hand, it has the advantage of being in conflict with the **naturalistic tendency** of the age. In the saints' lives that are written these days, people are very busily engaged in showing *the man's part,* the *role* of his natural qualities, of his mental capacity and of his surroundings. They are right here if they are not too exclusively satisfied with these points of view. But *God's part* must be shown also. The old writers often exaggerated in this respect. Extraordinary facts succeeded one another without interruption. The saint found himself endowed with the treasure, he had but to stretch out his hand to draw from it; and saving for certain violent temptations in which he came out victor by sheer force, he for the most part had merely to consent to the Divine advances. Do not let us fall into the opposite excess, but let us frankly recognise what God, *without any necessity,* has done for His friends.

**15.**—Now for the **proof of our thesis.** It stares us in the face when we glance through a collection of lives of the saints. If some seem to be lacking in the extraordinary graces, we see that it is because we have no records regarding them. So that there are no positive proofs to bring against the above conclusion.

This greater or lesser absence of documents is easily explained where priests are in question. By the help of their sacerdotal knowledge they find no difficulty in dispensing more or less with direction. If they have not arrived at ecstasy, which would have attracted attention, a number of facts of their inner lives remain necessarily unknown. Women have a greater difficulty in continuing unknown. They need to consult their directors. They have often even left detailed autobiographies, written against their will, by the director's orders.

**16.**—*Examples* of saints that have sometimes been thought less favoured. Let us begin with **St. Vincent of Paul.** Scarcely any extraordinary occurrences are related with regard to him. It is only known that he remained motionless for several hours together, his eyes fixed on the crucifix; which seems to indicate a prayer that was out of the ordinary. They also cite his two visions of St. Jane Frances de Chantal, one during her last illness, the other at the time of her death. This does not amount to much, I admit; but his first biographer, Abelly, recognises the fact that he allowed no one to penetrate into his soul.*

* "No one has ever been able to find out," he says, "what kind of prayer M. Vincent's was; nor if it was ordinary or extraordinary, his humility always having caused him to hide the gifts that he received from God" (*Vie*, Book III, ch. vii).

**17.**—In the same way very little is known of **St. Jean Baptise de la Salle's** prayer. Canon Blain, however, one of his first biographers, tells us that the saint, as a young priest, often fell into raptures while saying Mass. And, further, he never then suffered from distractions (Book I, ch. iv, §§ 4, 5). Although he was a man of action he passed a great part of his days and nights in prayer (Book II, ch. i, § 4). These last details are sufficient to make us hold that he passed out of the ordinary way.

**18.**—We can also cite the Blessed Curé d'Ars. He was several times questioned adroitly with the view of ascertaining the nature of his prayer; he always eluded his inquirers. But they had indirect proof of his being in the mystic state by seeing him at prayer, or hearing his prophetic words or the loving exclamations that he was unable to repress, such as: "One never wearies (in prayer); *the hours glide past like minutes;* in fact, *it is a foretaste of Heaven*"; or this: "*There are some priests* who see Our Lord every day in the Mass"; or again: "after communion, the soul revels in the balm of love like a bee amongst the flowers... After Holy Communion *we are conscious of something extraordinary,* a sensation of well-being that pervades the whole body... *It is Our Lord who communicates Himself to us.*"

**19.**—I have sometimes heard certain other saints quoted as having had no extraordinary states: Blessed Peter Faber, Blessed Peter Canisius, St. John Berchmans (all three of the Society of Jesus), and St. Francis of Sales.* Even were this true, the very moderate thesis that I have laid down would not be invalidated. For I have said that *nearly* all the saints have received these graces. I have admitted, therefore, the possibility of certain exceptions. But it happens that the four servants of God, just referred to, actually confirmed the general law.

**20.**—We have little information concerning the inner life of Blessed **Peter Faber**, although he wrote a *Memorial,* to which, during his thirty-sixth year, he consigned his reflections, resolutions, and petitions. This ignorance, says his biographer, Fr. Orlandini, is due "to the extreme modesty of his holy man, who has set down very little, and also to the multitudinous occupations which prevented his contemporaries from recording them... But it is a tradition, however,... that he had the gift of miraculous healing of the sick" (*Vie,* Book II, ch. xvi). In his *Memorial* he admits that he often heard supernatural utterances. He quotes a certain number of these locutions; one group constitutes a revelation occupying several pages.

**21.**—**St. Peter Canisius** has often shown that he was not in the ordinary way. One of his biographers tells us that in spite of all his occupations "he usually

* Bossuet says so of the last named (*États d'Oraison,* Book IX, No. 11). He wrongly concluded this from two letters of the saint (March 11, 1610; Feb. 26th, 1615), in which are found only vague expressions on his manner of prayer, such as saying that he likes the broad paths. But the souls most favoured with mystic graces would say as much.

devoted the first four hours of the day to meditation" and other pious exercises. "Numerous witnesses testify... to having on many occasions seen his face radiating such bright flames that the eyes were dazzled by them" (*Vie*, by Fr. Michel, Book VI, ch. ii). One evening in a church at Fribourg, he was perceived "in a rapture... a ball of fire above his head." After his Mass "he was seen going about the house as though in an ecstasy, his eyes bathed with tears, roaming hither and thither, without any object, and as it were beside himself. The supernatural impression lasted for several hours, and when he came out of it, he walked at such a pace that his companion, unable to follow him, was forced to shake him in order to bring him back to a normal state of consciousness" (*ibid.*). He himself tells us in his *Confessions* that on the eve of the day when he had made his solemn profession in the hands of St. Ignatius, he had a double apparition, one of the Saviour "showing him His most Sacred Heart, and inviting him to drink from the sacred source," the other of a second guardian-angel who was henceforth given to him "in order to aid and instruct him" (*ibid.,* Book I, ch. v). Another biographer tells us that "God had made known to him, more than once, the glory that certain holy souls enjoyed in Heaven and the pains that certain others suffered in purgatory" (*Vie,* by Fr. Dorigny, Book VI).

**22.**—Let us come to **St. John Berchmans**. In the Society of Jesus he has become the patron of fidelity to the ordinary life. But it would be an error to conclude from this that his prayer was ordinary also. The question was inquired into during the process of beatification, and the cardinal postulator concluded by saying that this young saint was an ecstatic. "Was it not," he says, "ecstasy, which, after transfiguring him during his prayer, rendered him insensible to cold and the stings of insects? Was it not ecstasy from which his brethren were forced to recall him by shaking him and calling him in a loud voice?" (quoted by Fr. Cros, *Vie,* Book II, ch. xviii). With the exception, perhaps, of certain periods of dryness, he "had no distractions" in prayer. Finally, the groans that he uttered were so loud at times that they awoke the occupants of the neighbouring rooms. If the saint had been the master of his actions he would have suppressed these cries through humility and the care that he always took to avoid all singularity (see *ibid.*, ch. ii).

Thus in the fourteen saints or Beati of the Society of Jesus who are not martyrs, we do not find a single exception to the thesis.

**23.**—As for **St. Francis of Sales,** our information as to his interior life is but scanty, because he refused to reply to the questions put to him. St. Jane Frances de Chantal interrogated him more than once; she relates in her depositions that the saint was satisfied with saying: "These things are *so simple and so delicate* that we cannot speak of them afterwards" (*Deposition,* art. xxxiii). She says again that: "What God wrought in him was by *lights* and *sentiments* which God shed in the *supreme* part of the soul; while *the inferior part did not participate* in it" (*ibid.*).

These characters do not belong to ordinary prayer; but we further note that the saint had the gift of prophecy, of the knowing of consciences and the gift of miracles (*ibid.*, art. xl). Finally, he had two ecstasies in the presence of witnesses: the first, that lasted for half an hour, took place during his episcopal consecration (1602). He then saw the three Divine Persons performing this consecration. This vision continued without an ecstasy during the remainder of the ceremony; he continued absorbed in this impression for six weeks. He had already had a vision of St. Anthony of Padua (*Vie*, by Perennes, Migne ed., Book V, ch. xi), and had brought a dead man to life (1698, *ibid.*, Book III, ch. xv).

In the second ecstasy (1604), God showed him the Order that he was to found, and who should be his coadjutor. He did not then know Mme. de Chantal (*ibid.*, Book VI, ch. i).

### § 3. Dispositions Favourable, or the Reverse, to the Mystic Union

**24.**—As I have said elsewhere (ch. xii, **11**), the practise of virtue is the best of dispositions for the mystic union.

Another excellent disposition is a life of **recollection** (ch. xii, **9**). The saints have nearly all practised *long* prayers; that is the way to an *exalted* form of prayer.

I do not say that our exercises must be long *in reality*. For obedience may lay employments upon us that necessarily restrict our prayer, if not to nothing, at any rate to what is strictly necessary. God owes it to Himself not to punish us for having obeyed Him. *

I merely said that we must *like* remaining for a long time with God. If the sentiment is sincere, we shall know how to find hours of leisure, we shall, above all, avoid throwing ourselves *of our own accord* into a whirlpool of occupations which obedience has not ordered and which it at times merely tolerates. We claim that we desire to do good to others; but would it not first be better to sanctify ourselves more by recollection? In reality we are following our natural tastes, and are very glad to have a pretext for flying from the trials of the life of prayer and the high virtues to which it leads us.

We must not fall, however, into the opposite illusion and sacrifice our duties to the love of solitude (see ch. xii, 9).

**24** *bis.*—**Objection**. It would seem that the mystic writers are more exacting. They appear to say that in order to arrive at supernatural contemplation or to

* St. Teresa: "... You may think you are injuring yourselves by leaving your prayer to perform any necessary duties; this is not the case. Our Lord will direct such things to our profit" (*Interior Castle*, second Mansion, ch. i, 18). But she says elsewhere: "It is most important to withdraw from all unnecessary cares and business... This is so essential, that unless done at first, I think it impossible for anyone ever to reach the principal room" (*ibid.*, First Mansion, ch. ii, 16).

maintain ourselves in it, we must renounce everything else, become as little children, who are incapable of anything. In a word, we must become hermits. St. John of the Cross seems to be of this opinion (*Ascent of Mount Carmel,* Book I, ch. xiii, p. 50) when he says: "That thou mayest know everything, seek to know nothing." What increases the difficulty is that the mystic is not only impelled by these reasons; but he feels an attraction which he regards as divine, and which leads him to forsake all for solitude in prayer. Hence a continual interior conflict.

**24** *ter.*—**Reply**. We must not take literally all that certain writers say of detachment. They are trying to impress us with an excellent tendency, but they do not contend that there is nothing that should counterbalance it. This, I think, is the wise principle: the mystic should have the *tendency* to leave all in order to occupy himself with God, but God, Who inspires it, wills that he should satisfy this tendency only when certain restrictions (that will be suggested by reason and necessity) have been taken into consideration.—In this case it is no longer nature that makes the man enter into the active life, but a supernatural motive. He then leaves all for God.

Let him therefore devote himself as zealously as others to those studies that are necessary for him, instead of counting foolishly on God's supplying all that is lacking (experience proving the contrary). On the other hand, he will do well, so it seems, to deprive himself of frivolities, for example all those items having no intellectual bearing, that fill the newspapers.

**25.**—The **obstacles** to the mystic union are negligence of the spiritual life, dissipation, contempt for or indifference with regard to these graces. Ignorances, prejudices, and bad direction are an indirect hindrance, because persons are thus led to repel these favours, or to turn away from the line of conduct necessary for their preservation (ch. xxvi, **6**).

Writers have insisted upon these causes, which are of the supernatural order, or are connected with it, as implying the action of the human will.

But it would be reasonable to ask if there are no obstacles of the purely natural order, independent of our own will; our type of mind, for instance. I have no answer to give to this question, interesting as it is; it has not, I think, been dealt with by any body.

**26.**—I have proved the following fact on several occasions: When persons have scarcely passed beyond the prayer of quiet, numerous occupations, and especially the **supervision of others,** produce a marked diminution in the mystic union. It would seem, then, that in this degree God requires, at any rate on certain days or hours, a calm and recollected life.

It may be that these souls acquire at these times as much merit as if they succeeded in their prayer, but of another kind. The Menologies of the Religious Orders prove that those who have attained to a very high degree of contemplation often enjoy certain privileges; for example, after having employed the day in the most fatiguing labours, they can pass almost the entire night in prayer. What a desirable grace is this!

**26** bis.—From what has already been said (§ 1), we see that if we consider the whole number of souls that seek, in a certain measure, at any rate, after perfection, those that attain to the mystic state are not rare, but neither are they very numerous. We should like to know the cause of this last circumstance.

Writers have given no very definite reply. This is understandable: it is a very difficult question, affecting God's plan of distributing graces. On this point He has not chosen to reveal to us all His secrets.

The Ven. Marina de Escobar thought that usually, although not always, it is, at any rate partly, the fault of the souls themselves if they do not receive some of these graces (see ch. xii, **22**).

St. Teresa, when dealing with this question, seems at first sight to contradict herself slightly. At one time she plainly states that everyone is called to these favours (see Extracts, ch. xxv, **19**, 2° and 3°; ch. iii, **12**). At another time she modifies her statement.*

These slight variations can be explained in two ways: 1° even when she was speaking positively, the saint perhaps admitted that in the case of those capable of aiming at perfection there were exceptions, but so rarely that it was not necessary to refer to them; 2° St. Teresa is very dependable and fully worthy of credence when she describes states of soul or gives rules of conduct. But we have just said that it is a question here of a different and much more difficult order. The saint does not say that she had received special revelations on this point. She was reduced, as we all are reduced, to relying upon reasons of probability. And then she inclines to one side or another, according as she wishes to arouse those who are not sufficiently hopeful or to calm those who are too sanguine.

**26** *ter*—The question may be restricted in the following manner. Suppose that all the obstacles opposed to the mystic union have been avoided, and that we have made use of every known means of obtaining it (striving after perfection, a life of recollection in prayer, the desire for these graces, recourse to an experienced director, etc.). Are we certain to obtain these favours—or to regain them, if they have disappeared, or to progress in them if we already possessed them?

Alas, experience seems to prove that this is not the case. God gives no undertaking on the subject, and He shows us that this is so. But at any rate our prayers will not useless: they will be granted under one form or another. What we actually aimed at were the graces of sanctification. God will grant them either directly or by other ways.

In other words, not everyone is called to the mystic union. God does not enable all souls to acquire merit by making use of the same means.

* "Do not imagine that it matters little whether you try to obtain these graces; if you are not to blame, the Lord is just; what He refuses in one way, His Majesty will give you in another, as He knows how" (*Interior Castle*, Third Mansion, ch. ii, 17. See also Fifth Mansion, ch. iii).

"So that, because all of this House give themselves to prayer, it follows not that all must be contemplative; that is impossible... Do what lies in you and dispose yourselves for contemplation with that perfection before mentioned, in case He bestow it not on you (though I suppose He will not fail of giving you it if there be true mortification, and humility) He reserves this regalo for you, to give it you all together in Heaven" (*Way of Perfection*, ch. xvii, pp. 50-52).

# CHAPTER XXIX

## Terminology, and That of St. Teresa in Particular

**1.**—Should infused contemplation be called a "**gratuitous**" **grace** [*gratia gratis data*]?

No. And I shall show that the writers who affirm the contrary are only in apparent disagreement with this reply.

Let us begin by noting that all grace may be called gratuitous, as signifying that God is not bound to grant it to us. It is the actual etymology of the word. But theologians take the expression: *gratuitous graces* in its more restricted sense. By this they mean those graces which, like the gift of tongues or of miracles, are given to us *principally* for our neighbour's spiritual good.

Certain visions and prophecies come under this category. But it is not so with infused contemplation. This is given to us first and foremost for our own good. Scaramelli disputes at great length the view of those who call it a gratuitous grace (Tr. 2, No. 147 and fol.), and of those also who give this name to all revelations and visions without any exceptions.

On the other hand, neither is this contemplation sanctifying grace, the grace that renders the soul formally pleasing to God. But *it is connected with it* as the means to the end, as is the case with actual grace, infused habits and the gifts of the Holy Ghost; in a word, all the *auxilia* (aids, auxiliary graces). The authors who describe contemplation as a gratuitous grace have merely meant to say that it is not sanctifying grace, nor is it therefore essential to sanctification.

If we would avoid all ambiguity, three kinds of graces must be distinguished instead of two; sanctifying grace, the graces that are auxiliary to it, and the gratuitous graces (see Soto, quoted by Suarez, *De gratia,* proleg. 3, ch. iv, Nos. 14, 15; and Joseph a Spiritu Sancto, Vol. II, disp. 11, No. 54).

**2.**—In order to describe the mystic states, St. Teresa employs only words that were already in use in her time: *contemplation, recollection, prayer of quiet, sleep, union, ecstasy, inebriation, espousals, marriage.* But she sometimes **restricts their sense,** as in the words prayer of quiet, for example (ch. v, **13**), and even contemplation (ch. iv, **5**).

Many authors have not been careful enough about this, and in quoting from writers, especially amongst the early writers who make use of the same words, they have not suspected that they employ them with different shades of meaning.

And further, the saint herself, as we shall see, has not always taken the words in precisely the same sense. Let us not be surprised. Innovators like herself cannot avoid certain hesitancies. It is always difficult to create a faultless language to express ideas that our predecessors have been unable to define clearly.

**3.**—Let us begin by studying the significations that the saint gives to the word **recollection**. With her it possesses two meanings, and we must know this if we would understand her writings. Certain authors do not seem to have remarked this fact. Their quotations thus confuse quite dissimilar things.

1° Let us remember, first, that the prayer of simplicity has sometimes been called the prayer of *active recollection.*

It is in this signification that St. Teresa takes the word recollection (without an adjective) in the *Way of Perfection;** it is, so it would seem, the same prayer that she describes at the end of her *Second Letter* to Fr. Rodrigo Alvarez, although she does not use the word recollection. She points out that this state comprises various ways of being which are merely shades of the same state. For example, it may come on suddenly, without any preceding causes, and thus manifest the divine action with greater clearness. Or again, it makes itself felt with much sweetness and devotion. All this occurs, in fact, in the prayer of simple regard.

**4.**—2° In the *Interior Castle* (Fourth Mansion, ch. iii, 1), on the contrary, the saint adds to the word recollection the epithet supernatural. It is the same at the beginning of the *Second Letter* to Fr. Rodrigo Alvarez. It is really a mystic state that she is describing.† It appears from the description that she gives this name to a prayer of quiet that is very weak and sudden, one that has not yet power to

* She is not thinking of a mystic state, because she says: "Whoever would attain this way of recollection (since, as I said, it is in our power) let him not be weary of inuring himself to what hath been spoken; which is by little and little, to get the mastery of himself, not losing himself for nothing, but wholly gaining himself to himself... and I know that if ye practise it for a year, yea, perhaps in half that time, with the favour of God ye shall attain it" (*Way of Perfection*, ch. xxx, p. 89).

† For she says that it in no way depends upon ourselves. "Do not fancy your mind can gain it [this recollection] by thinking of God dwelling within you... This is a good practice... It is not, however, the prayer of recollection, for by the divine assistance everyone can practise this, but what I mean is quite a different thing... I think I read somewhere that the soul is then like a tortoise or sea-urchin, which retreats into itself... but these creatures can withdraw into themselves at will, while it is not in our power to retire into ourselves unless God gives us grace to do so... On first speaking of the Fourth Mansions, I told you I had mentioned divine consolations before the prayer of recollection. The latter should have come first, as it is far inferior to consolations, of which it is the commencement" (*Interior Castle*, Fourth Mansion, ch. iii, 3, 4, 7).

hamper the understanding in its action, or in a slight degree only.* This is what is called *passive* recollection in certain treatises.

In her *Life,* the saint even goes further (ch. xv). She seems to regard the words recollection and prayer of quiet as synonymous, for she joins them together by saying: "The prayer of recollection and of quiet."

**5.**—Even when she speaks of passive recollection, the saint never presents it to us as a special degree, as a *stage* of the mystic life. Some writers have taken a contrary course. But to act thus is to endow this prayer with an importance that it neither theoretically nor practically possesses. By thus separating states which differ by insignificant shades only, mysticism is complicated.

To complete the misfortune, the definition given by certain authors is so vague that it applies to all the neighbouring states.

**6.**—Let us examine the word **union** as St. Teresa employs it in chapter xviii of her *Life.* The beginning of this chapter has given rise to divergences of interpretation. The saint, indeed, announces in the heading, which is her own composition, that she is about to speak of the "fourth state of prayer," and from her first sentence she also calls it "the fourth [supernatural] water," these expressions certainly refer to ecstasy.† Only, as she does not employ this last word in the first pages, but speaks of union, many modern writers have concluded that the saint begins by omitting to mention the subject that she had announced. They think that she has returned to the description of the degree below ecstasy, which she had been treating of before.

But we can prove that this was not the saint's meaning. What she here calls union, without any qualifying term, is simple ecstasy, that which does not grow to the strength of rapture. This word union, unfortunately serves her to describe several different things, according to the case in question. Here are the proofs of the accuracy of my interpretation of her words.

1° We should have to allow the existence of a grave fault in composition at the outset of this chapter; for it is a fault to announce one subject and then to deal at great length with another.

2° The same language being employed again in the succeeding chapters, it would follow that the saint continues for a considerable time to revert to a subject that she has already exhausted.

3° All the characters that she attributes to this *union* belong, by definition, to ecstasy; for she says: "In this fourth state there is no sense of anything, only

* The saint does not go to the point of asking that the understanding should then be excited to action, but merely that it should not be hindered.

† It must be so, since "the waters" number four only, and therefore the last must correspond with the highest degree of union. And further, the saint shows this clearly in ch. xx, 2, for she says: "Consider we now that this last water," etc., and some lines farther on she adds: "During rapture the soul does not seem to animate the body."

fruition... The senses are all occupied in this fruition in such a way that *not one of them is at liberty, so as to be able to attend to anything else, whether outward or inward*" (*Life,* ch. xviii, 2). In short, the internal criticism of the text decides the question.

4° Finally, there is an historic proof which is conclusive. It is a document of Fr. Gratian, who was a confidant of the saint. In 1608 he published a book (*Dilucidario,* etc.) in order to defend her against various accusations. He there shows that contemporaneous writers said that St. Teresa described ecstasy by the generic term of union. According to him, they lamented that confusion and misunderstandings resulted. Now Fr. Gratian is careful not to deny that the saint had made use of the language attributed to her. He merely undertakes to justify it (ch. iii; this passage is reproduced by la Fuente, with other long extracts; Vol. II of the *Escritos,* p. 505). He is persuaded, in particular, that this word will not cause any misunderstandings. It has since been proved to the contrary, and in our days also the true signification is not universally understood.

Fr. Gratian has only one good reason to give in support of his contention, namely, that St. Teresa "attached no importance to the use of this or that word," and that she had herself said that she would not restrict herself to the didactic and hampering methods that professors are obliged to employ. And before criticising the methods of a book we must ask ourselves to what kind of literature it belongs, and what liberties are allowed to this class of writing.

Let us add that the saint had a reason for avoiding the word ecstasy as much as possible. She explains this to Fr. Rodrigo Alvarez: "Raptures and trance, in my opinion, are all one, only I am in the habit of using the word trance instead of rapture, because the latter word frightens people" (*Second Letter, Life,* p. 457). The word union served her purpose equally.

**7.**—One word now regarding the expression: **prayer of union,** which refers to the state bordering upon ecstasy, which I have called the full union (ch. iii, **15**). The various French translators have been prodigal with its use in order to make their style more elegant and to avoid the words "the preceding state," which the saint so often employs.*

But above all, they have anticipated its use, permitting themselves an interpretation of which they should have warned the reader. It is a singular thing that in her *Life* the saint does not employ this expression when she describes *ex professo* the corresponding state; in the chapters xvi and xvii, that is to say. She only begins to use it much further on, in chapters xxii, xxiii, xxvii. It shows a want of fixed usage, with regard to terminology.

* Fr. Peyré, who has retouched the translation of Fr. Bouix, has counted that the expression *prayer of union* occurs five times only in the *Life,* twice in the *Interior Castle,* and not once in the *Way of Perfection.*

**8.**—A man who has made a profound study of the original text of St. Teresa's works has put the following question to me: It is generally admitted that what the saint calls the **third water** in her *Life* is the same state as that described in the *Interior Castle* as the *fifth mansion.* Is this quite accurate? May not the second state, instead of being identical with the first, be more nearly allied to ecstasy?

**9.**—**Reply**. This is a difficult problem, and it may be insoluble. But at least we may say that if there are differences between them, they affect insignificant shades only. The saint had already, in her *Life,* pointed distinctly to the character that I have used in order to define the full union, when she said: "The faculties of the soul now retain only the power of occupying themselves *wholly with God*" (*Life,* ch. xvi, 4).

Let us add that this question is of no importance either for the direction of souls or for establishing a reasonable classification in mysticism.

But it is of real utility to define and to give a name to an intermediary between those two widely divergent states, the prayer of quiet, and well-defined ecstasy. When two large towns are far apart, it is difficult to point out the road to be traversed, and to describe it, if we have no landmark between them, a village or a railway station or what not. It is of small importance whether this dividing point is a mile nearer or farther away from the centre. St. Teresa has made a wise innovation in creating this landmark. To determine whether she always kept it strictly in the same place is a problem for the learned only.

**10.**—What meaning has the saint given to the expression **spiritual sleep?**

This again is a question a clear solution of which it is not easy to give. In her *Second Letter* to Fr. Rodrigo Alvarez the saint speaks of this state as being situated between the prayer of quiet and the full union. It would then be a prayer of quiet that is strong and also silent, as the word sleep indicates. But the special characteristic is not, for all that, well defined. In her *Life* she was content to say: "the faculties are not lost, neither are they asleep" (ch. xiv, 3).

The saint speaks in the same way in the *Interior Castle* (Fourth Mansion, ch. iii, 11), when she says: "They call it [the prayer of quiet] spiritual sleep,—which is a more advanced stage of what I have described." St. Francis of Sales has adopted this interpretation (*Treatise on the Love of God,* Book VI, ch. viii).

It is sometimes objected that in her *Life* the saint, in describing the *third water,* that is to say the full union, calls it "a sleep of the powers of the soul" (ch. xvi, 1).

But this is a misunderstanding. The summary of the chapter contains this word, it is true, in Fr. Bouix's translation, but it is not in the summary composed by the saint herself. And then she does not give it the important place in the body of the chapter that he attributes to it. She uses it once only (and not twice, as her translator does), but without making it the name of the special state that she describes. It is in the same way that she says: It is an "agony," or "a glorious folly."

There is a more embarrassing passage (*Interior Castle,* Fifth Mansion, ch. 1). The saint here says twice over that the prayer of quiet is a sleep, and that it differs in this from the full union. The sole conclusion to be drawn from these conflicting statements is, as I have said, that it is not a question here of a very sharply defined state. Above all we must not make of it a degree, properly so-called; there is no need. The four degrees that I have adopted are sufficient for all descriptions.

**11.**—It has been stated elsewhere (ch. ii, **8**) that St. Francis of Sales has referred to a certain state of prayer by the name of prayer of **simple committal** to God. Relying upon St. Jane Frances de Chantal's explanations I have said that this state is nothing else than the prayer of simplicity.

Many writers have never thought of deciding this question by an historic argument. Interpreting the words in the sense that seemed most natural, they have supposed that the state thus designated consisted in *reflecting* upon resignation, upon abandonment.

The true interpretation of the saint's meaning, on the contrary, is that we reflect upon whatever subject we choose; but the prayer of simple regard being generally painful to human nature, we are indirectly led in it to *practise* resignation (ch. ii, **21**), and consequently to urge ourselves on thereto at times. St. Francis of Sales, then, has employed a word which indicates neither the subject that the mind considers nor the manner in which this consideration is performed; and this last point is a drawback; but on the other hand it reminds us clearly of what our line of conduct should be, namely submission.

Under the opposite system we are obliged to admit that meditation on abandonment,—on a special virtue, that is to say,—constitutes a special degree of prayer. But then it would be necessary to admit the same for each of the other virtues. St. Francis of Sales cannot have entertained such an absurd idea.

# CHAPTER XXX

## Scientific Methods in Descriptive Mysticism

### § 1. Progress of This Science: Its Sources

**1.**—With regard to descriptive mysticism (see first *preface,* No. 2) we can ask ourselves two questions which bear upon the methods by which we must treat it. 1° Has this science **progressed** with the ages, or has it stood still, immovable, after being permanently fixed by the first writers upon the subject? 2° Can we hope for fresh progress in the future?

*A priori,* we may reply that a constant perfecting has been going on in the past, and that it will be the same after our days. Otherwise mysticism would be an exception to the law that governs all the other sciences, secular or religious, and especially descriptive sciences. The art of seeing accurately and explaining accurately is a human work; it is capable, like all human achievements, of continual progress.

History, in fact, proves to us the existence of these successive developments.

**2.**—**General historical survey** of mysticism. All the sciences began with observations of facts which no one could fail to see. Mysticism did not issue forth fully equipped from the brain of a Jupiter any more than all the others. Two great epochs can be distinguished in its development, the one before and up to St. Teresa, the other from the saint's death to our own times.

During the first period, mystics were only concerned with three orders of facts that stared them in the face: ecstasies, visions of Our Lord or of the saints, and revelations (Examples: St. Gertrude, St. Bridget). But the states of union below ecstasy were more difficult to analyse, as is the case with all rudimentary things. So their ideas on these subjects were very vague, their descriptions were short and hazy and failed to distinguish between quite different kinds.* Thus

* To convince ourselves of this, it is sufficient to glance over the notes to Fr. Meynard's learned treatise. He gives an abundance of passages from the early writers. Many are not descriptive at all, and even treat of questions that are merely allied to his subject. For instance, when he wishes to prove that an

Blessed Angela of Foligno, whose writings contain such beautiful passages on the subject of raptures and visions, gives us nothing definite about the other states.* The same must be said about Dionysius the Areopagite, Ruysbroeck, etc. For the lower states they were sometimes content with such vague phrases as this: "You find yourself taken possession of by a certain sweetness."†

It was St. Teresa who was the first to take the trouble to study the states below ecstasy under the microscope. Her personal contribution amounts to just this, and in this respect she worked a true revolution. She rendered an immense service, for these states are the most common. And besides knowing how to describe, she knew how to classify.

At the same time, St. John of the Cross was an innovator, but in a narrower field. He analysed at great length certain spiritual destitutions, of which, although real, no one had hitherto seen the importance. The progress achieved by these two great masters will explain why later writers always come back to quoting them. In proving the omissions of the early writers, we shall feel neither astonishment nor scorn. They gave the utmost that their age was capable of, and rendered possible the progress of those who succeeded them; they deserve our gratitude.

Those who marvel at these slow advances of the human intellect, should also be surprised that St. Thomas' *Summa* and *The Imitation of Christ* were not written in the time of the Apostles.

Now that this great scientific work appears to be concluded, it all seems very easy to us. But how many obstacles have not its initiators had to overcome! For example, in order to distinguish clearly between the various mystic states, a very clear terminology would have been needed as a guide; but it was a vicious circle. For inversely, before they could coin this terminology rapidly, it was almost necessary to begin by distinguishing the states clearly one from another. It is only tentatively and slowly that the human intellect has been able to extract itself from this difficulty. Since St. Teresa's time, descriptive mysticism seems to have made but little progress. Scarcely any new facts have been discovered, and this condition has been acquiesced in rather too easily; but attention has been chiefly directed to another useful work: that of explaining and coordinating what was already known. An attempt has been made to bring more order into the explanations, to perfect the formulas by which known facts are expressed.

early author has spoken of the prayer of quiet in the same way as St. Teresa, he has to change the meaning of the word (Vol. II, No. 196). His proof is that this author, commenting on the *Canticle of Canticles,* says that the Bride, the type of the soul, has moments of repose. But then all other commentators would also be mystics, equally with St. Teresa.

* But for a description of all that ecstasy contains, Blessed Angela surpasses St. Teresa. Her book is of the highest order.

† Speaking of the prayer of quiet, St, Teresa says: "For though I read *many* spiritual *books,* wherein this very matter is discussed, they threw very little light upon it" (*Life,* ch. xiv, 10).

**2** *bis.*—The foregoing survey of mysticism furnishes the answer to an **objection** that has sometimes been made to me:* "The old writers have not referred to this or that delicate circumstance which you regard as important or even essential. There is reason, therefore, to think that you are mistaken."

This objection implies that the old writers have said everything, foreseen everything. This is an assertion without proofs. If it were thus, St. Teresa's contemporaries might have reproached her for believing that a weak woman, like herself, could add any new features to the descriptions left by eminent men.

The same objection has been made with regard to dogmatic theology. Many of the Fathers of the first few centuries have spoken but vaguely on certain points which have since come to be regarded as of capital importance. Protestants have wrongly concluded that these points are therefore not essential, and that the Church has changed the doctrine of the ancients. She has merely developed it and defined it.

Instead of saying that, for about the last three centuries, there has been a deviation from the traditional doctrine, we must say that we have at last emerged from the vagueness of tradition.

**3.**—**Sources** of descriptive mysticism. This science relies upon two kinds of documents: 1° The descriptions that are found in classical and approved writers; 2° those that can be supplied by living persons from their own experience. These two kinds of information are indispensable; each one throws light upon the other. There are many passages in the old writers, the real sense of which is only grasped when it is commented on by the living voice of a person who has passed through similar states, and the converse of this is also true.

Let us speak of each of these sources.

**4.**—**Descriptions** given by the old writers. Here are two precautions that should be taken when they are made use of:

(*a*) Not to be content to have recourse to the authors before St. Teresa only, under pretext that they are the great masters. For we have seen (**2**) that they are generally very vague with regard to the states inferior to ecstasy (including affective prayer and that of simplicity).

(*b*) Before making an accurate *inventory* of the definite facts that a book, or one of its chapters, contains, an analysis is necessary, and this is a longer and more difficult task than one would at first imagine. As a rule the facts are buried in a host of accessories: digressions, pious reflections, literary developments, useless repetitions, commentaries on the Holy Scriptures, etc. All this extraneous matter must be eliminated and only the *residue* that is based on experience left.

* We find it the ground of many of the Abbé Saudreau's arguments.

Sometimes this will be made up of very little; of a long chapter, only a few lines will remain. But at least the facts thus isolated will be very clear, very distinct.

I have devoted myself to this slow work of dissection, and my book is the result.

(*c*) In seeking to bring together these facts, the whole of which, combined, constitute a state of prayer, we must not at the same time concern ourselves with problems such as knowing what name should be given and what place assigned to it in our classification.

I have perceived that certain discussions on mysticism, in which I have taken part, would have been shortened if the various *questions had been separated* in this way. We should have begun by saying: Do we admit the existence or the frequency of such a state described in such or such terms? Without concerning ourselves with knowing if we should call it mystic, or give it such or such a classical name, we will call it the N state provisionally. When we are in accord on this point we can consider the others.

It will often be found that we are of the same mind as to the basis, that is to say the existence of this state; the divergence consists only in the choice of the label that is to be applied to N.

This separation of the description and the terminology will show us that many of the old writers have described the same things under different names—or on the other hand, different things under the same names.

**5.**—In descriptions of the mystic states, should we bring forward texts of **Holy Scripture** in support of our statements? St. Bernard and St. John of the Cross do so incessantly; Blessed Angela of Foligno, and St. Teresa (except in the case of her *Conceptions of Divine Love*) scarcely ever do so. Which method is the best?

The answer depends upon the object that we have in view. Either you wish to give a proof, properly so-called, that such or such a state exists with such a particular shade, or else you take it for granted that the reader accepts your ideas as already proved by other means.

In the first case, do not quote biblical texts. For they generally prove nothing, or almost nothing, in these matters. You are obliged to rely upon an interpretation that lends itself to your argument, but which will be disputed. The recalcitrant reader will say to you, "Many other interpretations have been given to this passage. You reverse the logical order of things; instead of basing your thesis upon a meaning, the correctness of which I dispute, you ought, on the contrary, to base its correctness on a thesis which has first been undeniably proved. You assign such a passage of the psalms to the mystic state. But it is applicable to other souls. Hence the great value of these texts and the part that the Church gives them in the Liturgy. In the same way you interpret such a scene in the *Canticle of Canticles* as belonging to the extraordinary states of prayer; but it may refer in a more general way to divine love."

If, on the other hand, a description is regarded as being established by observation, nothing prevents our resorting to passages of Holy Scripture, whether by way of an approximate confirmation, or as a mere literary device, in order to repeat the same things under another form.

This is what the Fathers have sometimes done with regard to dogmatic truths. In spite of appearances, they do not claim to prove such or such a proposition by the Bible; they take for granted that it is known and accepted, but they simply wish to find it stated more or less approximately in the divine book, and to formulate it in biblical style.*

**6.**—Let us give **two examples** of these quotations that prove nothing. In order to establish the fact that there is a state called the spiritual marriage, writers have the habit of relying upon the text in Osee: *Sponsabo te mihi in fide* (ii, 20), which they translate thus: "I will espouse thee to me in faith." But they forget to prove that this passage refers to marriage in the stricter sense of the mystics, that is to say, the transforming union, which is the whole question. The literal sense is very different and much more mysterious. *Fides* here means fidelity, as when you say: I will keep faith with you. In this passage God says to Israel: "I will violate my covenant, because thou has first abandoned me. Return to me and I will contract a *faithful alliance* with thee; one that is enduring, that is to say."

And so the text, taken alone, has no reference to prayer.

It will perhaps be objected that Our Lord has, nevertheless made use of it to announce His favours to certain of His servants such as the Ven. Mary of the Incarnation, Ursuline. But I have only asked that texts from Holy Scripture should be left out of the question in certain demonstrations. Our Lord is not seeking to prove a thesis here; He is making a promise. Nothing hinders Him from employing the biblical style that is used in books of piety of that period.

*Second example.* In treating this question: Can contemplation endure for some length of time? Instead of seeking the answer in a number of carefully weighed observations, there has been a repetition from age to age of the classical solution of St. Gregory the Great, saying that contemplation scarcely lasts more than half an hour, because of that text of the Apocalypse "there was silence in heaven, as it were for half an hour" (ch. viii, 1).

To begin with, this text proves nothing at all. It is a question of silence, as in some twenty places in Holy Scripture; but it is not the silence of contemplation, nor even of prayer. And then there is another question which should first have

* Through humility St. John of the Cross persuaded himself that he relied more upon Holy Scripture than upon his own experience: "Therefore, while touching but slightly on the subject of this dark night I trust neither to experience nor to knowledge, for both may mislead me; but solely to the Holy Scriptures, under the teaching of which I cannot err, because He who speaks therein is the Holy Ghost" (*Ascent of Mount Carmel*, Prologue, p. 3). Certainly Holy Scripture does not deceive us, but man may deceive himself by applying it in an arbitrary way.

been dealt with: Of what contemplation is St. Gregory speaking? Is it the simple regard of the prayer of simplicity? Is it of ecstasy generally, or ecstasy only at its maximum? And what, also, does he mean by "not lasting?" Is it cessation or a slight fluctuation? These are points that should have been decided.

If we want to write a trustworthy book on mysticism, it is not sufficient to take a pair of scissors and cut up passages of old books. A critical study of the text must be made.

7.—I have said that there is a **second source** of information with regard to descriptive mysticism: namely, accounts of experiences supplied by trustworthy persons who are now alive.*

There are two preliminary conditions to be fulfilled:

1° The director who collects these documents and criticises them, should have made a serious study of mysticism and be gifted with discernment, so as not to pin his faith to the first comer. When we wish to further any science, to make a "contribution" to it, we do not apply to an ignorant person or even to a beginner.

2° We should bear in mind that these researches cannot for the future aim at making any great discoveries. After so many centuries, during which people have observed, dissected, and discussed, it is clear that everything of importance has been recorded. It is a question now of modestly deciding certain *small circumstances,* detailed facts, that the old writers have not referred to from motives that we are ignorant of. Perhaps they overlooked them, or they wished to keep within certain boundaries.† How many writers, after publishing a book, realise that they have not said all that they knew or could easily have known?

These *minor facts,* overlooked by our predecessors, are but the crumbs from their table. But science loves to gather everything up. And further, these new facts may have useful consequences. They will assist us one day, either to outline a new theory or to refute certain free-thinkers, who, satisfied with noting superficial characters, liken the mystic states to morbid symptoms.

I have tried here and there in this book to point out several of these small facts of which no other writer has spoken, and I have asked that "researches" should be made on certain obscure points (see this word in the Analytical Index).

* I do not include here the question of the progress to be effected in laying down rules of conduct. We must ask for these rules, not any longer from persons receiving the graces of mental prayer, but from theologians. And then these principles were discovered a long time ago because we could not do without them, while detailed descriptions were not indispensable. It is only a question now, therefore, of clearness in explaining them.

† St. Teresa nearly omitted, designedly, in her *Life,* to describe the state which follows the prayer of quiet. This would have caused a great hiatus in her recital, "I never understood it and never could explain it; and so I was resolved, when I should come thus far in my story, to say very little or nothing at all... Our Lord, to-day, after Communion, admitted me to this state of prayer... and taught me how to speak of it "(*Life,* ch. xvi. 2-3).

It is very annoying for specialists to have to be always thus learning. But it is an evil that has no remedy; all the sciences suffer from it.

**8**.—This idea of interrogating living persons has not found favour with a contemporaneous writer, recently deceased. Under the cloak of anonymity, he attacked it in a Catholic Review (*L'Ami du Clergé* of September 26, 1901; reply December 5, 1901). Here are his **three objections:**

1° That the love of novelty will lead people to make light of the traditional descriptions.—We reply that this would be an anti-scientific disposition; that of the physician, who under the pretext of progress, would make a clean sweep of all previous research. I start from the quite different idea that we are not to destroy, but to complete; and this also with regard to the minor facts only.

Let us not oppose tradition to observation. The first is nothing but observation in the past; it cannot contradict that of the present. It should be the most precious in our eyes, because it is bequeathed to us by the saints and has borne the long test of time. For my part, no one will accuse me of having despised it, and especially of not having quoted St. Teresa. If I have done so, it is just because I have considered her as a mine of observation.

2° In order to give an account of our own states of prayer, it is necessary to examine ourselves, to become too introspective; which is attended with drawbacks.—To begin with, if the director has studied mysticism, he can question a person without it being necessary for the latter to make any examination beforehand. And then, we are never intended to begin examining ourselves during prayer, even when it is merely a question of ordinary prayer. This would be to make distractions for ourselves. But, afterwards, a moderate examination is permitted, otherwise St. Teresa and many others would not have been able to write their beautiful works.

3° Finally, the writer is afraid of meeting with those who are vain and will tell falsehoods; and others who will relate things that they have found in books. And then he rather unkindly says: "Everyone knows that no confidence can be placed in descriptions given by women; they lack the spirit of analysis and are ignorant of the exact terms in which to convey their impressions. St. Teresas are not met with every day."—This simply proves that the director, as I said further back, must have both knowledge and discernment. Such men have existed in the past; why not in the future?

Here is a convenient way of making researches. Let writers insert a series of questions in their books. They will get the answers eventually.

### § 2. Classifications

**9**.—We have seen that St. Teresa is satisfied with **reducing** the stages of the mystic union **to four**. These degrees subdivide themselves into further varieties according to divers circumstances. The saint has had the wisdom not to try to arrange all these shades of states so as to make one *unbroken series.*

Many writers have tried to do this, and have thus arrived at the most incongruous results. M. Ribet has shown us all these diverse classifications. They are so varied, and sometimes so irreconcilable, that it is enough to disgust with their subject those who are beginning to study mysticism. One reckons fifteen degrees, another twelve, another six, etc. —Who, then, is right? the beginner will ask. Whom are we to believe?

The answer is that no one is right. They have all tried to solve an impossible problem; and with this object they have forgotten a fundamental principle of all sound classification, namely, that it must start from one single point of view.

An illustration will show what I mean. One musical air can be played in various keys; in *sol,* in *fa,* etc.; and then by instruments of different tones, human voices, flutes, violins, and various organ-stops; lastly, it may be accompanied in many ways. Now it is *a priori* an impossible problem to wish to classify all these ways *on one single line.* If we persist we shall have arbitrary solutions, as many as we please. This is because there are three points of view instead of one; the *pitch,* the *tone,* and the *accompaniment.* It would be easy to make three classifications; they would never fall rationally into one alone.

Let us show the application of these remarks. We must not inquire whether the prayer of "supernatural silence" should come before or after the "spiritual inebriation." This is to ask whether a melody played in *fa* should be classed before the same air upon the flute. These two points of view have nothing in common. The name of the prayer of silence alludes to the intensity of the ligature; the term spiritual inebriation refers to something else: the state of the affective faculty, joy or sadness. Describe them in what order you choose, but do not persist in arranging them like the beads of a rosary!*

Will those who thus find a series of twelve or fifteen degrees, dare to affirm that the various persons whom they direct have passed through their gauge *exactly* in the order indicated? Schram himself, who subdivides so much, admits, when quoting Godinez, that these divisions make no claim to respond to the reality (No. 315 of the 1848 ed., 304 of the old ed.). It is therefore a purely arbitrary construction.

With regard to the four degrees of the *Interior Castle,* on the contrary, there can be no dispute. Since the first three are the weak state, the medium state and the strong state of a grace that is fundamentally one and the same, it is a hundred to one that they will be passed through in this order. But *when it is a question of variations of detail, there is no certain historic sequence.* One day you have the species A; to-morrow the species D, etc. They are not distinct stages. But you are allowed to gather now a rose, now a pink, *in the same garden.* Or, to

* M. Ribert has wisely bid us remark that the prayer of "spiritual silence" and of "spiritual sleep" are not degrees, but simple ways of being of different degrees (Vol I, ch. xi, No. 4. p. 186): "It is with sleep as with silence, it is to be met with in a different measure of intensity in several mystic states" (ch xii, No. 3).

go back to the comparison referred to above, to-day the air is played on the organ in *la,* and to-morrow on the harp in *sol.*

But how, then, do these authors construct their fanciful little classifications? I imagine that, instead of resorting to any investigations, they perform this operation quietly in their study; being guided merely by reasons of suitability. To one it seems, all things considered, that such a state *ought* only to arrive tardily, after such and such another state. And the matter is then settled! He never communicates his reasons to his readers, and does not trouble to enter upon a critical discussion. Others consider the requirements of symbolism. It is in this way that an idea of Richard of St.-Victor is adopted by St. Bonaventure—without either of them, perhaps, taking it very seriously; for they give another classification elsewhere. According to this conception the degrees of contemplation *should* correspond with the six days of creation, not only as a whole, which would be acceptable enough, but as to number. They correspond likewise with the six steps of King Solomon's throne (St. Bonaventure, *Commentary on the Gospel of St. Luke,* ch. ix, No. 47, Vol. XII, Quaracchi, new ed.). But another, with the same symbolism of the six or seven days of the creation, would prove just as legitimately that there must be twelve or fourteen degrees, since the Bible ascribes a morning and an evening to each day.

Brancati, without naming him, condemns another writer who has imagined nine degrees of contemplation, corresponding with the nine choirs of angels (op. vii, ch. xvi). This is a pure play of fancy.

Symbolism is an excellent thing, but as a supplement, in order to sum up in a more literary form results that have been definitely proved elsewhere. It cannot be the main foundation of a scientific work. It is an artificial process leading to the most widely differing results.

**10.**—Apart from the classification of the *Interior Castle,* we can find none that is scientifically tenable. From the practical standpoint it is **the most convenient.** For if the chief divisions are more than three or four, they no longer accomplish the end that we have in view. The first requirement is to aid directors, so that they may *quickly* understand the height to which any particular soul has attained. But for this you want divisions that are recognised as responding universally to the reality, and easy to retain. Broad lines suffice, from the point of view of the advice to be given. It is not necessary to classify persons in more than three or four degrees. For example, you must know whether they are, or are not, ecstatics. But you will have nothing special to say to them if they inform you that they experience the "spiritual inebriation" at times. Directors will be obliged to us for having economised their time.

Another object of classifications is a more theoretical one. The mind requires to be able to command a great subject by general surveys. But should we understand the plan of a sermon, if instead of three points it contained twelve? The fewer the principal divisions, the clearer and more agreeable is it to the mind, and the more easily are they remembered.

**11.**—Writers who, like Alvarez de Paz and so many others, have multiplied the degrees of prayer, would have been warned against this exaggeration if they had taken the precaution of **comparing** together all **the definitions** that they gave. They would have perceived that these only differed in appearance. You find always the same ideas, expressed at times in almost identical terms. In each one you are told: there are wonderful lights, a great peace, a great love, etc. But if such resemblances exist, why leave us to believe in the existence of frontiers separating quite distinct realms? Say merely that the same state is susceptible of certain different shades.

**12.**—Some writers have referred to a degree of prayer that they call the prayer of **active union** (Philip a SS. Trinitate, Part III, Tr. 1, d. iv, a. iii; Vallgornera, No. 1023; etc.). I think that this system is inadmissible. In fact: 1° according to these writers such a degree consists in conformity to the will of God. Now this is a virtue, not a state of prayer. At that rate we ought to give a special name to every state in which the soul practises each of the other virtues; they are quite as worthy of it. 2° It seems as if these writers had wished to push the parallelism between the ordinary and the extraordinary ways to undue lengths. Seeing that recollection was divided into active and passive (ch. xxix, 3), and the same with regard to the prayer of repose (we have noticed that the prayer styled active is the prayer of simplicity), they have said by analogy: Let us give a corresponding state to St. Teresa's prayer of union. Since it is a passive state, let us imagine an active union. But then, why stop there and not imagine two sorts of ecstasy, one active and the other passive? And the same with the spiritual marriage?—Let us not multiply divisions without necessity.

# CHAPTER XXXI

## A Discussion Regarding Some Theoretical Questions

**1.**—I will begin with the **three** following **questions:** Are there such things as natural levitation, natural stigmata, natural ecstasies? Free-thinkers answer yes, without any hesitation; and they cannot do otherwise, since they admit the existence of nothing supernatural in this world. The majority are satisfied with making this *a prioritistic* statement. Others, as we shall see, endeavour to bring proofs.

**2.**—Amongst Catholics, opinions are divided. I will not attempt to say on which side right lies. The psycho-physiological sciences do not seem to me to be sufficiently advanced to enable us to make any decisive pronouncements one way or the other. I will adopt a position which is intermediate, but which, however, appears to me unassailable, that of showing that the **proofs** brought in support of naturalistic explanations are **fallacious.** Sometimes they are arbitrary hypotheses, sometimes arguments founded upon facts that are either exaggerated or misconstrued.

Since the contrary theses have thus resisted all attacks, it follows that, until something fresh transpires, they are much the most probable. If ultimately, however, the advance of medical science and psycho-physiology were to bring serious objections against them, neither religion nor mysticism need be perturbed. They are not in any way dependent upon the solution of these questions.

### § 1.—Is There a Natural Levitation?

**3.**—Attempts have been made to prove **experimentally** that the human body, in certain super-normal cases, can diminish *slightly* in weight, and it has therefore been concluded that this diminution may *perhaps* become so complete that the body can remain suspended in the air.

But the experiment from which this conclusion proceeds is hotly contested. It is that in which Sir William Crookes weighed a magnetised person, and proved a loss of weight. It has been objected that this experiment, simple as it is, has not succeeded with other observers. No case of levitation has ever been known at the Salpetriere.

It is true that some neuropathic persons feel their bodies to be lighter at certain times than is normally the case. Scaramelli (Tr. 3, No. 275) says that ecstatics often have the same sensation when they come to themselves again. But there is reason to think that this is a purely subjective impression. There would only be one scientific way of deciding the matter, namely, to weigh the person in question. This is what M. Pierre Janet did with an ecstatic (real or otherwise?) who experienced this feeling. He found him to be of exactly the same weight as in the normal state (*Bulletin de L'lnstitut psychologique International*; Paris, 27 Rue Serpente, July, 1901).

**4.**—Another argument has been offered: that instances of levitation have been observed amongst Indian **Fakirs**. These phenomena, having no other object than the satisfaction of the operator's pride and the spectators' curiosity, cannot come from God, and the operator himself does not think of attributing them to Him. Therefore, it is said, they are natural. No; they may be diabolic, or the results of clever trickery. And further, the inquiry has not hitherto been of a really scientific character.

**5.**—Lastly, recourse has been had to *a prioritistic* arguments. The spiritualists and occultists have said: "Nothing could be simpler, It is a case of **electric attraction** or **repulsion,** of polarity, or the emission of vital fluid."

But if there is an electric current directed towards the ground, why does it recoil instead of burying itself in it? And why is there no sparking with neighbouring bodies?

If an attraction existed, it would be in connection with an electrified body placed above the saint, as in experiments made with electric puppets. Now no such condition is present. I have read many pamphlets on this subject. What has struck me is the charlatanism (sometimes unconscious, as I like to believe) of these tall talkers. Nothing is easier in physics than *to feign* an explanation. You let fall some big words, you suggest some gratuitous hypotheses, and conclude with a triumphant air, saying, like the *savant* in the comedy, " And that is why your daughter is dumb."

In order to have the right to affirm that it is *electricity* that raises up the ecstatic's body, you must have really disentangled the *how* of this action. And then why do you not explain it *in detail?* Better still, why do you not make the experiment (and under the same conditions of isolation) with a statue weighing sixty kilogrammes, or even one kilogramme, furnished with an apparatus for generating electricity? One must really count largely upon the ignorance of the public with regard to scientific processes, to try to dazzle them with fine words.

**6.**—Certain writers perceive that electricity, as a matter of fact, explains nothing. You must have recourse, they say, to the emission of the vital fluid.

This would-be explanation assumes that the following propositions are proved:

1° There is a vital fluid, which is distinct from the electric current (many persons deny it. It is merely a hypothesis);

2° This fluid can issue from the body, and "exteriorise itself;"

3° It can then exercise a motive power; now of attraction, now of repulsion;

4° This last may be strong enough to lift a body weighing sixty kilogrammes.

5° And this for several hours at a time, and sometimes to a great distance from the ground.

What a number of hypotheses! And not one experiment! And further, they forget to explain to us why, when this power of repulsion is exercised upon the ground, those who are looking on experience nothing similar. They feel no shock when they draw near. These are not the characteristics of a scientific theory.

I am quoting from memory only, those who say: Levitation is perhaps a phenomenon similar to that of the iron filings that are lifted up by the electro-magnet.—The case is very different. The electro-magnet is an apparatus outside of and distinct from the iron filings, just as the balloon is distinct from the aeronaut, and the hand from the weight that it lifts. The saint is not drawn up by an external apparatus.

**7.—Catholic writers** admit that the levitation of the saints is supernatural, but they have sometimes wished to tell us *how* God does it. The simplest explanation, and that most in conformity with the order of Providence, consists in saying: Since the angels have power to move corporeal objects, God makes use of their ministry, so as to avoid intervening Himself without necessity. He entrusts them with the task of raising the ecstatic's body; and this from motives derived* from the good of souls.

It is by virtue of the same power that Satan supported Simon Magus in the air.

Two other explanations have been given; I like to think that their inventors have not taken them seriously:

1° Fr. Séraphin (*Theol, myst.*, No. 205) follows Lopez de Ezquerra in explaining the fact by saying that the body has *really* lost its weight. This hypothesis is not tenable. For, to begin with, it supposes that God intervenes without necessity. For He alone can suppress one of the essential qualities of matter. And then, the body would act like the cork that rises to the surface of the water. According to the principle of Archimedes, it would fly like an arrow to the extreme limits of our atmosphere, more than 70 kilometres, that is to say. And who knows whether, as a result of its acquired velocity, it would not continue indefinitely to traverse the realms of space?

* Benedict XIV gives one of these motives: "By Divine power the body may be raised on high, not because this has any necessary connection with ecstasy or rapture resulting from a vehement divine contemplation, but because God—as this ecstatic contemplation is like to, and, as it were, a commencement of that which will be in the beatitude of souls—in order to instruct us therein, grants at times to the enraptured this special gift; which gift is a certain imperfect participation of the gift of fleetness, which will be bestowed on glorified bodies" (*De Canon.*, Book III, ch, xlix. No. 4, English: *Heroic Virtue*, Vol. III. ch, x, p. 242).

There is a simple explanation. The body is in conditions similar to those of the balloon which ascends, finds its equilibrium and oscillates. Nothing is *destroyed,* but something is *added;* a force, that is to say, equal but of a contrary nature to weight. St. Teresa seems to suggest this fact when she says: "It seemed to me, when I tried to make some resistance, as if *a great force beneath my feet* lifted me up. I know of nothing with which to compare it" (*Life,* ch. xx, 7).

2° Without being aware of it, hagiographers often allow themselves to represent levitation as a semi-natural state; as though it were the natural consequence of a divine action, only purely psychological. They say, for instance: "The soul, desirous of immersing herself more completely in God (whom she regards as being exterior to herself) precipitates herself towards Him, and *carries the body away* after her." These words are very poetic, but do not bear criticism. It would follow that, when the soul feels the desire for a closer acquaintance with some exterior object, she has the direct power of transporting her substance from one place to another, in which case the body, which is joined to her, ought to follow her. But this power is a mere hypothesis. On the contrary, experience teaches us that the soul has only one means of passing from one place to another, namely, by moving the bodily limbs and acting upon surrounding bodies by this means (see another refutation in Scaramelli, Tr. 3, No. 275).

Let us, then, content ourselves with more moderate expressions, which do not claim to give a scientific explanation, but which point to the harmony of things and their symbolism. Let us say: "It is all as though the soul, etc.," or: "It would seem that, etc."

### § 2.—Are There Natural Stigmata?

**8.—Definition.** The term natural stigmata is given to wounds that resemble those of crucifixion, or, more generally, of the Passion, and that are produced solely by the *natural* action of the imagination and vivid emotions (see ch. xiii, **15**). Being strongly impressed by the Saviour's sufferings, and inflamed with a great love, this preoccupation would act physically upon the person, by producing Our Lord's Wounds. This would diminish nothing of the merits. But the immediate cause would not be supernatural. It matters little to know how the imagination may have been excited, and whether the soul would have to be in a supernatural state, such as ecstasy. Finally, it would be this faculty, and not a special supernatural action which would produce the phenomenon. I repeat what has been said previously (**2**), that even if it were ever to be proved that the stigmata can be explained naturally, neither religion nor mysticism need be perturbed.

**9.**—Does the imagination possess such a power? That is the problem.

I reply, in the first place, that if it is a question of a person in the **normal state,** there is no reason for inclining to the affirmative. It would be contrary to all analogies. For in medicine we have no examples of a modification of the tissues produced by the imagination in these cases.

**10.**—The question is a more difficult one if it relates to persons in an **abnormal state,** such as the sleep of ecstasy or hypnotism. Certain physiologists, some Catholics, others Free-thinkers, admit that the imagination can produce wounds and bleedings. Some are content with affirming this, without giving the smallest proofs.* This is really too lax and unscientific.† Others, more conscientious, bring bring as an argument two celebrated experiments made upon hypnotised persons: one on a soldier of la Rochelle, whose arm actually bled upon the suggestion that it would do so (experiments made by Drs. Bourrut, Burot and Mabille, quoted by Bernheim, *De la Suggestion,* Part I, ch. iv); the other at Nancy, where vesication was brought about by suggestion (experiments made by M. Focachon, a chemist, of Charmes, in the presence of Drs. Beaunis, Bernheim, and Liegeois, 1885).

These experiments lose much weight from the fact that no one has since succeeded in reproducing them distinctly, notwithstanding numerous attempts. It is to be feared, therefore, that these first experimenters omitted to take certain circumstances into account. In the soldier's case trickery is probable. For the doctors recognised the fact that he was very untruthful. Now the bleeding did not occur until several hours after the suggestion, which gave the patient the opportunity for inducing it secretly. Finally, it did not appear upon the arm that had been selected by the doctor.

With regard to the Nancy experiment, it seems likely that the stigmatic haemorrhage was confused here with a particular malady that is seen at times in neuropathic and arthritic subjects. It is called *demography* or *pseudo-urticaria.*

Swellings encircled by rubefaction appear on the skin, and may remain for many days or even weeks. But they are due, not to an excitation of the imagination, but to an excitation of the skin, by pressure, friction, etc.‡ The

* Or again, certain unbelievers have constructed a vicious circle. They have begun by proving the power of the imagination, relying upon the existence of the saints' stigmata; and have afterwards explained the saints' stigmata by the power of the imagination.

† The same reproach can be made to an early writer quoted by the Bollandists in the seventeenth century (May 25th, p. 247, No. 8). Speaking of the seven instruments of the Passion that were found graven in the heart of St. Clare of Montefalco (see the picture reproduced by Dr. Imbert, Vol. II), he is satisfied, without basing his theory on any natural analogy, to attribute them to the action of her imagination. It is surprising that this faulty method should have been condemned neither by the Bollandists, nor Benedict XIV, who gives the conclusion of this quotation (*De Canon.*, Book III, ch. xliii, No. 17). Benedict XIV explains elsewhere the very restricted degree in which the action of the imagination may be admitted in the production or cure of diseases. According to him, it can at times produce a slight modification in the flow of the nervous fluid or liquids of the human body; it has no action upon the tissues (*De Canon.*, Book IV, Part I, ch. xxxiii, Nos. 21, 30, 31).

‡ This is so true, that the phenomenon is observed even in the case of neuropathic horses (as highly bred horses usually are).

doctors who examined Louise Lateau were careful to avoid this source of error. She could not touch her stigmata.

And further, it has been shown (see Imbert, Vol. II, ch. vi, xiv; Surbled, *La Morale*, Vol. IV, Part II, final chapter; Gombault, *L'Imagination,* Part IV, ch. ii, pp. 504, 514) that the saints' stigmata presented very great differences from those of the hypnotised persons of whom we have just been speaking.

1° With the first, there are true wounds; the flow of blood is often very abundant. There is nothing similar with the others. There has merely been a swelling or a more or less coloured exudation. It is a coarse imitation only.

2° The first often persist for several years, or reproduce themselves periodically every week. The others are transient;

3° It is not possible to cure the first by means of remedies;

4° The first are often very painful. This fact has not been noted with the others;

5° The first have always been accompanied by ecstasies;

6° Contrary to what is observed in all natural wounds of a certain duration, those of the saints exhibit no fetid odour* (sometimes they even emit a perfume), no suppuration, no morbid deterioration of the tissues. And the remarkable thing is that any non-stigmatic wounds from which they may suffer follow the normal course.

To sum up, if we say that the imagination is capable of producing the stigmatic wounds, we are forced to state it as a fact without any experimental proof.

**10** *bis.*—If anyone wishes to prove in a really scientific manner that the imagination, auto-suggestion, that is to say, can produce the stigmata, there is only one way of doing it: instead of proposing mere hypotheses, he must bring similar facts, only of *the natural order,* that is to say wounds produced by suggestion, *apart from any religious idea.* But none have ever been met with, notwithstanding the extreme goodwill of doctors and hypnotisers. There is not one example of a real wound produced in a hospital by the excitation of the imagination and the sensibility. Rubefaction, or, at the most, reddish sweats, have indeed, been obtained, although very rarely; but there has never been any flow of blood, and especially no punctures, no tearing of the tissues. And this not even on the soft parts of the skin, any more than those occupied by the stigmata of crucifixion, that is to say on the inner and very tough surfaces of the hands and feet.

Let us add that if the stigmatic wounds could be explained *a priori* by auto-suggestion, the same could be said of all diseases. When you have typhoid fever, a cold on the chest, cholera, corns or warts, nothing would hinder our attributing these modifications to the powerful action of the imagination. If it can perforate the hands, it can just as easily perforate, dilate, or contract the lungs or the other

* An exception is cited: St. Rita of Cassia received a supernatural wound in the centre of her forehead, due to a thorn from the crown of thorns on her crucifix. The odour was insupportable (Bolland. of May 22).

viscera! And inversely, auto-suggestion would explain all cures. With arbitrary hypotheses one can explain anything that one chooses.

**11.**—Several Catholic medical men have attempted to explain the stigmata by the fact of **blood-sweating.** There are natural examples of this phenomenon, they say, and these are caused by the emotions. It may be the same, therefore, with the stigmata.

Dr. Lefebvre, Professor of Medicine at Louvain, has refuted this argument by analogy at great length, entering into a number of technical details that cannot find a place here (*Louise Lateau, etude medicate*, Part III, art. I. Eng. Trans., by F. S. Northcote). It will be sufficient to notice:

1° That the authenticity of the greater number of blood-sweatings is disputed (see the word *Agony in* the Abbé Vacant's *Dictionary of Theology*), and that they are very rare. It is otherwise with the stigmata;

2° The sweats that have been subjected to examination by doctors are not due to a moral cause; it is a special illness. This would suffice to destroy the whole argument from its foundation;

3° In these diseases, it has often been proved by the microscope that the reddish liquid which exudes is not blood. The colour is due to a special substance;

4° The essential characters of the stigmata are these: they are wounds, they are *localised* in the same places as in Our Lord's Body, they bleed on fixed days, and they cause terrible sufferings. The haemorrhage is merely a secondary and intermittent phenomenon.** Finally, the wounds make their appearance in places places where the skin is thickest and most resistant, on the palms of the hands and the soles of the feet; which never occurs, says Dr. Lefebvre, with morbid haemorrhages (*ibid.*, § 1).

The blood-sweatings, on the contrary, do not imply the presence of wounds. They are due to a dilation of the pores of the skin, so as to allow the filtering through of liquids, as with ordinary perspiration; there is neither puncture nor rent.

**11** *bis.*—Instead of explaining the stigmata by the natural action of the imagination, an attempt has been made to achieve this by the hypothesis of an unconscious fraud. The ecstatic would have frequent attacks of somnambulism, and while in this state he would make the wounds himself.†

It is certain that directors should ascertain whether the stigmatics that they have under their observation are not somnambulists. But if this may have been the case at one time or another, to try to explain in this way all the hundreds of

* According to Dr. Lefebvre, the stigmatic haemorrhages that had come under his observation, proceeded in the following order: "First a vesicle is seen to form and rise little by little." This is the bullate period. "Directly after the rupture of the vesicle and the escape of the fluid, blood begins to ooze from the bare derma." This is the bleeding period.

† A phenomenon frequent amongst stigmatised ecstatics has been explained in the same way; they abstain, or almost entirely so, from food. It has been supposed that they go at night in a state of somnambulism to the larder! The housewife would certainly not be long before she discovered it!

cases of stigmatisation would be a too unlikely and convenient hypothesis (ch. xiii, **18**). And further, in modern times, doctors have taken many wise precautions to avoid the above-mentioned error. Sometimes they have watched the person in question night and day, sometimes they have enveloped the limbs with sealed bandages, or have enclosed them in transparent and sealed globes. Finally, even in the most distant times, they were not so ignorant or so simple as not to see if the subject suffered from somnambulism, and especially if he had frequent or periodical attacks of it.

**12.**—I have hitherto spoken of wounds and not of simple **stigmatic pains.** Can these last be produced by an inflamed imagination accompanied by a vehement love? St. Francis of Sales admitted this. Speaking of St. Francis of Assisi, he says: "Now the soul, as the form and mistress of the body, exercising *her authority over it*, impressed the *pains* of the wounds with which she was struck, on the parts corresponding to those wherein her beloved had endured them. Love is admirable in sharpening the imagination to penetrate to the exterior" (*Treatise on the Love of God*, Book VI, ch. xv). The holy doctor does not, however, wish to go too far, and he thinks that the wounds demand another origin. "But love being within, could not well make the *holes in the flesh* without, and therefore the burning seraph, coming to its help, darted rays of so penetrating a light, that it really made in the flesh the exterior wounds of the crucified" (*ibid.*).

The saint saw that the first of the two preceding propositions must at any rate be proved. He brings forward three facts which he appears to regard as analogous, for instance, that "a powerful imagination can turn a man white in a night." Unfortunately, in no one of these instances does any pain occur.

It was their possibility, however, that he wished to establish. And further, these examples would tend to overthrow the saint's second proposition, as in it we see the imagination working directly upon the body.

### § 3.—Are There Natural Ecstasies?

**13.**—This problem has again been dealt with, although briefly, in two fairly recent works: *Le Merveilleux divin*, by Dom Marechaux, O.S.B. (Book IV, ch. ii, p. 226), and *La Magie Moderne*, by Fr. Rolfi, O.S.F. (Part II, Appendix II, p. 258 263). Neitner of them settles the question, but they seem to incline, the first towards the negative, the second towards the affirmative.

To treat the problem by a **truly scientific method,** we must: 1° define exactly what we understand by natural ecstasy. People are too often satisfied with vague terms, and then the argument wanders away; an example of syncope is produced, and it is described as ecstasy. 2° rely upon facts, and undoubted, *accurately observed* facts, the details of which have been carefully noted, and this by persons who are competent to distinguish these states from others that are apparently exactly like them. For instance, how can any conclusion be drawn from a vague description which would be as applicable to catalepsy as to ecstasy? Facts alone, and not *a priori* ideas, can justify a solution. The latter do not count in questions of physiology. There must be a basis of experimental fact.

**14.**—Let us first consider the definition itself. The expression natural ecstasy has come to have one **wide sense** and another narrow. The first applies to all alienation of the sensible faculties, even when caused by illness, without reference to the question of whether the soul were occupied in any way during this time or no. Medical men often employ this language, each restricting the sense slightly, according to his own fancy. It is thus that they speak of hypnotic ecstasy and hysterical ecstasy.

Stated in this way, the question as to the existence of natural ecstasies is thus settled in advance; their existence has to be admitted. But the proposition thus affirmed is without interest. It resolves itself into the commonplace truth that certain diseases, or great fatigues, deprive the individual of the use of his faculties. And further, it is to lavish the term, ecstasy, upon states which already possess clearer and more definite titles in medical science. Finally, it is to combine under one name things that differ too widely in kind.

Those Catholic theologians who have studied this question have often adopted the same language. I do not blame them for this. In many cases they were not proposing to clear up any obscure problem of mysticism, but merely to determine in a practical way the value that should be attached to certain facts in the saints* lives. The only important point for them, therefore, was the separation of divine ecstasy from all other alienations of the senses, without subdividing the latter too minutely. Thus Benedict XIV (*De canon,*, Book III, ch. xlix) calls natural ecstasy the alienation of the senses "produced by natural causes such as the disease called catalepsy." Cardinal Bona (*De discret. spir.*, ch. xix, Nos. iv, v) does the same thing, as does also Schram (*Theol. myst.*, No. 586 of the 1848 edition, 577 of the old edition). Cardinal Brancati de Lauria relapses into this view, after having emancipated himself from it for a moment by dividing ecstasies into those that are healthy and those that are morbid (*De oratione*, op. 5, ch. vi). If we go back to St. Thomas, we see that he divides ecstasies into the natural, the demoniac, and the divine (2, 2, q. 175, a. 1). But he explains that by the first he means the state of those sick persons who lose the use of their senses. At the end of the next article he even applies the word rapture to great excesses of anger or terror. This, indeed, is what the Greek word ecstasy means, if we keep to the etymology. It is a state where the person is "beside himself."

As my aim is different from that of these great masters, no one will be surprised if I treat this question from a more restricted standpoint.

We have already seen that when we wish to invoke the authority of an early writer in favour of the existence of natural ecstasies, we must carefully examine the sense in which he has used this expression, bearing in mind not only his definitions but the considerations or historic traits that he brings forward and the end that he has in view. Otherwise we shall run the risk of misunderstandings. Here is a striking example of one: Suarez (*De oratione*, Book II, ch. xv, No. 6) quotes Gerson as being a believer in natural ecstasies. Now if we turn to Gerson's very brief words (*De monte contempl.* ch. xxi), we certainly find the word *raptus*, but used in the sense of a strong mental distraction. This makes it possible for him to enunciate the following proposition, which would otherwise be absurd: "This kind of rapture is *habitual* with painters and other artists who are absorbed in their own imaginations."

**15.**—Here is the **more restricted sense** in which I propose to use the expression natural ecstasy, and the following discussion will apply to this sense alone. It is a state which not only in its beginnings, but *in its whole duration*, includes two essential elements: the first, which is interior and invisible, is the *natural* concentration of the intellect, of the imagination, or of the affections upon one single object, and this with *considerable force;* the second which is corporeal and visible, is the alienation of the bodily senses; understanding by this, not only the cessation of their spontaneous activity, but a great difficulty in making them act if we endeavour to excite their organs to operation.* According as such a cessation is complete or nearly so, the ecstasy itself will be said to be either complete or partial.

This definition excludes deep sleep and syncope, because in them the mental faculties cease to operate. It excludes sleep mingled with dreams, and somnambulism, either natural or induced, because the mental faculties do not assume an extraordinary energy in these states. Thus an insignificant mental image is sufficient to occupy a hysterical patient during his attack. Finally, the definition leaves out of the question the bodily weakness or immobility that is only momentarily produced by a vigorous effort of thought, and which is soon replaced by a numbing of the faculties. To sum up, all the morbid states are excluded from the definition.

This view of natural ecstasy seems to me to be that held by Suarez (*loc. cit.*, and ch. xix, Nos. 29, 30), Scaramelli (*Direct myst.*, Tr. 3, No. 185), and many other modern writers, such as Dr. Lefebvre (*Louise Lateau, étude medicate*, second edition, Part IV, art. 3, § 3, p. 236).

**16.**—Another state, very like the preceding, can be imagined. I will call it natural ecstasy of the second kind, or, to put it more clearly, **semi-natural ecstasy.** Here the mind is no longer occupied with a purely natural subject, as was the case just now; it is concerned with the supernatural, but the ordinary and hidden supernatural. Its object is no longer a proposition of geometry or metaphysics, it is one of the truths of religion. This truth is considered with curiosity and love, but, save for the intensity of mental application, it in no way differs interiorly from the prayer of ordinary Christians. What we require to

* Those who wish for a general definition which includes at once both natural and supernatural ecstasies, can adopt the following, quoted by M. Ribot: "It is a *deep* contemplation, with abolition of sensibility and [most generally] suspension of the locomotive faculty" (*Psychologie de l'Attention* ch. ii, § 2; English, *Psychology of Attention*).

know is if the alienation of the bodily senses could be the consequence of an intellectual concentration of this nature. Suarez deals with this question (*loc, cit.*> ch. xiv).

**17.**—Let us begin by considering the problem of *purely natural* ecstasy, **that of philosophers** and mathematicians.

I put aside the question of whether there are any means of proving that it is *a priori possible.* For we can argue on this question for ever without coming to any definite conclusion. We may try, for example, to invoke this general principle that if our intellectual forces concentrate themselves upon one single object, the operation of the bodily senses is thereby hampered. But is this the case to the extent of their being suspended and of resisting all excitations from without? It is this, as Suarez says, that we do not know (ch. xv, end of No. 6). Theoretically we might conceive that our faculty of knowing, being finite, might find an object that totally exhausts its activity. But practically we cannot say whether God has made this absorption possible, naturally and without illness, in this world.

And still more we must put aside the explanations of the ancient natural philosophers, like that of Zacchias, which is given by several early writers, and notably by Brancati. According to him, "the immediate cause of the alienation of the bodily senses is that the animal spirits (the vital fluid, we should now say) which were destined for these senses and to act as their motor power, *all precipitate themselves towards the brain*" But this theory rests upon a gratuitous hypothesis, which is too easy a way of explaining or seeming to understand all the phenomena of nature. By what experiments has Zacchias proved this movement of the animal spirits? They forget to tell us.

**18.**—Let us therefore be satisfied with this more practical problem: has the existence of natural ecstasies, responding to the definition given above, been **proved?**

The reply seems to me to be in the negative. But I would add that I am not pledged to any special opinion. I say again, if the progress of knowledge were finally to bring proofs in its favour, I should accept them without repugnance.

**19.**—Let us examine the *facts* which people have brought forward. We will not linger unduly over those that Brancati, Schram, and others have endeavoured to find in **Holy Scripture.** They are only successful by dint of forced and arbitrary interpretations of the passages. They give the name of alienation of the senses to states of profound astonishment, such as that of the Queen of Saba, admiring Solomon's magnificence, or Jacob's stupefaction on learning that his beloved son Joseph was not dead. In these days also we should doubtless say that the Queen of Saba fell into an ecstasy, but we should know what we meant by it. As for Jacob, at the most it was the ailing condition of body that we call stupor. It is not an intense application of the faculties, but a kind of shock that is produced by unexpected news, paralysing the brain instead of stimulating it.* This case does not come within my definition.

**20.**—The facts drawn from **secular history** by these same writers are the three following in particular. They may be described as classical:

1° The case of the priest *Restitutus,* who, according to St. Augustine, was able to lose the use of his bodily senses at will;

2° *Archimedes,* who, according to Titus Livy, on the occasion of the taking of Syracuse, was so engrossed in a problem, that he allowed himself to be killed by a soldier without offering any resistance;

3° *Socrates,* who, as Alcibiades tells us (Plato's *Symposium*), remained for twenty-four hours motionless, lost in thought, in the camp that Potidsea was besieging.

I ask the reader's indulgence for certain all too convincing examples which Schram quotes, without believing them, from Marsilio Ficino, namely, that Pythagoras was in a kind of lethargy for ten years, Zoroaster for twenty, and Epimenides for fifty years.

Let us return to the other three examples, a Slender store of facts that have been carefully transmitted from author to author.

1° With regard to *Restiiutus,* we are not informed as to what his mind was occupied with during the alienation of his bodily senses. It cannot therefore be proved to have been a case of natural ecstasy in the meaning of my definition. In reality it may have been nothing but an attack of hysteria, or, again, a case of charlatanism, It is an instance of a fact that has been incompletely observed;

2° *Archimedes* was merely an absent-minded man. When the soldier advanced to kill him, all he thought of saying to him was: "Do not disturb the circles that I have traced on the ground!" A marked readiness to be convinced is required in order to call a man an ecstatic who thus keeps up his communications with the exterior world, traces figures and talks to a visitor.

We must form the same opinion with regard to his joyous progress through the city, crying: *Eureka!*

3° *Socrates* — Let us begin by being on our guard against the Greek passion for inventing fables, often from the right motive of giving an allegory in the form of an anecdote. They have told us that the bees constructed a honeycomb upon Plato's lips; this was to symbolise his eloquence. The ecstasy of Socrates is doubtless the symbol of the profundity of his thought.

But let us examine Plato's story more closely. He does not say whether he is giving us a legend or a fact, the reality of which is guaranteed. He is content to put into the mouth of Alcibiades a pompous eulogy of Socrates, addressed to Socrates himself, whom he wishes to gratify. And Alcibiades takes the disquieting precaution of warning his hearers that after the libations of the banquet there may

* See the description by Dr. Lefebvre (*Louise Lateau,* p, 242, English Trans., p. 145).

not perhaps be much sequence in his ideas. Finally, it is impossible to separate the true from the fictitious in such a literary composition.

Let us conclude with Lefebvre: "that history has not preserved us *one single* authentic example" of natural ecstasy.

**21.**— Fr. Rolfi cites two incidents relating to **St. Thomas Aquinas,** which have at least the merit of not going back to mythological times, but which are not conclusive. " One day, when, in conformity to the doctors' advice, his leg was to be cauterised, he began to meditate so profoundly that he did not perceive the operation. Another time, when he was writing in his cell, he was so absorbed in his reflections that the candle, burning away, burnt his hand without his noticing it" (p. 261).

But St. Thomas had divine ecstasies, which allow of this explanation being given for the cases just quoted.* He alone could know if the concentration of his faculties was purely natural. Has he been questioned on the subject? In the absence of any reply, we are leaving the domain of facts to rely upon hypothetical explanations, which is an unfortunate method. And then, with regard to the diseased leg, it would be necessary to know whether the infirmity did not consist exactly in an insensibility which they were endeavouring to combat by the use of actual cautery. Here again the observations are incomplete.

From these remarks we see that the thesis of the *existence* of natural ecstasies *has never been* historically *proved.* For reliance is placed upon an insignificant number of incidents, and none of them can withstand criticism.

**22.**—And, further, all the **probabilities** are against it. In fact, if human nature were really possessed of this power, we should not be reduced to relying upon three or four anecdotes, dating back fifteen hundred or two thousand years. We should have found a series of examples amongst great thinkers of all ages. We should also find other contemporaneous instances. Europe, during the last two or three centuries, has been full of scientific men of the first order, who have been profound thinkers in metaphysics and mathematics. Not once have they been found in the attitude of ecstasy, with eyes fixed and arms extended toward the theorem contemplated. There was never any mention of ecstasy in the case of Newton, Leibnitz, or Euler, nor of Lagrange, Laplace, or Gauss, nor of Rieman, Kronecker or Hermite, etc. If, in medical science, a theory was not better confirmed by experience, no one would venture even to enunciate it.

Dr. Lefebvre remarks that we ought also to find ecstasy in the " capitalist, calculating an operation which will place him on the highest summit of fortune, or precipitate him into the ignominy of poverty." Ecstasy should also occur constantly in the most ordinary conditions. "Do we not daily meet with instances of the strongest impetuosity in the case of affections which are purely human?

* In this hypothesis, these incidents would be similar to that quoted by André du Val in the *Life of Blessed Mary of the Incarnation, Carmelite.* For during a severe surgical operation she felt no pain, having been in an ecstasy all the time.

When the ardour of the senses is united to the ardour of the soul, does there not result a half animal, half human passion which terrifies us by its violence"?

Such passions as these should alienate the senses. "To sum up the whole briefly (he concludes) if ecstasy could be produced by overstrained attention, by a trick of the imagination, by a strong impulse of the thoughts or the senses, it would become a *common fact of daily life.* Medical men, who see human nature in all its weaknesses and all its mysteries, do not meet with it in our days... *Hence I conclude that true ecstasy, of purely psychical origin, independent of any disease of the nervous system, is a myth.*"

The rationalists are obliged by their system to proclaim that all kinds of ecstasy, even those of the saints, are natural, and the majority regard them as illnesses. Catholics are playing into their adversaries' hands when they admit the existence of natural ecstasies *without solid proof.*

I may repeat here, with regard to the saints' ecstasies, what I have said farther back about stigmatised persons (10 *bis*): if it is wished to prove in a really scientific manner that the phenomenon is due to the imagination, to auto-suggestion, there is but one way of doing so: instead of proposing simple hypotheses, let them bring analogous facts, only of the natural order; produced, that is to say, apart from any religious idea. But none such have ever been encountered.

**23.**—In order to explain mystical contemplation in a purely natural way, unbelievers have likened it to a mental exercise which certain **Hindu Buddhists** practise. They incorrectly describe this exercise as contemplation, for it is rather the diminution or cessation of thought. If it amounts to physical immobility, they call it ecstasy, although on the side of the soul it is merely a state of stupefaction. The only accurate fact is that this state is purely natural, for those who enter into it do not believe in a personal God, and therefore in no wise seek any union with Him.

This is how a traveller, M. J. Bois, describes these strange practices which he has studied at close quarters (*Revue des revues*, 1903). I summarise his results.

The *yogis* of India are men who endeavour to imitate ecstasy. Imbued with a belief in Pantheism, they desire to realise immersion in the great All, and to feel the sentiment of their own identity with the universal Being. This aim is called *Yoga*, communion. It is a pantheistic communion, therefore. To attain to it: 1° there are interior exercises: they try to establish a void in the mind, for the varied thoughts are the fugitive waves that trouble the surface of the great ocean of being, and these must be discarded if the soul would attain to the immutable depths; 2° there are further a number of strange bodily exercises. For instance, they concentrate the gaze upon a point between the eyebrows, in order to throw themselves into a kind of hypnotic sleep. But, above all, they practise for months *the art of breathing.* It consists in holding in the breath for ever increasing periods. Thus by a long training they arrive at its complete suspension, having previously stopped up the throat with the tongue (the string of which they have cut), turned over backwards. They thus produce a counterfeit of ecstasy, a comatose state that resembles the sleep, almost without respiration, of hibernating animals, such as bears and marmots. They are then immersed in the great All, that is to say into the great nothing. The limbs are also dislocated, so as to enable them to assume the attitude of various animals; they hope thus to get into communion with their mental powers, which, being very low, are regarded as more nearly akin to the Universal Being, whose activity is unconscious.

**24.**—Let us now speak of the ecstasy that I have called **seminatural,** that which consists in the alienation of the bodily senses during a prayer which, in itself, is not of an extraordinary nature, except with regard to the intensity of the attention. Have these ecstasies sometimes occurred?

Those who admit the existence of a purely natural ecstasy are obliged to answer yes; the problem is no longer quite the same, however.

Brancati puts this question, and he words it in his own fashion by speaking of *acquired contemplation,* of a prayer of an *ordinary* nature, that is to say, in which intuition, a simple regard, to a great extent takes the place of reasoning. He asks if it can produce alienation of the senses and answers that it does not produce it habitually, but that "it may sometimes occur." He offers no facts in support of this assertion, but only an *a priori* consideration regarding vital fluids. Benedict XIV accepts the same conclusion, but solely upon Brancati's testimony (*loc. cit.,* No. 14). These are not proofs.

**25.**—The two writers just quoted came to deal with this question as follows. They were studying the canonisation of saints. Brancati reminds us that he had been engaged in this study for thirty years. They had, therefore, to explain what part ecstasy played in these processes, and to state, in particular, whether alienation of the bodily senses occurring in a healthy man during prayer should be called a **miraculous fact.** Brancati and Benedict XIV reply that the Church never regards it as such, unless "it is accompanied by certain signs that are above the forces of nature, such as a resplendant countenance, and other similar things" (*loc. cii.*), No. 14). This last exception is intelligible. They said to themselves that high contemplation does not render the body luminous or fragrant, or raise it into the air. From this they have concluded that for these things God's direct intervention, or that of the angels, is required; that we have here a derogation from a physical or physiological law, and, consequently, a miracle.

If these supererogatory characters are wanting to the ecstasy, it is no miracle, and still less is it one that can be directly proved, since the alienation of the senses, the abolition of all sensation, may be produced merely by disease. It might even be said that natural sleep, especially when profound, is the beginning of this state. And this manner of looking at things should *a fortiori* be followed, if we allow (which I have not done) that contemplation can produce this same physiological effect *naturally.* This argument was put forward by the writers already quoted. Brancati concludes from it that "ecstasies should be called marvellous, but not miraculous, occurrences."

But, it will be objected, if the alienation of the senses is not to be classed amongst miracles, is not the interior state, if it has risen to a very high level, at least a miracle? No more than the other, for how is the level to be ascertained? Solely by the ecstatic's own testimony. Now he may have deluded himself, more or less, so that the miracle is not yet sufficiently proved. But another reason actually shows that there is no miracle. This interior state is the result of a grace, of a gift of the Holy Spirit. Now, although these interior graces, destined for our sanctification, require God's direct intervention, the Church has never called them miracles. For she reserves this last title for signs that are perceptible to the senses. And further, these interior graces are an addition to our nature, not a derogation from it. Finally, they are facts which are produced regularly, and many of them are capable of being predicted with certainty when certain conditions, such as the reception of the sacraments, are granted. We have here the characters of a law, one of the higher order, it is true, but still a law. It is the opposite of a miracle, therefore (Cf. Scaramelli, Tr. 3, No. 182).

**26.**—Having been led to speak of ecstasies with reference to beatifications and canonisations, I will add one more word in order to show the exact part attributed to them by the **Sacred Congregation of Rites.**

This Congregation always enters into two questions which it calls *dubia*. First *diibium majus:* Are there heroic virtues in this confessor's cause or a real martyrdom in this martyr's cause? Second *dubium majus:* Have there been two, three, or four miracles since his death? Each must be judicially attested by at least two eye-witnesses.

From what has been said, we see that ecstasy does not fall into the second category. The part it plays is purely indirect. As the servant of God's entire life has to be inquired into, his supernatural gifts must be considered. Now ecstasy forms part of them. But 1° the existence of these gifts cannot directly be the subject of a legal proof (but only moral), since the principal interior agent is invisible. 2° They may be proved *indirectly* if they are accompanied by a fulfilled prophecy, a healing, or other miraculous exterior occurrence. 3° In this case they merely serve to establish the heroic degree of charity, relying upon the fact that God has given an exterior approbation of it, or that He has granted a powerful means of attaining to it. 4° For the most part ecstasies only figure as an objection; for it may be asked whether the alienations of the senses were not merely maladies pointing to an unbalanced temperament. The contrary must be firmly established. And so the causes in which ecstasies were absent are the most easily brought to a successful conclusion.

Many rationalists imagine, on the contrary, that the saints have been canonised only because of their ecstasies.

**27.**—And so much the more, says Benedict XIV, should the examination of **revelations** and **visions** be preceded by that of the virtues, even if these revelations seem to bear the divine stamp. We should act "as though they were purely gratuitous graces," given, that is to say for the good of others and not because of the holiness of their subject. Indeed, these favours "can be proved in no other way than by his word who sees them and to whom the apparition was made; he, therefore, who is to give evidence in his own cause... and [be] believed, ought to be an unexceptionable witness and consequently endowed with heroic virtues... Heroic virtues alone can reveal and clearly show the character of the person, and the subsequent issues of them [visions and apparitions] " (*De Canon.*, Book III, ch. lii, No. 2. Eng, *Heroic Virtue,* Vol. Ill, ch. xiii, p. 348).

## § 4.—The Nature of the Union and of the Vision Of the Mystics

**28.**—Theologians are almost unanimous in affirming that mystic visions of the Divinity are not of the same kind as the **beatific vision**. I am with them in holding this opinion.

From the historic point of view, however, it is interesting to recall the fact that the two celebrated mystic theologians, Philippus a SS. Trinitate and Antonius a Spiritu Sancto, inclined to the opposite system, and it is curious to find that they were not impugned by anyone. According to this theory, the two kinds of vision would differ only in intensity, and therefore in clearness. In heaven there would be a plenitude of light and happiness; here below, the sole difference would be that the light would be faint and the happiness incomplete.**

This is what Philippus a SS. Trinitate says, in effect, when dealing with the whole of the mystic unions together (this last point stands out in Disc. I, Art. I, of the same treatise, and from the classification of *Disc.* III). The writer asks himself this question: How does the mind act during the mystic union? He willingly believes it to be a participation of the beatific vision. "From the point of view of the object of the vision, *we might say* that these divine things are perceived in the *media* of very sublime *species*, representing the object in a very eminent manner; but it would *perhaps he better* (*forte melius did potest*) to admit that the light of the higher order thus communicated to the mind, is a *certain participation of the light of glory;* consequently, it disposes the intellect so that God Himself may unite Himself to it, *after the manner of an intelligible species*, but in a diminished degree (*deficienter*). In this way God is seen in Himself (*in seipso*), but not with the clearness and perfection of the state of glory, either the disposition of the subject, or the restricted power of manifestation and elevation of this light being the cause of a deficiency. The resulting vision is then direct, as is the sight in heaven of God as seen *in Himself*, but it is not so clear; and it is called vision in darkness" (Part

* In the Lille *Revue des sciences ecclésiastiques* (July, 1905) I explained this theory, but without making myself responsible for it. I merely asked that it might be refuted by convincing reasons, and particularly that the arguments upon which it appears to rest might be answered. I do not know that they have been examined.

III, Tr. 1, disc, ii, art. i). Antonius a Spiritu Sancto transcribes this passage while approving of it (but without warning us that he is not its author) (Tr. 4, No. 61)

On the vision of God, see our Extracts elsewhere: Blessed Angela of Foligno (ch. xviii, **75**). St. Catherine of Siena (*ibid.*, **76**), Ven. Marina de Escobar (*ibid.*, **77**, and her vision, ch. v, **38**), Tauler (ch. v, **34** *bis*), St. Alphonsus Rodriguez (ch. xviii, **60**), St. John of the Cross (ch. xviii, **59**), St. Mary Magdalen of Pazzi (*ibid.*, **66**), Mère Suzanne Lévêque (*ibid.*, **63** *bis*), Ven. Anne Madeleine de Rémuzat (ch. xix, **31**).

**28** *bis.*—How is the nature of these visions, and more generally the mystic union, to be **explained?** I will imitate Alvarez de Paz, who does not attempt to explain them. He, however, was placed in exceptionally favourable circumstances, being both an ecstatic and a Professor of Theology. He says that the facts are very certain, but that they surpass our powers of understanding (see ch. xviii, **78**).

As a contemporary writer, however, has tried to prove that "the felt presence" and all experimental* knowledge of God is impossible here below (see ch. v, note), it will be well to give a rapid indication of a manner of conceiving of this presence, and to show its possibility.

Let us suppose that God gives a thought or a feeling (the thought of His presence, for instance). Can He, or can He not, by a supernatural and intellectual mode of sight, make known the *fact* that this action proceeds from Him? I can see no impossibility here. But if we grant that God has this power, it follows that we can have a knowledge of the presence of God that *includes* a perception which puts us into real communication with Him and which is therefore experimental and without reasoning.

Not only does this knowledge contain a perception, but we can admit that it merits this designation throughout. In fact, many Catholic doctors think that knowledge of a law implies knowledge of a law-giver; that we do not then pass from one idea to the other by reasoning: they are two aspects of one and the same idea. So, too, God's action manifested, implies His presence, and we therefore know this presence without reasoning and experimentally.

These few words do not claim to explain all the facts stated by the mystics. I have considered one of them only, that which is the starting-point.

**29.—First objection.** We have just said that the knowledge of God by mystic vision is experimental. But this word seems unsuitable, since God then manifests His nature, not immediately, but by *species.*

**30.—Reply.** The same difficulty might be urged with regard to the material eye. When it contemplates surrounding objects it is not united to them directly. It only enters into relations with them by way of species, and these are of the sensible, that is to say, the inferior order. And yet we say that this knowledge is

* We call that knowledge experimental, which comes from the object and manifests it, not only as possible, biri as existing, operating, in order to make itself known and generally as being present.

experimental. It goes far beyond knowledge which stops at a simple picture of the object.

The mystical vision of God is truly an experimental knowledge.

It is the same as with the interior touch which forms the basis of all the mystic states; it manifests, not the nature of God, like the vision, but His action of a special kind upon the soul.

**31.—Second objection.** When God grants us *species intelligibiles* only, we should not say that we see Him. We ought to reserve this expression for the beatific vision.

**32.**—Reply. If you are afraid of a confusion, add a qualifying adjective; say: *mystic vision.*

But there is no serious reason for forbidding the words: *see* and *vision.* The saints have always used them to describe the sublime, divine communications that they have received. They do not say: I see an image of God, but: I see God. The Church has never molested them; we need not be more severe.

And then such an argument would necessitate many other changes in language. We could no longer say: I see a tree, because it is not known in the depths of its nature, but only by certain qualities, made known to us by *species.* In the same way we should have to give up saying that in Heaven the angels are seen one by another and by the souls of the elect. For these spirits receive *species* only.

### § 5.—Causes of the Alienation of the Senses And Of the Ligature

**33.**—This problem may be profitably studied both as regards the prayer of quiet and ecstasy. Let us begin with the last-named case; the phenomena are more sharply defined here.

In ecstasy it has always been admitted that the alienation of the senses is a consequence of the **concentration of the faculties** upon their object. It would result either from the force of the person's attention to an idea or image, or from the vehemence of his love.

In order to prove this, we argue from an analogy with distractions. When the mind or the heart are deeply engrossed, a number of sensations seem unable to penetrate to the soul. It is the alienation of the senses in a lesser degree. If, further, the object of thought imposes itself upon us against our will, we find it difficult even to think of anything else; which is very like the ligature. We can imagine, then, that when God exercises upon the thoughts an action a thousand times more intense, a domination over the soul a thousandfold stronger, the effect upon the body and the play of the faculties would be *more striking*, so much so even that the sensibility might *perhaps* (it is prudent to introduce a *perhaps*) be reduced to zero, like the free passage of ideas.

This explanation can be summed up in a sentence. Ecstasy is regarded as a stronger distraction. When this is set forth in detail, as I have just done, we see more clearly the hypothetical element that it contains.

**34.**—While admitting the preceding cause, we may ask ourselves whether it is the only one.

I think I can prove that there is another, although we are completely ignorant of its nature, and that this **other cause** plays the principal part.

In fact, in the prayer of quiet, we again find phenomena of the same kind as in ecstasy, although in a lesser degree. There is an action of the mystic state upon the body and a ligature of the powers. Now it is evident that the cause given above no longer explains anything in the case of the prayer of quiet, for it is absent. The attention, far from being strong, is incessantly thwarted by distractions; and in the same way the love is usually calm. It is vain to object that during the distractions the soul continues to have a certain knowledge which is real although she is unconscious of it.** Apart from such a statement being purely hypothetical, the reasoning is not conclusive. For it would be necessary to prove that this knowledge produces a *very strong* attention, notably greater than that experienced in reading a very interesting book. And there is no sort of proof that this is so; nay more, it is not possible to imagine that the knowledge which is present so strongly should not resist wandering thoughts and should not become conscious.

The physiognomy of the prayer of quiet shows also that it differs greatly from the state of the absent-minded man. If this latter does not produce certain acts, it is that he does not think of them. Recall his attention, and he will make them immediately. The contemplative, on the contrary, thinks of these acts and feels powerless to carry them out. We have here all the difference between an absent-minded rnan and one who is powerless to act.

There is an unknown cause, therefore, that paralyses the man in the prayer of quiet. Analogy obliges us to admit that this cause exists and becomes stronger in ecstasy. And since it dispenses with all other aids in the prayer of quiet, we may with probability conclude that it could also dispense with them in ecstasy; which resolves itself into saying that it probably takes the principal part there.

* Authors often express this idea by saying: During the distractions, the soul produces *direct* acts. They contrast this word with conscious, *deliberate* acts. We produce them daily, but in the material order. For example, we engage "mechanically" in some exterior work, thinking of some other object, that is to say, so thoroughly that afterwards we do not even remember whether we completed it. It was only in the *direct* state that we were aware of it. And the same with the recitation of vocal prayers. In a word, we can associate ideas or images, and co-ordinate acts for a predetermined object, while thinking exclusively of something else. It is a case of automatic action, but not purely that of the mechanical apparatus; it is directed by a sensibility which takes the place of the absent attention.

This signification is the most usual. It is used notably by Bossuet (*États d'Oraison*, Book V, 20-1; and by Lopez de Ezquerra (*Lucerna*, Tr. II, ch. ix, No. 79).

Certain modern treatises on mysticism give also to the term, *direct acts*, another sense which is often not consistent with the first, and which may thus lead to confusion. They contrast it with *discursive acts*, with reasoning. It thus becomes the synonym of *intuitive* acts. Now the words *unconscious* and *intuitive* are far from being equivalents. For we can reason without being aware of it, and then we perform an unconscious act which is not intuitive; and inversely we may voluntarily think of some first principle, and then we make an intuitive act which is not unconscious. In order to avoid misunderstanding I have never made use of the term *direct acts*.

If authors have not thought of this cause, it is because they always study the case of ecstasy and never that of its lesser forms, which is the only one that solves the problem.

It is disagreeable thus to find ourselves confronted with an unexplained phenomenon. It hurts our self-love to admit our ignorance. We must learn, however, to resign ourselves to it. The greatest modern scientific men have set us the example. They have not been ashamed to say: I do not know. Let us not imitate the old natural philosophers, including those of the seventeenth century, who in the face of all phenomena had their explanation ready, at times a childish one.* St. Teresa displays a candour which it is good to imitate. Speaking of the ligature in the states below ecstasy, she says: "As I said, I do not know why, but as a general rule they are unable to do so" [meditate on the Passion] (*Interior Castle*, Sixth Mansion, eh. vii, 14).

**35.**—Writers often try to explain why it is that **ecstasies** become **rarer** when the soul has arrived at the transforming union. They have never given any satisfactory reasons. And this was to be expected: this problem is closely connected with the one just dealt with; the two phenomena depend upon the action of one and the same cause, which remains unknown. As I have just said, we do not rightly know why the mystic state produces alienation of the senses in certain cases; consequently we do not know why in other cases it does not produce it. In the same way if I did not know what makes a watch go, neither should I know why it stops or why it loses.

**36.—Another problem.** We have seen that the mystic union tends to produce immobility both of *body* and of *mind*, simultaneously. Since these two actions bear such a resemblance one to the other, may they not both be attributed to a *single* (although unknown) *cause?*

Certainly. I begin by saying that the thing is *possible*. It may be that the mystic union acts directly on the body only. And then, if it renders the mind inactive, it would be solely by rendering certain of our organs inactive. It is in this way that various beverages or drugs benumb or excite our faculties.

But if it is *possible* that the two phenomena should be produced by one cause, there is a certain probability that God has ordered things thus, for He does not multiply causes without necessity.

### §6.—Discussion Regarding the Two Nights Of St. John of the Cross

**37.**—In chapter xv, I think I have proved that the first night described by the saint is a latent prayer of quiet, having merely the appearances of a (usually arid)

* Descartes himself, who aimed at a reform in scientific methods, was unable to free himself from these deplorable habits. His admirers are too apt to conceal this fantastic side of his theories. See my article on *La physique de Descartes*, in the Review *Les Études* of September, 1892.

prayer of simplicity; and that the second night is composed of all the mystic states, properly so called, that are below the spiritual marriage.

Other authors have understood the saint in various ways differing from mine. It is well to examine these ways: they all suffer from one disadvantage: they explain certain clear passages and leave out others which would prove embarrassing.

Let us begin with **Fr. Berthier.** His analysis was published in 1790 under the form of eleven letters addressed to the Marquise de Créqui. "His interpretation is rather long (it has been said to me), but much easier to understand than yours. He must have been right, for they reprint his explanations as a preface to several French translations of St. John of the Cross's *Works.* And further, those who wish to expound the saint's doctrine, usually do so by summing up Fr. Berthier's analysis. Now the attractive feature in his explanation is that there is no longer any mystery left."

**38.—Reply.** I admit that there is no mystery left; but perhaps rather more is wanted. Yes, it is simple; a little too much so, it seems to me. I am certainly an ardent partisan of simplicity, but on condition that it should be in conformity with truth. If someone came and said to me: "I have a theory on electricity, quite the simplest possible," I should mistrust it; it would be too fine a programme.

Fr. Berthier is very pious and his instructions are excellent; we must not forget this. But, unlikely as it may seem, he has seen one thing only in these mystic books: *asceticism.* He develops its precepts at length and in the conviction that he has great secrets to teach us. These secrets resolve themselves into this, that pride and sensuality must be resisted. The saint would have been much astonished at finding that he was to receive so much gratitude for these ordinary truths. *If St. John of the Cross had not said a word about mysticism, Fr. Berthier's account of him could remain exactly the same.**

He is therefore incomplete. He regards the book from one very restricted point of view only, that of asceticism. *And it is just the chief point that he omits.* In this way all the mystery, all the difficulty disappear. He may have explained this omission to himself, and then no blame attaches to him. Perhaps he only wished to write an adaptation for the use of persons in the world?

To convince the reader of the truth of my contention without being obliged to compare Fr. Bertier's exposition with the whole work, it is only necessary to call to mind one evident fact, namely, that according to St. John of the Cross the two nights are two kinds of contemplation. Now Fr. Berthier *does not tell us what each of these is, from this point of view, and in what they differ one from the other.* He was free to speak of the remainder only, and he does it very well. But let it not be claimed that he gives the key to this mysterious book. He brings the saint within

* He speaks, however, of tending towards the "divine union." But we see that he does not understand this expression in the mystical sense. To him it is simply a virtue, "conformity to the divine will" (*Letter* 10).

the reach of all Christians, but it is by bringing him down to their level. It was the only way that it could be done.

And the question that must be put to anyone who wishes to explain St. John of the Cross too simply, is this: "In what way are his two nights not merely trials, but contemplations?" Do not hope to have a clear reply.

**39.**—And still more, Fr. Berthier has not seen that, in this book, asceticism takes on **a very special character** that is not found in Fr. Rodriguez and other classical treatises on the virtues. St. John of the Cross is not speaking, like these writers, to all pious Christians, but to a special class, those who aspire to the mystic union or who have already entered into it. And *he draws his arguments* not from the current truths of Christianity, but precisely from this union after which his readers are seeking.

For example, the ascetic writers hardly think of putting anyone on his guard against the abuse of objects of piety. But were they to do so, this is the argument that they would employ: "We must make use of these images because they serve to arouse in us the love of God and of the saints. But it would be an exaggeration to see in them the sole, or the chief, means of attaining to that love."

St. John of the Cross addresses himself to a more limited audience and gives a more special motive. We may sum up his counsels thus (see *Ascent of Mount Carmel*, Book III, ch. xiv, xxxiv). "Do not despise this means, to do so would be contrary to the spirit of the Church; but know that it is not a *proximate* means of arriving at the mystic union which you desire. Do not give it a greater importance than it merits."

Here are two very different arguments. The second alone gives a mystic colouring to an ascetic counsel.

So, too, if an ascetic writer were speaking of sensible devotion (that obtained by the aid of the sensible faculties), he would simply require that we should not be unduly attached to it. St. John of the Cross goes to the length of rejecting it altogether, for certain persons and at certain times. The first would give as a reason that this great attachment is an imperfection. The second says that this kind of devotion is not easily present at the same time with the mystic union, the only thing that he is concerned with, and that we must, when necessary, make it give way to the higher state.

Finally, if we make a general survey of the saint's work, we see that all the *active* part, the asceticism, that is to say, is linked to the *passive* part, and this again to the final goal, the spiritual marriage. It no longer resembles Rodriguez.

**40.**—This partly explains a **defect** with which St. John of the Cross has been reproached, namely, his obscurity. And the explanation is all in his favour. In his books the asceticism, such an easy thing to understand, is perpetually mingled with and linked on to another, which is very difficult: mysticism.

**41.—Another incomplete summing up** of the matter consists in saying: The First Night of St. John of the Cross subjects the senses to the intellect, the second subjects the intellect to God.

**42.—Reply.**—You are at liberty to think of the purgative life as being thus divided into two periods; although I am at a loss to understand how one can achieve the first conquest, in a supernatural way, without the second. But do not say that this represents *the whole* of St. John's teaching. The proof to the contrary is that this formula suits *all Christians.* All can understand and practise it. But the saint is only addressing a particular class (*Prologue, Ascent of Mount Carmel*).

It is true that he has himself made use of this formula, although very rarely. But the context restricts its meaning. For 1° he credits this double labour with *a special aim.* This is not only our salvation, nor even virtue, but the mystic union, and the most exalted part, "the summit of Carmel." 2° *As to the means*, he speaks above all of prayer and the very special manner in which the faculties should operate in it. Who would suspect all this in reading the formula given above? It is too simple, too general.

**43.—It would be** still more **incorrect** to say that the two nights are purifications, one active, the other passive. The saint expressly says the contrary. The second is only *more manifestly* passive than the first. Both belong to the purgative way, and both also to the unitive way.

Neither must we say: The two nights are simply two kinds of sufferings; the first made up of aridity, darkness, and coldness; the second by such or such a more painful ordeal.

I reply that these things are certainly present, but with something more, a certain contemplation to which the saint refers incessantly and as the chief element. You omit to speak of it. Do so, and if you believe that this contemplation is not mystical, try to define it.

**44.—A wrong point of departure.** To sum up, when we read St. John of the Cross, all the classical divisions of other writers, all the moulds into which they have cast their ideas, present themselves to our minds; and, whether we will or no, we try to fit the saint's ideas into them. It is time thrown away. He has his own mould. We must resign ourselves to it.

**45.—Example.** All the ascetic writers speak of the three ways, the purgative, the illuminative and the unitive, and they make them correspond, approximately, at all events, to the terms: way of beginners, of proficients and of the perfect. Some allow mysticism to play no part here; others, at the most, place it at the end of the third way only. The saint also employs these six terms, but giving them a meaning peculiar to himself. He looks at matters from the special point of view of mysticism and places it in the second and the third way (*Spiritual Canticle*, the argument preceding Stanza I, and Stanza XXII, line I). The illuminative way, that of Proficients, begins with him at the cessation of meditation (Stanza V) and ends before the raptures of the spiritual espousals (Stanza XIII).

He had already said elsewhere: "Souls enter this Obscure Night, when God is drawing them out of the state of *Beginners,* which is that of those who *meditate* in the spiritual way, and is leading them into that of *Proficients,* the state *of Contemplatives*" (*Obscure Night*, Book I, ch. i, p. 327). "The way of the spirit, the way of *proficients*, which is *also called the Illuminative Way*, or the way of *infused contemplation*" (*Obscure Night*, Book I, ch. xiv, p. 370).

Certainly this language is very different from that of other spiritual writers.

§ 7.—THE SCEPTICS CONFRONTED WITH THE MYSTICS

**46.**—Catholic mystics affirm that they receive purely intellectual perceptions and communications. For instance, in the mystic union, they are convinced that they enter into communication with God, really and without images; and in certain higher degrees they say that the Blessed Trinity is revealed to them without any admixture of material representations; they perceive the special relations of the three Divine Persons amongst Themselves.

The question has often been discussed; what is the value of this belief of the mystics? is it not a simple illusion on their part? This question divides itself again naturally into two others. How are they certain of the **objectivity** of this intellectual knowledge? and how can they make us share their certainty?

In the first place, they are certain; just as I am certain of having a book before my eyes. You may explain, as you like, by learned arguments, that I take as objective, a phenomenon which is only subjective; you will not succeed in convincing me.

If we go on to inquire how the mystics can convey a participation in their certainty to the uninitiated, I reply that they will be successful only with persons of good-will, those who are without prejudices, those who do not *a priori* deny the supernatural or one of its kinds. I admit that with free-thinkers there is no decisive means of convincing them.* Certain Catholics are actually in the same case. They take advantage of the circumstance that the Church imposes no obligation on this point; for the fact of revelation does not necessarily imply that the prophets' visions were intellectual; and I am speaking here of these visions alone.

Let us not be scandalised by this inability to convince. We can imagine a quite similar fact in daily life. We all admit that red is distinct from blue; and this because it is a matter of daily experience.

But let us suppose that a blind man should come and argue that it is an illusion; that this difference has no objective foundation. We reply that he is a bad judge of the question, and that we possess a sense of which he is deprived. "But (he will answer), it is just here that you make your mistake; it is the result of preconceived

* Professor William James recognises that free-thinkers, in their turn, have no arguments capable of confuting the mystics: " The [rationalist's] denials have no strength... It must always remain an open question whether mystical states may not possibly be... windows through which the mind looks out upon a more extensive and inclusive world... Mystical states, indeed, wield no authority due simply to their being mystical states. But the higher among them... offer us hypotheses, which we may voluntarily ignore, but which as thinkers we cannot possibly upset " ( *Varieties of Religious Experience,* Lect. XVII, p. 428).

ideas." We then call numerous witnesses: If he rejects them, we have no further unanswerable arguments to offer. For only one such can exist; namely, to communicate to him our impressions of red and blue, so that he may prove their differences for himself. This participation cannot be realised.

This simile may be given slightly differently, as follows. If the blind believe without any discussion what the sighted tell them with regard to light, colours and the visual faculty, it is because they form a very small minority in the world, and that before such a wealth of witnesses they feel that it would be senseless to deny it. But let us suppose that the proportions were reversed, and that the sighted were a small exception. The blind would generally refuse to believe them, and would invent various theories to explain what they would describe as their illusion. The discussion would never be closed.

It is the same if people dispute a fact that our memory certifies to us with extreme clearness. Our intuition is incommunicable. We can do one thing only: declare energetically that we are sure that it occurred; and the debate will be ended; each party will maintain his own position.

The great mystics are equally certain of their intuitions, but they cannot prove their objectivity. They do not even think of attempting it. They offer, not demonstrations, but accounts of their experiences. From the moment that the sceptics refuse to accept these testimonies, however numerous these may be, there is no way of arriving at a definite understanding.

Only we must note that this negation is not scientific. In any science where observations are recorded, we must trust to the numerous and concordant statements of those who make the experiments. It would be unreasonable to reject such an assemblage of evidence.

**47.**—With regard to **revelations** and imaginative visions, I will not deny that illusions may exist (see ch. xxi). But there are also cases where the mystic is absolutely certain of the reality of the phenomenon. Rationalists cannot allow this. They usually have recourse to the explanation by the **subconscious,** by the power, that is to say, which our faculties possess of working, without our being aware of it, upon data already in their possession.* It is the system now in vogue. But if this explanation is to be really scientific, an exact definition of the limits of the subconscious must first have been given, instead of bringing it forward, without any proof, as an unlimited power.† Everything is thus unerringly explained in accordance with their wishes. When a super-normal fact of

* The depository of the memory is another department of the unconscious (*inconscient*). It is static; the subconscious is dynamic; it co-ordinates and perhaps matures, elaborates the ideas, images, and feelings.

† M. Emile Boutroux recognises this: "The state of consciousness is composed of a focus and a margin, the perihelion of which is more or less fluctuating and undefined. Now this is what we learn (?), that this margin is itself connected continuously with a third region, which, unsuspected by our consciousness, and even obscure, *cannot in any degree be measured by us with regard to its scope and depth* " (*Revue de métaphysique et de morate*, January, 1907, p. 16).

psychology presents itself, the ignorant person feels no shadow of perplexity; he attributes it to the little subterranean workshop of the mind, and the thing is done. We can understand that with this very simple mode of procedure, the supernatural can be eliminated without difficulty. Such persons affirm without any proof that all religious sentiment and religious life are merely a development of human activity. St. Paul's revelations and those of the Bible prophets and the saints are attributed to eruptions of the subconscious. This is indeed a fruitful theory!

**48.**—If we are unable to achieve the victory of changing the sceptics' opinions, there is one point at least that we may require of them, namely, that they should have the honesty to quote the **mystic writings** as they are, instead of whittling them down, and changing them in order to make them more easy of explanation. Too great liberties have often been taken in this respect.

M. Darlu had the courage to complain of this at a meeting of the *Société française de philosophie*, at which twenty-five professors of the Sorbonne or the University were present. The entire meeting was occupied with *the development of the mystic states in St. Teresa*; the report filled the Society's *Bulletin* (January, 1906, Paris, Colin). "One of the uninitiated in these matters (said M. Darlu) may give his impressions. The history of mysticism is of the greatest interest; apart from the fact that it forms a notable portion of the history of thought, it makes us reflect upon our inner aspirations, or it may be upon our spiritual poverty. But this is on condition *of its being history*, of recording *impartially* what the mystics think, what they experience, or believe that they experience. The psychology of mysticism, on the contrary, substitutes itself for mysticism proper, it analyses, it claims to modify the interior states that it attests, classifying them under one or other of its own compartments. It is *brief*, it is *superficial* it is liable, from the bias of its methods, to *distort*, even to *debase* what it pretends to explain " (p. 41).

At the same meeting (p. 19), a letter was read from M. Blondel, drawing the attention of one of the readers of papers at the Conference (M. Delacroix) to the circumstance that he did not make a sufficient distinction between facts and his explanations of them, and that the explanations reacted in an adverse manner upon his descriptions of facts. "I am afraid," he said, "that in the essay which you submit to us today, a tacit or barely indicated postulate is implied, but one that is none the less liable to injure your method and to reverse several of your conclusions. You study the mystic phenomena indeed, as being *in* the person concerned (which is the indispensable condition of all positive research), but you study it also as being *of* the subject only, and we have here, under colour of scientific reserve, a foregone conclusion of the metaphysical order *which reacts upon your interpretation and even upon your description of the facts...* In the domain of the sensible faculties, do not perception and hallucination, although identical in many respects as far as consciousness goes, do they not, however, differ—I do not say here, in their real origin, but even from the point of view of phenomena? Should I for this reason ask you to set out from the hypothesis of a *divine action* upon souls, to admit a fostering *perception* and a dynamical sensation, so to speak, of this mysteriously afferent reality? In no wise. I merely ask you not to exclude implicitly by your systematic way of putting the problem and of *describing* the mystic states, a hypothesis which does not fit in with your methods. For you seem to exclude it... by *altering the nature and import of the facts*... By the manner in which you expound this succession of states [those of St. Teresa] you *imply that a solution* has been arrived at with regard to the actual question of their origin, and you reduce them, as hallucinations, to mere nervous diseases, mere efference without afference. And I say plainly, that your description of the facts themselves is thereby distorted. If I draw your attention, somewhat insistently, to a tendency that seems to me to make itself apparent in several of your expressions, you will pardon me, believing that it is a question here not only of the *method* that should be applied to the philosophic study of mysticism, but even, we must say it, of *all* religious philosophy... If we wish to avoid distorting facts, they must first be described without pronouncing even indirectly upon their deep-seated cause.*

To sum up, if the mystics cannot succeed in getting their testimony as to the objectivity of their intellectual knowledge accepted as true, we may at least require that people should no longer feign to ignore their formal declarations on this subject. I would point out that, at the meeting of which I have just spoken, certain members have at least recognised the existence of this conviction. Thus M. E. Boutroux, when endeavouring to sum up St. Teresa's teaching, said: "From this action of God within us, there results a supernatural knowledge that is obtained by way of intellectual intuition. St. Teresa has, with great clearness, the idea of a *perception* which is not that of the senses, one of which the senses are not capable and which is given to the *intellect alone*... Her doctrine is a mysticism which passes through contemplation in order to arrive at action, one in which the aim of contemplation is to put the soul *into possession* of the interior and divine cause by which her action will be made creative and all-powerful" (p. 17).

M. Lalande (p. 32) also quotes the testimony of the mystics, and shows whither the refusal to admit it leads. "We may make two hypotheses (he says) regarding the states in question. Either, *as the mystics claim to be the case*, it is a question of normal although rare states. These consist in the *experience of a reality* to which we do not habitually attain, *but which exists independently of them;* which they do not create, which can be known just in the same way by different minds. And *the perception of this reality* is an advantage, a power in practical life, as an extra sense would be... Or, they are sick people, sufferers from hallucinations, evolving everything *from their own centres*, and there is nothing real about their

* The writer of the paper naturally denied that he distorted any facts. He added that "the exclusion of transcendency," that is to say of objectivity, is for him "not a postulate, but a method" of explanation. This simply consists in affirming that the mystics are mistaken in "believing that they are subjected to any action."

experiences. What they believe themselves to perceive is merely a more or less copious invention of their own mind, like that which is created by an artist's imagination or the delirium of the insane."*

M. Belot, of whom I shall speak shortly, also states that "the mystics think and claim that they *make experience* of God, that they have a direct and interior contact with Him" (p. 37).

Finally, M. Lovel is of the same opinion: "I should like (he says) to call the Society's attention to a very large question that mysticism raises. I ask myself whether everything can be explained by psychological illusions, and if we ought not to *leave the door open* to metaphysical hypotheses, allowing us to attribute an *objective reality* to the cause of mystical *perceptions*... There might be something exterior that would set the sensibility of the mystics into motion; they have *no doubt* as to the reality of this exterior something and *their testimony should not be rejected without grave reasons*" (p. 26).

**49.**—During the meeting already referred to, M. Belot put another question which relates not to the existence of an object perceived by the mystics, but to **its precise nature.** They are sure "that they make experience of God." "By what right," the speaker asked, "is this God, or rather this confused, vague, inexpressible reality, the presence of which the mystics feel within them, by what right can this Being be, and, as a matter of fact, is He identified with one or other of the pre-existing conceptions of the divinity?" How, to be exact, do contemplative Catholics know that it is the God of the Christian tradition and not that of the Buddhists, or Pantheists, or one of those deities of whom various philosophers have dreamed? The speaker adds: "This is a problem which imposes itself from the first upon the student of mysticism, and which, although entirely positive, yet goes beyond a simple psychological description of the mystic states.† I have always been astonished at the facility with which mystics convince themselves that their ecstasies have God for their object, their contents or their cause,‡ and also at the complaisance with which observers and the least mystical analysers of mysticism let this affirmation pass without asking themselves what it really can mean, nor *on what, it is,* in fact, *founded* " (p. 37).

I think that M. Belot slightly exaggerates "the complaisance" of the sceptics. If they do not ask, as he does, the how of certain mysterious facts, it is because they prefer to deny them *a priori.* But let us return to the chief point of the problem. The question is on what the conviction, not of the public but of the mystics themselves, is based.

* The speaker goes on to refute this second hypothesis.

† It goes beyond simple description, because it seeks to find the *how.*

‡ The astonishment thus experienced is of the same kind as that of the blind man who should be surprised "at the facility with which the sighted convince themselves" that there is a difference between red and blue.

Let us first note that even in the natural order a similar very difficult problem exists, one which has greatly exercised the minds of philosophers; it is that of the origin of ideas. When we descend from general theories to detailed ideas and beliefs, it is in no wise easy to analyse their formation sufficiently to enable us to assign the exact part played by their diverse causes: intellectual intuitions, the mould of personal temperament, early education, the definite teachings received when of ripe years, the insensible influence due to surroundings, etc. Therefore if Catholic mystics were without an answer to the *how* put to them here, they would be in the same case as their neighbours.

But they have a reply, which is very clear in the case of ecstasy. They are already provided with a very definite *credo;* they know their catechism. But in the brilliant light by which they are inundated, they declare that they *recognise* the Sovereign Being of which this familiar work has spoken. To take one example only, they at times behold the Blessed Trinity. This does not consist, as M. Murisier very simply supposed, " in seeing three persons sculptured in a block of marble " (*Maladies du sentiment religieux*, ch. i, § 4, p. 62). Were it thus, they would have learned nothing new. They would have proved that God, or rather His image, is Three and One. But this is given at full length in the catechism. The ecstatic claims to go still further; at times he sees the mutual relations of the Three Divine Persons; he sees that the Word is the expression of the Father's thought and that the Holy Spirit is the expression of their mutual love.* They recognise clearly Him of whom they have been already told.

In the states below ecstasy, it must be admitted that the distinctness of the intellectual communications is less; there are hesitations, and these are the greater as the state is less elevated. Mystics are quite able to observe and describe this difficulty, but they rely upon the little light that still reaches them, and on the arguments that exclude every other cause except the action of the One true God; and finally on the traditional teaching, confirmed by their directors.

In his last sentence, M. Belot pointed out that amongst mystics and many of their readers, he finds a readiness to believe that astonishes him; they unhesitatingly admit the existence of the supernatural, and, in particular, of the supernatural as the Catholic religion conceives it. It is true that our theologians bring this last belief, which they regard as certain, into the woof of their definitions and explanations. But their case is quite different from the other. To begin with, they do not engage in a purely philosophic study or in polemics with the philosophers, for they would then have to set out from purely psychological or rationalist *data*. They address themselves to believers, to souls favoured with these graces and to their directors, and they utilise all the beliefs held by this class of reader. If they wrote for sceptics, their way of writing would be very different. Instead of saying, for instance: such a state is supernatural, they would make this

* Each one says it in his own way, but they say the same thing.

slight change, and say: such a state is believed to be a supernatural one by the mystic; and in this way their explanations could not be charged with implying a postulate. Sceptics may make this small modification of our definitions for themselves. And further, by writing in this fashion, theologians are only exactly reproducing the writings of the mystics; they speak their language; while there is a tendency to alter the documents when setting out from the opposite postulate.

These two reasons justify the method hitherto employed in all mystic treatises written by Catholics.

# CHAPTER XXXII

## Two Historical Monographs

### § 1.—A Protestant "Revival" With Mystic Tendencies

**1.** —Everyone has heard of those periods of religious exaltation observed from time to time, especially in America and England, and called *Revivals.* These occurrences show remarkable intensity in Wales; they reappear there at intervals of a few years. The two last revivals took place in 1859, lasting for three years, and in the winter of 1904-5. The more recent one has been carefully studied by several writers, notably by M. Henri Bois, Professor of Theology at the Protestant Faculty of Montauban.*

Following the documents, I purpose solely to describe the facts, without putting forward any theory. In the case of phenomena so complex and so little studied hitherto by psychologists, it would be very difficult to distinguish between the parts played by God and by human dispositions.

The **facts** are as follows. In 1904 a need for conversion passed over Wales. Laymen, men or girls, felt themselves inflamed with holy zeal to preach a return to God, and arranged meetings in the chapels, paying no attention to their sectarian differences. The Protestant ministers lent their buildings, likewise without regard to the creed of their congregations. Their particular role was a very small one. It did not even consist in presiding over the meeting. That was arranged for as might seem best. At most the pastor said a few words of welcome.

These meetings were attended almost entirely by the populace: shop-keepers, artisans, agricultural labourers. The rich and intellectual classes hardly appeared at them. In the northern districts, where English is the spoken language, their success was likewise small.

* *Le Réveil au pays de Galles,* Toulouse, 28, rue des Salenques, 8vo, 615 pp., 1906. The quotations are taken from this book.

Four kinds of exercises took place at these meetings, which were sometimes held every day; but without any previously arranged programme, and in any order: addresses, improvised prayer, hymns, "testimony."

1. The *addresses* had only a secondary place. The promoter of the meeting, even were it a girl or an artisan, mounted the pulpit. The address was an improvised one and its subject very restricted. There was no dogma. The preacher spoke with emotion of the necessity of forsaking sin, resisting the evil one, giving oneself up to Jesus for ever. The motives were drawn solely from the love which Jesus showed for us on Calvary. The other details of His life were passed over (a surprising fact). Hell was never spoken of. From time to time the speaker read a few verses from the Bible. But if the emotion reached a high level, those present replied with words of approval, or even familiarly cut short the discourse, beginning to sing hymns or to pray aloud.

2. This kind of *prayer* was greatly esteemed. It was always extempore, although generally based on reminiscences of the Bible or of hymns. They prayed for the conversion of sinners or gave thanks for their conversion. The first to feel the inspiration, even tiny girls of five or six, expressed their feelings thus without any constraint, and sometimes at a length that wearied the ordinary listener. Often others began to pray aloud, without attention to those who had already begun.

3. But the favourite exercise was the singing of *hymns*. The Welsh are a poetic and musical race. They know by heart about a thousand hymns in their own tongue; they sing them perfectly in part-time. Generally both words and music are the production of some artisan, and are of great beauty. Suddenly a bystander intoned one of these compositions. Sometimes the meeting joined in; sometimes another bystander began a different hymn, on another note; then each would continue without attending to the other; while a third would begin to pray in a loud voice. These exercises were so attractive to the Welsh that they sometimes prolonged them in the evening for eight or nine hours, that is, till 4 or 5 a.m.

At some moments the excitement would pass all bounds. When these great meetings were praying and singing thus, it was like "the voice of an ocean rising, always rising, its waves breaking, veritable ground-seas, up to the throne of God, in which a thousand human beings gave themselves wholly, body and soul, to agonised prayer for the conversion of sinners." The promoter himself could not overcome his emotion. He collapsed in the pulpit, crying: "Save, great Jesus, save!"

Sometimes this enthusiasm had its drawbacks in relation to the furniture of the chapels where the crowds gathered. One pastor closed his, because in two months sixty pounds' worth of damage had been done—without any bad intention, be it understood.

There is in this a fervour and power of prayer which we cannot but praise. Miners, on ending their day's work, rushed home, washed their grimy skin, put on their best clothes and hastened to the meeting.

4. *Testimony* is an exercise often renewed when the meeting is enkindled. The promoter gives an inventory of those who are really saved, more or less as in the Salvation Army. He asks all those who have given themselves to Jesus to stand up. Often there are some who hesitate: then the whole meeting fervently prays for them. Their neighbours exhort and implore them to be converted. As soon as their consent is obtained, it is proclaimed, and those present enthusiastically intone the refrain *Diolch iddo* (Thanks be to God). Then the siege of those who have resisted is begun again; and so on. Sometimes the leader declares that the sitting is over, but the audience does not listen and begins hymnsinging afresh.

2.—Among the impressionable and emotional Welsh we observe a phenomenon requiring special mention, which they call **the hwyl.*** When it comes about in its characteristic manner, he who is praying aloud or preaching becomes more and more excited and at last suddenly loses consciousness for several minutes, but continues to pray or preach. It is a kind of somnambulistic attack.† On coming to himself he remembers nothing. The voice has changed. It is a kind of improvised cantilena very like plain-chant. It is in the minor mode, and uses only three or four notes. Words and gestures often become rhythmic, and tears fall. The bystanders claim that this state proceeds from the action of the Holy Ghost.

M. Henri Bois adds a few detailed remarks. He has observed a revivalist who "at the end of each phrase of the hwyl, had a kind of sob closely resembling the nervous, hysterical sob." In the case of others "the fists closed, contracted, giving the appearance of a boxer; or the fist is thrown backward and forward, regularly and untiringly, as in the movement of a miner attacking the rock with his pick; or,

* This word means *sail*, more especially "a sail blown out by the breeze." The Welsh word *awel* (breeze) is sometimes used in the same sense.

† In the Revival of 1859, "physical manifestations were much more marked. The people frequently fell into delirium, giving vent to their emotion by leaping and crying Hosanna! alleluia! In hundreds of places the onlookers were carried outside the chapels, unable to move hand or foot."

In Wales glossolalia (the gift of tongues) has not been observed. The contrary is true of a revival of great force which spread from Christiania over Norway, 1907. The leader of the movement was a Methodist pastor named Barrat, who had received the gift on a voyage to America. He spoke eight different tongues which he did not himself understand. There is reason to believe that, as in similar cases (particularly that of Edward Irving, about 1830), these are but pseudo-tongues, imitated words which like music simply translate the emotional tempest by which the subject is shaken. (See *Archives de psychologie*, Geneva, July 1907, pp. 1 and 40.)

In 1907 there were also revivals with glossolalia in London, Calcutta and Tibet. Nervous agitation played a great part in that of Los Angeles. (See the review *Notre petite jeuille*, published at Rivaz in the Canton of Vaud, July and October 1907.)

It was the same with the revival at Cassel (Prussia, 1908), which has been described by Pastor Schrenck (*Die Casseler Bewegung*, Cassel, Rottger). He condemns the tumult which arose and proves that the unknown tongues which were spoken were mere sounds without meaning.—The *Gazette de Cassel* relates that in this town the police had the hall closed, because of the convulsive scenes and bizarre dances which took place there. But in the surrounding villages all went on as before.

On all sides Protestants are praying for a Revival throughout the world. At Geneva cards are published with the invocation: "O God, send a Revival and begin it in me for the love of Jesus."

if there is a table or a bench near, the hand is raised, and, as it falls again, gives two or three blows each time... or again, the body rises and falls on the toes in cadence; or the movement takes place not upwards and downwards, but to right and left... the varieties are many." When the speaker has finished his address, he often rests from his emotion by hiding his face for some time in his hands or his handkerchief.

"The Welsh hwyl is not confined to the religious field... It is no rare thing to hear it during the speeches at political meetings. It is thus one of the methods common to the temper and manners of the Welsh of giving vent to intense emotion." It is the same, it seems, with the Scottish Highlanders in their prayers. "It follows that we must neither condemn nor overvalue the hwyl. What is due to the action of the Holy Ghost is the emotion itself. The hwyl is only a quite accidental translation of it." It is partly the result of the poetical and musical aptitudes of the Welsh. They are a race which still possesses its bards and where the very labourers play the harp.

It would seem that meetings so long and turbulent would be fatiguing. We are assured that this is not so, if they are not too frequent. "Tiredness and hunger are forgotten." The hearers leave them "joyous, calm, cheerful, beaming. Joy is not tiring."

It is a strange fact that the promoters themselves never fall into the hwyl. Outside the meetings they are even "a little mournful and dull," without conversation. This is no doubt the result of the fatigue brought on by the numerous meetings. They need the stimulus of an excited crowd.

**3.**—We have now to ask whether these exercises have **good results** from the religious, moral and social points of view. Several Protestant writers or English-speaking observers have contested it.* But many judge these matters from a distance, without obtaining serious information. They gained a bad impression in advance from the excessive manifestations of piety which they might with more indulgence have attributed to the Welsh temperament, so different from that of the phlegmatic Englishman. Then some pastors themselves could not conceive meetings from which almost all doctrinal element was lacking, giving free play to the feelings. They called it "an emotional debauch." Others, on the other hand, strove to observe more closely the normal results and found them good. They were so at first, while the Revival was actually in progress. Many drunkards and gamblers gave up their vices, to the great despair of the publicans, who lost the greater part of their customers. The miners who drank half their wages brought the whole home to their families, and their households changed in appearance. All became well ordered; the children were well dressed. As a result, domestic quarrels grew less frequent; the wives stated that they were no longer beaten by their husbands. The workmen who still so far forgot themselves as to use bad

* The review *Foi et vie* has replied to them by giving details of the results of these and some former Revivals (Nov. 16, 1907).

language were rebuked by their comrades. Debts were paid. A doctor said: "I hardly know what to think of the Revival, but in any case it has been good for me; not that I have more patients, but they are paying off old debts of which I never expected to hear anymore. I have gained twenty pounds by it." A certain number of souls rose higher and were enkindled by a vivid love of God and zeal for their neighbour's salvation.

And when the excitement of the Revival has passed off, what fruits remain? We are assured that many of the converted persevered; their lives were completely changed. It is not surprising that there were relapses; one of the disadvantages of Revivals is that " under the influence of the environment sudden and sometimes temporary exaltations are produced. Those who have been thus converted, as if overheated, without the change taking deep root, are unconverted again as easily as they were converted. The direction of their feelings changes with remarkable ease, because these feelings are not so much the real expression of their inward being as the passing over them of a current of emotion from outside."

**4.**—The Revival had several **promoters,** of both sexes, almost simultaneously. I will speak only of Evan Roberts, the principal, especially as it is about him that we have most information. He was a working miner. He was twenty-six years old when, in December 1904, he took the lead of the new-born revivalist movement. His father, also a miner, was a pious man, who brought up his ten children in the fear of God. When Evan came into the world, his mother cried: "Another son for the Lord's service! Perhaps he will be a preacher one day!" On leaving the mine Evan used to hurry home and plunge deep into his books. His father used to complain that he could not drag him away from them before 3 or 4 a.m. He never wearied of studying his Bible, even at the bottom of the pit, using his miner's lamp for the purpose. He has composed some fine hymns and plays the harmonium; he also uses the violin and the mandoline. For thirteen years "he had prayed to receive the Holy Ghost" that is, for more than a conversion, and for ten years he had besought a Revival: "I could spend whole nights" he used to say, "reading stories of Revivals and talking of Revivals. It was the Spirit that was thus urging me to think about a Revival." At last, one day, no longer able to withstand the inward urge, he preached to his old comrades in the village school hall. From that moment, for more than six months, he gave himself up to meetings. Everywhere an unknown power accompanied his words, "His speech is that of familiar conversation. What he says is very simple and hardly ever rises above a commonplace level... He often begins his addresses by saying that he does not know what he is going to say, but that the Holy Spirit will dictate his words... He takes as the subject of his sermons some incident that has just happened, a verse that has just been sung, a text painted on the chapel wall. Save for a few moments when he grows a little more heated, he speaks with a very calm air, standing, one hand in the pocket of his jacket or trousers, the other holding his Bible... He says all that crosses his mind, without previous thought on the connection of his discourse. His manner is essentially fragmentary, discontinuous. And he often ends abruptly with the words: 'I have nothing more to say to you now.'" Like the other revivalist leaders, it is his practice never to appear in a meeting save when it has already begun; they sometimes wait over two hours; this gives both the meeting and themselves time to become heated, to rise to a high pitch. After having mounted the pulpit, Evan sometimes remains long in silent prayer. "His silence sometimes works miracles. His mere presence causes a shudder to run through a vast assemblage of people of both sexes and every age. He possesses that prestige, that mysterious something, that nameless faculty devoid of all authority which some few folk possess, enabling them to exercise a real magnetic fascination on those who are about them... In the taverns there are many discussions about the mysterious powers of Evan Roberts." It has been said of him that he can throw a meeting outside itself by merely uttering the word "Mesopotamia."

In the long run Evan's nervous system has shown signs of overwork. The emotions he manifests in the pulpit, his contortions, his sobs at the thought of sinners, and his subsequent outbursts of joy at noting conversions, have been found excessive. Thinking to bear the sins of the meeting after the fashion of the dying Jesus, he falls into a kind of intense agony, sinks down in the pulpit, where he disappears for several minutes, writhes about, and then reappears transfigured.

An equally displeasing feature is that, as a result of his growing nervousness, he has tended to become irritable; persuading himself that many persons come merely in a spirit of curiosity, he scolds the audience, threatens it and makes motiveless scenes.

Evan is believed to read the thoughts of his hearers. The fact has been explained by the remarkable and ceaselessly developed ability with which his piercing eyes search faces, especially those ranged near his pulpit. He also hears very acutely conversations carried on in a low voice.

Evan believes that he has heavenly visions, and especially that he receives from the Holy Ghost admonitions which guide him in his everyday life. If he had read and accepted Catholic treatises on mysticism, he would have learnt that such monitions must be rejected for some time until their divine origin has become quite clear. He has himself confessed that it is not easy to "discern between the voice of the devil and the voice of God... If there is any rule for distinguishing this difference, I have so far not discovered it." M. Bois rightly adds: "God's voice or the devil's— these are for Roberts the sole alternatives. He does not perceive that there is a third possibility: man's voice." This absurd confidence in his revelations has brought Roberts to perform strange acts which have distressed his friends. They fear that his nervous tension may lead to madness. Sometimes he refuses to attend a great meeting where all sorts of preparations have been made to receive him. He is satisfied with saying: "I have prayed for guidance, and the Spirit's reply is: You must not go." Sometimes, after rising to speak, he reseats himself, engulfs himself in the pulpit where he remains invisible for a couple of hours; and this before 2,500 huddled and over-excited people. Already in the middle of his wanderings surprise had been aroused by Evan ceasing them to make a seven days' retreat in his room, during which time the Spirit had forbidden him to speak except in writing. One person alone brought him his food in silence.

After the Revival, Evan observed a long period of rest.

### § 2.—THE MUSULMAN CONCEPTION OF ECSTASY

**5.**—For an exact understanding of the Musulman conception of ecstasy it is best to portray the exercises in use in certain associations with ecstatic tendencies. To this end, we will begin by presenting a few ideas on the **Musulman confraternities.***

The islamic countries are filled with a multitude of religious associations, many of which are also political and give rise to considerable uneasiness for the future.† They surround themselves with more or less secrecy. The oldest, that of the *Kadriya,* dates from the twelfth century of our era, and was called into being by the need of union in opposition to the first crusades. Its name is taken from that of its founder, the Persian Sidi Abd-el-Rader el-Jilani, who died at Bagdad in 1166, His followers call him the *Sultan of the Saints.*

One of the more recent and rapidly growing associations, that of the *Senussiya,* was founded by an Algerian, Sheikh Senussi, who died in 1859. As opposed to the exclusive tendency of the other orders, he had opened his to them, allowing them to keep their names, doctrines, usages and privileges. This concentration took place round a common hate of the Christians. It keeps aloof from them and prepares for the revolt which, on the day the Lord has appointed, will chase them from " the land of islam " (*dar-el-islam,* the opposite of *dar-el-harb,* the land of the infidels: literally, country of the holy war). Its device is " Both Turks and Christians I will break with a single blow.11

Those affiliated to the confraternities are called *Khuan* (brethren)‡ in North Africa, *dervishes* (poor men) in Turkey and Central Asia, *fakirs* (beggars) in India, *murids* (disciples) in Egypt, Arabia and Syria.

Since the French conquest of Algeria in 1830, the confraternities have, as a reaction, taken on an immense development in all islamic countries. Very few Musulmans are not included in them, apart from the rich and sceptical elements of the large cities. M. Pommerol estimates their numbers at 170 millions.

* Bibliography.—Rinn, *Marabouts ei Khouan* (Algiers, Jourdan, 1884); Le Chatelier, *Les confréries musulmanes* (Paris, Leroux, 1887); Depont and Coppolani, *Les confréries religieuses musulmanes* (Algiers, Jourdan, 1897); Pommerol, *Chez ceux qui guettent* (Paris, Fontemoing, 1902); Fr. Petit, Superior of the Assumptionists at Constantinople, *Les confréries musulmanes* (an excellent summary, Paris, Bloud, 1902).

† Morocco is the centre of several very military confraternities. They are credited with the rising of 1907.

‡ The plural of *akku.*

Leaving on one side the excellent administrative and financial organisation of these groups, I will speak only of their religious aspect.

We know that every day each Musulman has to recite certain prayers at fixed times; the muezzins announce them from the 'minarets. The Khuan are bound to follow them with other prayers, peculiar to their association. One of the principal is a sort of litany, called *dikr* (*repeated enunciation*) for which a chaplet is used. The basis of this is the same in all the orders, but with small variations which enable the initiates to recognise each other with ease. Generally they include the creed, the fundamental formula of islam: "There is no God but God" (*La ilaha ill' Allah*: literally, No God or divinity, except God), which is repeated, for example, a hundred times. To this are added other phrases or short invocations, such as "God sees me," "May God pardon," or a fragment of a verse from the Koran, or names of divine attributes: "O living One," a hundred times; "O changeless One," a hundred times; or simply the syllable *Hua* (He). When the rhythm of the common recitation quickens, the first syllables of "La ilaha ill' Allah" successively disappear, and are reduced to *lahu, la ha, la hi,* or even to *hu$_t$ ha, hi,* or *hu-hu.*

The phrase *La ilaha*... has to be repeated by the *Kadriya* 165 times after each of the five daily prayers; by the *Kerzaziya,* 500 times; for the *Aissaua,* the daily total is 13,600 times.

**6.**—Given these preliminaries we come to the question of Musulman **pseudo-ecstasy.**

Among all the confraternities of which we have just spoken, many have mystical tendencies and their end is to procure, on certain days and for a few moments, a profound union with God. This union (*ittisâl*), described by the Persian and Hindu Sufis of the ninth century, resembles the Buddhist *nirvana,* It is the annihilation of personality by identification (*jam'* or *ittihad*) of the subject with God. Sidi Abd-el-Kader el-Jilani proclaimed that "happiness lies in forgetting existence." Sheikh Senussi thus defined ecstasy: "The annihilation of man's individuality in the divine essence," and Abdul-Kerim has summed up this state in two words: "unconsciousness and insensibility." Such a doctrine cannot shock the Musulmans, for they venerate madmen as saints and think that God dwells in these empty brains. This explains the liberty they leave them, which seems excessive to us.*

Sometimes the initiate strives especially to unite himself with the founder of his order, whom he regards as a higher emanation of the Divinity and his all-powerful intermediary. Thus the *Repaya.*

* M. Asin y Palacios, Professor of Arabic at the University of Madrid and editor of *Cultura española,* published in his review (Feb. 1906) a scholarly article on the idea of ecstasy among the Musulmans. He chose two typical writers, who had an immense influence, the Persian Ghazzali (Al-Gazel, twelfth century) and the Murcian Mohidin Abenarabi (thirteenth century). The highest degree described by these teachers is absolute unconsciousness; they seek to arrive thereat by the moral and physiological processes I am about to indicate.

7.—Let us now see **by what road** the pseudo-ecstatic union is reached. Sufism, which preceded the confraternities, and from which many of them are derived, was satisfied to counsel the moral means of renunciation, detachment pushed as far as possible. In its primitive stages this was the essence of Sufism, which was simply a way (*tariqâ*), a method of sanctification, not a dogmatic system or an association. But the confraternities have added special exercises. Henceforth there is a great difference from Christian mysticism. The latter admits that it is impossible, even indirectly, to procure a true mystic state by one's own efforts. God must produce it, and then it comes unexpectedly, whether in the midst of prayer or a secular occupation. No preparation can lead to it.

The Musulman thinks otherwise. He has a physical procedure, which consists in the manner of reciting the *dikr* in common; this is especially done on Friday, the weekly islamic religious festival.

Various prescriptions set forth as to how the breath may be held and prolonged. There is a more important point, namely an exhaustive gymnastic, which is compulsory, and has as its result the production of a kind of giddiness, hysterical inebriation, followed either by convulsions or by a profound weakness. Thus, among the *Kadriya*, says Le Chatelier, "the Khuan give themselves up to a rhythmic and rapid balancing of the upper part of the body, which is favourable to congestion of the cerebro-spinal system. Under the twofold influence of this purely physical cause and of an extreme mental tension, of the convergence of all the intellectual faculties on a single idea, that of God's majesty, the phenomena of religious hysteria are produced in many of the adepts... they are very marked in the convents of the order" (p. 29). The founder had laid it down that the disciple must limit his recitation "to repeating *ha* while turning the head to the right, *hu* while turning it to the left, *hi* while lowering it, prolonging each sound as long as his breathing allows. We can imagine the effect which the repetition of these syllables must produce on the best constituted temperament, accompanied as it is by violent motions of the head" (*ibid.*, p. 33).

In our days the *Zaheriya* perform the same movements slowly with the formula *La ilaha ill' Allah*, uttered in one breath, sometimes twenty-one times without taking breath.

The *Serehurdiya*, founded in the thirteenth century, repeat indefinitely and without interruption the phrase *La ilaha*, etc., moving the head from the navel to the right shoulder, and thus fall into a dumb unconsciousness. The *Zaheriya* add the left shoulder. The *Nakeshabendiya* sometimes have recourse to the assistance of opium or one of its substitutes. Among the *Beiumiya*, at each invocation, the body is bent as far as the waist, the arms being crossed; they are uncrossed as the erect posture is resumed, and the hands clapped together at the height of the face.

Some of the confraternities deserve special mention, because of the strong nervous excitement to which their members attain.

Firstly that of the *Kheluatiya*; it dates from the fourteenth century. The members retire from time to time into a profound solitude; hence their name

(*Khelua*, retreat). While thus separated from the world, the adept may speak to others only by signs or in writing. He fasts from sunrise to sunset and takes only what nourishment is strictly necessary. Thanks to the use of coffee, he sleeps two or three hours only. He recites certain sacred names, such as *Hua* (He), *Qayyum* (changeless), *Haqq* (truth), which must be repeated ten, twenty or thirty thousand times a day, according to the instructions of the teacher. "The upper eyelid is pressed firmly upon the lower, so as to produce in the visual organ a muscular excitement which acts on the optic nerve and consequently upon the cerebral system... For example, *Qayyum* is recited twenty thousand times while the head is balanced and lowered in a vertical plane, the eyes being closed. The speed of the recitation can hardly exceed once per second, and the duration of such a prayer is five or six hours. Supposing that the initiate is given three names to repeat in like manner, he needs eighteen hours a day... The doctors of the order compare the initiation of the Khelua to a poison, which is deadly if it be taken in too big doses at the start, and to which one must grow accustomed by progressive use... All the members who make frequent retreats are, even if their duration is not prolonged, in a serious mental state. Pale, gaunt, haggard-eyed, they always preserve the traces of these sharp experiences when returning to ordinary life... An extreme exaltation is the characteristic of this order, and more than any other it must be regarded as the shrine of an intense fanaticism" (*ibid.*, pp. 62 ff.).

Another very remarkable confraternity is that of the *Aissaua*, founded in the fifteenth century by Sidi Mohammed ben-Aïssa. The *dikr* is transformed into raucous cries, "cadenced by a dull music, in very rapid time. To each of them correspond very deep and rapid bendings of the body as far as the waist, or circular movements of the head, also calculated to overthrow the nervous system. The crises thus brought about are soon betrayed by a cerebral inebriation and anaesthesia variously localised according to the subject. As these phenomena become manifest to the practised eye of the presiding Sheikh, the Khuan, at a sign from him, pierce their hands, arms and cheeks with slender darts. Others cut their throats or breasts with sharpened sabres, eat poisonous animals, chew cactus- leaves bristling with spikes. All, little by little, fall exhausted, in a torpor which a touch from the *moqaddem* (president, initiator) transforms, in some cases, into an hypnotic sleep" (*ibid,*). Some grind pieces of glass between their teeth (p. 101).

In another confraternity, that of the *Refaya*, founded in the twelfth century by Rafaï, nephew of Sidi Abd-el-Kader, the majority collapse when the hysteric inebriation supervenes. The others "swallow serpents or burning coals, or roll amid burning brands. Moreover they accustom themselves to falling upon sharp spears, piercing their arms and cheeks with the like implements, and being trodden under the feet of their Sheikh" (*ibid.*, pp, 204, 206). The howling dervishes, who, like the dancing dervishes, give public sittings at Constantinople and Cairo, belong to the order of the *Refaya*. The ceremony opens with cries accompanied by tremblings and somersaults timed by drums. "Forming a chain" says Théophile Gautier, "they drag from the base of their chests a raucous and prolonged shout, *Allah hu!* which seems not to be a product of the human voice. The whole band, moving together, steps back a pace, throws itself forward with a simultaneous movement and howls in a deep, hoarse tone which resembles the growling of a menagerie in a bad humour, when lions, tigers, panthers and hyenas find that their feeding time is delayed. Then little by little the inspiration comes, their eyes shine like the pupils of wild beasts in the depths of a cavern; an epileptic foam froths at their lips, their faces are distorted and shine lividly under the sweat; the whole file crouches down and rises again under an invisible breath, like ears of corn in a storm, and always, at each movement, the terrible *Allah hu* is repeated with growing energy. How can such howlings, repeated for more than an hour, fail to break the bony case of the chest and make the blood flow forth from its broken vessels?" (*Constantinople,* ch. xii).

The dancing dervishes (founded in the thirteenth century) are *Maulaniya.* They are also called *Mevlevis.* "They waltz, their arms stretched out in the form of a cross, their heads bent on to their shoulders, their eyes half closed, their mouths half open, like trusting swimmers who let themselves he carried along on the wave of ecstasy... Sometimes their head turns right up, showing the whites of their eyes, their lips flecked by a light foam" (*ibid.,* ch. x). Finally they fall on their knees, worn out, faces to the ground, until they are touched by their chief, who sometimes has to massage their arms and legs.

An uninstructed spectator would not suspect that these physical exercises have for the howling or dancing dervishes a religious significance, and constitute a process for arriving at union with the divinity. This profound union does not consist, as with our saints, in knowing and loving God in a higher manner, in repose and silence. In the orders with ecstatic tendencies, the Khuan are content, on the other hand, with a low idea, and violently procure physiological impressions leading like drunkenness to unconsciousness. The physiognomy of these two kinds of ecstasy is profoundly different.

# THE MYSTIC UNION

## CANTICLE

Who tastes Thee, Jesus, hungers for Thee sore!
Who drinks deep draughts of Thee still craves for more,*
Nor shall his burning longing e'er grow cold
Thy Sacred Heart, O Lord, close claspt to hold.

Yea more: to enter in.† It calls us. See
That blest abyss of the Divinity!
Chained to the flesh, the soul yet yearns to rise
And lose herself a space in those fair skies.

The Master smiles on this desire of love;
And to the soul's so ardent cry: "My dove,
Come, enter through My riven Wound, saith He,
The hidd'n abyss lies open now to thee."

Then His caressing Hands extending wide,
He bears the dove towards His piercèd Side.
She enters in! O joy! O life! I hold
The treasure sweet, possess'd by saints of old!

O life, my thirsting spirit's hidden need!
I knew thee not, but sought for thee indeed;
But still a secret call, the Voice Divine,
Impelled me to the joys that should be mine.

Profound the mystery of this blest place!
Two spirits claspt in a most sweet embrace;
And with the flash of their commingling fires
She breathes,—grasps,—sees the God of her desires.

* Qui te gustant esurient;
Qui bibunt adhuc sitiunt.
(***Hymn*** Jesu, decus angelicum.)

† Et corde in isto seligat
Æterna tabernacula!
(***Hymn*** Cor Arca.)

Nos intimis recessibus
Semel receptos contine!
(*Hymn* O Cor, Amoris Victima.)

But now, alas l the too brief time is o'er,
Transformed, the dove descends to earth once more;
A double fire enkindled in her soul,
To suffer and to love, her spirit's goal.

Let the great waters flow! they shall not quench
Her love for Christ, nor shall her courage blench
Though spurn'd and trodden; seeking but to share
The shameful Cross, that once her Lord did bear.

Who tastes Thee, Jesus, hungers for Thee sore!
Who drinks deep draughts of Thee, but craves for more
Nor shall his burning longing e'er grow cold
The Well-Beloved's Cross close claspt to hold.

## THE MYSTIC UNION

# BIOGRAPHICAL INDEX*

## I

### Medieval Authors

**1. St. Gregory the Great,** Pope (a. d. 540-604). Exposition of the Book of Job (commonly called *Moralia*). "Those who love an interior life may still read it with great advantage" (Schmid, Patrology, ed. by Schobel, p. 330).

**2. Dionysius the pseudo-Areopagite.** It is now almost universally admitted that the writings attributed to the Areopagite were the work of "a priest and monk trained in the Neo-Platonic school, in the interval between the Councils of Ephesus and Chalcedon (431-451); their author was a man of great talent, depth and subtlety, but humble and pious withal; they quickly attained great celebrity, were repeatedly translated into Latin, commented upon by the most renowned theologians, and became, to the Scholastics of the Middle Ages an aid to their speculations; to mystics, a light in contemplation, and to ascetics, a guide on the threefold way of perfection" (Schmid, l.c. p. 218). The works which concern us here are: (1) *De divinis nominibus,* an explanation of the names by which God is called in Holy Scripture; (2) *De cælesti hierarchia,* a treatise on the names, office, and order of the angels; (3) *De ecclesiastica hierarchia,* on the Sacraments, their ministers, and those that receive them; (4) *De mystica theologia ad Timotheum,* on union with God, the supreme object of our knowledge and love. English translations by J. Parker, m. a., 1897; A. B. Sharpe, m. a., 1910.

**3. Hugh of St. Victor** (a. d. 1097-1141), Canon Regular. Prefect of the monastic school of St. Victor at Paris, was an intimate friend of St. Bernard. His minor works, *De arca Noë mysticâ, De arca Noë morali, De arrhâ animæ, De vanitate mundi,* etc., are almost entirely devoted to mystic speculations.

**4. St. Bernard, Abbot of Clairvaux** (a. d. 1091-1153). Among his mystical writings the following are the most prominent: Eighty-six sermons on the

* The Bibliographical Index, which has been partly re-written for the English edition, contains a good deal of additional matter, including all information relating to English translations of works written in other languages. Some duplicated French translations of foreign works have been omitted [Translator].

Canticle of Canticles; *De consideratione, de diligendo Deo, de gradibus humilitatis,* etc.

English: *Life and Works,* by S. J. Eales, 4 vols., 1889-1896; *The Song of Songs,* selections from the above-mentioned sermons, 1901; *Sermons on Advent and Christmas,* 1909.

**5.** Works of his disciples and contemporaries (**Guigo**, fifth prior of the Grande Chartreuse, William of St. Thiery, etc.) have sometimes been erroneously attributed to St. Bernard.

**6. Richard of St. Victor**, Canon Regular, a Scotchman, successor of Hugh of St. Victor (d. 1173). The best known of his mystical works are: *Benjamin minor* and *Benjamin major, de statu interioris hominis.* English: *A very devout treatise, named Benjamin. The Cell of Self-knowledge* (Tr. I), Gardner, 1910.

**7. St. Hildegard,** Benedictine abbess of Rupertsberg, near Bingen (a. d. 1099-1179). Her influence on contemporaries was very great. Her writings, partly printed in Migne's P. L. CXCVII, have been critically edited by Cardinal Pitra, Spicil. Solesm. VIII. 1882.

**8, 9, 10. St. Bonaventure,** Friar-Minor. General of the Franciscans, *Doctor Seraphicus* (b. Bagnarea, Tuscany, a. d. 1221, d. Lyons 1274). He chiefly deals with mystical theology in the *Itinerarium mentis ad Deum, de sex alis Seraphim, de septem gradibus contemplationis,* etc. The work *De theologia mystica* is often attributed to the Friar-Minor **Henricus de Palma**; while *De septem itineribus æternitatis* was written by **Rudolph de Bibrach,** a Franciscan of Suabia, who lived about 1360. Three of these "Ways" belong to mystic contemplation, one of them, the fifth, describing experimental knowledge; but it is difficult to see what precise distinction he makes between the various "ways."

**11. St. Thomas Aquinas,** *Doctor Angelicus* (b. Rocca-Sicca a. d. 1225, d. Fossa-Nuova 1274), Dominican. His chief work, the *Summa Theologiae,* has been called the grandest monument of thought which the Middle Ages have produced. *Opera omnia,* Rome, 1570. 17 vols., folio. Passim. See **Vallgornera** (No. 68). English: The *Summa Theologica* of St. Thomas Aquinas, tr. by the English Dominicans. Edited by Wilfred Lescher, O. P., in 3 parts. Part I. 1910.

**12. Blessed Albertus Magnus,** Dominican. For a short time Bishop of Ratisbon. He held the post for three years only, and resigned that he might be free to continue his work at the school of his Order at Cologne (b. Lauengen in Suabia a. d. 1193, d. Cologne 1280). St. Thomas Aquinas was his pupil. Among his works, which fill 21 volumes in folio, is the treatise on mystical theology: *De Adhaerendo Deo,* in which he dissuades from the use of the imagination and the thought of created things as aids to attaining to union with God. This may have been intended only for such souls as have arrived at the mystic state; but he does not say so, and in his translation of this work (*De l'union a Dieu*), 1896, Fr. Bertier, O. P., credits him with the opposite intention. "We notice the difference between this method and that which prevailed later. In the XIIIth Century we are to strip ourselves of the phantoms of the imagination; in the

XVIIth, on the contrary, the tendency is to make the utmost use of this faculty" (*Opera omnia,* Lyons, 1651). English: *The Treatise of Albertus Magnus... de adhaerendo Deo.* London, 1850.

**13, 14, 15. St. Gertrude,** Benedictine (b. Germany a. d. 1256, d. Helfta, Saxony, 1303). *Insinuationes Divinae Pietatis.* Two editions of her revelations have been published by the Benedictine Fathers of Solesmes. Latin, Oudin, 1875. French, Poictiers, 1863. They have also edited the revelations of her Novice-Mistress, **St. Mechtildis of Hackeborn** (a. d. 1241-1298).

To St. Mechtildis' revelations are further added those of Sister **Mechtildis of Madeburg,** who lived for many years as a Beguine in that town (d. 1280). St. Gertrude has often been confused with Abbess Gertrude of Hackeborn, her contemporary and namesake, a religious of the same convent of Helfta. Abbess Gertrude was sister to St. Mechtildis, and was St. Gertrude's Superior for thirty years. For two hundred and fifty years after her death St. Gertrude's influence was very slight; her writings became widely known only when printed, first in German (1505), and then in Latin, by the Carthusian, Lansbergius (1536). See also G. Ledos' excellent French life: *Ste Gertrude* (1901). English: *Life of St. Gertrude the Great* (C.T.S.); *Life and Revelations of St. Gertrude,* by Sister M. Frances Clare, 1865; *Select Revelations of St. Mechtild,* Tr. by Dr. Cruikshank, 1875.

**15** *bis.* Richard **Rolle**, of Hampole, Hermit (b. a. d. 1290 (?), d. Hampole, near Doncaster, 1349). *De Emendatione Vitae* and *De Incendio Amoris,* translated into English by Richard Misyn, 1334-1345, *The fire of love* and *The mending of life, or the rule of living* (Early English Text Society), 1896. *The Form of Perfect Living,* ed. Hodgson, 1910. *The Fire of Love and the Mending of Life* (Misyn's trans.), ed. Comper, 1914. *Some Minor Works of Richard Rolle,* ed. Hodgson, 1923. *The Amending of Life,* ed A.P., 1927. *The Life and Lyrics of Richard Rolle,* Comper, 1928. *Selected Works of Richard Rolle,* ed. Heseltine, 1930.

**16.** Blessed **Angela of Foligno,** of the Third Order of St. Francis (a. d. 1248-1309). *B. Angelæ de Fulgineo Visionum et Instructionum Liber.* Paris, 1598; re-edited, Bolland., Jan. 4. The revelations were taken down from her lips by Fra Arnaldo, Friar-Minor, the saint's confessor. The Bollandists suppressed Fra Arnaldo's headings of the chapters, printing them on the margin only; but the original arrangement is followed both by M. Hello and in the English translation which has been quoted in this work.

French translation, *Visions et Instructions de Ste Angèle de Foligno,* by E. Hello, 1868. *Le Livre de la Bse. Angèle de Foligno,* ed. Doncœur, 1925. English: *The Book of the Visions and Instructions of Blessed Angela of Foligno,* translated from the original Latin by a Secular Priest, 1880; *The Book of the Divine Consolation of the B. Angela of Foligno,* translated from the first Italian version by Mary G. Steegman, 1909.

**17. John Tauler,** Dominican (b. Strasburg (about) a. d. 1300, d. Strasburg 1361). *Sermons,* Leipsic, 1498; reprinted Basle, 1521, 1522; Cologne, 1543. English: *The History and Life of Tauler,* with twenty-five of his Sermons; translated by S. Winkworth (Anglican), 1857; reprinted 1905. *The Inner Way:* thirty-six Sermons for Festivals (Anglican). The series of fourteenth-century meditations on the Passion, *Meditations on the Life and Passion of our Lord* (1875, reprinted 1904), and attributed to Tauler, is not considered as the production of his pen. Another work, translated into English and published under his name: *The Imitation of the Poor Life of Christ,* or *Spiritual Poverty,* is certainly spurious. "It is full of heresy and nonsense, abhorrent to the soul of holy John Tauler" (Fr. Wilberforce, O.P., in his Preface to *Meditations on the Life and Passion,* etc.).

Fr. H. S. Denifle, O. P., has shown that the story of Tauler's conversion to the perfect life by a layman, the so-called "Friend of God from the Oberland," is the invention of Rulman Merswin, author of the *Dialogue of the Nine Rocks.*

**18.** Blessed **Heinrich Suso,** Dominican, of Suabia (b. (about) a. d. 1296, d. Ulm 1365). Has been called "The Minnesinger of the love of God." His autobiography, which he published shortly before his death, is a document of great importance for the psychology of mysticism.

*Leben,* Augsburg, 1482; *Leben,* Breslau, 1828; *Leben u. Schriften,* Breslau, 1828; Augsburg, 1854. *Œuvres Mystiques,* translated by Fr. Thiriot, O. P., Paris, 1899. English: *The Life of Blessed Henry Suso, by himself,* translated by Fr. Knox, Cong. Orat., 1865. *Little Book of Eternal Wisdom,* 1910. The *Buch der Neun Felsen* (Dialogue of the Nine Rocks) is now known to be not by Suso, but by Rulman Merswin, a merchant of Strasburg (1307-1382), an author of not unimpeachable orthodoxy. It is omitted from Fr. Thiriot's translation of his works. The Nine Rocks signify successive stages in the spiritual life; the last alone deals, and this briefly, with questions of mysticism. It is difficult to follow the author in his differentiation of the various stages; his treatise would have gained in precision if he had divided it into three parts: the flight from mortal sin, from venial sin, and the pursuit of virtue.

**19, 20, 21, 22**. St. **Bridget**, of Sweden (b. in the Province of Upland, Sweden, a. d. 1302, d. Rome 1373). Foundress of the Order of St. Saviour, commonly called the Brigittines. *Revelationes Sanctæ Birgittae Sueciae,* Nuremberg, 1500; Rome, 1628. Contains (1) a Preface by Card. Juan **de Torquemada,** O. P. (b. Valladolid 1388, d. Rome 1468). (2) A preliminary Treatise by Gonsalvo **Durand**, Bishop of Montefeltro. (3) A Preface to Book VIII by Alphonsus **de Vadatera,** Bishop of Jaen, and afterwards an Augustinian Hermit. As the saint's confessor and secretary he assisted Fr. Peter Olafson, Cistercian, Prior of Alvastra, who spent thirty years in collecting the revelations and translating them from Swedish into Latin (*Revelationes Extravagantes,* ch. XLVIII). The revelations were attacked when the Council of Constance was sitting (1414-1418), and a controversy arose concerning them, giving occasion to Gerson to write his treatise on *The Discernment of Spirits,* reserving his judgment, however, regarding the revelations in dispute. At the Council of Basel (1431-1443) a fresh dispute arose concerning their orthodoxy. A committee was appointed, with Juan (afterwards Card.) Torquemada as President, to examine the revelations and to report to the Council. The report was favourable, and the committee's view was endorsed by the Council. The revelations had already been approved by Gregory XI (1377), by Urban VI (1379), and praised by Boniface IX in his Bull of canonisation (1391).

They were divided into eight books by Alphonsus de Vadatera, the ninth (*Revelationes Extravagantes*) being collected and arranged by Fr. Peter of Alvastra. English: *Select Revelations of St. Bridget,* with an Introduction by Card. Manning, 1874, 1892; *St. Bridget of Sweden,* by F. M. Steele, 1909. There is a good French life, *Ste Brigitte de Suede,* by la Comtesse de Flavigny, Paris, 1892.

**23. St. Catherine of Siena,** Dominican Tertiary (b. Siena a. d. 1347, d. Rome 1380). The *Dialogo,* "the Book of the Divine Doctrine," a treatise on the spiritual life in the form of colloquies between the Eternal Father and the human soul (represented by Catherine), was taken down from the saint's lips when in ecstasy. It was divided into five parts by Fr. Raimondo, O. P., the saint's confessor and editor: *l'Opere della serafica Santa Caterina da Siena,* edited by Girolamo Gigli, Lucca and Siena, 1707-1713; French translation by E. Cartier, 1855. English: *The Dialogue of St. Catherine of Siena,* translated by Algar Thorold, 1907; *The History of St. Catherine of Siena and her Companions,* A. T. Drane, 1880; *St. Catherine of Siena,* Gardner, 1907; *St. Catherine of Siena,* Curtayne, 1929.

**24.** The Blessed Jan van **Ruysbroeck** (Rusbrochius), surnamed *Doctor Admirabilis* (b. Ruysbroeck, near Brussels, a. d. 1293, d. Groenendael 1381). *Opera Omnia,* translated from the Flemish into Latin by Laurence Surius, a Carthusian of Cologne (d. 1578), Cologne, 1652. Originally a secular priest, Ruysbroeck founded a monastery of contemplative Augustinians at Groenendael, near Brussels, and became their first Prior. Tauler was either his disciple or his friend. His mystical writings abound with passages on the happiness of ecstasy. Some of his translators, failing to reproduce the exact shades of the original, have rendered his work unnecessarily obscure and disturbed the sequence of thought. Ruysbroeck knows nothing of the art of composition; his distinctions are often imperfect and obscure, his explanations incomplete. His style is rugged at the best, but he has magnificent flights. He had a large following; but to understand the popularity of his writings we must read him in the original; much is lost in a translation. The immemorial *cultus* paid to Ruysbroeck has been confirmed by a decree of the Sacred Congregation of Rites (Dec. 9th, 1908). Twenty years after his death his writings were attacked by Gerson and defended by Denis the Carthusian (*De contemplatione,* Book III, a. 25), who calls him a "Second Areopagite," and then again by Lessius (*De summo bono,* Book II, ch. I, No. 7) and Bellarmine (*De script. eccl.,* p. 366). E. Hello has translated some selected passages into French (1869), rather exaggerating the lyrical nature of the text. There is another translation by Maeterlinck: *l'Ornement des Noces spirituelles,* Brussels, 1891. English: *Reflections from the Mirror of a Mystic,* from the French of Hello, by Earle Baillie, 1905; *Ruysbroeck and the Mystics,* from the French of Maeterlinck, by J. T. Stoddart, 1894; *Light, Life, and Love,* selections from the German mystics of the Middle Ages (Anglican), W. R. Inge, 1904. *The Book of the Twelve Beguines* (tr. Francis), 1913. Ruysbroeck , by E. Underhill, 1914. *The Adornment of the Spiritual Marriage, The Sparkling Stone, The Book of Supreme Truth* (tr. Dom), 1916. *The Kingdom of the Lovers of God* (tr. Hyde), 1919. *Ruysbroeck the Admirable,* by d Aygalliers (tr. Rothwell), 1925.

**24** *bis.* Walter **Hilton**, Augustinian Canon of Thurgarton, Notts (d. a. d. 1393). *Scala Perfectionis* (English) was printed by Wynkyn de Worde, 1494, 1519, and 1525. *The Scale of Perfection,* reprinted from the 1659 edition, with a Preface by Fr. Dalgairns, Cong. Orat., 1870. New edition, 1908. *A Devout Treatise, compiled by Master Walter Hylton of the Song of Angels. The Cell of Self-Knowledge,* seven early English mystical treatises, with Introduction and notes by Edmund Gardner (Tr. IV), 1910. *Minor Works of Walter Hilton,* edited by Dorothy Jones, 1929.

**25.** Jean **Gerson** (le Charlier de), Canon of Notre Dame and Chancellor of the University of Paris (b. Gerson, near Rheims, 1363, d. Lyons 1429). Surnamed "the very Christian Doctor." His works fill five volumes, folio. *Opera Omnia,* Antwerp, 1706; *Opera Mystica.*

**25** *bis.* Mother **Juliana of Norwich** (b. a. d. 1342, d. Norwich 1442). An anchoress who lived in a cell in the churchyard of St. Julian's Church, Norwich. *Sixteen Revelations of Divine Love,* first published by Fr. Serenus Cressy, Benedictine, of Douai, 1770; reprinted 1843. *Revelations of Divine Love,* 1902. New ed. (ed. Hudleston) , 1927. The Lady Julian, A Psychological Study (Thouless), 1924.

**26. Denis the Carthusian** (Denis of Ryckel) (a. d. 1402-1471), surnamed *Doctor ecstaticus.* He lived at the charter-house of Roermond (Diocese of Liège). *De contemplatione; De fonte lucis* (Nuremberg, 1495). His complete works, in forty quarto volumes, have been republished by the Carthusian Fathers of Montreuil-sur-mer.

**27.** Henry **Harphius** (Henry Herp), Provincial of the Franciscans of the Strict Observance in the Province of Cologne, and Guardian at the Convent at Mechlin. Place and date of birth unknown (d. Mechlin a. d. 1478). *Theologia Mystica,* edited by the Carthusian, Fr. Loher, Cologne, 1538. Corrected ed., Rome, 1586. The work is divided into three books. Brother Gerard d'Hamont, quoted by Abbé Auger, says: "If all the passages borrowed from Ruysbroeck were omitted, scarcely anything would remain" (*Les Mystiques des Pays Bas*).

## II

## AUTHORS OF THE SIXTEENTH CENTURY

**28.** St. **Catherine of Genoa,** of the Third Order of St. Francis (b. Genoa a. d. 1447, d. Genoa 1510). Surnamed "the Seraph of Genoa. *Trattato del Purgatorio. Libro de la Vita,* including *del Purgatorio,* Genoa, 1551. French translation by Fr. Bouix, Ruffet, 1863. English: *Treatise on Purgatory,* with Preface by Card. Manning, 1858. *Treatise of St. Catherine on Purgatory,* Tr. by J. M. A., 1878.

**29.** John **Landsberge** (Lanspergius). Styled the Just. A Carthusian of Cologne (b. Landsberge in Bavaria a. d. 1490, d. Cologne 1525). *Opuscula spiritualia,* 2 vols., Cologne, 1630. He deals only occasionally with questions of mysticism. Republished by the Carthusian Fathers of Montreuil-sur-mer. *Opera omnia,* Monsterollii, 1888.

**30.** Ven. **Blosius** (Louis de Blois) (b. Donstienne, near Liège, 1506, d. Liessies 1565). Benedictine, Abbot of Liessies in Hainault. Formerly page of honour to the Emperor Charles V, he entered the Abbey at the age of fourteen. *Opera,* published by his disciple, Jacques Frojus, Cologne, 1571. Reprinted, Cologne, 1589; Paris, 1606. *Opera,* Ingolstadt, 1631 and 1728. He belongs to the same school as Ruysbroeck. *Collected Works,* published by the Plantin Press, Antwerp, 1632; reprinted 1669; again reprinted by the monks of Kempton, S. Bavaria, 1672. English: translated from the Latin, by Fr. Bertrand Wilberforce, O. P., *A Book of Spiritual Instruction* (*Institutio Spiritualis*), 1900; *Comfort for the Faint-hearted* (*Consolatio Pusillanimium*), 1902; *A Mirror for Monks* (*Speculum Monachorum*), 1901; *The Sanctuary of the Faithful Soul* (*Conclave animae fidelis*), 1904. *Collected Works* (7 vols.), 1924, etc.

**31.** Fr. **Balthasar Alvarez,** Jesuit (b. Cervera, Spain, a. d. 1533, d. Belmonte 1580), Spiritual director and confessor to St. Teresa. See **43**, Ven. Louis du Pont. *Vida del P. Balthasar Alvarez,* by da Ponte, Madrid, 1615. French translation by Bouix, Regis Ruffet, 1873. English: *Life of Father Balthasar Alvarez,* from the French of da Ponte, 1868.

**32.** St. **Teresa** (b. Avila a. d. 1515, d. Alva 1582). *Escritos,* published by Fra Luis de Leon, Augustinian, Professor at Salamanca; 4to, Salamanca, 1588; *Escritos de Santa Teresa,* edited by Don Vicente de la Fuente, Madrid, Rivadeneira, 1877 and 1881, 2 vols. French translation by Fr. Bouix, S. J., 1852, 6 vols. Lecoffre. Fr. Peyré, S. J., has revised the translation of the *Life,* so as to bring it nearer to the original, 1904. In 1908 the same writer published, with slight alterations, *Le Chemin de la Perfection, Le Château,* and the *Cantique des Cantiques.* A new French translation, far superior to that of Bouix, is now in course of publication: *Œuvres de Ste Thérèse,* by the Carmelite nuns of the Convent of the Incarnation, Paris. Vol. I and Vol. II, *Life* and *Relations;* Vol. III and Vol. IV, *Foundations,* with documents; Vol. V and Vol. VI, *Way of Perfection, Interior Castle,* and *Opuscula.*

English: *The Life of the Holy Mother St. Teresa,* Foundress of the Discalced Carmelites according to the Primitive Rule. Translated by Abraham Woodhead, MDCLXXI; 4to, 3 vols. Vol. I, *Life;* Vol. II, *Foundations;* Vol. III, *Way of Perfection, Interior Castle, Conceptions of the Love of God. Life of St. Teresa of Jesus,* written by herself. Translated by David Lewis, 1870; 2nd ed., 1888; 3rd ed., with notes and Introduction by Benedict Zimmerman, Prior, O. C. D., 1904. *The Life and Letters of St. Teresa,* Fr. H. S. Coleridge, S. J., Quarterly Series, 3 vols., 1881, 1887, 1888. *The Book of the Foundations,* David Lewis, 1871. *The Interior Castle,* translated by the Benedictines of Stanbrook; revised, with an Introduction and notes by Benedict Zimmerman, Prior, O.C.D., 1906. *Letters of St. Teresa,* Dalton, 1853; reprinted 1902. *Minor Works,* translated by the Benedictines of Stanbrook, 1913. *The Way of Perfection,* translated by Benedictines of Stanbrook, 1925.

The saint wrote her Life in 1565. Afterwards she composed the *Way of Perfection* (Escurial Manuscript), which she re-wrote in 1569 (Valladolid Manuscript). Although the Valladolid Manuscript contains the work in the form in which St. Teresa wished it to be published, the earlier manuscript contains many passages of such beauty that editors and translators have thought it advisable to incorporate them in their editions of the revised text. Hence the great difficulty in references, as the numeration of the chapters differs greatly in the various editions. About the year 1569 the saint composed her *Conceptions of Divine Love,* a commentary upon the Canticle of Canticles. Five years before her death, and having reached the highest degree of the mystical life, she wrote the *Interior Castle.* For her services in furthering the progress of mysticism, see *Graces of Interior Prayer,* ch. XXX, 2. Many French Lives of St. Teresa have been written. One of the most interesting is that by *La Carmelite de Caen* (Mère Marie du Sacré Coeur), Retaux, 2 vols. (2nd ed.), 1892. M. de Curzon has published a Bibliographic Thérèsienne, 1902.*)

It is usual amongst free-thinkers to call the saint hysterical and to account thus for her ecstasies. M. Pierre Janet, who had adopted this thesis, was shown by a priest that the saint possessed none of the characteristics that he had assigned to hysteria in one of his books. He investigated the question again, and retracted his earlier conclusions at a public Conference (Bulletin de l'Institut psychologique international: Paris, 28, Rue Serpente, July, 1901). Dr. Imbert has also shown that this theory is contradicted by medical science (Vol. II, Appendix). Dr. Goix proved that the saint's illnesses were due to intermittent fever, caught from the marshes, from which she suffered all her life. It was a common ailment in her country (*Annales de philosophie chrétienne,* June, 1896). See also Fr. de San's *Étude pathologico-théologique* (Louvain, Fonteyn, 1886), and M. de Montmorand's article in the Revue philosophique, March, 1906.

In *Le Miracle et ses contrefaçons,* art. II, ch. VII, § 3, by Fr. de Bonniot, there is a chapter headed: The saints cannot be hysterical subjects. He starts from the certain principle that this malady is primarily psychic. "Disorders of the will that have passed into habits are, if not the cause, at least an essential element in hysteria. This neurotic condition either results from, or causes, enfeeblement of the will, so that habitual organic disorder is not found without mental disorder being present also." On the other hand, "virtue is merely the will that has acquired the habit of controlling both itself and the impulses of its nature, whether healthy or diseased. The hysterical subject, even when most obstinate, never controls himself." All this is true *a fortiori* with regard to the holiness which consists in the practice of all the virtues, and this in a heroic degree. A saint may be anæmic; he may be ill; but he is not mentally unbalanced.

**33, 34, 35, 36, 37. St. John of the Cross** (b. Hontiveros, Old Castille, a. d. 1542, d. Ubeda 1591). *Escritos,* first edition (incomplete), published at Barcelona, 1619.

* In his introduction to the *Life of St. Teresa of Jesus,* Benedict Zimmerman, Prior, O. C. D., says: "The Bibliographie Teresienne, by Henry de Curzon (Paris, 1902), is unfortunately too incomplete, not to say slovenly, to be of much use." [Translator.]

The first complete edition is that of Seville, 1702. The earliest French translators were not aware of its existence. Republished by Don Juan Orti, Madrid, 1872. French translation, by Fr. Cyprian of the Nativity, 1641, with an Introduction by Fr. Maillard, Provincial of the Jesuits, 1694; republished by Regis Ruffet, 1864; and by Mother Teresa of Jesus, Prioress of the Carmelite nuns of the Rue de Menin, 5 vols, Oudin, 1880. Fr. Cyprian's translation (1641) has an introduction by Fr. **Jerome of St. Joseph** (Madrid, 1629), a "commentary" of 224 pages by Fr. **Nicholas of Jesus-Mary**, Professor of Theology at Salamanca (Madrid, 1630), and three addresses by Fr. **James of Jesus.** The 1630 edition further contains a "Treatise on the soul's union with God," by Fr. **Louis of St. Teresa.** Instead of mysticism we find, however, a study on the three theological virtues. English: *Complete Works,* translated by David Lewis, with a Preface by Card. Wiseman, 2 vols., 1864. Reissue of complete Works, edited and with Introductory essay by Benedict Zimmerman, Prior, O. C. D., 1906-9. *Life of St. John of the Cross,* compiled and translated by David Lewis, 1888.

## III

## Authors of the Seventeenth Century

**38.** Ven. **Jerome-Gratian of the Mother of God**. First Provincial of the Discalced Carmelites; collaborator with St. Teresa (b. Valladolid a. d. 1545, d. Brussels 1614). *Dilucidario del verdadero spiritu,* etc. (Explanation of the true spirit of Mother Teresa of Jesus, Brussels, 1608). La Fuente quotes long extracts from this work at the end of his Vol. II.

**39.** Fr. Franciscus **Suarez**, Jesuit (b. Granada a. d. 1548, d. Lisbo 1617). His theological and philosophical writings amount to twenty three folio volumes. *De Religione,* Tr. 4; *De Oratione,* 1609. In his treatise, *De Religione Societatis Jesu,* Book IX, ch. VI, he refutes the objections brought against the Exercises of St. Ignatius. His biographers say that he had occasional ecstasies. *Collected Works,* Mainz and Lyons (1630); Venice (1740); Besançon (1856-62).

**40. Jeanne de Cambry** (Sister Jeanne Marie of the Presentation) (a. d. 1581-1639), Augustinian nun, Prioress of Saint Georges, at Menin, Belgium, and afterwards a Recluse. *Œuvres Spirituelles,* 4to, Tournay, 1665 (some of her works were published as early as 1620). Her *Life* (French) has been written by Fr. Saintrain, Redemptorist, Casterman, 1899.

**41.** Ven. Father **John of Jesus-Mary,** third General of the Discalced Carmelites (b. Calahora, Spain, 1564, d. Genoa 1615). *Opera Ascetica,* folio, Cologne, 1622. A small and incomplete treatise on mysticism. His *Schola orationis* also contains a chapter on the same subject. There is a French translation of this treatise by Fr. Cyprian of the Nativity (Paris, 1650). He is called Calaguritanus, from his birthplace.

**42.** The Ven. **Louis du Pont** (de la Puente), Jesuit (b. Valladolid a. d. 1554, d. Valladolid 1624). *Vida del P. Balthasar Alvarez,* Madrid, 1615. French translations by Abbé Piot (1842); by Fr. Bouix, Regis Ruffet (1873). Bossuet constantly quotes this work. The *Life* contains an explanation of his prayer by Fr. Balthasar Alvarez; but in chapters XIII and XLI, in which he solves seven difficulties, it is not always clear whether he is speaking of the prayer of simplicity or of the mystic state; he dwells only on the qualities that are common to both these degrees. The last is, however, clearly referred to in chapters XIV and XV. *Guia espiritual,* Valladolid, 1609. French translation: *Guide espiritual,* Perisse, 1863. English: *Life of the Ven. Louis de Ponte, S. J.* 1882.

**43.** St. **Francis of Sales,** Bishop of Geneva (b. Château de Sales, near Annecy, a. d. 1567, d. Geneva 1622). *Traité de l'amour de Dieu,* Lyons, 1616. The first six chapters treat of meditation and ordinary contemplation only; interior prayer is dealt with from Book VI onwards. The saint was not acquainted with the works of St. John of the Cross; they were only published three years later, and were not translated into French until sixteen years after his death. *Œuvres Complètes,* 16 vols., Paris, 1821. English: Library of St. Francis of Sales: Vol. II, *Treatise on the Love of God,* translated by Dom Mackey, O. S. B., London, 1884. The first English translation was printed at Douai, 1630.

**44.** Fr. **Alvarez de Paz,** Jesuit (b. Toledo a. d. 1560, d. Potosi 1620). Professor of theology at Lima, and then Provincial of Peru. Vol. III of his complete works, entitled *De Inquisitione pacis sive de studio oratione,* folio, Lyons, 1617, 1619, 1623; Mayence, 1619; Cologne, 1620, 1628. Reprinted by Vivés, Paris, 1875. This holy man had frequent ecstasies. According to his own admission to his Confessor, his union of heart and mind with God was so profound that amidst the most distracting occupations it was never suspended for a moment during twenty-five years. See P. Poulain, on de Paz, in Vacant's *Dictionnaire de Théologie.* His classification has the same defects as Scaramelli's. He does not name the transforming union, although he employs the words spiritual marriage; but he uses them in the sense of continual union with God (Vol. III, Book V, Part III, ch. XIV). He does not appear to have read St. Teresa's works, which were too recent in date, but only her *Life,* by a Carmelite Father whose name he does not give (Vol. III, Book V, Part III, ch. IX, para. 2).

**45.** St. **Alphonsus Rodriguez,** Lay-brother of the Society of Jesus (b. Segovia a. d. 1531, d. Majorca 1617). French translation of the Spanish *Life* (compiled from his Memoirs) by Fr. de Benaze, Retaux, 1890. The saint left twenty-one volumes of these memoranda; he wrote the first in 1604, at the age of seventy-three, and the last in 1616 at eighty-five. He must not be confused with Fr. Alphonsus Rodriguez (1537-1616), the author of a fine, purely ascetical treatise: *Esercizio di Perfezione.* English: *Christian Perfection,* 3 vols., 1843. This latter writer frankly admits his ignorance, if not of mysticism, at all events to a part of its terminology. Speaking of the terminology, he says: “Some persons may understand something of it. For myself, I frankly confess I understand nothing" (*On Prayer,* ch. IV). He was wrong in speaking thus, but several modern writers err when they say he was condemning mysticism. English: *Life of St. Alphonsus Rodriguez,* by Fr. Goldie, S. J., 1889.

**46.** Fr. Constantin de **Barbançon**, Capuchin. Guardian at the Monastery at Cologne. *Secrets Sentiers de l'Amour Divine,* Paris, 1622 and 1649. A very diffuse writer, giving no definitions. *The Secret Paths of Divine Love* (tr. Touchet), 1928.

**47.** Fr. **Joseph of Tremblay** (a. d. 1577-1638), Capuchin; surnamed l'Eminence Grise; the confidant of Richelieu. Founder of the Benedictines du Calvaire. *Introduction à la vie spirituelle.* Republished under the title of *Méthode d'oraison,* 3rd ed., 1626; and again by Fr. Apollinaire de Valence (Le Mans; Œuvre de St. F. d'Assise), 1897. There is a manuscript of his on prayer in the Mazarine Library, Paris. This writer does not speak of mysticism, properly so called, but merely of the prayer of simplicity, which he calls the prayer of quiet.

**48.** Ven. Father **Thomas of Jesus**, Discalced Carmelite (1564-1627). *Summary of the Degrees of Prayer* (in Spanish), Rome (?), 1609. The French translation by G.C.T.A., the King's interpreter, Paris, 1612, is merely a collection of extracts from St. Teresa, arranged in chapters. The translation is very careless both as regards matter and style. The volume concludes with a *Treatise on Mental Prayer* by the same author (Paris, 1612), which treats of the ordinary way of prayer only. *Traité de la contemplation divine* (Liège, l675).

**49.** Fr. Maximilian **Sandæus** (van der Sandt), Jesuit (a. d. 1578-1650). *Theologia mystica,* contains a number of short theses, the scheme of which is difficult to follow. He does not appear to have made use of St. Teresa's works or those of St. John of the Cross, whose names are, however, given in his Bibliographical Index.

**50, 51, 51** *bis.* The Ven. **Marina de Escobar** (b. Valladolid a. d. 1554, d. Valladolid 1633). She was a friend of St. Teresa (*Vida,* Vol. I, Book IV, ch. XXVII), Foundress of the Order of the Holy Saviour or Brigittines of the Recollection. *Vida,* etc..., compiled from her writings, Madrid, 1665-1673; Latin translation by Fr. Melchior **Hanel**, S. J., Prague, 1672-1688, 2 vols. folio. The first volume was compiled by the Ven. Louis du Pont (da Ponte), who was her confessor for thirty years; the second by Fr. André **Pinto Ramirez,** S. J.; the Preface is by Fr. Tanner, S. J. The Dominican Fathers were also in constant communication with the Ven. Marina, especially Fr. André du Pont, who took his brother's place when he was absent, and acted as Secretary in connection with her revelations. He was thus engaged for thirty-six years (Tanner, *Prudentia,* p. 80).

**52.** Fr. Louis **Lallemant**, Jesuit (b. Chalons-sur-Marne a. d. 1578, d. Bourges 1635). Master of Novices to Frs. Surin and Rigoleuc, at Lyons, during their second Noviciate. *Maximes,* compiled by Fr. Rigoleuc, Paris, 1694; reprinted, Lecoffre, 1892, under the title *La Doctrine Spirituelle.* The three writers referred to have sometimes been said to represent a school apart in the Society of Jesus with regard to their spirituality. Fr. Balthasar Alvarez had to defend himself from a similar accusation (see *Graces of Interior Prayer,* ch. XIV, 32). Such an error is easily understood. They wrote on the subject of mysticism, while the bulk of their brethren taught ascetic theology, reducing it to a method. The subjects treated were different, but not opposed one to the other, as many of those who have not studied these questions have supposed. Mysticism does not contradict asceticism; it completes it. English: *Spiritual Doctrine,* edited by Fr. Faber, 1855; new ed., 1928.

**53.** Ven. **John of Saint-Sampson,** a blind Lay-brother of the Calced Carmelites (b. a. d. 1571, d. Rennes 1636). *Maximes et Œuvres,* published by Fr. Donatien of St. Nicholas, Paris, 1651, 1656. There are separate later editions of the Life and the Maxims, by Fr. Sernin de St. André, Poussielgue, 1881-1883. *Œuvres completes,* 2 vols. folio, Rennes, 1658.

**54.** St. **Jane Frances de Chantal,** Co-foundress with St. Francis de Sales and first Superior of the Order of the Visitation (b. Dijon a. d. 1572, d. Moulins 1641). *Ste Jeanne Françoise de Chantal, sa Vie et ses Œuvres,* by Mère de Chaugy, 8 vols., Paris, 1874. *Œuvres,* Migne, 2 vols. folio, 1862; Plon, 8 vols. 8vo, 1877-1893. It is to be regretted that a chronological table of the saint's interior life has not yet been drawn up, showing the development and alternations of her state of prayer and her trials (see **74** and **89**). English: *Life of St. Jane Frances de Chantal,* Orat. Series, 2 vols. *Life of* Coombs, 2 vols., 1847; *Life of,* E. Bowles, Quart. Series, 1874; *Life of* from the French of Mgr. Bougaud, New York, 1896.

**55.** Dom **Augustine Baker,** English Benedictine (b. Abergavenny 1575, d. 1641). A convert from Protestantism. Was for nine years spiritual director to the Benedictine nuns at Cambrai, after which he was removed to the Monastery of St. Gregory at Douai, and became a conventual. In 1638 he joined the English Mission, and died of a fever when on the point of being taken by the pursuivants. *Sancta Sophia,* edited by Fr. Serenus Cressy, Benedictine, Douai, 1657. New edition by Dom Norbert Sweeney, London, 1876; reprinted 1905. *Confessions* (ed. McCann), 1922.

**56.** Cardinal **de Richelieu** (b. Paris a. d. 1585, d. Paris 1642). *Traité de la perfection du chrétien,* Paris, 1646; reprinted in Migne's *Dictionnaire d'ascétisme* (1865). This must not be confused with another work by the same writer: *L'Instruction du chrétien.*

**57.** Fr. Miguel **Godinez** (real name Wading), Jesuit. Professor of Theology in Mexico (a. d. 1591-1644). *Pratica de la teologia mistica,* Puebla de los Angelos, 1681. Has gone into many editions. See de la Reguera, **104**; also Schram, **114**. He divides contemplation into the cherubic and the seraphic. This distinction has not the importance attributed to it. It would have been correct if he merely meant to say that now the will and now the intellect predominates. But he further implies that each contemplation has an object which is peculiar to it alone. Thus the contemplation of the Blessed Sacrament would be cherubic. This is a purely arbitrary distinction.

**58.** Blessed Fra Carlo **da Sezze**, Franciscan Lay-brother (d. 1670). He was favoured with the Stigmata. *Trattato delle santa contemplazione,* 1650; Rome, 1742. He adopts a complicated form of classification.

**59.** Fr. **Maurus of the Infant Jesus,** Ex-Provincial of the Discalced Carmelites of Gascony (d. 1690). *L'Entrée à la divine sagesse* (4th ed.), Paris, 1678. He quotes neither St. Teresa nor St. John of the Cross, but appears to have intended to make a further subdivision of the trials described by the latter writer. The eight degrees of his Mount Carmel are fantastic.

**60.** Fr. **Philippus a SS. Trinitate,** General of the Discalced Carmelites (b. Avignon A.D. 1603, d. 1671). *Summa theologiæ mysticæ,* Lyons, 1656, folio; reprinted Brussels, 3 vols., 1874. He is also the author of a Latin life of the Ven. Fr. Dominic of Jesus Mary, third General of the Discalced Carmelites, translated into French by Fr. Pierre de Saint-André, Lyons, 1668.

**61.** Fr. **Simon of Bourg-en-Bresse,** Capuchin. *Les saintes elevations de l'âme en Dieu* (1657). His classification resembles Courbon's, but is less clear. Some of his descriptions contain certain exaggerations.

**62.** Fr. **Jean Chéron,** Provincial of the Calced Carmelites of Gascony. *Examen de la théologie mystique,* Paris, 1637. In chapters XXVI, XXVII, and XXVIII he brings a somewhat violent indictment against the language of the mystics and against ideas which are nevertheless those of St. Teresa. "I deny," he says, "that the soul has several faculties" (p. 362). He considers it ridiculous to say that distractions occur in the mystic state (p. 361), or that the soul contemplates God "in the darkness" (p. 393), etc. These remarks may be directed against John of Saint-Sampson.

**63. Desmarets de Saint-Borlin,** first Chancellor of the Académie Française (a. d. 1595-1676). *Les délices de l'esprit,* 1658. A strange book, and written in bad taste, but showing a certain knowledge of the states of prayer. He explains them as symbolised by facts in the Old Testament. He is somewhat tainted with quietistic ideas.

**64.** Fr. J. **Rigoleuc,** Jesuit (b. Quintin, Britanny, a. d. 1595, d. Vannes 1658). *Vie et Œuvres,* compiled by Fr. Pierre Champion, 1686; republished, Lecoffre, 1868. *L'oraison sans illusion* (Paris, 1687), often attributed to Fr. Rapin, S. J., which appeared anonymously, merely consists of four treatises taken from Fr. Rigoleuc's works.

**65.** Fr. Jean-Joseph **Surin**, Jesuit (b. Bordeaux a. d. 1600, d. 1665). *Catéchisme spirituel,* 1659. *Les Fondements de la vie spirituelle,* 1667. English: *The Foundations of the Spiritual Life,* translated by E. B. Pusey (Anglican), 1844. See also **52.**

**66.** Fr. **Lupi de Bergamo,** Friar-Minor of the Observance. *Teologia mistica insegnata co' suoi tocchi interni* (Mystic Theology, taught... with its interior touches). Bergamo, 1659.

**67. De Bernières-Louvigny,** of Caen, Treasurer of France (b. a. d. 1602, d. Caen 1659). The numerous letters written to him from Canada by the Ven.

Mary of the Incarnation, Ursuline, have been lost. He died suddenly while at prayer. *Le chrétien interieur,* 2 vols., 1659, 1674. *Œuvres spirituelles,* 2 vols., 1679. De Bernières published nothing himself. These books were produced after his death, being compiled from his notes and letters. Fr. Franois d'Argentin contributed to the first work, which by 1690 had gone into twelve editions, 30,000 copies having sold. The manner in which these books were compiled explains their want of order and maturity, and we find occasional unconsidered expressions, showing quietistic tendencies, which, however, are contradicted in other passages. In the Italian translation of *Œuvres Spirituelles,* put upon the Index in 1682, these defects were doubtless accentuated. English: *The Interior Christian* (extracted from the writings of de Bernières-Louvigny), 1684.

**67** *bis.* Fr. Eloy **Hardouin** of St. Jacques, Recollect Friar, Definitor of the Paris Province. *Conduite de l'âme dans l'oraison depuis les premiers jours jusqu'aux plus sublimes degrés,* Paris, 1661.

**68.** Fr. **de Vallgornera**, Dominican (a. d. 1595-1665). *Mystica Theologia divi Thomae,* Barcelona, 1662, 1672, folio; reprinted, Turin, 1891. Being chiefly composed of extracts from the works of St. Thomas Aquinas and his predecessors, this book is instructive for students who wish to reconstruct the state of mysticism as it was in the thirteenth century. It is unfortunate that the passages are often but distantly connected with mysticism. The plan of the work is modelled upon that of Philippus a SS. Trinitate. Even the titles of chapters are often identical. It is to be regretted that the extracts were not given between quotation marks. It is not always easy to know where they end.

**69, 70.** The Ven. **Mary of Jesus** (Mary of Agreda) (b. Agreda, on the frontiers of Aragon, a. d. 1602, d. Agreda 1665), Discalced Franciscan nun. Foundress and first Abbess of the Franciscan Recollects at Agreda. *La mistica ciudad de Dios, historia divina de la Virgen Madre de Dios,* Madrid, 1670; republished by Francis Silvela, 1890. The French translation of this work (*La Mystique Cité de Dieu*), by Fr. Thomas Croset, Recollect Friar, Marseilles, 1696, contains a general Preface on the subject of revelations, drawing the conclusion that these are divine, and also a life of Ven. Mary of Agreda by Joseph Ximines Samaniego, General of the Franciscans, and later Bishop of Palentia. It has been republished by Poussielgue and by Berche. There is also a partial (French) translation of Samaniego's *Life,* Poussielgue, 1857. The Roman authorities have repeatedly shown themselves adverse to this work, which was first condemned in 1681. See Mgr. Chaillot's *Theol. Myst.,* 123; also *Graces of Interior Prayer,* ch. XXI, **30**. Bossuet describes the work as "an impious impertinence and a trick of the devil."

**71.** The Ven. **Boudon**, Archdeacon of Évreux (b. La Fère, Picardy, a. d. 1624, d. Évreux 1702). *Le régne de Dieu en l'oraison mentale,* Paris, 1671. After the condemnation of quietism he issued an amended edition of this work, which appears to be that which Migne included, without any explanatory note, in his edition of **Boudon's** *Works,* 3 vols. folio, 1856. In 1823 and 1837 other publishers were unfortunately content to reissue the original edition as it stood. Migne gives the *Life* of Boudon by the Lazarist, Fr. Collet, 1754; reprinted 1828. English: *Life,* by Healy-Thompson, 1880.

**72.** Fr. **Pierre de Poitiers** (P. de P.), Capuchin. Provincial of Tourraine. *Le jour mystique,* 3 vols., Paris, 1671. He evidently understands the "mystic repose," but we lose our way when he further subdivides it into twenty-one kinds, all "essentially different," not counting secondary subdivisions (Vol. III, p. 279). This unwieldy classification is derived from the consideration of the *appetitus concupiscibilis* and *appetitus irascibilis,* and so on.

**73.** Fr. **Tanner**, Jesuit (a. d. 1623-1694). *Prudentia in examinandis... Marinæ de Escobar revelationibus,* Prague, 1698; also a similar treatise as Preface to the Latin Works of the Ven. Marina de Escobar, 1672.

**74.** The Ven. **Mary of the Incarnation,** an Ursuline of Tours, afterwards of Quebec (b. Tours a. d. 1599, d. Quebec 1672). Bossuet has called her "the Teresa of our times and of the New World" (*États d'oraison,* Book XIX, 3). *Life and Letters* (French), by her son, Dom Claud Martin, Benedictine Abbot of Saint-Germain des Près, Paris. 2 vols., Paris, 1677, The *Life,* revised, was published by Abbé Chapôt, 2 vols., Poussielgue, 1892. Another remarkable *Life* is that by an Ursuline of Nantes (Mère Marie de Chantal), Retaux, 1895. This writer is to be congratulated upon showing clearly the dates of the supernatural graces received, and not intermingling descriptions of different periods. Many hagiographers omit thus to show the evolution of the mystic life in the soul. English: *Life of the Ven. Mother Mary of the Incarnation,* by a religious of the Ursuline Community, 1888.

**75.** Cardinal **Bona**, General of the Cistertian Order (b. Mondovi, Piedmont, a. d. 1609, d. Rome 1674). *Lapis Lydius* (on the Discernment of Spirits), Rome, 1672. *Via compendii ad Deum.* English: *The Easy Way to God,* translated by H. Collins, 1876.

**76.** Fr. **Antonius a Spiritu Sancto,** Definitor-General of the Carmelites and Bishop of Angola (d. 1674). *Directorium mysticum.* Printed by decision of the General Chapter of the Order and designed for the instruction of scholastics, Lyons, 1677, folio; Venice, 1732; Seville (under the title *Cursus theologiæ mystico-scholasticæ*), 1732. Reprinted, Vivés, 1904.

**77.** Fr. Jacques **Nouet** (b. Mans a. d. 1605, d. 1687). *L'Homme d'oraison, sa conduite dans les voies de Dieu,* 2 vols., Paris, 1674. Reprinted, Lecoffre, 1893.

**78.** Fr. **Joseph a Spiritu Sancto,** first of the name (see **100**). *Cadena mistica carmelitana de les autores carmelitas,* folio, Madrid, 1678.

**79.** Fr. Paul **Segneri**, Jesuit (b. Nettuno, a. d. 1624, d. Rome 1694). *Concordia,* etc. (*the accord between work and repose in prayer*), 1680. Translated into several languages from the Italian. Latin translation by Fr. Rassler, S. J., Augsburg; 1707. This writer was the first to censure the errors of Molinos, who was condemned in 1687. *Setti Principi,* Venice, 1682, published under the name of Francisco Pace, is also attributed to Fr. Segneri. It refutes seven illusions in the teaching of Molinos, and has been translated into French under the title: *Le quiétism, ou les illusions de la nouvelle oraison,* Paris, 1687. The anonymous translator is believed to be the Abbé Dumas. English: *Life of Fr. Paul Segnery,* Orat. Series, 1861.

**80. Lebrun**, Canon, *Éclarcissement de la théologie mystique,* Rouen, 1681.

**81. Anonymous**, of the Society of Jesus. *Traité pour conduire les âmes a l'etroite union d'amour avec Dieu... contre les fausses et trompeuses devotions,* Douai, 1680 (2nd ed.).

**82.** Fr. Jean **Crasset**, Jesuit (b. Dieppe a. d. 1618, d. Paris 1692). Lecturer on the Humanities and Philosophy in the colleges of his Order. *La vie de Madame Hélyot,* Paris, 1683.

**83. Renée de Lorraine,** Abbess of Montmartre. *Conclusion des retraites,* Paris, 1684.

**84.** Fr. **Courbon**, Doctor of the Sorbonne. Curé of Saint-Cyr, near Paris, in the seventeenth century. *Instructions familières sur l'oraison mentale,* Paris, 1685. Reprinted 1874 (4th ed., Gaume). A very instructive book in spite of inaccuracies. One of the chief of these consists in attributing to affective prayer gifts which imply a higher state. *Entretiens spirituels,* Casterman, 1867, is a re-issue of some ascetical works by the same author. One amongst these, *Bonheur d'une âme qui a trouve Dieu dans l'oraison,* deals with mysticism, but it is not of much interest. English: *Familiar Instructions on Mental Prayer,* edited by W. W. Richards, 1852. *Mental Prayer,* edited by Fr. Gordon, Cong. Orat., 1871.

**85.** Fr. **Maximien de Bernezay,** Recollect Friar. *Traité de la vie interieure,* 3rd ed., Paris, 1687. A few chapters only deal with questions of mysticism.

**86.** Cardinal **Brancati da Lauria,** Friar-Minor, Conventual (b. Lauria a. d. 1616, d. Rome 1693). *De oratione christiana,* Venice, 1687; republished by the Carthusian Fathers of Montreuil-sur-mer, 1896. He does not distinguish the real difference between the prayer of simplicity and the prayer of quiet, understood in St. Teresa's sense (see *Graces of Interior Prayer,* ch. V, and the article by P. A. Poulain in the review *Les Études,* April 20, 1899). He admits that these graces are "an unknown country" to him (Op. VII, Preface). This book consists almost wholly of writings prior to the fifteenth century, and for this reason alone it is interesting as showing the less accurate knowledge of those times (see a similar remark regarding Vallgornera, **68**).

**87. St. Margaret Mary** Alacoque, Nun of the Order of the Visitation (b. Louthecour, in Burgundy, a. d. 1647, d. Paray-le-Monial 1690). *Vie et Œuvres,* published by the Convent of Paray-le-Monial, 2 vols., Poussielgue, 1867; 2nd ed., 1876. English: *Life of Blessed Margaret Mary,* Orat. Series, 2 vols., 1850.

**88. Fléchier**, of the Académie Française. Member of the Congregation of Christian Doctrine, Bishop of Nîmes (b. Pernes a. d. 1632, d. Montpellier 1710). Vol. V of his Complete Works, 1782; *Dialogues en vers sur le quiétisme; mémoires sur les faux prophètes du Vivarais* (written about 1690). New edition of his Works by Migne.

**89.** *Le charme du divin amour, ou Vie... de la Soeur* **Bénigne Gojoz**, Lay-sister of the Visitation of Turin (b. Viuz, Geneva, a. d. 1615, d. Turin 1692), by Mother M.-Q. de Provane. The date of the manuscript is 1693. 1st ed., Turin, 1846; 2nd ed. completed by Canon Peletin, Besançon, 1901. Mother de Provane distinguishes fifteen successive states of soul in her *Life*, but the majority are not degrees of prayer. They are merely different thoughts that predominated in Sister Benigne's mind during long periods of her life. This writer pays no attention to chronology. English: *Life of Jeanne Benigne Gojoz*, from the French of Mother M.-G. de Provane, 1878.

**90. Lopez de Ezquerra,** Priest, *Lucerna mystica*, Venice, 1692 and 1702.

**91. Nicole.** *Réfutation des erreurs des quiétistes*, Paris, 1695.

**92.** De **la Bruyière,** Jean, of the Académie Française (b. near Dourlay, Normandy, 1646, d. Versailles 1696). Acted as teacher of history to the young Duke of Burgundy under Bossuet. Author of many satires. *Dialogues posthumes... sur le quiétisme*, Paris, 1699. (*Œuvres*, Vol. III (Hachette et cie, 1895), contains a new edition of the *Dialogues*. Quietism is refuted here with an irony sparkling with wit.

**93. Bossuet**, Bishop of Meaux (b. Dijon a. d. 1627, d. Paris 1704). In his first treatise, *Instruction sur les états d'oraison*, 1697, Bossuet is conspicuous for knowledge, lucidity, and good sense. His second treatise (Firmin-Didot, 1897), which was rediscovered and published in our own time by Fr. Levesque, of Saint-Sulpice, speaks of ordinary prayer only—*Lettres* and various works; *Mystici in tuto; Schola in tuto.*

**94.** Fr. Antony **Massouli**, Dominican (a. d. 1632-1706). *Traité de la véritable oraison* (against quietistic teaching), Paris, 1699. We have also from his pen an admirable *Traité de l'amour de Dieu* (written with the same object), 1703. Reprinted, Paris, 1866.

**95.** Domenique **Bernino**, Bishop of Osimo (a. d. 1603-1663). *Life of St. Joseph of Cupertino* (Italian), French translation (*Vie*, etc.), 1856.

## IV

## Authors of the Eighteenth Century

**96.** Gottfried **Arnold**, Lutheran (b. Annaberg, Austria, a. d. 1665, d. 1714). *Historia et descriptio theologiæ mysticæ*, Frankfort, 1702.

**96.** *bis.* Fr. **Francis of St. Thomas,** Discalced Carmelite, Prior of the "desert" of Bolarque. *Medula mystica*, Coïmbre, 1705.

**97.** Fr. **Honoré de Ste. Marie,** Definitor-Provincial of the Discalced Carmelites of Aquitaine (a. d. 1651-1729). *Tradition des Pères et des auteurs écclésiastiques sur la contemplation*, 3 vols., Paris, 1708. Contains much information. *Dissertation apologétique*, Bordeaux, 1701; No. in Paris Bibliothèque Nationale, D. No. 37803.

**98.** Fr. **Rousseau**. *Avis sur les differents états de l'oraisonmentale,* 1710. Reprinted under the title of *Directions pratiques,* Lethielleux, 1903.

**99.** Blessed **Mary of the Angels,** Carmelite (b. Turin a. d. 1661, d. Santa Christina 1717). *Vita,* by Fr. Elias of St. Teresa, Turin, 1729. French: *Vie,* by Fr. Sernin de Saint-André, 2nd ed., Regis Ruffet, 1868. English: *Blessed Mary of the Angels,* by Fr. O'Neil, S. J., 1909.

**100.** Fr. **Joseph a Spiritu Sancto,** Definitor-General of the Discalced Carmelites (d. 1639). *Cursus theologiae mystico-scolasticae,* 6 vols. folio, Seville, 1710-1740. Vol. VI is very scarce. See above, his namesake (**78**). Quotations always refer to the second of the name.

**101.** Sister **Mary of St. Teresa,** Carmelite Lay-sister of Bordeaux. *Lettres spirituelles,* edited by Abbé de Brion, 2 vols., Paris, 1720.

**102.** Ven. **Anne Madeleine de Rémuzat** (b. Marseilles, a. d. 1696, d. Marseilles 1730). *Vie,* published by the Visitation Convent at Marseilles, 1st *Life,* 1760, 2nd *Life,* 1868; (2nd ed.) Vitte, 1894. Anne Madeleine has been called the Second Margaret-Mary. It was Margaret Mary who instituted the devotion to the Sacred Heart, and Anne Madeleine who propagated it. English: *The Nun of the Order of the Visitation,* Mgr. van den Berghe, 1879.

**103.** St. **John Baptist de la Salle** (b. Rheims a. d. 1651, d. St. Yon, near Arpajon, 1719), Founder of the Brothers of the Christian Schools. *Explication de la méthode d'oraison,* 1739; new edition at the Mother House, 1898. The author speaks continually of the prayer of simple regard.

**104.** Fr. Emanuel de la **Reguera**, Jesuit (b. a-d. 1668, d. 1747). *Praxis theologiæ mysticæ,* Rome, 1740-1745. This is a Latin translation of Godinez's little book, expanded into two enormous folios. See Schram (**114**). It contains much *ascetic* erudition regarding the early writers. It is not until p. 800 of Vol. I that he begins to ask himself in what ordinary and extraordinary contemplations differ one from the other (No. 147), and he leaves the question undecided.

**105.** Fr. **de Caussade,** Jesuit (a.d. 1693-1751). *Instructions spirituelles... sur les divers états d'oraison* (27 Dialogues), Perpignan, 1741. Reprinted, 2 vols., Lecoffre, 1892-95, with notes by Canon Bussenot of Rheims.

**106.** Eusebius **Amort** (b. Toebz, Bavaria, A.d. 1692, d. 1795), Canon-Regular, Theologian to Cardinal Lercari. *De revelationibus visionibus et apparitionibus privatis regulae tutae,* etc., Augsburg, 1744; Venice, 1750. A very instructive book as a collection of documents, from which he deduces a number (125) of rules for the discernment of spirits (Part I, ch. XXII), and applies them more especially, and sometimes with great severity, to St. Gertrude, Blessed Veronica of Binasco, and to about four hundred of Mary of Agreda's propositions. With regard to the last named, his *Nova Demonstratio de falsitate revelationum,* etc., Augsburg, 1751, was answered by Fr. Diego Matheo, Franciscan, Madrid, 1747, showing that in eighty places Amort had misunderstood the Spanish text of Mary of Agreda's book.

**107.** Pope **Benedict XIV** (when still Cardinal Lambertini) (b. Bologna 1675, d. Rome 1758). *De servorum Dei... canonizatione,* Rome, 1767. English: *Heroic Virtue,* translated from the Latin, 3 vols. Edited Cong. Orat., 1847.

**108.** Fr. Casimiro **Tempesti**, Friar-Minor, Conventual. *Mistica teologia,* from St. Bonaventure, etc., 2 vols., Venice, 1748.

**109.** Pietro **Gianotti**, Curé of Città di Castello. *Teologia mistica,* 3 vols., Lucca, 1751; *Ristretto di mistica,* Perugia, 1758.

**110.** Fr. Jean Baptiste **Scaramelli**, Jesuit (b. Rome a. d. 1687, d. Macerata 1752). *Directorio mistico,* Venice, 1754. French translation, *Directoire mystique,* by Fr. Catoire, 2 vols., Casterman, 1865. The clearest and most complete treatise on mysticism existing. It has often been imitated or abridged. From the descriptive point of view it is, I think, the best work of the eighteenth century; but with regard to theory, I have had to dissociate myself from him more than once. His classification, in particular, which has been adopted by Frs. Séraphin , Verhaege, Voss, etc., is somewhat defective, for it gives as distinct *degrees,* having a fixed place in the mystic ladder, conditions which are simply manners of being of the prayer of quiet, as well as of ecstasy (silence, inebriation, the anguish of love, touches, etc.). It is true, however, that these graces are received in a *higher measure* in the more exalted unions. The book contains discussions which give it a special interest for theologians.

**111.** **Lafiteau**, Bishop of Sisteron (a. d. 1685-1708). *Lettres spirituelles,* Paris.

**112.** Nicholas **Terzage**, Bishop of Marni. *Theologia historico-mystica,* folio, Venice, 1766. A refutation in detail of the teaching of Molinos. See Chaillot, 123.

**113.** Fra **Bernardo of Castelveture, Capuchin**, of Calabria, *Directorio mistico,* Venice, 1774 (3rd ed.).

**114.** Fr. **Schram**, Benedictine (a. d. 1658-1720). *Institutiones theologicæ mysticæ,* Augsburg, 1777. As he says in the Preface, his idea was to condense Reguera's two folio volumes into octavos. Some pages are transcribed verbatim (Aphorismi, Arcana). It contains good ascetical matter, but the classification of the mystic states leaves much to be desired. The writer seems to think that, in employing different terms, his predecessors were intending to designate different states. It is to be consulted for its learning. This work has been several times re-edited in the nineteenth century. First in Paris (Vol. I, 1845; Vol. II, 1847) by M. Schwertfeger, a Curé of the Diocese of Lausanne. With the exception of some unimportant suppressions, and that of the author's name, the edition seems to conform to the original. The numeration of the paragraphs is retained. It was reprinted at Lièges, 1860; but in the 1848 edition M. Schwertfeger had the unfortunate idea of altering the numeration and retouching the translation. The French translation (Vivés, 4th ed., 1891) is from the original text, but the numeration is changed. English: *Little Manual of Direction for Priests,* translated by H. Collins, 1882.

**115.** St. **Alphonsus Liguori** (b. Naples a. d. 1696, d. Nocera de Pagani 1787). *Homo Apostolicus,* Ap. 1, Venice, 1782, is a short summary of mysticism for the use of missionaries. It is to be found in full in *Praxis confessarii,* by the same holy Doctor.

**116.** Fr. Michael **Marciani**. *Trattato di mistica teologia,* Foligno, 1790.

## V

## Authors of the Nineteenth and Twentieth Centuries

**117.** Fr. Pierre Joseph **Picot de Clorivière** (b. Brittany 1735. d. Paris 1820), Restorer and first Superior of the Society of Jesus in France, after the Brief of re-establishment given by Pius VII. *Considérations sur l'exercise de la prière,* 1802 and (Devalois) 1887. A short and comprehensive summary of everything relating to prayer, both ordinary and extraordinary. Fr. de Clorivière possessed this last prayer in a high degree. His Life has been written by Fr. Jacques Terrien, Poussielgue, 1892.

**118.** Fr. **Grou**, Jesuit (b. in the Calaisis a. d. 1731, d. Lulworth, Dorset, 1803). *L'Interieure de Jésus et de Marie,* published from his manuscripts, by Fr. Cadres, S.J., 2 vols., 1845; reprinted 1862. He speaks of the prayer of simplicity (see *Graces of Interior Prayer,* ch. II, **75**). New and revised edition, Haton, 1909. *Maximes spirituelles,* Belin, 1789 (see Maxims, 2, 10, 14). English: *The Interior of Jesus and Mary,* 1891; *Spiritual Maxims,* 1898.

**119.** Johann Joseph **von Görres** (b. Coblentz a. d. 1776, d. Munich 1848). *Die Christliche Mystik,* 4 vols., Ratisbon, 1836-1842. French translation by Charles Sainte-Foi, *La Mystique chrétienne,* Poussielgue, 1854. His writings are interesting, but overweighted with endless pseudo-scientific dissertations; the authorities are not, as a rule, indicated. English: *The Stigmata,* a history of various cases. Translated from the *Mystik* of Görres, 1883.

**120.** *Dictionnaire de mystique,* in the Abbé **Migne's** third *Enyclopédie théologique,* 1858, folio. The author gives no authorities, which detracts very much from the value of the book.

**121.** Sister **Saint-Martinien,** of the Congregation of St. Charles. *Lettres,* Angers, Lacheze, 1863, 2 vols.

**122.** **Bizouard**. *Des rapports de l'homme avec le démon,* 6 vols., Gaume, 1863. Written in a good spirit and full of facts and authorities.

**123.** Mgr. **Chaillot**, a Roman Prelate. *Principes de théologie mystique;* Paris, Herve, 1866. The first two-thirds of the book is a refutation of Quietism; it is an abridged translation of Terzago. This work first appeared without the author's name, in the *Analecta Juris pontificii* of 1863. The remainder is a refutation of Mary of Agreda, as affecting sixty articles, condemned by Cardinal Gotti, whom Clement XII had charged with this examination (1734). *Analecta* (1855-1863).

The Preface gives a short history of the censures of which the *Mistica Città di Dio* had been the object in Rome.

**124.** Fr. Augustine **Hewitt** (b. Fairfield, Conn., U.S.A., a. d. 1820, d. New York 1891). One of the Founders and second General of the Institute of St. Paul the Apostle in New York. A convert from Anglicanism. *Light and Darkness,* New York, 1871, 1896.

**125.** Fr. **C. P. Séraphin**, Passionist (d. a. d. 1879). *Principes de théologie mystique,* Casterman, 1873. He has made great use of Scaramelli; *Grandeurs de Marie,* 5 vols., de Lossy, 1860. Vol. I is an apology for Mary of Agreda. The writer maintains this, when taken alone, inadequate rule, that we should "judge the revelations by the life" (p. 25). He applies it so as to leave it to be supposed that the *holiness* of the life proves the complete truth of the revelations. Fr. Séraphin thinks that he is giving a guarantee of Mary of Agreda's inspiration when he says that without having learnt the natural sciences she spoke on these subjects with an accuracy that was the admiration of all hearers. But this admiration is in itself a rather unfavourable note. For her contemporaries were full of misconceptions regarding physics, chemistry, medicine, etc. If she pleased them so greatly, it was that their views were identical. The truth in physics or physiology would have repelled them (see *Graces of Interior Prayer,* ch. XXI, 26, a similar remark regarding St. Hildegard).

**126.** Dr. **Lefebvre**, Professor of General Pathology and Therapeutics at the Catholic University of Louvain. *Louise Lateau; étude médicale,* Louvain, 1870-1873. It contains much information on ecstasy and the stigmata, treated in a scientific way. *Vie* of the same, by Dr. Rohling, translated from Dr. de Noue, Douniol, 1874. English: *Life of Louise Lateau,* translated by Northcott, d. d., 1873.

**127.** Fr. **Verhaege**, a Picpus Father. *Manuel de théologie mystique,* Palme, 1877. He adopts Scaramelli's classification.

**128.** M. **Griveau**, Judge of the Court at Nevers. *Étude sur la condemnation du livre de Fénelon,* 2 vols., Poussielgue, 1878.

**129.** Fr. de **Benniot**, Jesuit. *Le miracle et les sciences médicales,* Didier-Perrin, 1879; *Le miracle et ses contrefaçons* (5th ed.), Retaux, 1895.

**130.** Abbé **Ribet**. *La mystique divine,* Poussielgue, 3 vols., 1879, 1895.

**131.** Fr. **Voss**, Picpus Father. *Scaramelli directorium mysticum in compendum redactum,* Lecoffre, 1881

**132.** Fr. Pierre Xavier **Pouplard**, Jesuit. *Un mot sur les visions,* Palmé, 1883; Téqui, 1897.

**133, 134.** Fr. **Jeiler**, Franciscan. On the word contemplation (Beschauung), *Kirchenlexicon,* 1883. **Pruner's** article on *mysticism* in the same dictionary is merely a summary of Schram.

**135.** Fr. **Seisdedos Sanz**, Jesuit. *Estudios sobre las obras de Santa Teresa,* Madrid, Library of *Ciencia cristiana,* 1886.

**136.** Fr. André-Marie **Meynard**, Dominican. *Traité de la vie interieure,* 2 vols., 1889; 3rd ed., Amat, 1899. He makes great use of Vallgornera (**68**). It is incomprehensible that this learned writer should say "as a general rule the prayer of quiet does not endure a minute" (Vol. II, 208). Also that the soul "may be raised to extraordinary, perfect contemplation by means of created things" (*Ibid.,* 36. The example that he quotes is simply ordinary meditation); also that "the contemplative act, even the most perfect act of the spiritual marriage, does not, ordinarily, last more than half an hour" (*Ibid.,* 18). See also *Graces of Interior Prayer,* ch. XXX, **2,** note.

**137.** Abbé **Auger**. *Étude sur les mystiques des Pays-Bas.* This very instructive treatise occurs in the *Memoirs* crowned by the Belgian Academy, Brussels, April, 1892. *De doctrina et meritis Joannis van Ruysbroeck,* thesis for the Doctor's Degree, Louvain, Valinthout, 1892.

**138.** Fr. Aug. **Poulain**, Jesuit. Various review articles, particularly *La mystique de Saint Jean de la Croix,* in *La Messager du Coeur de Jésus,* 1893 (the separate issue is out of print). *Les desiderata de la mystique, Les Études,* for March 20, 1898 (out of print).

**139.** Dr. **Imbert-Goubeyre,** Professor at the Clermont School of Medicine. *La stigmatisation et l'extaste divine,* 2 vols., Amat, 1894. *L'hypnotisme et la stigmatisation,* leaflet, Bloud, 1899. The first of these works contains many of the statistics quoted throughout this book.

**140.** Abbé **Saudreau**, first Chaplain of the Bon-Pasteur at Angers. *Les degrees de la Vie spirituelle,* Vic et Amat, 1896, 1897. A book full of unction. *La Vie d'union à Dieu,* Amat, 1900. At the end of his chapter x, the author criticises, without giving any names, "certain modern writers" (I am amongst them), and endeavours to some extent to combat the thesis of the felt presence of God laid down in my chapters V and VI. Already, in his first work, he failed to recognise any line of demarcation between the prayer of simple regard and St. Teresa's prayer of quiet. This explains why, in the first edition of *The Degrees,* he finds fault with the classification of contemplation as being either acquired or infused. He returns to this position in his next work (No. 128), *L'état mystique,* Amat, 1903. The writer explains in ch. VIII, No. 69, that the mystic state is, in his opinion, composed of two elements: 1° a knowledge of God which is confused and which surpasses our intelligence (he does not further define its object and mode); 2° an unreasoned but very intense love. He evidently takes it for granted here that he is defining the mystic state in an advanced and highly developed stage only. In ch. XII, § 6, 141, he, like Fr. Ludovic de Besse, gives the name mystic to a prayer which is that of simple regard only. These writers fix the frontier separating the ordinary way and the mystic way at an earlier point than I have done.

M. Saudreau's method consists in quoting the writers prior to St. Teresa in particular. As he indicates no very clear line of demarcation (see *Graces,* etc., ch.

XXX) between the various states of prayer, he wishes this system to be followed, regarding the tendency of the moderns to be more precise as a mistake.

This writer's conception of mysticism has led him (No. 145, ch. XIII) to a proposition which no one accepts: "The words mystic way, contemplative way, unitive way, perfect way, refer to the same state." This would be true only if, with him, we were to regard the mystic state and contemplation as beginning at a very low degree of prayer.

In so far as it is *positive,* M. Saudreau's system is not opposed to mine with reference to mystic knowledge. We both hold that it is of a higher nature than the knowledge acquired in ordinary prayer, and that it comes directly from God, instead of being produced by reasoning or by the memory.* But he wishes to stop there, thinking that experience teaches nothing more and that everything is said. Personally I think I can define things more minutely. His system will often be preferred by those who require, first and foremost, a simple theory. This one is as simple as can be desired. It can be expressed in two lines, and adds no new mystery to the mysteries of faith. And, further, M. Saudreau says repeatedly that his view alone represents the "traditional teaching," that of the "Great Masters" (with capitals.) This repeated declaration, given with great assurance, ends by impressing certain minds who have not enquired whether the opposite doctrine could not say as much. M. Saudreau has published another work: *Les faits extraordinaires de la Vie spirituelle,* Amat, 1908. For the reply, see A. Poulain in the *Revue du Clergé Français* (June 15, 1908) and Fr. de Seguier in *Les Études* (Oct. 20, 1908, and Jan. 5, 1909) See also *Graces of Interior Prayer,* ch. V, **5,** note.

The better to prepare the mind for the reception of some of his ideas, M. Saudreau will not allow the name extraordinary to be applied to the mystic states of union below ecstasy. This is contrary to tradition. At the beginning of the seventeenth century Fr. du Pont applies this description to the prayer of quiet "and of silence" (*Meditations,* Introduction, § 1), and a little later Philippus a SS. Trinitate also makes use of this term, which has become usual (Part I, Tr. 1, disc. III, art. 1).

M. Saudreau also states that the ligature is not met with in the mystic unions below ecstasy (p. 199), and he confuses it with the action on the body. He adds: "Not one of the Masters attributes such effects to the prayer of quiet." Such assertions are incomprehensible when we read the extracts at the close of ch. XIV (*Graces*). English: *The Degrees of the Spiritual Life,* translated by Dom Bede

* Let us note that even in the most ordinary prayer, God can give direct lights. This character could therefore only mark the degree of distance between it and the mystic state. Let us also notice that M. Saudreau separates this character from those with which I associate it. Now, thus isolated, this sign cannot be identified with any certainty, for our natural intelligence produces acts that seem quite similar: it has its intuitions and, apparently, at least, its creations. Thus the character which M. Saudreau gives as distinctive of the mystic state, is practically unverifiable. It is the same with those who claim that an act is mystic when it results from a gift of the Holy Ghost (see ch. VI, 19 *bis*.)

Camm, O. S. B., 2 vols., 1907. *The Way that leads to God,* translated by L. L. Yorke Smith, 1910.

**141.** Fr. **Ludovic** de Besse, Capuchin. *L'Eclaircissements sur les œuvres de Saint Jean de la Croix,* Oudin, 1893; *La science de la priere,* Annat, 1903. He wishes to popularise the prayer of simplicity, which design is excellent; but he is wrong to call it a mystic state and to speak of the states described by St. Teresa as miraculous. I have pointed out many other inaccuracies in *Les Etudes,* Nov. 5, 1903. This book attacks me more than once—not by name, however.

**142.** M. Henry **Joly**. *Psychologie des saints,* 1897. English: *The Psychology of the Saints,* with Preface and notes by H. Tyrrell, 1898.

**143.** Abbé **Lejeune**, Cure of Charleville. *Manuel de théologie mystique,* Poussielgue, 1897; *Introduction à la vie mystique,* Lethielleux, 1899. The author deals briefly here with mysticism; in his first and last chapters he gives just what is strictly necessary for beginners. *L'oraison rendue facile,* Lethielleux, 1904, treats of ordinary prayer only, but contains some excellent chapters for souls needing encouragement. Note those on *petitions, false abandonment, spiritual sweetness, aridities.* Lastly, the article *Contemplation* in M. Vacant's *Dictionnaire de théologie;* it is short and pithy.

**144.** Anonymous (Rev. Mother **Cécile**, Abbess of Solesmes). *La Vie spirituelle et l'oraison,* Retaux, 1899. See especially chapters IX, X, XI, on the prayer of the ancients. English: *The Spiritual Life and Prayer,* 1900.

**145.** Abbé **Gombault**, Curé of Montlivaux, Loir-et-Cher. *L'Imagination et les états preturnaturels* (from the author), 1899. Work crowned by the Institut Catholique de Paris, 1899. Also articles published in *La Science Catholique,* Oct., 1907; Nov., 1908.

**146.** M. **Estrade**. *Les apparitions de Lourdes,* Mame, 1899. The author describes the counterfeits by which the devil endeavours to discredit true apparitions.

**147.** Mgr. Elie **Méric**. *L'autre Vie,* 2 vols., Téqui (11th ed.), 1900. A refutation of spiritualism. His Review (*Revue du monde invisible*) sometimes deals with questions of true mysticism; but more often with its counterfeits, human or diabolic. *L'Imagination et sesprodigues,* Téqui, 2 vols., 1905.

**148.** Fr. Ernest Dubois, Redemptorist. *De exemplarismo divino,* 4 vols. folio, Rome, Cuggiani, 1900. He deals with mysticism in Vol. IV, Books III and IV. He agrees with my interpretation of Bossuet's opuscule on the prayer of simplicity (Book III, p. 507).

**148.** *bis.* Algar Thorold. *Catholic Mysticism,* 1900.

**149.** Abbé Charles **Sauve**. *États Mystiques.* Appendix to *L'homme intime,* Amat, 1901.

**150.** Abbé Jules **Pacheu.** *Introduction à la psychologie des mystiques,* Oudin, 1901.

**151.** Dom **Marechaux**, Benedictine. *Le merveilleux divin et le mereilleux démoniaque,* Bloud, 1901.

**152.** Adrien **Arcelin**. *La dissociation psychologique; A study of unconscious phenomena,* Bloud, 1901. The separate reprints of a very striking article, published Oct., in the Brussels *Revue des questions scientifiques.*

**153.** Fr. **Dublanchy**, Marist. Article on *L'Ascetique* in Vacant's *Dictionnaire de théologie,* 1903.*

**153.** *bis.* Fr. Pius **Devine**, English Passionist. *A Manual of Mystical Theology,* 1903. He follows Scaramelli.

**154.** Fr. **Maumigny**, Jesuit. *Pratique de l'oraison mentale,* 2 vols., sold separately, Beauchesne, 1905 (Vol. I, ordinary prayer; Vol. II extraordinary prayer).

**155.** Cardinal **Gennari**. *Del falso misticismo,* Rome, Descleé (2nd ed.), 1907. It is a refutation of Molinos and Fénelon.

**156.** Dom Vital **Lehodey**, Abbot of the Trappist Monastery at Bricquebec (Manche). *Les Voies de l'oraison mentale,* Lecoffre, 1908.

**157.** Fr. **Vermeersch**, Jesuit, Professor of Theology at Louvain. *Quaestiones morales selectae,* Vol. I, Part II. Bruges, Beyaert, 1909. Note the thesis on the felt presence of God and the spiritual senses (No. 78).

**158.** Fr. A. B. **Sharpe**, M. A. *Mysticism, its true nature and value,* 1910. A clear exposition of mysticism, treated from the objective standpoint.

* In his Bibliography (col. 2053), he refers to the following books, the titles of which seem to be related to mysticism. I have not included them in my own list because, not having had the opportunity of examining them, I have been unable to determine whether the word *mysticism* is employed by their authors in its proper sense. I have omitted Martin Gerbert d'Hornau (*Principia théologies mysticm,* Abbey of St. Blaise, 1758), as the author speaks of asceticism only.

Sixteenth Century, (*a*) Sebastian Toscano, Augustinian. *Theologia mystica,* Lisbon, 1568; Venice, 1573.

(*b*) The Ven. Bartholomew of the Martyrs, Dominican (1514-1590), *Compendium doctrinæ spiritualis,* Lisbon, 1582. Republished in Venice, 1711, under the title *Compendium mysticm doctrinæ.*

Seventeenth century, (*c*) Ven. John of Jesus-Mary, Discalced Carmelite. *Theologia mystica,* Naples, 1607.

(*d*) Ven. Jerome of the Mother of God, Discalced Carmelite. *Theologia mystica,* Brussels, 1609.

(*e*) Leo of Saint-John, Carmelite. *Théologie mystique,* Paris, 2 vols., 1654.

(*f*) Dominic of the Holy Trinity. The Seventh Treatise of his *Bibliotheca theologica,* Rome, 1665-1676.

(*g*) Michael of St. Augustine, Calced Carmelite. *Institutionum mysticarum libri quatuor,* Anvers, 1671.

Eighteenth century, (*h*) Haver. *Theologia mystica,* Paderborn, 1708.

(*i*) John of Ascargorta, Franciscan. *Lecciones de Télogia mistica,* Granada, 1712.

(*j*) Anthony of the Annunciation, Discalced Carmelite. *Disceptatie mystica de oratione et contemplatione scolastico stylo,* Alcala, 1683; *Quodlibeta theologica mystica,* Madrid, 1712.

(*k*) Diago (Didacus) of the Mother of God. Franciscan, *Ars mystica,* Salamanca, 1713.

(*l*) Casimir de Marsala, Capuchin. *Dissertationes mystico-scholasticæ adversus pseudo-mysticos hujus ævi,* Palermo, folio, 1748; *Crisis mystico-dogmatica,* Palermo, 2 vols., folio, 1751.

## Some Biographies *

(*a*) *Fleurs dominicaines*, ou *les mystiques* **d'Unterlinden** (a. d. 1230-1330), by the Ven. de Bussieres, Poussielgue, 1864.

(*b*) **Sainte Lidwine** *de Schiedam* (b. Schiedam a. d. 1380, d. Schiedam 1433), by Huysmans; Stock, 1901. Chapter XI sets forth very clearly the part played in God's providence by sufferings.

(*c*) *Vie de Sainte* **Françoise Romaine** (b. Rome a. d. 1384, d. Rome 1440), by Dom Rabory, Benedictine of Solesmes. *Œuvre de Saint Paul,* 1884.

(*d*) *Vie de Sainte* **Catherine de Ricci** (b. Florence a. d. 1522, d. Florence 1590), by Fr. Bayonne, O. P., 2 vols. 12mo; Poussielgue, 1873. English: *Saint Catherine of Ricci,* with a treatise on the Mystical Life by Fr. Bertrand Wilberforce, O. P.; F. M. Capes.

(*e*) *Vie de la Vénérable* **Agnès de Jésus**, Dominican of Langeac (a. d. 1602-1634), by de Lantages; new edition by Abbé Lucot, 2 vols., Poussielgue, 1863. Another Life, by Vicontesse d'Ussel, Bloud, 1889.

(*f*) *Vie de la Bienheureuse* **Marie de l'Incarnation,** Carmelite (Mme. Acarie) (a. d. 1564-1638), by André du Val, Doctor at the Sorbonne, second Superior of the French Carmelites, 8vo, Paris, 1621; republished by Lecoffre, 1893. This writer lived in a close intimacy with Blessed Mary of the Incarnation, and gives us many facts concerning her inner life. He saw the foundation of more than fifty Carmelite houses, which were under his control. English: *A Gracious Life,* E. Bowles, 1879.

(*g*) *La Mère* **Jeanne Delaloë,** a Belgian Benedictine (a. d. 1620-1660), by Dom Bruno Destrée; Desclée, 1905. This book is chiefly composed of the Journal in which the servant of God entered (in a very simple style) the great graces that she received. She had much to put up with from an ignorant director.

(*h*) Venerable **Jeanne-Marie de la Croix** (a. d. 1603-1673), by Bede Weber, translated from the German into French by Charles Sainte-Foi; Poussielgue, 1856.

(*i*) *Vie de la Vénérable* **Marie Crescence Hoess,** of Kaufbeuren, in Bavaria, Religious of the Third Order of St. Francis (beatified 1902) (a. d. 1682-1744), by Fr. Jeiler, O. S. F. Rendered into French by Fr. Rugemer, O. S. C.; Casterman, 1896.

(*j*) *Vie de* **Catherine Emmerich** (a. d. 1774-1824), by Fr. Schmoeger, Redemptorist. Translated from the German by Abbé de Calzales; 3 vols., Bray,

* The writers referred to in the above list, either present different characteristics or they contain autobiographies that are interesting from the point of view of mysticism. Or, again, they are given incidentally, in connection with the *Works* of some saint, or, lastly, they are more widely known.

1868. In the *Revue des sciences ecclesiastiques* of 1889, Vol. II, certain errors, contradictory statements, and puerilities occuring in Catherine Emmerich's revelations are pointed out.

(*k*) **Les stigmatisées du Tyrol** (Maria von Moerl) (a. d. 1812-1868), Domenica Lazzari (1815-1848), by Leon Bore, 2nd edition, Lecoffre, 1846.

(*l*) *La Soeur* **Apolline Andriveau,** Sister of Charity (1810-1895), Poussielgue, 1896. English: *Sister Apolline Andriveau and the Scapular of the Passion.* Translated by Lady Herbert, 1887.

## List of Quietist Writers

**1.** Fr. **Benedict Fytche** (Canfield), Capuchin. Convert from Anglicanism (a. d. 1563-1610). *Regula Perfectionis;* sen breve *totius vitm spiritualis compendium,* Cologne, 1610. English: *The Ride of Perfection,* containing a brief and perspicuous abridgement of all the wholle spirituall life, reduced to only this point, of the Will of God (Rouen, 1609). Printed by order of his General, 1625. Numerous editions have appeared. Condemned 1689. St. Francis of Sales had already remarked that Book III "could be misinterpreted." *Œuvres,* edited by Dom Mackey, Vol. IV, p. 9.

**2.** Antonio **de Roias**, Secular Priest. *Vita dello Spirito ove s'impara a par orazione, ed unirsi con dio,* Madrid, 1620. It contains approbations by nine Bishops. French translation by Fr. Cyprien of the Nativity, *La Vie de l'esprit, pour s'avancer en l'oraison,* 1649, 1652. Condemned 1689. While recommending prayer without acts, and this to all persons alike, he introduces a number of acts, as a prelude, at any rate. See his final summary.

**3.** Fr. John **Falconi**, of the Order of Mercy (b. a. d. 1596, d. Madrid 1638). *Lettre a une fille spirituelle,* Madrid, 1657. Condemned 1688, 1689. This letter, dated 1628, was circulated in manuscript for thirty years. *Lettre a un Religieux;* condemned 1688. [First and second] *Alphabet (cartilla) teaching how to read in the Book of Life Eternal which is Jesus Christ* (Barcelona; the first in 1637, the two in 1676). Condemned in 1687, Molinos relied upon his writings (*Guida Spirituale,* Book I, ch. XIII, Nos. 86, 88).

**4.** Francis **Malaval**, a Layman of Marseilles (a. d. 1627-1719). He lost his sight at the age of nine months. After completing his studies, he became a Doctor of Theology and of Canon Law, and the fame of his vast knowledge procured him the title of Doctor at the Sorbonne. He published, under his initials only (F. M.), the first part of his *Pratique facile pour elever l'ame a la contemplation* (1664), and the complete work later (1669). At the request of his friend, Cardinal Bona, Pope Clement X allowed Malaval to receive the tonsure in 1674, and wear ecclesiastical dress. In 1680, Fr. Paul Segneri wrote against the *Pratique facile* in his book *Setti Principi,* which a commission of three Cardinals condemned in 1682. But, finally, Malaval was vanquished, and in

1688 his book was placed on the Index. He submitted in 1695 in a *Letter* addressed to his friend, the Abbé de Foresta, Provost of the Cathedral; he refuted Molinos' sixty-eight Propositions—incompletely, alas! for his *Letter* was also put on the Index in 1703. He made a pious death, however, at the age of ninety-two, in the arms of Mgr. de Belzunse, a year before the plague of Marseilles, and was buried in the Dominican Church, of which his nephew was Prior. His life has been written by the learned Abbé Dassy (Marseilles, 12mo, 1869).

Notwithstanding Malaval's good intentions, his writings have done immense harm, both by the numerous editions of his works that have appeared in France and Italy, and by the two books which he inspired: Epiphane Louis' *Conferences,* and Mme. Guyon's *Moyen Court.* Bourdaloue considered that this last work was substantially a reproduction of Malaval's *Letter* to Madame de Maintenon, July 10, 1694 (see the defence in Cardinal de Bausset's *Vie de Fénelon,* Vol. II). It is very likely that Molinos himself was inspired by Malaval's book.

**5.** Fr. Epiphane **Louis**, Abbé of Estival, in Lorraine, Procurator-General of the Premonstratensian Reform. *Conferences mystiques sur le recueillement,* Paris, 1676, 1684. It was composed at the request of the Benedictine Nuns of the *Saint-Sacrament* of Paris, of which the author was Superior.

**6. Molinos**, a Spanish priest (a. d. 1627-1696), lived for twenty years in Rome. *Guida spirituale,* Rome, 1675. Sixty-eight of his propositions were condemned by a Bull of Innocent XI, 1687. In the beginning Molinos presented his doctrines with such skill that he received the eulogistic approbations of four Inquisitors of the Holy Office and seven Cardinals (see *Vie de Madame Guyon,* by Guerrier). One of these, Innocent XI, on becoming Pope, had given Molinos rooms at the Vatican. For ten years the Dominicans and Jesuits protested; they proved that whole Convents were discarding vocal prayers and confession in order to give themselves up to a state of contemplative idleness of a wrong kind. But the partisans of Molinos were so adroit as to turn the tables, and they persuaded the Inquisition to censure the Jesuit writings. Fr. Paul Segneri narrowly escaped being put to death. Finally, Molinos' hypocrisy came to light. Twelve thousand letters referring to his direction of souls were found in his house, and his trial lasted for two years. Two hundred of his disciples were afterwards arrested. He confessed his immorality (Terzago, p. 15), abjured his doctrines, and was condemned to perpetual imprisonment. He died nine years later, aged sixty-nine. English: *The Spiritual Guide,* translated from the Italian reprint of 1690, Glasgow, 1885. *The Spiritual Guide,* by Michael de Molinos, translated by Kathleen Lyttelton, 1888.

**7. Mme. Guyon** de la Mothe (a. d. 1648-1717). Her writings amount to forty volumes. The chief are: *Moyen Court et tres facile defaire oraison;* Grenoble, 1685. Condemned in 1689. When the book appeared, some Religious of Grenoble bought fifteen hundred copies for distribution. *Les torrents* *spirituels* appeared at Cologne in 1720, after a long circulation in manuscript. The *Regle des associes a l'enfance de Jesus* (Lyons, 1685; condemned in 1689) is by Madame Guyon (see the preface to the *Opuscules,* Cologne, 1720), and not by de Bernieres, as the compilers of the Index of 1900 supposed. This last writer died twenty-six years earlier. See *Mme. Guyon, Sa Vie,* by M. Guerrier, Professor at the College (Lycee) at Orleans; Didier, 1881. Mme. Guyon was lacking in judgment. Her works show that she was satisfied with the falsest of arguments. But she possessed qualities calculated to gain her many partisans. She preached incessantly, spoke only of God and of prayer; the ladies of the Court felt fired by contact with such a holy soul. She was pliant, insinuating, fascinating, and at the same time obstinate, showing unwearying tenacity with regard to the resumption of opinions which she had seemed to retract. These opinions were reduced to one only: abandonment carried to its extremest limits, to annihilation, exhortations to this spiritual "death" and the subtle analysis of the endless degrees leading up to it, appear on every page with tiresome monotony, since imitated by certain apostles of abandonment. In her letters to Fénelon she takes the tone of a professor who finds that his pupil has still very much to learn, but she feels that he will accomplish it, thanks to his good-will. English: *Autobiography of Mme. Guyon,* 2 vols., translated by J. T. Allen, 1898; *A Short Method of Prayer and Spiritual Torrents,* translated by Marston, 1875.

**8.** Fr. Francis **La Combe,** Barnabite, Mme. Guyon's director. *Orationis mentalis analysis,* Verceil, 1686. Condemned in 1688.

**8.** *bis.* Abbé **Bertôt** (d. 1681), one of Mme. Guyon's first directors and for twenty years Chaplain to the Benedictine Nuns at Montmartre. *Le directeur mystique,* 4 vols., Cologne, 1726. It is the model of a weak and attenuated style. These volumes consist of the perpetual repetition of three or four obscure ideas.

**9.** Mère **Sainte-Thérèse de Jésus,** Abbess of the Convent at Lavaur (a. d. 18281884). *Vie,* written by herself and published under the title *Aimer a Souffrir,* by Abbé Roques, her director (3rd ed.), Toulouse, 1886. Condemned in 1894, with *Vues sur le Sacerdoce.* Mother St.-Teresa began her ecstasies at the age of forty, and they may have been real. But her revelations contained errors; at the age of fifty she made a vow never to desire or to ask God for any particular thing for herself until her death. This resembles the quietists' exaggerations. She believed that she knew by revelation that she would be "the mother of a great [spiritual] people," and that she would thus be the cause of a great revival in the Church. I have known several seers of visions with this illusion.

END OF BIOGRAPHICAL INDEX

[*Translation*]

LETTER FROM HIS EMINENCE, CARDINAL STEINHUBER,
PREFECT OF THE SACRED CONGREGATION OF THE INDEX

REVEREND FATHER,

—It is with real satisfaction that I have read your Reverence's book on Les Grâces d'Oraison. I cannot resist the desire to congratulate you with all my heart upon this fine and useful work. Directors of souls and the masters of the spiritual life will draw from it abundant supplies of enlightenment and the counsels necessary to enable them to solve the many complicated questions that they will encounter. What pleases me is the simplicity, the clearness, and the precision of your exposition, and still more, the solidity of the teaching. I can say that same for the care that you have taken to rely upon the old and approved masters who have written on the subject of mysticism. You dispel their obscurities, you reconcile their apparent contradictions, and you give their language the turn that the spirit and the speech of modern times demand. I pray God ardently to bless the labour that you have undergone in order to aid and console so many souls. May He assure an ever-increasing circulation to your book.

I salute you in Our Lord.

Your devoted servant in Christ,

✠ A. CARDINAL STEINHUBER.

Rome, *March* 16, 1904.

# AUTHOR'S PREFACE TO THE SIXTH EDITION

**1.**—In this sixth edition the numeration is the same as in the earlier editions, although certain paragraphs have been added. In order that the reader may distinguish these more readily, their numbers are usually followed by the word *bis;* the remainder of the book is but little altered.

**2.**—In the Preface to the first edition (No. **3**) I asked that competent persons, those who have studied mysticism or who have experienced certain of its graces, should kindly send me their observations. This request has been complied with. I thank my kind correspondents, and I beg them to continue to render me their assistance.*

The numerous letters thus received, or the conversations that have resulted, have served either to confirm the details of my descriptions or to point out some slight variations. Above all, questions have been put to me, and these have suggested fresh points to be dealt with.

**3.**—There is a somewhat widespread impression that mystical books may turn the heads of certain persons of heated imaginations, and suggest to them that God and the saints may come and converse with them and direct their conduct. It is recognised that my book, far from presenting this danger, is a vigorous remedy against these flights, whether because it dwells upon the illusions that such a way entails, or because it reverts constantly to the great truth that abnegation and love of the Cross must be the soul's great preoccupations. Those high-flown and restless spirits of which we speak are usually without this attraction.

The danger lies, not in speaking of revelations, but in doing so in a way that leads to their being desired. It is seen that I incline to the opposite tendency.

**4.**—Readers who wish to get a rapid general idea of my book will do well to omit the Extracts at the end of the chapters. This is a work of verification which is best carried out later.

NOTE

References to the Works of St. John of the Cross and St. Teresa relate, unless otherwise stated, to the following translations and editions: *Works of St. John of the Cross*, David Lewis, 1864. *Life of St. Teresa of Jesus*, David Lewis, 1904. *Interior*

* Those who have not my address can send their letters c/o my publishers (Gabriel Beauchesne et Cie, 117, Rue de Rennes, Paris).

*Castle*, Stanbrook ed., 1906. *Way of Perfection, Conceptions of the Love of God, Book of Foundations*, Abraham Woodhead, 1675. Letters of St.Teresa, Dalton, 1902. With regard to the extracts and quotations from other works, where an English translation was available, it has been utilised, and references are then given both to the English and the original titles. Where no such translation was available, the French title only is given, as *Vie, Œuvres*, etc.

[*Translator.*]

# INTRODUCTION TO THE TENTH EDITION

WITH BIOGRAPHICAL INDEX

BY J. V. BAINVEL

*Professor of Theology at the Institut Catholique of Paris*

THE author of this book having died three years ago, in 1919, the publisher has asked me to prepare a new edition for the press. It has seemed to me that the best way of doing so was to add an introduction to the work.

This Introduction comprises eight sections: I. The Author and his Work. II. The Matter of the Book. III. Criticisms and Controversies. IV, Poulain and Maumigny. V. Present State of Mystical Studies, VI. Practical Questions and Remarks. VII. The Present Edition. VIII. Additional Remarks.

## I
## THE AUTHOR AND HIS WORK

Before speaking of the book of which a new edition is here presented to the reader, it seems well to devote a few words to its author. I therefore first present his curriculum *vitae,* with the outstanding characteristics of his character and personality, following the short semi-official account of the *Litterae annuae.*

### *1. Life and Career of Père Poulain*

Père Augustin Francois Poulain was born at Cherbourg on December 15, 1836. After four years' studies with two companions in his native town, he was sent to the Jesuit college at Brugelette, where he finished his elementary course and took his humanities and rhetoric, all *mediocri successu,* as the writer of his biographical notice tells us: to be translated, I suppose, as "with middling success," in the Latin sense of *mediocris.* He did very well in philosophy, and at the end of the year obtained his B.-ès-L. After five years at Brugelette he went in 1854 to the ficole Sainte-Geneviève, where he did a year's science with like success, also gaining the baccalaureate. After a second year of scientific study he was admitted to the ficole Centrale.* But another way opened before him.

On October 25, 1858, he entered the Jesuit noviciate at Angers. After his two years' probation he made his vows at the ficole Sainte-Genevieve, and devoted another year to the study of mathematics.

From 1861 to 1870 he was successively supervisor at Metz, theological student at Laval (1867), and then, while continuing his theological studies, professor of mathematics at the École Sainte-Geneviève.

From October 1870 to 1881 he was twice sub-minister, once minister, four years supervisor, three years teacher of mathematics to candidates for the B.-es-Sc. His third year of probation was made at Laon in 1870-1, and he pronounced his final vows at the École Sainte-Genevieve on February 2, 1877.

From 1881 to 1897 he was sub-director at the Internat of the Catholic Faculties of Angers. In 1897-8 he taught mathematics at the scholasticate in Jersey.

In October 1898 he returned to Paris, to the residence in the rue de Sevres, and remained there until 1918, fulfilling various offices: sub-director of the artists' guild from 1898 to 1903; then director 1903-7. From 1898 to 1907 he was librarian, and in this office, after the dispersion of 1901, displayed a most praiseworthy and meritorious activity in satisfying the desires of all.

He published, among other works, *The Graces of Interior Prayer,* which has been several times reissued.

In August 1918, his strength failing, he retired to the hospital in the rue de Dantzig, where he died a holy death on July 19 of the following year, 1919.

He was naturally of a witty and happy disposition and diffused gladness all around him; the clearness of his mind is manifest in all he wrote.

### *2. Writings of Père Poulain*

On reading this dry resume of a well-filled religious life, one question at once presents itself to the reader's mind. How could a man so fully occupied in scientific teaching and supervision at the École Saint-Clement at Metz and at the École Sainte-Genevieve in Paris; so taken up by the material cares and discipline of a large house at Angers, in the midst of continually recurring difficulties whose vicissitudes he records with a wit and humour which charmed all without ever involving a breach of charity; devoted as he was, in his capacity of sub-director or director, to his artists, whose often irregular habits and unforeseen adventures caused him much worry and anxiety, and among whom he needed all his presence of mind and ingenuity to give effectual help to these young folk, often wilful and imprudent; how could this man have conceived the idea of compiling a treatise on mysticism, how did he prepare himself for the task and bring it to

* It is not very clear from the information in my possession whether he gained his B.-ès-Sc in 1855 or 1856, nor whether he spent a year at the Centrale.

conclusion? That as a supervisor he could issue a charming little booklet on *The Art of Skating*, that as professor of mathematics he could compose a *Treatise on Geometry** or brilliant talks on the teaching of mathematics,† we can understand. But a work on *The Mysticism of St. John of the Cross*, a large volume on *The Graces of Interior Prayer*! His friends could not get over it. He had so little of "the mystical look"! And then he had done comparatively so little theology! But facts must be faced.

And it was no joke, none of those witty efforts to which he unexpectedly gave vent so appositely and almost without thought. He meant it to be a serious work. Fond of a joke as he was, both for himself and in others, he would allow of no joking on these subjects, which he evidently had very much at heart. In this matter he meant to be taken seriously.

*3. His Studies of and Interest in Mysticism*

He had, in fact, long been interested in these questions. Probably his attention had been drawn to them in the first years of his religious life; it certainly was in his "third year." And everything goes to show that this attention was not a matter of purely speculative curiosity. In spite of his jealous care never to open his soul to profane eyes, it may be guessed that he had himself felt the mystical touch. Once at least he confided in a young religious capable of understanding him that his mystical experience had gone as far as the prayer of quiet, no farther. This confession seems to be confirmed by a number of convergent indications. The author, then, is expressing no mere abstract maxim when he says that, far from being proud of the prayer of quiet, he who has attained it should rather only feel humbled, and say: "I have only got so far."‡

It is an evident fact that the little work on *The Mysticism oj St. John of the Cross*, first published serially in the *Messager du Coeur de Jésus*, in 1893, presupposes a long familiarity not only with the writer who is its subject, but with the whole field of mystical questions. As for *The Graces of Interior Prayer*, it bore witness from its first edition in 1901 to a knowledge of mystical authors and a mastery of the subject which were not those of a mere amateur or curious enquirer.§

* He used in fun to call this work the "Poor Man's Geometry" for he had devoted all his ingenious and inventive wit to simplifying the theorems so as to bring them within the reach of the meanest intelligence.

† Especially in his *Causeries pidagogiques*, edited by J. V. Bainvel, 1898.

‡ "Those who remain stationary would do well to ponder a thought that should engender humility; it is that God has perhaps called them to mount up higher..., Instead of feeling a certain pride because we have arrived at the prayer of quiet, we ought to ask ourselves fearfully why we have not gone beyond it." Ill, **12**..

§ When the book first appeared, Père Poulain had already been in contact with many prayerful souls. In a letter written in 1901, some extracts from which are given in the *RAM* of Jan. 1921, II, 67-8, he wrote to one of his friends: "In thirty years I have come to know 33 persons who seem to have real supernatural graces, and nine who have false visions." M, Saudreau is mistaken in saying the contrary.

The author did not cease work on it until his death. In the notes which have kindly been put at my disposal with a view to the present edition, I have found no trace of this work, but only numerous letters addressed to the author either with regard to translations—these have appeared in four or five languages at least—or to ask him questions, discuss some point or other, suggest ideas, etc.

### *4. The first Edition of The Graces of Interior Prayer*

The first edition was not issued without difficulty. The wind had not yet set in the direction of works on mysticism. More than one person doubted whether it were prudent to popularise these matters; they feared, not without some apparent reason, that such a book might turn weak heads. Moreover, the author's theological studies seemed to have been insufficient, and the first edition bore traces of this insufficiency. An eminent professor of theology, Père J.-B. Terrien, without imposing an absolute veto, and recognising the great merit of the work, required corrections before which the author recoiled, not from conceit, but by reason of his attachment to ideas which he considered right and practical—and he was in some degree right. An umpire was appointed who, by limiting the theologian's requirements to what was purely matter of doctrine Père Terrien was as good and condescending as could be), made them more acceptable to the author, and by obtaining from the latter the sacrifice of some cherished ideas and the insertion of certain formulas designed to guard against false interpretations or misleading applications, brought about a sufficient agreement. The theologian was glad to be able to pass a book which he valued; the author, while keenly feeling some of the sacrifices, was glad to be able to take wing at the cost of a few feathers.

### *5. The Success, Diffusion and Influence of the Book*

The success of the book is well known. In twenty years nine editions have appeared, comprising twenty thousand copies. Several of these new editions show a noteworthy progress. The author was careful to profit by everything; criticisms, the questions which were put to him from all directions, new experiences, contact with a larger number of souls, the growing number of publications and courses of lectures, both on mysticism and on kindred questions (lives of the Saints or pious persons, studies of experimental psychology or pathology, rationalist schemes and explanations or the replies of Christian apologists); he managed to bring all these within his wide and elastic framework, like a collector labelling, classifying and enriching his collection. The book thus grew considerably in size between the first and the ninth editions. There is no doubt that the work played a great part in the popularisation of mystical studies and the ever-quickening interest manifested in them on all hands, not only in France, but throughout the world. I have already mentioned that it has been translated into four or five languages. The author, in his ninth edition, 1914, mentions four translations: English, German, Italian and Spanish. We need not mention the works of all kinds which were inspired or influenced by it, particularly the *Dictionnaire de theologie catholique*, the American *Catholic Encyclopaedia*, the *Dictionnaire apologetique*, etc. Specially connected with this influence was the publication of the *Journal intime de Lucie-Chrisiine*, which was placed in his hands as a result of the fame his book had gained him.

### *6. Qualities and Defects of the Book. The Author's Purpose*

Its success was well deserved. He had succeeded, with his rare talent for popularisation, in writing a clear, didactic treatise on delicate and difficult subjects, a treatise comparatively short, very up-to-date in its presentation, within the capacity of all, giving everyone the impression that they understood what had until then been considered as beyond the reach of most. We feel that the author always had in view, when speaking of mystical things, readers—especially women readers—of moderate intelligence and culture, pious folk who do not speak for themselves, cloistered religious, humble and modest souls. Even in learned discussions, or with those who are called "scholars," he remains accessible to all—a perfect populariser. In this work we see once more the author of the "Poor Man's Geometry," with its short phrases, its explanations simple sometimes almost to the point of naive, its clear divisions, its many paragraphs, its clever typographical devices, all the professor's condescension to the willing pupil. These advantages, as often happens in such cases, are not without corresponding drawbacks; extreme subdivision, which sometimes interferes with a complete view; classifications that are somewhat artificial, in which definitions and formulas correspond only imperfectly with concrete reality; dissections of living activity in which the soul, the principle of unity, of continuity, even of life, is somewhat withdrawn from the observer's sight. We must none the less recognise that the author has done all he could to lessen or avoid these drawbacks, which are a condition of all scientific analysis and observation. He warns us repeatedly that in the mystical life everything holds together; that the various states follow without any abrupt transition, are incessantly fused and mingled with each other.*

This combination of advantages and drawbacks is particularly to be observed in the relegation to the end of the chapters of the extracts from mystical writers. Its advantages are very great. The reader is not being continually distracted by footnotes; the movement and sequence of thought is more obvious; the extracts, given at length and following on each other without interruption, form a kind of anthology of mysticism, of which each chapter is a garland composed of the most characteristic or finest passages that have been written on each of the subjects treated. On the other hand, immediate verification is less easy, the text is a little dry and meagre, the relation between a statement and the authorities supporting

* See, in the Analytical Index, the entries *Continuity, Unity, Degrees, Transitions.*

it is not so close (especially as at times the quotations do not prove quite what they are asked to prove).

However, all things considered, the advantages seem to outweigh the disadvantages, the more so as we see in the book what the author himself principally saw in it, a practical guide "for those souls who are beginning to receive mystical graces and who do not know how to find their way in this new world," and also for those "who are drawing near and who have entered a state bordering on it," seeing that "the same difficulties present themselves to these souls also."*

True, it is not under this practical aspect that most of its readers consider the book. But even for those who seek in it not so much a rule for their personal conduct as a manual of mystical knowledge, we must, I think, recognise that the author has been well served by his pedagogical instinct in the ordering and arrangement of the book and in all that concerns its editing. It remains to be seen whether the matter corresponds to the form.

## II
## The Matter of the Book

### *7. Descriptive Process*

I said just now that in this book we have a real treatise on mysticism. The author wished above all to provide a practical handbook. Actually he has written a substantial work in which the chief questions connected with this delicate and difficult subject are clearly and skilfully propounded. As he himself says, his book is descriptive rather than doctrinal. Rightly or wrongly, he believed that "the speculative school has produced masterpieces which could probably not be surpassed"†; "one would prefer to re-edit their immense labours rather than begin the work all over again"; "mysticism cannot make any advance on that side"; that "the future of mysticism" lies in the progress of observation, and that (doubtless in this direction) "our successors will do better than ourselves," as happens "in all the descriptive sciences," and as has happened in mysticism itself, where authors are distinguishing, " although very slowly, states which had previously been confused."‡ In any case he has concentrated on the facts in order to study, distinguish and classify them. This work he has performed in a masterly manner. He studied first and foremost, St. Teresa, then St. John of the Cross, but he neglected no mystical writer, at any rate among those who were Catholics. The earlier writers gave him excellent general ideas, but for exact and clear

* Preface to the First Edition, **2**.

† The masters of whom the author seems specially to be thinking are Alvarez de Paz, Vallgornera, Philippas de SS. Trinitate, Antonins a Spiritu Sancto, and La Reguera. I think he would also include, though separately, St. Thomas and St. Bonaventure.

‡ Preface, **2**.

classification he turned to St. Teresa, especially to the *Interior Castle*, supplementing her on some points of detail* by St. John of the Cross. But St. Teresa herself is not very methodical; from the play of her mobile thoughts and the imagery flowering in her descriptive passages the movement as a whole and its governing lines must be disentangled. This he has done. Let us follow the author in his task, rapidly indicating his main arguments and conclusions, and adding a few remarks and explanations where these are called for.

### 8. *Analysis of the Book*

Chapter I begins by distinguishing between ordinary prayer and extraordinary or mystical prayer. Grace is necessary for both, for both are supernatural; but the former is active, and depends on ourselves, the second is passive, and depends on a special movement of God which is not ours to command.† Those acts or states are therefore mystical which could not be produced by our own effort and industry, even in a slight degree or for a single moment. To distinguish still more clearly, he proposes to give the name of *mystic* "to supernatural states containing a *knowledge* of a kind that our own efforts and our own exertions could never succeed in producing " (I, **9**). But we shall see that this element of *knowledge* is not admitted by all, at any rate in the sense in which our author uses it.

To distinguish better between mystic and ordinary prayer, the author in Chapter II gives a rapid sketch of the latter, dividing it into four degrees: vocal prayer, meditation or methodical or discursive prayer,‡ affective prayer, the

* For instance, on the prayer of mystical aridity.

† The author is careful to avoid the phrase "passive states" as equivocal. It is true that this expression needs explanation; nevertheless I think it should be preserved, not only because it is consecrated by long usage (we know that it goes back at least to Dionysius the mystic, fifth or sixth century), but also because it indicates very well the difference between ascetic activity, which is chiefly our own with God's help, and mystical passivity, which is chiefly God's action in us and consists above all in the reception of this action, without our having any other personal share in it than the vital reaction.

‡ Contemplation in the sense in which St. Ignatius uses the word in his Exercises, although an ordinary and active form of prayer, is none the less clearly to be distinguished from discursive or reflective meditation. It is, to use the Saint's words, "visual meditation," and its proper procedure consists not in discoursing or reasoning in the strict sense, but in looking and listening, making some practical reflections and applications of what is seen and heard, extracting the lesson from the facts, "drawing some profit from them," as the Saint puts it. Would that this contemplation, as St. Ignatius understands it, were better understood and practised by those good folk who go in for prayer! It withdraws us from the vague and abstract and accustoms us to live in close touch with our Lord, to absorb His spirit, to enter into intimacy with Him.—into His heart, as we may say. As a method, nothing could be simpler than this, no application more elastic, no study more interesting, nothing helps us to know our Lord better and attach ourselves to Him more closely. He becomes a living reality, the Gospel a spectacle unrolling itself before the eyes of our mind, enlightened by faith and love, as it was unrolled before the eyes of the disciples and the multitudes, and in this familiar contact with our divine Master we take on ourselves, as it were, His thoughts, His feelings, His habits and His life. As for meditation, we must not see this either as a matter of reasoning pure and simple; it also visualises, applies and relishes the truth which it contemplates. The whole soul gives itself and acts normally in it.

prayer of simplicity or of simple regard.* The two latter, the second especially, are very close to mystical prayer, although they do not so far contain any mystical element. We now understand why the author speaks of them at length; he explains them thoroughly, and defends them against their detractors, while pointing out their possible abuses. The advice he gives on this subject is excellent, and, although it contains no element of Quietism, it reacts against the excesses of those who see Quietism everywhere. Before leaving the region of ordinary prayer, the author glances at the history of mental prayer, indicating some interesting details and pointing out several current errors.†

After these preliminaries comes "General Ideas on Mystical Union." This is the second part. The author begins in Chapter III by distinguishing, according to the nature of the object that is presented to the mystical contemplation, those graces which he calls *deific* (because it is God himself who is manifested in them, and they afford a means of entering into the Divinity) from those which he calls *ex-deific*, visions or revelations having some object other than God.‡ The former are are the principal, and constitute the mystical union or infused contemplation in the strict sense.

He goes on to distinguish the four degrees of this mystical union as St. Teresa describes them in the *Interior Castle*: incomplete mystical union, or *prayer of quiet*; full or semi-ecstatic union, which the saint calls the *prayer of union;* ecstatic union or ecstasy§; transforming or deifying union, generally known as spiritual marriage. The author sees in the first three degrees one and the same grace—divine union in the weak, medium and strong states respectively. In the prayer of quiet the mind is joined to God, but the imagination is free**; the union is therefore incomplete, and distractions are possible. In the full union the imagination itself is taken captive, and distractions no longer intervene; but the action of the senses is not suspended, and one can, though not without effort,

* The application of the senses, as St. Ignatius understands it, is at once affective prayer and prayer of simple regard, but without mingling with any other: it is *sui generis*, and requires a separate classification. This prayer is much like certain forms of mystical prayer, and real mystical touches may be mingled with it, as also happens moreover in contemplation or even meditation.—One word more on this matter. [The *Exercises* of St. Ignatius are *written after the ascetic manner*, but they might have been *made* by the Saint *after the mystic manner*, and often are so by many who hardly realise it.] He did not consider these questions as we do nowadays, and did not worry himself much with such distinctions.

† I presume that the date 1868 given in paragraph **66** *bis* is erroneous. Should it be 1688?

‡ These terms are not elegant. But the author does not examine them too carefully. Like the scientist, he is ready to coin new terms in order to explain new facts and new relations. He bases the word *deific* on the authority of Dante, but I doubt whether Dante, who used the word *s'india* of the Seraph who plunges into God, had the same sort of idea in mind.

§ Ecstasy, considered as alienation of the senses, is not so much a fact of the mystical order properly speaking, as an epiphenomenon; but the "prayer of ecstasy" implies something more, in *the union itself*, than the "prayer of union." This latter is called *simple* union as opposed to *ecstatic* union, and *full* union as opposed to union of *quiet*.

** I take it that the action of the senses is joined to that of the imagination and goes with it step by step, but the author does not say so.

communicate with the outside world and withdraw from prayer.* In ecstasy there there is in addition complete alienation of the senses, and all voluntary movement is impossible.

There are therefore, before the spiritual marriage, three quite distinct degrees of mystical union, though these are themselves of varying intensity and joined to each other by an imperceptible transition.

From these three degrees of union, which differ only in intensity, the spiritual marriage is distinguished as a stable and constant *state,* making the whole life a life of prayer, and putting the soul into continual communion of thought and action with the divine Spouse—though here again there are numerous variations.

The author remarks, and he seems to be right in doing so, that many words used by the mystics (prayer of silence, mystical sleep, inebriation, jubilation, wound of love, flight of the spirit, rapture, etc.) are not *successive degrees* of mystical development, rather *different conditions of experiencing* the four preceding degrees.

In order to illuminate the road by explaining terms and classifying ideas, we must make clear the different meanings attached to the word *contemplation* (chapter IV). It is usually defined as a *simple regard accompanied by love.* But what variety we find in its application! At one time the word is synonymous, with the mystical state, at another it signifies mystic prayer, at another the intuition evoked by the ordinary exercise of our natural faculties, etc. Hence arises the necessity for an historical explanation of the term. Let us especially note two things:

1. The distinction, already of long standing, between *acquired* and *infused* contemplation, the former meaning the prayer of simplicity, the normal end of discursive meditation, the latter meaning mystical prayer. This acquired contemplation is no invention of Père Poulain. He shows that the word was used as far back as the seventeenth century in the sense in which he uses it. As for the thing itself, and the distinction between the two kinds of contemplation, that is traditional, and is to be found clearly indicated by Richard of St. Victor.†

2. The use or abuse by the seventeenth-century quietists of both the word and the thing; of the word, by speaking of contemplation acquired by the cessation of all mental activity; of the thing, by regarding this state of acquired contemplation

* The possibility of this effort implies that the will is free, and can work on the senses and motor forces.

† In the ninth edition the author has given in an Appendix (*Appendix I* of the present work) a list of authors who have spoken of *acquired* as distinct from *infused* contemplation. Some few errors have been observed in this list; but Père Poulain's teaching seems certain. In this same ninth edition the author has suppressed (IV, 7) the line where it had been stated that the words *acquired contemplation* are to be found in Denis the Carthusian, *De fonte lucis,* ch. viii; but the reference in the Table of Proper Names remained. I have suppressed it.

as the highest perfection, dispensing us from all activity and preserving us from all sin or imperfection.*

After these preliminaries, the author studies in chaps. V and VI the *inner nature* of the mystic union, of the mystic act or state as such, independently of its diversity of degrees or mode of being. He sees in it two fundamental characteristics: the *felt presence* of God, in place of the abstract *thought* of God; the *interior possession* of God by a *spiritual sensation*, analogous to bodily sensation.† This analogy is based on the five bodily senses, so that the mystics commonly speak of spiritual *sight*, *hearing*, *touch*, *taste* and *odour*. There are, then, for the mystics, as it were spiritual senses by which they touch God, taste God, and so on.

In the lower states, they make use particularly of the words *touching*, *tasting*, *feeling* or *inbreathing* God present within them: they do not speak of *hearing*, nor, more especially, of *seeing*, save in the higher states. What they mean to express thus is an experimental and concrete knowledge, different from the abstract knowledge which we have when we think of God. God thus felt is within the soul, and it is by *introversion*, by turning upon ourselves or by profound recollection, that we attain to this feeling of Him. Hence the name of *interior senses* which they give to these spiritual senses, and the feeling of *possession* which is attached thereto for them; *they feel God present within them*. This feeling of presence is associated in particular with the sense of touch, and implies *saturation* with God, *immersion* in God, *fusion* in God; sometimes, especially in the higher states, a divine *touch*, a divine *embrace*, a divine *kiss*, and analogous effects, the part the soul plays being more prominent in the first, that of God in the others.

To these fundamental characters the author adds ten other "subsidiary" ones, which complete the description of the mystic phenomenon or state. They are as follows, in the author's own words (VII, 1).

1. The mystic union does not depend upon our own will.
2. The knowledge of God accompanying it is obscure and confused;
3. The mode of communication is partially incomprehensible;
4. The union is produced neither by reasonings, nor by the consideration of creatures, nor by sensible images;
5. It varies incessantly in intensity;
6. It demands less effort than meditation;

* The word *acquired* seems not to be used in quite the same way by the quietists as by current usage. For us it signifies the result of an effort; for them, the divine gift attached to cessation from all effort, the divine action substituting itself once for.all for human activity and crowning this cessation from all activity, even mystical.

† It is not an imagined sensation, as when we see, hear, taste, touch in imagination something perceptible to the bodily senses. This imagined sensation is of the bodily senses, not spiritual.

7. It is accompanied by sentiments of love, of repose, of pleasure, and often of suffering;

8. It inclines the soul of itself and very efficaciously to the different virtues*;

virtues*;

9. It acts upon the body and is acted upon in return;

10. It impedes to a greater or less extent the production of certain interior acts; this is what is called the ligature.

After having studied (in chaps. VII-XIV) these general characteristics of the mystic union, the author goes on to the detailed examination of each degree of the union (prayer of quiet, full union, ecstasy, spiritual marriage). We need not follow him in detail (chaps. XV-XIX). He must be read. But I must call attention to chap. XV, devoted to the two Nights of St. John of the Cross. This is one of the most original and personal sections of the book. If the interpreter has seen correctly, we have in it a precious key with which to enter into the thought of the great mystic. St. John of the Cross, in the *Ascent of Mount Carmel* and in the *Dark Night*, considers the mystical states (and also the period preparatory to them) under their negative or privative aspect, under the form of nights; the night of the senses, the night of the spirit. What exactly does he mean by these two nights? Two successive states of prayer, two degrees of contemplation of God.

The first night is specially marked: (1) by a state of aridity, sometimes calm and tranquil, more often bitter and painful; (2) by a simple gaze directed almost wholly and uninterruptedly towards God. The state thus described is at "the extreme borderland separating ordinary prayer from the mystic union, properly so called" (XV, **1** and **20**): a prayer of simple regard, but already including, though it be hardly sensible as yet, some degree of the prayer of quiet, a veiled manifestation of God who alone produces this arid but beloved remembrance, this persevering attraction to the Great Unknown, a painful desire of drawing near to Him in spite of the pain that His approach causes, and of self-purification so as to be less unworthy of His presence, a kind of polarisation of the whole spiritual being towards this all-powerful magnet, and other feelings of the same kind. It is therefore already, on its obscurer side, a prayer of union. The author proposes to call it a *sub-mystic union* (XV, **20**). "Before St. John of the Cross's time thousands of souls had passed through this arid contemplation. But... no one had distinguished it either from common aridity or from the neighbouring mystic states. *They did not perceive the hidden element* which gives it all its value... St. John of the Cross made this most helpful discovery " (XV, **24**). If the interpreter is right—and he seems to be so—he has himself a claim to our gratitude for having discovered in the great mystic a preparation of purification

* The mystics go further and speak at this point of infused virtues, not in the theological sense of the word (in which sense all supernatural virtues are infused), but in the experimental sense; they feel, as it were, humility, gentleness, charity, increase in them, invade their soul, take root therein, etc.

and a hidden call to the mystic state. He has made another discovery if, as he tells us, the second night, the night of the spirit, should be understood of the three other mystic states inferior to the spiritual marriage, these themselves also being considered as together forming a purificatory preparation and painful progress (though one not lacking in an element of sweetness) "in the divine darkness/' towards the summit of the mystic state.*

It is the spiritual marriage, with its joy and splendour, which is sung of in the *Living Flame of Love* and in the *Canticle.*

All who have read St. John of the Cross know that ascetic counsels play a large part in his writings; but this asceticism is itself entirely directed to the mystical life, and to see in it only an ordinary asceticism is a strange misunderstanding. (See XXXI, **37-45.**) The *Ascent of Mount Carmel* describes especially "the active part of the first two purifications (the struggle against the passions and habits, even those good in themselves but which form an obstacle to the mystic union)... The *passive* part is principally described in the *Obscure Night of the Soul*" (XV, **2**, note).

We see from this study of St. John of the Cross that between the prayer of simple regard, in which no mystical element is to be found, and the prayer of quiet, which is wholly mystical, a place must be left for this prayer of aridity directed towards God which is as it were on the threshold of the mystical state.

We can now pass at once to the fourth part, devoted to those visions and revelations which the author calls *ex-deific.* The matter is treated at length, in four chapters, XX-XXIII; description, illusions to be feared, procedure in judging them, rules of conduct for directors and directed. In the hundred and more pages which the author devotes to this section I find nothing which needs special mention or might cause difficulty to the reader.

The fifth part (ch. XXIV) deals with the "trials sent to contemplative souls." The author remarks that, "with the exception of St. John of the Cross' first *night* of the soul and certain obsessions," these trials are not confined to mystics; but that they often reach in the case of the latter an exceptional degree of acuteness. He demonstrates this fact, points out five reasons for which God sends (or, as I would add, *permits*) them, indicates some errors to which beginners are subject,

* The author tells us (XV, **2**, note) that once at least (*Ascent of Mount Carmel*, I, 2, *cf.* II, 2) St. John gave the name *night* to the spiritual marriage itself when compared with the beatific vision, of which it is only the pale dawn.—The painful character of this aridity seems to be due in part to the weakness of the intellectual eye, not yet prepared for this higher light and new mode of knowledge; in part also to the impurity of the soul in face of that infinite purity which it glimpses in an implacable light and under an implacable eye. There is an affective element in this prayer, which the author has noticed and on which he says a few words, though perhaps without giving it the attention it deserves.—It would be interesting to compare the explanations of Père Poulain on this subject with those of Fr. Gerard of the Cross, the scholarly editor of the great Spanish mystic in the *Preface to the Dark Night and the Ascent of Mount Carmel*, which may be read in French in *EC*, Jan. 1920.

and says in what sense they may be laid to the account of the devil. He divides them into four groups; sickness, persecutions from our fellow-men, interior sufferings or spiritual desolation, visible assaults of demons (possession and obsession). The interior sufferings are classified under fourteen headings (§ 8). On most of these points the author gives interesting information and practical counsels.

In the sixth part (chs. XXV-XXXIII), under the title of "Mysticism; some supplementary questions," various points are examined which touch upon the subject either directly or indirectly: desire for the mystical union, the qualities needed by a director, quietism, the rarity or frequency of the mystical states, terminology, especially that of St. Teresa, scientific methods in descriptive mysticism, various discussions, two historical monographs (a Protestant Revival, the Musulman conception of ecstasy).

Among the various discussions (ch. XXXI) some questions merit our attention for a moment. is there a natural levitation, natural stigmata, natural ecstasies? The author divides the question: *is there?* into three parts. On each of these points he replies: (i) is it possible? I do not know. (2) Are there such things? I do not know. (3) What is to be thought of the alleged cases? In fact, either such levitation, stigmata, or ecstasy are not real, or it is not proved that they are natural (§ 1-3).

Nature of the union and vision of the mystics (§ 4). I draw attention to this question, because frequently people attribute or seem to attribute to the author an opinion which he does not hold.

"Theologians," he says, "are almost unanimous in affirming that mystic visions of the Divinity are not of the same kind as the beatific vision, I am with them in holding this opinion" (XXXI, **28**).

The bibliography with which the volume closes, copious, interesting for the personal remarks introduced, and well arranged in chronological order, bears witness to the great mystical learning of Père Poulain—all the more so as he seems to have been in touch with all or nearly all the works he quotes.*

The reader will remark for himself the deep feeling which runs through the *Canticle* of the Mystic Union, at the end of the volume, and the high poetic level in which that feeling is expressed. This is the one page in the book which throws some direct light for us on the writer's soul. The *man* may be glimpsed here and there in the course of the work; but the poet and the mystic are seen here alone.†

The three indices—analytical, of the principal proper names, and of the contents—make the use of the book relatively easy.

* There are, however, gaps and errors. Fr. Scheuer, S.J., Professor at the Scholasticate of Louvain, had collected copious bibliographical data; but they were scattered by the ravages of the 1914-18 War. See below, No. 38.

† Save, so far as the mystic goes, for the rare passages like that which I have quoted at the beginning of the present study, in which we may see, if we will, a reference to the writer himself.

## III

## CRITICISMS AND CONTROVERSIES

### *9. Some Remarks and Reservations of the Editor concerning Researches, the Reading of the Mystics, Desire for Mystical Graces*

I will not stop to criticise the part which the character of the author has played in the composition of the work, I have mentioned a few points in No. 6 of this Introduction. It might be added that the style is a little loose, that the order and arrangement of the chapters is, here and there, a little disconcerting at first sight, that there are sometimes remarks which are a little naive or "homely," etc. One also gets the impression that the author's range of experience is comparatively restricted, that the higher states are described mostly from books,* that the souls with whom he was in touch hardly seem to have been what we call great and holy souls, but generally good and devout folk, slightly out of the common, not too detached from self, nor always exempt from illusion. On some points of detail I cannot associate myself without reservation with the way in which the author sees things, or at least with his tendencies and mode of expression. This is particularly the case as concerns research, the desire of or request for the mystical states, the reading of mystical books. Not that he says anything false: but he does not seem to show things in their true light, and thus runs the risk of being misunderstood or misapplied. I feel, therefore, that I must on these matters supplement the author or rectify the tendency by a few brief remarks.†

It seems to me necessary to add something to what is said about *research* (see *Analytical Index*). We may profit by the experience we gain of souls, and cause others to profit thereby: we may impart this experience to the public, and competent Reviews may (as the *Revue d'ascetique et de mystique* does) appeal to this experience, and call attention to such and such a point for purposes of study. But we must be careful to do nothing which might lead souls to think that we seek or see in them *interesting cases;* we must never regard them as such, never question them or act with study or experiment as our principal intention. The dignity of souls, respect for God and His action in them forbid it. No scientific interest can prevail against this consideration. Moreover science itself would lose thereby; for the souls would perceive it; from that time forward we should either wound them and cause them to be shut to us, or else warp them; and that would be the end of all advantage to science, not to speak of the evil brought upon the souls themselves. If a doctor may not make experiments upon his patients, how much less a director on the souls in his charge!

* The author himself tells us that he had known but few souls who had passed beyond the prayer of quiet.

† On these points I follow Père de Maumigny rather than Père Poulain.

To what is said of the *desire* for mystical graces (see *Analytical Index*) we would add this. When a soul is in the mystical states or is visibly called to them, we may tell it to pray that it may be faithful to grace. If it guesses that it is called or inquires,. we may reply in the affirmative, drawing its attention according to the need of the moment either to the responsibility which this grace imposes on it or to the divine help which will not fail it. If it is in a state of expectation of or desire for a higher grace, it should be drawn to pray for that grace and to prepare for its reception. If it relaxes, or is tempted to do so, if it is weary of waiting, it should be supported, encouraged and stimulated by showing it the value of the grace which God is reserving for it provided it deserves to receive it or can wait in patience.

When nothing indicates or allows us to suspect that a soul is called to these states, there is no occasion to arouse such a desire in it or to urge it in that direction. Better to put it on its guard against chimerical desires which are subject to illusion, recommending it to be faithful to the grace it already possesses, without wasting time over dreaming of graces it has not; showing it Christian perfection in the practice of solid virtues, the duties of its state, and so on.

The first three points of No. **4** of the first Preface* ought always to be kept in mind by the director in his dealings with souls.

May we take advantage of the illusory aspirations of a soul which is not called to these states, in order to urge it to go on toiling at its own perfection? Yes, not by encouraging it in such desires, but by using them as a starting-point in urging it to struggle and practical effort; by showing it that the perfection of which it dreams and for which it searches in the clouds is within its grasp if it so wills, in the path of duty and of fidelity to the graces of the moment.

May we leave in its state of illusion a soul which thinks that it is called without being really so, or which wrongly thinks that it has already entered upon the mystical state? Evidently not, if there is a chance of leading it back to the truth without grave inconvenience; but if it is probable that it will not emerge from its illusion, or that it will only do so at the cost of all its courage and energy, we must seek to get something out of it by taking it as it is, without wanting to heal it at any price.

What is to be done and what advice given about reading mystical books? For directors of souls such reading may be necessary; it will generally be useful. As for the directed, the author sometimes speaks as if they were left to themselves: "I am writing especially for those souls who are beginning to receive the mystic graces and who do not know how to find their way in this new world... I address myself to those also who are drawing near and who have entered into a state bordering on it. The same difficulties present themselves to these souls also" (*Preface*, I, **2**). He says again later; " It is necessary to have a director " (*Preface*, I, **4**, 5°); which, indeed, hardly needs saying. But he is a little afraid of directors. Books like his

* And also the subject of the fourth, abstracting from St. Ignatius.

own are made to help them. Now the question of reading the mystics concerns the director more than the directed. This is the first principle in the matter. The second is—and the author, without making it his own, dares not deny it—" that mystical books may turn the heads of certain persons " (*Preface,* II, **3**). "It is recognised," he adds, " that my book, far from presenting this danger, is a vigorous remedy against these flights," He warns his readers, it is true, against illusions, and often repeats that "abnegation and love of the Cross must be the soul's great preoccupations." All things considered, however, I do not think it wise to place such books in the hands of everyone, especially when, as in this case, there is frequent mention of visions, revelations, possession and obsession, and many things which excite curiosity, especially with women.

The following seems right and practical in the matter. First, we must distinguish between books in which mystical matters are mentioned, and books which treat solely and *ex professo* of such questions.

Many books which refer to mystical matters (the writings of the saints, particularly St. Teresa, St. Margaret Mary, etc.; similar writings by devout but uncanonised persons, lives of the saints, ascetic or historical works, etc.) can be read without danger and with great profit by the great bulk of devout readers. There are, however, some reservations to make as to certain biographies of pious persons.*

Popular manuals of mysticism—such as the present book—may be useful, edifying and instructive, to all who have charge of souls, to students, to all pious and instructed persons, well grounded in solid piety and without any pretensions to mysticism, capable of being edified by the great things God works in souls, and of drawing profit therefrom whether for themselves in their own path or for others with whom they are in contact.

The director may usefully bring them to the notice of every healthy and judicious soul who is already in the mystic ways or who may be called thereto, in order to help it to self-realisation and to recognise the touch of grace; sometimes also in order to test the ground, to stimulate or raise up some good and generous soul, which is already firmly established and practical-minded, but does not yet seem to be giving to God all that might seem rightly expected of it.

I think I have included within one or other of these categories —which, as will be seen, are very wide—almost all those persons to whom books involving mystical considerations, or those which deal *ex professo* and exclusively with mysticism, might be useful. I have preferred widening the road, by pointing out

* I mean especially certain contemporary lives, where there is little else but visions and revelations, wherein Our Lord is continually on the scene, gossiping, if I may use such a word, with the soul, telling it many good and pious but commonplace things, and even others not so commonplace but extremely doubtful, the whole written perhaps more to tickle curiosity and to nourish a vain and sometimes morbid sentimentality than to instruct and edify.— When writing these words I had specially in mind a book which has since been condemned by the Holy Office—*Soeur Gertrude-Marie.*

their usefulness for many, to narrowing it, while at the same time pointing out the limits and restrictions called for in regard to certain souls to whom they might do harm.

I have perhaps dwelt too long on these secondary questions, which have only a very small place in the book, and my remarks may perhaps seem a little quibbling. But such questions are practical questions, and of an order which seem to me to demand precision in their treatment.

### *10. The Definition of the Mystical States*

I now come to questions of the speculative order. The most important of those on which I have some reservations to make or further points to add touches on the very essence of the mystical state, its two fundamental characters, as the author presents them to us in chapters V and VI.

The first is "God's presence felt"; the second is the feeling of a "kind of interior possession of God" by a deep sensation of imbibition or saturation, of fusion, of immersion," by a kind of "interior touch."

What the author says seems to me to be true and to correspond for him to an experience which has been lived through, to an experimental demonstration. The texts quoted at the end of the two chapters fully confirm the two theses. I should have, then, only one small remark to make, if I did not think that I ought to call attention to one essential element.

The remark is as follows. There is something obscure and inexact in the distinction of the two "fundamental" characters, something awkward in the enunciation of the second thesis (VI, **8**) and in the way in which the spiritual senses are brought into the preliminary exposition. Perhaps it is a mere question of editing. The author wishes, I take it, to develop more exactly in this thesis what he has put forward more vaguely in the first. It is as if he had said: "The mystical state consists in the *felt* presence of God. How do we *feel* this presence? By a kind of spiritual sensation. This spiritual sensation is analogous to that which we have by one or other of the five bodily senses. Yet the mystics do not use the words *see* or *hear* for the degrees below ecstasy, but only *taste, smell, touch*. It is this spiritual touch which seems to be the first fundamental act of the mystical experience, anterior to taste or smell, to which it acts as a *substratum*." We can then compare this first feeling of God (analogous, the author says, to that which we have of our body when we close our eyes and remain motionless) to a kind of spiritual touch. In this way, it seems that the two characteristics set forth by our author constitute only one, indicated by the words *felt presence* and explained by the analogy of the spiritual senses, particularly that of touch. It is true that the author speaks in his second thesis of an *inward possession* of God by a feeling of *imbibition, immersion, fusion*; but all this is nothing more than a description of that *felt presence* with which the first thesis deals.

### *11. The Affective Element in the Mystical States*

To this remark on the expression, I will now, like a blind man discussing colours, add a few reflections on the thing itself.

Père Poulain has been reproached for not mentioning love in his definition of the mystic state. He has himself dealt with this objection in the ninth edition, by adding a paragraph on this point (V, **21** *bis*). "I have been asked" he says, "why I do not speak at this point of the feelings of love which accompany the mystic union, why I wait until chapter XL These feelings, I am told, form an essential part of this union; they are a fundamental element of it. It seems therefore that they should be mentioned at the start. I reply that one cannot speak of everything at once. And then these feelings are only the consequence of the new kind of knowledge which marks the mystic union. It is this knowledge which is the real fundamental element, the necessary starting-point of the description. We must begin by concentrating our attention on this all-important and difficult subject."

This reply is not without value. None the less the reproach seems to me well founded, in part at any rate. Love is not forgotten; but it comes a little late, overshadowed, as the ninth "subsidiary character" in the description of the mystic union. The author, it is true, is *describing*, not *defining*; he does not say "accessory" or "secondary" character; and he considers it, like the nine others to which he joins it, as forming an integral part of that concrete whole which is the mystic state. I think, however, that he ought to have put it among the fundamental characters, not as first or second or third—for, as we have seen, the first and second are but one—but as the necessary determinant of the sensation (or feeling) which is given us, in chapter V, as constituting the mystic state, and explained, in chapter VI, by the idea of the spiritual senses. He would then have said something like this:

"The mystical state consists above all in a loving feeling of the divine presence or action in us which may be compared to a sensation": or, to keep more closely to the author's formulas, "The fundamental fact of the mystic union is the presence or action of God in us, felt and tasted by the heart."* The knowledge which the soul has of God is not an abstract knowledge; it is experimental, analogous to that which we have through the senses, and this is what is expressed by the word *felt presence* or *action*; but it is not *any* kind of experimental knowledge; it is a knowledge that is loving, tasted by the heart, enjoyable and enjoyed. We might say, with Pascal, that it is *God sensible to the heart*, giving the word *sensible* its etymological meaning. The mystics understand their state as an affective one, and if the word love is not always on their lips or under their pens, it is always in their thoughts. To realise this we need only run over the quotations of chapters V and VI.† This presence is only felt in the depths of the soul, when it

* Fr. de Maumigny, as we shall see, has given loye its place in the actual definition of mystic contemplation.

† The author himself defines the mystic aridity of St. John of the Cross as "a loving memory of God" (XV, **29**); "a loving attention, to God" (XV, **34**).

is profoundly recollected and as it were wholly concentrated about the divine Guest; but this condition is always presupposed, and it does not seem necessary to express it. Likewise it is unnecessary to say that this knowledge is not abstract, nor discursive, as when one *thinks of God* or *meditates* on His essence or attributes; the word *feeling* implies this. The whole of the mystic life is not contained in this loving feeling of presence; but the author might have been satisfied to point out this felt presence, this intimate and loving possession of God as the fundamental characteristic which is at the basis of the mystic acts and states.*

*12. Consciousness of the Supernatural in the Mystical States*

I think, however, that we might take for starting-point a wider idea than this purely descriptive notion of the initial fact. I proposed one, twenty years ago, which seems to me to go deeper to the root of things, by defining the mystical life as " the life of grace which is becoming conscious, known experimentally."† By this I mean that God gives to the mystical soul something like a new sense, the consciousness of its life in God and of His life in itself. This consciousness itself develops little by little, follow^ ing the development of the mystical life, from the feeling of the presence or of a loving touch of God in the soul to that of the divine participation in all our supernatural acts and of union— accidental of course, but immediate—between Himself and us, between His substance and ours, in such a way as to embrace God's life and operations in us, our life and operations in Him. It would be knowledge and love both at once, sometimes the one coming to the fore and sometimes the other.‡

I think that this definition, or an analogous one, the formula whereof could be brought to perfection little by little, would give an exact idea of the mystic life, and would apply to all its manifestations, from the first impressions of knowledge or of love to the full development of the mystic union in the spiritual marriage,

* Note that this *felt presence* or *action* of God does not of itself imply any distinct vision of the Beloved, or any other positive knowledge than that of an intimate *presence,* sometimes of a *touch* or a *look.* Hence astonishment, sometimes mixed with terror, before this *obscure transcendence* (if I may so call it). This terror is distinct from the fear of illusions or diabolic deceit (which comes only on reflection). It may happen—and it does happen in the passive purifications—that this *look* takes on a certain penetrating and implacable element, revealing the soul to itself, with all its dirt, ugliness, fundamental egoism, its nothingness and evil, making such a contrast to the greatness and purity of God that the soul is in torment therefrom, and would, if possible, flee, or hide, to escape from the gaze.

† In *Nature et surnaturel,* II, 5, p. 62.

‡ This is the idea of Gerson, and as it would seem, more or less explicitly, of all the mystics. M. Pacheu, in a series of articles on this question, has energetically claimed for the affective element the first place in the very definition of the mystic state. Père de la Taille, in a study which will be analysed below, also places the affective element, the act of will, at the origin of the mystic state, as at that of the act of faith. Why not accept the opinion of Gerson, who seems to reconcile the various statements of the mystics? Sometimes they feel themselves inflamed with love without at first knowing whence this love comes, save that it is infused and does not come from themselves; sometimes they have a feeling of loving presence, a feeling which is itself wholly impregnated with love, but, *natura prior,* anterior to love, knowledge and love always inseparable and each implying the other.

without excluding the objective elements which seem to come as if from outside in visions or revelations.

Whence comes this broadening of consciousness, this kind of hypersesthesia of mind and heart? In what does it consist? The mystics tell us, and we must believe them, that it is a special gift of God, a mode of knowledge by spiritual sensation, without image or sensible object. Mystical theologians add that it comes about, at least in some cases, by means of infused ideas, being in this similar to the knowledge of the angels, midway between the obscure knowledge of faith and the beatific vision. The author does not speak, so far as I know—not, at least, by that name— of the analogy with the knowledge of the angels, and I seem to remember that he excused himself from doing so on the ground of our ignorance of the nature of this knowledge. This excuse is only partly valid: however obscure this knowledge is to us, it is something to know that mystical knowledge is comparable with it, and to be able to apply thereto the explanations on the subject with which St. Thomas has provided us.*

When it is said to be a gratuitous gift from God, this is not to put it in the category of the gratuitous graces, which are so called because they are not sanctifying grace, nor in direct relation therewith, but are given for the advantage of others rather than that of the recipient; fundamentally mystic grace is to be regarded as in intimate relation with sanctifying grace and its connected benefits, the virtues or gifts of the Holy Ghost, with our own supernatural life.

### *13. The Mystical Ways and the Ordinary Way*

Although it is a gratuitous gift, it does not therefore follow that it comes entirely from without; it may be a special blossoming of the supernatural life under a particular influence of God and His grace.

is this special blossoming in the direct line of the supernatural life, a normal development thereof, as it were, so that all spiritual life is destined to attain to it,

* In many cases of mystical knowledge we must admit, in accordance with the scholastic theory, these infused ideas or "species impressæ," produced directly by God in our souls. But the theory of "species impressæ," and therefore that of infused ideas, seems to me to be somewhat hard put to it to explain the primary and fundamental fact of the mystic state: this feeling of presence, of possession, of living and immediate contact between God and the soul, this love felt in the depths of the soul, at its centre, as the mystics say, without any distinct intellectual perception of a determinate object, this intimate experience (at once cognitive and affective, yet sometimes more the one, sometimes more the other), this idealess sensation, this live passivity, of which the mystics often tell us without being able to explain it. It will be seen that this difficulty is likewise felt in the natural order, when we have to explain by the "species" theory sensible knowledge, especially by touch, or the facts of immediate consciousness. I cannot see why a special infused light (*influxus luminis intellectualis*) dimly resembling the *light of glory*, and raising and fortifying the understanding, could not enable it to lay hold on, directly, without infused "species," the supernatural realities inherent in the soul and forming part of its life: its supernatural acts, the graces and infused virtues, with the gifts of the Holy Ghost, the obscure presence of God and His intimate contact with the substance of the soul, the effects of divine action in the depths of that soul. I do not therefore think that knowledge by infused "species " is essential to the mystic state.

and we must impute its failure to blossom either to the subject himself, or to unfavourable external circumstances? From the seventeenth century to our own day the negative reply has, I think, been the commoner, both on the part of the mystics themselves and on that of theologians and directors of souls. The mystic ways were usually regarded as exceptional, as ways which the soul could not enter for itself without a special call accompanied by graces not vouchsafed to everyone and to which it would be imprudent to aspire without this special call. That many were so called and did not enter or attain them through their own fault is—both mystics and directors have told us—a common experience; but it was hardly laid down as a general rule that whoever is faithful to grace is destined to embark upon them, and that to proceed on the path to holiness, to Christian perfection, and to prepare oneself for the mystic graces if they are not already possessed, is all one. Some theorists seem to have been of the contrary opinion, but their view was seldom listened to.

Since the reawakening of interest in mystic studies many theologians and enquirers have appealed from this judgment, and have supported their opinion by facts and authorities which cannot be neglected. We shall return to this question later: it deserves to be studied at length and impartially. In order to clear the ground, a few remarks may be useful.

1. We should not hold as *a priori* certain the opinion that the mystic ways are the natural continuation of the ordinary ways of Christian asceticism, and that they alone can lead the soul to sanctity; but neither must we regard it as *a priori* false.

2. We must remember that the scholastic theories of contemplation, perfection, the virtues with their many divisions (particularly the division of the virtues into *exemplares, politic#, purgatoriae, purgati animi* of which St. Thomas speaks, I-II, q. lxi, a. 5) are ancient in origin and are not specifically Christian or supernatural. It would therefore be an abuse to seek in them direct lights on Christian mysticism, let alone formulas of mysticism.

3. If the perfection of the spiritual life is likewise a perfection of love, it is natural to connect the spiritual ways with the degrees of this love (the purgative way with the love of the beginner, the illuminative way with that of the proficient, the unitive with that of the perfect, II—II, q. xxv, a. 9): but who does not know that these degrees apply equally in the ordinary and in the mystic ways?

4. We must not deny that the mystic ways can take us farther in a shorter time; but we must not assert confidently that the *De perfectione vitæ spiritualis* of St. Thomas, for instance, implies fixed ideas on the distinction or non-distinction between the ascetic *ways* and the mystic *ways,* or on the necessity of the mystic ways for arriving at this perfection.

5. The questions which so occupy us nowadays as to this distinction between the mystic and non-mystic ways, the possibility of arriving at perfection without passing through the former, and other similar questions, did not

present themselves in former days as they do now. We must therefore be prudent in applying old texts to modern questions.

6. Above all, we must try to agree on the use of our terms, particularly on the definition of the mystic touch and the mystic state,

It must be remembered, on both sides, that the question is not solved, that it is not even properly put; that some people put it chiefly from the point of view of mystical theology, that is to say, from the standpoint of principles, others from the point of view of experimental mysticism, that is, from the standpoint of fact; that the field of discussion is encumbered with confused notions and vague ideas, and considerations irrelevant to the questions under discussion. Its study must therefore be taken up methodically, without preconceived solutions, and taking care to put the question in proper terms, to define the positions, to distinguish between what is determined and what is not, not to claim for oneself or to strain in one's own favour texts, facts, principles which are admitted on all hands, but which do not count on either side when the question is correctly stated. Cf. Sec. 40, 4.

### *14. The Mystical Graces and the Gifts of the Holy Ghost*

The mystic graces are ordinarily attached to the operations of the Holy Ghost in us and, more particularly, to His gifts; some authors connect them specially with the gift of wisdom, others with all the gifts in general or one of them in particular, according to the nature of the particular case. But they do not explain themselves very clearly on this point. Those who appeal to the gift of wisdom content themselves with attributing thereto that enjoyable knowledge of God which seems to be the fundamental act of the mystic state and which, without any doubt, holds a large place therein. Others are even less precise: among them Fr. Poulain, who only says a word about the matter in passing, VI, **19**, **20**, and XXV, **9**. It seems to me worth while to dwell on the matter a little.

This connection of the mystical operations with the gifts of the Holy Ghost, without being strictly proved, is legitimate, and seems founded on the nature of things. But the same idea of these gifts is not held by all. The clearest and most coherent system is that of St. Thomas, in the *Summa* (for the gifts in general, I—II, q. 68; for each gift in particular, II-II, after each of the virtues to which it is attached; those of understanding and knowledge to faith, that of fear to hope, that of wisdom to charity, that of counsel to prudence, that of piety to justice, that of fortitude to the virtue of the same name).

It may be said in a true sense that St. Thomas laid down the principle of the relation of the gifts to the mystic state when, on the one hand, he made his own the formula of Dionysius presenting to us "Hierotheus perfect both inasmuch as he knows divine things and also inasmuch as God works divine things in him" (*non solum discens, sed et pattens divina*), and on the other, he made of the gifts dispositions which make us supple and ready for the divine motion, so that, as the virtues perfect our active powers to make us act according to the lights of reason and faith, the gifts perfect our faculties in order to make them supple and docile under the divine motion. Now this passivity under divine action being one of the elements of the mystic state, it is natural to attach these states or operations to the gifts which put us in the hands of the divine mover.

We cannot conclude from this that the domain of the gifts is limited to the mystic states, for this reason among others, that St. Thomas regards the gifts as necessary to salvation, "because no one can arrive at this habitation of the blessed unless he be moved and guided by the Holy Ghost" (I—II, q, 68, a, 2). What, then, is the special exercise of the gifts in the mystic state, or to what special acts is it attached? Fr. Garrigou-Lagrange replies: "What characterises the mystic state and distinguishes it from the ascetic life is the *special passivity* which is found in the *supra-human mode* of the gifts of the Holy Ghost, when this mode of knowing and loving God has become *frequent* and *manifest.*"* Let us be content, at least provisionally, with this formula and this explanation; but not without adding a word on the gift of wisdom and the special part which many think it plays in the mystical state.

There seems to be a certain difference of opinion as to the nature of the gift of wisdom among both mystical and theological authors. Some hold to the word *sapere, sapor,* and stop at the idea of spiritual *taste,* of *enjoyable* knowledge, and understand it either of the mystical or of the ordinary order; but they apply it particularly to the former, as designating a higher and in particular an affective knowledge. St. Thomas explains the word a little differently. Firstly the holy Doctor relates it to the *σοφία* of Aristotle, knowledge by first causes, philosophical knowledge, which has as its object God and divine or transcendent things. Then he attaches to it the idea of knowledge by a certain sympathy or *connaturality* between the knowing subject and the object known. This is not a purely abstract knowledge; it comes about by a kind of return upon oneself, to feel or verify in oneself the truth of the thing said. When we speak of filial love, of filial duty, to a child who loves its parents as it ought, he judges of our remarks by an inward sense, which causes him to understand and taste the principles and their applications according to the inner echo, according to the agreement between what he hears and what he feels in himself. This knowledge by *connaturality,* by sympathy, holds a large place in St. Thomas' teaching. M. Ollé-Laprune has rediscovered it, so to speak, and analysed it extensively in his book on *Moral Certitude.*†

If I have rightly understood certain explanations given by Fr. Gillet, O.P., it is to this mode of knowledge, in great part, that he would attach mystic knowledge. I think, too, that there is here a vein to be exploited, some light to be gained. Yet I do not think it is necessary that the whole question of mysticism should be bound

* *LVS*, Feb. 1922, vol, 5, p. 384; cf, March, 462-5.

† I have often spoken of it myself: in *Nature et surnaturel,* X, 2; in the *Vie intime du catholique,* VII, 93 sq., and elsewhere. Cf. *Summa,* II-II, q. 45, a. 2.

up with this. This knowledge by *connaturaliiy* is found in the ordinary Christian life, and if, as I have done myself,* we call this life a mystic life, and this knowledge a sort of mystic knowledge, it can only be, it seems to me, in an analogical or weakened sense, mystical knowledge and the mystical state not being considered, whether by the mystics or by mystical theologians, as the normal condition of all Christian life.

When the mystics describe their state as an experimental knowledge of God, they certainly mean something different, both as to the object known and as to the mode of knowledge, from this knowledge by connaturality. It remains to be seen whether the word *experimental* is relevant in the matter, and what this experimental knowledge of God really is.

### *15. The Mystical Life, an Experimental Knowledge of God in Ourselves and of our Life in God*

It cannot be doubted that the mystics mean to affirm that they have an experimental knowledge of God and of their supernatural life. All their descriptions and statements point in this direction. To see nothing more in them than modes of expression is to overthrow the whole science of mysticism at its base or to make it merely the science of ordinary Christian life.

But what exactly do they mean by this experimental knowledge, by this sense of God and of divine things, this touch, this taste, this sight? To know it with exactness we must have experienced it, just as to know the taste of honey we must have tasted it for ourselves, or to know the meaning of love or sight we must ourselves have loved or seen.

Must we, then, believe them when they tell us that they have seen God?†

### *16. The Mystical Life and the Vision of God*

Do they claim to have had the beatific vision? We should sometimes think so, if we took them literally. Blessed Angela of Foligno: "It was also said unto me that the aforesaid unutterable manifestation of God is the same good which the saints

* In the Vie intime du catholique, l.c.

† The question is twofold: (1) Does this feeling of presence or divine touch which we have placed at the basis of mysticism, this consciousness of the divine in us, imply an obscure perception of God, analogous to that which is maintained by the ontologists? Some authors think so, and perhaps Père Poulain might have been drawn to think so by his philosophical upbringing; but of this thought there remains hardly a trace, if so much, in his book. Faithful to his method, he is content to state the facts and quote the sayings of the mystics, without attempting to give them any philosophical interpretation. I think M. Saudreau has been led into misunderstanding him on this point. Fr. Lahousse, on the other hand, seems to have admitted this obscure perception of God, and M. Saudreau is not wrong in attributing it to him. It is also, I think, the view of Fr. Marshal in his penetrating studies (see *Bibliographical Index*). One may differ from his opinion, as I do myself; but it cannot be condemned *a priori*, nor can it be denied that his reasons deserve examination.—(2) The mystics, not at the beginning of their course, where they speak particularly of contact, of spiritual taste, etc., but in the higher states, say that they have *seen* God. Can we find out exactly what they mean by this word?

possess in life eternal—nor is this good other than the aforesaid, but there it is another kind of experience and only different from the aforesaid that the least saint who possesses least thereof in life eternal hath more than can be given unto any soul in this present life, before the death of the body" (XVIII, **75**). And she says that she has had "more than a thousand times this supreme manifestation of God." There is an analogous, though less explicit, assertion by St. Catherine of Siena. God is speaking: "Burning with the fire of love, they taste in Me the eternal Deity, who am to them a sea pacific, with whom the soul has made so great union, that she has no movement except in Me. And being yet mortal, they taste the good of the immortals."* Still more explicit is the Ven. Marina de Escobar, according to the testimony of her confessor, Fr. Louis du Pont: "She told me that she had seen clearly the divine essence and the face of God, one in three Persons, as well as the beatitude of the saints, and the manner in which it takes place, I asked her what kind of clearness she was speaking of: Was it that of the Blessed, and that which St. Paul is said to have had in his rapture? Or was it a clearness of a lesser kind?... This is what she answered me in writing: 'The light that my soul received for the understanding of these mysteries was as great as is possible during this life; but with this characteristic, that the knowledge was extremely clear and distinct. I know with certainty that I see exactly the same object as the inhabitants of the heavenly Jerusalem; but the revelation has not told me whether it is with the same force and in the same manner. However, here is one fact: I have seen the interior beatitude of several, saints, and how God brings it about. And I have compared it with what I experience when the divine Majesty manifests to me the greatness of His essence, and it has seemed to me that these divers manifestations were absolutely identical. I even believe that on one or two occasions I have not been far from that clearness of vision of which you speak, and with regard to which you quote St. Paul's example to me.'"† Fr. du Pont would have liked her to consult her angels on the matter; but she never had the opportunity. "God," the venerable director concludes, "may not wish us to know more on the subject."

To St. Catherine of Siena, who, as is well known, generally reflects the ideas of the Dominican theologians, God clearly said that the soul "burning with the fire of love, tastes.., the eternal Deity"; that, "being yet mortal, they taste the good of the immortals"; but He explains to her afterwards that, when "tasting and seeing Him," neither Paul nor anyone on earth tastes and sees Him" in essence, but only in the virtue of charity," and that all such sight, while the soul is within a mortal

* *Dialogue,* trans. Thorold, London, 1925. p. 150.

† The formula of St. Paul, in the passage to which allusion is here made, 2 Cor. xii, 1-4, does not give the impression of the beatific vision, *face to face,* as he describes it elsewhere, opposing it to the knowledge of faith, which is *per speculum, in ænigmate* (1 Cor. xiii, 12). *Understanding* is not *seeing.*

body, "is a darkness compared to that sight which the soul has who is separated from the body."*

Fr. Alvarez de Paz, one of the masters of mystical theology, also affirms that in the highest degree of contemplation "eyes are given unto the soul by which she may see God. God manifests himself to the soul by an image that represents Him very perfectly... It is a new infusion made to the mind... Thus furnished and strengthened by the highest help, the mind sees God... not by denying... or affirming something of Him, but by regarding the divine greatness without any admixture of anything else, in the tranquillity of a calm day. Certainly, O reader, when you see the light with the bodily eyes... you see light."† In the same way the soul, in this degree of contemplation, sees God. It will be said: this is astonishing, or rather unbelievable. For we take it as indisputable that God is not seen here intuitively. If, then, the soul does not see God, how can we say nevertheless that she sees Him; and if she sees Him, in what sense is it that she does not see Him? I admit that it is astonishing. The fact, however, is very certain... The soul knows God in the depths of her being,‡ and she sees Him, so to say, more clearly than she sees the material light with the eyes of the body... Neither the senses nor the imagination have the least part in this vision; all takes place in the summit of the spirit (XVIII, **78**). The author, we see, without himself pronouncing against the beatific vision, seems to hold that God is not seen *intuitively* here on earth; but he firmly upholds the vision of God by the understanding, as distinct from all abstract knowledge.§

* *Dialogue,* 79, trans. Thorold, pp. 150, 151. Cf. Poulain, XVIII, **76**.

† I confess that I do not understand what this seeing of light means. We see *luminous* or *illuminated bodies;* but *light*? The author is speaking, I take it, of the sun and other luminous centres.

‡ Note these words: "In the depths of her being"; the mystic soul sees God as if *present in itself.*

§ Mystical authors insist sometimes on the vision of God, the clearness of this vision occasionally going so far as to suppress in some sort the obscurity of faith, sometimes on the obscurity, the darkness in which the soul is lost before the Great Unknown. They have then a kind of obscure intuition of God, revealing to them what He is not still more than what He is, His infinite transcendence. This is for them the highest degree of the knowledge of God on earth, below the beatific vision. See on this point the valuable study of Fr. Joret, O.P., *L'intuition obscure de Dieu,* in *LVS,* Oct 1921, vol. 5, pp. 5-57. There we find collected a considerable number of texts from the mystics on this vision of the divine transcendence, from Dionysius the Areopagite, Tauler, Ruysbroeck, etc., to St. John of the Cross, St. Mary Magdalen de Pazzi, Mme. Helyot, etc., with the excellent commentaries and explanations of St. Thomas. To show the mingling of light and darkness which is found in this knowledge, I quote a few lines from St. Mary Magdalen de Pazzi, *l.c.,* pp. 55, 56. They are from a dialogue between the soul and God the Father. "The Father: Another fruit of the communication of My essence is a kind of disappearance of faith in souls.—The Soul: How can this be, O Father, since without faith we cannot be saved?—The Father: Behold, My daughter. By the communication of My essence I shed upon you a knowledge of Myself so deep, so clear and so intimate that it forces you after a fashion to confess that you no longer have faith... because this knowledge is so clear that it seems to belong less to faith than to sight. This most faithful loss of faith is a kind of wedding garment... woven (who would believe it?) of light and darkness, like that which is attributed to Me when it is said that I am clothed with light as with a garment, and that I dwell in the midst of darkness inaccessible. The more My immensity makes Me clear and knowable in Myself, the more am I incomprehensible to creatures because of their incapacity, and in this I resemble the sun,

We must then recognise that in mystic contemplation there is an intellectual knowledge of God, generally regarded as distinct from the beatific vision, not only in *degree*, but in *kind* ) and on the other hand, no less distinct from all abstract knowledge.

### *17. Some Remarks on this Vision of God*

Can we reach any greater exactness? Yes, on some points.

1. If this knowledge is by "species impressae," by intellectual image, as Fr. Alvarez believes, we must conclude that it is not the intuitive vision of God; for, as St. Thomas explains, no created image, no distinct *species impressæ* of God can enable us to see God *in Himself, facie ad faciem.*

2. If, with some mystics, we consider that this vision of God may be, in some cases, a face to face vision, though diminished, we must conclude that it is then without image. Whence comes it that it is, as Blessed Angela of Foligno says, much less beatific than that of the least infant dying after Baptism? We must, it would seem, seek for the reason on the side of the knowing faculty, or rather of the light infused into this faculty to make it capable of this immediate knowledge of God. This light is not the light of glory, but an intermediate light, higher than that of faith, inferior to that of glory. In this case as in lower ones, the gift of wisdom is called in; but we have remarked already that the action of this gift is asserted rather than explained.* Fr. Alvarez de Paz says that he does not know what this light is; and Fr. Arintero wisely remarks that we must not wish at all costs to force into our human schemes of classification the thousandfold varieties of God's activity.

### *18. The Spiritual Senses*

What we must hold to, on the unanimous testimony of mystics and mystical writers, is that in contemplation the soul has something like spiritual senses, which put us in relation with the concrete realities of the spiritual world, as the bodily senses do with those of the sensible world.† These spiritual senses are not

which is never less visible than when it shines most strongly... (The soul) exults at not knowing God: that is the darkness; and yet it knows Him so well that in a certain manner it loses its faith in Him."

Sometimes this knowledge is presented as something purely negative, like pure darkness. This is inexact. It is also very positive, a blinding light.

* The authors invoke it particularly to explain the affective, relishing (*sapere*) element of mystical knowledge. See Sec. 14.

† M. Saudreau has keenly contested this doctrine, not, as it seems to me without somewhat misrepresenting Fr. Poulain's thought. The *feeling of divine presence* can, in a real sense, be put at the basis of the mystical state, inasmuch as it is implied in the "divine effects" which M. Saudreau admits. Now there is, in this feeling, a certain "perception" of God, distinct from ordinary abstractive knowledge. Of what nature this perception is is a controverted question; but the fact is recognised or supposed by all the mystics. The explanations which the latter afterwards give, do not exclude it: they imply it. Now M. Saudreau, who quotes a number of texts concerned with knowledge and love, often forgets in his explanations the element of *knowledge* and retains only the *affective* element.

distinct faculties; the "piritual sensations" are special operations of our ordinary faculties, cognitive or affective. It is impossible to obtain at one's own will these perceptions, tastes, touches, odours; impossible to procure their object for them. They are not, therefore, natural senses, exercised naturally and at our own pleasure.

We do not place ourselves in the mystic states; they are passive rather than active. That is why they are related more to the gifts of the Holy Ghost than to the virtues. For the gifts, according to St. Thomas, are placed in us by God with grace and the infused virtues, not to perfect our faculties with a view to the supernatural act—that is the business of the virtues—but to make them supple and docile to the action of grace, at the touch of the Holy Ghost.

It remains to complete this rapid account of the principal questions treated by Fr. Poulain by comparing him with Fr. de Maumigny, and afterwards to say a word or two on the progress of these studies since the sixth edition (1906) and their present state.

## IV

## Poulain and Maumigny

### *19. The Two Men*

We can hardly think about Fr. Poulain and his *Graces of Interior Prayer* without also thinking of Fr. de Maumigny and his *Pratique de L'oraison mentale.* Moreover the comparison will help to give us a more exact and precise idea of the book that is here republished.

Fr. Antoine Malvy has thrown into bold relief the contrast between the two men. Fr. de Maumigny, who himself was also formerly a professor of mathematics at the rue des Postes and in the Jersey scholasticate, "a man of most austere virtue and very watchful against possible illusions, seemed to have been moved to write somewhat in spite of himself... He did not encourage without

In this connection he often reproaches Fr. Poulain with having truncated his texts. Is the reproach sometimes well founded? I do not know; but usually it is not. The great object of M. Poulain being to show that the mystics have a knowledge of God of a peculiar kind, he stops his quotation when the fact is proved, without concerning himself with the affective element, which is not in doubt and which he studies separately. Now the whole of M. Saudreau's attention is fixed on the affective element. If he were content with proving this, all would be well; but his explanation tends to diminish or suppress the element of *Knowledge*, either by confusing it with the affective element, or by reducing it to nothing but the consciousness of a purely *subjective* effect, a profound joy, a delicious love, interior tastes. He therefore excludes from the mystic life properly so called all experimental knowledge of the cause itself, God. He does not, it is true, reject the knowledge of God by infused ideas; but he reserves it for the angelic state, an extraordinary state, much superior, according to him, to the mystic state, which he regards as ordinary. Cf. Arintero, l.c., pp. 51 and 56, some extracts from which will be found below, Sec. 23. Fr. Arintero, who echoes M. Saudreau, ends by admitting that, in spite of Fr. Poulain's excesses—as he understands them, after (and following?) M. Saudreau—he comes closer to him than to his assailant. *Cuestioms místicas,* p. 63.

careful appraisal the call to the extraordinary ways, but among the immediate witnesses of his life he passed for having had close personal experience of them... Fr. Poulain formed a perfect contrast to him. His knowledge of the ways of the spirit was concealed beneath a charming simplicity, wherein the acute, cutting Norman mind was easily to be found."*

At the beginning of this introduction I expressed my conviction that Fr. Poulain was drawn towards mystical studies by some personal experiences. He seems to have been, from his youthful years in religion, an enquirer into mysticism, "a seeker for rare spiritual plants," as Fr. Malvy says. Fr. de Maumigny, would, I think, have been scrupulous about such curiosity. I do not know whether he read the mystics in his early years; but if he did so, it must have been for a practical end, firstly for his own spiritual good (ascetical profit or mystical necessity, I cannot say), later from "the necessities of the direction of souls and of more advanced spiritual instruction,"† which he had to give as instructor in the third year of probation (the second novitiate which St. Ignatius established for his religious at the end of their studies, before sending them out on apostolic work).

Among the causes which led him to publication, it would not be rash to allow some part, direct or indirect, to the book of Fr. Poulain. This book raised many questions, theoretical and practical, and seemed, on many points, in disagreement with the oral teaching of Fr. de Maumigny. He was therefore consulted, and asked to publish his conferences. He at last decided to do so. The work appeared in 1905, four years after that of Fr. Poulain.

### *20. The Two Books*

The two books, like the two men, differ considerably from each other. It is a difference of spirit, tone and manner rather than of doctrinal basis. There is more soul and life in Fr. de Maumigny; there is more of the practical common sense of a director of souls, more contact with reality. Even when he is giving practical advice, Fr. Poulain is the man of theory; even when he theorises, Fr. de Maumigny has his eye on the practical. On one side we see the professor explaining and studying; on the other the priest concerned with good and its application.

The titles themselves indicate the two tendencies: *The Graces of Interior Prayer,* telling us of studies and considerations; *The Practice of Mental Prayer* (*Pratique de L'oraison mentale*), a guide to direct us in prayer. Even in his mysticism Fr. de Maumigny is an ascetical teacher; even in his asceticism Fr. Poulain is more of a speculative thinker. Poulain is rather a seeker and scholar, a theorist; Maumigny, much less learned, not at all enquiring, is rather a practitioner, a director.

* *RAM*, 1920, I, 102.—See *Le P, R. de Maumigny*, by A. Hamon, 1921.

† Malvy, *l.c*,—Fr. Hamon thinks that Maumigny was a great mystic.

Fundamentally the doctrinal differences reduce themselves to very little, especially in the later editions.* I pointed out the principal ones, when I made my reservations in the matter of the reading of mystical books, researches, the desire for the mystic graces, the call to extraordinary prayer, the place which belongs to love in the definition of the mystic phenomenon. For on all these points I have left Poulain for Maumigny, or rather I have remained with Maumigny; for, if I had learnt much from the former, I have always desired to be the disciple of the second, the master who has done me much good.

I said above: *especially in the later editions.* On many points, in fact, Fr. Maumigny was, at the start, further from Fr. Poulain, both in ideas and tendencies. These differences concerned not mystical prayer itself so much as the intermediate states, and the manner of approaching it; affective prayer, acquired contemplation or prayer of simple regard. Fr. de Maumigny was at first very hostile to these forms of prayer, which he considered as of small use, or even harmful, because they seemed to him unlikely to lead to practical results, subject to illusion, and too quietist. Little by little, he had to admit that Poulain had behind him an array of texts and facts, a whole tradition, of which account had to be taken, and that daily experience itself bore witness in favour of these forms of prayer. Hence arose the explanations and developments concerning affective prayer in the third part of vol. I, chapter vii of the sixth part†; in the first part of vol. II, the explanations concerning the distinction between perfect and imperfect contemplation, chap, xi, and on the difference between acquired and infused contemplation, chap. xiv. On his side Fr. Poulain profited by the criticisms made on certain tendencies in his book in relation to the same intermediary prayers. Without clashing or assimilation with each other they were mutually influenced to their common good (perhaps rather by indirect action than immediate contact).

A definite example, all to the advantage of Fr. de Maumigny, will help the reader to appreciate better the relations and the differences between the two masters. Compare the chapters given up to the definition of the exact nature of the mystic union or extraordinary prayer, Poulain, chaps. V-XIV; Maumigny, vol. II, chaps, iii~x. The analysis reveals to the two writers the same or almost the same characteristic traits; but Fr. de Maumigny has then concentrated his analysis in a definition full of life and warmth, little resembling the style of Poulain: "Contemplation may be defined as a simple and loving gaze on God, wherein the soul, upheld by admiration and love, knows Him experimentally, and, in

* Without forgetting, however, that Fr. Maumigny gives up a whole volume to ordinary prayer, studied for its own sake and with a practical end, while Fr. Poulain concerns himself with it only in passing and in order to introduce ns to the study of mystical prayer. We might add that even in Maumigny's second volume, devoted to Extraordinary Prayer, the ascetic preoccupation is dominant.

† "The rule which ought to govern everything in prayer is to follow the fading of grace, controlled by an experienced director."

profound peace, enjoys a foretaste of eternal blessedness." Poulain, as it were, anatomises the mystic state; Maumigny looks at it and describes it like an astonished spectator who sees a soul in ecstasy. They say the same thing, or almost the same*; but what a difference in tone! is it that Poulain does not possess possess the *feeling* of mystic reality and its beauty? He does; but he does not give it rein in the course of the book; at most we may here and there feel a hardly perceptible breath of it. It is only in the *Canticle of the Mystic Union* that, while remaining purely objective, he lets us see the depth of his feeling, as in the following verses:

Who tastes thee, Jesus, hungers for thee sore!
Who drinks deep draughts of thee still craves for more,
Nor shall his burning longing e'er grow cold
Thy Sacred Heart, O Lord, close elaspt to hold.

Yea more: to enter in. It calls us. See
That blest abyss of the Divinity!
Chained to the flesh, the soul yet yearns to rise
And lose herself a space in those fair skies...

O life, my thirsting spirit's hidden need!
I knew thee not, but sought for thee indeed;
But still a secret call, the Voice Divine,
Impelled me to the joys that should be mine...

But now, alas! the too brief time is o'er,
Transformed, the dove descends to earth once more;
A double fire enkindled in her soul,
To suffer and to love, her spirit's goal.

Who tastes Thee, Jesus, hungers for Thee sore!
Who drinks deep draughts of Thee, but craves for more;
Nor shall his burning longing e'er grow cold
The Well-Beloved's Cross close elaspt to hold.

* The reader will have noticed that Maumigny brings love into his definition, while Poulain classes it among the "subsidiary characters." See above, Sec. II.

## V

## Present State of Mystical Studies*

### *21. The Movement of Mystical Studies.—The Teresian Group*†

Fr. Poulain's book, the chronicler of the *RAM* in the article quoted above tells us, "was a real revelation to many people. We may say that it popularised mysticism... It reduced to easy formulas the experiences of St. Teresa and St. John of the Cross." He did not claim to have performed a final work; but he opened, or rather reopened, a road almost closed to the great majority since the seventeenth century. His book, we have already said, has played a great part in the renewal of interest in these questions shown in the last twenty years. Several have walked in his footsteps; some as pupils following their master (among them MM. Caudron and Lejeune); others as masters themselves, but generally agreeing with him in their conclusions (among them Fr. Roure, in his articles in *Etudes*; Dom Vital Lehodey, in *The Ways of Mental Prayer*; Fr. Vermeersch, in his *Quasstiones morales selectee*; and more recently Mgr. Farges, in his excellent book *Mystical Phenomena*). Independent enquirers, like M. Pacheu, Fr. Marechal, Fr. de Grandmaison, Fr. de la Taille, M. Tanquerey, have brought keen attention to bear on certain delicate problems— the feeling of presence, the affective element in the mystic states, contemplative prayer; but, while explaining one fact or another differently, they are almost in agreement on some fundamental points: the specific distinction between mystic and non-mystic states, and the existence of an *acquired* as distinct from mystic contemplation; the current notion of the mystic state as implying an experimental knowledge of God and of divine things; the transcendental, psychologically unique and divino-passive character of this state; the degrees, classical since St. Teresa, of quiet, full union, ecstatic union, as the normal development of a single series; the spiritual marriage, crowning and consummating, so far as is possible here on earth, the union between God and the chosen soul, a union marked in this highest state by an habitual vision of God, in an infused light, more or less vivid but without total eclipse (in conscious life) and by a stable love virtually always in act (in this conscious life).

* The following pages, Secs. 21-26, published in the *RA*, Dec. 1 and 15, 1921, have called forth protests from M. Saudreau, some explanations by Fr. M. de la Taille, reflections and criticisms by Fr. Garrigou-Lagrange. The protests of M. Saudreau appeared, with my reply, in the *RA*, June 15, 1922; the explanations of Fr. de la Taille appeared, at my request and with his permission, in the *RA*, April 1, 1922, and are reprinted here, Sec. 39; the criticisms and reflections of Fr. Garrigou-Lagrange are in the *LVS*, March 1922, and are in Part discussed below, Sec. 40. I have taken advantage of the lights thus offered me to attempt to make these pages a little less imperfect.

† I realise how very artificial is the formation of these unhomogeneous groups. It is a first attempt to help the reader to find his way about and to gain a preliminary idea of the movement and its various tendencies. I give the first group the name "Teresian" because the greater number of its representatives gravitate towards St. Teresa and use her classification. Cf. Sec. 40, 1°.

*22. The Ascetico-mystical Group: M. Saudreau, etc.*

Opposed to this group, which is itself not at all homogeneous, there is another, which, while appealing to tradition and the great teachers of the past, calls into question several conclusions which might have been considered as definitely established.

M. Saudreau, who may be regarded as the leader or principal representative of this group, refuses to recognise two specifically distinct ways in the spiritual life. In his view, all spiritual life is normally intended to expand by a continuous progress from the first efforts to pray from the heart and bring about intimate relations with God to the spiritual marriage—at the risk of considering as accidental phenomena, all equally accessory and outside the normal course of the spiritual life, not only visions, revelations, prophecies, and other so-called gratuitous graces, but ecstasy itself. Moreover, M. Saudreau does not admit that there is in the mystic states that experimental knowledge of God, that angelic mode of knowledge without sensible images, by infused intellectual "species," of which the mystical theologians speak.* The very explicit expressions of the mystics on this special mode of knowledge, which seems so strange to themselves in their first experiences, are, in his eyes, only metaphors, manners of speaking. All the more does he exclude the immediate and almost intuitive vision of the divine essence without "species," admitted by certain mystic theologians, at least in regard to the highest degree of contemplation,† an opinion which sometimes he seems to regard as irreconcilable with the faith. He shows Fr. Poulain no mercy for what he says about the "spiritual senses," reproaching him for having thus made mystic knowledge a sort of intuitive vision of God.

M. Saudreau has a deep sense of spiritual things, and he brings excellently before us the *passivity* of the mystic states. But he refuses to go into further details. Without seeing anything *extraordinary* in the degrees of prayer inferior to ecstasy, he considers as mystic prayers not only the prayer of quiet, but also that of simple regard (which we call *acquired* contemplation and he holds to be *infused*)—but not affective prayer. As for the higher states, he characterises them, without other details, as marked by a confused knowledge of God, surpassing our understanding, and by an intense love whose reason escapes us. For him the words "Mystic way, contemplative way, unitive way, perfect way" all mean the same thing; as for ecstasies, visions, revelations, and other extraordinary phenomena, they are not in the direct line of the mystic life.‡

* M. Saudreau admits knowledge by infused species, but he makes it the property of the "angelic" state, which he distinguishes from the "mystical" state, the latter according to him having no characteristic of its own save a special passivity, of the affective order, without any particular feature in the intellectual mode of acting save a special influx of light, which otherwise he does not characterise. See Sec. 40, 2.

† Fr. Arintero, who will shortly be considered, does not hide his sympathy with this opinion, when so limited to the highest degree of mystical knowledge.

‡ About this it would be easy to come to an understanding.

The difference between him and Fr. Poulain (or Fr. de Maumigny) is, in large part, that between the inexact and the exact; he is content with the rather vague assertions of the old writers, while the two Jesuits base themselves on the clearer explanations of St. Teresa, St. John of the Cross, the great mystic theologians of the seventeenth century (such as Alvarez de Paz, Philip of the Holy Trinity, Vallgornera, Antony of the Holy Ghost), and still more upon the experiences and descriptions of mystic souls (from Blessed Angela of Foligno to St. Alphonsus Rodriguez or Marina de Escobar). It cannot be denied that these descriptions or explanations enable us to be much more definite about many things left vague, even by great mystic writers such as Ruysbroeck and Tauler,* or by the great mystics of the Middle Ages, such as St. Gertrude, St. Mechtilde, St. Bridget (whose writings relate especially *ex-deific* visions and revelations, as Poulain calls them), or as St. Catherine of Siena, whose *Dialogue* consists in large part of doctrinal explanations, pious reflections, practical exhortations.†

By the side of M. Saudreau we may place Fr. Ludovic de Besse, Capuchin, Fr. Lamballe, Eudist, and a goodly number of writers who distinguish the mystic from the ascetic life only by accidental or secondary features.

Along the road opened by M. Saudreau, its ascetical and mystical editor, went the *Ami du clerge,* with Fr. Lamballe, Eudist, lately dead, who published his studies in a work entitled *La contemplation* (*Mystical Contemplation*, London, 1913); Fr. Ludovic de Besse, Capuchin, in *Etudes franciscaines;* and also, I think, a certain number of Benedictine authors, who, like those already mentioned, do not recognise any clear distinction, *so far as the spiritual life is concerned*, between the ascetic and the mystic ways. Like M. Saudreau, they connect with the mystic ways all the prayer of simple regard and contemplation, deny, like him, the existence of an *acquired* contemplation, distinct from mystical contemplation, and reduce the mystical life to the unitive way. They hold to the formulas of the writers before the sixteenth century or those who agree or seem to agree with them (such as Blosius), and refuse to see any progress in the distinctions and analyses of the moderns, regarding as *extraordinary* only interior locutions, ecstasies, visions and revelations.‡

*23. The Dominican Group: Fr. Arintero, Fr. Garrigou-Lagrange, etc.*

Can we speak of a Dominican school in mysticism? I think so, at least for some time past. I concern myself here only with Fr. Garrigou-Lagrange and Fr.

* All the same it must be recognised that Ruysbroeck and Tauler are very precise on certain points of the first importance and in full agreement on these points of SS. Teresa and John of the Cross, notably upon the vision of God in mystic knowledge and on the supra-human character of this knowledge. See Fr. Hugueny's fine study on *La doctrine mystique de Tauler.*

† See fuller explanations on the position of M. Saudreau in *RA*, June 1922. See also the chronicle in *RAM*, April 1922, III, 207-11, the reflections and remarks of Fr. J. de Guibert on M. Saudreau's manner.

‡ We might also mention, as attached to M. Saudreau's group, Dimmler and Krebs in Germany; Lercher in Austria; Louismet in England; Vicente de Peralta in Spain. See Sec. 40, I.

Arintero. Both are on good terms with M. Saudreau and agree with him on several points. Fr. Arintero, however, reproaches him especially with two things: (1) that he excludes from the mystic state, in order to attribute them to the state which, "by a rather new-fangled name, he calls the angelic state, all those divine communications in which the imagination does not intervene, and which by that very fact are not in agreement with the normal mode of action of the human understanding, but with that of the angels," that is to say, "the thing which is most characteristic of the mystic life"; (2) that he rejects or minimises the spiritual senses" by which, "according to the teaching of the best masters and the experience of the great contemplatives, through the veils of faith the divine is in some way seen—going sometimes so far as to appear entirely to deny* that marvellous and undeniable supernatural perception, as if it were incompatible with the state of 'wayfarer'... maintaining that all this is pure metaphor; that, according to tradition, there is no other knowledge of God than the abstract and the face to face, and that thus no place remains for concrete perception by spiritual sensations."† But, like Fr. Garrigou-Lagrange, he is in agreement with him in considering the mystic states as the normal development of the spiritual life, of the striving after the perfection of charity, so that every soul which labours hard to purify itself from its faults and defects, follows generously after Jesus in the practice of the Christian virtues, strives after union with God in fidelity to grace and perfect conformity of will with the divine will, and is going along the unitive way, is by that very fact proceeding towards the mystic union, which is nothing else than the perfection of charity. We give on this subject the actual formulas of Fr. Arintero, who says that he differs from Mgr. Farges (and Fr. Poulain) on the three following points, which may be reduced to a single one:

"1. Our Lord makes the offer to all men to manifest Himself to them and to give them the reward of a beginning of their beatitude,‡ if they have a real love for for Him.

"2. We all possess the seven gifts of the Holy Ghost, with which we can arrive, by being faithful and docile, at the fulness of life and understanding, and thus to the union of 'fruition' (*L'union fruitive*) or mystic union. And without that, we shall always be children who never reach the age of discretion, or that of the perfect man, *qui exercitatos habet sensus* (the spiritual senses). More: we shall be the 'slothful servants' (of the Gospel), through not having cultivated the talents we received at baptism.

"3. The transition from the ascetic to the mystic life is quite gradual, imperceptible, like that from childhood to full age; and perfection can only lie in the full development of baptismal grace: *perfectum, cut nihil deest.*

* A note explains that he does not deny it absolutely.

† Cuestiones m ísticas, pp. 51 and 56.

‡ That is, the mystic state.

"Hence (it follows) that the perfect in Christ are treated as close friends and receive great supernatural communications, which cause them to enjoy a beginning of beatitude, and even an intermediate vision, the mystic vision: *Eliam in hac vita, pur gate oculo per donum intellecius, Deus... videri potest*, says the Angelic Doctor.

"This, it seems to me, is very important in order that all those who thirst may take courage to *come to the waters* and to *find* in Jesus the desired *rest* and the *light of life* which they need in order not to *walk in darkness*, to know and practise what St. Teresa calls real truth, that is, truth exempt from all illusions, such as can arise in the exercise of virtue, as, indeed, cannot be otherwise if we allow ourselves to be guided by ordinary lights alone, without the supernatural enlightenment of the Holy Ghost. Hence St. Thomas: *In vita spirituali omnis motus esse debet a Spiritu Sancto.*

"This is what I have particularly desired to bring out in the *Cuestiones*. This it is which, though not in agreement with the pseudo-tradition of these last centuries, was the teaching current in all the (religious) Orders up to the eighteenth century, as many on all sides are coming to recognise who formerly, confiding in current opinions, Supposed the contrary."*

Fr. Garrigou-Lagrange, in a series of articles on *La mystique et les doctrines fondamentales de saint Thomas*, is of the same mind as Fr. Arintero on this point. For him also the mystic states stand in regular relationship to the development of charity; "There are not," he says, "two unitive ways, one ordinary, the other *in itself* extraordinary, to which not all fervent souls can aspire. There is but one unitive way, which, by a docility to the Holy Ghost that becomes more perfect day by day, leads to a closer mystic union. This latter is *extraordinary in fact*, because of the small number of fully docile souls, but it is not *extraordinary in itself* or *of its own nature*, like miracles or prophecy. On the contrary, it is, *in itself, the perfect order*, the full development of charity realised *de facto* in all truly generous souls, at least at the end of their lives, if they live long enough. It may indeed be that, for lack of appropriate direction or favourable surroundings, or again as a result of a nature too given to turn to outward things, certain generous souls only attain the mystic life after a time longer than the ordinary duration of life here on earth. But these are accidental circumstances, and, however frequent they may be, they do so without prejudice to the fundamental law of the full development of the life of grace... This summit is not arrived at without infused contemplation. And assuredly this is not the fruit of our own labours; it surpasses the human mode of Christian virtues. We cannot have it when we will; it comes from a special grace, an inspiration and enlightenment to which the gifts of the Holy Ghost make us docile. But, although we cannot have this inspiration when we

* Extract from a letter to Mgr. Farges, kindly shown me by the latter, I do not scruple to publish it, as it is only a resume or copy of what Fr. Arintero says in his *Cuestiones*.

will, we can hold ourselves in readiness to receive it, ask for it and merit it, at least in the wider sense of the word *merit*. Every soul in a state of grace has in fact received the gifts of the Holy Ghost, which are developed with charity, and generally the Holy Ghost moves us according to the degree of our habitual docility."*

In accordance with these principles, Fr. Garrigou-Lagrange replies to the three questions recently asked by Fr. de Guibert in the *RAM*:

"1. What is it that characterises the mystic life?—A special Passivity or predominance of the gifts of the Holy Ghost, the supra-human mode of which is specifically distinct from the human mode of the Christian virtues without however their being confounded with the graces *gratis datae*.

"2. When does the mystic life begin in the course of the spiritual life?—Normally with the passive purification of the senses and the prayer of passive recollection.

"3. is a special vocation necessary in principle to attain to it?—*In principle*, no, 'the grace of the virtues and the gifts' suffices *of itself* by its normal development to dispose us thereto, and mystical contemplation is necessary for the full perfection of the Christian life. Yet *in fact*, when certain conditions, sometimes independent of our own will, are lacking, very generous souls would only reach it after a time longer than the ordinary duration of our earthly existence; just as, certain conditions lacking, some understandings capable of a higher intellectual formation do not reach it." (*L.c.*, 7-8.)

These answers are interesting, and while they agree on the whole with those of Fr. Arintero, they tone down the hard and discouraging element in the Spanish writer, which makes us responsible, as "slothful servants," for not having made sufficiently good use of the talent we received at baptism.

is this to say that these answers are fully satisfying? Alas, no. I confine myself to pointing out a few remarks and difficulties.

*Ad* 1: There is room for greater exactness. Neither the Church nor St. Thomas seem to reserve the intervention of the gifts in the Christian life for the mystic states. The teaching of St. Thomas on the gifts is very clear. They are, according to him, in strict correlation with the virtues, the latter helping us to perform the supernatural act *connaturaliter* in so far as it is our own (with the help of grace), the former preparing us to receive the movement of the Holy Ghost and rendering the soul supple to the divine touch, like a horse to the touch of the rider to whom and by whom he is known. Hence it seems that the gifts ought to come

* *La perfection de la charité*, *LVS*, April 1921, II, 5. In his studies on *The call to the mystic life*, the author has made his position more clear by distinguishing between a general and remote call, a call proximate and personal, and between that which is normal and that which is extraordinary. This is an important step in the direction of a possible agreement. But many things remain to be defined and stated exactly. Even in his nominal definitions Fr. Garrigou-Lagrange too often introduces his personal views, as he introduces his personal opinions into the texts of St. Thomas and the old writers. See the remarks of Fr. de Guibert in *RAM*, April 1922, *Trois définitions de théologie mystique*.—-Cf. Sec. 40.

into play whenever the soul receives an actual grace, a special touch of God.* It is true, St. Thomas sometimes, especially in the *Sentences*, connects the gifts with a mode of action that is divine or supra-human, wherein the soul is passive rather than active. But if that is the special domain of the Holy Ghost, which He reserves to Himself, His action in it is neither restricted nor isolated; ordinary grace also comes from Him. This supra-human mode of action is not necessarily the *mystic* mode, in the strict sense of the word. Fr. Garrigou-Lagrange speaks of "predominance"; but is it then a question of degree?—See some further explanations, Sec. 14 and Sec. 40, 8.

*Ad2:* So be it; but where do these passive purifications, this passive recollection, begin, in what exactly do they consist and by what are they distinguished? With and by passivity, no doubt; but is not this a definition *idem per idem*?—See some further explanations, Sec. 14, and also Sec. 40, 8.

*Ad3*: Here especially the question becomes delicate and difficult. We can see, either here, in chaps, xxv and xxvii, or in Fr. de Maumigny, or Mgr. Farges, formal texts of St. Francis de Sales, St. Alphonsus Liguori, Fr. Balthazar Alvarez, St. Teresa, Benedict XIV, where the thought seems directly opposed to the statement of the learned theologian. He says: "There are not two unitive ways... There is only one... which by a docility to the Holy Ghost that becomes more perfect day by day, leads to a closer mystic union." They say: "There are very perfect persons to whom our Lord never gives such delights... Not all the perfect are raised to perfect contemplation... God has a thousand ways of enriching souls and of leading them into his dwellings without making them pass through this short cut... Many perfect men are canonised by the Church without there being in their process the slightest mention of infused contemplation."† Not to speak of so many other warnings as to the necessity of the call, the dangers of illusion, etc.

From another angle: does not daily experience seem to show that the mystic ways and progress in the road of perfection are not functions of one another?

True that in favourable surroundings the mystic graces flourish almost naturally; but that mystic souls are always the most perfect, and that a Carmelite convent, for example, is the more fervent the greater the number of mystic souls it contains, and the more mystic the more fervent souls there are, that is not so clear.

We see that many questions remain to be answered before mystic science is an exact science, as, in many points, theology is. Cf. Sec. 40, 11.

* I know that this is not the teaching of St. Thomas' brethren. Fr. Froget, for example, seems to restrict the intervention of the gifts to cases where the mode of acting is divine rather than human. See Gardeil, *BTC,* art. *Dons,* 1779-81. Cf. Sec. 40, 9.

† It is true that the opinion of SS. Teresa and Francis de Sales remains open to discussion. Cf L. de Grandmaison, *Études,* CXXXV, 333-4.

### *24. Fr. Maréchal's Philosophico-mystical Synthesis*

We may conclude from this that the time for a definitive synthesis has not arrived. Attempts at synthesis may none the less have their usefulness, at least provisional, were it only to establish some guiding principles, as is said today.

Beside that which Fr. Garrigou-Lagrange has sketched out by making mysticism a sort of annex to a treatise on Charity, I know of two other relatively short but powerful ones: that of Fr. J. Marechal in the *RP,* 1912, II, 416-88, and that of Fr. de la Taille, in the *RSR,* Sept-Dec. 1919, 273-92.* Though they are very condensed and difficult to follow, in the nature of things, they should themselves be read in addition to my present summary of them.

Fr. Marechal, writing for the *Revue de philosophic* an article on experimental religious psychology, proceeds by observation and analysis. He begins by placing the mystic life in the general *processus* first of our psychological, then of our spiritual life. Of the latter he follows the stages, from ritual and vocal prayer, by the paths of the interior life, up to contemplation, which he divides into sensible, imaginative and intellectual. In the last he notes on the one side (in morbid phenomena) a simplification which impoverishes the personality; on the other (in the intense and normally evolving intellectual life) a simplification which enriches it—whether in the profane or the mystic order—and he studies, in the light of this distinction, Neoplatonism, the Hindu Musulman and profane mystics, and lastly medieval Christian mysticism and that of the Renaissance. Arriving thus at the problem of ecstasy, he rejects two *interpretative* solutions; that which denies the real absence of multiplicity in ecstasy, and that which sees in it only complete unconsciousness. In their place he substitutes the *literal* solution, founded on the facts, according to which ecstasy is "the synthesis of an empirical negativity and a transcendent positivity." This vigorous study, which is at once that of a scholar, a philosopher and a theologian, boldly integrates the mystic way into our psychological life, all of whose activity, from the first awakening of reason up to ecstasy, is dominated by a primary orientation of heart and mind towards the good and the true, that is towards God, whom the soul finds here on earth in the obscure union of ecstasy and the spiritual marriage, while waiting to find Him *in* the beatific light of heaven. Without, of course, being an ontologist, the writer, here as in his penetrating study of *Le sentiment de présence* (though in this perhaps less clearly), sees in the first fact of the mystic life a certain loving perception of God in an intuition, which, at first obscure and confused, ends by opening upon the beatific vision. This intuition is accompanied by, even if it does not in some manner suppose, a loving striving after God—a striving which itself is only the first natural orientation of our soul towards God, becoming explicit in

* The study of Fr. de la Taille has been published in separate form, with slight alterations, by Beauchesne, Paris, and in English by Burns Oates & ash bourne, London {*Contemplative Prayer*).

the new species of precise and supernatural striving. Hence the interdependence between knowledge and love in mystic activity.

The author does not dare to say that this mystic activity, up to ecstasy inclusive, is impossible—under the action of grace, needless to say—outside the Christian religion, in a soul (such as that of Plotinus) which lives an intense supernatural life. Natural ecstasy, if it exists at all, is something quite different.

### *25. Fr. de la Taille's Theologico-mystical Synthesis*

Fr. Marechal's procedure is that of philosophical and experimental analysis which leads to the transcendence of mystic contemplation; that of Fr. de la Taille, in his study on *Contemplative Prayer*, is an explanation of the facts by the application of theological data. The author desires "to indicate briefly the nature of the general solution which traditional theology appears to offer to certain questions touching passive contemplation." Five questions are in turn examined, those which must first of all be answered in order to obtain clear ideas on the facts of contemplation, taken as known according to the descriptions of the mystics, especially St. Catherine of Genoa.

1. *Its object and medium, its process.* Contemplation is "a loving fixing of the gaze on the Sovereign Good in the medium at once luminous and dark of faith... a particular exercise of the virtue of faith" (p. 10), but beneath a particular touch of the Holy Ghost, causing the contemplative soul to vibrate at one aspect or another of the divine object which desires to reveal Himself to her in an obscure image of Himself. "It is known as unknown... and contemplation becomes higher and... purer in proportion as it further reveals and makes this transcendent darkness shine more splendidly " (p. 3). Its process is a simple regard, analogous to the knowledge of the angels.

2. *The Way In.* The act of faith is made under the urge of love (perfect or imperfect). " The light of faith, although residing in the spirit, did not enter man by way of the spirit, but by way of the heart." Likewise, contemplation comes from love; it is a loving gaze. But what is it that distinguishes this love from the love implied in every act of faith? It is not its perfection or its intensity. The love of the contemplative may be less than that of the ordinary Christian. But this love is a love "consciously infused... The mystic has the consciousness of receiving from God a 'ready-made' love... The soul knows and feels itself invested with this love by God. And this is why... she attains the presence of God in herself... She receives the gift *from the hand* of the Giver, who is, therefore, present in a manner perceptible to the soul" (p. 13). The origin of contemplation is "in this love which is passively received, and in the consciousness of this passivity, which swoops on the intelligence and carries it above itself towards the Sovereign Good, to which it attaches it in a dark light" (p. 13).

3. *Trials.* This refers to sufferings "inherent in the contemplative life by its very nature." The first is "that of the progressive and laborious birth of contemplation." It must adapt itself to this new life, this obscure light, this night

of the senses and the spirit, this apparent inactivity. This does not happen without effort, trouble, suffering; the light itself "will wound her eyes at first, this new and obscure light, which only adapts itself well to eyes purified from the world of the senses, and from everything issuing from that world " (p. 15). "It should be noted," says the author, "that these initial sufferings are spared to children when God presents them with contemplative grace, because the child's soul, fresh and new, has not yet any acquired habits to confine the exercise of the gifts and to obscure the light of faith " (p. 15).

This adaptation to a new life already implies many renunciations. To develop the contemplative light it must "emancipate itself more and more from all servitude and dependence and constraint coming from the nature of the senses." It must therefore strip itself of all the impurity of the human and natural, and subject everything to the exacting demands of the supernatural. And often this "purification of the human element has to go on either without any correlative enjoyment... or in a state of torment and desolation due to the painful character of the contemplation itself" (p. 17).

This is only the suffering of the natural man; much deeper and keener is that of the spiritual man, which is attached to the divine gift itself. God appears, so good, so lovable... and he is loved so little by men; loved so little, in relation to his infinite lovableness, by the contemplative soul itself, whether owing to the fundamental powerlessness of a limited nature, or still more to that obstacle which the self unceasingly opposes to perfect union, the unity of love, the loss of self in the infinite Love.

4. *Place in the economy of the spiritual life,* (*a*) Contemplation "transcends... the natural man and the means at his disposal, even when helped by grace." This is evident, since it implies a mode of knowledge superior to the human mode. But it does not follow therefrom that it must "be classed among phenomena which are exceptions to the divine law, and in consequence miraculous." The creation of the soul, although it transcends all created causality, is not miraculous, since it is according to the law of God, as a completion required by the natural operation of secondary causes. is it so with the mystic states? The author replies in the affirmative.

(*b*) "Granted the law of Providence on the growth and development of grace, we can say in the case of a given subject, that when he has passed to a certain point to which he can attain by his human exercise of virtue there will be no more regular and normal progress for him except by the path of passivity" (p. 22).

(*c*) "This point of juncture is far from being the same for all souls. For some it is close to the beginnings of the Christian life; for others it is situated on a higher level of spirituality...* Perhaps even this point may be further on the way than the

* In an explanatory letter, inserted in Sec. 39 below, Fr. de la Taille writes: I have not maintained in my little book that man can without the grace of contemplation 'arrive at very high summits of grace and

last stage of their journey in this world, however faithful they may have been to the grace which was given them: the moment of the change [in their life of prayer] had not arrived for them when death faced them " (p. 23).

(*d*) "The ground on which these two different relations, the one to the subject, the other to the Ordainer of grace, meet, is that of the gifts of the Holy Spirit, of those passivities mobile under the touch of God, which are already in the just man before he receives the gift of contemplation, and which in the contemplative state are moved by God in the special manner required to cause the light of faith to emerge in its 'nudity' before the soul, as a new and henceforward an independent medium, self-sufficing as regards both information and evidence concerning the God who emits it" (p. 24).

Thus for the author contemplation is, in relation to the just man, "at once both supernatural and yet, in a certain sense, connatural" (p. 24).

5. *Consequences for direction,* (*a*) "Since the soul, even in a state of grace, cannot obtain for herself contemplation by the exercise of her own faculties, it is useless for her to make efforts with that intention.

(*b*) "Since contemplation occurs in the course of the normal prolongation of the life of grace, it is right that the soul should dispose herself towards it.

(*c*) "As to desiring the arrival of this light as a proximate event, and asking God expressly for it as we ask for the things necessary or advantageous for us at the moment, it would be as if a child on going to bed at night were to ask God to wake him the next morning ten inches taller" (p. 25). Prayers and desires are at least indiscreet and useless.

(*d*) "Once, however, contemplation has been constated, the soul should be urged to feed upon it and make progress in it" (p. 25). This comes about by the exercise of contemplation itself, and could not happen without renunciation and humility, without the cultivation of the virtues, notably charity.

(*e*) In the period when contemplation invades the whole soul and, so to speak, lays hold of the whole human activity, in the period of crucifying purifications, " the task of the director is not so much to direct as to sustain, to comfort, one can hardly say to console..." He may present to the mind and heart "objects and truths the memory of which may bring a motive of action, or rather of power to suffer, an encouragement to self-abandonment, to peaceful acquiescence and repose in union with the will of God. As to the direction of such a soul in her interior in which the divine light dwells, there is no need to trouble about it, for God takes charge of it" (p. 28).

(*f*) If, as usually happens, this state of trial resolves itself into a higher state, "in which the contemplative light, fully mistress of a fully purified soul, far from diminishing or countering her natural activity, marvellously helps it and multiplies its fertility," then "charity towards the neighbour reaches its height...

sanctity' but only 'at a higher level of spirituality.' The former expression exceeds what I think I can certainly affirm; not the second, which is more temperate."

under the rule of the law of love." This last state, the author remarks in conclusion, was, from the first moment of her life, that of our Blessed Lady, "for she was all pure and perfectly governed from the first instant of her existence by the law of love and charity."

I have summed up at length, and so far as possible in the writer's own words, this fine and weighty study. But to be fully understood it must be read entire. Faithful to his word, the author has made every effort to explain "the experience of contemplatives" by "the principles of the theologian," It was difficult to say so much, on such a complicated subject, in so few words. The study is a masterly one, and one is captivated, in reading it, by the serene and powerful light thrown on all the great problems of the mystic life. It is good to see the facts grow clearer and fall into order by the intuitive penetration of a writer who seems to have merely to read (shall I say within himself or in others' writings?) in order to present them to us, explaining them after the principles of theology and the data of experience. But we must give ourselves a shake, break the charming spell, verify and criticise. Are these explanations true? is the construction solid? is it anything more than a clever hypothesis? Even as an explanatory hypothesis, does not the explanation give rise to some objections? It raises fewer than that of Fr. Garrigou-Lagrange, of whom we spoke above; for it is more subtly detailed, takes more account of the facts, and in particular it does not take for granted identity between the passive ways and the unitive way. But it does raise some.

I have nothing but praise for paragraphs 3 and 5, on trials and direction, save to note in them a few gaps, of no great importance. Paragraphs 1 and 2 on the process of contemplation (by concrete intuition, not by abstraction or reasoning) and its origin (in charity *felt* as infused) are powerfully conceived and presented; but some doubts or obscurities may remain as to the ingenious manner in which contemplation is explained as an act of the virtue of faith put in action by the Holy Ghost, whose touch sets the gifts in motion. That it is exercised in the world of faith, not in that of direct and immediate vision, well and good; that it is merely a special act of the virtue of faith, is possible; but, as Fr. Arintero says, is our analysis of the possible activities of the human soul under divine action so perfect that we have to reduce them all to the operation of the virtues and the gifts? If the reduction of the act of contemplation to an act of faith remains doubtful, that of infused love (inherent in and inseparable from the contemplative act) to an act of will which commands this act of contemplative faith remains doubtful also, for more than one reason. These are powerful constructions; let us guard against taking them for assured explanations, for established truths See Sec. 39, 2.

The same remark applies in greater degree to par. 4, on the place of mystical contemplation in the economy of the spiritual life. The author takes account of the facts, and among these facts I select three which certain theorists of mysticism seem to overlook or contradict:

1. For some souls the mystic states begin almost together with the Christian life; for others they may commence only at "a higher level of spirituality" (p. 22). Sanctity then is not a function of the mystic states. But see 4, *c*, note.

2. Many die without reaching the mystic states, "however faithful they may have been to the grace which was given them."

3. This grace given on earth to non-mystics, and to which they have been faithful, may exceed the grace given to mystics "already advanced in the contemplative way," since such a non-mystic is supposed to be more holy in purgatory than an advanced mystic.

Let us look at these concessions. They enable us to be more sympathetic to the opinion of our author and to follow him with more interest when he explains to us how, in his eyes, mystic contemplation is a normal development of the spiritual life.

"Contemplation, in relation to the just man," he says, "is at once both supernatural and connatural" (p. 24). Why so? By virtue of a "law of Providence on the growth and development of grace," in accordance with which, "in the case of a given subject, when he has passed a certain point to which he can attain by his human exercise of the virtues and supernatural gifts, there will be no more regular and normal progress for him, except by the path of passivity" (p. 22). is there such a law of Providence? In what does it consist? This is explained in a note. It "consists in this, that man progresses by his victories over self-love... for the advantage of his love of God, so that his self-love ends, if not by dying, at least in being separated from that inaccessible term by only a negligible distance." Here indeed I see a law of Providence, but quite a different one from that set forth in the text. The author brings the two laws together thus: "One can see that the continuous heroism implied in such a conquest growing more and more complete, and more and more stable, will not be able to maintain itself beyond a certain point, given human weakness, unless by means of the help beyond all price derived from contemplative love... But since in all men there exists the weakness inherent in fallen nature, it is evident that in every case moral forces have a practical limit, and contemplation and increasing contemplation may well be needed to surpass and advance beyondit." In this I see a new enunciation of the law, but nothing resembling a proof. It is indeed true that grace is necessary, continual and abundant grace; an exceptional grace, if you like; but it remains to be proved that this exceptional grace must be the mystic grace. All that the author says by way of proof is that "It is sufficient to read on this point the Dialogues of St. Catherine of Genoa." This is a little summary for so important a question. Even were it true for St. Catherine or for every other mystic soul, it does not follow that it is a general law. Of this general law neither the theologians nor the ascetics nor the mystics themselves tell us anything, nor do they prove its necessity.* The Church supposes the contrary: when it beatifies and canonises, it has no concern with the mystic ways, or does not concern itself with them otherwise than it does with miracles, that is, as a sign which manifests sanctity in a given case, proves it, if you like, indirectly, but not as an element which constitutes or conditions it.† See No. 39, x.

To this proof from authority I add one from reason and experience. "It is the first step that counts," the proverb says. And another proverb has it that "sewing makes the tailor." This is verified in the spiritual life. The difficulty, instead of increasing as we advance, seems rather to diminish. The exercise of a virtue makes the virtue more easy; the will is tempered by its own activity and its victories. On the other hand, the passions grow feebler as we resist them, virtuous habits are acquired which counterbalance the weight of natural inclination. All philosophical and Christian asceticism confirms this fact of everyday experience. Whence the observation that virtue becomes little by little second nature. Habituated to following the movements of grace, the soul follows them as it were naturally. The author seems to have forgotten this fact, when he establishes a kind of law of increasing difficulty to which he attaches the necessity for a special grace. It is true that, as against this fact of common experience, we can observe another in the case of certain souls, at some critical or decisive moment in the spiritual life, when God demands that the soul cast off all its ropes and let the ship ride without sail, oar or rudder at the mercy of the wind of grace, which urges it out to the open sea: *Due in altum.* He demands from it complete and blind abandonment to the great Unknown who is calling to it. And the soul is powerless to give itself, to get clear of itself, to forget itself. A wonderful prayer of Blessed Claude de la Colombiere to the Sacred Heart expresses this powerlessness very well: "Sacred Heart of Jesus, teach me perfect forgetfulness of myself... I feel in myself a great will to please Thee and a greater powerlessness to succeed, without a very special light and help which I can only hope for from Thy grace. Let Thy will be done in me, Lord Jesus. I oppose myself to it, and I know well that I do so; but gladly, as I think, would I not oppose myself to it. It is for Thee, O divine Heart of Jesus, to do everything," etc.—Cf. Sec. 39, I.

In similar cases, then, the soul needs a "very special help." God must, in a way, do everything. is a mystic grace necessary for this? Yes, for mystic souls. But must this special intervention of God always be a mystic grace? Perhaps: but this has not so far been proved.

* The texts cited on this subject are either not general in their bearing, or can be understood in another sense, or have only a limited authority.

† St. John Berchmans is often quoted as an example of a saint who was canonised without any trace of mystic grace in his interior life, which in other respects is well known. Such is the feeling of M, Delehaye himself in the delightful portrait of him which he has given us in the series *Les saints.* But Fr. L. Peeters gives, in *RAM,* April 1922, a collection of facts and considerations which lead us rather to conclude that the saint enjoyed a mystic prayer.

May the author of this beautiful study forgive me for thus examining him with a lens, dissecting him, showing myself, here and there, *tardus ad credendum*. But the question is a grave one, of great consequence for many souls.

Even from the scientific point of view it is fatal to take hypotheses for realities, assertions for proofs. Now from our examination it must be evident, if I am not mistaken, that this powerful attempt—the most powerful that I know—to mingle together in a definitive synthesis mystic experiences and theological principles, does not succeed in reaching irrefragable proofs and irresistible conclusions.* Let us admit that "from a comparison between these two sources of information... light may break forth." But to that end let us take account of facts no less than of principles; it is the facts that quicken and nourish the principles. The old writers traced the main lines of *Mystical theology*; but a place remains for studies of *Experimental mysticism*, to which the greater part of the problems at present under discussion belong. To solve them, we must consider mystic phenomena in themselves and for themselves, without stretching them to fit preconceived ideas, without grouping them in ready-made schemes. We must proceed as in the observational sciences, while illuminating and guiding our studies by the light of principles and acquired data. We must treat of experimental mysticism as a special science, the handmaid of theology in the sense that it borrows its principles therefrom, not that the principles are sufficient to decide questions of fact.†

### *26. Present Problems and Questions of Method according to Fr. J. de Guibert*

It is to this work that Fr. J, de Guibert refers specialists in mystical studies in an article in the *RAM*, "A propos de la contemplation mystique," putting them on their guard against hasty generalisations, against preconceived ideas, against the application to a science *in fieri* of the principles of an entirely different one. The sub-title, *Problemes aciuels et questions de methode*, indicates the exact object of his work.

After remarking on the luxuriant flowering of mystical literature, of which we are witnesses, he points out the wide divergences of view between men "all of

* I have recognised, it is true (see Sec. 39), and am glad to recognise that the eminent theologian has replied well to my questions and objections. But I have not been able to feel that his construction, splendid as it is, carries its proof with it.

† Cf. Sec. 40, 13 and 14.—While not a synthesis, in the proper sense of the word, Fr. de Grand maison's fine study on *L'élan mystique* should be singled out for special notice as giving a general view of the principal problems to be solved in mysticism, and offering just and profound observations which may be of use in the solution.—For special mention, also, are the scholarly works of Dom Mager, O.S.B., which on important points open out new roads to research, notably those in which he shows us the speculative theorists of the Middle Ages deviating to some small extent, in their theories of the Christian life, from the Pauline and Johannine direction. This had reduced the Christian life to the life of Christ in us and ours in Him; their theory, following Denis and the Neoplatonists, gave a preponderating influence in this life, to the aspect of *contemplation*.

whom are versed in the practice of direction and in the knowledge of ascetic and mystical literature, all having a long personal practice of the interior and sometimes of the mystical life." Instead of "adding one more to the already long list of proposed theories," and seeking to answer questions which do not yet seem ripe for solution, whose very statement is in dispute, he wished "to limit the exact point of debate, mark off the *real* problems, by distinguishing them from questions of words, point out the source of the confusion which all experience in these discussions, indicate some of the means which seem calculated to throw light upon and advance the discussion" (331). An exercise in method, as we see, and one that needed doing.

Leaving on one side the questions of *practical conduct* and of *application*, he confines himself to *theoretical* problems, which he reduces to three principal heads: "1. What is the *nature* of the mystic states? 2. is there a *frontier* or *boundary* which separates them from more ordinary, lower states, and where must this boundary be placed? 3. Who is called upon to cross it? Can we speak of a *mystical vocation*, as a particular vocation in the path of Christian perfection?" (331).

1. Nature and constitutive element of the mystical states. After pointing out some concrete solutions, differing greatly among themselves, the author, classifying them considerably, as he himself remarks, reduces the answers to four types, each with numerous varieties:

(*a*) Special *infused knowledge* of God and divine things.

(*b*) *Infused love* produced by the soul under a more immediate and powerful action of God drawing it to Himself.

(*c*) Greater *passivity* of the soul, *acted upon* rather than *acting*.

(*d*) *Simple and loving* attention to God. The author connects with this the opinion of Fr. Lercher and others, who seem to identify the mystic state with the *unitive way*. This opinion might make a fifth category.

2. Where does the mystic life, in the strict sense of the word, properly speaking, begin?—It is generally agreed to exclude from it *discursive* meditation and so-called *affective* prayer; and to include in it the higher states of prayer, including the prayer of quiet. There is a division of opinion as to the prayer of simple regard, as to the existence of an *acquired contemplation* which is not mystical, and of *psychologically* mystic states which are purely natural.

3. What relation is there between the moral, ascetic life and the mystic life? Between progress in holiness and the graces of prayer?—The question in this respect is largely whether the mystic states are the normal term of all fervent interior life, if Christian perfection can be found apart from the mystic states, or if these are the necessary condition for reaching this perfection, or one of its constituents.

On many of these questions not only is there no understanding, but we have an impression of vagueness in the ideas, of misunderstanding in the discussions, of blows dealt awry. Whence does this confusion arise? In part from the fact that some transfer into this field the divergences of theological schools and systems. And in this there is a defect of method graver than might appear at first sight, all the graver for being unconscious; we think we are speaking of grace as Holy Scripture and the Church understand it, when we are speaking of efficacious grace in the "Thomist" sense of the word.

In part, too, it arises from inexactitudes whether of words, or of descriptions of mystic states; the same words are used in varymg senses, things are described in confused and vague terms, which are not applicable either *soli* or *omni.*

In part, again, from difference of procedure; some start from theological principles and introduce mystical phenomena as best they can; others start with the facts, describing and classifying them, as is done for a separate science, which has its own province, its own methods, its own language.

How can this confusion be remedied, the discussions simplified and set in order?—First of all, it is necessary to fix and determine the terminology.—Then, to study both doctrines and facts *systematically*; for example, the *doctrine* of St. Francis de Sales or St. Bonaventure, the *false* mystics, so finely described and analysed by St. Teresa.—To put the questions in order, beginning with those on which the others depend; to establish and verify the data before drawing conclusions, etc. Not to reject *a priori* the principle of progress, trying to square St. Teresa with Dionysius the Areopagite, or, in spite of his protestations, Tauler with St. Thomas. In a word, to proceed methodically, treating questions of theology by theological methods, questions of fact by positive methods.

We can but subscribe to counsels so wise and practical, by hoping that they will be followed, for the greater good of mystical studies.*

Fr. Poulain, we may say with all truth, had done in advance in his book what Fr. de Guibert asks; he had chosen the descriptive method, and kept to it.

Before presenting to the reader this new edition of an almost classical work, I think that I should add to Fr. de Guibert's counsels on theoretical study a few remarks of a practical order.

* Fr. de Guibert published, in the *RAM*, April 1922, a study of *practical* terminology, entitled *Trois définitions de théologie mystique,* corresponding with the programme here outlined, defining the words: *acquired* and *infused* contemplation, *ordinary* and *extraordinary* in the ways of holiness, *remote* or *proximate* call, *sufficient* or *efficacious*, in order to arrive at an understanding on these words, independently of the various systems, eliminating from the nominal definition the elements of the systematic order which Fr. Garrigou-Lagrange had introduced.

## VI
## Practical Questions and Remarks*

Without seeking at present to solve all questions of theory and method, can we not arrive at a practical understanding on some few points?

We must be glad to see that mystical studies are today being taken up widely, not to say becoming fashionable. But, without warding off souls capable of profiting by them, let us recall a few truths which should not be forgotten either by those who write on mystical subjects or by their readers.

### *27. Distinction between Asceticism and Mysticism*

Agreement has been reached, it seems, on the distinction to be made between speculative theology, historical theology, practical theology, and the like. It would seem that it could equally be reached for moral theology and ascetical or mystical theology. These disciplines are not always adequately distinguished from one another; but they must be distinguished in practice, so that the same work need not be constantly being repeated. The principles of speculative morals are admirably set forth, discussed and coordinated in the I—II of St. Thomas, and applied, in the II—II, to the principal objects considered by theology. This work has been done, and neither the moralist nor the catechist has to bring it into question; he has only to make use of it, by remembering and applying it. In morals, the casuist has not to establish his principles; he has only to make use of them in practical applications. Ascetics differs from morals in that it has not to concern itself with what is licit or illicit, but with the practical exercise of the virtues, with turning the attention to the better thing. Ought not ascetic and mystical theology likewise to be distinguished? The one has as its principal object *our action* under that of God, the other *God's action* in us. Ascetic theology has not to study speculatively and for their own sake either the operation of our psychological activity or the divine concurrence, but to make use of what is known of it for the direction of the ascetic life; mystical theology has not to refashion the theory of grace, the virtues, the gifts, etc., but to make use of it to explain mystical phenomena in the degree in which they spring from grace, the virtues, or the gifts. The ascetic author will say, for example: Pray, and pray always; for you can do nothing without grace, and grace is assured only to prayer. He will say, on the other hand: Act so as to correspond with grace; for if grace sometimes acts without action of ours, it is certain that it will not sanctify us without action of ours. These principles will apply in the mystical order; in a different fashion perhaps, but the *action* of the mystic is subject to the general

* These sections, Nos. 27-37 (with the addition of par. 9), have already appeared in the *RAM*, Jan. 1922. The teaching of Sec. 27 has been criticised by Fr. Garrigou-Lagrange. This has afforded opportunity for a short explanation, completing a note.

laws of asceticism. More: mysticism and asceticism are, as it were, two aspects of the same spiritual life; asceticism considers that life so far as it is our own personal effort; mysticism, so far as it is the work of God in us. The two disciplines, then, are inseparable *ex parte objecti*; but they are distinct *secundum diversam objecti considerationem.* And mark well, this distinct consideration has as correlatives distinct formal objects, irreducible the one to the other *in eadem linea.* Whence the distinction to be maintained between the two sciences, the one having as its object the moral and supernatural man as *acting,* the other as *acted upon* or *passive.* *

There is nothing astonishing, then, in our speaking, in the two disciplines, of the purgative, illuminative, unitive *way* (or *life*); but ascetic or active purification is one thing, mystical or passive purification another, and thus of the other ways. We must not then, without distinction or explanation, reduce the unitive way to the mystic life, any more than we may the purgative way to the ascetic life. Reserve, if you like, a *supra-human* perfection to the mystic union, not to be arrived at merely by the ascetic ways—ways of *human* perfection, in which we work after the human fashion (though, of course, under the action of grace): but note at the same time that this perfection of the action or of the mode of operation (according as it is rather human or divine) is not reserved to the unitive way, but is found equally in the purgative and in the illuminative way.

To connect the purgative way with the ascetic life and the unitive way with the mystic life would therefore be to unite things which are disparate. Each of these two "lives" has its three stages, or "moments" or "aspects" (for it is not only a matter of succession in time), and to take for granted that the *virtutes purgati animi* are the virtues of the mystic states is to beg the question.

The distinction between the ascetic and the mystic ways is thus largely a distinction of their modes of operation. In both of them the action is God's and

* In thus reducing mysticism to the study of the supernatural life considered as *passive*, I do not forget what I have said above, Sec. 12, on the mystical state as specified by the *consciousness of the supernatural in us.* There it was a question of the specific difference which constitutes the mystical state in the full and precise sense of the word. Now passivity alone does not constitute this difference; for there is an element of passivity in all human activity (under the action of the secondary or of the primary cause), and especially in all supernatural activity (under the action of grace); but the proper object of mystical study is not *all* supernatural passivity, but only the *conscious* passivity of the supernatural as such, or, what comes to the same thing, the supernatural state and supernatural phenomena so far as they fall under consciousness. All supernatural life is mystical, in the objective sense of the word, inasmuch as it is constituted by supernatural realities inaccessible, as such, to our natural reason and consciousness; but supernatural life only in so far as it falls under consciousness is mystical in the full and precise, specific sense of the word. Fr. Garrigou-Lagrange peremptorily denies that there is any duality of formal objects, *LVS,* March 1922, p. 473. No duality which cannot be reduced to the higher unity of the principles of speculative theology, true; but that there is no duality, if we consider them *præcisive* in themselves, as special sciences of the spiritual life, both subordinate to theology, but distinct from each other, as particular sciences, studied for their own sakes, I deny. Everyone knows that all the sciences, in the degree that they progress and in order to progress more freely, need to specialise by becoming distinct from each other and specifying their object.

also our own; in both the act is supernatural; but in the former it is after the human mode, God is moving the soul after the fashion of human activity; in the latter it is after the divine mode, God is moving the soul in the divine fashion.

In other words, in the ascetic ways we are more active than passive; in the mystic ways more passive than active.

We might add that in the former the action follows the mode of the virtues; in the latter that of the gifts. But this does not mean that the gifts are not concerned in ascetic activity or the virtues in mystical.

### *28. Asceticism of the Ordinary Ways and that of the Mystical Ways*

It might be said with equal truth either that there are or that there are not two forms of Christian asceticism. There is but one, that of the Gospel, which merely completes asceticism based on human philosophy, raising it to a higher level, attaching it, not to the law of human nature nor to an abstract ideal, but to the positive commandment of God or of Our Lord, to the example of the divine Master or the Heavenly Father, to the demands of more abundant grace and to the divine life within us. There are two, or several, according to the ways wherein the soul may be found, the degrees at which it has arrived, according to the special demands of grace on each soul. It seems better, truer and surer, as well as more practical, to say that there is only one. It is the way of combat and renunciation through love in order to establish the reign of love, implying prayer to obtain grace and effort to use it, and all, from first to last, in accordance with the divine intentions and in conformity with God's will. We know that the Quietists and other false mystics regarded things differently; but neither God nor His Church absolves anyone from the practice of the virtues, from struggle against himself, from renunciation, imitation of our Lord, patience in bearing the Cross with Him and like Him.

### *29. The Mystical Ways and Christian Perfection*

The mystic graces are a powerful method of sanctification; this is beyond all question. We might quibble by saying that in the mystic act the soul is passive rather than active, and that it is not our *being moved* that sanctifies us, but *our own movement* towards God. True, it is not grace alone which does everything, but the grace to which we correspond, or, if we prefer, our correspondence to grace. No one, therefore, would try to make out that the mystic graces sanctify us without our aid: the mystics are there to remind us of this if anyone were tempted to forget it. But it remains that these graces attract the soul, uplift it, draw it to a world so beautiful, bring it into contact with a force so gentle, provide it with such great lights on God and the nothingness of all that is not God, that, carried by the divine hand, leaning upon the Beloved, whom it feels as its sole possession and its all, the soul runs in the odour of those ointments, escapes from everything and even from itself, so as to belong entirely to Him, see nought but Him, and love none but Him.

Must we conclude from this that there is no such Christian perfection save in the mystic way? We have already said that this assertion rests either on a confusion between the mystic ways and the perfection of charity, or on the gratuitous hypothesis of their practical identity. That it is a short cut to arrive there, as St. Teresa says, is true; but this short cut has its pitfalls, as she repeats *ad nauseam*, and the other mystics with her. All complain that, in the ways themselves, many, nay, the majority, stay by the wayside.* Lastly, neither the Gospel nor the Church, as we have seen, say anything of the necessity of the mystic ways for Christian perfection, or of a special perfection which should be the possession of mystic souls alone. There is a special way of tending towards perfection in the practice of the evangelical counsels; but the attempt has never been made to identify this special way with that of the mystic states.† The remembrance of these principles will perhaps help us to understand better the position maintained in the course of this *Introduction* on the question of desire for mystic graces, etc. So, too, we must not forget that God does not lead all souls by the same way, that there are saints in the world who might not have been saints in the cloister, and that the soul must take care above all to use the graces it receives to go faithfully on in the way on which God has placed it.

### *30. Mystical Graces or Touches, Mystical Ways or States*

It may be useful, and make for greater exactness, to distinguish between mystical graces or touches, mystical ways and states. By mystical graces or touches is generally meant special interventions of God in a soul, which are of the mystical order, even when such a soul is not ordinarily led by the mystic ways and is not in the mystic states. A soul can receive mystic touches in a given case without for all that being specially called by God to follow the mystic way or to

* St. Ignatius wrote to St. Francis Borgia in 1545 with regard to obstacles: "which prevent God from bringing to perfection at His own good pleasure the gifts which He has already placed in the soul: and it is not only before he has been loaded with benefits in the divine service, with particular gifts, and with the consolations of the Holy Ghost, that man sets up such obstacles; he does so also after having received the graces and signal favours of God, and when as the result of these favours his soul, illumined by lights from on high, freed from all darkness and delivered from distress and anxiety, is flooded with joy and unspeakable happiness. Yes, when this soul has so many helps for salvation by which it is wholly carried away, not without a sovereign pleasure, towards the love of eternal things and the desire for unending glory, it is then that, allowing itself to be distracted by the most trivial thoughts—tragic proof of the lightness of our nature-—it lets slip, through its imprudence, the abundance of so many heavenly goods." *Lettres de saint Ignace de Loyola*, French trans. Bouix, Paris, 1870, Letter 34, pp. 154-5.

† We mean the mystic states *properly so-called*, not the states or exercises through which the soul (under the influence of grace which is not mystic) prepares itself in a fashion, disposes itself *negatively*—by the prayer of the heart and of simple regard, by the spirit of prayer, by an intensely ascetic life, by a great desire for perfection, for belonging wholly to God, for intimate union with Him—for the reception of the mystic graces (should it please God to give them) despite the fact that, or perhaps because, it is most unworthy and would not dare to aspire to them explicitly. See L. de Grandmaison, *Études*, cxxxv, 315-19 (on the *mystical exercises*), and 332-4 (on the predisposition, preparation and aspiration for the mystic graces).

lead the mystic life. There is nothing, in consequence, to prove that a soul is unfaithful to God in the *sole fact* that it has had some mystic touches in particular circumstances. God might have His reasons, for the soul's own good or that of others, for making her taste this inebriating wine on one or more occasions, without wishing to make it her ordinary drink.

It might perhaps be well to distinguish also between mystic *graces* and *touches*, mystic *states* and *ways*, since the words *touches* and *states* are often taken in a more exact, less general sense than the words *graces* and *ways*.

### *31. Mystic and Gratuitous Graces*

It is of the nature of grace to be gratuitous. Yet theologians distinguish graces into graces of sanctification (*gratum facientes*) and gratuitous graces (*gratis datse*). The former all relate to sanctifying grace and are given to the soul for its personal sanctification; beside sanctifying grace properly so-called, they are the virtues, the gifts of the Holy Ghost, actual graces (light, love, etc.). The latter are given for the advantage of our neighbour; the gifts of miracles, prophecy, tongues, etc.

The mystical graces are fundamentally graces of personal sanctification. Yet often, and this seems to be in the Providential order, they have a close relation with our neighbour's good, especially in the degree in which they become *extraordinary, striking, miraculous.* This firstly in themselves; when they are eminent, they attract attention, and exercise a salutary influence; the speech, the action of a saint, the passing encounter, are something divine; God is to be found in them. In the second place, they sometimes have miraculous effects or accompaniments; for example, ecstasy, and other analogous effects. Lastly, they are often accompanied by gratuitous graces; the gift of prophecy, miracles, reading hearts, etc.

This remark may help us better to understand the current language and to explain certain divergences among writers, differences rather in expression and viewpoint than in doctrine.

### *32. Mystical Souls*

It seems impossible to deny that certain temperaments seem more fitted for the unfolding of the mystic states. By this I mean not only the physical temperament, but the moral, the turn of mind, the dispositions of the heart. Affective souls, delicate and refined, reflective and interior, of nervous temperament, almost morbid, are not all mystics; but they show some mystic tendency, in the profane sense of the word, in their bearing and their affections; and it seems that, if there are fields predisposed, as it were, for the graces of mystic prayer—and everything shows that this is so—these are such in a special degree. In what do these predispositions consist and how far do they go? Insoluble questions perhaps, but questions which force themselves on us and cannot be escaped. They must therefore be studied. If an attentive and serious study does not succeed in answering them all, it will at least help to discern better— a thing which is possible in principle and attainable in practice— supernatural from natural or diabolical mysticism.

The same remarks apply with regard to the influence of the environment, of reading, of exterior circumstances on the blossoming (or atrophy) of the mystic graces. This influence is not always sensible, but it often is so, just like that of temperament—and it is not only an influence of the environment, it is often entirely personal.

### *33. Counsels of Discretion*

To this favourable or unfavourable influence of the environment or of persons, we must attach a counsel—on which we cannot insist too much—of extreme discretion in these matters. This counsel applies especially to directors of souls, and to superiors of nuns; but it concerns everyone. The more discreet one is in these matters —whether pro or contra—the better.

It is not good for mystic souls to feel that we are concerning ourselves specially with them, or are talking about them. The more they forget themselves the better. And they will forget themselves all the better the more they are treated like everyone else, All this, of course, without any affectation; for such affectation would itself be a special treatment, which they would soon notice.

The same applies to special trials. We must ordinarily leave to God the business of putting them to the test. The human hand is too clumsy for the purpose—and moreover it has not grace at its disposal.

They must open themselves—and thus they must have someone to whom they can do so. Moreover, they have a wonderful instinct for knowing with whom to speak and with whom to be silent. But they should not feel curiosity. While sometimes helping them to speak—for it is sometimes difficult for them—we must not chatter about these divine things. They must indeed be spoken of: but, even in cases of practical necessity, they should be spoken of briefly and rarely. Let us, in accordance with the excellent formula of St. Ignatius, "let the Creator act with His creature," and intervene only as little as possible; so far as the necessities of direction compel us, no farther.

In particular I cannot unreservedly approve the endless writings sometimes demanded or encouraged by directors without sufficient reason. It is true that without these demands or encouragements we should perhaps know less of the marvels of divine action in certain wonderful souls. But, on the other hand, how many souls have been spoilt! What an amount of useless chatter, to say the least! I cannot help saying that I am not without some apprehension at seeing the popularisation of mystic studies. This popularisation has its advantages—especially, if I may say so, for non-mystic souls, for writers or directors who concern themselves with these matters for the advantage of others—but mystic souls themselves should be concerned with these things as little as possible, and not at all *for their own sake*; souls who *seek themselves* should guard against illusion: they will *find themselves,* and not in the good sense.

### *34. Allowances must be made for Nature in the Mystics*

It is also important in judging or directing mystic souls to take account of what is *natural* in them; for their nature remains unchanged. And in this nature there may be morbid elements, some of which are independent of the mystic states, while others are perhaps their result (if not fundamentally, at any rate in their mode of action and reaction). Now the more insight one has into a mystic soul, the more we seem to see how much there is in it that is characteristic of the individual nature in its manner of thinking, feeling, expressing itself, even in its mode of reaction to an otherwise supernatural action. We must then, while compelling ourselves to treat mystic souls (when they are truly mystic) according to the touches of grace, also treat them according to the conditions and demands of their nature. It is always necessary, even when they are supernatural and in supernatural states, not to forget that they have their particular nature and temperament, their idiosyncrasy (as doctors say), their special personality. God takes account of all this in His action on them and in them. The director should follow God's example; but he should keep in mind that God can change and remake nature, whereas he cannot.

### *35. What must Always be Remembered*

In these matters above all, it is not *knowledge* which matters, but *action*. It is of action, then, that we must think rather than study; of practice rather than theory. We must remember the words of the *Imitation*: "Many hear the Gospel often, yet are not moved thereby to a better life; for they have not the spirit of Christ. He who would fully and with delight understand the words of Christ, should strive in all things to conform his life to that of Christ... It is not fine words which make the just man and the saint; it is the life of virtue which makes them friends of God, I would rather feel compunction than know its definition. Even when you know the whole Bible and all the maxims of the philosophers by heart, what good is it all without charity and the grace of God?"

What is to be said, in practice, in the present case? There is a danger that souls will give themselves to study instead of striving after practice; that they will examine themselves to find out where they are and by what "ways" they are being led instead of labouring to make themselves better and to progress in the way in which God has placed them; that they will seek graces they have not instead of making use of those which God has given them.

The important thing is not that we are in one way rather than another, at one degree rather than another; but to walk in the way on which we are, to mount always higher, and to lose nothing of the graces received.

The ways may be diverse; but the principles of progress and perfection are the same for all. "To love God with all thy heart and with all thy mind and with all thy strength" is the great commandment, given to all. We strive after this perfection of love in the degree in which we renounce ourselves, in which we apply ourselves to doing what pleases God, putting our will in union with His, practising the virtues, as Jesus and Mary practised them, doing our duty as they did theirs, suffering as they suffered—all in loving conformity of our will with the will of God.

If mystical science is still largely in the making, Christian asceticism has its principles and directions well known to all. And this asceticism is the same for all, in whatever way we walk, at whatever step we stand on the ladder whereon none can ascend to God save by withdrawing from self and from earthly things. Let each be persuaded that he will advance in all spiritual things in the measure in which he frees himself from his self-love, his own will, his own interest." The formula is that of St. Ignatius*; but the thought is everywhere in the Gospel, everywhere in the *Imitation,* everywhere in Christian asceticism, everywhere in the mystics.

## VII

## The Present Edition

### *36. This Edition and the Preceding Ones*

A word on this point will be enough. I have not thought it right to tamper with Fr. Poulain's text. The body of the book, including the Prefaces, Indexes, Appendix I, is thus an exact reproduction of the ninth (French) edition. I have had in my possession the copy of this edition which the author kept by him until his death. In this he had written, on the back of the half-title;

"Additions made to the 8th edition, 1909†: pp. 13, 50, 72, 190, 256, 291, 483, 531 (+ the Bibliographical Appendix)."‡

On turning to the pages indicated, I have found these additions marked in red pencil. They are, on pp. 13, 50, 72, 190, the paragraphs numbered with a *bis* (**14** *bis,* etc.). As to the other pages, there are sentences added at the end of a paragraph: p. 256, **39** (If no merit were acquired); p, 291, **22** (In the Old Testament); p. 483, **18** (See in the Bollandists); p. 531, **26** *ter* (In other words), with, in the margin, a pencil note; " St. J(ohn) of the Cross, *Night*, bk. I, c. 9, end, p. 290."—This is specially noted for those who do not possess the ninth edition. Here and there, throughout the volume, the author has marked a few typographical corrections, noted in the margin. These corrections have been made in the present edition, with a few others, which I have myself noticed.

* It is shorter and more to the point in Spanish: Piense cada uno que tanto se aprovechara en todas cosas espirituales cuanto saliere de su proprio amor, querer, é interese.

† The sixth edition is in fact already dated 1909, the Imprimatur bearing date 1908. I presume that the 7th and 8th editions were new impressions only.

‡ In this edition these and other page references have been adapted to the English text. (Tr.)

### *37. What the Editor has done*

Without interfering with the text, I have thought it well to improve the work by two editions:

1. At the end of the book, and Appendix on *The Discernment of Spirits*. On this subject., so important, as we all know, in the spiritual and especially the mystic life, the author certainly gave a little information, but scattered and incomplete, I have thought that it would be useful to the reader if I put before him three documents of the greatest value; the rules given by St. Ignatius in the *Spiritual Exercises*; the reflections of St. Teresa on illusions and temptations, drawn from *The Way of Perfection*, at the chapters on the *Pater noster* where she comments on *Lead us not into temptation*; and lastly, some remarks of St. Margaret Mary on the marks of the spirit of God. With these three pieces, joined with chapter 54 of the third book of the *Imitation* entitled *Of the various movements of nature and grace* (which I have not thought it necessary to add, since the *Imitation* is in the hands of all), we have the best that has been said on these difficult matters.

2. An *Introduction* to make clear the main issues of the work. This Introduction, as will be seen, has reached the proportions of a small book by itself.

While feeling, both in the course of editing and now that it is finished, how ambitious it was, and how insufficient it must be and in fact is, I have none the less continued, and offer it as it is, hoping that it may and will, in spite of its drawbacks, render some service to the ordinary reader, who wishes to be rapidly put into touch with the movement and present state of these studies, and to other workers in this field of study, who may perhaps find in it some useful notes for deeper research.

The *Canticle of the Mystic Union* was inserted without pagination before the *Biographical Index*, I have thought it better to number its pages, which causes no change in the numbering of the pages which follow it, as allowance had been made for it.

It will be remarked that I have allowed myself to criticise the author and have not always followed his opinion. All the same, the differences are but slight. Without considering his book as the last word on mystical science, how can we help but appreciate the author's immense effort to initiate us into these difficult studies, and—even if we do not in all respects think with him—not do justice to his continual care to keep his book up to date and make it more and more perfect? It is in this sentiment of esteem and sympathy that I have pointed out my *desiderata* and suggested my own ideas, which, in fact, are not so much my own as those of my venerated teacher, Fr. de Maumigny, whose memory I am happy to unite with that of him whose work, with the corrections I have indicated, will more and more produce the same fruits as his own, and supply what is lacking in it. The two books, in fact, complete and throw light on each other.

The author's bibliography is not quite up to date, for two reasons: 1, because it stops, save for a few rare indications, at the year 1909, the date of the sixth (French) edition. The author, in the years that followed, must have kept in touch with and noted the various books and articles and all else that came to his knowledge on the questions which he had so much at heart. But so far no such notes have been brought to my notice. It seems, indeed, that the ninth edition, save for the Bibliographical Appendix, bearing specially on the question of *Acquired contemplation*, contained nothing new on this head; for none of the additions, carefully indicated in the MS. note which I have reproduced above, bears on the bibliography of the subject. I have already said that Fr. Scheuer had gathered together valuable corrective or supplementary notes on this point, but they were mislaid during the War. At my request he has been good enough to take up the work once more, not without success. He has already made a rich collection of valuable data. I have inserted some of them in the Bibliographical Index which precedes this Introduction. I hope that his whole work will soon be published in the *RAM*, to the great profit of enquirers. Moreover, Fr. Scheuer has pointed out to me a few mistakes in Fr. Poulain's bibliography, and his corrections are given below.

A copious bibliography will be found in the article by Fr. Marechal analysed above, and especially in the *RAM.* I have thought it well to add to this Introduction a Bibliographical Index supplementary to Fr. Poulain's; but this Index, in no wise exhaustive or methodical, claims to give no more than a general idea of present-day activities in this field. I do not mention what is already included by Fr. Poulain.

### *38. Bibliographical Note by Fr. Scheuer*

I have inserted in my memoranda the authors which Fr. Poulain has rejected in a note on p. 615 as doubtful, with the exception of Casimir de Marsala. Our library contains the first of this writer's two works: there is no, question of mysticism there. The same may apply to the second.

Under Nos. 39 and 49, Fr. Poulain mentions two writers named Thomas of Jesus, I do not know on what foundation.* Villers (*Bill. Carmelitana*) does not distinguish between them. He only knows the one numbered 49, Definitor General (1564-1627); he attributes to him the work given under No. 39, which is found in Vol. Ill of his *Opera omnia.* The principal mystical works of Thomas of Jesus are as follows:

De contemplatione divina libri VI, Antwerp, 1620;—Divinae seu a Deo infusse orationis methodus, natura, gradus, libri IV, Antwerp, 1623;—Commentarius in

* The mistake is corrected in the ninth edition. The old No. 39 is suppressed, which moves the following numbers one forward: 39 instead of *40*, etc., *48* instead of 40. Beginning with 51, the numbers again agree, thanks to the use of *bis* or *ter*. Thomas of Jesus, with Fr. Scheuer's dates, is No. 48. But Fr. Poulain ignores the *Opera omnia*.—J. V. B.

qusestionem CLXXV, XI—II, De raptu et extasi, printed after the author's death in Vol. II of the Opera. The Opera omnia (3 vols., Cologne, 1684) were collected by Fr. Paul of All Saints, at the desire, according to Villers, of Urban VIII expressed at the General Chapter of the Order.

Joseph a Spiritu Sancto, No, 100, died in 1739, not 1639. His six volumes were republished partly at Seville, partly at Madrid. The two first were republished at Naples, 1724. The sixth is no rarer than the others, which all are so to an extraordinary degree.

Joseph a Spiritu Sancto (Portuguese), the first of the name (No. 78), died in 1674. He is also the author of a considerable work: *Enucleatio mysticæ theologæ S. Dionysii Areopagitæ*, a posthumous work published in the second volume of the *Opera omnia* of Thomas of Jesus, Cologne, 1684, pp, 455-602.

Nicholas of Jesus, No. 35. Correct: Nicholas of Jesus-Mary.

P. SCHEUER, S.J.

LOUVAIN, *August* 6, 1921.

## VIII

### ADDITIONAL REMARKS*

*39. Two Letters of Fr. de la Taille,—1. Why the Mystic Graces at a given moment become practically necessary. 2. How mystical contemplation is connected with the virtue of Faith*

I

UNIVERSITA GREGORIANA, 120, VIA DEL SEMINARIO, ROMA.

*Dec*, 22, 1921.

DEAR AND REVEREND FATHER, PAX CHRISTI!

I owe you a thousand thanks for the far too kind things that you have said about my study in the last number of the *Revue apologetique.* Had I an ounce of humility, I ought to be very overcome. But I feel that the public can largely supply what is lacking in my astonishment. It is because it does not know you so well as I do.

It would certainly please me, if we were still side by side, to continue the conversation so agreeably begun. I would then, so far as I could, come to the help of the argument which, you say, is no argument, since it is only the statement of

* I have said in two notes, Secs. 21 and 27, that certain pages of this Introduction, published in the *RA* or the *RAM,* called forth protests, explanations, and criticisms. I think that I ought to give here, with the writer's kind permission, the explanations of Fr. M. de la Taille, and to discuss, at least in part, the criticisms of Fr. Garrigou-Lagrange. The explanations of Fr. de la Taille have given me full satisfaction, inasmuch as they answer my objections and difficulties, but without having positively convinced me that his magnificent synthesis compels the adherence of all, as definitive, on every point.

the thesis. I would say substantially this: Ordinary grace (by this name I mean non-mystical grace) never, by definition, does more than use, by supernaturalising them, the means and resources of our human, specifically human, psychology. But in each man human psychology has limited resources and means, be it a matter of the actual sum of his affective and mental dispositions or of the potentiality in reserve. When it is a matter of passing the limits accessible to this sum of forces, even when supernaturalised (that is, when the struggle of charity against self-love has attained the point which calls into operation the maximum of the human resources of a given individual, and it is necessary to pass still further, to gain a further victory over self-love in the interests of God and his kingdom), it is then necessary, *normally*, that the divine action should bring into play something other than strictly human elements, and consequently call into being new and ultra-human states of soul. This amounts to saying that ordinary grace must give place to mystic or contemplative grace. Once more, the boundary of the two realms is not the same for every man; it varies from man to man according to temperament, character and outward circumstances. But can it be denied that for every man it exists somewhere or other? Otherwise we should have to suppose that the human make-up has an infinite potential energy; and this is not credible, or even possible.

Will you say that grace supplies for the insufficiency of nature? But once more, *ordinary* grace (understood as above) only supernaturalises means borrowed from nature; turns the direction of our affections and strivings towards our Last End, and immerses them in the divine element which will carry them thereto. It raises what we have already acquired, and causes what so far was only in our latent reserve to spring forth; raising alone in the former case, raising and strengthening in the latter; but in both making use of the elements of nature; here adorning with its splendour the moral forces at our disposal, there bringing to light those concealed in our unexplored depths. If we compare it not only with what.we at present possess, but with the sum-total of our possessions actual and potential, we must say that it does not increase the moral forces of our nature. It increases them only by comparison with our moral state at the moment. This refers to ordinary grace, and not, certainly, to contemplative grace, which makes use of resources foreign and superior to our nature. It is thus that it increases our moral forces by comparison with the whole sum of our psychological resources, whether actual or potential. And that is why it will carry us further when ordinary grace has to stop short, at least in the normal and regular course of things.

I am always careful to add *regularly*, *normally* (p. 22 of my little book, "regular and normal progress") since we must always leave room for the sovereign interventions of divine omnipotence, which is sometimes pleased (in the physical course of things, at any rate) to make secondary causes produce disproportionate effects, not by increasing their productive capacity, but by supplying a substitute for it by the introduction of a divine virtue, to which they allow passage; and this constitutes a miracle. But the miracle is outside the ordinary course of providence, which indeed is defined by its care to adapt proportionate causes to effects. Miracles are by definition extraordinary; and to claim for the regular and normal course of things the process from which they are excluded is not to derogate from its excellence. In short, apart from instances of miracle, which belong to extraordinary Providence, contemplation is required to raise man beyond the limits which human moral strength can reach, limits which vary according to the individual, but are in all cases real, and consequently are destined to be passed by all who have reached them, under penalty of making no further progress in the illimitable way of grace and holiness. This, reverend Father, is what it seems possible for me to oppose to your principal complaint against my modest attempt to sketch the conditions of supernatural progress.

It remains, you say, that the further one advances the easier virtue becomes, and consequently progress is less difficult. Then there is no need of the grace of contemplation to finish the course in the case of the man who has completed the first and most difficult stages. is there not a misunderstanding here? Assuredly the long and laborious practice of a virtue will often bestow a growing facility in performing acts of the virtue already acquired. But for that which still remains to be acquired, the part of the progress not yet achieved, is it the same? It would then, to be logical, be necessary to maintain that the first polishing of a soul which has but just returned from a state of mortal sin, and is raising itself to a certain degree of spiritual life and inward comeliness (that very commonplace thing which we see every day) represents a greater moral effort, the overcoming of a greater difficulty, than those last and sublime purifications from self-love whereby the soul is prepared for final and perfect union with God in heaven. Who will believe this? Why then are there so many souls who afford us the spectacle of a beginning in virtue, and so few that of its consummation? Why that feeling of powerlessness, which affects us in quite another way after years of effort, before the task in prospect, than in the first steps by which we journeyed up to the foot of that so rugged and steep mountain? What may sometimes cause illusion in the observer is that the help of God is poured into souls with such abundance and superabundance that for a time it takes away the feeling of a difficulty to be overcome. But this does not mean that the difficulty is not there, and that it is not great relatively to the agent considered in himself; but rather that the divine succour is so strong that in comparison the difficulty is a bagatelle. Let this profuse succour come in more sparing measure, and you would see the soul panting, sinking under its burden, beseeching for grace. Let us not say, then, that the difficulty was smaller, and therefore required less aid: but rather that if the difficulty were relatively smaller, it is because the help was more abundant. This lessening of the difficulty, this growth, if you like, of relative facility, does not enable us to say that there is less need of divine help. No: for, if there is facility, it is thanks to an excess of divine help. Now what is the quality of this divine help? This is the former question arising once more.

Besides, if the facility of the progress increases with the progress itself, why should the last stage of this progress, which is the annihilation of self-love in favour of charity, be, regularly speaking, reserved for the future life? Now that this is the case is the teaching of the most reliable doctors of the spiritual life, St. Augustine and St. Francis de Sales. Does not this also follow from the liturgical prayers in which the Church makes us constantly beseech God to deign to heal the impurity of our hearts, a perpetual paraphrase of the verse *Cor mundum area in me Deus, et spiritum rectum innova in visceribus meis*? And that is for all. But this last stage ought to be a small affair for those who are so near to it. The truth is that the last stage is the most difficult one. To achieve it the light of a soul cast by death into the element of purest truth is not too much. And that is why in this world the first commandment, which includes the whole law, is not fully accomplished. To love God, truly and literally, with all our heart, with all our strength, with all our mind and with all our soul, is the business of heaven. On the way thither there will always be some gap in God's empire over our mind, our soul, our strength, our heart. Our dispositions will never be those of heaven; a friendship with God so sovereign, that not only does it take precedence of all else, but entirely subordinates all else, becoming itself the sole principle of all our acts of will, our affections, our strivings and inclinations. That is the unit which is inaccessible in time, So true is it that the difficulty of making further progress in the victory over self-love grows in proportion to the efforts already made.

You say again: If contemplative grace were normally necessary for the consummation of sanctity, it ought to be the object of an enquiry during the process of canonisation; and this is contrary to the Church's practice.—I heard this objection raised, twenty years ago, by a canonist particularly expert in these matters, who had been postulator in a large number of causes. And as he had before him only my inexperienced youth, quite incapable of finding a reply, he took it upon himself to refute it: "You might have answered," he told me, "that the processes of canonisation are entirely based upon testimony. Now since the grace of contemplation is wholly interior, the only person who can testify to it is the subject himself, whose evidence is inadmissible in his own cause. And this reply," he added, "is a satisfactory one." I believe it is: and it seems too that it can be completed. The grace of contemplation, even on the understanding that it is necessary for unlimited progress in sanctity, is not sanctity itself. It is a means directed to the practice of the virtues, especially charity; but it is not that virtue itself. Now the process is concerned (as it ought to be) with the virtues. The question is not whether a man has had the means of practising the virtues, but whether he has in fact practised them. When I have ascertained that he has practised them, and that in the required degree, I know all I need to know; I am free to infer therefrom that he has certainly not lacked the necessary means, whatever they are. *Ab actu valet ad posse.*

Lastly you raise doubts as to the relation of contemplation to faith. At this I am more surprised. But as I have already indicated a few headings of proofs in my little book, I refrain from returning to the matter, save to note my surprise; for nothing in mystical theology seems to me more certain than this.

I think I have covered almost the whole field of your criticisms. Pardon my impertinence: that of a theologian, who firmly believes that passive prayer, as much as the other kind, belongs to his province, and claims it all with equal right as subject for his enquiry. You will say that competence does not always go with right; and there I give way to you, protesting that I have not the least pretension to competence, but merely the desire to submit my views to those who are competent. If you have had the patience to read these lines to the end, you will at least have seen the very keen interest that I have taken in your article, which certainly merits my most entire gratitude. To which I join the humble homage of my religious and affectionate respect.

MAURICE DE LA TAILLE.

P.S.—Will you allow me to point out an apparently insignificant *erratum*? I did not write of the origin of contemplation that it is "in this love which is passively received and in the consciousness of this passivity, which swoops on the intelligence and carries it above itself towards the Sovereign Good, to which it attaches it in a dark light"; but this: "it is in this love which is passively received, and, in the consciousness of this passivity, swoops on the intelligence," etc. It is love which carries off the understanding and attaches it to its object: a mere affair of commas.

Moreover, I did not maintain in my work that man can without the grace of contemplation arrive "at very high summits of grace and sanctity" but only "at a higher level of spirituality." The former expression exceeds what I think I can certainly affirm; not the second, which is more temperate.

II

ROMA, 120 VIA DEL SEMINARIO,

3.1.22.

Dear and Reverend Father, Pax Christi!

Certainly I am flattered that you should insert my reflections in the *RA* and in your *Introduction*. But as I do not want this letter to have the air of a protest, but to remain what it is, an exchange of ideas, motivated by the thanks I owe you for your kind criticism, it seems well to me that the beginning and end of the letter should not be suppressed.

The heads of the argument of which I speak relatively to contemplative faith are identically the same in the book and in the article. As for the question you put to me, my reply is this. Contemplation is, in my sense, a true act of the theological virtue of faith; it is found in it: an adhesion *to* the last end, *on the testimony* the last end gives to itself, and *by love for* the last end. It belongs to the economy of which faith forms part—as is normally the case with intellectual visions, which are not acts of faith, but regularly speaking are conditioned by the presence of faith. Then, strictly speaking, contemplation is an act of faith, because in it is found the very essence of theological faith. But if anyone by an act of faith understands what is commonly called the act of faith, something supported by the imagination, conditioned by acquired knowledge of historical motives of credibility and terminating in abstractions, assuredly it could not be said that contemplation is an act of faith. But all these circumstances of common faith are not intrinsically necessary to the operation of the *instinctus fidei.* It does without them when the divine object of faith becomes present in the gift of that additional love, that divinely rooted love wherein it reveals itself. That is what I have attempted to explain by the distinction between the theologian's and the philosopher's points of view. There seems to me no doubt that in his teaching on this point St. John of the Cross could not be more certain of himself. It is where he exalts contemplation above all the other so-called mystical phenomena (including intellectual visions or revelations). All those graces "gratis datæ" being exterior to the faith, may do harm to the faith; contemplation or passive prayer cannot, because it is an exercise of faith. We must cultivate it as much as we must on the other hand free ourselves from the others. But upon this point one might quote indefinitely, and I have not my authors at hand. But I must remark that it would be a great pity for contemplatives if their prayer were not, could no longer be, an exercise of the theological virtue. It would then be necessary to urge them to sacrifice everything and to strain every nerve to practise by preference the theological virtue to which prayer belongs, which is that of faith.

MAURICE DE LA TAILLE, S.J.

*40. Brief of Pope Benedict XV to the Editor of LVS.—Fr. Garrigou-Lagrange's Criticisms—Detailed Discussions*

Fr. Garrigou-Lagrange has done me the honour of devoting 22 pages of *La vie spirituelle* (March 1922, vol. 5, pp. 459-80) to a critical examination of my article on *The Present State of Mystical Studies,* an extract from the present *Introduction,* published in the *RA,* Dec. 1921, and of another, published in the *RAM,* Jan. 1922. As I said above, I have taken advantage of his criticism, as of that of M. Saudreau and the progress of my own thought, to improve my work. But there remain many points in dispute, on which I owe the reader some explanation or enlightenment.

First, may I be allowed to congratulate the eminent Professor of the Collegio Angelico, who takes so great a part in the editing of *LVS,* on the Brief addressed to Fr. Bernadot, the director of that review, by His Holiness Benedict XV, Sept. 15, 1921. It is a great joy to me to hear proclaimed from so high a place "the exceptional value of St. Thomas' teaching regarding the spiritual life, both ascetical and mystical," and I associate myself with all my heart in the praise given to *LVS* for "its efforts to show what light the Prince of Scholastic philosophers throws on these abstruse questions." There is still more in the Brief. Firstly, a warning for everyone. "Many, in our days, neglect the supernatural life or confuse it with some vain and soft pious sentimentalism. We must then remember unceasingly what the Holy Scriptures and the Fathers say on this subject, and this especially of the school of St. Thomas, who has so luminously explained their teaching on elevation to the supernatural life; and remember also the conditions requisite for progress in the grace of the virtues and gifts of the Holy Ghost." The Brief then goes on to eulogise the Review, which "is very learnedly devoted to the exposition of these teachings," and expresses the desire that it may do much good. Humbly, but with all my heart, I unite myself with these praises and desires.*—Now let us examine the criticisms of Fr. Garrigou-Lagrange.

1. I admit the foundation of the remarks on p. 459 as to my attempt at classification. I have taken advantage of them to express certain points more exactly; but I have kept to the grouping previously adopted, because it gives a first conspectus of the field to the outside onlooker, who is trying to find his way about in a world new to him.

It must be added that a great change is taking place in the constitution of the groups, and that with extreme rapidity. Two years ago the points of division were many: where the mystic state begins, in what it consists, who are called to it, its relation with the perfection of the spiritual life. Now a sort of coalition has been brought about between all those who, while remaining divided on other points, regard the mystic life properly so-called, "in its essentials," to use the formula of the writer now being considered, p, 459, " as the normal blossoming of the interior life." This is a concentrated formula to which everyone may subscribe.

2. When I said that the difference between M. Saudreau and Fr. Poulain "is in large part that between the inexact and the exact," I meant as regards the proper constituent of the mystical state, the essential difference between what is properly speaking mystical and what is not, and not, as Fr. Garrigou-Lagrange understands, p. 460, "facts relatively exterior to the mystic life, such as ligature and ecstasy." This difference is, for Fr. Poulain, the experimental perception of God present in the soul, or, what comes to the same thing, of the divine presence. Now this seems to me very precise, much more precise than M. Saudreau's definition, as given in *LVS*, vol. 5, p. 381: "A higher knowledge of God which, although general and confused, gives a very high idea of His incomprehensible greatness, by an unreasoning but very precious love, which God Himself communicates and to which the soul, for all its efforts, can never raise itself "; more precise even than that of Fr. Garrigou-Lagrange, *ibid.*, 382, given here, Sec. 14. I cannot then find "in M. Saudreau more doctrinal precision

* Latin Text and French translation in *LVS*, Dec. 1921.

than in Fr. Poulain," *ibid,*, 469. As for Fr. Poulain's formula, quoted *ibid.*, "This doctrine of the role of the gifts of the Holy Ghost has hardly more than an historical interest," I myself find it a little blunt. But we must not forget that the author professes that he wished to write a treatise on experimental mysticism, not a mystical theology.

3. The writer correctly states that I avoid pronouncing on what he calls "the main thesis of (Fr. Poulain's) book, which considers the mystical state as a state extraordinary in itself, outside the *full* and *normal* development of the interior life, as a grace in no way necessary to sanctity, even great sanctity." A few remarks on this point.

Firstly, this is hardly the main thesis of the book. It held a comparatively small place in the author's interests. I should even think that he would rather have been inclined towards a close connection between the mystical graces and sanctity. But he vaguely felt the difficulty of the problem, and it is possible that practical considerations led him to use here and there a somewhat restrained phraseology. All the same, if there is a main thesis in his book, it is not this, but rather that of a special knowledge of God, as characteristic of the mystic state: experimental knowledge.

As for myself, this question of the relations between mysticism and asceticism seems to me a very complex one, involving many others, and by that very fact requiring many distinctions and definitions. I do not claim to solve them or even to separate them out in their entirety. A few remarks alone, to dispel or prevent, if possible, a few confusions and misunderstandings.*

(*a*) In a treatise on theology both speculative and practical, a complete theory of human acts, such as St. Thomas has so wonderfully provided in the Second Part of the *Summa,* it is evident that mysticism finds as much place as asceticism, St. Thomas gave it its place, without otherwise occupying himself directly with either mysticism or asceticism. He is concerned with the turning of the soul towards God, as he says, by the good use to which it puts its manifold activities, whether in the active life, which is that of everyone, or in the contemplative life, which is that of those who are specially taken up with God and divine things.

(*b*) If it is a question *in abstracto* of the full normal development of the interior life, as Fr. Garrigou-Lagrange says (p. 460), the mystical life has its place in this development as being the perfect earthly blossoming of this interior life; similarly, if it be question of the divine action or the operations of grace in the human soul, of man's co-operation in the divine action, or of the ascents of the soul to God. Now it is from one or other of these points of view, often both, that the older writers, with their almost instinctive search for synthesis and views of things in the round, wrote their treatises on the spiritual life. They could not therefore separate mysticism from asceticism. Generally they did not even dream of

* See also Sec. 13, above.

distinguishing them, apart from some special reason for marking the distinction. Not that they could not recognise and describe the mystic states; but they regarded asceticism and mysticism as elements of one whole, the whole which they had in view.

(*c*) Similar remarks apply to treatises on direction, states of life, exhortations to perfection, etc. When St. Thomas wrote the *De perfections vitae spiritualis*, when Tauler or Lallemant spoke to chosen audiences, who had to be raised to the highest perfection possible for them, it was no time for distinguishing between ascetical and mystical ways, unless this distinction formed part of the instruction itself or was introduced for some special reason.

These remarks, taken together with what will be found in Sec. 13 of this Introduction, will help us to understand how prudent we must be in applying old texts to questions which were not then asked, as they are asked today.

4. They will also help us to understand somewhat better the delicate question of the call to the mystical life, Fr. Garrigou-Lagrange has made an interesting and conciliatory distinction on this point: between the general call, which is for everyone, and the special call, which is for elect souls only. This distinction, if it does not fully solve the question, none the less helps towards an understanding. I find it applied by Fr. Lehmkuhl, in his *Theologia moralis,* to the no less delicate question of religious vocation. There is a call to all men to Christian perfection, since to all it was said: *Estote perfecti, sicut et Pater vaster caelestis perfectus est.* There is, on the other hand, a special call to perfection in the way of the counsels, addressed to the Apostles, addressed in a particularly clear fashion to the young man in the Gospel (Mark x, 17-22). We may then say something similar here. In pursuing the analogy, we can, it seems to me, make the following points:

(*a*) Evangelical perfection (or Christian perfection) is for everyone. All can reach it.

(*b*) There is a special call to this perfection, addressed to a few souls whom Jesus invites to follow Him in what is called the way of the counsels, poverty, chastity, religious obedience.

(*c*) The Gospel ideal is the same for all: a life of love for God, m the footsteps of our Lord, in inner detachment from all that is not God, in self-renunciation.

(*d*) To this ideal we tend or ought to tend as it were naturally, by the way of the counsels. And sanctity seems in fact to be more frequent in this way. But one may be holy, even a canonised saint, in the ordinary way, more of a saint perhaps than one would have been in the other, which, though more perfect in itself, may be less suited to the nature or condition of a particular person.

All this seems to me to apply, point by point, to the question of the mystic and the so-called ordinary ways.

Christian perfection is in theory within the reach of all, and it is the same for all. We can reach it whether by the ordinary or by the mystic ways. We shall reach it perhaps more quickly, and as it were *connaturally*, by the mystic way; but there is nothing to prove that we shall not reach it by the common way. All the more as exterior trials well borne may take the place of the mystic trials which, according to St. John of the Cross, are necessary, at any rate to mystics, for their arrival at perfection.

So much, it seems to me, can be said *a priori* on these delicate questions, so far as we are allowed to scrutinise the inscrutable ways of God.

After these explanations, a few words will suffice to take up our position as against Fr. Garrigou-Lagrange.

5. He speaks on page 461 of "concessions" being made to him. This word supposes in me a state of mind which, in fact, does not exist. I have no ready-made system nor position laid down for all the questions of mysticism. I am a seeker, and take to myself gladly the scraps of truth which are offered me, wherever they come from.

6. He seems to think that I look upon the mystic life as "outside the normal way which leads to holiness." If I have ever—and it would astonish me to know that I had done so—used any formula like this, it is certainly not in the sense which he gives it.

7. He defends himself, *ibid.*, from the charge of having ever maintained "that mystic souls are always the most perfect." It never came into my head to impute such an idea to him.

8. He does not admit that "The gifts must come into play whenever the soul receives an actual grace." The opinion here rebutted is that which I myself expressed as a probable consequence of the idea St. Thomas has given us of the gifts of the Holy Ghost, while remarking that not all St. Thomas' brethren were of his opinion.* I think it well to bring before the reader St. Thomas' answer to the question: "Are the gifts necessary to man for his salvation?" Reply: "The gifts are, as it is said in the preceding article, perfections of man, disposing him to follow the divine inspiration. Thus wherever the inspirations of reason are not sufficient, but the inspiration of the Holy Ghost is necessary, then the gift is necessary... Now in the things belonging to human reason, that is in all that concerns man's natural end, man can act by the judgment of reason... But in the supernatural order, and of the supernatural end towards which reason moves us inasmuch as it is stirred in a certain imperfect fashion (*aliqualiter et imperfede informata*) by the theological virtues, the movement of reason, even when supernaturalised by the virtues, does not suffice unless there be added to it from on high the inspiration and movement of the Holy Ghost... For none can arrive at this land of the blessed except he be moved and guided by the Holy Ghost. And that is why, to arrive at this end, it is necessary for man to have the gift of the Holy Ghost."

This may not be as explicit and clear as we would like. Yet it seems to me plausible, if not necessary, to see set forth here as a principle the necessity of an

* See *Introduction*, Sec. 23.

actual grace to supply what is lacking to our natural faculties, even when stirred up by the virtues, and to put them in a condition to act supernaturally. This necessity carries with it the necessity of the gifts, these being conceived by the Angelic Doctor as correlative with this actual grace, which he calls according to the traditional usage, by the names *instinctus, inspiratio, motto Spiritus sancti.* And notice, as is explained *Ad primum*, that this necessity does not stop at certain kinds of more excellent works which surpass the capacity of the virtues; it pertains to the radical insufficiency of our natural faculties, even when elevated by the infused virtues, before the supernatural act proceeding under the movement of a higher principle: *Dona excedunt communem perfectionem virtutum, non quantum ad genus operum... sed quantum ad modum operandi, secundum quod homo movetur ab altiori principio.* I have no wish to say anything different from St. Thomas.

9. I gladly pay my homage to the labours of the authors quoted by Fr. Garrigou-Lagrange, p. 466; I doubt, however, whether the interpretation of St. Teresa's "short cut," given by M. Saudreau, even were it perfectly correct, cuts all the ground away from under those who consider the saint's thought as at least open to discussion. Also are we not far from an understanding when, like my critic, on a single page, we make one part of the texts mean a "general and remote call" and recognise in the others "relative exceptions to the individual proximate call"?

10. The statement that, for certain souls, the mystic states only begin at "very high summits of grace and sanctity" is not mine, but Fr. de la Taille's.*

To this formula Fr. Garrigou-Lagrange opposes that "according to St. John of the Cross, the passive purification of the senses is common to beginners." I do not see the bearing of the objection, if it be admitted that by "beginners" St. John means beginners in the mystical life. It may be said in general that to arrive at these "very high summits of grace and sanctity" which have been referred to, we must pass through trials; but is it proved that these trials must be those of the mystical purifications?

11. I have said in this Introduction, Secs, 23-24, that mystical science is not yet complete and that the time for a definitive synthesis has not yet come. Fr. Garrigou-Lagrange (pp. 468-70) is astonished and offended at this. He recognises that there is still much to be done; but he considers "the initial and fundamental problem of mystical theology" as solved.

This problem is, in his view, "whether or no the *mystic* state is fundamentally by its very nature ordinary or extraordinary." To say that the greatest Doctors of the Church have not clearly put this capital question of spirituality or that they have remained undecided about it, that at least they have not expressed themselves clearly and that their teaching on this most important point is open to

* I did not know that the latter had changed, or was going to change, this formula into another more circumspect one. See *Introduction,* Sec. 39, I *ad finem*, and *cf.* Sec. 25, 4, c.

discussion... all that amounts to saying that after nineteen centuries of Christianity mystical science still remains to be defined... In reality this question must have been very simple for these great saints; it is we who complicate it, because we see not from above, but from below; what is divided in the lower order is one single thing in a higher order, as Dionysius often repeats."

Everyone will see how vague this is, and full of misunderstandings. Before saying whether the mystic state is *ordinary* or *extraordinary*, we must be agreed about the meaning of these words. Now there is no agreement on this point.* No one that I know of calls in question what Dionysius, St. Augustine, St. Thomas have said on mysticism; but to suppose that these great masters have answered the questions with which we are occupied today, we must first of all know whether they asked them. Let us agree that they saw things from above and we from below. We bow before what they say when looking from above; but we must also maintain that they have not answered the questions which we ask while looking from below.

I do not deny that these great masters were great mystics, or that they set forth, at least implicitly, the principles of mystical theology, were it only by describing the full blossoming of human life according to the ancients, or of the supernatural and Christian life according to Scripture and Tradition; but Fr. Garrigou-Lagrange himself doubtless does not claim that they meant to compose *ex professo* treatises on experimental mysticism.

12. As for the scientific systematisation of data and principles, Fr. Garrigou-Legrange and the *LVS* daily make meritorious contributions thereto, which I applaud with all my heart. I should do so all the more were it not the tendency of Fr. Garrigou-Lagrange to confiscate St. Thomas and the older writers for himself, as if the older writers and St. Thomas had taken sides in the matters that divide us.

It is painful to see introduced into these matters theological disputes from which mysticism has nothing to gain. On this head I have alluded (*Introd.,* Sec. 26) to an article by Fr. Garrigou-Lagrange in which, speaking of grace, he understands and explains it in the specifically Thomistic sense. On this he returns to the battle, pp. 474-80, Certainly I will be careful not to renew the Thomist-Molinist dispute here. But who can think that these quarrels on disputed points of theology will assist the progress of mysticism, or the insinuations that accompany them charity and good understanding?

13. Fr. Garrigou-Lagrange quotes, p. 470, certain words of mine in the *RA,* Dec, 15, 1921, pp. 351-2, I recognise that, in the passages quoted, my pen has tended to misrepresent my thought, and I have retouched my text, Sec. 25 *ad finem.*

* For the word *mystic,* I have already said this, Sec. 40, 2; *cf.* Secs. 10-12, Sec. 22, etc. For the words *ordinary* and *extraordinary,* see J. de Guibert, *Trois définitions, l.c.*

14. I have never claimed to make mysticism a science independent of theology, or *mystical theology* a science "quite different from" theology. I have retouched or explained on this subject what shocks my critic. I grant that he is right, or nearly so, so far as concerns *mystical theology*; but from *mystical theology* I distinguish *experimental mysticism*, which I regard as a science to be subsumed under theology (*ut Musica Arithmeticae*); an observational science, as is *experimental psychology* in relation to *metaphysical psychology*. See the explanation added to Sec. 27, note. May these explanations and details help towards that understanding that is so desirable!

15. It is indeed Fr. Garrigou-Lagrange that I had in mind when, Sec. 26, speaking of the writer who, when treating of *grace*, means *Thomistic* grace. It is vain to feel sure of his opinions. When the Church, which has a very clear doctrine on grace, refuses to identify with this doctrine of the Christian community and the teaching authority the particular features of either the Thomist or the Molinist system, there is nothing for us to do but to respect her refusal.

16. There follow pp. 476-9, where I find nothing that concerns me, nor even directly mystical questions. I come then to the end of the article, and transcribe its last sentence, which I make fully my own: "It is not enough to read the works of the great Doctor attentively and to meditate on them. We must pray that while granting us his own habitual serenity he will obtain for us grace to understand whatever is highest and most living in his teaching which is of a nature to bring souls to God and to open to the greatest number the ways to the interior knowledge of God."

J. V. BAINVEL.

PARIS, *August 4th*, 1922.
*Feast of St. Dominic.*

## BIBLIOGRAPHICAL INDEX TO THIS INTRODUCTION

ABBREVIATIONS

CB *Collationes Brugenses*, Bruges.

DA *Dictionnaire apologétique de la foi catholique*, Jaugey-d'Alès.

DTC *Dictionnaire de théologie catholique*, Vacant-Mangenot.

EC *Éludes carmélitaines.*
LVS *La Vie spirituelle.*
MCJ *Messager du Cœur de Jésus,* Toulouse.
RAM *Revue d'ascétique et de mystique,* Toulouse.
RP *Revue de philosophie.*
RPA *Revue pratique d'apologétique;* now RA = *Revue apologétique.* RQS *Revue des questions scientifiques,* Bruxelles.
RSPT *Revue des sciences philosophiques et théologiques.*
RSR *Recherches de science religieuse.*

THE Dictionaries or Reviews concerned with religious matters usually allot some space to mystical questions. Among them, to quote French publications alone, are the *Dictionnaire apologétique,* the *Dictionnaire dé théologie,* the *Ami du clergé. Études, Études carmélitaines,* the *Messager du Cœur de Jésus,* the *Polybiblion, Recherches de science religieuse,* the *Revue de philosophie,* the *Revue pratique d'apologétique,* the *Revue des sciences philosophiques et théologiques.* Since 1920 two reviews have been in existence in France, devoted exclusively to questions of the spiritual life, asceticism and mysticism: *La vie spirituelle. Ascétique et mystique,* a monthly publication, having a group of professors of the Collegio Angelico at Rome as its editorial committee and Fr. M. V. Bernadot, O.P., as editorial Secretary; and *La revue d'ascétique et de mystique,* Toulouse, appearing quarterly, and edited by Fr. J. de Guibert, S.J. This Index is greatly indebted to the copious bibliography of the RAM and to the MS. notes of its editor; and, also to the records of the learned Fr. Scheuer, Professor at the Scholasticate of Louvain. See also the *Indications bibliographiques* of Fr. Maréchal, in the RP, 1912, II, 483-8,—I quote only what is not included in Fr. Poulain's Biographical Index.

Alphonsus of the Mother of Sorrows, O.C.D., *Pratique de l'oraison mentale et de la perfection, d'après sainte Thérèse et saint Jean de la Croix.* 8 vols, Bruges, 1909-14.

Balthazar Alvarez. See *Dudon.*

AMI DU CLERGE, Dec. 8, 1921, vol. 38, pp. 689-702, *Chronique de théologie ascétique et mystique* (less uncompromising in tendency than when the chronicler was Fr. Saudreau or even Fr. Lainballe). Blessed Angela of Foligno. See *Thorold.*

J. G. Arintero, *Cuestiones místicas,* Salamanca, 1920. Of. RAM, April 1921, II, 178-87;—*La Evolución mística, ibid.,* 1921. Aurelian of the Blessed Sacrament, O.D.C., *Cursus ascéticas,* Ernakulam, 3 vols., I, Via purgativa, 1917; II, Via illuminativa, 1918; III, Via unitiva, 1919.

André Paiole, S.J., *De la vie intérieure,* 1659. Cf. *Valensin.*

St. Bernard. See *J. Ries.*

Bover, *De mystica unione "in Christo Jesu" secundum B, Paulum.* BIBLICA, 1920, Rome, I, 309-26.

H. Bremond, *Histoire littéraire du sentiment religieux en France depuis là fin des guerres de religion jusqu'à nos jours,* 1916-22. 5 vols. English: *A Literary History of Religious Thought in France,* 1928 ff.

Mgr. Castellan, Archbishop of Chambéry. Address delivered at the reopening session of the Catholic Faculties of Lyons on the large place held by mystical studies in present-day religious thought, Nov. 19, 1919.

J. Chatel, *De l'oraison mentale et de la contemplation. Théorie et pratique,* Louvain, 1915.

Denifle, O.P., *La vie spirituelle d'après les mystiques allemands du XIVe siècle* (French trans, by the Comtesse de Flavigny, 1903).

P. de Puniet, O.S.B., *La contemplation d'après Louis de Blois,* LVS, 1920, II, 463.

E. Dimmler, *Mystik, Gedanken über eine Frage der Zeit,* Gunzburg, 1919;—*Wandel in Licht. Einzelzüge mystichen Gedankenslebens,* Kempten, 1920;—*Der brennende Dornbusch. Gedanken über den Weg zu Gott,* Kempten, 1920.

Fr. Dudon, S.J., *Michel Molinos,* 1921;—*Les leçons d'oraison du P. Balthazar Alvarez,* RAM, Jan. 1921, II, 36-57.

J. M. Dumas, S.M., *L'ascétique et la mystique de l'Imitation,* LVS, 1922, II, 433-48.

Mgr. A. Farges, *Les phénomènes mystiques distingués de leurs contrefaçons humaines et diaboliques. Traité de théologie mystique* (1921). Cf. *Roure* and *Guibert,* English: *Mystical Phenomena* (London, 1926).

Fr. Garrigou-Lagrange, O.P., *L'ascétique et la mystique. Leur distinction et l'unité de la doctrine spirituelle,* LVS, 1920, I, 145-65;— *La mystique et les doctrines fondamentales de saint Thomas,* LVS, 1920, I, 217-28 sq;—*La perfection de la charité,* LVS, 1921, II, 1-20;—*L'appel à la vie mystique. Pour fixer le vocabulaire,* Nov. 1921, V, 80-99;—*L'appel général et l'appel individuel,* Dec. 1921, Jan. 1922, V, 165-87, 241-70.

Mgr. Gauthey. See *Margaret Mary.*

L. de Grandmaison, S.J., *L'élément mystique dans la religion,* RSR, 110, I, 180-208;—*La vie religieuse au grand siècle. La tradition mystique dans la Compagnie de Jésus,* ÉTUDES, 1921, CLXVI, 129-56. Relates to Bremond, above, vol. 5.—*La religion personnelle. L'élan mystique,* ÉTUDES, 1913, CXXXV, 309-35. English: *Personal Religion,* London, 1929.

J. de Guibert, S.J., Numerous articles and reviews in the RAM, especially: *Les études de théologie ascétique et mystique,* Jan. 1920. I, 5-19;—*A propos de la contemplation mystique. Problèmes et méthodes,* Oct. 1920, I, 329-50;—*Trois définitions de théologie mystique,* April 1922, III, 162-79. See *Arintero, Saudreau, Naval, Farges,* etc.

F. Hatheycr, *Die Lehre des P. Suarez über Beschauung und Ex stase,* in P. *Franz Suarez, Gedenkblätter,* Innsbruck, 1917, pp. 75 -122. Howley, *Psychology and Mystical Experience,* London, 1920.

J. Huby, S.J., *Foi et contemplation d'après saint Thomas,* RSR, 1919, X, 137-61.

F. von Hügel, *The Mystical Element in Religion as studied in Saint Catherine of Genoa and her Friends,* London, 1908, 2 vols, (new ed. 1923). Cf. *Grandmaison.*

Huguony, O.P., *La doctrine mystique de Tauler,* RSPT, April 1921, X, 194-221.

Mgr. Ighina, *Cours de théologie ascétique et mystique,* French trans. by Abbé Dorangeon, Bourges, 1904.

St. Ignatius Loyola, *Exercices Spirituels,* French trans. by Père Debuchy, S.J., 1910.

St. John Of the Cross, Critical Edition by Fr. Gérard of the Cross, 3 vols., Toledo, commencing 1912, French trans. by Canon Hoornaert, Bruges, 1915-18. Cf. J. de Tonquedec, RPA, May 1919, p. 165.

D. Joret, O.P., *L'élément fondamental de l'état mystique,* LVS, 1921.

II, 283 sq;—Many other articles: *Les dons du Saint-Esprit;—. A l'école du Maître intérieur L'intuition obscure de Dieu;—- L'extase.*

E. Krebs, *Grundfragen der kirchlichen Mystik,* Freiburg im. Breisgau, 1921.

Fr. Lamballe, Eudist, *La contemplation ou Principes de vie mystique,* 1912. English; *Mystical Contemplation,* London, tr. Mitchell, 1913.

R. Langenberg, *Quelle und Forschungen zur Geschichte der deutschen Mystik,* Bonn, 1902.

La Reguera, *Praxis theologiæ mysticæ,* 1921. This is the work of Godinez, translated into Latin by La Reguera and republished by Watrigant.

M. de la Taille. See under T, below.

L. Leleu, *La mystique divine et sa psychologie générale,* ANNALES DE PHILOSOPHIE CHRÉTIENNE, July, Sept., Nov. 1906;—-*La mystique et ses attaches ontologiques, ibid,,* Aug., Dec. 1907

Lercher, S.J., *Grundsätzliches über Mystik aus Theologie und Philosophie,* ZEITSCHRIFT FÜR KATH. THEOLOGIE, Innsbruck, 1918.

Letourneau, *Disputes mystiques et questions de mots,* LIBRE PAROLE, Dec. 22, 1921;—-*Disputes mystiques et resultats pratiques,* LIBRE PAROLE, Jan. 5, 1922.

E. Longpré, *La mystique de saint Bonaventure,* ARCHIVUM FRANCISC. HIST. 1921, XIV, 36-108.

S. Louismet, O.S.B., *Mysticism,. True and False,* London, 1919;—*Divine Contemplation for All, London, 1920;—The Mystical Knowledge of God, 3rd ed., London, 1920;—The Mystical Life, London, 1917;—The Mystery of Jesus, London, 1922;—Mystical Initiation, London, 1923;—The Burning Bush, London, 1926.*

A. Mager, O.S.B., *Zur Wesensbestimmung der Mystik;—Alte und Neue in der Mystik;—Zur Stufenfrage in der Mystik.* BENEDIK- TINISCHE MONATSCHRIFT, Beuron, 1919, 1920;—*Aus der mystischen Litteratur der Gegenwart,* PASTOR BONUS, Trêves, 1920, 143-9. Cf. RAM, Jan. 1921, II, 196.

J. Mahieu, Collection *La vie spirituelle,* Bruges, beginning 1919;— *Les travaux de Mgr. Waffelaert, Evêque de Bruges, sur la théologie mystique,* RAM, 1920, II, 377-81.

A. M. = Ant. Malvy, *Chronique* in RAM, 1920.

J. Maréchal, S.J., *A propos du sentiment de présence chez les profanes et chez les mystiques,* Louvain, 1909. Reprinted from RQS, 1908-9; *Sur quelques traits distinctifs de la mystique chrétienne,* RP, 1912, II, 416-88; —*Science empirique et psychologie religieuse,* RSR, 1912; —*L'intuition de Dieu dans la mystique chrétienne,* RSR, 1914, V, 145- 62. English: *Studies in the Psychology of the Mystics,* London, 1927.

St. Margaret Mary, *Vie et œuvres,* 3rd ed., by Mgr. Gauthey, 1915.

Fr. Marie-Joseph, O.D.C., *Il existe une contemplation acquise,* EC, Jan. 1920.

R. de Maumigny, S.J., *Pratique de l'oraison mentale,* 2 vols., 1oth ed., 1916 and 1918.

M. Meschler, S.J., *Aszese und Mystik,* Freiburg im Breisgau, 1917.

M. de Montmorand, *Psychologie des mystiques catholiques orthodoxes,* 1920. See RAM, Jan. 1921, II, 63-9.

Fr. Naval, *Theologiæ asceticæ et mysticæ cursus* (trans. from Spanish), Rome, 1920. Cf. J. de Guibert, RAM, 1920, II, 177-82.

J. Pacheu, *L'expérience mystique et l'activité subconsciente,* 1911;— *Quelques réflexions sur la méthode en psychologie religieuse,* RP. 1912, II, 371-91;—*Les mystiques interprétés par les mystiques,* RP, 1913, I, 616-60;—*L'expérience mystique de Macaire l'Egyptien,* RP, 1920, 109-36; —*L'école du cœur,* 40, May 1921, 278-88.

L. Peeters, *Le surnaturel dans la vie de saint Jean Berchmans,* RAM, April 1922, III, 1x3-33.

H. Pinard, S.J., *L'expérience, la raison, les normes extérieures dans le catholicisme,* RP, 1912, II, 489-529.

Pourrat, *La spiritualité chrétienne,* 4 vols., 1919 ff.; English: *Christian Spirituality,* London, vol. I, 1922; vol. II, 1924; vol. III, 1927.

Ch. Rieder, *Der Gottesfreund der Oberland,* Innsbruck, 1905.

J. Ries, *Das Geistliche Leben in seinen Entwicklungstufen, nach der Lehre des hl. Bernardus,* Freiburg im Breisgau, 1906.

L. Roure, S.J., *Mysticisme,* in DA;—numerous articles in ÉTUDES, particularly concerning Farges and Montmorand, April 16, 1921.

Ruysbroeck, Translation by the Benedictines of Wisques, Brussels, 1919-20. 3 vols. issued.

Saudreau, *Manuel de spiritualité,* 2nd ed., Angers, 1920;— *L'idéal de l'âme fervente,* Angers, 1920. Cf. RAM, 1920, I, 382-4;—*L'état mystique et les faits extraordinaires de la vie spirituelle,* 2nd ed., Angers, 1921;—*La vie d'union à Dieu d'après les grands maîtres.* 3rd ed., *ibid.,* 1921 English: *The Ideal of the Fervent Soul,* London, 1927; *The Mystical State,* London, 1924; *The Life of Union with God,* London, 1927.

Seisdedos y Sanz, S.J., *Principios fundamentales de la mística,* Madrid, 1913 sq. 5 vols. issued.

L. Sempé, S.J., *L'aboutissement de l'oraison: l'état contemplatif,* MCJ, 1920, XCV, 621 sq;—*Contemplation mystique et sainteté,* MCJ, 1921, XCVI, 102-6.

Silverio de Sta Teresa, *Obras de S. Teresa de Jesus editadas y anotadas,* Burgos, 19x5-20. 6 vols. issued; the Letters are lacking.

R. H. J. Steuart, S.J., *The Prayer of Simplicity,* MESSENGER OF THE SACRED HEART, NOV. 1920, 187;—*A Note on Mysticism,* MONTH, 1920, CXXXVI, 447-52.

M. de la Taille, S.J., *L'oraison contemplative,* RSR, 1919. X, 273-92. Published in booklet form, 1921. English: *Contemplative Prayer,* London, 1926.

A. Tanquerey, S.S. *L'oraison de simplicité dans ses rapports avec la contemplation,* LVS, 1921, I, 161-74;—*Un plan de théologie ascétique et mystique,* RAM, Jan. 1921, II, 23-35.

St. Teresa. See *Silverio de Sta Teresa.* French translations: Bouix- Peyré; Carmelites-Polit.

Algar Thorold, *An Essay in Aid of the Better Appreciation of Catholic Mysticism, illustrated from the Writings of Blessed Angela of Foligno,* London, 1900.

H. Thurston, S.J., *Some Physical Phenomena of Mysticism,* MONTH, 1919-21.

J. de Tonquedec, S.J., *Le mot " Mystique ",* RPA, 1919, vol. 28, pp. 547-56.

A. Valensin, S.J., *Une étude synthétique de la vie intérieure au début du XVIIe siècle,* RAM, April 1921, II, 161-77. See *Baiole.*

Vicente de Peralta, O.M.C., *Místicos franciscanos,* series in ESTUDIOS FRANCISCANOS, 1919, 1920, 1921.

Villada, S.J., *De mística,* series in RAZON Y FE, 19x9, 1920.

Mgr. Waffelaert, Bishop of Bruges, *Prospectus generalis in theologiam mysticam, seu manuductio ad praxim unionis contemplativæ,* CB, 1911, XVI, 321 sq, published in French in the collection of M. Mathieu, under the title: *La mystique et la perfection chrétienne,* 1911; —*Notanda quaedam utilissima ad rite intelligenda opera scriptorum contemplativorum, adque ipsam divinam contemplationem exercendam,* a series of articles on mysticism, especially comparing Bl. John Ruysbroeck with St. John of the Cross, CB, beginning 1912, XVII, XVIII, XIX;—*La colombe spirituelle prenant son essor vers Dieu, ou Les trois voies du chemin de la perfection,* Bruges, 1919; *Analecta ascetica et mystica. De ipsa contemplatione,* CB, 1920, XX, 446-9; 1921, XXI, 58 sq.

E. I. Watkin, *The Philosophy of Mysticism,* London, 1919. See THE MONTH, 1919, CXXXVI, 274-8.

H. Watrigant, S.J. See *La Reguera.*

B. Williamson, *Supernatural Mysticism,* London, 1921.

J. Zahn, *Einführung in die Christliche Mystik,* Paderbom, 1908.

In. addition to the works listed by Fr. Bainvel, a few others, principally in English, are also Worthy of notice. Certain additional information as to

English translations, etc., has been added in Fr. Poulain's *Biographical Index* at the end of the present volume. The following may be specially mentioned: [TR.]

Butler, Cuthbcrt, *Western Mysticism,* 2nd ed., London, 1927. Knowles, David,
*The English Mystics,* London, 1927.

Baruzi, Jean, *Saint Jean de la Croix et le problème de l'expérience mystique,* Paris, 1924.

Peers, E. Allison, *Spanish Mysticism: A Preliminary Survey,* London, 1924. *Studies of the Spanish Mystics,* 2 vols., London, 1927-30. (translator) *The Works of St. John of the Cross,* 3 vols., London, 1934-5. (translator) *The Complete Works of St. Teresa of Jesus,* 3 vols., London, 1946.

Sainz Rodriguez, Pedro, *Introducción a la historia de la literatura mística en España,* Madrid, 1927.

Nicholson, Reynold A., *Studies in islamic Mysticism,* Cambridge, 1921

# APPENDIX I

## ACQUIRED AND INFUSED CONTEMPLATION*

WE have seen above (chap. iv, **8**) that there are two kinds of contemplation. From the beginning of the seventeenth century the one has been called *acquired, active* or *ordinary* contemplation, the other *infused, passive, supereminent, mystical* contemplation. The great thing is to remember that there are two. This fact has been denied by a contemporary writer and his followers. This denial had never been previously put forward. This is in itself sufficient to prove that the writer in question does not represent the mystic tradition, whatever he may say to the contrary. To establish the fact with certainty, it is enough to give a list of mystical writers who have admitted without any hesitation that there are two kinds of contemplation. The list, which includes 63 names, is as follows.†

Richard of St. Victor (see chap. iv, **8,** above)
Walter Hilton (part I, chap. v)
St. Teresa‡
The Ven. Louis du Pont (Preface to the *Méditations,* §§ x, xi)
Alvarez de Paz (*De perfecta contemplatione,* bk. V, part I, chap. i)
Thomas of Jesus (*De Oratione*, bk. I, chap. iii)
Lallemant (Fifth principle, chap. iv)
Sandæus (pp. 68, 76, 81)
St. Jane de Chantal (see chap. ii, **72,** above)
Nicholas of Jesus (part II, chap. iii; § 1)
Cardinal de Richelieu (chap. xxxi)
Godinez (bk. VI, chap. xvii, at the end, quoted by la Reguera, vol. II, p. 209)
Philippus a SS. Trinitate (part II, tract. I, disc, ii)
Rigoleuc (*Traité de Vhomme d'oraison,* chap. III, § 1ii)
Surin (*Catéchisme spirituel*, part I, chap. iii) de Vallgornera (q. iii, disp. i, art. iii)

* This Appendix was added by the author in the ninth edition.—J. V. B.

† I do not quote the titles of treatises in the references, for they will be found sufficiently indicated in the Biographical Index.

‡ See my chap. xxix, **3**. The saint distinguishes between two kinds of recollection, one which depends on our own will, the other which does not. This amounts to distinguishing between two kinds of contemplation, for the word *recollection* never being used to mean meditation, it must refer to the state above it, that is, to contemplation.

Boudon (*Le Règne de Dieu,* bk. I, chap. viii)
Morotius, Cistercian (*Cursus vitæ spiritualis,* 1674; Ratisbon ed., 1891; p. 291)
John of St. Thomas (quoted by Fr. Meynard, vol. I, No. 126)
Camus, Bishop of Belley; quoted by Boudon.
Cardinal Bona (*Via compendii,* chap. x)
Antony of the Holy Spirit (Tr. III, disp, i, sect, vii)
Nouet (bk. V, entretien iii)
Renée de Lorraine, p. 33 Segneri (*Concordia,* part I, chap. i)
Balthasar of St. Catherine (*Splendori di sapienza celeste,* Bologna, 1671; pp, 239, 393)
Courbon (part III)
Cardinal. Brancati (see chap. iv, **8,** above)
Lopez de Ezquerra (*ibid.*)
Grandeolas (*Le Quiétisme,* Paris, 1695, p. 71)
Massoulié (*Traité de Voraison,* part III, chap. x)
Dom de la Grange, Canon of St. Victor (*Vidée veritable de Voraison,* Paris, 1699, p. 114)
Honorius of St. Mary (see chap. iv, **8**, above)
Fr. Rousseau (Prelim., and letter xi)
Arbiol (*Desengaños místicos,* Madrid, 1733, p. 385)
Cherubino da Sancta Teresa, Carmelite (*Sancta Teresa maestra di Spirito,* Venice, 1736, p. 153)
Joseph of the Holy Spirit (vol. I, p. 125; vol. II, p. 228)
St. John Baptist de la Salle (part II, chap. i, § 1)
de la Reguera (vol. I, p. 788, No. 79; vol. II, p. 209)
Calatayud, Oratorian (*Divus Thomas,* Valencia; 1744-52; vol. III, pp. 81-4)
Benedict XIV (*De Canon.,* bk. III, ch. xxvi, No. 7)
Tempesti (Traité III)
Gianotti (vol. Il, p. 9)
Scaramelli (See chap. iv, **6**, above)
Terzago (Dissert, vii, § 3)
Joseph of Jesus-Mary (quoted by Terzago)
Dominic of the Holy Trinity, General of the Discalced Carmelites (vol. VII of the *Biblioth. Theol.,* Rome, 1776; bk. VII, sect, iii, chap. xiv, § 1)
Schram (Original edition, No. 240); 1848 ed., No. 250)
St. Alphonsus Liguori (Append. I, No. 7)
de Clorivière (chaps. xxiv, xxv)
The anonymous authors of the *Dictionnaire d'Ascétisme* of Migne (at the word *Contemplation*)
Séraphin (part I, chap. ii)
Verhaege (bk. I, sect, i, chap. i)
Ribet (vol. I, chap. iii)
Voss (bk. I, part i, chap. 3)

Jeiler (p. 498)
Meynard (vol. I, Nos. 126, 128)
Aguillo Lopez de Turiso, Franciscan (*Theologia mistica,* Barcelona, 1893, p. 147)
Lejeune (*Introduction to the Mystical Life*, chap. vii, anD *Dictionnaire de théologie*)
Fr. Dublanchy (see chap. v, 34, above)
Devine (part I, chap. iv)
Dom Vital (part II, chap. ix)
Fr. Vermeersch (Nos. 65, 70)

# APPENDIX II*

## ON THE DISCERNMENT OF SPIRITS

### I
### RULES OF ST. IGNATIUS†

RULES

for feeling and recognising in some sort the various motions that are excited in the soul,—the good, that they may be taken up; the evil, that they may be rejected. And these Rules are more suited for the First Week.

The first rule: in those persons who are going from mortal sin to mortal sin, the enemy is wont commonly to put before them apparent pleasures, causing them to imagine sensual delights and pleasures, the better to maintain and further them in their vices and sins. In the case of these persons the good spirit applies the contrary method, pricking their consciences and causing in them remorse by the selfaccusation of reason.

The second: in those persons who are proceeding earnestly with the work of clearing off their sins, and are mounting in the service of God our Lord from good to better, there obtains the contrary method to that in the first rule: for then it is the way of the evil spirit to sting, to sadden, and raise obstacles, making the soul restless by false reasonings that it may get on no further. And it is the way of the good spirit to give courage and strength, consolations, tears, inspirations, and repose of mind, making things easy and removing all obstacles to the end that the soul may go on further in doing good.

The third, of spiritual consolation: I call it "consolation" when there is set up in the soul some inward motion, whereby the soul begins to be on fire with the love of her Creator and Lord; and, consequently, when she can love no created thing on the face of the earth in itself, but only in the Creator of them all. Likewise when she bursts forth into tears out of love of her Lord, be it for grief over her sins, or over the Passion of Christ our Lord, or over other matters directly ordered to His service and praise. In short I call "consolation" any increase of hope, faith and charity, and any inward joy that calls and attracts to heavenly

* Added in the tenth French edition. See *Introduction,* Sec. 37.

† *Spiritual Exercises*. The translation in the English edition is that of Fr. Rickaby, S.J., London, Burns Oates & Washbourne, 1923.

things and to the salvation of one's own soul, rendering her restful and pacifying her in her Creator and Lord.

The fourth, of spiritual desolation: I call "desolation" everything that is contrary to the third rule,—as a darkening of the soul, trouble of mind, movement to base and earthly things, restlessness of various agitations and temptations, moving to distrust, loss of hope, loss of love; when the soul feels herself thoroughly apathetic, tepid, sad, and as it were separated from her Creator and Lord; because, as consolation is contrary to desolation, in the same way the thoughts that spring from consolation are contrary to the thoughts that spring from desolation.

The fifth: in time of desolation one ought never to make a change, but to stand firm and steady in the resolutions and determination in which one was on the day previous to such desolation, or in the determination in which one was in the previous consolation; because, as in consolation the good spirit rather leads us and directs us by his counsel, so in desolation does the evil spirit, by whose counsels we cannot find the way to any right resolve.

The sixth: though in desolation we ought not to change our previous purposes, it is very helpful heartily to change ourselves in the direction contrary to the said desolation—for instance, by insisting more on prayer, meditation, much examination, and putting out our strength in some suitable manner of doing penance.

The seventh: let him who is in desolation consider how God is leaving him by way of probation to his natural powers, that he may stand out against the various agitations and temptations of the enemy; for he can stand out with the divine aid, which ever attends upon him, although he does not manifestly feel it, because the Lord has withdrawn from Him his high fervour, strong love, and intense grace, yet leaving him grace enough for eternal salvation.

The eighth: let him who is in desolation labour to hold on in patience, such patience as makes against the vexations that harass him; let him consider that soon he shall be consoled, using diligent efforts against such desolation, as is enjoined in the sixth rule.

The ninth: there are three chief causes why we find ourselves in desolation. The first is, by reason of our being tepid, indolent, or negligent in our spiritual exercises; and so for our faults spiritual consolation goes away. The second, to prove us, what we are worth and how far we will hold on in His service and praise without so much remuneration of consolations and ample graces. The third, to give us a true knowledge and understanding whereby we may inwardly feel that it is not in our power to bring on or maintain a flood of devotion, intense love, tears, nor any other spiritual consolation, but that it is all a gift and grace of God our Lord; and that we may not build our nest in another man's house, lifting up our intellect to some pride or vainglory, attributing to ourselves devotion or other parts of spiritual consolation.

The tenth: let him who is in consolation think how he shall carry himself in the desolation that will come on afterwards, gathering new strength for that time.

The eleventh: let him who is in consolation take care to humble and abase himself as much as he can, thinking how little he is worth in time of desolation, without such grace or consolation. On the other hand, let him who is in desolation think that he can do much with the grace that he has, sufficient to withstand all his enemies, taking strength in his Creator and Lord.

The twelfth: the enemy is as a woman in being weak perforce of circumstances, but strong of bent and purpose of will. For as it is the way of a woman in a broil with any man to lose heart and take to flight when the man shows her a bold face; and contrariwise, if the man begins to lose courage and take to his heels, the anger, vengeance and ferocity of the woman runs very high and passes all measure; in like manner, it is the way of the enemy to flag and lose heart, his temptations taking flight when the person who is exercising himself in spiritual things shows a bold face against the temptations of the enemy and does the diametrical opposite to what they suggest. And contrariwise, if the person who is malting his exercises begins to take fright and to lose heart in suffering temptations, there is no wild beast so fierce on the face of the earth as is the enemy of human nature in the following out of his wicked intention with ever such enormous malice.

The thirteenth: he also behaves like a false lover in wishing to lie low and not be discovered. For as such an empty fellow who is paying his addresses with evil intent to the daughter of a good father, or the wife of a good husband, wishes his words and entreaties to be secret: and, on the contrary, it is great displeasure to him when the daughter discloses to her father, or the wife to her husband his glozing words and wicked intention, because he readily gathers that he shall not be able to succeed with the enterprise commenced; in the same way, when the enemy of human nature brings in his cunning persuasions upon the just soul, he wishes and desires them to be received and kept secret; but when the person solicited discloses them to his good confessor, or other spiritual person, who knows his machinations and malicious intents, it displeases him vastly, because he gathers that he shall not be able to succeed with his malicious design which he had entered upon, seeing that his machinations are discovered manifestly.

The fourteenth: in like manner he behaves as a brigand-chief to subdue and plunder what he desires: for as a captain and chief of an army pitches his camp and reconnoitres the strength and lines of defence of a fortification, and then attacks it on the weaker side; in like manner the enemy of human nature, going round, looks at every side of all our theological, cardinal and moral virtues; and on whatever side he finds us weaker and more ill off for our eternal salvation, on that side he attacks and endeavours to take us by storm.

## RULES

to the same effect with greater discernment of spirits, and they are suitable more for the Second Week.

The first: it is the way of God and His angels in their motions to give true gladness and spiritual joy, removing all sadness and trouble which the enemy brings on, whose way it is to fight against such gladness and spiritual consolation, bringing up apparent reasons, subtleties, and never-ending fallacies.

The second: it is of God our Lord alone to give consolation to the soul without previous cause: because it is proper to the Creator to come in, to go out, to set up a movement in the soul, drawing her wholly to the love of His Divine Majesty. I say, "without cause"—without any previous sense or knowledge of any object, whereby any such consolation as that should come by her acts of understanding and will.

The third: with a cause the good angel and the evil one equally may console the soul, to contrary ends; the good angel for the advancement of the soul, that she may grow and ascend from good to better; and the evil angel to the contrary effect, and thereafter to draw her to his own wicked intention and malice.

The fourth: it is the way of the evil angel, who transforms himself into an angel of light, to go in with the devout soul and come out with himself, that is to say, to bring in good and holy thoughts, conformable to the said just soul; and afterwards he gradually contrives to arrive at his own end, dragging on the soul to his secret machinations and perverse intentions.

The fifth: we ought much to attend to the course or current of the thoughts: and if the beginning, middle and end are all good, tending to entire good, it is a sign of the good angel; but if in the course of the thoughts that he suggests the thing comes to end in something evil, or distracting, or less good than what the soul had previously proposed to herself to do; or if it weakens her, or renders her restless, or troubles the soul, taking away from her that peace, tranquillity, and quiet which she had before, it is a clear sign that the thoughts proceed from the evil spirit, the enemy of our advancement and eternal salvation.

The sixth: when the enemy of human nature shall have been felt and recognised by his serpent's tail, and the evil end to which he leads on, it is useful for him who has been tempted by him to look afterwards at the course of the good thoughts that he suggested to him, and the beginning of them, and how he (the Evil One) gradually managed to make him come down from that sweetness and spiritual joy in which he was, till he led him on to his perverse intention,—to the end that by such experience, observed and noted down, he may be on his guard in future against his customary machinations.

The seventh: in those who are going forward from good to better, the good angel touches such a soul sweetly, lightly, and pleasantly, as a drop of water that enters into a sponge; and the evil angel touches so as to sting, and with a patter and disturbance, as when a drop of water falls upon a rock; but those who are going on from bad to worse the above-named spirits touch contrariwise. The cause of which is this, that the disposition of the soul is contrary to the said angels, or like; for when it is contrary, they enter with a din and sensational accompaniments, so that their entry may easily be perceived; but when it is like, the entry is in silence, as of one coming into his own house by an open door.

The eighth: when the consolation is without cause, though there be no deception in it, since it proceeds from God our Lord alone, as has been said, nevertheless the spiritual person, to whom God gives such consolation, ought to look with much watchfulness and attention to discern the proper time of such actual consolation from the following, in which the soul remains aglow and favoured with the favour and remnants of the consolation that is past; because often in this second period, by her own proper activity, working upon habits and consequences of concepts and judgments, she comes, either through the good spirit or through the evil spirit, to form various purposes and opinions, which are not given immediately by God our Lord; and therefore they must needs be very well discussed before entire credence is given to them and they are carried into effect.

## II

## Counsels of St. Teresa On Temptations and Illusions*

*Extracts from Chapter XXXVII*

It is certain that He for His own part will not fail us. Oh, how well He pays us and how limitless are His rewards!...

We must never be insincere with Him, for He loves us... treat Him frankly and openly, never saying one thing and meaning another; and then He will always give us more than we ask for.

The Lord, then, saw it was necessary to awaken such souls and to remind them that they have enemies, and how much greater danger they are in if they are unprepared, and, since if they fall it will be from a greater height, how much more help they need from the Eternal Father. So, lest they should fail to realise their danger and suffer deception, He offers these petitions so necessary to us all while we live in this exile: "And lead us not, Lord, into temptation, but deliver us from evil."

*Extracts from Chapter XXXVIII*

There are great things here for us to meditate upon, sisters, and to learn to understand as we pray. Remember I consider it quite certain that those who

* *Way of Perfection*. Relating to the petition of the *Paternoster: Lead us not into temptation.* (From Professor Allison Peers' translation in *The Complete Works of St. Teresa of Jesus,* published by Sheed & Ward.)

attain perfection do not ask the Lord to deliver them from trials, temptations, persecutions and conflicts—and that is another sure and striking sign that these favours and this contemplation which His Majesty gives them are coming from the Spirit of the Lord and are not illusions. For, as I said a little way back, perfect souls *are in no way repelled by trials, but rather* desire them and pray for them and love them. They are like soldiers: the more wars there are, the better they are pleased, because they hope to emerge from them with the greater riches. If there are no wars, they serve for their pay, but they know they will not get very far on that.

Believe me, sisters, the soldiers of Christ—namely, those who experience contemplation and practise prayer—are always ready for the hour of conflict. They are never very much afraid of their open enemies, for they know who they are and are sure that their strength can never prevail against the strength which they themselves have been given by the Lord: they will always be victorious and gain great riches, so they will never turn their backs on the battle. Those whom they fear, and fear rightly, and from whom they always beg the Lord to deliver them, are enemies who are treacherous, devils who transform themselves and come and visit them in the disguise of angels of light. The soul fails to recognise them until they have done it a great deal of harm; they suck our life-blood and put an end to our virtues and we go on yielding to temptation without knowing it. From these enemies let us pray the Lord often, in the *Paternoster*, to deliver us: may He not allow us to run into temptations which deceive us; may their poison be detected; and may light and truth not be hidden from us. How rightly does our good Master teach us to pray for this and pray for it in our name!

Consider, daughters, in how many ways these enemies do us harm. Do not suppose that the sole danger lies in their making us believe that the consolations and the favours which they can counterfeit to us come from God. This, I think, in a way, is the least harmful thing they can do; it may even help some whom this sensible devotion entices to spend more time in prayer and thus to make greater progress. Being ignorant that these consolations come from the devil, and knowing themselves to be unworthy of such favours, they will never cease to give thanks to God and will feel the greater obligation to serve Him; further, they will strive to prepare themselves for more favours which the Lord may grant them, since they believe them to come from His hand.

Always strive after humility, sisters, and try to realise that you are not worthy of these graces, and do not seek them. It is because many souls do this, I feel sure, that the devil loses them: he thinks that he has caused their ruin, but out of the evil which he has been trying to do the Lord brings good. For His Majesty regards our intention, which is to please Him and serve Him and keep near to Him in prayer, and the Lord is faithful. We shall do well to be cautious, and not to let our humility break down or to become in any way vainglorious. Entreat the Lord to deliver you from this, daughters, and you need then have no fear that His Majesty will allow you to be comforted much by anyone but Himself.

Where the devil can do great harm without our realising it is in making us believe that we possess virtues which we do not: that is pestilential. For, when consolations and favours come to us, we feel that we are doing nothing but receive, and have the greater obligation to serve; but when we suffer from this other delusion we think that we are giving and serving, and that the Lord will be obliged to reward us; and this, little by little, does us a great deal of harm. On the one hand, our humility is weakened, while, on the other, we neglect to cultivate that virtue, believing we have already acquired it. *We think we are walking safely, when, without realising it, we stumble, and fall into a pit from which we cannot escape. Though we may not consciously have committed any mortal sin which would have sent us infallibly to hell, we have sprained our ankles and cannot continue on that road which I began to speak about and which I have not forgotten... But I warn you that this temptation is full of peril...* What can we do about it, sisters? To me the best thing seems to be what our Master teaches us: to pray, and to beseech the Eternal Father not to allow us to fall into temptation.

There is something else, too, which I want to tell you. If we think the Lord has given us a certain grace, we must understand that it is a blessing which we have received but which He may take away from us again, as indeed, in the great providence of God, often happens. Have you never observed this yourselves, sisters?... I am not the only person to be like this, for I have noticed the same thing in many people better than myself, so I know it can happen.

That being so, who can say that he possesses any virtue, or that he is rich, if at the time when he most needs this virtue he finds himself devoid of it?... The truth is that, if we serve the Lord with humility, He will sooner or later succour us in our needs. But, if we are not strong in this virtue, the Lord will leave us to ourselves, as they say, at every step. This is a great favour on His part, for it helps us to realise fully that we have nothing which has not been given us.

And now you must take note of this other piece of advice. The devil makes us believe that we have some virtue—patience, let us say— because we have determination and make continual resolutions to suffer a great deal for God's sake. We really and truly believe that we would suffer all this, and the devil encourages us in the belief, and so we are very pleased. I advise you to place no reliance on these virtues: we ought not to think that we know anything about them beyond their names, or to imagine that the Lord has given them to us, until we come to the test. For it may be that at the first annoying word which people say to you your patience will fall to the ground. Whenever you have frequently to suffer, praise God for beginning to teach you this virtue, and force yourself to suffer patiently, for this is a sign that He wants you to repay Him for the virtue which He is giving you, and you must think of it only as a deposit, as has already been said...

It is very important always to be on the watch and to realise that this is a temptation, both in the things I have referred to and in many others. For when The Lord really gives one of these solid virtues, it seems to bring all the rest in its train: that is a very well-known fact. But I advise you once more, even if you think you possess it, to suspect that you may be mistaken; for the person who is truly humble is always doubtful about his own virtues; very often they seem more genuine and of greater worth when he sees them in his neighbours.

*Extracts from Chapter XXXIX*

Beware also, daughters, of certain kinds of humility which the devil inculcates in us and which make us very uneasy about the gravity of our *past* sins. There are many ways in which he is accustomed to depress us so that in time we withdraw from Communion and give up our private prayer, because the devil suggests to us that we are not worthy to engage in it. When we come to the Most Holy Sacrament, we spend the time during which we ought to be receiving grace in wondering whether we are properly prepared or no. The thing gets to such a pass that a soul can be made to believe that, through being what it is, it has been forsaken by God, and thus it almost doubts His mercy. Everything such a person does appear to her to be dangerous, and all the service she renders, however good it may be, seems to her fruitless. She loses confidence and sits with her hands in her lap because she thinks she can do nothing well and that what is good in others is wrong in herself.

Pay great attention, daughters, to this point which I shall now make, because sometimes thinking yourselves so wicked may be humility and virtue and at other times a very great temptation. I have had experience of this, so I know it is true. Humility, however deep it be, neither disquiets nor troubles nor disturbs the soul; it is accompanied by peace, joy and tranquillity. Although, on realising how wicked we are, we can see clearly that we deserve to be in hell, and are distressed by our sinfulness, and rightly think that everyone should hate us, yet, if our humility is true, this distress is accompanied by an interior peace and joy of which we should not like to be deprived. Far from disturbing or depressing the soul, it enlarges it and makes it fit to serve God better. The other kind of distress only disturbs and upsets the mind and troubles the soul, so grievous is it. I think the devil is anxious for us to believe that we are humble, and, if he can, to lead us to distrust God.

When you find yourselves in this state, cease thinking, so far as you can, of your own wretchedness, and think of the mercy of God and of His love and His sufferings for us. If your state of mind is the result of temptation, you will be unable to do even this, for it will not allow you to quiet your thoughts or to fix them on anything, but will only weary you the more: it will be a great thing if you can recognise it as a temptation. This is what happens when we perform excessive penances in order to make ourselves believe that, because of what we are doing, we are more penitent than others. If we conceal our penances from our confessor or superior, or if we are told to give them up and do not obey, that is a clear case of temptation. Always try to obey, however much it may hurt you to do so, for that is the greatest possible perfection.

There is another very dangerous kind of temptation: a feeling of security caused by the belief that we shall never again return to our past faults and to the pleasures of the world. "I know all about these things now," we say, "and I realise that they all come to an end and I get more pleasure from the things of God." If this temptation comes to beginners it is very serious; for, having this sense of security, they think nothing of running once more into occasions of sin. They soon come up against these—and then God preserve them from falling back farther than before! The devil, seeing that here are souls which may do him harm and be of great help to others, does all in his power to prevent them from rising again. However many consolations and pledges of love the Lord may give you, therefore, you must never be so sure of yourselves that you cease to be afraid of falling back again, and you must keep yourselves from occasions of sin.

Do all you can to discuss these graces and favours with someone who can give you light and have no secrets from him. However sublime your contemplation may be, take great care both to begin and to end every period of prayer with self-examination. If these favours come from God, you will do this more frequently, without either taking or needing any advice from me, for such favours bring humility with them and always leave us with more light by which we may see our own unworthiness. I will say no more here, for you will find many books which give this kind of advice. I have said all this because I have had experience of the matter and have sometimes found myself in difficulties of this nature. Nothing that can be said about it, however, will give us complete security.

What, then, Eternal Father, can we do but flee to Thee and beg Thee not to allow these enemies of ours to lead, us into temptation? If attacks are made upon us publicly, we shall easily surmount them, with Thy help. But how can we be ready for these treacherous assaults, my God? We need constantly to pray for Thy help. Show us, Lord, some way of recognising them and guarding against them. Thou knowest that there are not many who walk along this road, and if so many fears are to beset them, there will be far fewer.

What a strange thing it is! You might suppose that the devil never tempted those who do not walk along the road of prayer! People get a greater shock when deception overtakes a single one of the many persons who are striving to be perfect than when a hundred thousand others are deceived and fall into open sin...

Do not be afraid to walk on these roads, sisters, for there are many of them in the life of prayer—and some people get most help by using one of them and others by using another.

## III

## Marks to Discern the Spirit of God, According to St. Margaret Mary*

Vive ✠ Jesus!

In that great fear which I have always had of being deceived among the graces and favours I have received from my sovereign Lord: here are the marks which He has given me whereby to know what comes from Him and what comes from Satan, self-love or some other natural movement.

In the first place, these favours and particular graces will always be accompanied in me by some humiliation, contradiction or contempt from creatures.

In the second place, after having received any of these favours or divine communications, whereof I am so unworthy, I shall be plunged into an abyss of nothingness and interior confusion, which will cause me to feel as great pain at the sight of my own unworthiness as I have received pleasure from the enjoyment of the merits and liberality of my sovereign Lord, who will thus extinguish in me all vain complacency, and every motion of self-esteem and vanity.

Moreover these graces and knowledge, whether given me for myself or some other, will never produce in me any feeling of contempt for my neighbour, however great his wretchedness appears in the light of them. This will only move me to feelings of compassion and charity, to give him all the aid in my power.

These graces will not prevent me from observing my rule and from obedience, since He has so rigorously submitted them to obedience that should I happen to depart therefrom, He would withdraw from me with all His favours.

Moreover this Spirit which guides me, from whom I receive them and who is beyond all that can be expressed, has established such rule over me that it seems that I can say that He rules and governs me inwardly as it pleases Him, for I cannot resist Him, since it is His life that quickens me. He raises me and abases me, consoles and afflicts me, without my doing aught else than adore and love Him and give myself up entirely to Him. This is all that He wills of me: that I love, act, and suffer in silence, and He makes me enjoy an unchangeable peace among these three desires which He has enkindled in my heart, which incessantly torment me, namely, to love Him, to suffer for His love and to die, for life would be unbearable for me without the cross. The whole of my earthly happiness is to be able to suffer.

Moreover this Spirit which leads me gives me an insatiable hunger to communicate, to be humiliated, to live in poverty, unknown, despised and at last to die bowed down under the burden of every misery. These are the notes which

* *Vie et Œuvres de la Bienheureuse Marguerite-Marie Alacoque*, par Gauthey, Paris, de Gigord, 1915, vol. II, pp. 181-3.

my sovereign Master has deigned in His mercy to give me as an assurance of His graces and of their coming from the good Spirit, and, if I mistake not, all the graces that He works in me produce in me all these effects. And were I permitted to be afflicted it would only be from the fear of having unwittingly deceived creatures, as has happened. The smallest esteem they have for me is a torment I cannot bear. For it is true that were I known with all my wickedness, I should be held only in horror and hate and all that comes from me would be contemned. Were that so, it would be the greatest consolation that could happen to me, since I see that I have performed no action that is not worthy of punishment. And then, when one hears of a life without the love of God, that is the sum of all possible evils. And although the Sacred Heart of Jesus has become my Master and my Director, yet He does not will that I should do anything that He commands me without the consent of my superior, which He wills me to obey more exactly even than His own. This is what He teaches me: to distrust myself as my own most cruel and powerful enemy;— but if I place all my confidence in Him, He will defend me therefrom; —never to be disturbed at anything whatever that may happen, considering all events in the order of His holy Providence and will, which, when it pleases Him, is able to turn all things to His glory.

# ANALYTICAL INDEX

# INDEX OF PROPER NAMES

(The letter B before a number refers to the Bibliographical Index)

# ABOUT THE AUTHOR

Fr. Augustin Poulain, SJ (1836-1919)

Reverend Père Augustin Francois Poulain was born at Cherbourg, France, on December 15, 1836. After pursuing higher studies in philosophy and science, in 1858 he entered the Jesuit novitiate at Angers. He made his final vows at the École Sainte-Geneviève in 1877.

Jesuits receive many years of higher education, and Poulain did well in philosophy and science, while pursuing further studies in theology and mathematics. He was ordained a priest in 1870, and served in the Jesuits with various duties, including professor, supervisor, director of an artists' guild, and librarian. He died a holy death on July 19, 1919.

He was of a naturally witty and happy disposition and diffused gladness all around him; the clearness of his mind is manifest in all he wrote.